STO

ACPL ITEM
DISCARDED

Y0-AAB-608

1-3-61

Market Power: Size and Shape
Under the Sherman Act

THE TRADE REGULATION SERIES

S. CHESTERFIELD OPPENHEIM, Editor

TRADE ASSOCIATION LAW AND PRACTICE
George P. Lamb *and* Sumner S. Kittelle
assisted by Carrington Shields

FOREIGN COMMERCE AND THE ANTITRUST LAWS
Wilbur Lindsay Fugate

MARKET POWER: SIZE AND SHAPE UNDER THE
SHERMAN ACT
G. E. Hale *and* Rosemary D. Hale

THE TRADE REGULATION SERIES

S. CHESTERFIELD OPPENHEIM, Editor

MARKET POWER

Size and Shape
Under the Sherman Act

by

G. E. HALE

OF THE ILLINOIS BAR

and

ROSEMARY D. HALE

LECTURER IN ECONOMICS
LAKE FOREST COLLEGE

LITTLE, BROWN AND COMPANY

Boston · Toronto   1958

COPYRIGHT, © , 1958, BY G. E. HALE AND ROSEMARY D. HALE

ALL RIGHTS RESERVED, INCLUDING THE RIGHT
TO REPRODUCE THIS BOOK OR PORTIONS
THEREOF IN ANY FORM

LIBRARY OF CONGRESS CATALOG CARD NO. 58-10708

Published simultaneously in Canada
by Little, Brown & Company (Canada) Limited

PRINTED IN THE UNITED STATES OF AMERICA

1142145

IN MEMORY OF

GEORGE ELLERY HALE
1868-1938

WILLIAM BROWNE HALE
1875-1944

JAMES T. DANES
1890-1955

Trade Regulation Series

EDITOR'S FOREWORD

This Trade Regulation Series was initiated in recognition of the continuing need for practical guides to good faith compliance with antitrust and cognate trade regulation laws. The Series designation is used in a broad sense to cover two main branches of law related to the general objectives of American competitive enterprise.

One of these branches is antitrust law, commonly understood as a set of legal controls designed to preserve and promote competition and to prohibit unreasonable restraints of trade, monopolization, and potential threats to the vigor of competition. In the federal sphere, the Sherman, Federal Trade Commission, and Clayton Acts are the major statutes embodying congressional expression of this national antitrust policy.

A second branch is a set of laws aimed at regulating the plane of competition. In this area a wide range of business behavior is subjected to prohibitions against unfair competition and unfair trade practices as developed at common law and in courts of equity. Prohibitions also stem from state and federal statutes, such as the bans on unfair methods of competition and unfair or deceptive acts or practices in the Federal Trade Commission Act, the prohibitions against price discriminations in the Robinson-Patman Act, and the state "Fair Trade" Acts.

These two sets of laws do not operate as water-tight compartments, one insulated from the other. They may be invoked separately or concurrently, and they often supplement each other. Moreover, many governmental policies directly or indirectly affect the over-all reliance upon competition as the general regulator of the American economy. The patent laws, public utility regulation, and fiscal, monetary, tariff, and tax policies also bear upon the primacy of the objectives of competitive enterprise.

The purpose of the Series is to provide legal handbooks containing systematic statements of legal principles applicable to typical problems in specific segments of this field of law, but characterizing these productions as legal handbooks requires explanatory comment. The well-known generality of the standards of law in this field and the frequent uncertainty as to the state of the law obviously limit presentation in the hornbook style of neat and simplified summations of existing legal rules and precedents. Yet the goal set for each author is a text designed to present the law with the greatest possible clarification, as a guide for the general practitioner who has little experience in this field, for the economist or business executive who wants to be quickly oriented in one of the areas covered, and for the specialist who desires a ready reference tool.

Since each author has been asked to tailor his text to the nature and scope of his particular subject, no rigid pattern of presentation has been adopted for the Series. Allowance is made for differences in style and diction of the individual authors, and for the requirements of the various subjects covered.

S. CHESTERFIELD OPPENHEIM

Ann Arbor, Michigan
May 14, 1956

PREFACE

In December, 1943, the American Law Institute abandoned William B. Hale's project for a group study of the antitrust laws. We then resolved to carry forward his program as best we could by our own efforts. Many kind persons have helped us along the way. Unfortunately, their number is too great for individual mention. We must, however, acknowledge the perceptive assistance of the Editor of this Series, Professor S. Chesterfield Oppenheim. He does not necessarily agree with all that is said within these covers but he has patiently examined the entire text and made many helpful suggestions. And we must name Miss Emily J. Niemet, a member of the Illinois Bar, for whose painstaking editorial assistance we are tremendously grateful. Numerous other friends have assisted in the arduous task of gathering factual data. From others, and particularly colleagues on the Attorney General's National Committee to Study the Antitrust Laws, fellow members of the Lake Forest College faculty, and members of the firm founded by a leading antitrust lawyer, John P. Wilson, we have gleaned ideas which illuminate every section of our book. Our heartfelt thanks go to all these friendly helpers.

Portions of this work have previously been published as articles in legal periodicals. Acknowledgment is made to the publishers of those journals for their courtesy in permitting reproduction of their copyright material (the identity of the journals is indicated in footnotes to several chapters and the appendixes). Some of the text has been abstracted from briefs and memoranda prepared for clients. We have, however, taken pains carefully to conceal their identity. We are also indebted to our publisher, Little, Brown and Company, for the cooperation of its staff in the preparation of the manuscript and the several stages of proof.

Some decades ago a sanguine jurist wrote:

> The anti-trust laws of the state and the United States have been so frequently before the state and federal tribunals, and every phase and feature so ably and exhaustively discussed, that any attempt to improve on these discussions would be vain. [Mayes, C.J., in Cumberland Telephone & Telegraph Co. v. State, 100 Miss. 102, 54 So. 670, 674 (1911).]

Despite that admonition, we have attempted to "improve upon" the discussion in the cases. We do not hope to have provided

answers for all problems but we have tried to restate the arguments
in coherent form and to bring the authorities within easy grasp of
the practitioner.   The result is a volume of some bulk.   If the
Southern justice was correct, we have indeed labored many years
in vain.   We think more appropriate, however, the instruction of
the novelist:

> It takes space to feel, it takes time to know, and great organisms
> as well as small have to pause, more or less, to possess themselves
> and to be aware.

— Henry James

G. E. H.
R. D. H.

Chicago, Illinois
December, 1957

SUMMARY OF CONTENTS

TABLE OF CONTENTS

CHAPTER 1

INTRODUCTION

CHAPTER 2

HORIZONTAL SIZE: THE ABUSE THEORY

CHAPTER 3

HORIZONTAL SIZE: THE STRUCTURE THEORY

CHAPTER 4

HORIZONTAL SIZE: OTHER THEORIES

CHAPTER 5

VERTICAL INTEGRATION

CHAPTER 6

DIVERSIFICATION: IMPACT OF MONOPOLY POLICY
UPON MULTIPRODUCT FIRMS

CHAPTER 7

DISPERSION: MONOPOLY AND GEOGRAPHIC INTEGRATION

CHAPTER 8

WEALTH

CHAPTER 9

ATTEMPTS TO MONOPOLIZE

CHAPTER 10
REMEDIES

CHAPTER 11
IN ENDING

Appendixes

APPENDIX A

MARKET IMPERFECTIONS: ENFORCEMENT OF THE ANTITRUST LAWS IN A FRICTION-AFFLICTED ECONOMY

APPENDIX B

MONOPOLY IN MOTION: DYNAMIC ECONOMICS IN ANTITRUST ENFORCEMENT

LIST OF ABBREVIATIONS

Atty. Gen. Nat. Com. Rep.	Report of the Attorney General's National Committee to Study the Antitrust Laws (1955)
Celler Committee I	Hearings Before the Subcommittee on the Study of Monopoly Power of the House Committee on the Judiciary, Serial No. 14, 81st Cong., 1st Sess., 2d Sess.; Serial No. 1, 82d Cong., 1st Sess.; Serial No. 12, 82d Cong., 2d Sess. (1949-1952)
Celler Committee II	Hearings Before the Antitrust Subcommittee of the House Committee on the Judiciary, 84th Cong., 1st Sess. (1955)
Kilgore Committee	Hearings Before the Subcommittee on Antitrust and Monopoly of the Senate Committee on the Judiciary, 84th Cong., 1st Sess. (1955-1956)
O'Mahoney Committee I	Hearings Before a Subcommittee on Federal Licensing of Corporations of the Senate Committee on the Judiciary, 75th Cong., 3d Sess. (1938)
Roosevelt Committee	Hearings Before Subcommittee No. 5 of the House Select Committee on Small Business, 84th Cong., 1st Sess. (1955)
TNEC, Final Rep.	Final Report and Recommendations of the Temporary National Economic Committee, Sen. Doc. No. 35, 77th Cong., 1st Sess. (1941)
TNEC, Final Rep. of Exec. Secy.	Temporary National Economic Committee, Final Report of the Executive Secretary, 77th Cong., 1st Sess. (1941)
TNEC Hearings	Hearings Before the Temporary National Economic Committee Pursuant to Public Resolution No. 113 (75th Cong.), 75th Cong., 3d Sess.; 76th Cong. 1st Sess., 2d Sess., 3d Sess. (1939-1940)

Market Power: Size and Shape
Under the Sherman Act

CHAPTER 1

Introduction

§1.1. Subject matter of this work. This book is a study of the law of market power prevailing in the United States in the middle of the twentieth century. It is chiefly concerned with the size and shape of single enterprises. Many business ventures are now carried on in corporate form; for purposes of this study, however, it is immaterial whether the business is conducted by a proprietorship, a partnership, a joint venture,[1] a joint stock company or a corporation.[2] Similarly, we consider the single enterprise both as a buyer and a seller because it is well established that the law affects both monopoly and monopsony.[3] On the other hand, we do not deal with relations among business rivals[4] nor do we attempt an analysis of "trade practices" except insofar as they may bear upon the existence of monopoly or attempts to monopolize.[5] This study therefore does not cover the full range of those statutes commonly referred to as the "antitrust laws"; at the same time many of the questions beyond the scope of this volume are intimately connected with our concepts of the law of monopoly.[6] Here, indeed, law is a seamless web: even within the covers of this work every problem is related to every other and the reader is duly warned against reliance upon a single portion of the analysis. We have attempted to suggest the more obvious points of cross reference but it is hazardous to try any antitrust case without at least nodding acquaintance with the entire topic.

§1.2. Other areas of law bearing upon the subject. Many other types of governmental action profoundly affect the problem

§1.1. [1] Nichols, Joint Ventures, 36 Va. L. Rev. 425 (1950).

[2] In §3.9 *infra,* however, we consider to what extent activities by a number of persons, organized into a corporation or otherwise, should be considered the activities of a "single trader."

[3] E.g., Hood Rubber Co. v. United States Rubber Co., 229 Fed. 583, 587-588 (D. Mass. 1916). Debates on the basic federal legislation indicated a concern over the activities of buyers as well as sellers. Walker, History of the Sherman Law 15 (1910).

[4] Hale, Agreements Among Competitors, 33 Minn. L. Rev. 331 (1949).

[5] It is contemplated that other volumes in this series, under the editorship of Professor S. Chesterfield Oppenheim, will cover such subjects.

[6] In this work the word "monopoly" is often used in its economic sense to include a degree of monopoly rather than that full monopoly contemplated by the law.

of monopoly. Statutes may directly create public or private monopolies; the much debated patent laws[1] furnish a prominent example. Interventionist legislation may have similar effects; statutes designed to regulate prices and production, either throughout the economy or in special fields known as "public utilities," may have a heavy impact upon the competitive system.[2] The tariff is often called the "mother of trusts";[3] local counterparts, disguised as licensing restrictions, building codes and the like, afford sturdy shelter from the blasts of competition.[4] Particularistic legislation, reflecting the interests of organized minorities, frequently grants express or implied exemption from the operation of statutes designed to encourage competition. Labor unions, for example, are now free under federal law to exercise economic power without regard to the Sherman Act.[5] Internal taxation, again, has far-reaching effects upon competitive conditions. The burden of such taxes may carry far more important implications for economic growth and rising living standards than any amount of antitrust litigation.[6] Obviously, however, this study cannot en-

§1.2. [1] Patent Code of 1952, 66 Stat. 792, 35 U.S.C.A. §§1 et seq.

[2] Wilcox, On the Alleged Ubiquity of Oligopoly, 40 Proceedings Am. Econ. Assn. 67, 70 (1950). The antitrust laws should not be applied to regulated business. Hale and Hale, Monopoly and Mobilization, 47 Nw. U.L. Rev. 606 (1952). But compare, e.g., Gibbs v. Consolidated Gas Co., 130 U.S. 396 (1889).

[3] Occasionally, the relationship between tariffs and monopolies has achieved legal recognition. Bladen, Monopoly and Competition in Canada, in Chamberlin, ed., Monopoly and Competition and Their Regulation 3, 15 (International Economic Assn. 1954); McLean and Haigh, How Business Corporations Grow, 32 Harv. Bus. Rev. No. 6, 81, 86-87 (1954) (conservation laws which prohibit distress production and hence bargain sales to refiners).

[4] Stone and Denton, Toward More Housing 100-101 (TNEC Monograph No. 8, 1940); Edwards, Legal Requirements that Building Contractors Be Licensed, 12 Law & Contemp. Prob. 76, 77, 81 (1947); Clark, Monopolistic Tendencies, Their Character and Consequences, 18 Proceedings Acad. Pol. Sci. 124, 127 (1939).

[5] United States v. Hutcheson, 312 U.S. 219 (1941); Milk Wagon Drivers' Union v. Lake Valley Farm Products, Inc., 311 U.S. 91 (1940). A different rule may obtain if the labor union combines with one or more employers to restrict markets. Allen Bradley Co. v. Local Union No. 3, 325 U.S. 797 (1945). Compare Scoville, Revolution in Glass Making 219, 271, 303 (1948); Celler Committee I, ser. 14, pt. 4A, at 241. Federal legislation appears to apply to noncommercial organizations. American Medical Assn. v. United States, 317 U.S. 519 (1943). Query, however, if it would be applied universally to educational, religious and similar institutions.

[6] Terborgh, Capitalism and Innovation, 40 Proceedings Am. Econ. Assn. 118, 123 (1950); Noyes, The Prospect for Economic Growth, 37 id. 13 (1947); Edwards, Maintaining Competition 150 (1949); Celler Committee I, pt. 2B, at 1034, 1045; Jacoby, Anti-Trust Policy Re-examined, 58 J. Pol. Econ. 61 (1950); Slichter, The Conditions of Expansion, 32 Am. Econ. Rev. 1 (1942); Wright, Capitalism 193 (1951); Hoover, Capital Accumulation and Progress, 40 Proceedings Am. Econ. Assn. 124, 135 (1950); House Select Committee on Small Business, Review of Small Business, H.R. Rep. No. 2513, 82d Cong., 2d Sess. 106, 113, 119 (1952). Compare Aubert-Krier, Monopolistic and Imperfect Competition in Retail Trade, in Chamberlin, ed., Monopoly and Competition and Their Regulation 281, 285 (International Economic Assn. 1954); Goetz-Girey, Monopoly and Competition in France, id. at 21, 28; Johr,

compass any such vast territory as that covered by the foregoing statutes. Nor have we attempted, except for a brief recommendation by way of conclusion, to evaluate the general antimonopoly policy of the United States. There is a good deal to be said against competition, particularly in relationship to such topics as the business cycle,[7] but we have assumed that monopoly (or monopolization) is and will remain illegal.[8] Our task, therefore, is to define what is meant by "monopoly."

§1.3. **Pleading and practice.** This study deals with questions of substantive law and does not refer to the many procedural problems which arise in every antitrust case. For the most part, such matters of procedure are not unique to the law of monopoly: most of the questions of pleading, proof and practice are shared with many other branches of the law. Accordingly, the practitioner is referred to works on those topics. It is true, however, that several procedural questions arise with particular urgency in the antitrust field. One which has been much discussed relates to the mechanical problems of the "big case": in monopoly litigation the size of the record is often notoriously large and techniques for coping with its sheer bulk are undoubtedly necessary.[1] Likewise antitrust cases share with those in the public utility rate and some other fields serious problems of applying the ordinary rules of evidence to complicated situations.[2] One question, for example, is whether evidence of ancient acts is admissible to prove a conspiracy and, if so, under what conditions.[3] It is also true that there are specialized rules with respect to venue in antitrust proceedings.[4] Again, the practitioner must consider the closely allied

---

Regulation of Competition, id. at 338, 349, 351; Hansen, Economic Policy and Full Employment 133 (1947). Lintner and Butters, Effects of Taxes on Concentration, in Business Concentration and Price Policy 239 (Stigler ed. 1955).

[7] E.g., Rostow, Market Organization and Stabilization Policy, in Income Stabilization for a Developing Economy, c. 10 (Millikan ed. 1954); Boulding, In Defense of Monopoly, 59 Q.J. Econ. 524, 541 (1945).

[8] Evaluation of our antimonopoly policy would require comparison with conceivable alternatives such as interventionist regulation of prices and production. Such alternative programs raise large questions of both an economic and a political character. See, e.g., Hayek, The Road to Serfdom (1944); Stone, The Myths of Planning and Laissez Faire, 18 Geo. Wash. L. Rev. 1 (1949).

§1.3. [1] McAllister, The Big Case: Procedural Problems in Anti-Trust Litigation, 64 Harv. L. Rev. 27 (1950); A.B.A., Section of Antitrust Law, Committee on Practice and Procedure, Report (May 1, 1954).

[2] See, e.g., Dession, The Trial of Economic and Technological Issues of Fact, 58 Yale L.J. 1019, 1242 (1949).

[3] See, e.g., United States v. Pullman Co., 50 F. Supp. 123, 126 (E.D. Pa. 1943), aff'd per curiam, 330 U.S. 806 (1947); Chadwell, Pre-Trial, Proceedings A.B.A., Section of Antitrust Law, 52, 57 (Aug. 18, 1954); Day, Trial, id. at 65, 69.

[4] Venue in the federal courts is controlled by §§4 and 12 of the Clayton Act, 38 Stat. 731 (1914), 15 U.S.C.A. §§15, 22. The leading cases interpreting those sec-

doctrine of forum non conveniens.[5] We fully recognize the importance of both general and specialized questions of pleading and practice involved in all antitrust litigation. Our study, however, cannot encompass all those vital topics and only touches thereon at peripheral points.

§1.4. **A page of history.** Anglo-American law on the subject of monopolies can be traced back many centuries: even in Blackstone's day, treble damages could be recovered.[1] Both statutes and common law doctrines find their origins in the Elizabethan era.[2] Of greater interest today, however, are the statutes enacted in the United States after the middle of the nineteenth century. First, many states took action;[3] the federal government followed with the famous Sherman Act of 1890.[4] Doubts concerning the scope of federal power[5] rendered the latter legislation of little moment until 1911 when two large "trusts" were demolished under its impact.[6] In 1914 dissatisfaction with the administration

---

tions are Eastman Kodak Co. v. Southern Photo Materials Co., 273 U.S. 359 (1927), and United States v. Scophony Corp., 333 U.S. 795 (1948). Note the interesting quirk with respect to service of process. Id. at 809.

[5] Braucher, The Inconvenient Federal Forum, 60 Harv. L. Rev. 908 (1947); United States v. National City Lines, 334 U.S. 573, 580 (1948); United States v. National City Lines, 337 U.S. 78 (1949).

§1.4. [1] 4 Blackstone, Commentaries on the Laws of England* 159 (Cooley's 3d ed. 1884).

[2] Butchers' Union v. Crescent City Co., 111 U.S. 746, 761-762 (1884) (concurring opinion); Chicago, Wilmington & Vermillion Coal Co. v. People, 114 Ill. App. 75, 106 (1904), aff'd, 214 Ill. 421, 73 N.E. 770 (1905); Letwin, The English Common Law Concerning Monopolies, 21 U. Chi. L. Rev. 355 (1954); Adler, Monopolizing at Common Law and Under Section Two of the Sherman Act, 31 Harv. L. Rev. 246, 256 (1917); Dana, "Monopoly" Under the National Anti-Trust Act, 7 Harv. L. Rev. 338-339, 348 et seq. (1894).

[3] Martin, ed., State Anti-Trust Laws xlvii (WPA, 1940).

[4] Limbaugh, Historic Origins of Anti-Trust Legislation, 18 Mo. L. Rev. 215, 230 et seq. (1953); Stocking and Watkins, Monopoly and Free Enterprise, c. 9 (Twentieth Century Fund, 1951). Federal statute needed: (1) for interstate commerce, as to which no common law exists; and (2) for enforcement mechanisms. Letwin, Congress and the Sherman Antitrust Law, 23 U. Chi. L. Rev. 221 (1956); Thorelli, The Federal Antitrust Policy (1955); Letwin, The Origins of Antitrust Policy, 64 J. Pol. Econ. 156 et seq. (1956); Dewey, The Common Law Background of Antitrust Policy, 41 Va. L. Rev. 759 (1955) (history of law of restraint of trade in Great Britain and United States prior to legislation; takes somewhat different view than Letwin supra). A brief historical review of litigation against monopolies under the federal statute is found in Rostow, Monopoly Under the Sherman Act, 43 Ill. L. Rev. 745, 748 et seq. (1949).

[5] United States v. E. C. Knight Co., 156 U.S. 1 (1895).

[6] Standard Oil Co. of New Jersey v. United States, 221 U.S. 1 (1911); United States v. American Tobacco Co., 221 U.S. 106 (1911). Much of the early litigation under the federal legislation was concerned with the adoption and scope of the so-called "rule of reason" applicable to agreements among competitors. Handler, A Study of the Construction and Enforcement of the Federal Anti-Trust Laws 5 et seq. (TNEC Monograph No. 38, 1941).

of the basic federal statute led to additional congressional action.[7] Despite the enactment of the Clayton and Federal Trade Commission Acts, administration of the federal prohibition upon "monopolization" was not vigorous during the next two decades;[8] and in 1933 there intervened the NRA experiment which, in effect, relaxed federal legislation against monopolists.[9]

After the collapse of the NRA the federal government exhibited a considerably increased interest in the enforcement of the antitrust statutes. That interest was heightened by the extensive investigation by the Temporary National Economic Committee, which sat from 1938 until 1940, working in a climate of economic opinion hostile to big business.[10] In the litigation which followed (after the interruption of World War II) there was a tendency to apply the statutes stringently against many forms of business organization.[11] So far, indeed, did the courts go that [12] many observers found the decisions had taken on a protectionist hue.[13] In 1953, recognizing complaints concerning the administration of the statutes, the federal Attorney General appointed a committee to analyze the state of the law and to make recommendations with respect thereto. That committee's report, published in 1955,[14] represents a consensus of informed opinion with respect to the enforcement of the antitrust laws.

This study does not proceed upon an historical basis. We have

---

[7] Stocking and Watkins, Monopoly and Free Enterprise 351 (Twentieth Century Fund, 1951). The 1914 legislation is a half-step toward the public utility type of regulation.

[8] Id. at 274; United States v. United States Steel Corp., 251 U.S. 417 (1920). At the same time the courts were not inclined to be lenient in cases involving arrangements between independent business entities. See, e.g., American Column & Lumber Co. v. United States, 257 U.S. 377 (1921).

[9] Lyon, The National Recovery Administration 672 (1935); Roos, NRA Economic Planning 93, 343 (1937).

[10] TNEC, Final Rep. of Exec. Secy. The committee sponsored a series of important monographs, many of which are cited in this book. It also held extensive hearings, some portions of which are valuable in understanding the antitrust laws. The committee's Final Report and Recommendations was a distinct disappointment. After the end of World War II the Celler Committee held extensive hearings on the monopoly problem. There have, of course, been other congressional investigations and reports, some of which are referred to hereinafter.

[11] Stocking and Watkins, Monopoly and Free Enterprise 288 et seq. (Twentieth Century Fund, 1951).

[12] E.g., United States v. Griffith, 334 U.S. 100 (1948); United States v. New York Great Atlantic & Pacific Tea Co., 173 F.2d 79 (7th Cir. 1949).

[13] E.g., Griffin, An Economic Approach to Anti-Trust Problems 35 (American Enterprise Assn. 1951).

[14] Atty. Gen. Nat. Com. Rep. Judge Stanley N. Barnes, the Assistant Attorney General in charge of the Antitrust Division of the Department of Justice, and Professor S. Chesterfield Oppenheim of the University of Michigan were cochairmen of the committee. Many references to the work of that group will be found in this book.

believed, with Mr. Justice Holmes, that it is revolting to have no better reason for a rule of law than that so it was laid down in the time of Henry IV.[15] We have thought it preferable to proceed analytically and to attempt to shed such light as we could upon antitrust enforcement in that manner. True, history gives us a perspective on the flow of judicial decisions and may permit some useful speculation with respect to swings of the pendulum of opinion. We recognize also that it is "delusive to treat opinions written by different judges at different times as pieces of a jig-saw puzzle which can, by effort, be fitted correctly into a single pattern." [16] At the same time, we do not believe that a purely historical study would shed much light upon the rational administration of our antimonopoly statutes.[17]

§1.5. **Legislation and adjudication.** Our modern law of monopoly embraces an unusual combination of statute and judge-made law. In almost every jurisdiction monopoly (or monopolization) is illegal even in the absence of legislation. Thus in 1884, Mr. Justice Bradley was able to state:

> I hold it to be an incontrovertible proposition in both English and American public law that all *mere* monopolies are odious and against common right. The practice of granting them in the time of Elizabeth came near creating a revolution. . . .[1]

and a state court has declared:

15 Holmes, Collected Legal Papers 187 (1920). The Justice also said: "Most of the things we do, we do for no better reason than that our fathers have done them or that our neighbors do them, and the same is true of a larger part than we suspect of what we think. The reason is a good one, because our short life gives us no time for a better, but it is not the best . . ." Id. at 185.

16 Wyzanski, J., in United States v. United Shoe Machinery Corp., 110 F. Supp. 295, 342 (D. Mass. 1953). We have, to borrow a phrase, attempted to separate the "is" from the "ought," although on a different plane from that indicated by Pound, Scope and Purpose of Sociological Jurisprudence, 25 Harv. L. Rev. 489, 513 (1912). See Dorr, Philosophy of the Sherman Law, Proceedings A.B.A., Section on Antitrust Law, 14 (Aug. 22, 1955) (history of judicial opinion regarding Sherman Act, showing swings of pendulum).

17 But compare §1.9 infra. Another possibility may lie in the comparative approach to the problem of monopoly. Some of the papers collected in Chamberlin, ed., Monopoly and Competition and Their Regulation (International Economic Assn. 1954) afford a good starting point for investigation of the situation in Italy, France and other foreign states. Account should also be taken of the compilation in Friedmann, ed., Anti-Trust Laws: A Comparative Symposium (University of Toronto Faculty of Law Comparative Law Series, Vol. 3, 1956), outlining statutes and practice in ten foreign states. Another excellent study is found in Reynolds, The Control of Competition in Canada (1940). Differences in legal systems and economic conditions, however, would raise extraordinary difficulties in the path of one attempting such a comparative study.

§1.5. 1Concurring in Butchers' Union v. Crescent City Co., 111 U.S. 746, 761 (1884). Note the concurring opinion of Field, J., at 755-756. Note also the learned review of the early British and American authorities in Field, J., dissenting in the Slaughter-House Cases, 16 Wall. 36, 102 et seq. (U.S. 1872). Judge Taft's

Monopolies in their very nature are opposed to the genius and principles of a Republican form of government, and require neither express statutes nor constitutional prohibitions to make them illegal.[2]

In the absence of statute, however, the principal means for enforcing the common law's policy is merely to refuse enforcement of contracts in violation thereof.[3] Other remedies appearing desirable, most states of the Union adopted constitutional or statutory provisions with respect to the monopoly problem in the period following the War Between the States.[4] While state legislation has largely fallen into disuse,[5] the federal statutes of 1890 [6]

---

famous review of the common law authorities is found in his opinion in United States v. Addyston Pipe Co., 85 Fed. 271 (6th Cir. 1898), aff'd, 175 U.S. 211 (1899). See also Apex Hosiery Co. v. Leader, 310 U.S. 469, 497 (1940).

[2] Georgia Fruit Exchange v. Turnipseed, 9 Ala. App. 123, 62 So. 542, 545 (1913). Accord: City of Chicago v. Rumpff, 45 Ill. 90, 95 (1867); Bishop v. American Preservers' Co., 157 Ill. 284, 41 N.E. 765 (1895); Chicago, Wilmington & Vermillion Coal Co. v. People, 214 Ill. 421, 444, 73 N.E. 770, 777 (1905); State v. Nebraska Distilling Co., 29 Neb. 700, 46 N.W. 155, 161 (1890); Distilling & Cattle Feeding Co. v. People ex rel. Moloney, 156 Ill. 448, 41 N.E. 188 (1895); Adler, Monopolizing at Common Law, 31 Harv. L. Rev. 246 (1917) (legislation and adjudication of Sherman Act). In Central Ohio Salt Co. v. Guthrie, 35 Ohio St. 666 (1880), the court said at page 672: "Public policy unquestionably . . . is opposed to monopolies. . . . The clear tendency of such an agreement is to establish monopoly, and to destroy competition in trade, and for that reason, on grounds of public policy, courts will not aid in its enforcement."

In State v. Central of Georgia Railway, 109 Ga. 716, 35 S.E. 37 (1900), it was said at page 38: "The common law has always abhorred a monopoly, and has encouraged competition in all legitimate businesses of the people, whether followed by individuals or corporations." In some jurisdictions the prohibition extends only to monopolies of "necessities" as opposed to "luxuries." Foster v. Shubert Holding Co., 316 Mass. 470, 55 N.E.2d 772, 775 (1944).

[3] State v. Black, 5 N.J. Misc. 639, 138 Atl. 513, 514-515 (1927); Aetna Insurance Co. v. Commonwealth, 106 Ky. 864, 51 S.W. 624 (1899). There are, however, situations in which the common law affords a remedy other than mere refusal to enforce contracts. Such is the case, for example, when the acts of a monopolist constitute one of the recognized common law torts. 4 Restatement of Torts §759. In such situations, of course, damages may be recovered under the common law.

[4] Martin, ed., State Anti-Trust Laws (WPA, 1940). A current collection of such statutes is maintained in CCH Trade Reg. Rep. ¶¶10,000 et seq. (10th ed.). In Illinois, for example, Article IV, §22 of the Constitution provides that the General Assembly shall not pass any local or special law granting to any corporation or individual any special or exclusive privilege, immunity or franchise whatever. The basic statute of June 11, 1891, entitled "An Act to provide for the punishment of persons, co-partnerships or corporations forming pools, trusts and combines . . . ," prohibits combinations to affect the price of any article of merchandise or commodity. Laws 1891, p. 206, Ill. Rev. Stat., c. 38, §§569 et seq. Note also the special legislation applicable to "cornering" grain, stocks of railroad or other corporations, and gold. Id. §328. Compare Note, Illinois Anti-Trust Act Disinterred, 43 Ill. L. Rev. 205 (1948).

[5] Id. at 213; Nutting, The Texas Anti-Trust Law, 14 Texas L. Rev. 293, 300 (1936). Oblique evidence as to the enforcement of state statutes is provided by the opinion in Cleaning Assn. v. Sterling Cleaners, 285 Ill. App. 336, 2 N.E.2d 149 (1936).

[6] Act of July 2, 1890, 26 Stat. 209, 15 U.S.C.A. §§1 et seq. (commonly known as the Sherman Act).

and 1914 [7] have been widely applied. The basic monopoly provision is found in Section 2 of the Sherman Act, reading as follows:

> Every person who shall monopolize, or attempt to monopolize, or combine or conspire with any other person or persons, to monopolize any part of the trade or commerce among the several States, or with foreign nations, shall be deemed guilty of a misdemeanor . . .

Obviously, the language quoted is broad and ill-defined. Our federal Supreme Court itself has said with respect to the Sherman Act:

> As a charter of freedom, the Act has a generality and adaptability comparable to that found to be desirable in constitutional provisions. It does not go into detailed definitions which might either work injury to legitimate enterprise or through particularization defeat its purposes by providing loopholes for escape.[8]

Thus while judicial discretion, in the first instance, is relegated to a subordinate position by reason of the existence of legislation, it appears in the guise of interpretation and plays a prominent role in antitrust enforcement.[9] Indeed, so wide is the range of judicial discretion that there have been many complaints with respect to the vagueness of the statutes. Woodrow Wilson, for example, argued that business had suffered from the vagueness of the antitrust legislation. "Nothing hampers business like uncertainty . . . ," he said.[10] It is often argued that reduction of uncertainty can only be had at the expense of arbitrary (per se) rules.[11] Such rules would, no doubt, produce harsh and undesirable consequences in many of their applications. In part this study constitutes an attempt to find an underlying rationale for the law's attitude toward monopoly in the hope of reducing uncertainty: development of such a rationale might permit a predic-

---

[7] Act of Oct. 15, 1914, 38 Stat. 730, 15 U.S.C.A. §§12 et seq. (commonly known as the Clayton Act); Federal Trade Commission Act of Sept. 26, 1914, 38 Stat. 717, 15 U.S.C.A. §§41 et seq. There have been several amendments to the 1914 legislation, notably the Act of June 19, 1936 (Robinson-Patman), 49 Stat. 1526, 15 U.S.C.A. §13, amending §2 of the Clayton Act.

[8] Appalachian Coals, Inc. v. United States, 288 U.S. 344, 359 et seq. (1933).

[9] Johnston, Monopolize or Attempt to Monopolize, Proceedings A.B.A., Section of Antitrust Law 72 (Aug. 26, 1953). We shall not discuss the constitutionality of the legislation except to offer some comments upon its asserted want of due process by reason of its vagueness. See §11.3 infra and compare §1.7 infra.

[10] Address by President Wilson, 51 Cong. Rec. 1962, 1963 (1914). Accord: Pope, The Reason for the Continued Uncertainty of the Sherman Act, 7 Ill. L. Rev. 201 (1912); Young, Who Shall Administer the Anti-Trust Laws? 147 Annals 171 (1930); Jackson, Enforcement of Anti-Trust Laws, 3 Fed. B.A.J. 71, 128 (1937); O'Mahoney Committee I, pt. 4, 593, 595.

[11] Edwards, Public Policy and Business Size, 24 J. Business 280 (1951).

table application of the relevant statutes. Whether such a hope can be realized is, however, open to serious question.

§1.6. Federal jurisdiction. At one time the rival jurisdiction of state and federal authorities was hotly debated. In almost every case brought under the antitrust statutes that issue of jurisdiction was raised and contested, often to the higher courts. In the last decade, however, the problem has become far less important. Sweeping decisions of the federal Supreme Court have established the existence of national power over almost every aspect of economic life. In one decision it was held that the Congress might prohibit a farmer from planting a few bushels of wheat upon his own acres as chicken feed.[1] Shortly thereafter in an antitrust case the Court announced:

> . . . Congress wanted to go to the utmost extent of its Constitutional power in restraining trust and monopoly agreements such as the indictment here charges. . . . The purpose was to use that power to make of ours, so far as Congress could under our dual system, a competitive business economy.[2]

Probably the all-inclusive character of federal regulation is somewhat overstated in the foregoing quotation because the Court has subsequently found occasion to deal again with the scope of national power and to indicate that at least a few small transactions are beyond the reach of the Sherman Act.[3] We cannot here, however, attempt to delineate the precise scope of the federal power under the commerce clause of the United States Constitution. That question is largely one of constitutional law, extending far beyond the confines of antitrust.[4] Furthermore, state legislation

---

§1.6. [1] Wickard v. Filburn, 317 U.S. 111, 128-129 (1942), citing cases under the antitrust statutes.

[2] United States v. South-Eastern Underwriters Assn., 322 U.S. 533, 558-559 (1944). Compare Mandeville Island Farms, Inc. v. American Crystal Sugar Co., 334 U.S. 219, 234 et seq. (1948); Apex Hosiery Co. v. Leader, 310 U.S. 469, 485 (1940); United States v. Frankfort Distilleries Inc., 324 U.S. 293, 297-298 (1945).

[3] United States v. Yellow Cab Co., 332 U.S. 218, 230 et seq. (1947); Lorain Journal Co. v. United States, 342 U.S. 143, 146, 151-152 (1951); United States v. Employing Plasterers' Assn., 347 U.S. 186 (1954). In the last case it was said at page 189: "Under such circumstances it goes too far to say that the Government could not possibly produce enough evidence to show that these local restraints caused unreasonable burdens on the free and uninterrupted flow of plastering materials into Illinois. That wholly local business restraints can produce the effects condemned by the Sherman Act is no longer open to question. . . ." As to the sweep of federal power under the Clayton Act, consult Moore v. Mead's Fine Bread Co., 348 U.S. 115 (1954); Sawyer, The Commerce Scope of the Robinson-Patman Act, 38 Calif. L. Rev. 343, 345 (1950).

[4] Attention is invited to the sweeping views of federal power presented in 1 Crosskey, Politics and the Constitution 17 et seq. (1953); Berle, Banking under the Anti-Trust Laws, 49 Colum. L. Rev. 589, 596 (1949) (only safe course is to assume that all banking is subject to federal regulation under commerce clause).

is rarely utilized[5] and, to the extent it bears upon current problems, will probably be interpreted in the light of the more numerous federal decisions.[6] Procedural matters, including the vital subject of remedies, will continue to be influenced by the division of power between the nation and the states. Substantive questions, however, are likely to be resolved without reference to the jurisdictional issue.[7]

Many interesting and difficult questions arise out of attempts to apply the antitrust laws to foreign nationals and transactions abroad. For the most part, however, those questions involve possible restraints of trade rather than monopolies; further, they are heavily weighted with jurisdictional and kindred problems. Accordingly, we have not here attempted to deal with the international aspects of antitrust enforcement.[8]

§1.7. **Relationship of the several antitrust statutes.** As indicated above, our primary concern is with the interpretation of Section 2 of the Sherman Act and comparable state legislation. The inquiry, however, must touch upon other portions of the antitrust statutes. In the first place, we must be cognizant of Section 1 of the Sherman Act, which prohibits every contract, combination or conspiracy in restraint of trade. Such statutes,[1] aimed at combinations among business rivals, are intimately related to the monopoly problem: putting the matter another way, the difference between monopoly and restraint of trade may depend upon our conception of legal and economic entities in modern enterprise. Account must also be taken of more specific legislation, particularly the federal Clayton Act, which prohibits

5 Note, Illinois Anti-Trust Act Disinterred, 43 Ill. L. Rev. 205, 219, 222 (1948). Examination of the reports of the Attorney General of Illinois for the years 1936 through 1942 revealed no mention of the state antitrust law. There is, however, some occasional activity in the states. See, e.g., N.Y. Atty. Gen. Ann. Rep. 81 (Dec. 31, 1942). A valuable survey of the antitrust law of New York, together with a compilation of activity in other states, will be found in Handler (chairman), Committee to Study New York Antitrust Laws of New York State Bar Association, Report (1957).

6 Moody & Waters Co. v. Case-Moody Pie Corp., 354 Ill. 82, 92, 187 N.E. 813, 818 (1933).

7 In this book we have attempted to record state as well as federal decisions bearing upon the monopoly issue. State statutes, however, vary from one jurisdiction to another. As indicated in the text, the law has largely developed under federal auspices and it is entirely possible that decisions in one or more of the forty-eight states have escaped our attention. For such reasons, the practitioner whose problem is controlled by state law should carefully check the statutes of that jurisdiction and the decisions thereunder. As indicated above, we take no account of the law outside the United States of America.

8 Another volume in this series deals with the subject referred to in the text: Fugate, Foreign Commerce and the Antitrust Laws (1958). Our own analysis is presented in Monopoly Abroad, 31 Texas L. Rev. 493 (1953).

§1.7. 1 Prohibitions similar to those of §1 of the Sherman Act are frequently found in state legislation. Note also the prohibition against conspiracies to monopolize found in §2 of the Sherman Act itself.

several trade practices.[2] We cannot pause to consider the interpretation of that supplementary legislation since each section thereof is encrusted with a heavy annotation of judicial review.[3] We must, however, take account of the statutes as indicative of legislative purpose and as casting light upon the proper interpretation of the more sweeping prohibitions against monopoly or monopolization.

§1.8. **The contribution of the economists.** Lawyers and judges can ignore the work of economists so long as — and just so long as — they are willing to endure the embarrassment which may result from their ignorance of economic theory.[1] The truth of the matter is that the law of monopoly has always dealt with economic matters; lawyers and judges have been talking economics for centuries without realizing it.[2] No doubt Mr. Justice Holmes had that fact in mind when he wrote:

[2] Sections 2, 3, 7 and 8 of the Clayton Act (15 U.S.C.A. §§13, 14, 18, 19) deal with price discrimination, exclusive arrangements, mergers and interlocking directorates. Several states have enacted similar measures. Account must also be taken of §5 of the Federal Trade Commission Act (15 U.S.C.A. §45), prohibiting unfair methods of competition and unfair or deceptive acts or practices. For the most part that statute has been applied against misrepresentations and other market "imperfections." Henderson, The Federal Trade Commission 339 (1925); Blaisdell, The Federal Trade Commission 308 (1932). It is, however, well established that all acts and practices violating the Sherman Act also constitute violations of §5 of the Federal Trade Commission Act. FTC v. Cement Institute, 333 U.S. 683, 691, 694 (1948); FTC v. Motion Picture Advertising Service, Inc., 344 U.S. 392, 395 (1953); Times-Picayune Publishing Co. v. United States, 345 U.S. 594, 609 (1953). On the other hand, violations of §5 of the Federal Trade Commission Act do not necessarily constitute infringements of the Sherman Act. It is often said that the Federal Trade Commission Act was designed to stop practices "in their incipiency" which, when full blown, would violate the other antitrust laws. FTC v. Motion Picture Advertising Service, Inc., *supra*, at 394-395; Oppenheim, ed., Lectures on Federal Antitrust Laws 164 (University of Michigan, 1953). This so-called "incipiency doctrine," if meaningful at all, can be used to differentiate the statutes in order to prevent redundancy. In any event, the old rule that the Federal Trade Commission Act was limited to practices characterized by deception, bad faith, fraud or oppression has probably been repudiated. FTC v. Gratz, 253 U.S. 421, 427-428 (1920).

[3] Both books of official reports and legal periodicals, for example, are choked with discussion of the Robinson-Patman Act, which superseded §2 of the Clayton Act. E.g., Rowe, Price Discrimination, Competition and Confusion, 60 Yale L.J. 929 (1951).

§1.8. [1] The classic example of the hazards of ignoring the economists is found in the opinion in United States v. New York Great Atlantic & Pacific Tea Co., 173 F.2d 79 (7th Cir. 1949). Compare Adelman, The A & P Case: A Study in Applied Economic Theory, 63 Q.J. Econ. 238 (1949). On the relationship between economic theory and the actual workings of the economic system, see §1.11 *infra*. Compare Moulton, Controlling Factors in Economic Development (Brookings Institution, 1949).

[2] Molière, Le Bourgeois Gentilhomme, act II, scene iv (1670):

M. JOURDAIN. Par ma foi! il y a plus de quarante ans que je dis de la prose sans que j'en susse rien, et je suis le plus obligé du mond de m'avoir appris cela.

I look forward to a time when the part played by history in the explanation of dogma shall be very small, and instead of ingenious research we shall spend our energy on a study of the ends sought to be attained and the reasons for desiring them. As a step toward that ideal it seems to me that every lawyer ought to seek an understanding of economics.[3]

About half a century after Mr. Justice Holmes so expressed himself, the courts began to take formal cognizance of economic theory in antitrust decisions;[4] today only the careless practitioner will hazard his reputation in an antitrust case without acquaintance with the relevant economic theory. For the economists have thought long and hard about monopoly. Often their contributions consist of little more than refinements of language; to speak precisely, however, is, in the phrase of a famous teacher of law,[5] to "make a noise like a lawyer," and a primary purpose of this volume is to introduce practitioners to the outlines of economic thinking about monopoly.

Lawyers should observe carefully some of the fundamental distinctions drawn by the economists. They divide impediments to an efficient allocation of resources into two broad categories of "impurities" and "imperfections." The "impurities" are the monopoly elements, public or private, which prevent the attainment of "pure" competition. "Imperfections" are other obstacles to the "perfect" deployment of labor and materials. They are found in ignorance, indivisibility, inertia and immobility.[6] Ignorance, for example, upon the part of the consumers, producers or investors, hinders the flow of resources into channels where they might be more productive.[7] Indivisibility (economies of scale)[8] is closely

---

[3] Holmes, Collected Legal Papers 195 (1920). Note also his dissent in Vegelahn v. Guntner, 167 Mass. 892, 44 N.E. 1077, 1080 (1896), wherein he said: "Propositions as to public policy rarely are unanimously accepted, and still more rarely, if ever, are capable of unanswerable proof. They require a special training to enable any one even to form an intelligent opinion about them." Lawyers seeking to follow the analysis of the economists should equip themselves with some volume such as Crum and Schumpeter, Rudimentary Mathematics for Economists and Statisticians (1946).

[4] Times-Picayune Publishing Co. v. United States, 345 U.S. 594, 612 n.31 (1953); United States v. E. I. Du Pont de Nemours & Co., 118 F. Supp. 41, 49 (D. Del. 1953), aff'd, 351 U.S. 377, 380, 392, 394 (1956).

[5] Professor Austin W. Scott.

[6] Thus in Machlup, The Political Economy of Monopoly 19 (1952) it was said: "Perfect competition requires that everybody is free to move unlimited amounts of productive resources into any field that looks promising to him, and that there are no man-made obstacles to the movement of factors of production into and out of particular employment." See also Machlup, The Economics of Sellers' Competition 119 et seq., 221n (1952); Abramovitz, An Approach to Price Theory for a Changing Economy 24 (1939). See Appendix A infra.

[7] Lyon, The National Recovery Administration 678 et seq. (Brookings Institution, 1935); Svennilson, Monopoly, Efficiency and the Structure of Industry, in Chamberlin, ed., Monopoly and Competition and Their Regulation 271, 279 (International

connected with ease of entry, an important concept in the economics of monopoly. Occasions may thus arise in which removal of the imperfections becomes more important than reduction of the impurities.[9] Economists lay much stress, too, upon distinguishing "short-run" periods of time from those involving the "long term." They emphasize the slope of the demand curve and the shape of the cost curves. Fundamental, too, is the distinction between dynamic and static analysis of economic phenomenon.[10] There is, however, no ultimate magic in economic theory. Eventually the rails run out in sand drifts[11] and before we reach the end of the track we find that many competing considerations[12] prevent the lawyer from placing complete reliance upon the teachings of the economist.[13]

Economic Assn. 1954). But compare Abramovitz, Monopolistic Selling in a Changing Economy, 52 Q.J. Econ. 191, 212 (1938). Much of our legal structure, particularly that in the field of commercial law, is intimately related to such imperfections. Goods can only be sold, for example, if the law will enforce contracts with respect thereto.

8 The difficulty, of course, is to find the level of output at which economies of scale are fully realized. Economists usually conceive of costs as a U-shaped curve which declines with increasing output until capacity is fully utilized and then rises as diminishing returns set in. The reality of diminishing returns is vividly illustrated by the alleged fact that the International Harvester Company produced steel for sixteen cents a ton less than the United States Steel Corporation, which, of course, has far larger steel-making capacity. O'Mahoney Committee I, pt. 4, at 519.

9 The problem is not confined to the antitrust laws. See, e.g., Pacific States Basket Co. v. White, 296 U.S. 176 (1935). Note also that the issuance of patents is conditioned upon the disclosure of processes which might otherwise remain secret. Machlup, The Political Economy of Monopoly 281 (1952). Note also the following statement by a leading economist: ". . . there are many reasons why a customer buys from one producer rather than another besides the simple one of a difference in prices which they charge, and since the rival producers make it their business to exploit all these influences upon the customer's choice, the very existence of competition, in the plain sense of the word, insures that the market will not be perfect." Robinson, The Economics of Imperfect Competition 90 (1933).

10 See Appendix B. Compare, Steindl, Maturity and Stagnation in American Capitalism 52 (Oxford University Institute of Statistics Monograph No. 4, 1952). More fundamentally, all economic problems arise as a consequence of change. Hayek, Individualism and Economic Order 82 (1948).

11 Edwards, Issues in the Monopoly Problem, in Chamberlin, ed., Monopoly and Competition and Their Regulation 188 (International Economic Assn. 1954).

12 Among the competing considerations are the requirements of due process of law guaranteed by state and federal constitutions: lawyers cannot assume facts to exist, they must plead and prove matters which economists are privileged to postulate. In economic theory, for example, it is permissible to assume that the most efficient size of steel mill is one which will produce x tons of steel per day. To prove that assumption as a fact might well raise insuperable problems.

13 In United States v. Richfield Oil Corp., 99 F. Supp. 280 (S.D. Cal. 1951), aff'd per curiam, 343 U.S. 922 (1952), it was said at page 287: "Economic considerations are relevant in determining legislative policy. They may be important in interpreting the limit of that policy. They do not constitute an excuse for the violation of the legislative policy declared in a statute." We do not think that the foregoing statement means that the teachings of the economists are to be disregarded. For it

§1.9. **Other social sciences.** Economists claim to be rational and lawyers assert that they are practical. That there should be a gulf between rationality and practicality is attributable in part to the fact that lawyers must take account of factors lying outside the economists' sphere. As indicated above, the law cannot simply parrot the teachings of economic theory because it is also strictly bounded by considerations derived from other social sciences.[1] Political science[2] and sociology[3] are perhaps the most obvious other categories of formal learning applicable to antitrust proceedings. Unfortunately, scholars in those disciplines do not yet appear to have addressed themselves to a detailed study of the monopoly problem. When the law has fully assimilated the teachings of the economists, however, it will be desirable to turn for additional guidance to the political scientist and the sociologist.

§1.10. **Ethical concepts.** Law cannot rest solely upon scientific foundations. Experience indicates that both legislation and adjudication depend heavily upon concepts of "fairness."[1] It is easy to argue that such ethical concepts are deeply flavored with emotional content and so vague as to be easily warped into the mold of political expediency. Partisan enforcement of the laws, based on the voting strength of pressure blocks, is far from unknown in the antitrust field.[2] Nevertheless, philosophers, moralists, theologians and others concerned with man's spiritual welfare

---

is through study of economic theory — and in some instances only through such study — that we can determine whether there has been a violation of rational legislative policy.

§1.9. [1] United States v. Aluminum Co. of America, 148 F.2d 416, 427 (2d Cir. 1945).

[2] Political science is not, of course, to be confused with "politics" in the partisan sense. There has been an abundance of the latter commodity in the administration of the antitrust laws, and one of our chief objectives is to reduce the vagueness now afflicting the statutes and hence to curb the demagoguery with which we have been so surfeited. When we speak of "political science" we are thinking of such factors as the ability of business managers to take over functions of controlling others which might well be exercised by government. Compare Hale, Agreements Among Competitors, 33 Minn. L. Rev. 331, 386-387 (1949).

[3] The libraries, of course, are full of books containing loose, emotional tirades on the subject of monopoly. Consider, for example, the following statement by a trained economist who should have known better: "Feudalism is the power of wealth to rob the business world. . . . Feudalism devours capitalism by seizing markets through the power of money and predatory business practices, destroys free enterprise, and takes tribute at every corner." O'Mahoney Committee I, pt. 4, at 524. What little we have been able to learn on this subject from the sociological point of view is recorded in Chapter 8, dealing with wealth.

§1.10. [1] Dirlam and Kahn, Fair Competition 14 (1954).

[2] Griffin, An Economic Approach to Anti-Trust Problems 47 (American Enterprise Assn. 1951). The importance of economics to a study of the law of monopoly is largely derived from the fact that it indicates the cost of ethical concepts and sociological ideals. In other words, it tells us when consumers are being compelled to subsidize various classes of producers.

could no doubt offer constructive suggestions with respect to the interpretation of our antimonopoly policy. Unfortunately, important contributions in this field of law do not yet appear to have emanated from such sources.[3]

§1.11. **Empirical investigation.** In a field of the law characterized by so much unsupported assertion, no apology is required for extensive documentation of the propositions submitted. Indeed, the subject is so controversial that it has seemed desirable to search hard for factual checks upon the legal theories advanced. To that end the authors have read through thousands of pages of congressional hearings, examined dozens of business histories, scanned hundreds of corporate reports and digested a multitude of articles in business, investment and trade journals.[1] Unfortunately, time and facilities have not been available for quantitative studies of business behavior. In fact, were unlimited resources at hand, it would be difficult to organize statistical studies to which exception could not be taken.[2] The empirical investigation recorded in this volume is therefore of a purely qualitative character.[3] Its value is obviously less than that of quantitative analysis. Perhaps, however, it may create a presumption as to the operations of our economic system which can be taken as correct until disproven. Furthermore, it may provide a starting point for that more careful combing of the facts which future research should emphasize.

[3] Some theological thought is collected in Glover, The Attack on Big Business (1954). Professor Wilber G. Katz of the University of Chicago is leading an interesting movement looking toward the linking of law and theology. Katz, Natural Law and Human Nature, 3 U. Chi. L. Rec. No. 3, 1 (1954); Katz, Law, Christianity and the University, 40 The Christian Scholar 164 (1957). Note also the other articles in the same issue of The Christian Scholar. In 1949 the Federal Council of the Churches of Christ in America, supported by the Rockefeller Foundation, commenced a series of studies on ethics and economic life. The studies were conducted under the general supervision of Charles P. Taft, chairman of the Council's Department of the Church and Economic Life. Several volumes embodying the studies to date have been published (under the auspices of the National Council of the Churches of Christ in the United States of America, into which the Federal Council merged) and more are in preparation. Some of those studies are cited in this volume. The series promises an auspicious start in the investigation of problems mentioned in the text.

§1.11. [1] Antitrust litigation itself generates a tremendous amount of information concerning the actual operation of our economy. See, e.g., United States v. Aluminum Co. of America, 44 F. Supp. 97 (S.D.N.Y. 1941), rev'd, 148 F.2d 416 (2d Cir. 1945).

[2] The basic difficulty is that cause and effect cannot be isolated and identified: so many factors affect the functioning of markets that we can never be sure which one produces a particular result. Another difficulty is that we have not yet developed techniques for measuring some of the most important concepts developed by the economists (e.g. demand).

[3] Compare the techniques employed in Note, Functional Discounts Under the Robinson-Patman Act, 67 Harv. L. Rev. 294 (1953).

CHAPTER 2

Horizontal Size: The Abuse Theory

§2.1. The meaning of horizontal size. By "horizontal size" we mean the proportion of a specific commodity or service supplied (or procured) by a single firm. Other phrases are often used to describe the same phenomena. It is, for example, common to speak of "concentration" within an "industry." Horizontal size is the common garden form of monopoly both to the lawyer and to the economist.[1] It is easily distinguished from "vertical integration," in which a firm enlarges its operations to include more successive steps in the production or marketing of a commodity or service. Different, too, is "diversification," wherein an enterprise enters upon the production of new and different products. We may also differentiate the case of "dispersion," in which the firm enlarges the geographical scope of its activity and enters new markets.[2] Today two legal tests for the existence of objectionable monopoly are commonly used.[3] One is the "abuse" theory, which emphasizes the conduct of the firm in question. The other is the "structure" theory, which finds illegality in the mere existence of a firm whose horizontal size is great. In that connection, however, we should carefully distinguish "horizontal size" from "wealth." Frequently the courts say that mere size is not an offense; or, that mere size, while not outlawed by the Sherman Act, is

§2.1. [1] E.g., FTC, The Present Trend of Corporate Mergers and Acquisitions 11 (1947); Thorp and Crowder, The Structure of Industry 163 (TNEC Monograph No. 27, 1941).

[2] The various "shapes" mentioned in the text are discussed in Chapters 5, 6 and 7. In any one antitrust suit, however, both horizontal size and "shape" may become relevant. E.g., United States v. Columbia Steel Co., 334 U.S. 495 (1948).

[3] There may be a third and possibly obsolete test for the existence of monopoly. That third test might be related to the concept of a governmental grant or patent excluding all but a single firm from a given area. Consider, for example, the following language in United Shoe Machinery Co. v. La Chapelle, 212 Mass. 467, 99 N.E. 289, 291 (1912): "The earlier conception of a monopoly was a grant of an exclusive right from the sovereign power. This still defines with accuracy that which an inventor receives under the patent laws. But in a wider sense monopoly denotes a combination, organization or entity so extensive, exclusive and unified, that its tendency is to prevent competition in its comprehensive sense with the consequent power to control prices to the public harm."

an earmark of monopoly power.[4] Such statements almost invariably refer to horizontal size and not to that pure size embodied in the term "wealth." An investment trust, for example, may be wealthy in that its total assets are large in terms of dollars. Unless its investments are concentrated in some one industry, however, it is unlikely that the investment trust will achieve much horizontal size. When we speak of horizontal size and the abuse or structure tests of its legality, we refer to a single firm (e.g., the Aluminum Company of America) producing a single commodity (e.g., aluminum ingot) within a defined geographic area. This is, as indicated above, the common concept of monopoly and thus deserves our first attention.

§2.2. **Extent of concentration.** Some empirical evidence exists on a quantitative basis with respect to the "concentration" problem. We are, of course, here concerned only with concentration in terms of horizontal size and not with those statistics which tend to show that the wealth of the nation is concentrated in the hands of a few persons or corporations.[1] Studies of horizontal size have indicated a startling condition of oligopoly (few sellers) in many industries. Thus Thorp and Crowder found that about half the products they analyzed were manufactured under conditions wherein the four largest producers controlled 75 per cent of the supply.[2] A famous catalog of "concentration" prepared by Professor Wilcox listed industry after industry dominated by one, two, three or four firms.[3] Observers who fail to find universal concentration in manufacturing or other broad categories nevertheless have taken the position that specific industries were sharply af-

[4] United States v. United States Steel Corp., 251 U.S. 417, 451 (1920); United States v. Griffith, 334 U.S. 100, 107n (1948). Consider also the following statement made by an Assistant Attorney General of the United States in charge of the Antitrust Division of the Department of Justice: "Do not misunderstand me. I am not condemning bigness as such. We have never attacked bigness as such and our enforcement program does not contemplate such an attack . . ." Celler Committee I, pt. 1, at 364.

§2.2. [1] See Chapter 8.
[2] The Structure of Industry 408, 412 (TNEC Monograph No. 27, 1941); see also Houghton, The Growth of Big Business, 38 Proceedings Am. Econ. Assn. 72, 80 (1948).
[3] Wilcox, Competition and Monopoly in American Industry 65 et seq. (TNEC Monograph No. 21, 1940). Federal Trade Commission figures are presented in Celler Committee I, pt. 1, at 563 et seq. Such findings have been given wide publicity in college texts and other publications, e.g., Purdy, Lindahl and Carter, Corporate Concentration and Public Policy 467 (1942). Such statistical findings are at least emotionally connected with relatively new economic theories relating to "monopolistic competition." Galbraith, Monopoly and the Concentration of Economic Power, in Ellis, ed., A Survey of Contemporary Economics 99, 106-107 (American Economic Assn. 1949). Compare E. B. Muller & Co. v. FTC, 142 F.2d 511, 514, 518 (6th Cir. 1944).

fected.[4]   Other observers have reached different results.   They have found fault with the methods of computation employed by Thorp and Crowder and others.   In particular, they have objected to the product classification and to a tendency to disregard the spatial limits of market areas.[5]   Professor Wilcox, whose pre-war study has often been cited as evidence of high concentration in the economy, subsequently took a wholly different stand on the question.   Statements that oligopoly was characteristic of the economy as a whole, he declared, were founded upon studies which did not afford a basis for definite conclusions on that subject.   His own conclusion was wholly different: "It may safely be concluded that oligopoly is not, by all evidence, the ruling market form in the modern economy and that it does not, in fact, comprehend the great majority of actual cases." [6]

§2.3.   **Observations on the trend of concentration.**   One might expect that statistics with respect to the extent of concentration at any particular time would be open to technical objection, and at the same time believe it possible to measure the trend in such figures.   Compare, for example, our view of corporate balance sheets: we admit that the balance sheet in and of itself does not, as of the end of any specific year, tell an investor much about the business it purports to describe; at the same time, we can believe that study of a series of annual balance sheets will indicate important trends.   Similarly, the literature with respect to oligopoly contains many allegations of a trend away from competition.[1]   Perhaps it is significant that such statements are often found in publications prepared by governmental agencies.[2]   From time to

---

4 E.g., Edwards, Four Comments, 34 Rev. Econ. & Stat. 156, 158 (1952).

5 Stigler, The Extent and Bases of Monopoly, 32 Am. Econ. Rev. Sup. No. 2, pp. 1, 6 (1942); Wilcox, On the Alleged Ubiquity of Oligopoly, 40 Proceedings Am. Econ. Assn. 67, 68-69, 72 (1950); Mund, Book Review, 40 Am. Econ. Rev. 454, 456 (1950); Adelman, Measurement of Industrial Concentration, 33 Rev. Econ. & Stat. 269 (1951); Adelman, Rejoinder, 34 id. 174 (1952); Hoover, Institutional and Theoretical Implications of Economic Change, 44 Am. Econ. Rev. 1, 6 (1954).   But compare George, The Measurement of Industrial Concentration, 34 Rev. Econ. & Stat. 168 (1952); Edwards, Comment, id. at 156; Blair, The Measurement of Industrial Concentration, id. at 343.   Note the interesting comparison in Rosenbluth, Industrial Concentration in Canada and the United States, 20 Can. J. Econ. & Pol. Sci. 332, 336 (1954).

6 Wilcox, On the Alleged Ubiquity of Oligopoly, 40 Proceedings Am. Econ. Assn. 67, 73 (1950).   Compare Bernheim, ed., Big Business: Its Growth and Place 98-99 (Twentieth Century Fund, 1937).

§2.3.   1 Veblen, Absentee Ownership 77 (1923); Faulkner, The Decline of Laissez Faire 172 (1951).

2 E.g., Smaller War Plants Corporation, Economic Concentration and World War II, Sen. Doc. No. 206, 79th Cong., 2d Sess. 6, 11, 20, 25 (1946); House Select Committee on Small Business, Subcommittee on Monopoly, United States v. Economic Concentration and Monopoly, 79th Cong. vii (1947); House Committee on the

time, there have been particularly positive assertions with respect to the so-called "merger movement," the theme of which is that big business is gobbling up all the small firms.[3]   Again, however, other observers have called attention to technical defects in the statistics upon which such claims are based.[4]   Many have found that there is no compelling evidence of increasing monopoly power, pointing to the general growth of the economy, changes in transportation, marketing, and an increase in the number of commodities as affecting the problem.[5]   One of the most competent studies suggests that mergers have been more important among small than large concerns.[6]   Furthermore, there is respectable data indicating that concentration is on the decline.   A recent and careful study, for example, suggests that smaller corporations, taken as a whole, probably improved their relative position in the economy between 1929 and 1948.[7]   In that connection attention has been invited to improvements in communication and transportation with resultant breakdown of local barriers which formerly insulated many sellers.[8]   Some studies of specific industries have reached similar results[9] and the over-all figures suggest that small business continues to exist and even prospers.[10]

Judiciary, Subcommittee No. 5, Bank Mergers and Concentration of Banking Facilities, 82d Cong., 2d Sess. 29 et seq. (1952); N.Y. Times, Feb. 6, 1945, p. 24, col. 3.

[3] FTC, The Present Trend of Corporate Mergers and Acquisitions 9 (1947); Faulkner, The Decline of Laissez Faire 153 (1951); Blair, The Measurement of Industrial Concentration, 34 Rev. Econ. & Stat. 343, 352 (1952).

[4] Lintner and Butters, Effect of Mergers on Industrial Concentration, 32 id. 30, 33 (1950); Adelman, Measurement of Industrial Concentration, 33 id. 269, 295 (1951); Jacoby, Anti-Trust Policy Re-examined, 58 J. Pol. Econ. 61, 65 (1950); Adelman, Rejoinder, 34 Rev. Econ. & Stat. 356 (1952); Adelman, Federal Trade Commission Report on Changes in Concentration in Manufacturing, 50 J. Am. Stat. Assn. 660-664 (1955).

[5] Mason, Methods of Developing a Proper Control of Big Business, 18 Proceedings Acad. Pol. Sci. 162, 169-170 (1939); Wallace, Industrial Markets and Public Policy, in Public Policy 59, 73 (Friedrich and Mason ed. 1940); Mason, Economic Concentration and the Monopoly Problem 23 et seq. (1957).

[6] Lintner and Butters, Effect of Mergers on Industrial Concentration, 32 Rev. Econ. & Stat. 30, 48 (1950). Compare Stocking, Comment, 34 id. 161 (1952); Lintner and Butters, Further Rejoinder, id. at 364.

[7] Kaplan, Big Enterprise in a Competitive System 124 (Brookings Institution, 1954); see also Patinkin, Multiple-Plant Firms, Cartels and Imperfect Competition, 61 Q.J. Econ. 173, 201 (1947). Compare Schumpeter, Capitalism, Socialism and Democracy 81 (3d ed. 1950); TNEC Hearings, pt. 1, at 88; Stigler, The Statistics of Monopoly and Merger, 64 J. Pol. Econ. 33, 35-37 (1956); Prais, The Financial Experience of Giant Companies, 67 Econ. J. 249, 262 (1957).

[8] Machlup, The Economics of Sellers' Competition 203-204 (1952); Celler Committee I, pt. 2B, at 814.

[9] Markham, Competition in the Rayon Industry 48 (1952); Adelman, Measurement of Industrial Concentration, 33 Rev. Econ. & Stat. 269, 293 (1951).

[10] Kaplan, Small Business: Its Place and Problems 53, 74 (Committee for Economic Development, 1948); Adams, Is Bigness Bad? 13 (Republic Steel Corp. 1950). Attempts have also been made to measure the trend in price rigidity, a matter

§2.4.   **Self-correction in the economy.**   In the preceding sections, we have referred to quantitative studies both of the economy as a whole and of specific industries.   There is also evidence of a qualitative character, gathered on a slightly different plane, indicating that strong forces within the economy operate to correct monopoly situations.   Under both static[1] and dynamic[2] theories of competition, there is ample room for market forces to correct whatever "impurities" may arise.   Empirical evidence supports both the static and dynamic views on that subject.[3]   Perhaps most vivid is the effect of "creative destruction," the process whereby new products displace old-fashioned commodities and methods.[4]

---

which is, of course, closely related to the concentration problem. Careful observers find no evidence of increasing inflexibility.   Mason, Price Inflexibility, 20 Rev. Econ. & Stat. 53, 55, 59 (1938); Humphrey, The Nature and Meaning of Rigid Prices, 45 J. Pol. Econ. 651, 658 (1937).

§2.4. [1] Simons, Economic Policy for a Free Society 87 (1948); Wilcox, Competition and Monopoly in American Industry 315 (TNEC Monograph No. 21, 1940); Celler Committee I, pt. 2A, at 539. But compare Robinson, Imperfect Competition Re-visited, 63 Econ. J. 579, 592 (1953).

[2] Schumpeter, Capitalism, Socialism and Democracy 99 (3d ed. 1950); Hildebrand, Monopolization and the Decline of Investment Opportunities, 33 Am. Econ. Rev. 591, 592 (1943); Mason, Schumpeter on Monopoly and the Large Firm, in Schumpeter: Social Scientist 89, 93 (Harris ed. 1951); Chamberlin, The Impact of Recent Monopoly Theory on the Schumpeterian System, id. at 83. Perhaps Browning had some vision of Schumpeter's "creative destruction" when he wrote:

There are flashes struck from midnights,
There are fire-flames noondays kindle,
Whereby piled-up honors perish,
Whereby swollen ambitions dwindle. . . .
                    Cristina IV (1842)

[3] United States v. American Can Co., 230 Fed. 859, 879-880, 234 Fed. 1019 (D. Md. 1916), *appeal dismissed,* 256 U.S. 706 (1921); United States v. American Can Co., 87 F. Supp. 18, 23 (N.D. Cal. 1949); United States v. Aluminum Co. of America, 44 F. Supp. 97, 183 (S.D.N.Y. 1941), *rev'd,* 148 F.2d 416 (2d Cir. 1945), 91 F. Supp. 333, 364, 394, 398 (S.D.N.Y. 1950); Abbott Laboratories, Inc., Ann. Rep. 1949, 2, 4, 8 (North Chicago, 1950); Parke, Davis & Co., 86th Ann. Rep. 3-4 (Detroit, 1953); Argus Research Corp., Ethical Drug Industry (1952); Six in the Money, 40 Fortune No. 2, pp. 68, 72 (1949); Celluloid Corporation, 8 id. No. 4, pp. 144, 145 (1933); Dry Ice, 6 id. No. 1, pp. 74, 78 (1932); 1 Nevins, Study in Power 15, 195 (1953); Wilcox, Competition and Monopoly in American Industry 309 (TNEC Monograph No. 21, 1940); Bernheim, ed., Big Business: Its Growth and Place 101-102 (Twentieth Century Fund, 1937); Nicholls, Some Economic Aspects of the Margarine Industry, 54 J. Pol. Econ. 221, 233-234 (1946); Patinkin, Multiple-Plant Firms, Cartels and Imperfect Competition, 61 Q.J. Econ. 173, 201 (1947); Scoville, Revolution in Glassmaking 219 et seq. (1948); U.S. Rubber, 9 Fortune No. 2, pp. 52, 54 (1934); American Ice, 7 id. No. 5, pp. 73, 75 (1933); Bicycles, 8 id. No. 3, pp. 49, 51 (1933); Bright and Maclaurin, Economic Factors Influencing the Development and Introduction of the Fluorescent Lamp, 51 J. Pol. Econ. 429, 431 (1943); Gillette Review, 4 Fortune No. 4, pp. 46, 147 (1931); Durrance, Spark in Brimstone, 35 Barron's No. 10, p. 3 (1955); Corporate Management, 7 Fortune No. 6, p. 47 (1933).

[4] Some of the effects of "creative destruction" upon established concerns are recorded in Appendix B, page 455.

§2.5. **Conclusions with respect to concentration.** As pointed out above, the quantitative studies are not conclusive with respect to the present state of concentration. Neither do they indicate a trend toward or away from monopolistic conditions in the United States during the last century. Techniques of measurement, particularly with reference to the definition of commodities and of geographic markets,[1] have proven inadequate. Even if we could overcome such difficulties, we still probably would not know to what extent the concentration shown was caused by factors of indivisibility. By that we mean that some degree of concentration may be rendered "technologically inevitable"[2] by the economies of large-scale production and distribution. Witness, for example, the apparent tendency toward contraction in the number of makers of automobiles. In short, so far as concentration is concerned, we do not know where we are and we do not know where we are going; such is the flimsy factual foundation of our antimonopoly policy.

§2.6. **The abuse theory: Its nature.** The first test of illegal monopoly which we shall consider is based upon conduct rather than upon horizontal size: no matter how large a firm may have grown, it is not considered to have violated the statutory prohibitions unless it has misbehaved. The misbehavior in question is commonly termed an "abuse." We shall shortly explore the specific nature of the abuses. Here we state only that the "abuse" test as opposed to the "structure" test is related to misconduct rather than to economic power. As phrased by one court,

> . . . monopoly is the power acquired over the traffic, sale and purchase of a commodity, . . . by which the free flow of such commerce and competition . . . is necessarily crushed. . . . Since the size of the business alone is not necessarily illegal, it is the crushing of competition, by means of force, threats, intimidation, fraud, or artful and deceitful means and practices, which violates the law.[1]

Note that the abuses are conceived of as directed against business rivals. In the language of an acute observer,

> The abuse theory which the *Steel* and *Harvester* cases fastened on to the act was really the notion that only alarming and un-

§2.5. [1] Thorp and Crowder, The Structure of Industry 13 (TNEC Monograph No. 27, 1941); Mund, Book Review, 40 Am. Econ. Rev. 454, 457 (1950).
[2] Fellner, Collusion and Its Limits Under Oligopoly, 40 Proceedings Am. Econ. Assn. 54, 61 (1950). Compare Kaplan, Big Enterprise in a Competitive System 117 (Brookings Institution, 1954).

§2.6. [1] United States v. American Naval Stores Co., 172 Fed. 455, 458 (S.D. Ga. 1909).

gentlemanly conduct — involving, for example, the use of slander
concerning one's competitors . . . would be sufficient to invoke
the Sherman Act against the crime of monopolizing.[2]

It followed that under the abuse test there could be "good" and
"bad" monopolies: their legality depended upon their behavior.[3]

§2.7. **Adoption of the abuse theory by the courts.** It is difficult to say what test the law follows today. At the same time, it is
clear that the courts used the abuse test for at least several decades.
It is commonly thought that the adoption of the abuse theory can
be traced to the 1911 decisions in the *Standard Oil*[1] and *Tobacco*[2]
cases. Whether that be true or not, the *Steel* and *Harvester* decisions, announced about a decade later, made it plain that the
abuse test was to prevail. Thus, in the latter opinion it was said:

> The law, however, does not make the mere size of a corporation,
> however impressive, or the existence of unexerted power on its
> part, an offense, when unaccompanied by unlawful conduct in the
> exercise of its power.[3]

[2] Levi, The Antitrust Laws and Monopoly, 14 U. Chi. L. Rev. 153, 160 (1947).
[3] Kales, Contracts and Combinations in Restraint of Trade §49 (1918).

§2.7. [1] Standard Oil Co. of New Jersey v. United States, 221 U.S. 1, 55 et seq.
(1911). But compare Atty. Gen. Nat. Com. Rep. 50-51 (1955).

[2] United States v. American Tobacco Co., 221 U.S. 106 (1911); Levi, The Antitrust
Laws and Monopoly, 14 U. Chi. L. Rev. 153, 157-158 (1947); Rostow, Monopoly
Under the Sherman Act, 43 Ill. L. Rev. 745, 759 (1949); Johnston and Stevens,
Monopoly or Monopolization, 44 id. 269, 274 et seq. (1949); Kahn, A Legal and
Economic Appraisal of the "New" Sherman and Clayton Acts, 63 Yale L.J. 293,
296 (1954). Compare Pope, The Legal Aspect of Monopoly, 20 Harv. L. Rev. 167,
186-187 (1907); Walker, History of the Sherman Law 297 (1910). In Martin, ed.,
State Antitrust Laws xlviii (WPA, 1940), it was said: "General [state] antitrust laws,
while doubtless promoted in part by popular distrust of big business, make no
reference to the absolute or relative size of permissible combinations in the form
of corporations or otherwise."

[3] United States v. International Harvester Co., 274 U.S. 693, 708 (1927). Language in several other cases supports similar views. Thus, in United States v.
United States Steel Corp., 223 Fed. 55 (D.N.J. 1915), aff'd, 251 U.S. 417 (1920), it
was said at page 104: "The question is one of undue restriction or obstruction of
trade, and not of undue volume of trade. If mere size were the test of monopoly
and trade restraint, we have not one, but a half dozen unlawful monopolies in
the large department stores of a single city. . . . the normal and necessary expansion of business to any size is not forbidden by the Sherman Law, unless such expansion is accompanied or accomplished by an undue restrain [*sic*] or obstruction
of trade . . ." In United States v. American Naval Stores Co., 172 Fed. 455 (S.D.
Ga. 1909), it was said at page 459: "The size of business, and the gaining of
business popularity, fair dealing, sagacity, foresight, and honest business methods,
even if it should result in acquiring the business of competitors, would not make
an illegal monopoly. It is the acquisition and use of unfair and illegal power in
defeating competition which makes such illegal monopoly." *Accord:* United States
v. United Shoe Machinery Co., 222 Fed. 349, 357 (D. Mass. 1915), aff'd, 247 U.S. 32
(1918); compare Moody & Waters Co. v. Case-Moody Pie Corp., 354 Ill. 82, 187
N.E. 813 (1933). As recently as United States v. Pullman Co., 64 F. Supp. 108 (E.D.
Pa. 1946), aff'd *per curiam*, 330 U.S. 806 (1947), it was said at page 112: "If there

This result, based upon a construction of Section 2 of the Sherman Act, finds foundation in the legislative history of the statute[4] and may continue to command some adherence to this day.

It is now widely assumed that the abuse test has been abandoned. Since the decision in the *Alcoa* case[5] in 1945, most observers have thought that the structure test is now in vogue. We shall examine the adoption of the structure test at a later point.[6] Meanwhile, however, we note that some life remains in the abuse theory. Numerous opinions, ostensibly based upon the structure theory, contain more than a hint that vestiges of the abuse doctrine are retained. Thus, in the leading case of *United States v. Griffith* the Court said:

> It is indeed "unreasonable, *per se,* to foreclose competitors from any substantial market." . . . The anti-trust laws are as much violated by the prevention of competition as by its destruction. . . . It follows *a fortiori* that the use of monopoly power, however lawfully acquired, to foreclose competition, to gain a competitive advantage, or to destroy a competitor, is unlawful.[7]

Reference to the "use" of monopoly power in the foregoing quotation suggests that even under the structure theory the conduct of the defendant is not immaterial. Furthermore, the school of thought which stresses the ethical content of the antitrust laws comes close to rejecting the structure test in favor of the older doctrine. For example, in a recent book it was said:

> The only circumstances in which antitrust proceedings against big business units . . . are warranted are when the units over-step

---

is only one store in a town at which every one trades, that fact does not itself constitute a monopoly in the legal sense. It is only when the merchant maintains his position by devices which compel every one to trade with him exclusively that the situation becomes legally objectionable."

4 Canfield, Is a Large Corporation an Illegal Combination or Monopoly Under the Sherman Anti-Trust Act? 9 Colum. L. Rev. 95, 104, 106 (1909); Adler, Monopolizing at Common Law and Under Section 2 of the Sherman Act, 31 Harv. L. Rev. 246, 248 (1917). See also authorities collected in §2.8 *infra.*

5 United States v. Aluminum Co. of America, 148 F.2d 416 (2d Cir. 1945).

6 §3.2 *infra.*

7 United States v. Griffith, 334 U.S. 100, 107 (1948). In the same opinion it was said at page 106: "Any one who owns and operates the single theater in a town, or who acquires the exclusive right to exhibit a film, has a monopoly in the popular sense. But he usually does not violate §2 of the Sherman Act unless he has acquired or maintained his strategic position, or sought to expand his monopoly, or expanded it by means of those restraints of trade which are cognizable under §1 . . ." Compare United States v. United Shoe Machinery Corp., 110 F. Supp. 295 (D. Mass. 1953), *aff'd per curiam,* 347 U.S. 521 (1954); United States v. E. I. Du Pont de Nemours & Co., 118 F. Supp. 41 (D. Del. 1953), *aff'd,* 351 U.S. 377 (1956). Note that recent British legislation appears to be based at least in part on the abuse test. Harbury and Raskind, The British Approach to Monopoly Control, 67 Q.J. Econ. 380, 402 (1953).

the rules of a free enterprise system: rules prohibiting monopolizing, either by collusion or by exclusion (which is, by definition, unreasonable). This is our thesis.[8]

§2.8. **The language of the statute.** As indicated above, our primary concern is with Section 2 of the Sherman Act. The important parts of that section read as follows:

> Every person who shall monopolize, or attempt to monopolize, or combine or conspire with any other person or persons, to monopolize any part of the trade or commerce among the several States, or with foreign nations, shall be deemed guilty of a misdemeanor . . .[1]

It will be noted at once that the statute does not refer to "monopoly" but prohibits monopolization. The verb "monopolize" in the section is, of course, used in its active form, with the result that a passive situation does not appear to fall within the terms of the prohibition. This interpretation of the Sherman Act was pointed out in the *Standard Oil* decision of 1911, wherein it was said:

> . . . it is worthy of observation . . . that although the statute by the comprehensiveness of the enumerations embodied in both the first and second sections makes it certain that its purpose was to prevent undue restraints of every kind or nature, nevertheless by the omission of any direct prohibition against monopoly in the concrete it indicates a consciousness that in the freedom of the individual right to contract when not unduly or improperly exercised was the most efficient means for the prevention of monopoly. . . .[2]

Mr. Justice Holmes, dissenting in another case, put the matter even more succinctly:

> . . . the act of Congress makes no discrimination according to size. Size has nothing to do with the matter. A monopoly of "any part" of commerce among the States is unlawful.
>
> There is a natural feeling that somehow or other the statute meant to strike at combinations great enough to cause just anxiety on the part of those who love their country more than money, while it viewed such little ones as I have supposed with just indifference. This notion, it may be said, somehow breathes from the pores of the act, although it seems to be contradicted in every way by the words in detail.[3]

---

[8] Dirlam and Kahn, Fair Competition 44 (1954).

§2.8. [1] 26 Stat. 209 (1890), 15 U.S.C.A. §2.
[2] Standard Oil Co. of New Jersey v. United States, 221 U.S. 1, 62 (1911).
[3] Dissent in Northern Securities Co. v. United States, 193 U.S. 197, 407 (1904); see also Levi, A Two Level Anti-Monopoly Law, 47 Nw. U.L. Rev. 567, 574 (1952).

For the most part, the legislative history of the statute sustains the view that it was not aimed at mere horizontal size. Thus one student of the subject reached the following conclusion:

The word "monopolize" was a suitable term for describing the common-law offenses. The term "engrossing" alone was not satisfactory, for, as has been noted, the circumstances had to be taken into account in determining whether mere forestalling, engrossing and regrating should be held to violate the common-law. "Monopolize," on the other hand, indicated the evil as such, not the mere possession of a monopoly, both the commission of those acts of extortion and oppression which brought the monopolists of Elizabeth into disrepute, by the enhancement of prices and the interference with the freedom and due course of trade.[4]

There has been much adverse criticism of the 1920 decision of the United States Supreme Court holding that the United States Steel Corporation had not infringed Section 2 of the Sherman Act. Whatever the merits of that contention — and we do not pause here to review all the facts placed before the Court in that case — it is apparent that the language of the statute afforded considerable support for the Court's determination. Finding that the defendant was not guilty of bad behavior in the recent past, the Court felt obliged to absolve it of the misdemeanor declared in the act. In the opinion it was said:

The Corporation is undoubtedly of impressive size and it takes an effort of resolution not to be affected by it or to exaggerate its influence. But we must adhere to the law and the law does not make mere size an offence or the existence of unexerted power an offence. It, we repeat, requires overt acts and trusts to its pro-

[4] Adler, Monopolizing at Common Law and Under Section 2 of the Sherman Act, 31 Harv. L. Rev. 246, 259 (1917). See also id. at 247-248, 249, 250 and at 258, where it is said: "There is not and never was a common-law offense known as 'monopoly' apart from all consideration of subject-matter and means employed." *Accord:* Canfield, Is a Large Corporation an Illegal Combination or Monopoly Under the Sherman Anti-Trust Act? 9 Colum. L. Rev. 95, 96-97 (1909). Mr. Pope, however, pointed out that the question of whether a corporation was an illegal monopoly scarcely arose at common law because the remedy afforded was solely refusal to enforce contracts. Pope, The Legal Aspect of Monopoly, 20 Harv. L. Rev. 167, 182 (1907). See also Walker, History of the Sherman Law 33 (1910). In the latter work it was said at page 58: "No Senator or Representative expressed any view different from that of Senators Edmunds and Hoar relevant to the meaning of the word 'monopolize' . . . therefore we are justified in provisionally holding that Section 2 of the Sherman Law does not prohibit a complete acquirement of the whole or any part of interstate or international commerce, except where that complete acquirement results from efforts of the monopolizer to prevent other parties from competing with him in achieving that complete acquirement." See also id. at 96. Compare United States v. Aluminum Co. of America, 148 F.2d 416, 429 (2d Cir. 1945), with United States v. E. I. Du Pont de Nemours & Co., 118 F. Supp. 41 (D. Del. 1953), *aff'd*, 351 U.S. 377 (1956).

hibition of them and its power to repress or punish them. It does
not compel competition nor require all that is possible.[5]

Adoption of the abuse theory, in short, cannot be attributed
wholly to the courts: the legislative branch of government must
share whatever blame may be involved.

§2.9. **Abuses and other concepts.** Before considering specific
acts which constitute the abuses, we should attempt to delineate
the relationship of the abuse doctrine to other concepts under the
antitrust laws. It will be noted that the word "abuse" does not
appear in Section 2 of the Sherman Act, whereas that statute does
expressly prohibit "attempts" to monopolize. Abuses and attempts are doubtless closely related. Indeed, it is often difficult to
distinguish them.[1] Both suggest that the defendant is attempting
to gain monopoly control in some area of commerce. Note, for
example, the way in which Professor Kales spoke of the subject:

> Since the Standard Oil and Tobacco Cases, it has become articu-
> late that a combination of properties . . . which, by reason of its
> size and preponderant position in the business, has the power and
> purpose, or uses its power to exclude others from the business by
> illegal acts and unlawful and unfair methods of competition, is
> an attempt at monopoly . . . it is what may be called a bad trust.[2]

Note that Mr. Kales, in describing the abuse doctrine, refers to it
as an "attempt." The distinction between the abuse and the
attempt probably lies only in the fact that the firm guilty of an
abuse already has some degree of market power in the field of
commerce in question. He who "attempts" to monopolize, however, need not have such a foothold in that market. He may either
be generally wealthy or have some degree of market control in
another market. The concept of "attempt," however, does not
necessarily include any element of market power in the field
where monopolization is sought.

---

[5] United States v. United States Steel Corp., 251 U.S. 417, 451 (1920). In United
States v. American Naval Stores Co., 172 Fed. 455 (S.D. Ga. 1909), it was said at
page 458: ". . . the essence of the monopoly 'is found not so much in the creating
of a very extensive business in the hands of a single control.' The size of a
business is not in itself a violation of this law . . . the criminal act in the
statute [Sherman Act] is the certain and necessary prevention of all other persons
from engaging in such business, and thereby stifling competition. The evil is not
the enlargement of the trade of one person or corporation, but the destruction
of the trade of all other persons in the same commodity." Note that the courts
adopting such views apparently place considerable reliance upon that self-correction
of the market referred to in §2.4 *supra*.

§2.9. [1] E.g., Lorain Journal Co. v. United States, 342 U.S. 143 (1951); Hughes
Tool Co. v. Ford, 114 F. Supp. 525 (E.D. Okla. 1953), *rev'd*, 215 F.2d 924 (10th
Cir. 1954), *cert. denied*, 348 U.S. 927, 965 (1955).
[2] Kales, Contracts and Combinations in Restraint of Trade §49 (1918).

We shall later[3] have occasion to examine the general relationship between Sections 1 and 2 of the Sherman Act. Here we point out merely that an abuse may be closely related to those "restraints of trade" prohibited by Section 1. Indeed, a court has said: "The statute prohibits only such monopolies as are unjust and unreasonable restraints of trade. . . ."[4] The language of the quoted sentence suggests that a monopoly is a species of restraint; and since under the abuse theory only misbehaving monopolists infringe Section 2 of the Sherman Act, it follows that those acts (the abuses) are types of restraints of trade. Under the structure theory, as adopted by the United States Supreme Court, the situation is only slightly different. Thus, in *United States v. Griffith* it was said:

> Any one who owns and operates the single theater in a town, or who acquires the exclusive right to exhibit a film, has a monopoly in the popular sense. But he usually does not violate §2 of the Sherman Act unless he has acquired or maintained his strategic position, or sought to expand his monopoly, or expanded it by means of those restraints of trade which are cognizable under §1. . . .[5]

The foregoing language suggests that whatever applications are made of the abuse doctrine under the current decisions are, again, closely related to restraints of trade within the meaning of Section 1 of the Sherman Act.[6]

At first impression one might suppose that the specific prohibitions of the Clayton Act[7] were not directed at the abuses familiar under the earlier legislation. One would assume that the 1914 statute was not intended to duplicate the Sherman Act of 1890 and hence that the Clayton Act must be given a meaning apart from the content of the abuses. On the other hand, the subject matter of the Clayton Act's prohibitions appears to be largely the same as that reached under the abuse doctrine. Accordingly, it is probably preferable to regard the Clayton Act as making more specific the already existing rules of law laid down under the

---

3 §3.9 *infra.*

4 United States v. Eastman Kodak Co., 226 Fed. 62, 65 (W.D.N.Y. 1915), *appeal dismissed,* 255 U.S. 578 (1921); Johnston, Monopolize or Attempt to Monopolize, Proceedings A.B.A., Section of Antitrust Law, 72, 80-81 (Aug. 26, 1953).

5 334 U.S. 100, 106 (1948).

6 Compare United States v. United Shoe Machinery Corp., 110 F. Supp. 295, 342 (D. Mass. 1953), *aff'd per curiam,* 347 U.S. 521 (1954).

7 38 Stat. 730 (1914), 15 U.S.C.A. §12. Oddly enough, as mentioned in §2.13 *infra,* the Clayton Act prohibits certain conduct and leaves untouched other activities which produce the same economic result.

abuse test.[8] Such a view is consistent, furthermore, with the notion that both the abuse doctrine and the Clayton Act constitute the regulation of excessive market power rather than its prohibition.

§2.10. **Price discrimination.** The practice of charging varying prices to different customers is, of course, specifically prohibited by Section 2 of the Clayton Act (Robinson-Patman Act).[1] We leave interpretation of that miracle of draftsmanship to hardier students of the antitrust laws. It is nevertheless plain that the practice of cutting prices with an intent to drive out one's competitors has long constituted a prime abuse within the meaning of Section 2 of the Sherman Act. It was, indeed, one of the practices which aroused public feeling against the "trusts" before the enactment of the law bearing Senator Sherman's name.[2] It continues to be unlawful under the Sherman Act as presently interpreted.[3] In fact, a question exists as to whether any form of price-cutting can escape the statute's terms. Apparently there can be lawful price reduction, for the Supreme Court said not long ago:

> . . . price cutting without more is not a violation of the Sherman Act. It is indeed a competitive practice which this record shows to have been common in the industry. It may be used in violation of the Act. . . . But since it is not unlawful *per se,* facts and cir-

[8] In Handler, The Legal Aspects of Industrial Mergers in Handler, ed., The Federal Anti-Trust Laws 173 (Columbia University, 1931), it was said at page 200: "By predatory practices I would include not only price cutting, temporary competition, and the exclusion of competitors, but any violation of the anti-trust laws as well. This would add new teeth to the present acts. . . ." Compare the doctrine of "incipiency." Corn Products Refining Co. v. FTC, 324 U.S. 726, 738 (1945). The theory of the incipiency doctrine is that the Clayton Act was designed to put a halt to practices which could lead to monopoly and thus have a preventive effect. In that connection attention is invited to the desirability of distinguishing between the acquisition of an original monopoly power and its spreading into other products or geographic areas by one of the practices condemned by the statute.

§2.10. [1] 49 Stat. 1526 (1936), 15 U.S.C.A. §13; Austin, Price Discrimination and Related Problems Under the Robinson-Patman Act (A.L.I. 1950). In application the Robinson-Patman Act appears to protect competitors rather than consumers, the theory being that unless rival firms are kept in business consumers ultimately will suffer. Compare United States v. Corn Products Refining Co., 234 Fed. 964, 1012 (S.D.N.Y. 1916), with United States v. New York Great Atlantic & Pacific Tea Co., 67 F. Supp. 626, 676 (E.D. Ill. 1946), aff'd, 173 F.2d 79 (7th Cir. 1949).

[2] 1 Nevins, Study in Power 228 (1953). Price-cutting with intent to run another out of business is actionable apart from statute today. Mackey v. Sears, Roebuck & Co., 237 F.2d 869, 874-875 (7th Cir. 1956).

[3] United States v. American Tobacco Co., 221 U.S. 106, 160-161 (1911); American Tobacco Co. v. United States, 328 U.S. 781, 808 (1946); Complaint ¶48(a) in United States v. International Business Machine Corp., No. C-72-344, S.D.N.Y. (1952).

cumstances must be adduced to show that it was in purpose or effect employed as an instrument of monopoly power.[4]

Recently, a lower court struggled with the problem of price reduction and, while it found that practice not absolutely illegal, yet came up with a formula suggesting that business firms no longer enjoy much leeway to move their prices downward:

> . . . no case exists in which the courts have held that a price reduction, in itself, not having as its purpose the destruction of a competitor or the monopolization of trade or commerce, but made to meet competition in the field or to retain trade or custom or to gain new custom, is *illegal as such*.[5]

Originally, objectionable price discrimination took the form of a geographic differential directed at rivals having only a local business. By undercutting a competitor within some relatively small territory, an attempt was made to drive him out of business and to monopolize the trade.[6] Indeed, in some instances, the discrimination was refined to the point where it extended only to individual customers of the rival and did not even include other consumers within the affected area. If anything, the latter practice has impressed the courts as more reprehensible than the former.[7]

[4] Schine Chain Theatres, Inc. v. United States, 334 U.S. 110, 120 (1948). The conventional view in the older cases was that underselling in ordinary competition did not constitute a violation of the law, provided it was not part of a plan to drive rivals out of business and to obtain a monopoly. American Steel Co. v. American Steel & Wire Co., 244 Fed. 300, 302 (D. Mass. 1916).

[5] Balian Ice Cream Co. v. Arden Farms Co., 104 F. Supp. 796, 801 (S.D. Cal. 1952), aff'd, 231 F.2d 356 (9th Cir. 1955), cert. denied, 350 U.S. 991 (1956). In the same case it was said at page 807: ". . . the price reduction here was (a) long in contemplation; (b) it bore a realistic relation to previous changes by others in the field, either in the locality or elsewhere; (c) it corresponded to factors relating to cost of production and demand for the article. . . . These are legitimate criteria for legal price reduction." Compare Feddersen Motors, Inc. v. Ward, 180 F.2d 519 (10th Cir. 1950); United States v. New York Great Atlantic & Pacific Tea Co., 173 F.2d 79 (7th Cir. 1949); Sunbeam Corp. v. Payless Drug Stores, 113 F. Supp. 31, 42 (N.D. Cal. 1953).

[6] Standard Oil Co. of New Jersey v. United States, 221 U.S. 1, 43 (1911); United States v. Great Lakes Towing Co., 208 Fed. 733, 745 (N.D. Ohio, 1913), 217 Fed. 656 (N.D. Ohio, 1914); 2 Nevins, Study in Power 226-227, 370 (1953). As indicated in the text, such conduct constitutes an attempt as well as an abuse. State v. Atlantic Ice & Coal Co., 210 N.C. 742, 188 S.E. 412 (1936); Tooke & Reynolds v. Bastrop Ice Co., 172 La. 781, 135 So. 239, 241 (1931). But cf. Balian Ice Cream Co. v. Arden Farms Co., 104 F. Supp. 796, 801 (S.D. Cal. 1952), aff'd, 231 F.2d 356, 367 (9th Cir. 1955), cert. denied, 350 U.S. 991 (1956) (antitrust laws do not require one who reduces prices in one area to make similar reduction in all areas).

[7] State ex Information Hadley v. Standard Oil Co., 218 Mo. 1, 116 S.W. 902, 1025 (1909), aff'd, 224 U.S. 270 (1912); Ware-Kramer Tobacco Co. v. American Tobacco Co., 180 Fed. 160 (E.D.N.C. 1910); People v. American Ice Co. 135 App. Div. 180, 120 N.Y. Supp. 41, 443, 452 (1st Dept. 1909), aff'd mem., 140 App. Div. 912, 125 N.Y. Supp. 1136 (1st Dept. 1910).

The practice of "freight absorption" has been attacked under the Robinson-

Today, the abuse of price discrimination is greatly enlarged in
scope. It extends to the so-called "squeeze" exercised by a vertically integrated firm selling raw material to a competing fabricator
at prices so high that the rival cannot meet the integrated firm's
prices on final products.[8] In the recent *United Shoe Machinery*
litigation the court held that it was illegal for the defendant to
lease its machines for a charge which included both the use of
the machinery and its upkeep. That practice, the court held, constituted a discrimination against those shoe manufacturers who
required less maintenance service than their rivals.[9] In the same
case, the court objected to the defendant's practice of reducing
prices on types of machines upon which it met stiffer competition.[10] Such a holding suggests that "margins" must be uniform
for all products of the seller in question.

The abuse of price discrimination extends to situations in which
prices are formally equal but actually different in that the quality
of the product is varied. Hence a firm which renders special
services to its more important customers may be guilty of an abuse
even though its prices are equal to all comers.[11] Similarly, abuses
arise out of preferential treatment secured by the defendant in

Patman Act and also when indulged in by a group of rival firms. FTC v. Staley
Manufacturing Co., 324 U.S. 746 (1945); FTC v. Cement Institute, 333 U.S. 683
(1948). Even individually arrived at "delivered prices" are questionable under the
decision in Triangle Conduit & Cable Co. v. FTC, 168 F.2d 175 (7th Cir. 1948),
aff'd per curiam, 336 U.S. 956 (1949). Freight absorption, however, has not usually
been considered an abuse under §2 of the Sherman Act. United States v. Corn
Products Refining Co., 234 Fed. 964, 994 (S.D.N.Y. 1916). Economic aspects of freight
absorption are discussed in Stigler, A Theory of Delivered Price Systems, 39 Am.
Econ. Rev. 1143 (1949); Fellner, Competition Among the Few 298, 302 (1949);
Stocking, The Economics of Basing Point Pricing, 15 Law & Contemp. Prob. 159
(1950); TNEC Hearings, pt. 19, at 10,654.

8 United States v. Aluminum Co. of America, 148 F.2d 416, 436 (2d Cir. 1945).

9 United States v. United Shoe Machinery Corp., 110 F. Supp. 295, 322, 326 (D.
Mass. 1953), *aff'd per curiam*, 347 U.S. 521 (1954).

10 110 F. Supp. at 343. Compare United States v. Griffith, 334 U.S. 100 (1948).
Note also the reference to quantity discounts in the United Shoe Machinery case
(at 336) suggesting that such discounts, if not justified by savings in costs, will
constitute "abuses" under the Sherman Act.

11 United States v. American Can Co., 87 F. Supp. 18, 28 (N.D. Cal. 1949); United
States v. Paramount Pictures, Inc., 66 F. Supp. 323, 352 (S.D.N.Y. 1946), *rev'd*, 334
U.S. 131 (1948); United States v. General Electric Co., 82 F. Supp. 753, 899 (D.N.J.
1949). But compare id. at 855-856; United States v. American Can Co., 230 Fed.
859, 897, 234 Fed. 1019 (D. Md. 1916), *appeal dismissed*, 256 U.S. 706 (1921). An
example of quality improvement rather than price reduction as a competitive
method is set forth in Hower, History of Macy's of New York 381 (1943).

A restraint upon alienation might be imposed by a seller in the hope of aiding
his program of price discrimination (by keeping favored customers from selling
to others). The practice, however, appears to have been held legal. Gano v. Del-
mas, 140 Miss. 323, 105 So. 535, 537 (1925); see Crystal Ice Co. v. San Antonio
Brewing Assn., 8 Tex. Civ. App. 1, 27 S.W. 210, 211 (1894).

buying its raw materials.   Rebates from railroads constituted a major cause of complaint against the old-fashioned trusts.[12]   Indeed, it has been said that no more powerful instrument of monopoly could be devised than the securing of such preferences,[13] and the courts have condemned similar arrangements in the recent past.[14]

§2.11.   Analysis of price discrimination.   It is elementary economic doctrine that a monopolist will discriminate among his customers in order to maximize his revenues.   It is also well established that a seller without monopoly power cannot long engage in price discrimination.[1]   It would seem to follow that price discrimination should be unlawful and that firms which cut prices and drive their rivals out of business should be held to have infringed Section 2 of the Sherman Act.   As our sad experience with the Robinson-Patman legislation indicates,[2] however, the matter is not nearly so simple as the foregoing statement would suggest.

In the real world of business, we cannot have competition unless there is rivalry among sellers.   Such rivalry inevitably includes freedom to meet the lower price of a competitor.   Meeting that lower price may mean discrimination against other customers of the seller.   As stated by the Attorney General's Committee,

> It is of the essence of effective competition that competitors should try to meet, or offer an equivalent for, any superior inducement which one of them offers.
>
> . . . effective competition also involves freedom to undercut rivals' prices. . . .

[12] 2 Nevins, Study in Power 132 (1953).   Considerable stress was laid upon the fact that the freight concessions were secret in character.   1 id. at 260; United States v. Corn Products Refining Co., 234 Fed. 964, 1001 (S.D.N.Y. 1916).   It is not wholly clear why secrecy added to the gravity of the complaint.   It is true that rival shippers would have demanded equally low rates had they known of the concessions but it is likely that they were negotiating for similar concessions even in the absence of such information.   The secrecy, of course, did add to the imperfections in the market place.

[13] United States v. United States Steel Corp., 223 Fed. 55, 76 (D.N.J. 1915), aff'd, 251 U.S. 417 (1920).   But compare 1 Nevins, Study in Power 89 (1953); Hower, History of Macy's of New York 51-52 (1943).

[14] Schine Chain Theatres, Inc. v. United States, 334 U.S. 110, 116-117 (1948); United States v. New York Great Atlantic & Pacific Tea Co., 173 F.2d 79, 88 (7th Cir. 1949).

§2.11.   [1] Watkins, Price Discrimination, 12 Encyc. Soc. Sci. 350, 352 (1934); compare Bailey, Price and Output Determination by a Firm Selling Related Products, 44 Am. Econ. Rev. 82 (1954).

[2] Rowe, Price Discrimination, Competition and Confusion, 60 Yale L.J. 929 (1951); Levi, The Robinson-Patman Act — Is It in the Public Interest? Proceedings A.B.A., Section of Antitrust Law, 60 (Sept. 17, 1953).

Effective competition is therefore compatible either with meeting (or matching) the prices of rivals, or with undercutting them. . . .[3]

Existence of price competition in an industry is often evidenced by deviation from published price lists[4] (which are presumably followed in quotations to some customers). Indeed, litigation charging illegal price-cutting can actually constitute an attempt to enforce a system of horizontal price-fixing.[5] Again, looking at the matter from the standpoint of the initiator of the price reduction, discrimination can constitute one of the most effective forces making for competitive markets. The Attorney General's Committee stated:

> . . . price discrimination may be the force which can increase the number of effective sellers in a market, or disrupt an otherwise effective system of monopoly pricing.[6]

[3] Atty. Gen. Nat. Com. Rep. 331, (8).

[4] TNEC Hearings, pt. 19, at 10,499, 10,506, 10,659; pt. 27, at 14,165, 14,260-14,261; Celler Committee I, pt. 4A, at page 948.

[5] State v. Atlantic Ice & Coal Co., 210 N.C. 742, 188 S.E. 412, 417 (1936) (semble); Williams v. Standard Oil Co., 278 U.S. 235, 244 (1929). Compare Balian Ice Cream Co. v. Arden Farms Co., 104 F. Supp. 796, 802 (S.D. Cal. 1952), aff'd, 231 F.2d 356 (9th Cir. 1955), cert. denied, 350 U.S. 991 (1956); United States v. United Shoe Machinery Corp., 110 F. Supp. 295, 326, 329 (D. Mass. 1953), aff'd per curiam, 347 U.S. 521 (1954); United States v. New York Great Atlantic & Pacific Tea Co., 173 F.2d 79 (7th Cir. 1949). It has been reported that an important oil company lacks the courage to initiate price reductions simply because it is afraid of political repercussions (perhaps in the form of antitrust litigation). Learned, Pricing of Gasoline, 26 Harv. Bus. Rev. No. 6, pp. 723, 731 (1948).

[6] Atty. Gen. Nat. Com. Rep. 336. Accord: Adelman, Effective Competition and the Antitrust Laws, 61 Harv. L. Rev. 1289, 1332 (1948); Dirlam and Kahn, Price Discrimination in Law and Economics, 11 Am. J. Econ. & Sociol. 281, 289 (1952); Machlup, The Political Economy of Monopoly 100 (1952); O'Mahoney Committee I, pt. 4, at 602; Machlup, Characteristics and Types of Price Discrimination, in Business Concentration and Price Policy 397 et seq. (Stigler ed. 1955) (catalog of different types of price discrimination and hints as to effects thereof). Various market imperfections may have a profound effect upon price discrimination. If, for example, entry into competition is easy, efforts to drive rivals from the field by price-cutting will not only prove fruitless but needlessly expensive. Note, for instance, the experience of the old Standard Oil Company. 2 Nevins, Study in Power 62, 66 (1953). Once the contemporary competitor has been driven from the field and prices raised to a monopolistic level, new rivals appear upon the scene. Compare Abramovitz, An Approach to Price Theory for a Changing Economy 6 (1939). In Dirlam and Kahn, Price Discrimination in Law and Economics, 11 Am. J. Econ. & Sociol. 281, 291 (1952), there is cited a case in which a maker of spark plugs sold those commodities to automobile manufacturers at about 25 per cent of the price for which similar plugs were sold for replacement purposes. The theory of the seller apparently was that he secured valuable advertising by having his plugs part of the original equipment of the automobile. To reap rewards from that type of advertising, however, requires a considerable lapse of time: in such circumstances disparities of wealth between the rival firms in the field may cause the less wealthy companies to drop out before the advertising

Price discrimination is more than an incentive to competition. It may constitute one of the principal stimulants to growth and innovation in the economy. Introduction of new products may be impossible without vigorous price reductions.[7] Many illustrations can be found in which such lower prices were necessary in order to secure acceptance of new products. The Aluminum Company of America, for example, in order to enter into markets then wholly supplied by copper producers, cut the price on its aluminum conductors without making equivalent reductions on other aluminum products. Henry Ford was well known for his practice of cutting prices in an attempt to increase the volume of his production — an attempt in which he succeeded spectacularly.[8] Price reductions themselves may be regarded as innovations as well as stimulants to new developments.[9]

The notion that every sale must return the same margin of profit to the seller is incompatible with the existence of a competitive system. Elimination of all price discrimination would either result in uniform artificially high prices, probably maintained by agreements among competitors, or else in pricing all products at

---

benefits can be realized. In Appendix A, *infra,* will be found some discussion of the problem of consumer ignorance and its effect upon price discrimination. Compare Morgenstern, Oligopoly, Monopolistic Competition and the Theory of Games, 38 Am. Econ. Rev. 10, 17 (1948). Again, since factors of indivisibility render it inevitable that competition will vary in intensity from one geographic market to another, a firm selling in several such markets may be compelled to discriminate in order to compete.

[7] Schumpeter, The Instability of Capitalism, 28 Econ. J. 361, 380-381 (1928); Nourse and Drury, Industrial Price Policies and Economic Progress 254-255 (Brookings Institution, 1938); Wright, Some Pitfalls of Economic Theory as a Guide to the Law of Competition, 37 Va. L. Rev. 1083, 1091 (1951); Adelman, Effective Competition and the Antitrust Laws, 61 Harv. L. Rev. 1289, 1330 (1948). In Nourse and Drury, *supra,* it was said at pages 253-254: "An essential feature of industrial price-making lies in the fact that, instead of passively accepting the market's pricing of a supply subject to no central control, it sets a price objective and directs a control production mechanism toward the attainment of that price level." See also Machlup, Characteristics and Types of Price Discrimination, in Business Concentration and Price Policy 397, 427 (Stigler ed. 1955).

[8] Wallace, Market Control in the Aluminum Industry 15, 256, 390, 392-393 (1937); Nevins, Ford: The Times, the Man, the Company 282 (1954); Brems, Product Equilibrium Under Monopolistic Competition 138 (1951); Monsanto Chemical Co., 51st Ann. Rep. 22 (St. Louis, 1953); Air Reduction, 8 Fortune No. 1, pp. 24, 117 (1933); Nourse and Drury, Industrial Price Policies and Economic Progress 262-263 (Brookings Institution, 1938). But compare Williamson, Winchester: The Gun That Won the West 179 (1952). Note the different approaches taken by two courts in United States v. Aluminum Co. of America, 44 F. Supp. 97, 218-219, 221 (S.D.N.Y. 1941), *rev'd,* 148 F.2d 416 (2d Cir. 1945), and in United States v. New York Great Atlantic & Pacific Tea Co., 67 F. Supp. 626, 640 et seq., 664 et seq., 678 (E.D. Ill. 1946), *aff'd,* 173 F.2d 79 (7th Cir. 1949).

[9] A publisher, for example, offered reprints of formerly popular works at greatly reduced prices and tapped a wholly new market for literature. Doubleday-Doran, 13 Fortune No. 2, pp. 73, 166 (1936).

marginal cost.[10] If all sales were made upon a marginal cost basis, there would be no discrimination whatever, but the result would be bankruptcy or state subsidies for some sellers.[11] The reason for that result is simple: by making all sales at marginal cost levels, there would be nothing to apply against overhead costs, and total expenses would not be covered by all sellers. Public utility regulation has often started with the premise that all discrimination should be eliminated. For the reasons indicated, it has as frequently ended in creating more discrimination than existed in the free-market situation.[12]

Amid such considerations it is clear that price discrimination cannot be universally condemned. Application of the antitrust laws to cases of underselling is hazardous unless the court is satisfied that the defendant's conduct constitutes an effort to use superior resources substantially to handicap less fortunate rivals.[13] Hence, in distinguishing "good" from "bad" price discrimination, considerable reliance must be placed upon the intent of the de-

[10] In United States v. United States Steel Corp., 223 Fed. 55, 79 (D.N.J. 1915). aff'd, 251 U.S. 417 (1920), the district court noted that the combination of competitors into the defendant had resulted in a firm less likely to vary prices among customers than competing independent steelmakers. The court went on to say at page 96: ". . . the strong trend of the steel business at the close of the last century was toward driving competitors out of business by cutting prices, and that the business policy inaugurated by the Steel Corporation . . . has resulted . . . in a more general division of business between all competitors in the steel business than under the old system . . ." The foregoing findings appear to sustain the view that price discrimination is more characteristic of competition than of combination.

[11] Clemens, Price Discrimination in Decreasing Cost Industries, 31 Am. Econ. Rev. 794, 797-798, 801 (1941); Tyndal, The Relative Merits of Average Cost Pricing, Marginal Cost Pricing and Price Discrimination, 65 Q.J. Econ. 342, 344 et seq. 355 et seq., 370 (1951). Compare Nelson, The Role of Regulation Re-examined in National Resources Planning Board, Transportation and National Policy 197, 201 (1942).

[12] 3-B Sharfman, The Interstate Commerce Commission 300 (1931) (freight vs. passenger traffic); Ritz, War Time Subsidies and Food Price Stabilization, in Problems in Price Control, pt. II, 93, 182-183 (Franck ed. 1947); Letzler, Price-Supply Problems in Building Materials, in Problems in Price Control: Changing Production Patterns 293, 322 (Caplan ed. 1947); Office of Price Stabilization, General Overriding Regulation No. 18, 17 Fed. Reg. 4236 (May 7, 1952). Compare United States v. United Shoe Machinery Corp., 110 F. Supp. 295, 349 (D. Mass. 1953), aff'd per curiam, 347 U.S. 521 (1954). An interesting controversy has been raised with respect to the practice of public utility companies selling appliances below "cost." Behling, Competition and Monopoly in Public Utility Industries 50 (Illinois Studies in Social Sciences, Vol. 23, No. 1, 1938). The public utility companies take the position that such sales are promotional in character and hence that they should be permitted to make them at whatever figures they choose.

[13] Wright, Mr. Harrod and Growth Economics, in Readings in Business Cycles and National Income 220, 222 (Hansen and Clemence ed. 1953); Mason, Schumpeter on Monopoly and the Large Firm, in Schumpeter: Social Scientist 89, 90 (Harris ed. 1951).

fendant. Some of the problems encountered in that process are discussed below.[14]

§2.12. Exclusive arrangements: Requirements contracts. Many types of exclusive arrangements have been held to constitute abuses. One of the most prominent types of such agreements is a "requirements" contract. Typically, a distributor undertakes to buy his "requirements" of a named commodity from a certain manufacturer.[1] The implication, of course, is that the distributor cannot buy that commodity from other manufacturers during the term of the agreement. Such requirements contracts have frequently been held to constitute abuses,[2] sometimes on the theory that rival manufacturers were "foreclosed" from markets by that means.[3] In other instances the challenged arrangements have been held legal, either because the court failed to find any actual contract in existence[4] or because it appeared that application of the statute to such exclusive agreements would thwart the de-

14 §2.30 *infra.*

§2.12. 1 Often a requirements contract is phrased in terms of a rebate at the end of a year or some other period of time, provided that the customer has not bought from rival firms. Obviously, any such arrangement may involve questions of price discrimination discussed in the preceding section.

2 Eastman Kodak Co. v. Southern Photo Materials Co., 273 U.S. 359, 368 (1927); United States v. Corn Products Refining Co., 234 Fed. 964, 979 (S.D.N.Y. 1916); United States v. Pullman Co., 64 F. Supp. 108, 111 et seq. (E.D. Pa. 1946), *aff'd per curiam,* 330 U.S. 806 (1946); United States v. American Can Co., 87 F. Supp. 18, 29-30 (N.D. Cal. 1949). In the last case it was indicated that the test under the Sherman Act was no different from that applied under §3 of the Clayton Act. Compare FTC v. Motion Picture Advertising Service Co., 344 U.S. 392, 395 (1953); United States v. Philco Corp., No. 18216, E.D. Pa., consent decree entered July 13, 1956, CCH Trade Reg. Serv. ¶68,409. Older decisions are collected in Hale, Control over Distribution, 14 Miss. L.J. 170, 171 (1942); Levi, The Antitrust Laws and Monopoly, 14 U. Chi. L. Rev. 153, 154 (1947). Similar rules are applied, apparently independently of the antitrust laws, under the patent statutes of the United States. National Lockwasher Co. v. Garrett Co., 137 F.2d 255 (3d Cir. 1943); McCullough v. Kammerer Corp., 166 F.2d 759 (9th Cir. 1948), *cert. denied,* 335 U.S. 813 (1948). A requirements contract coupled with an intent to maintain a monopoly constitutes an attempt forbidden by §2 of the Sherman Act. Lorain Journal Co. v. United States, 342 U.S. 143, 150, 154-155 (1951).

3 United States v. National City Lines, Inc., 186 F.2d 562, 567 (7th Cir. 1951), *cert. denied,* 341 U.S. 916 (1951).

4 United States v. J. I. Case Co., 101 F. Supp. 856, 863, 868 (D. Minn. 1951); Leo J. Meyberg Co. v. Eureka Williams Corp., 215 F.2d 100 (9th Cir. 1954), *cert. denied,* 348 U.S. 875 (1954); Hudson Sales Corp. v. Waldrip, 211 F.2d 268, 272-273 (5th Cir. 1954), *cert. denied,* 348 U.S. 821 (1954). In the Court of Appeals it was said at page 274: ". . . plaintiff has sought in vain to make a cause of action out of the fact that the defendant, after a full trial, became completely dissatisfied with plaintiff's representation of its interests and refused to renew the contract . . . because, in its opinion, he was not affording adequate representation." But compare United States v. General Motors Corp., 121 F.2d 376 (7th Cir. 1941), *cert. denied,* 314 U.S. 618 (1941).

fendant's right to select its own customers in the absence of a scheme to effect a monopoly.[5]

In most situations today, the question of whether a requirements contract constitutes an abuse is academic, since Section 3 of the Clayton Act specifically applies to such arrangements[6] when the proscribed competitive effects are proven. Recent decisions under Section 3 have applied that rule stringently[7] — to the dismay of many observers.[8] It is also possible that requirements contracts may violate other statutes.[9] Under the abuse test of monopolization, legality may depend upon several factors. It has been said that the ultimate problem is whether the contracts unreasonably restrict the opportunities of competitors to market

[5] Whitwell v. Continental Tobacco Co., 125 Fed. 454, 463 (8th Cir. 1903); Corn Products Refining Co. v. Oriental Candy Co., 168 Ill. App. 585, 590 et seq. (1912); Brosious v. Pepsi-Cola Co., 59 F. Supp. 429, 482 (M.D. Pa. 1945), aff'd, 155 F.2d 99, 102 (3d Cir. 1946). Compare United States v. American Can Co., 87 F. Supp. 18, 31 (N.D. Cal. 1949); United States v. J. I. Case Co., 101 F. Supp. 856, 863, 866 (D. Minn. 1951); Park-In Theatres, Inc. v. Loew's Theatres, Inc., 70 F. Supp. 880, 887 (D.R.I. 1947), rev'd on other grounds, 174 F.2d 547 (1st Cir. 1949), cert. denied, 338 U.S. 822 (1949). Campbell v. Automatic Products Co., 162 Ohio St. 321, 123 N.E. 2d 401 (1954) (new product being put on market).

[6] Hale, Control Over Distribution, 14 Miss. L.J. 170, 172 et seq. (1942); Note, Section 3 of the Clayton Act, 22 U. Chi. L. Rev. 233 (1954).

[7] Standard Oil Co. of California v. United States, 337 U.S. 293 (1949); United States v. Richfield Oil Corp., 99 F. Supp. 280 (S.D. Cal. 1951), aff'd per curiam, 343 U.S. 922 (1952); FTC v. Motion Picture Advertising Service, Inc., 344 U.S. 392 (1953); Dictograph Products, Inc. v. FTC, 217 F.2d 821 (2d Cir. 1954). See United States v. E. I. Du Pont de Nemours & Co., 353 U.S. 586, 593n (1957). But compare New Orleans Cigarette Service Corp. v. Sicarelli, 73 So.2d 339, 341 (La. App. 1954); Johnson v. Shell Oil Co., 274 Wis. 375, 80 N.W.2d 426 (1957) (contract to buy specific number of gallons of gasoline per month sustained with some effort). See Chaffetz, Report of Chairman of Clayton Act Committee, Proceedings A.B.A., Section of Antitrust law, 149, 159 (Aug. 26, 1953); Hodson, The Manufacturer's Right to His Dealer's Loyalty, Symposium, N.Y. State Bar Assn., Section on Antitrust Law, 186 (CCH, 1953). The effect of the recent decisions is to forbid requirements contracts whenever any substantial amount of commerce is involved, regardless of other considerations.

[8] Lockhart and Sacks, The Relevance of Economic Factors in Determining Whether Exclusive Arrangements Violate Section 3 of the Clayton Act, 65 Harv. L. Rev. 913 (1952); McAllister, Where the Effect May Be to Substantially Lessen Competition or Tend to Create a Monopoly, Proceedings A.B.A., Section of Antitrust Law, 124 (Aug. 27, 1953); Austern, The Supreme Court and Section 3 of the Clayton Act, Symposium, N.Y. State Bar Assn., Section on Antitrust Law, 43 (CCH, 1950); Rahl, Antitrust Policy in Distribution, 104 U. Pa. L. Rev. 185, 198 (1955). But compare Schwartz, Potential Impairment of Competition, 98 U. Pa. L. Rev. 10 (1949). Several recent attempts have been made to "explain" the stringent rule of "quantitative substantiality." Stewart and Turner, The Significance of Oligopoly in Acquisitions and Exclusive Dealing Situations under the Clayton Act, 25 U. Cincinnati L. Rev. 427, 435 et seq. (1957); Kintner, Exclusive Dealing, 3 Practical Lawyer 69, 74 (1957).

[9] Thomsen v. Cayser, 243 U.S. 66 (1917); International Salt Co. v. United States, 332 U.S. 392 (1947); FTC v. Motion Picture Advertising Service, Inc., 344 U.S. 392 (1953); Menacho v. Ward, 27 Fed. 529 (S.D.N.Y. 1886) (common law decision).

their products.[10]   That may in turn depend upon the economic power of the defendant, the length of the term of the arrangement and the availability of other distributors.   One also has the feeling from reading the opinions that the intent of the defendant is relevant.[11]

§2.13.   Exclusive arrangements: Output contracts.   Another form of exclusive arrangement is the contract whereby the output of a manufacturer is to be sold to a single distributor.   Such arrangements may relate to the entire output of the manufacturer or merely to such part of his output as may be available for a specific geographic area.   In the latter event, it is more customary to refer to the arrangement as one whereby the distributor secures an "exclusive sales territory."   Oddly enough, Section 3 of the Clayton Act does not apply to output agreements of either type, although some state statutes do so.[1]

There are decisions in which output contracts have been held to constitute abuses and hence infringements of Section 2 of the Sherman Act or similar legislation.[2]   More commonly, however, such contracts are sustained,[3] perhaps because it is more difficult

[10] United States v. Columbia Steel Co., 334 U.S. 495, 523-524 (1948).

[11] 2 Restatement of Contracts §516.   In Comment g to that section it is said: "An agreement providing for exclusive dealing between the parties, while not in itself necessarily illegal, is not unlikely to involve an attempt to obtain a monopoly. In such a case the agreement is illegal."   See also Hale, Control Over Distribution, 14 Miss. L.J. 170, 171 (1942).

§2.13.   [1] Patrizi v. McAninch, 153 Tex. 389, 269 S.W.2d 343 (1954); Grand Prize Distributing Co. v. Gulf Brewing Co., 267 S.W.2d 906 (Tex. Civ. App. 1954).   There is no decision squarely holding that §3 of the Clayton Act does not apply to such an arrangement but the language of the statute seems plainly to indicate that it does not.

[2] United States v. Crescent Amusement Co., 323 U.S. 173, 186 (1944); United States v. Griffith, 334 U.S. 100, 109 (1948); Arnot v. Pittston & Elmira Coal Co., 68 N.Y. 558, 565 (1876); Dunbar v. American Telephone & Telegraph Co., 238 Ill. 456, 483, 486, 87 N.E. 521 (1909); United States v. International Boxing Club, 150 F. Supp. 397, 417 (S.D.N.Y. 1957).   Compare Schine Chain Theatres, Inc. v. United States, 334 U.S. 110, 118, 121-122 (1948).   Earlier decisions are collected in Hale, Control Over Distribution, 14 Miss. L.J. 170, 180 et seq. (1942).

[3] Virtue v. Creamery Package Manufacturing Co., 227 U.S. 8, 32-33 (1913); Carter-Crume Co. v. Peurring, 86 Fed. 439, 441 (6th Cir. 1898); Fargo Glass & Paint Co. v. Globe American Corp., 201 F.2d 534 (7th Cir. 1953), cert. denied, 345 U.S. 942 (1953); Bascom Launder Corp. v. Telecoin Corp., 204 F.2d 331, 335 (2d Cir. 1953), cert. denied, 345 U.S. 994 (1953); United States v. Bausch & Lomb Co., 45 F. Supp. 387, 399 (S.D.N.Y. 1942), aff'd, 321 U.S. 707 (1944); United States v. Imperial Chemical Industries, Ltd., 105 F. Supp. 215, 244 (S.D.N.Y. 1952); Schwing Motor Co. v. Hudson Sales Corp., 138 F. Supp. 899 (D. Md. 1956), aff'd, 239 F.2d 176 (4th Cir. 1956), cert. denied, 355 U.S. 823 (1957); Packard Motor Car Co. v. Webster Co., 243 F.2d 418, 420 (D.C. Cir. 1957), cert. denied, 355 U.S. 900 (1957).   Compare Lawlor v. National Screen Service Co., 238 F.2d 59, 65 (3d Cir. 1956), rev'd on other grounds, 352 U.S. 992 (1957).   See McLaren, Related Problems of "Requirements" Contracts and Acquisitions in Vertical Integration under the Anti-Trust Laws, 45 Ill. L. Rev. 141, 144 (1950); Note, Refusals to Sell and Public Control of Competition, 58 Yale L.J.

to find an intent to monopolize in the ordinary exclusive sales area agreement. When groups of competitors have been involved on a "horizontal" plane, a much more stringent rule has been applied under Section 1 of the Sherman Act [4] and a similar result might follow, even though the contract were exclusively "vertical" in character, if an attempt to enforce resale price maintenance could be established.[5]

Undoubtedly the decisions place considerable weight upon the intent of the defendant. The Attorney General's Committee took the position that a contract for an exclusive sales area should be legal if the manufacturer does not enjoy monopoly power and if the contract does not constitute part of an attempt to monopolize or an unreasonable restraint of trade.[6] It is not wholly clear what the first part of that test means: if the manufacturer already enjoys monopoly, there can be little harm in moving that monopoly power from the manufacturer to the distributor by an exclusive arrangement of the type here in question. Existing competitors of the distributor may be injured temporarily but a converse reaction will probably be experienced at the manufacturing level and there should be only a slight long-run difference in the allocation of resources. Eureka Williams, for example, offered many of its retailers exclusive sales territories in order to permit each such dealer to reap the benefit of his own promotion of Eureka's vac-

1121, 1122-1123 (1949); Handler, Annual Antitrust Review, 12 Record 1, 2 (Oct. 1957); Note, The Resurgence of the Exclusive Territorial Distributorship as an Anti-Trust Problem, 40 Minn. L. Rev. 853, 856 (1956). Perhaps the foregoing decisions reflect a belief that manufacturers normally possess more market power than distributors. It might not be easy to support that position by proof. Note the approval of "clearance" in the motion picture industry. Paramount Film Co. v. Village Theatre, Inc., 228 F.2d 721, 726 (10th Cir. 1956); United States v. Twentieth Century Fox Film Corp., 137 F. Supp. 78, 85 (S.D. Cal. 1956). Compare Inge v. Twentieth Century Fox Film Corp., 143 F. Supp. 294, 298 (S.D.N.Y. 1956). The notion in the Paramount case that the jury should pass upon the reasonableness of the restraint seems dubious.

[4] Eastern States Retail Lumber Dealers' Assn. v. United States, 234 U.S. 600 (1914); Associated Press v. United States, 326 U.S. 1 (1945); Interocean Publishing Co. v. Associated Press, 184 Ill. 438, 449, 453-454, 56 N.E. 822 (1900); Alexander's Stores v. Ohrbach's Inc., 266 App. Div. 535, 42 N.Y.S.2d 703 (1st Dept. 1943); Fashion Originators' Guild v. FTC, 312 U.S. 457 (1941). But compare Appalachian Coals, Inc. v. United States, 288 U.S. 344 (1933); Bascom Launder Corp. v. Telecoin Corp., 204 F.2d 331, 335 (2d Cir. 1953), cert. denied, 345 U.S. 994 (1953). See McLaren, Related Problems of "Requirements" Contracts and Acquisitions in Vertical Integration Under the Anti-Trust Laws, 45 Ill. L. Rev. 141, 157 (1950); Handler, A Study of the Construction and Enforcement of the Federal Anti-Trust Laws 13-14 (TNEC Monograph No. 38, 1941).

[5] United States v. Bausch & Lomb Co., 321 U.S. 707 (1944); United States v. Frankfort Distilleries, Inc., 324 U.S. 293 (1945); Note, Resale Price Maintenance and the Anti-Trust Laws, 18 U. Chi. L. Rev. 369, 370-371 (1951).

[6] Atty. Gen. Nat. Com. Rep. 30, e.

uum cleaners.[7] Such an arrangement necessarily excluded other retailers who might have sold Eureka cleaners. At the same time the concession made by the manufacturer undoubtedly weakened it by the amount of sales which might have been made to the excluded dealers. Eureka's hope lay in the possibility that the incentive offered by the exclusive sales territory would more than compensate for the lost sales. Accordingly, the matter is likely to boil down to a determination of the defendant's intent.[8]

§2.14. **Exclusive arrangements: Restricted sales areas.** If a manufacturer agrees with a number of distributors to grant them individually exclusive sales areas, the agreements will almost inevitably also restrict the distributors to the specific areas in question. Without such a provision it would be impossible to assure other distributors that their areas would remain exclusive. Hence it is common for a manufacturer to agree that a distributor may handle the entire output of a commodity in State X, while the distributor at the same time agrees not to sell in other states.

Section 3 of the Clayton Act does not apply to a restricted sales area, although several state statutes may do so.[1] Furthermore, it does not appear that such arrangements have ever been held to constitute an abuse under the Sherman Act.[2] There has been considerable litigation on a closely allied question, namely, whether a patent license may be restricted to a particular field of application. The decisions sustain the validity of such licenses by a

[7] Eureka Williams, 36 Fortune No. 6, pp. 108, 184 (1947). In the introduction of a new product, it is important that the retailer not only display the commodity but demonstrate it with assurance in its performance. Such tactics may require a knowledgeable sales staff and preacceptance by the consumer of the retail outlet. To provide such facilities the retailer may demand exclusive privileges. Bliss, Preretailing and Consumer Buying Patterns over Time, 21 J. Marketing 83, 84-85 (1956).

[8] Hale, Control over Distribution 14 Miss. L.J. 170, 180-181 (1942). Note the close connection between an "abuse" and an "attempt." An attempt, of course, requires a specific intent. See §9.3 infra. Accordingly, when the courts say that an exclusive sales area is lawful in the absence of an intent to monopolize, they have assimilated the "abuse" into the "attempt" for all practical purposes. Compare Note, Dealer Franchise Agreements, 63 Harv. L. Rev. 1010, 1022 (1950). The possibility of an adverse effect upon competition would appear to depend upon the existence of market friction: if the rival distributors can quickly obtain the capital to set up a new manufacturing enterprise, the output agreement will not hurt them or the ultimate consumer.

§2.14. [1] Hale, Control over Distribution, 14 Miss. L.J. 170, 183n (1942).
[2] Boro Hall Corp. v. General Motors Corp., 124 F.2d 822 (2d Cir. 1942); Hale, Control over Distribution, 14 Miss L.J. 170, 182-183 (1942). But cf. United States v. Philco Corp., No. 18216, E.D. Pa., consent decree entered July 13, 1956, CCH Trade Reg. Serv. ¶68,409. See Handler, Annual Antitrust Review, 12 Record 1, 5 (Oct. 1957). Contra: Rifkind, Divisions of Territory under the Antitrust Laws, Symposium, N.Y. State Bar Assn., Section on Antitrust Law, 173, 177, 181 (CCH 1953).

narrow margin.[3] Such a patent license, of course, does not prevent the licensee from manufacturing within the restricted area: he is only prevented from using or marketing the licensed patent in that area.   In view of the fact that the validity of such restricted licenses has been in doubt from time to time, it is not impossible that the restricted sales area practice will some day be held to constitute an abuse.

§2.15.   **Exclusive arrangements: Leasing.**   For many decades it was supposed that a seller of goods was free to lease them if he chose to do so.   It is, of course, not practical to lease commodities which are directly consumed by customers; one could scarcely conceive of a refiner "leasing" the sugar he sells to candymakers, bakers or housewives.   Machinery, however, has been made the subject of lease by manufacturers, particularly to other manufacturers.   For many years no one supposed the practice to be either unlawful or immoral.[1]

In several recent decisions, however, the practice of leasing machinery has been condemned.   In some degree leasing has been found akin to a requirements contract on the theory that the lessee may be "psychologically or economically" prevented from changing to a rival brand of machinery.   It has been said that leasing contains "exclusionary features," and there has been some complaint that the rentals charged for the machines were too low, and were made up by higher profits on supplies used with those machines and also sold by the same manufacturer.[2]   It is not clear

3 General Talking Pictures, Inc. v. Western Electric Co., 304 U.S. 175, 305 U.S. 124 (1938); Automatic Radio Co. v. Hazeltine Research, Inc., 176 F.2d 799, 803 (1st Cir. 1949), aff'd, 339 U.S. 827, 831 (1950); Vulcan Manufacturing Co. v. Maytag Co., 73 F.2d 136, 138-139 (8th Cir. 1934), cert. dismissed, 294 U.S. 734 (1935); Folk, The Relation of Patents to the Antitrust Laws, 13 Law & Contemp. Prob. 278, 283 (1948); Note, Legality of Patent License Requiring Assignment of Improvement Patents to Licensor, 47 Colum. L. Rev. 321, 322 (1947).   As noted in the last-cited article, the foregoing results appear to be inconsistent with other decisions of recent years narrowing the bargaining power of the patentee.   As to the impact of a combination among rivals to bring about a similar result, and the effect of §1 of the Sherman Act thereon, consult Hartford-Empire Co. v. United States, 323 U.S. 386, 324 U.S. 570 (1945); United States v. National Lead Co., 63 F. Supp. 513, 523-524 (S.D.N.Y. 1945), aff'd, 332 U.S. 319 (1947).

Vertical integration, of course, presents many problems similar to those involved in exclusive arrangements of the type discussed in the text.   See Chapter 5.

§2.15. 1 Williams v. Hughes Tool Co., 186 F.2d 278, 285 (10th Cir. 1950), cert. denied, 341 U.S. 903 (1951); Hughes Tool Co. v. Cole, 113 F. Supp. 519, 522 (W.D. Okla. 1953), aff'd, 215 F.2d 924 (10th Cir. 1954), cert. denied, 348 U.S. 927 (1955). An example of leasing in practice is described in Loehwing, Rented Car Race, 37 Barron's No. 17, p. 3 (1957).

2 United States v. United Shoe Machinery Corp., 110 F. Supp. 295, 321, 324-325, 344 (D. Mass. 1953), aff'd per curiam, 347 U.S. 521 (1954); United States v. American Can Co., 87 F. Supp. 18, 23-24 (N.D. Cal. 1949); Hughes Tool Co. v. Ford, 114 F. Supp. 525, 544 et seq. (E.D. Okla. 1953), rev'd, 215 F.2d 924 (10th Cir. 1954), cert.

that the cases condemning the practice of leasing have relied upon the abuse test of monopoly; if the decisions were based upon some different test, however, it would appear to follow a fortiori that leasing should be prohibited under the abuse doctrine. In these circumstances, it is not at all clear whether the practice of leasing is to be condemned universally, partially or rarely. In the leading case on the subject it was said:

> . . . this Court does not rule that leases of that type are in every context restraints of trade, or otherwise unlawful. All that this opinion has ruled is that when control of the market has been obtained in large part by such leases, the market power cannot be said to have been thrust upon its holder . . . the leases themselves are not forbidden; only when they are used as an instrument for seeking market control is the lessor to be charged with using them in an attempt to monopolize.[3]

§2.16. **Exclusive arrangements: Patent grant-backs.** Another recently recognized abuse lies in the field of patent licensing. Formerly, it was understood that a patentee might license others on condition that they grant him a license on such patents as they might own or thereafter acquire. Indeed, it appeared to be the law that the patentee could bargain for the assignment of all so-called "improvement patents" secured by the licensee.[1] In any event, such a transaction appeared to be lawful if entered into by

---

denied, 348 U.S. 927, 965 (1955); Complaint ¶¶25, 26, 47(a)(5) in United States v. International Business Machines Corp., No. C-72-344, S.D.N.Y. (1952). In the United Shoe Machinery Company case the trial court said at page 344: "Much of United's market power is traceable to the magnetic ties inherent in its system of leasing, and not selling, its more important machines. The lease-only system of distributing complicated machines has many 'partnership' aspects, and it has exclusionary features such as the 10-year term, the full capacity clause, and return charges, and the failure to segregate service charges from machine charges. Moreover, the leasing system has aided United in maintaining a pricing system which discriminates between machine types." In the American Can case the trial court said at page 23: "It is the fixed and uniform policy of American to lease rather than sell its closing machines . . . Therefore, the two independent can-closing machine makers . . . have a market limited to the small canmakers, for the ordinary canner will not purchase a can-closing machine as long as he can lease it from his can supplier . . ."

3 United States v. United Shoe Machinery Corp., 110 F. Supp. 295, 346 (D. Mass. 1953), *aff'd per curiam,* 347 U.S. 521 (1954). The difficulty with the statement quoted in the text, of course, is that every seller leases his products in the expectation of doing a larger volume of business than he could by outright sales alone. Doing more business is a step toward "market control." At some point in time, therefore, the successful seller must, under the rule quoted in the text, stop indulging in the practice of leasing. Query when that point is reached.

§2.16. 1 Transparent-Wrap Machine Corp. v. Stokes & Smith Co., 329 U.S. 637, 648 (1947); Ellis, Patent Assignments and Licenses 231 (1936).

a sole patentee[2] and without intent to monopolize. More recent decisions, however, cast doubt upon the grant-back practice. In several cases involving a patentee bargaining for a mere nonexclusive license, the practice has been held to violate the Sherman Act.[3] In part, those decisions are based on the ground that the patentee was a leading producer in its industry and that such a firm should not be permitted to use a patent to "extend" the statutory monopoly into another area. The Attorney General's Committee, rejecting the view that every violation of patent law constituted a per se offense under the antitrust laws,[4] concluded that the legality of the grant-back of patent rights should depend upon the circumstances involved. If the license running back to the original patentee were nonexclusive and the original licensee's incentive to carry on technological research were not dampened, the Committee apparently would find no fault with the grant-backs.[5]

§2.17. Exclusive arrangements: Tying clauses. Still another type of exclusive arrangement is found in the "tying" clauses whereby a seller refuses to dispose of two commodities separately but insists that they be purchased in combination. In the older cases, the practice was sometimes referred to as "full line forcing," [1] meaning that the distributor or customer could not obtain one commodity alone but was compelled to buy all of the manufacturer's products or none.

United Shoe Machinery Company formerly insisted that shoe manufacturers lease from it all the different machines required for use in their factories. The Shoe Machinery Company's practice gave rise to widespread complaint, and litigation under the Sherman Act was instituted with a view to penalizing the company's method of doing business. The court held, however, that leases were simply bargains not different from any others; that the Shoe Machinery Company enjoyed the privilege of offering to sell (or lease) all of its machines or none of them and that the tying in-

---

2 Compare United States v. National Lead Co., 63 F. Supp. 513, 524, 531-532 (S.D.N.Y. 1945), aff'd, 332 U.S. 319 (1947); Winkler-Koch Engineering Co. v. Universal Oil Products Co., 79 F. Supp. 1013, 1018 (S.D.N.Y. 1947).

3 United States v. General Electric Co., 80 F. Supp. 989, 1006 (S.D.N.Y. 1948); United States v. General Electric Co., 82 F. Supp. 753, 816 (D.N.J. 1949); Jessup, Agreement to Assign Improvement Patents, 21 So. Calif. L. Rev. 285, 287 (1948); Note, Legality of Patent License Requiring Assignment of Improvement Patents to Licensor, 47 Colum. L. Rev. 321, 322 (1947).

4 Atty. Gen. Nat. Com. Rep. 250, 6.

5 Id. at 227, 3.

§2.17. 1 Compare Davies, Joseph E. (Commissioner of Corporations), Trust Laws and Unfair Competition 322 (March 5, 1915).

volved did not fall within the prohibitions of the Sherman Act.[2] The Congress, displeased by the decision, sought to reach such tying arrangements in Section 3 of the Clayton Act. Decisions interpreting that statute make it plain that it will be enforced stringently[3] — perhaps beyond the original congressional intent. Meanwhile a number of cases involving attempts by patentees to compel licensees to purchase unpatented supplies along with the patented products had rendered it impossible for a seller to "tie" two products together if one was patented.[4]

Hostility to the tying practice has recently resulted in decisions holding it illegal under the Sherman Act. Most of the cases, it is true, purport to rely on Section 1 of that measure, since it is conceived that the seller enters into an agreement with the buyer which restrains trade. The view that "tying" two commodities together is thus illegal has been applied to a manufacturer of motor cars who attempted to induce its customers to use a financing service offered by its wholly owned subsidiary. In that opinion the court laid stress upon the "dominant" position of the automobile manufacturer, saying:

> . . . behind it all lay the might of GMC which had achieved a dominant position in the automobile industry as manufacturer of cars desired by dealer-purchasers and many members of the retail public. Of course, the utilization of the manufacturer's dominant position and the tremendous popularity of General Motors automobiles . . . made it possible for the appellants to force the sale of the related finance service.[5]

[2] United States v. United Shoe Machinery Co., 247 U.S. 32, 66 (1918). Older decisions are collected in Hale, Control over Distribution, 14 Miss. L.J. 170, 177 et seq. (1942). Compare Times-Picayune Publishing Co. v. United States, 345 U.S. 594 (1953); Pick Manufacturing Co. v. General Motors Corp., 80 F.2d 641 (7th Cir. 1935), aff'd per curiam, 299 U.S. 3 (1936). At one time the same view prevailed under §5 of the Federal Trade Commission Act. FTC v. Gratz, 253 U.S. 421 (1920). Note, however, that the opinion in that case (at 428-429) is expressly grounded on the condition that the seller did not enjoy monopoly power.

[3] International Salt Co. v. United States, 332 U.S. 392 (1947); Oxford Varnish Corp. v. Ault & Wiborg Corp., 83 F.2d 764 (6th Cir. 1936); see Standard Oil Co. of California v. United States, 337 U.S. 293, 305-306 (1949); Times-Picayune Publishing Co. v. United States, 345 U.S. 594, 608-609 (1953).

[4] Motion Picture Patents Co. v. Universal Film Manufacturing Co., 243 U.S. 502 (1917); Mercoid Corp. v. Mid-Continent Co., 320 U.S. 661, 666 (1944); Atty. Gen. Nat. Com. Rep. 250, 6; Note, Tying Restrictions: Changing Standards of Legality, 48 Colum. L. Rev. 733, 739 (1948). Compare Consumers Coffee Stores v. Illinois Commerce Commission, 348 Ill. 615, 181 N.E. 411 (1932). Note that in the patent cases it is not impossible to determine whether one product is "tied" to another because the patent claims define one of the commodities involved.

[5] United States v. General Motors Corp., 121 F.2d 376, 400 (7th Cir. 1941), cert. denied, 314 U.S. 618 (1941). In the Court of Appeals it was also said, at page 398: ". . . appellants were in a position to impose and did impose their will on the independent dealer-purchaser, not only as to how he was to conduct his business but

Several similar decisions have involved owners of chains of motion picture theaters.   In those cases it has been held illegal for the chain theater owners to bargain for the licensing of films upon a chain-wide basis, some stress being laid on the fact that a portion of the defendants' theaters were without local competition in the towns where they were located.[6]

It is not difficult to summarize the present state of the law with respect to tying because the Supreme Court has conveniently stated its views in succinct form.   The law now is:

> From the "tying" cases a perceptible pattern of illegality emerges: When the seller enjoys a monopolistic position in the market for the "tying" product, *or* if a substantial volume of commerce in the "tied" product is restrained, a tying arrangement violates the narrower standards expressed in §3 of the Clayton Act because from either factor the requisite potential lessening of competition is inferred.   And because for even a lawful monopolist it is "unreasonable, *per se*, to foreclose competitors from any substantial market," a tying arrangement is banned by §1 of the Sherman Act whenever *both* conditions are met.   In either case, the arrangement transgresses §5 of the Federal Trade Commission Act, since minimally that section registers violations of the Clayton and Sherman Acts.[7]

As indicated above, the recent Sherman Act decisions with respect to tying have been based upon Section 1 of that legislation. It is believed, however, that tying which infringes Section 1[8] would constitute an abuse within the meaning of Section 2 of the

---

also as to whether he would conduct it at all . . ."; and at page 403: ". . . GMC has always dominated the market for General Motors cars to a considerable extent, but it was only when control of the marketing process was perfected by the appellants and was directed at the creation of an artificial non-competitive market for GMAC, that it extended beyond legitimate business demands and became a menace to the interest of the public."

  [6] United States v. Crescent Amusement Co., 323 U.S. 173, 187-188 (1944); Schine Chain Theatres, Inc. v. United States, 334 U.S. 110, 116 (1948); United States v. Griffith, 334 U.S. 100 (1948).   Some of the amazing implications of those decisions are discussed in Chapter 7.   The practices of "block-booking," "package licensing" and charging one fee for two services were condemned in United States v. Paramount Pictures, Inc., 66 F. Supp. 323, 348 (S.D.N.Y. 1946), *modified*, 334 U.S. 131 (1948) (making of "franchise" agreements, however, involving contract whereby motion picture exhibitor obtains all "features" of given film producer, held lawful, 334 U.S. 131, 155; relief afforded in 85 F. Supp. 881, 897 (S.D.N.Y. 1949)); United States v. General Electric Co., 82 F. Supp. 753, 859 (D.N.J. 1949); United States v. United Shoe Machinery Corp., 110 F. Supp. 295, 322-323 (D. Mass. 1953), *aff'd per curiam*, 347 U.S. 521 (1954); Kansas City Star Co. v. United States, 240 F.2d 643, 656 (8th Cir. 1957).   Compare Miller Motors, Inc. v. Ford Motor Co., 149 F. Supp. 790, 805 et seq. (M.D.N.C. 1957).

  [7] Times-Picayune Publishing Co. v. United States, 345 U.S. 594, 608-609 (1953). Cf. Standard Oil Co. of California v. United States, 337 U.S. 293 (1949), *aff'g* 78 F. Supp. 850 (1948).

  [8] International Salt Co. v. United States, 332 U.S. 392, 396 (1947).

Sherman Act on the theory that such a restraint would automatically constitute an abuse. Accordingly, the practice of tying appears to be illegal in the circumstances outlined in the above quotation.[9]

§2.18. **Exclusive arrangements: Analysis.** In the preceding sections we have outlined various types of exclusive arrangements held to constitute abuses under Section 2 of the Sherman Act or similar legislation. The courts have used a number of phrases to suggest the underlying rationale of those decisions. It has been said, for example, that it is unreasonable to "foreclose" competitors from any substantial market.[1] In that connection the word "exclusion" is often stressed.[2] Another way of explaining the decisions is to say that the defendant has attempted to use "leverage" so as to exploit a dominant position in one market by expanding into another.[3] In a leading case it was said: "If monopoly power can be used to beget monopoly, the Act becomes a feeble instrument indeed." [4] In other decisions emphasis is placed on the theory that the seller "compels" or "forces" his customers to take products which they do not wish to buy.[5] In this section, we

---

[9] The decisions in United States v. United Shoe Machinery Co., 247 U.S. 32 (1918), and FTC v. Gratz, 253 U.S. 421 (1920), should be regarded as overruled.

The practice of reciprocity (sometimes called "back-scratching") is believed to be widespread in business. It does not, however, appear to have been attacked under the antitrust laws. But see FTC, Monopolistic Practices and Small Business 87 (Report to Subcommittee on Monopoly, Senate Select Committee on Small Business, Feb. 21, 1952); Kansas City Star Co. v. United States, 240 F.2d 643, 656 (8th Cir. 1957); compare 4 Restatement of Torts §768, Comment *f*. Reciprocity, however, appears to be a form of tying and presumably could be so treated in the courts.

§2.18. [1] International Salt Co. v. United States, 332 U.S. 392, 396 (1947); United States v. Griffith, 334 U.S. 100, 107 (1948). Compare Lorain Journal Co. v. United States, 342 U.S. 143 (1951). In United States v. Columbia Steel Co., 334 U.S. 495, 524 (1948), the phrase used was: "to unreasonably restrict the opportunities of competitors to market their product . . ."

[2] United States v. Pullman Co., 64 F. Supp. 108, 134 (E.D. Pa. 1946), *aff'd per curiam*, 330 U.S. 806 (1947); McLaren, Related Problems of "Requirements" Contracts and Acquisitions in Vertical Integration Under the Anti-Trust Laws, 45 Ill. L. Rev. 141, 155 (1950). Note here how close the abuse is to an "attempt."

[3] In Times-Picayune Publishing Co. v. United States, 345 U.S. 594, 611 (1953), the language of the Court was: ". . . the essence of illegality in tying agreements is the wielding of monopolistic leverage; a seller exploits his dominant position in one market to expand his empire into the next." Note the theory expressed in the dissenting opinion (at 628) that the defendant in that case had a "monopoly" in the morning newspaper field and was exerting "leverage" to enlarge his position in the evening newspaper market.

[4] United States v. Griffith, 334 U.S. 100, 108 (1948).

[5] United States v. Pullman Co., 64 F. Supp. 108, 112 (E.D. Pa. 1946), *aff'd per curiam*, 330 U.S. 806 (1947); Remarks by Senator Reed, 51 Cong. Rec. 14,091, 14,099 (1914); Lewis, Motion Pictures, 11 Encyc. Soc. Sci. 58, 62 (1933). At times somewhat fantastic characterizations have been applied to the restrictive arrangements referred to herein. For example, it has been said that they reflect a differential in

attempt to determine whether one or more of those concepts is
soundly conceived.

Characterization of exclusive arrangements as arising out of
"coercion," "compulsion" and the like suggests that there is
something unfair about the practices. Frequently it is said that
such agreements are "forced" on unwilling distributors,[6] who
thereby are robbed of a "free decision." [7] Such characterization
raises the question of why the exclusive arrangement is any more
unfair than the price agreed upon between the parties. Presumably the party benefiting from the exclusive arrangement suffers
a detriment in the price agreed upon (or some other term of the
transaction): that is, absent the exclusive arrangement, that party
presumptively could secure a more favorable price. It is therefore difficult to understand why there is any more coercion in the
transaction than in any other contract between parties similarly
situated. It is, of course, true, in the short run at least, that
wealthy firms have more bargaining power than poor ones. Some
of the discussions of exclusive arrangements speak of "channelling
of the profit motive into socially constructive channels, distributive
justice, and the diffusion of economic power." [8] The suggestion
appears to be that all bargains between persons of unequal wealth
should be controlled by the state in a program of universal intervention.[9] Condemnation of exclusive arrangements on the
ground that they constitute "unfairly exclusive tactics" [10] thus

---

bargaining power or that local dealers are compelled to supply capital to manufacturers. Note, Tying Restrictions, 48 Colum. L. Rev. 733, 737 (1948).

[6] Stockhausen, The Commercial and Anti-Trust Aspects of Term Requirements
Contracts, 23 N.Y.U.L.Q. Rev. 412, 415 (1948). Compare United States v. American
Naval Stores Co., 172 Fed. 455, 462 (S.D. Ga. 1909).

[7] Thus, in Dirlam and Kahn, Fair Competition 118 (1954) it was said: "The
prime question is whether the exclusion, i.e., the *act*, is unreasonable, or stems
merely from socially acceptable methods of vying for consumer patronage and from
the free decision of the buyer or dealer. If the former, the only relevant test of
competitive impact is whether competitors have been subjected to an appreciable
handicap." Query what is meant by "socially acceptable" methods. Cf. United
States v. J. I. Case Co., 101 F. Supp. 856 (D. Minn. 1951).

[8] Dirlam and Kahn, Fair Competition 39 (1954).

[9] Note the suggestion in Dirlam and Kahn, id. at 179, that disputes between
farm implement menufacturers and their distributors should be settled by compulsory arbitration. Note, too, the effect of immobility of one party's resources:
a farm implement retailer may have a large inventory of replacement parts, a
considerable investment in good will in the trade-mark of the manufacturer whom
he has represented, and the like, which make it difficult for him to change brands.
Id. at 176-177. Compare Miller Motors, Inc. v. Ford Motor Co., 149 F. Supp. 790,
811 (M.D.N.C. 1957). Note the surprising automobile dealers' protective act of
August 8, 1956, 70 Stat. 1125, 15 U.S.C.A. §§1221 et seq. Similar legislation exists
in several states.

[10] Dirlam and Kahn, id. at 55. Mr. Justice Holmes wrote: "I hope that my illustrations have shown the danger, both to speculation and to practice, of confounding
morality with law, and the trap which legal language lays for us on that side of our

comes perilously close to a policy of protectionism — which, of course, is the antithesis of competition.

Moving from the ethical to the economic realm, the notion that rivals are "foreclosed" by exclusive arrangements is worthy of careful analysis.[11] It is true that there are many instances in which such exclusion appears to have taken place. Both in the reported decisions of antitrust cases[12] and in economic literature,[13] instances can be found in which such foreclosure appears to have been real. It is submitted, however, that the notion of exclusion arising out of exclusive arrangements confuses the malady with its symptoms. Unless there is an element of horizontal monopoly at one level or another, there can be no exclusion: if there are many filling stations in a given area, the making of a requirements contract between the proprietor of one of them and a refiner of gasoline will not foreclose rival refiners because they may turn to the remaining stations. Instances of actual exclusion will be found to rest upon some such monopoly element at one horizontal level or another. Frequently monopoly elements arise out of indivisibility: economies of scale, for example, prevent the construction of more than one railroad in an area and hence an exclusive arrangement with such a railroad will effectively foreclose rival shippers.[14] It is probably true that an exclusive ar-

---

way. For my own part, I often doubt whether it would not be a gain if every word of moral significance could be banished from the law altogether . . ." Collected Legal Papers 179 (1920). Take, for example, United States v. National Retail Lumber Dealers Assn., 40 F. Supp. 448 (D. Colo. 1941). In that case the retail lumber dealers argued (at 456-457) that they were morally entitled to the exclusive sale of lumber at retail; and that the method of distributing lumber should be "fair," meaning that wholesalers should not be permitted to sell to ultimate consumers.

11 Compare Lockhart and Sacks, The Relevance of Economic Factors in Determining Whether Exclusive Arrangements Violate Section 3 of the Clayton Act, 65 Harv. L. Rev. 913 (1952); Director and Levi, Trade Regulation, 51 Nw. U.L. Rev. 281, 293 (1956).

12 United States v. American Tobacco Co., 221 U.S. 106 (1911); United States v. Corn Products Refining Co., 234 Fed. 964, 980, 1013 (S.D.N.Y. 1916); United States v. Pullman Co., 64 F. Supp. 108, 112 (E.D. Pa. 1946), aff'd per curiam, 330 U.S. 806 (1947).

13 1 Nevins, Study in Power 299-300, 356, 365 (1953); Oxenfeldt, Industrial Pricing and Market Practices 282 (1951). But cf. Kilgore Committee, pt. 3, at 1098.

14 1 Nevins, Study in Power 223, 299-300 (1953). Investor ignorance may also play a large role in such a situation: until the true market condition is made known to persons with savings one firm may be placed at a competitive disadvantage because it cannot raise additional capital. On the other hand, the "imperfections" cannot work in both directions at once. It has been urged, for example, that control of pipelines by oil companies results in those companies being "favored" over their rivals and, conversely, that the control over the refineries gives the oil companies preferential access to a "lucrative" pipeline business. Dirlam and Kahn, Fair Competition 150 (1954). Such a dual effect seems beyond the realm of possibility. Similarly, when a requirements contract is coupled with an exclusive sales area, it follows that competing manufacturers and distributors are left with a clear

rangement may, in the short run at least, increase the cost of entering into competition: if each existing filling station signs a requirements contract with a refiner, then another refiner attempting to
enter the market may well have to supply the capital for a new
filling station.[15] Whether that effect actually impairs competition
will depend upon factors of indivisibility and investor ignorance.
If a town is not large enough to support a second gasoline dis-
penser, then a requirements contract will raise a substantial barrier
to entry. Similarly, if investors are unaware of the possibilities of
profit for the rival refiner, they may not supply the necessary capital to construct another filling station. Apparently some such
factors influenced the recent decision in the *Shoe Machinery* case.
There it was held that the leasing of machines, rather than their
sale, "psychologically or economically" impeded the shoemaker
from using rival brands.[16] Offhand, one might suppose that the
shoemaker, not having had to invest capital in the leased machinery, might be more willing to replace it with the product of a
rival. Apparently, however, the court felt that leasing created
barriers to entry because other manufacturers of shoe machinery
would have to offer equally good terms to shoemakers in order to
meet the competition of the defendant. Viewed in that light, leasing appears to be little more than that extension of credit which
is commonly practiced in many lines of commerce.[17] It would
seem to be deleterious only if investors could not be made to
realize that the rival manufacturers could profitably utilize additional capital to finance similar extensions of credit.

In its essence, competition is simply "getting the business";
every sale forecloses a competitor and business could not go on
without continuous foreclosures of this type. An exclusive arrangement is simply "getting the business" for a period of time.[18]
It follows that an exclusive arrangement may well promote com-

---

field with respect to each other, since the "tied" manufacturer and distributor cannot deal with them.

[15] Atty. Gen. Nat. Com. Rep. 137, B. Compare United States v. Great Lakes
Towing Co., 208 Fed. 733, 745-746 (N.D. Ohio, 1913).

[16] United States v. United Shoe Machinery Co., 110 F. Supp. 295, 324, 344, 346
(D. Mass. 1953), aff'd *per curiam*, 347 U.S. 521 (1954). One of the few reasons given
for the court's conclusion in that case, which appears convincing, relates to the
provision for servicing of the leased machinery. Id. at 325. Apparently the defendant had developed such an efficient servicing organization that no independent
servicing firms had been developed by others. Accordingly, any rival shoe machinery
manufacturer would have to provide such servicing facilities himself, and hence
his capital requirements would be increased. Note, however, that the difficulty
mentioned appears to arise out of a monopoly in the business of providing service
for machinery and not out of the leasing practice itself.

[17] E.g., Gibb, The Saco-Lowell Shops 398 (1950).

[18] 4 Restatement of Torts §768.

petion, rather than discourage it.[19]   An output contract, for example, relieving a manufacturer of sales costs, could permit the distributor to cut prices and thus secure larger sales.[20]   Some such economy, often disregarded because distribution (as opposed to production) involves no tangible change in the commodities involved,[21] together with factors of indivisibility, may account for considerable cost savings which contribute to more effective competition.   Again, therefore, emphasis upon foreclosure shades rapidly into protectionism.[22]   In that connection it is interesting to note that the early British statutes against "forestalling," "regrating" and the like were partly price control mechanisms designed to protect existing monopolies and were ultimately abolished by believers in free trade.[23]

Restrictive arrangements, moreover, are important tools in the introduction of innovations.   In order to induce distributors, for example, to push a new product, it is often necessary to assure them exclusive rights within their respective areas: a monopoly element is created in order to induce effort to overcome consumer

[19] Compare Excelsior Motor Manufacturing & Supply Co. v. Sound Equipment, Inc., 73 F.2d 725, 728 (7th Cir. 1934). Even in Dirlam and Kahn, Fair Competition 194 (1954), the foregoing factor appears to be recognized.

[20] Numerous other possibilities suggest themselves. Exclusive arrangements may reduce risks involved in meeting future obligations and hence permit the undertaking of contracts otherwise too risky for the parties to contemplate; in other words, the parties to the arrangement share the risks of failure to produce on time and the like. Again, it is well understood that the practice of leasing machinery can reduce capital requirements at the lessee's level and hence encourage free entry into his business. Note also the possibility that economies of scale available to one party may be shared with the other. Such factors have been recognized in the courts. Standard Oil Co. of California v. United States, 337 U.S. 293, 307 (1949); United States v. J. I. Case Co., 101 F. Supp. 856, 862-863 (D. Minn. 1951); Stockhausen. The Commercial and Anti-Trust Aspects of Term Requirements Contracts, 23 N.Y.U.L.Q. Rev. 412, 421 (1948).

[21] Compare Roos, Dynamic Economics 6-7 (1934). Note the legality of "ancillary" restraints of trade. 2 Restatement of Contracts §515; Note, Illinois Anti-Trust Law Disinterred, 43 Ill. L. Rev. 205, 214 (1948). A restrictive covenant to protect the good will involved in the sale of a going concern, for example, is generally sustained. The reason is that the freedom of alienation thus encouraged is believed more important than the restraint imposed upon the vendor: in other words, the courts believe the "imperfections" are more deleterious than the "impurities." Note, similarly, the rule that one who induces another to breach his contract with a third party is liable to that third party. 4 Restatement of Torts §766.

[22] Compare Lorain Journal Co. v. United States, 342 U.S. 143, 153 (1951) (relief to be here provided may yet save injured competitor), with FTC v. Morton Salt Co., 334 U.S. 37, 46 (1948) (mere possibility that competitor may be injured will bring Robinson-Patman Act into play); Dirlam and Kahn, Fair Competition 117 (1954); Griffin, An Economic Approach to Anti-Trust Problems, 35-36 (American Enterprise Assn. 1951).

[23] Letwin, The English Common Law Concerning Monopolies, 21 U. Chi. L. Rev. 355, 369-370, 372 (1954).

ignorance and inertia. Often marketing of a new product requires "missionary work" of an expensive character.[24] Practical experience suggests that mere inducements in price are not always sufficient to produce such effects.[25]

From the foregoing discussion, it is plain that exclusive arrangements are not nearly so pernicious as sometimes supposed. As the discussion suggests, whether such practices should constitute abuses may depend upon many factors. Unless those factors, including indivisibility, investor and consumer ignorance and inertia, immobility and innovation, are carefully examined, a court is likely to condemn restrictive arrangements which are actually beneficial in character.[26] Obviously, the length of the contract's term is an important factor to be considered. Here again, however, we should be careful not to overlook the fundamental proposition that foreclosure can only result when there is some degree of monopoly power at a horizontal level.[27] Prohibition of restrictive arrangements may often, therefore, consist of little more than short-run regulation which does not dissipate the malady but only eliminates a portion of its symptoms.

§2.19. **Analysis of tying.** Because it raises questions somewhat different from those considered under the heading of "exclusive arrangements," we consider separately the issues raised by "tying" one product to another.[1] Frequently the decisions simply assume that tying is a practice in restraint of trade, deleterious to

[24] Compare Bascom Launder Corp. v. Telecoin Corp., 204 F.2d 311, 335 (2d Cir. 1953), *cert. denied,* 345 U.S. 994 (1953); Hudson Sales Corp. v. Waldrip, 211 F.2d 268, 274 (5th Cir. 1954), *cert. denied,* 348 U.S. 821 (1954); Atty. Gen. Nat. Com. Rep. 137, B; Dirlam and Kahn, Fair Competition 183-184 (1954). Examples of such "missionary work" are found in Longstreet, A Century on Wheels: The Story of Studebaker 37 (1952); The Borden Co., Ann. Rep. 1952, 16 (New York City, 1953); Sharp & Dohme, Inc., 1952 Ann. Rep. 23 (Philadelphia, 1953); Best-selling Bendix, 36 Fortune No. 5, pp. 133, 168, 171 (1947). Note the use of the leasing technique when the Dixie Cup Company developed a new line of machinery to fill containers with ice cream, Dixie always having furnished the containers. New Product Development Spurring Dixie Cup Co., 35 Barron's No. 14, p. 35 (1955).

[25] Compare Foundry Services v. Beneflux Corp., 110 F. Supp. 857, 861 (S.D.N.Y. 1953), *rev'd on other grounds,* 206 F.2d 214 (2d Cir. 1953).

[26] Lockhart and Sacks, The Relevance of Economic Factors in Determining Whether Exclusive Arrangements Violate Section 3 of the Clayton Act, 65 Harv. L. Rev. 913, 921, 933 (1952); Austern, The Supreme Court and Section 3 of the Clayton Act, Symposium, N.Y. State Bar Assn., Section on Antitrust Law, 43, 44, 47 (CCH, 1950). But compare McLaren, Related Problems of "Requirements" Contracts and Acquisitions in Vertical Integration under the Anti-Trust Laws, 45 Ill. L. Rev. 141, 156 (1950).

[27] Schwartz, Potential Impairment of Competition, 98 U. Pa. L. Rev. 10, 18-19 (1949). Compare Machlup, The Political Economy of Monopoly 122 (1952).

§2.19. [1] Standard Oil Co. of California v. United States, 337 U.S. 293, 305 et seq. (1949).

the public interest. They flatly say that tying agreements must necessarily lessen competition and tend to monopoly.[2] Section 3 of the Clayton Act, of course, takes a comparable position.[3] Upon analysis, however, the practice of tying is found to have far less obvious effects than those commonly attributed to it. Indeed, tying is a mysterious phenomenon which is not wholly understood by anyone.[4]

The notion that tying involves an exercise of "leverage" whereby a defendant "forces" a second product upon an unwilling customer[5] is built upon foundations of sand. So far as the "fairness" aspects of the matter are concerned we have indicated above that the notion of "coercion" would logically require the reduction of all disparity in economic resources.[6] Otherwise, no regularly employed adult could buy a paper from a newsboy without the hazard of rescission of the sale.[7] In economic terms, the notions of "leverage" and "coercion" are even more flimsy. Take, for example, the *General Motors* case, in which it was held illegal for that defendant to "tie" sales of its automobiles to the financing service provided by a wholly owned subsidiary corporation. What the courts obviously underestimated [8] was that sales of the automobiles were impeded by the tying provision. It is true that we do not know to what extent the tying arrangement affected the sales of automobiles. It is easy, however, to visualize a situation in which so many additional goods and services are "tied" to the car that sales of the principal product drop to nothing. If, for example, General Motors attempted to "compel" its dealers to purchase a house trailer with each automobile, many dealers would find it advantageous to switch to another manufacturer. Furthermore, the court also forgot that to the extent the tying arrangement hampered independent banks and financiers it pro

2 Mr. Justice Day dissenting in United States v. United Shoe Machinery Co., 247 U.S. 32, 70 (1918); Mr. Justice Day writing the opinion of the Court in United Shoe Machinery Corp. v. United States, 258 U.S. 451, 457-458 (1922). Compare Lorain Journal Co. v. United States, 342 U.S. 143, 152-153 (1951); Atty. Gen. Nat. Com. Rep. 137, B.

3 Compare Civil Aeronautics Act of 1938, §409, 52 Stat. 000 49 U.S.C.A. §489.

4 A comparable question is why labor unions engage in restrictive practices such as refusing to use labor-saving devices. E.g., Harper v. Hoecherl, 153 Fla. 29, 14 So.2d 179 (1943). One might well suppose that the unions would prefer to exercise their power by raising wages.

5 E.g., Stevens, Unfair Competition 75 (1917).

6 §2.18 *supra.*

7 Mere disparity of economic resources is not such duress as will make a contract voidable. 2 Restatement of Contracts §493. In any event the amount of "free will" involved in making the arrangements is not necessarily relevant to the economic effects thereof.

8 United States v. General Motors Corp., 121 F.2d 376, 399 (7th Cir. 1941), *cert. denied,* 314 U.S. 618 (1941).

tanto probably assisted competing manufacturers of automobiles and their dealers.[9]

Refutation of the "coercion" theory does not necessarily involve acceptance of the countervailing "freedom of choice" theory. Professor Kales and others, including Mr. Justice Holmes, have taken the position that there is no such thing as a tying arrangement: the seller simply offers one commodity and the buyer has a choice of taking it (i.e., the two commodities wrapped in one package) or nothing. It is a question of free choice with which the law should remain unconcerned.[10] The difficulty with Professor Kales' theory is simply this: both in law and in economics it is assumed that the defendant has some degree of monopoly power in the principal product.[11] Without such monopoly power, he simply cannot "tie" another product to the principal one. If, for example, I try to sell a hundred shares of American Telephone & Telegraph stock on the New York Stock Exchange, a purely competitive market, I

---

[9] Compare 121 F.2d at 399; Burns, The Decline of Competition 452-453 (1936).

[10] Kales, Contracts and Combinations in Restraint of Trade §45 (1918); Holmes, J., dissenting in Motion Picture Patents Co. v. Universal Film Manufacturing Co., 243 U.S. 502, 519 (1917); United States v. United Shoe Machinery Co., 247 U.S. 32, 66 (1918); United Shoe Machinery Co. v. Brunet, [1909] A.C. 330, 343; Whitwell v. Continental Tobacco Co., 125 Fed. 454, 461 (8th Cir. 1903); FTC v. Paramount Famous-Lasky Corp., 57 F.2d 152, 156 (2d Cir. 1932). In the Motion Picture Patents case, the language of Mr. Justice Holmes at page 519 was: ". . . a patentee has no less property in his patented machine than any other owner, and that in addition to keeping the machine to himself the patent gives him the further right to forbid the rest of the world from making others like it. In short, for whatever motive, he may keep his device wholly out of use . . . so much being undisputed, I cannot understand why he may not keep it out of use unless the licensee, or, for the matter of that, the buyer will use some unpatented thing in connection with it. Generally speaking the measure of a condition is the consequence of a breach, and if that consequence is one that the owner may impose unconditionally, he may impose it conditionally upon a certain event." In United States v. United Shoe Machinery Corp., supra, Mr. Justice McKenna said at page 66: "It approaches declamation to say that the lessees were coerced . . . it is easy to say that the leases are against the policy of the law. But when one tries to be definite one comes back to the rights and obligations of the parties. There is no question in the case of the use of circumstances to compel or restrain; the leases are simply bargains, not different from others, moved upon calculated considerations, and, whether provident or improvident, are entitled nevertheless to the sanctions of the law." In FTC v. Paramount Famous-Lasky Corp., supra, there was involved the validity of the block-booking practice in the motion picture industry. Whether such block booking constitutes tying depends upon whether the separate films are regarded as different commodities; unless the commodities are different the concept of tying is not applicable. Times-Picayune Publishing Co. v. United States, 345 U.S. 594, 614 (1953).

[11] Times-Picayune Publishing Co. v. United States 345 U.S. 594, 608-609 (1953); Miller, Unfair Competition 194, 199 (1941). Compare FTC v. Gratz, 253 U.S. 421, 428 (1920); FTC v. Paramount Famous-Lasky Corp., 57 F.2d 152, 157 (2d Cir. 1932). It has also been said that tying cannot be employed unless demand for the two products is "joint." Miller, Unfair Competition 201 (1941). Query whether that is correct.

cannot insist that the buyer also take fifty shares of United States Steel stock in the same transaction. Hence, since the "tie" implies some degree of monopoly power in the seller, it is not wholly correct to say that the buyer has complete freedom of choice.

It is now apparent why tying is a mysterious practice. As we have seen, there is no presumption that a seller stands to gain anything by "tying" one product to another and it follows that no worse allocation of resources can be presumed to flow from the tying arrangement. A question then arises as to why a seller may seek to "tie" one product to another. An easy explanation is found in situations wherein the principal product is subject to governmental price-fixing. If, for example, the principal product has its price fixed by interventionist legislation at levels below those which would be achieved on the free market, the seller can "tie" another product to it and thereby exploit the monopoly power in the principal product. During the World War II price control era, for example, the government held the price of whiskey below free-market levels. Accordingly, attempts were made to dispose of combinations of whiskey and rum because the price controls did not force rum below free-market levels.[12] Even in the absence of legislation, fear of intervention by the state may produce similar results. Again, the seller may be sensitive to public opinion and seek to camouflage higher prices for the principal product by the tying arrangement.[13] Or, he may simply seek to conceal his monopoly profits on the principal product from potential rivals.

Absent such price controls on the principal product, explana-

---

[12] Coffin-Redington Co. v. Porter, 156 F.2d 113, 114 (9th Cir. 1946); United States v. Fish, 154 F.2d 798 (2d Cir. 1946), *cert. denied*, 328 U.S. 869 (1946). Compare Porter v. Cole, 66 F. Supp. 11 (N.D. Tex. 1946), *aff'd per curiam*, 157 F.2d 856 (5th Cir. 1946).

[13] For whatever reason, it is apparent that many businessmen are afraid to raise their prices up to free-market levels. Note, for example, the following statement by a leading industrialist: "I believe that the steel industry as a whole, and particularly the old established companies, deserve great credit for the character of the services which they have given their customers during this period of a seller's market. They have maintained and even improved the high quality of their products. At the same time, they have exercised commendable restraint in maintaining prices at a level far below the prices which were asked and received for steel products in the so-called gray or black market . . ." Moreell, J & L and Competition, 2 Men & Steel No. 7, p. 2 (1949). In Acme Steel Co., Ann. Rep. 1948, 3 (Chicago, 1949) the following appeared: "Limitation of raw material was the only factor preventing our showing a large increase for the sale of our basic product . . . the demand for these items was so great that price was of little importance and had we elected to do so, we could have received premium prices for nearly every ton sold. We believe that our policy of charging only public market prices will be to our benefit in the future when competition for customer orders will again prevail." Cf. §§4.12, 8.2 *infra*.

tions of tying become less simple. Professor Stigler has attempted to explain tying in terms of price discrimination. In the *International Business Machines* situation, for example, he found that leases based on the amount of use of the machinery discriminated against customers with larger volume and thus enabled the lessor to divide his markets and collect higher rentals from those able to pay more.[14] Another conceivable explanation, akin to vertical integration, lies in the possibility that tying raises barriers to entry. In other words, potential rivals must also produce the ancillary product in order to enter the market: thus would-be competitors are required to raise more capital.[15] Such considerations basically involve indivisibility, which in turn may be found in many guises in explaining the phenomenon of tying. An example is found in a situation wherein expense is reduced by distributing two products in a single package. This, of course, amounts to indivisibility in distribution.[16] Another possibility is that the ancillary product requires larger volume than it could achieve in a free market in order to achieve economies of scale. The tying device may overcome that imperfection. Other imperfections, such as consumer inertia and the like, may well be involved. Investor ignorance is also an important factor.[17] In a

---

[14] Stigler, The Theory of Price 217-218 (rev. ed. 1952); Bork, Vertical Integration and the Sherman Act, 22 U. Chi. L. Rev. 157, 196 n.129 (1954); Pope, Vertical Forestalling Under the Anti-Trust Laws, 19 id. 583, 613 (1952). Director and Levi, Trade Regulation, 51 Nw. U.L. Rev. 281, 290 (1956). Note that the price discrimination involved is unusual: prices are reduced in favor of small customers and raised to large customers. Compare International Business Machines Corp. v. United States, 298 U.S. 131 (1936).

[15] Such may have been the case, for example, in Deon v. Kirby Lumber Co., 162 La. 671, 111 So. 55, 58 (1926). The court said, however, that the operator of a sawmill and general store might forbid his employees to patronize a rival retail establishment.

[16] Miller, Unfair Competition 203 (1941); Campbell and Hatton, Herbert H. Dow, Pioneer in Creative Chemistry 111 (1951). Compare Kansas City Star Co. v. United States, 240 F.2d 643, 658 (8th Cir. 1957). Consumer inertia and ignorance may play an important role. Consumers, for example, may wish much service (e.g., delivery, extension of credit on charge account, return privilege) and yet be unwilling to pay for it if the price is stated separately. Accordingly, the merchant must charge a single price for the commodity plus the services. In Porter v. Cole, 66 F. Supp. 11 (N.D. Tex. 1946), aff'd per curiam, 157 F.2d 856 (5th Cir. 1946), the court said at page 12: "The common practice of the trade to attract customers by uniting what is thought to be an attractive figure for two articles, may not be branded as either unfair competition, or, as fraudulent and improper . . ."

[17] In United States v. General Motors Corp., 121 F.2d 376 (7th Cir. 1941), cert. denied, 314 U.S. 618 (1941), it appeared that General Motors had gone into the business of financing its own cars because bankers were originally unwilling to engage in that business. Later, when the financing business had become established and the ignorance of the bankers thus dissipated, a question may have arisen as to whether General Motors should continue in that business or incur the losses incident to dissolution thereof. As the term "forced sale" indicates, frictions involved in winding up the going concern may result in sharp losses of value. Note that in United States v. United Shoe Machinery Corp., 110 F. Supp. 295 (D. Mass.

number of cases, the courts have recognized a manufacturer's desire to protect the good will of its principal product, by permitting him to "tie" repair parts and the like to it for fear that consumers would become disgusted with the basic machine if faulty parts or supplies were used.[18] Still another possible explanation for tying lies in the dynamic character of markets. The seller who "ties" an ancillary product to his principal product (in which he enjoys some measure of monopoly power) will find that monopoly element diminished by the "tie." He may, however, be willing to suffer that detriment in order to shift his strength into a field which appears to hold more promise for the future. Furthermore, various market frictions (imperfections) may conceivably operate to give the seller a net gain from the "shift"; he may somehow acquire more power in the new field than he loses in the old.[19]

In view of the foregoing considerations, it is apparent that wholesale prohibitions against tying can hardly be justified. In a number of the explanations offered above, it is difficult to see that there is any worse allocation of resources than would exist without the "tie." As the factor of indivisibility suggests, it would be extremely difficult to enforce a prohibition against tying to its rational conclusion: to do so would probably require that cameras be sold without lenses, that cars be sold without tires, and that credit never be extended to any customer.[20] Furthermore, the prohibition would be ineffective so long as the seller with some

---

1953), *aff'd per curiam*, 347 U.S. 521 (1954), the leasing practice there found to be deleterious was essentially an extension of credit. In both cases, the courts condemned the extension of credit but for different reasons, and it is not clear that the grounds of the two decisions are compatible. Note also that the practice of tying may increase consumer ignorance by concealing the separate prices which would be charged for the two commodities involved.

[18] Pick Manufacturing Co. v. General Motors Corp., 80 F.2d 641 (7th Cir. 1935), *aff'd per curiam*, 299 U.S. 3 (1936). Compare FTC v. Sinclair Refining Co., 261 U.S. 463 (1923). But see International Business Machines Corp. v. United States, 298 U.S. 131, 138-139 (1936); United States v. General Motors Corp., 121 F.2d 376, 400 (7th Cir. 1941), *cert. denied*, 314 U.S. 618 (1941). An interesting discussion of the last-cited case will be found in Birnbaum, The Auto-Finance Consent Decree, 24 Wash. L.Q. 525, 547-548 (1939).

[19] Part of what the seller gains may be "security." He may be spreading his risks by taking a weaker position in two fields, rather than holding a stronger one in a single line. Involved, of course, are all the frictions of entering and retiring from a market.

[20] Hale, Control over Distribution, 14 Miss. L.J. 170, 180 (1942). In April, 1955, a manufacturer of corn flakes started inserting six marbles in each box of his product. Three children of our acquaintance implored their parents to buy that brand of cereal. The children were indifferent to the corn flakes but eager for the marbles; their parents approved the flakes but feared the marbles were indigestible. Other cereal makers, whose boxes only contained space ships, rocket guns and the like, were no doubt dismayed by their rival's successful appeal to consumers. There is, however, no record that anyone complained to the Federal Trade Commission about the "tying" involved.

degree of monopoly power remained free to raise his price or otherwise exploit that power.[21]   In other words, a prohibition upon tying constitutes regulation of some degree of market power, rather than its eradication, and courts should be careful not to confuse protection of consumers and the economy as a whole with sheltering of rival firms.

§2.20.   **Refusals to deal.**   A fundamental rule of the common law, preserved under modern statutes, permits individual business firms to choose their own customers.   So long as the firm does not enjoy a monopoly and is not classified as a public utility it may refuse to deal with anyone whom it dislikes.   A New York court put the matter succinctly:

> It is the well-settled law of this state that the refusal to maintain trade relations with any individual is an inherent right which every person may exercise lawfully, for reasons he deems sufficient or for no reasons whatever; and it is immaterial whether such refusal is based upon reason or is the result of mere caprice, prejudice, or malice. . . .[1]

That general rule, however, is subject to severe qualification. Obviously it is not applicable to situations in which several competitors enter into a "horizontal" agreement not to deal with a customer or supplier; in such instances, Section 1 of the Sherman Act is violated by the boycott.[2]

21 United States v. General Motors Corp., 121 F.2d 376 (7th Cir. 1941), *cert. denied,* 314 U.S. 618 (1941); United States v. Griffith, 334 U.S. 100 (1948).   In cases wherein the fear of adverse legislation or the like prevents the raising of prices, the prohibition against tying may constitute effective regulation.   The foregoing idea was given orally to the authors by Professor Morris Adelman early in 1954.

§2.20.   1 Locker v. American Tobacco Co., 121 App. Div. 443, 106 N.Y. Supp. 115, 121 (2d Dept. 1907).   To the same effect see Barish v. Chrysler Corp., 141 Neb. 157, 3 N.W.2d 91, 95 (1942).   *Accord:* 4 Restatement of Torts §762; United States v. Colgate & Co., 250 U.S. 300 (1919); FTC v. Raymond Brothers-Clark Co., 263 U.S. 565, 573 (1924); United States v. Bausch & Lomb Co., 321 U.S. 707, 728 (1944); Chicago Seating Co. v. S. Karpen & Brothers, 177 F.2d 863, 867 (7th Cir. 1949); United States v. Imperial Chemical Industries, Ltd., 105 F. Supp. 215, 244 (S.D.N.Y. 1952); Times-Picayune Publishing Co. v. United States, 345 U.S. 594, 626 (1953); Barber, Refusals to Deal Under the Federal Anti-Trust Laws, 103 U. Pa. L. Rev. 847 (1955); Naifeh v. Ronson Art Metal Works, Inc., 111 F. Supp. 491 (W.D. Okla. 1953), *aff'd,* 218 F.2d 202, 207 (10th Cir. 1954); United States v. Twentieth Century Fox Film Corp., 137 F. Supp. 78, 85, 104 (S.D. Cal. 1956); Miller Motors, Inc. v. Ford Motor Co., 149 F. Supp. 790, 808 (M.D.N.C. 1957); Whitely v. Foremost Dairies, 151 F. Supp. 914, 924 (W.D. Ark. 1957).

2 Eastern States Retail Lumber Assn. v. United States, 234 U.S. 600 (1914); United States v. Frankfort Distilleries, 324 U.S. 293 (1945); Foster v. Shubert Holding Co., 316 Mass. 470, 55 N.E.2d 772, 776 (1944); see William Goldman Theatres, Inc. v. Loew's Inc., 150 F.2d 738, 743 (3d Cir. 1945).   Compare Gamco, Inc. v. Providence

Exceptions to the rule permitting choice of suppliers and customers, however, extend to the activities of single firms. Thus a refusal to deal in aid of a scheme of resale price maintenance may be unlawful,[3] and similar results have been achieved with respect to refusals engendered by a desire to conclude exclusive arrangements.[4] Indeed, in recent cases there is some suggestion that almost any attempt to gain an advantage over rivals may constitute an unlawful refusal to deal. In litigation involving a chain of grocery stores, for example, it was held unlawful to refuse to deal with a supplier who would not reduce his prices.[5]

Recently the Supreme Court of the United States summarized the law on this subject as follows:

Refusals to sell, without more, do not violate the law. Though group boycotts, or concerted refusals to deal, clearly run afoul of §1 . . . different criteria have long applied to qualify the rights of an individual seller. Beginning with *United States v. Colgate & Co.* . . . this Court's decisions have recognized individual refusals to sell as a general right, though "neither absolute nor exempt from regulation." . . . If accompanied by unlawful conduct or agreement, or conceived in monopolistic purpose or market control, even individual sellers' refusals to deal have transgressed the Act. . . . Still, although much hedged about by later cases, *Colgate*'s principle protects the Times-Picayune Publishing Company's simple refusal to sell advertising space in the Times-Pi-

---

Fruit & Produce Building, Inc., 194 F.2d 484, 486-487 (1st Cir. 1952), *cert. denied*, 344 U.S. 817 (1952); Providence Fruit & Produce Building, Inc. v. Gamco, Inc., 76 R.I. 54, 68 A.2d 20 (1949); Union Pacific Coal Co. v. United States, 173 Fed. 737 (8th Cir. 1909); Shotkin v. General Electric Co., 171 F.2d 236, 239 (10th Cir. 1948); Riedley v. Hudson Motor Car Co., 82 F. Supp. 8 (W.D. Ky. 1949). In the last two cases the courts refused to apply the usual rule stated in the text, on the grounds that a mere private injury had been pleaded and that there was no showing of injury to the general public interest. Query whether such grounds are supportable.

[3] FTC v. Beech-Nut Packing Co., 257 U.S. 441 (1922); United States v. Bausch & Lomb Co., 321 U.S. 707, 720-721 (1944). Cf. Harbury and Raskind, The British Approach to Monopoly Control, 67 Q.J. Econ. 380, 403 (1953).

[4] Lorain Journal Co. v. United States, 342 U.S. 143, 149-150, 154-155 (1951). But compare FTC v. Raymond Bros.-Clark Co., 263 U.S. 565, 572 (1924); Nelson Radio & Supply Co. v. Motorola, Inc., 200 F.2d 911, 915 (5th Cir. 1952), *cert. denied*, 345 U.S. 925 (1953); Leo J. Meyberg Co. v. Eureka Williams Corp., 215 F.2d 100 (9th Cir. 1954), *cert. denied*, 348 U.S. 875 (1954).

[5] United States v. New York Great Atlantic & Pacific Tea Co., 173 F.2d 79, 87 (7th Cir. 1949). Compare United States v. Klearfax Looms, Inc., 63 F. Supp. 32 (D. Minn. 1945). If an intent to establish or maintain an illegal monopoly can be proven, it is, of course, settled law that the refusal is unlawful. 4 Restatement of Torts §764; Eastman Kodak Co. v. Southern Photo Materials Co., 273 U.S. 359, 375 (1927); Kansas City Star Co. v. United States, 240 F.2d 643 (8th Cir. 1957). Such a refusal may also amount to an attempt to monopolize. Handler, Recent Anti-Trust Developments, 9 Record 171, 185 (April, 1954); Barber, Refusals to Deal Under the Federal Anti-Trust Laws, 103 U. Pa. L. Rev. 847, 849 (1955).

cayune or States separately unless other factors destroy the limited dispensation which that case confers.[6]

It will be noted that the foregoing quotation does not offer much specific guidance as to the legality of refusals to deal.

§2.21. **Analysis of refusals to deal.** Selection of one's own suppliers or customers is, as indicated above, a phenomenon associated with several trade practices. We have merely mentioned those most commonly associated with refusals to deal. So intimate, however, is the relationship between other practices and refusals to deal that we can scarcely consider the refusal separately. Often it must be viewed merely as a step toward some other abuse.[1] Obviously, for example, such is the case with exclusive arrangements because these arrangements always involve a refusal to deal with some existing or potential trader.

From the economic point of view a refusal to deal indicates the possession of some degree of market power. A seller in a purely competitive market (wheat before 1933, for example) will never refuse to deal because there is no advantage to be gained in so doing. He may, of course, withhold his supplies from the market in the hope that prices will advance. The identity of his customers, however, is a matter of indifference to him and, as we see in organized exchanges, frequently unknown. Accordingly, the law is on sound ground when it holds that a refusal to deal upon the part of one without monopoly power is never actionable. Correspondingly, a duty to serve all comers is imposed upon public utility concerns.[2]

The difficulty, of course, arises with respect to firms which enjoy some degree of market power but have not been classified as "public utilities." The fact that they do enjoy some degree of market power, whether arising out of governmental protection, time lags, self-achieved status or other factors, permits such firms to engage in practices, not available to others, which may be deleterious to the economy as a whole. On the other hand, if every effort to gain an advantage in trade constitutes an illegal refusal to deal, the end of competition is clearly in sight. As the public utility experience indicates, once a duty to serve all comers

---

[6] Times-Picayune Publishing Co. v. United States, 345 U.S. 594, 625 (1953); Barber, Refusals to Deal Under the Federal Anti-Trust Laws, 103 U. Pa. L. Rev. 847, 862 et seq. (1955).

§2.21. [1] Comment, Refusals to Sell and Public Control of Competition, 58 Yale L.J. 1121, 1123 (1949).

[2] Compare Whitwell v. Continental Tobacco Co., 125 Fed. 454, 460 (8th Cir. 1903). Note, too, the relationship between §1 and §2 of the Sherman Act. Lorain Journal Co. v. United States, 342 U.S. 143, 154 (1951).

is imposed upon the business firm, government must step in to fix the price at which sales will be made. For such reasons the Supreme Court once said: "If real competition is to continue, the right of the individual to exercise reasonable discretion in respect of his own business methods, must be preserved. . . ."[3] In those circumstances the legal test of a refusal to deal becomes dependent upon intent. Thus the Attorney General's Committee concluded that a refusal to deal by an individual firm might violate Section 2 of the Sherman Act if conceived in monopolistic purpose.[4] Presumably, the "monopolistic purpose" relates to some field of business not encompassed in the original enterprise operated by the defendant: otherwise the reasoning would be as circular as it is vague.

§2.22.   **Common law torts.**   Some of the abuses share the characteristic of being illegal in and of themselves. By that we mean that the acts constituting the wrongs involved are illegal at common law or under statutes unrelated to the monopoly problem. An obvious example is found in physical violence. Smashing windows of rival firms, ramming a competitor's vehicles in order to injure his business, distracting customers by blocking entrances to stores and the like, all constitute actionable torts wholly apart from the law of monopoly.[1] They are, however, also well-recognized abuses.[2] Another equally obvious category involves the use of bribery to learn the secrets of a rival's business or to induce his

[3] FTC v. Raymond Bros.-Clark Co., 263 U.S. 565, 572 (1924). Recently it was said that the mere denial of licenses under patents issued to the General Electric Co. did not constitute a violation of the Sherman Act; that the violation grew out of dominance of the industry and other factors. United States v. General Electric Co., 82 F. Supp. 753, 900 (D.N.J. 1949). Note also that in some instances "good" motives have actuated refusals to sell (as, for example, to maintain the quality of the defendant's products). Comment, Refusals to Sell and Public Control of Competition, 58 Yale L.J. 1121, 1124 n.17 (1949). The suggestion that refusals to sell should almost always be illegal is vigorously presented in Timberg, The Rights of Customer-Seller Selection, N.Y. State Bar Assn., Section on Antitrust Law, Third Annual Meeting, 151, 155-156 (CCH, 1951); Mund, The Right to Buy, Report to Senate Committee on Small Business, Sen. Doc. No. 32, 85th Cong., 1st Sess. (1957).

[4] Atty. Gen. Nat. Com. Rep. 132, A. As to the legality of "threats" and "compulsion," see the dissenting opinion of Mr. Justice Holmes in Vegelahn v. Guntner, 167 Mass. 92, 44 N.E. 1077, 1081 (1896).

§2.22.   [1] Meadowmoor Dairies, Inc. v. Milk Wagon Drivers' Union, 371 Ill. 377, 21 N.E.2d 308 (1939), aff'd, 312 U.S. 287, 386 (1941); see Fleetway, Inc. v. Public Service Transport Co., 72 F.2d 761, 762, 764 (3d Cir. 1934). Consult the pioneering and brilliant exposition in Handler, Unfair Competition, 21 Iowa L. Rev. 175, 201 (1936). Vivid instances of rough and tumble events are set forth in Thompson, Since Spindle Top 11 (Gulf Oil Corp. 1951) and Wilcox, Competition and Monopoly in American Industry 296-297 (TNEC Monograph No. 21, 1940).

[2] No case directly in point has been found but the result stated in the text is believed to follow the principle of decisions such as that in Mitchell Woodbury Corp. v. Albert Pick Barth Co., 41 F.2d 148 (1st Cir. 1930).

employees to commit acts of sabotage and the like.[3] Similarly, it is unlawful, wholly apart from the law of monopoly, to induce a breach of contract; again, it is well recognized that such conduct may give rise to a finding of abuses within the meaning of the law of monopoly.[4]

Somewhat more subtle are various forms of misrepresentation. A competitor may, for example, disparage his rival. That practice has been described by Professor Handler as follows:

> Disparagement is the legal name for the familiar practice of "knocking" competitive products. Sales are induced not on the merits of the article offered but on the alleged demerits of its rivals. It is not the product before the parties which is misrepresented but that of competitors . . . the tort stems from the law of personal defamation. Unlike defamation, it is an attack upon property or goods rather than upon the person.[5]

As Professor Handler has pointed out, such disparagement may be particularly effective as a weapon in the competitive struggle when used to suggest the insolvency or financial irresponsibility of the rival trader.[6] Accordingly, it is well established that disparagement is a tort wholly apart from the law of monopoly, and one court went so far as to say:

> We know of no jurisdiction in the United States in which trade libel or disparagement of goods will not create a cause of action.[7]

[3] 4 Restatement of Torts §759; Jones v. Baker, 7 Cowen 445 (N.Y. Sup. Ct. 1827); Monarch Tobacco Works v. American Tobacco Co., 165 Fed. 774 (W.D. Ky. 1908); American Steel Co. v. American Steel & Wire Co., 244 Fed. 300 (D. Mass. 1916); Mitchell Woodbury Corp. v. Albert Pick Barth Co., 41 F.2d 148, 150 (1st Cir. 1930). But cf. Dewey, the Common Law Background of Anti-Trust Policy, 41 Va. L. Rev. 759, 784 et seq. (1955). In a good many decisions there is talk of "espionage" and "surveillance." The "espionage" appears to have involved shadowing salesmen of a rival firm in order to identify his customers and then making drastic price concessions to such buyers in an effort to crush the rival. Standard Oil Co. of New Jersey v. United States, 221 U.S. 1, 43 (1911). "Surveillance" has a broader connotation, possibly suggesting threats to retaliate should rivals cut prices. It is not believed that mere observation of the behavior of competing firms should constitute an abuse or an attempt. Indeed, it would be difficult for firms to compete unless they were aware of each others' activities. The Sherman Act does not require competition to be pursued blindly. See the dissenting opinion in American Column & Lumber Co. v. United States, 257 U.S. 377, 412, 415-416 (1921). Compare United States v. General Electric Co., 82 F. Supp. 753, 901 (D.N.J. 1949).

[4] Handler, Unfair Competition, 21 Iowa L. Rev. 175, 211, 215-216 (1936). In Bender v. Hearst Corp., 152 F. Supp. 569 (D. Conn. 1957), the court appears to have overlooked the prior decisions on the subject. Compare the practice of buying up raw materials in order to raise the costs of competitors and thus reduce their profit margins. American Tobacco Co. v. United States, 328 U.S. 781, 801, 803 (1946).

[5] Handler, Unfair Competition, 21 Iowa L. Rev. 175, 197 (1936).

[6] Id. at 215.

[7] Black & Yates, Inc. v. Mahogany Assn., 129 F.2d 227, 233 (3d Cir. 1942), cert. denied, 317 U.S. 672 (1942). Accord: 3 Restatement of Torts §§573, 624, 626, 629, 632; 4 id. §§767, 768; State v. Dalton, 168 N.C. 204, 83 S.E. 693 (1914); Marr v. Putnam,

That rule does not mean, of course, that one cannot compare his own products favorably to those of rivals: "puffing" is a familiar commercial practice condoned by the law, which does not penalize comparisons unless they contain specific misstatements of fact with respect to the competitor's products.[8]

It is likewise established that disparagement may give rise to liability under the law of monopoly. Some of the most picturesque practices questioned under the antitrust laws relate to the activities of the old National Cash Register Company. In attempting to destroy the business of its rivals that concern bought up machines produced by others, smashed them into pieces and then offered them for sale prominently at nominal prices under the label of "junk." [9] Less fantastic practices were involved in litigation between two prominent manufacturers of breakfast food, in which one was alleged to have disparaged the other by saying that it had no right to use a trade-mark. With respect to the question of the effect of the law of monopoly on such disparagement the court said:

> The question arising upon the trial of the present action will be of the sufficiency of proof of acts showing an attempt to effect a monopoly and substantially to restrain competition in shredded wheat. To bring the defendant under the Anti-Trust Acts . . . the plaintiff may show that the defendant has threatened to cease dealings with its customers unless they decline to deal with plaintiff, has falsely represented plaintiff's goods to be inferior . . .[10]

---

196 Ore. 1, 246 P.2d 509 (1952). But compare Syracuse Broadcasting Corp. v. Newhouse, 236 F.2d 522, 526 (2d Cir. 1956); Advance Music Corp. v. American Tobacco Co., 268 App. Div. 707, 53 N.Y.S.2d 337, 341 (1st Dept. 1945). In the last-cited case, recovery was denied to a plaintiff who alleged that it had sustained injury because its songs were not listed on a "hit parade" of most popular music published by the defendant. The so-called "Printer's Ink" statutes seem largely aimed at exaggerated claims for the advertiser's own product and not designed to discourage disparagement. Note, Statutory Attacks on Deceptive Advertising, 43 Harv. L. Rev. 945, 946 (1930).

[8] 4 Restatement of Torts §649. Considerable difficulty has been encountered in securing equitable relief by way of injunction against disparagement because of the old rule that the chancellor will not enjoin a libel. Maytag Co. v. Meadows Manufacturing Co., 35 F.2d 403, 408 (7th Cir. 1929), cert. denied, 281 U.S. 737 (1930); Pound, Equitable Relief Against Defamation and Injuries to Personality, 29 Harv. L. Rev. 640, 655, 668 (1916); Nims, The Law of Unfair Competition and Trade-Marks 845 (4th ed. 1947); Callmann, The Law of Unfair Competition and Trade-Marks §§41.1, 41.2 (1945).

[9] Attorney General ex rel. James v. National Cash Register Co., 182 Mich. 99, 148 N.W. 420 (1914); Patterson v. United States, 222 Fed. 599, 612, 637 (6th Cir. 1915), cert. denied, 238 U.S. 635 (1915); Standard Oil Co. v. Doyle, 118 Ky. 662, 82 S.W. 271, 273 (1904); Handler, Unfair Competition, 21 Iowa L. Rev. 175, 182n, 215-216, 249-250 (1936); Callmann, The Law of Unfair Competition and Trade-Marks §§15.4, 41 (1945).

[10] Kellogg Co. v. National Biscuit Co., 71 F.2d 662, 665 (2d Cir. 1934). Accord: Stewart-Warner Corp. v. Staley, 42 F. Supp. 140, 147 (W.D. Pa. 1941); United States v. Pullman Co., 64 F. Supp. 108, 126 (E.D. Pa. 1946), aff'd per curiam, 330 U.S. 806

That such activities constitute abuses does not seem open to question at this time.

Oddly enough, both the general law of torts and the law of monopoly reach a different conclusion with respect to false advertising of the defendant's own products. The accepted rule is that a competitor may make false claims for his own products without giving rise to liability apart from the law of monopoly.[11] Thus Professor Handler has said:

> . . . a campaign of false advertising may completely discredit the product of an industry, destroy the confidence of consumers and impair a communal or trade good will. . . .
>
> Notwithstanding the manifest harm caused by these deceitful practices, the courts, in the main, have denied relief to the aggrieved competitor. . . .[12]

Similarly, the deceit involved in false advertising of one's own products does not appear ever to have given rise to a finding of an abuse under the Sherman Act.[13] The Federal Trade Commission, however, acting under Section 5 of its organic statute, has been preoccupied with the prevention of such misrepresentations and has entered a flood of cease and desist orders against them.[14]

(1947); Caldwell-Clements v. McGraw-Hill Publishing Co., 12 F.R.D. 531, 538-539 (S.D.N.Y. 1952). See also the opinion in the dubious case of Kobe, Inc. v. Dempsey Pump Co., 198 F.2d 416, 424 (10th Cir. 1952), *cert. denied,* 344 U.S. 837 (1952).

11 American Washboard Co. v. Saginaw Manufacturing Co., 103 Fed. 281 (6th Cir. 1900); Motor Improvements Co. v. A.C. Spark Plug Co., 5 F. Supp. 712, 714 (E.D. Mich. 1934); Callmann, The Law of Unfair Competition and Trade-Marks §18.1 (1945); Handler, Unfair Competition, 21 Iowa L. Rev. 175, 193-194 (1936).

12 Id. at 193. See also Handler, False and Misleading Advertising, 39 Yale L.J. 22, 37 (1929). The rule adopted by the American Law Institute appears to go beyond the decided cases in the direction advocated by Professor Handler. 4 Restatement of Torts §761; 3 id. §525. In many states so-called "Printer's Ink" statutes have been adopted against false and deceptive advertising of the seller's own wares. Note, Statutory Attacks on Deceptive Advertising, 43 Harv. L. Rev. 945 (1930). It has also been suggested that violation of any type of a penal or regulatory statute by a business rival should be enjoinable at the suit of competitors. Note, Enjoining the Violation of a Penal Statute as Being an Unfair Method of Competition, 42 Harv. L. Rev. 693 (1929); 2 Restatement of Torts §286. There is, therefore, room for the belief that the law stated in the text may soon be changed.

13 A survey of remedies against false advertising by customers and competitors does not mention relief under the antitrust laws. Handler, False and Misleading Advertising, 39 Yale L.J. 22 (1929). But compare the interesting decision in Boggs v. Duncan-Schell Furniture Co., 163 Iowa 106, 143 N.W. 482 (1913), wherein relief was granted on allegations that the defendant had falsely represented itself to be selling a new style of sewing machine previously advertised by the plaintiff.

14 E.g., FTC v. Standard Education Society, 302 U.S. 112 (1937); Book-of-the-Month Club v. FTC, 202 F.2d 486 (2d Cir. 1953); Rothschild v. FTC, 200 F.2d 39 (7th Cir. 1952). Misrepresentations would, of course, be ineffective were consumers fully informed. A discussion of the "imperfection" of consumer ignorance will be found in Appendix A *infra.* The materials there presented suggest the importance of

Since disparagement and false advertising both constitute attempts to mislead customers as to the relative merits of rival products, it is apparent that the courts must someday face the question of reconciling the decisions on those two subjects.

Another interesting problem arises out of conduct constituting unfair competition. It is well established that use of another's trade-mark or trade name constitutes an actionable wrong.[15] Such "palming off" has not, however, been held to constitute an abuse under the law of monopoly.[16] Strangely enough, almost the opposite result has been achieved, in that courts sometimes speak of the plaintiff in such litigation as one who attempts to "monopolize" his trade-mark or trade name.[17] This somewhat paradoxical situation is probably explained by the fact that the usual defendant in an unfair competition action is a marginal firm without significant economic resources and wholly lacking in monopoly power.[18]

Another practice which may give rise to liability wholly apart from the law of monopoly is that of instituting harassing litigation. One who initiates civil proceedings without probable cause, and for an ulterior motive, may be liable to the defendant in such a cause. Most of the reported decisions involve a multiplicity of suits brought by patentees against alleged infringers but the principle is equally applicable to any type of litigation.[19] Liabil-

---

eradicating misrepresentations in the market place and hence that false advertising should constitute an abuse.

Attention is further invited to the possibility that a rival might secure relief under the provisions of §43(a) of the Lanham Act (Trade-Mark), Act of July 5, 1946, 60 Stat. 441, 15 U.S.C.A. §§1051 et seq. But compare Chamberlain v. Columbia Pictures Corp., 186 F.2d 923, 925 (9th Cir. 1951), with L'Aiglon Apparel, Inc. v. Lana Lobell, Inc., 214 F.2d 649 (3d Cir. 1954).

[15] 4 Restatement of Torts §711. The tort is broader than mere appropriation of the trade-mark; it extends to imitation of nonfunctional features of a rival's products. Ross-Whitney Corp. v. Smith, Kline & French, 207 F.2d 190 (9th Cir. 1953).

[16] Compare Callmann, The Law of Unfair Competition and Trade-Marks §15.4 (1945). Note also that §5 of the Federal Trade Commission Act has been applied against unfair competition. E.g., Juvenile Shoe Co. v. FTC, 289 Fed. 57 (9th Cir. 1923).

[17] E.g., California Fruit Growers' Exchange v. Sunkist Baking Co., 166 F.2d 971 (7th Cir. 1947). Compare Pettishall, Trade-Marks and the Monopoly Phobia, 50 Mich. L. Rev. 967 (1952); Note, Developments in the Law: Trade-Marks and Unfair Competition, 68 Harv. L. Rev. 814, 895 et seq. (1955). An analysis based upon imperfections in the market place will be found in Appendix A, *infra*, pages 431 et seq.

[18] The suggestion is that trade-mark infringement could constitute an abuse under the antitrust laws if it were practiced by a defendant with some economic strength.

[19] 4 Restatement of Torts §§674, 767; Nims, Unfair Competition and Trade-Marks 857 (4th ed. 1947); Adriance, Platt & Co. v. National Harrow Co., 121 Fed. 827 (2d Cir. 1903); Racine Paper Goods Co. v. Dittgen, 171 Fed. 631, 633 (7th Cir.

ity, of course, depends upon a showing that the suits are oppressive in character and were instituted in bad faith: otherwise, it would be impossible for patentees and others to protect their rights in the courts.[20] Similar results have been achieved under the antitrust laws and it seems clearly established that the bringing of unfounded suits and the institution of harassing litigation constitute abuses under the Sherman Act.[21] Again, obviously, it must be established that the litigation was instituted for ulterior purposes or else the Sherman Act would constitute a bar to bona fide litigation.[22]

No great significance should be attached to the fact that an abuse within the meaning of the law of monopoly also constitutes an independent tort at common law.[23] Perhaps it should be noted, however, that while some of the abuses do not constitute ordinary torts, most of the business wrongs cognizable outside the law of

---

1909). The tort extends to false statements with respect to patent infringement as well as to the actual institution of litigation. E.g., Maytag Co. v. Meadows Manufacturing Co., 35 F.2d 403, 408 (7th Cir. 1929), *cert. denied*, 281 U.S. 737 (1930). Note the interesting decision in Angle v. Chicago, St. Paul, Minneapolis & Omaha Ry., 151 U.S. 1 (1894). In that case Angle was a contractor building a railway line for the Portage Railway Co. He brought suit alleging that the defendant, which conducted a rival railway, had bribed certain officers of the Portage Company to abandon construction of its line and had obtained an injunction against other officers on the basis of a misrepresentation to the court. Furthermore, it was alleged that the defendant had misrepresented the facts to a state legislature, which had then revoked a land grant to the Portage Company. The court held, on demurrer, that the defendant was guilty of the tort of inducing breach of contract. Had suit been brought by the Portage Company itself, perhaps a different theory of recovery would have been followed. In any event, the allegations paint a vivid picture of predatory practices.

20 Oil Conservation Co. v. Brooks Co., 52 F.2d 783, 785-786 (6th Cir. 1931); Western Electric Co. v. Hammond, 135 F.2d 283, 285 (1st Cir. 1943); A. Hollander & Son, Inc. v. Imperial Fur Corp., 2 N.J. Eq. 235, 66 A.2d 319, 324 (1949); Callmann, The Law of Unfair Competition and Trade-Marks §42.4 (1945); Handler, Unfair Competition, 21 Iowa L. Rev. 175, 200-201 (1936). Note how the foregoing rule makes proof of the tort depend heavily upon evidence of the defendant's intent.

21 United States v. Besser Manufacturing Co., 96 F. Supp. 304, 312 (E.D. Mich. 1951), *aff'd*, 343 U.S. 444 (1952); Darden v. Besser, 147 F. Supp. 376, 380 (E.D. Mich. 1956); Stewart-Warner Corp. v. Staley, 42 F. Supp. 140, 146 (W.D. Pa. 1941); Forgett v. Scharf, 181 F.2d 754, 755 (3d Cir. 1950), *cert. denied*, 340 U.S. 825 (1950); Kobe, Inc. v. Dempsey Pump Co., 198 F.2d 416, 424 (10th Cir. 1952), *cert. denied*, 344 U.S. 837 (1952); see Patterson v. United States, 222 Fed. 599, 613, 643 (6th Cir. 1915), *cert. denied*, 238 U.S. 635 (1915); Timberg, Trade-Marks, Monopoly and the Restraint of Competition, 14 Law & Contemp. Prob., 323, 331, 345 (1949). But compare Flynn & Emrich Co. v. FTC, 52 F.2d 836 (4th Cir. 1931). A striking example of predatory tactics involving an attempt to have a rival thrown into receivership is recounted in 1 Nevins, Study in Power 378 (1953).

22 Straus v. Victor Talking Machine Co., 297 Fed. 791, 799 (2d Cir. 1924); Morny v. Western Union Telegraph Co., 40 F. Supp. 193, 202 (S.D.N.Y. 1940).

23 Perhaps the most significant result attaching to the statement in the text is the availability of treble damages when the business tort also constitutes an abuse or an attempt. See §10.8 *infra*.

monopoly would also constitute abuses.[24]   As we have seen, there is at least one obvious deviation from the foregoing rule, namely, the fact that the tort of unfair competition does not appear to have been held either an abuse or an attempt to monopolize under the antitrust laws.   Yet, if we are to recognize abuses at all, it seems odd that practices so deleterious that they constitute wrongs apart from the law of monopoly should not be considered actionable under the antitrust laws.   Basically, the problem is akin to the fundamental question whether the law recognizes as torts merely those acts falling within the narrow categories of ancient writs. Under the more modern view, any intentional interference with another's business or property which causes injury is actionable unless the interference can be justified.   Such a "prima facie" rule broadens the scope of tort law and tends to make it a coherent whole.[25]

§2.23.   **Truthful advertising.**   As we have seen, neither the general law nor the law of monopoly prevents a business firm from making false statements concerning the merits of its own product.[1] It would seem to follow a fortiori that truthful advertising should be considered to be lawful in every respect and never to constitute an abuse.   Such a conclusion, however, should not be reached too readily.   It is true that truthful advertising does not find a place in the roster of established abuses.   On the other hand, in recent economic literature advertising is frequently seen as an important cause of consumer ignorance and hence of imperfections in the market place.   Furthermore, advertising has played an important role in the economist's concept of "monopolistic competition." It assists in the differentiation of otherwise identical commodities and thus permits sellers to discriminate among groups of buyers.[2]

24 Another common law tort closely related to §1 of the Sherman Act is the conspiracy to injure a third person in his trade or business.   Standard Oil Co. v. Doyle, 118 Ky. 662, 82 S.W.271 (1904); Willett v. Herrick, 242 Mass. 471, 136 N.E. 366 (1922); Carlson v. Carpenter Contractors' Assn., 305 Ill. 331, 137 N.E. 222 (1922); Manning v. Kennedy, 320 Ill. App. 11, 49 N.E.2d 658 (1943).

25 Oppenheim, Cases on Trade Regulation 58 et seq. (1936) (". . . a second view recognizes a general principle of tort liability, namely, an intentional interference by conduct which causes temporary injury to the interest of the plaintiff is tortious, unless the defendant can show that his interference is justified.   What constitutes justification is the crucial inquiry.   It raises questions of economic and social policy. It makes great demands upon the 'good sense' of the tribunal to determine whether under the circumstances the justification exists.   In trade relations cases this technique is particularly significant, albeit difficult, in connection with the determination of the scope of the privilege to compete, in marking a line between fair and unfair competition.").

§2.23.   1 §2.22 *supra.*
2 Brown, Advertising and the Public Interest, 57 Yale L.J. 1165 (1948).   But compare Marshall, Monopolistic Competition and Self-Alienation, 72 Pol. Sci. Q. 340, 341 (1957).   Additional discussion will be found in Appendix A *infra.*

So heavy have been the expenditures for advertising of cigarettes
and tooth paste, for example, and so great is the attachment of
consumers to the established brands, that it has become more difficult and expensive for new producers to enter into those fields.[3]
Accordingly, there has been considerable agitation against truthful advertising of the merely persuasive type, and in one opinion
the United States Supreme Court used language hinting that such
advertising might constitute an abuse (or at least some type of
wrong) under the antitrust laws.[4]

Whether truthful advertising should ever thus stand condemned
as an abuse cannot be decided purely on a basis of a program for
eliminating "impurities" from the market place. We must also
take account of market "imperfections," including consumer ignorance and the difficulty of rational choice by uninformed buyers.
Here advertising plays an informative as well as a purely persuasive
role and the distinction between the two is not altogether clear.[5]
Under "dynamic" economic theory, a measure of advertising —
even of a purely persuasive character — may be helpful in the introduction of new products and the promotion of new ways of
doing business. Absent such advertising, it might take a considerably longer period of time to overcome inertia and ignorance and
secure that general acceptance of new products essential to economies of scale. Indeed, without persuasive advertising some innovations might not "catch on" at all.[6]

§2.24. **Technological research.** Many lawyers will be sur-
prised, not to say shocked, to learn that promotion of technological
research by business firms may possibly amount to an abuse within
the meaning of the antitrust laws. Such, however, is the implication in the recent *Shoe Machinery* opinion. In that case the lower
court said:

> No doubt it was legitimate to spend something on research in
> connection with a new process, if that expense could be recovered
> within a reasonable time through the development of several
> machine types. But here expense was incurred without much re-

[3] Oxenfeldt, Industrial Pricing and Market Practices 283 (1951).

[4] American Tobacco Co. v. United States, 328 U.S. 781, 797 (1946). In that case
the Court said: "Such tremendous advertising . . . is . . . a widely published
warning that these companies possess and know how to use a powerful offensive
and defensive weapon against new competition. New competition dare not enter
such a field, unless it be well supported by comparable national advertising."

[5] See Appendix A, pages 419, 421, 431.

[6] See Appendix B, page 476. Examples are found in MacLaurin, Invention and
Innovation in the Radio Industry 148 (1949); R. J. Reynolds Tobacco Co., Ann.
Rep. 1950, 13 (Winston-Salem, 1951).

gard to its ultimate recovery, or indeed to anything but the need of meeting competition.[1]

According to the foregoing statement of the law, technological research could be limited to purely engineering matters promising short-term developments of immediate commercial value. Furthermore, the quoted language suggests that there is something improper in developing machinery to equal that of a rival firm. Such a decision, of course, is not wholly surprising in view of the recent hostility exhibited by the courts to patents[2] and the rigid rules narrowing the bargaining power of a patentee.[3] It is also undoubtedly true that money wisely spent on technological research can give rise to competitive advantages and that there is little distinction in the long run between improving products and reducing prices. Since price reductions (of certain types) can easily constitute abuses, there may be no reason to question the possibility that technological research could similarly violate the statute. On the other hand, any such rule appears to fly in the

§2.24. [1] United States v. United Shoe Machinery Corp., 110 F. Supp. 295, 329 (D. Mass. 1953), aff'd per curiam, 347 U.S. 521 (1954). Apparently the Attorney General had taken the position that the defendant had used technological research as a predatory practice both in getting ahead of rivals and in delaying or suppressing new devices. Id. at 331-332. It does not seem possible that the defendant could have done both of those things with respect to the same commodity. The court, however, appeared to frown on technological research motivated by a need of meeting the competition of others. Id. at 329. On the other hand, it said that the defendant's activities in some research fields did not reveal an exclusionary purpose because it was evenly spread over all subjects and not concentrated at competitive points. Id. at 332. Furthermore, the court said at page 344: ". . . beyond criticism is the high quality of United's products, its understanding of the techniques of shoemaking and the needs of shoe manufacturers, its efficient design and improvement of machines, and its prompt and knowledgeable service . . ." Compare Hughes Tool Co. v. Ford, 114 F. Supp. 525, 553 (E.D. Okla. 1953), rev'd, 215 F.2d 924 (10th Cir. 1954), cert. denied, 348 U.S. 927, 965 (1955).

[2] Kobe, Inc. v. Dempsey Pump Co., 198 F.2d 416 (10th Cir. 1952), cert. denied, 344 U.S. 837 (1952); Hughes Tool Co. v. Ford, 114 F. Supp. 525, 553-554 (E.D. Okla. 1953), rev'd, 215 F.2d 924 (10th Cir. 1954), cert. denied, 348 U.S. 927, 965 (1955); Oppenheim, ed., Lectures on Federal Anti-Trust Laws 53 (University of Michigan, 1953). But compare Patterson v. United States, 222 Fed. 599, 625, 646 (6th Cir. 1915), cert. denied, 238 U.S. 635 (1915).

[3] Folk, The Relation of Patents to the Anti-Trust Laws, 13 Law & Contemp. Prob. 278, 285, 287 et seq. (1948); Note, Patent Abuses and Anti-Trust, 64 Harv. L. Rev. 626, 629 (1951); Note, Contributory Infringement and Misuse, 66 Harv. L. Rev. 909, 913, 914 (1953); compare Wood, Unenforcible Contracts and Other Consequences, Proceedings A.B.A., Section of Antitrust Law, 159, 168 (Aug. 18, 1954). Note also the antagonism to acquisition of additional patents by a firm already considered "dominant." United States v. General Electric Co., 82 F. Supp. 753, 816 (D.N.J. 1949). It was also recently suggested for the first time that failure to work the patents might constitute an attempt or an abuse. United States v. United Shoe Machinery Corp., 110 F. Supp. 295, 333 (D. Mass. 1953), aff'd per curiam, 347 U.S. 521 (1954).

face of the policy expressed in the patent laws[4] and also to discourage innovation and growth.[5] Accordingly, it does not seem likely that the courts will adopt a universal prohibition upon technological research.

§2.25. **Acquisition of rival firms.** One of the best established abuses consists of the combination of competing concerns.[1] Typically, a large firm buys out one or more smaller rivals. Such acquisitions occurred with considerable frequency both before and after the passage of the Sherman Act in 1890. Some observers have found that mergers are relatively more popular in the eras of prosperity, and it has become fashionable to identify the periods from 1897 to 1904 and from 1922 to 1929 as times of particular activity in the merger field.[2] While Section 2 of the Sherman Act has always affected combinations, Section 7 of the Clayton Act was designed to put a stop to the practice of acquiring rival firms and that statute was tightened in 1950.[3] Since such acquisitions

[4] In United States v. National Lead Co., 332 U.S. 319 (1947), the Court said at page 359: "The attempt of the Government to throw the field of technical knowledge in the titanium pigment industry wide-open would reduce the competitive value of the independent research of the parties. It would discourage rather than encourage competitive research. It would be contrary to, rather than in conformity with, the policy of the patent laws now enforced. Changes in the underlying policies of the patent laws frequently have been presented to Congress, but Congress, by its failure to accept those changes, has added to, rather than detracted from, the strength of the present and traditional patent policies."

[5] Note that the language quoted in the text, *supra,* from United States v. United Shoe Machinery Co. suggests that business corporations should not engage in research in pure science but should limit themselves to technological matters promising immediate returns. This suggestion raises interesting questions with respect to the role of corporations in our society. Cf. §8.4 *infra.*

A somewhat similar question is whether superior management in a corporation might constitute an abuse or an attempt. Compare United States v. Aluminum Co. of America, 148 F.2d 416 (2d Cir. 1945). Perhaps the orthodox view of the economist is that the skill of management is something inherent in the enterprise and not a commodity which can be bought and sold. But compare Cochran, History of the Pabst Brewing Company 58 (1948). On the other hand, it might be possible to consider managerial talent simply another raw material which could be bought and sold in the market place. Many frictions, of course, prevent the free flow of managerial talent from one firm to another and it is doubtful whether the antitrust laws should attempt to equalize firms in this respect by holding back those which are more effectively managed than their rivals.

§2.25. [1] Discussion of the acquisition of noncompeting firms is dealt with herein under the headings of "vertical integration," "diversification" and "dispersion." See Chapters 5, 6 and 7. But compare Atty. Gen. Nat. Com. Rep., c. 3.

[2] Stigler, Monopoly and Oligopoly by Merger, 40 Proceedings Am. Econ. Assn. 23, 27 et seq. (1950); Faulkner, The Decline of Laissez Faire 156, 161 (1951). A real question may be raised as to whether the acquisition of a rival firm should be considered an abuse or an attempt to monopolize. Compare United States v. American Tobacco Co., 221 U.S. 106 (1911), with United States v. Quaker Oats Co., 232 Fed. 499, 506 (N.D. Ill. 1916) (dissenting opinion). As to the contention that the mergers have lead to concentration, see §2.2 *supra.*

[3] 38 Stat. 731 (1914), as amended, 64 Stat. 1125, 15 U.S.C.A. §18; Van Cise, Understanding the Anti-Trust Laws 20 (Practising Law Institute, 1955). In a proceeding under §7 the court must inquire into the tendency to create monopoly

are commonly preceded by contracts between the two affected concerns, Section 1 of the Sherman Act may also play a role in such cases.[4]   A combination of competitors may also be illegal at common law.[5]

Despite the existence of the more specific legislation embodied in Section 7 of the Clayton Act, merger or consolidation with a rival firm may still constitute an abuse under Section 2 of the Sherman Act.   Indeed, the public outcry against the "trusts" of the last century was largely based upon the buying up of competitors and their consolidation into the giant oil and tobacco firms successfully attacked under the 1890 legislation.[6]   More recent decisions make it clear that the prohibitions of Section 2 continue to apply to such acquisitions.[7]

Until its amendment in 1950, Section 7 of the Clayton Act reached only acquisitions achieved through particular means prohibited by that legislation.   Section 2 of the Sherman Act has

and lessen competition.   Aluminum Co. of America v. FTC, 284 Fed. 401, 405 (3d Cir. 1922), cert. denied, 261 U.S. 616 (1923).   But compare the drastic decision in United States v. E. I. Du Pont de Nemours & Co., 353 U.S. 586, 589 (1957).   Effects of the 1950 amendment are outlined in H.R. Rep. No. 1191, 81st Cong., 1st Sess. (1949).

[4] Northern Securities Co. v. United States, 193 U.S. 197 (1904); State v. Creamery Package Manufacturing Co., 110 Minn. 415, 126 N.W. 126 (1910).   The tests laid down by the several statutes may not differ materially.   United States v. Columbia Steel Co., 334 U.S. 495, 507n (1948).

[5] Bishop v. American Preservers' Co., 157 Ill. 284, 41 N.E. 765 (1895); State v. Creamery Package Manufacturing Co., 110 Minn. 415, 126 N.W. 126, 129 (1910).   State constitutions may effect a similar result.   Langdon v. Branch, 37 Fed. 449, 462 (S.D. Ga. 1888).

[6] Standard Oil Co. of New Jersey v. United States, 221 U.S. 1, 74 (1911); 1 Nevins, Study in Power 223, 260 et seq. (1953); United States v. American Tobacco Co., 164 Fed. 700, 702 (S.D.N.Y. 1908), aff'd, 221 U.S. 106, 157 et seq., 163, 166, 183 (1911); Patterson v. United States, 222 Fed. 599, 620 (6th Cir. 1915), cert. denied, 238 U.S. 635 (1915).

[7] United States v. Union Pacific Railroad Co., 226 U.S. 61 (1912); United States v. Southern Pacific Co., 259 U.S. 214, 229 (1922); Steele v. United Fruit Co., 190 Fed. 631, 633 (E.D. La. 1911); United States v. Great Lakes Towing Co., 208 Fed. 733, 744-745 (N.D. Ohio, 1913), 217 Fed. 656 (N.D. Ohio, 1914); United States v. New England Fish Exchange, 258 Fed. 732, 751 (D. Mass. 1919), 292 Fed. 511 (D. Mass. 1923); United States v. Pullman Co., 50 F. Supp. 123, 126 (E.D. Pa. 1943), aff'd per curiam, 330 U.S. 806 (1947); United States v. General Electric Co., 82 F. Supp. 753, 816 (D.N.J. 1949); United States v. United Shoe Machinery Corp., 110 F. Supp. 295, 313 (D. Mass. 1953), aff'd per curiam, 347 U.S. 521 (1954).   In the last case it was said at page 313: "This acquisition taken with all other acquisitions of patents and other kinds of property, shows that to some extent United has maintained its position through acquisitions of patents."   See Johnston and Stevens, Monopoly or Monopolization, 44 Ill. L. Rev. 269, 282 (1949).   But compare United States v. United States Steel Corp., 251 U.S. 417, 452 (1920); United States v. American Can Co., 230 Fed. 859, 861, 234 Fed. 1019 (D. Md. 1916), appeal dismissed, 256 U.S. 706 (1921); Moody & Waters Co. v. Case-Moody Pie Corp., 354 Ill. 82, 187 N.E. 813 (1933); Bender v. Hearst Corp., 152 F. Supp. 569, 577-578 (D. Conn. 1957); Kales, Contracts and Combinations in Restraint of Trade §53 (1918).   An acquisition may, of course, also constitute an attempt to monopolize.   Baush Machine Tool Co. v. Aluminum Co. of America, 72 F.2d 236, 239 (2d Cir. 1934).

never been so limited. Under the latter measure it is immaterial whether the acquisitions take place by way of stock purchase, merger, consolidation or the buying of tangible assets.[8] On the other hand, it has been tremendously difficult to determine when the Sherman Act would be so applied. Some years ago a distinguished authority carefully reviewed all the cases involving industrial combinations. He was unable to find any rationale running through the decisions.[9] Today we are educated by the more recent opinion of the United States Supreme Court in the *Columbia Steel* case.[10] There it was held that the acquisition of a steel fabricator in the West Coast area by the United States Steel Corporation was not illegal. That holding was predicated on a finding that United States Steel had been doing some 13 per cent of the structural steel products business in the territory prior to the acquisition. The acquired firm had been doing about 11 per cent of that same business. Accordingly, the law today appears to be that a consolidation involving no more than 24 per cent of the business in the relevant geographic market does not constitute an infringement of Section 2 of the Sherman Act. On that subject the Supreme Court said:

> The same tests which measure the legality of vertical integration by acquisition are also applicable to the acquisition of competitors in identical or similar lines of merchandise. It is first necessary to delimit the market in which the concerns compete and then determine the extent to which the concerns are in competition in that market. If such acquisition results in or is aimed at unreasonable restraint, then the purchase is forbidden by the Sherman Act. In determining what constitutes unreasonable restraint, we do not think the dollar volume is in itself of compelling significance; we look rather to the percentage of business controlled, the strength of the remaining competition, whether the action springs from business requirements or purpose to monopolize, the probable development of the industry, consumer demands, and other characteristics of the market. We do not undertake to prescribe any set of percentage figures by which to measure the reasonableness of a corporation's enlargement of its activities by the purchase of the assets of a competitor. The relative effect of percentage command of a market varies with the setting in which that factor is placed.[11]

[8] Handler, A Study of the Construction and Enforcement of the Federal Anti-Trust Laws 82 (TNEC Monograph No. 38, 1941).

[9] Id. at 74; see also Handler, Industrial Mergers and the Anti-Trust Laws, 32 Colum. L. Rev. 179 (1932).

[10] United States v. Columbia Steel Co., 334 U.S. 495 (1948).

[11] 334 U.S. at 527-528. Compare United States v. Associated Press, 52 F. Supp. 362, 374 (S.D.N.Y. 1943), *aff'd,* 326 U.S. 1 (1945).

Although not mentioned in the *Columbia Steel* opinion, two other factors may be of considerable importance. In the first place, if it can be shown that the acquiring concern has dismantled the plants of its former rival after taking possession of them, application of the statute is more likely.[12] A similar result will follow if it can be shown that the acquiring concern has secured restrictive covenants from the sellers whereby the latter agree not to compete[13] — and this although such restrictive covenants are common means of protecting the good will conveyed.[14] In any event, it is clear that the legal tests of the validity of an acquisition under Section 2 of the Sherman Act are far from precise in character.

§2.26. **Analysis of acquisitions.** Acquisition of a competitive concern removes one rival from the market place and hence, by definition, pro tanto reduces competition. Accordingly, it appears entirely proper to treat proof of the consolidation of two rivals as giving rise to a presumption of an abuse. Such a presumption is supported by the history of several important industries,[1] by legislative debates[2] and, as indicated above, by many decisions.[3] There has also been a contention, largely emanating from the

---

Several years ago the decision in Standard Oil Co. of California v. United States, 337 U.S. 293 (1949), applied a stringent test to §3 of the Clayton Act. Several observers at once suggested that the almost identical language of §7 of the Clayton Act should be affected thereby. Worth, Anti-Trust Law as Affected by Standard Oil Company of California v. United States, 48 Mich. L. Rev. 505, 517 (1950); Schwartz, Potential Impairment of Competition, 98 U. Pa. L. Rev. 10, 30-31 (1949); Comment, Corporate Consolidation and the Concentration of Economic Power, 57 Yale L.J. 613, 619-620 (1948); Note, The Amendment to Section 7 of the Clayton Act, 46 Ill. L. Rev. 444, 452 (1951). Such a view could, of course, render academic the discussion in the text. Note, however, that the Attorney General's Committee disapproved application of such a strenuous rule under §7 of the Clayton Act. Atty. Gen. Nat. Com. Rep. 122.

[12] United States v. American Tobacco Co., 221 U.S. 106, 157 (1911); United States v. Eastman Kodak Co., 226 Fed. 62, 69 et seq. (W.D.N.Y. 1915), 230 Fed. 522 (W.D. N.Y. 1916), *appeal dismissed,* 255 U.S. 578 (1921); Distilling & Cattle Feeding Co. v. People ex rel. Moloney, 156 Ill. 448, 41 N.E. 188 (1895).

[13] Shawnee Compress Co. v. Anderson, 209 U.S. 423, 433-434 (1908); Schine Chain Theatres, Inc. v. United States, 334 U.S. 110, 119 (1948); United States v. Great Lakes Towing Co., 208 Fed. 733, 745 (N.D. Ohio, 1913), 217 Fed. 656 (N.D. Ohio, 1914).

[14] Compare 2 Restatement of Contracts §516(a).

§2.26. [1] 1 Nevins, Study in Power, c. 9, pp. 256, 285 (1953); Williamson, Winchester: The Gun That Won the West 58-59 (1952).

[2] Walker, History of the Sherman Law 6 (1910). But cf. Letwin, Congress and the Sherman Antitrust Law, 23 U. Chi. L. Rev. 221, 257 (1956).

[3] The notion that acquisitions may give rise to a presumption of an abuse is specifically mentioned in United States v. Great Lakes Towing Co., 208 Fed. 733, 742 (N.D. Ohio, 1913), 217 Fed. 656 (N.D. Ohio, 1914). Compare United States v. United Shoe Machinery Co., 110 F. Supp. 295, 312 (D. Mass. 1953), *aff'd per curiam,* 347 U.S. 521 (1954).

Federal Trade Commission, that an alleged current "merger movement" is substantially reducing competition in many areas.[4]

It is interesting to note that this abuse is closely related to the structure theory of monopoly: application of Section 2 of the Sherman Act to acquisitions tends to curb horizontal size in its "incipiency" and does not constitute mere regulation of large firms.[5] On the other hand, under either the abuse or structure theory it would scarcely seem possible for small firms wholly without monopoly power to infringe the statute.[6] Indeed, plain as the presumption of reducing competition may appear, there are circumstances in which the acquisition of rival firms may not be harmful to the economy as a whole.

One of the situations in which no economic damage will result from a merger of rival firms is that involving easy entry into the industry. Both in theory and in practice the higher prices (and profits) achieved after the merger of rival firms will attract new entrants into the field.[7] By definition those new competitors will reduce the monopoly power achieved by the combination. An instructive example is found in the history of the old American Can Company. That combination paid extravagant prices to secure practically all the can-making plants in the United States. To remain solvent it then had to raise prices and no sooner had it done so than new competitors sprang up on all sides. The combination then tried buying them all out, found that process too expensive, attempted buying part of their output in order to maintain prices, and finally gave up the struggle.[8] There are many other examples of self-correction in the market place when

---

[4] FTC, The Present Trend of Corporate Mergers and Acquisitions 5 (1947); Stigler, The Statistics of Monopoly and Merger, 64 J. Pol. Econ. 33-40 (1956). But compare Lintner and Butters, Effect of Mergers on Industrial Concentration, 32 Rev. Econ. & Stat. 30, 32 (1950); Weston, The Role of Mergers in the Growth of Large Firms 101-102 (1953). The whole topic of whether concentration is increasing is discussed in §2.3 *supra*.

[5] Half a century ago a leader of the bar asked: "Does the law object to size, control of the market, in itself, or only to particular methods of accomplishing size, or is size not taken into account at all?" Pope, The Legal Aspect of Monopoly, 20 Harv. L. Rev. 167, 168 (1907). Unfortunately, as the discussion in the text indicates, Mr. Pope's question remains unanswered.

[6] In United States v. Corn Products Refining Co., 234 Fed. 964, 1012 (S.D.N.Y. 1916), Judge Learned Hand wrote: ". . . it is the mere possession of an economic power, acquired by some form of combination, and capable, by its own variation in production, of changing and controlling price, that is illegal." See also Celler, The New Antimerger Statute, 37 A.B.A.J. 897, 900 (1951); H.R. Rep. No. 1191, 81st Cong., 1st Sess. 7-8 (1949). But compare Schwartz, Potential Impairment of Competition, 98 U. Pa. L. Rev. 10, 32 (1949).

[7] See §3.12 *infra*. Note also §2.4 *supra*, where the self-correcting character of monopoly is discussed.

[8] United States v. American Can Co., 230 Fed. 859, 879-880, 234 Fed. 1019 (D. Md. 1916), *appeal dismissed*, 256 U.S. 706 (1921).

conditions of entry are easy.[9] It does not, of course, follow that the law should not punish those who attempt to monopolize by acquiring rival concerns even though their efforts are foredoomed to failure. Such penalties may accomplish nothing in the way of a better allocation of economic resources but may operate as a deterrent to other businessmen engaged in fields where entry is not easy.

A more troublesome question may arise if factors of indivisibility are present. If, for example, the rival firms are both too small to take advantage of technological advances, a prohibition of their merger will result in some loss of efficiency. One of the great difficulties involved is that we do not know how to measure the economies of scale in such a situation.[10] Even if we could measure indivisibility, a great question would remain as to whether we preferred the additional efficiency which the combination might achieve to the extra competition which might otherwise prevail in the market place. Again, there is the situation in which two small firms join forces in order to compete more effectively against giants in the same industry. Such a consolidation raises questions of "countervailing power" and is open to all the objections thereto.[11]

Another situation which tends to excuse the combination of rival firms is found when one of the concerns is about to fail and it can be urged that the acquisition of the firm by its competitor will avoid the frictions incident to bankruptcy. That situation has been recognized by the courts, which usually hold that such an acquisition does not infringe the relevant statutes. Even under Section 7 of the Clayton Act, the courts are apt to say that the consolidation does no harm to competition because one firm is about to drop out of the market place in any event.[12] Such rea-

9 United States v. Corn Products Refining Co., 234 Fed. 964, 970-971, 971-972 (S.D.N.Y. 1916); 2 Nevins, Study in Power 76 (1953); Bicycles, 8 Fortune No. 3, pp. 49, 51 (1933); American Ice, 7 id. No. 5, pp. 73, 75 (1933); U.S. Rubber, 9 id. No. 2, pp. 52, 54 (1934). Even the backing of J. P. Morgan & Co. has not always assured financial success to manufacturing concerns. Corporate Management, 7 id. No. 6, p. 47 (1933).

10 See §3.13 infra. Compare Atty. Gen. Nat. Com. Rep. 125 et seq. Note that about 1878, when the Standard Oil Company was busy buying out most of its competitors, it was looked upon with favor by banks because it was financially responsible and enjoyed widespread respect for its efficiency and dependability. 1 Nevins, Study in Power 266 (1953). But compare McDonald, Strategy in Poker, Business and War 100 (1950).

11 See §4.4 infra. Compare Note, The Amendment to Section 7 of the Clayton Act, 46 Ill. L. Rev. 444, 453 (1951). Note the experience recorded in Gibb, The Whitesmiths of Taunton 171-172 (1943). Cf. Stigler, Mergers and Preventive Antitrust Policy, 104 U. Pa. L. Rev. 176, 181 (1955).

12 International Shoe Co. v. FTC, 280 U.S. 291 (1930); Pitts v. Mississippi Power Co., 177 Miss. 288, 170 So. 817 (1936); Industrial Finance & Thrift Corp. v.

soning appears to be sound, although it may be difficult to say in any given case when prospective failure has been sufficiently established.[13]

More fundamental questions arise out of dynamic considerations. As indicated by the foregoing discussion, the courts have attempted a distinction between the internal growth of a business firm and the acquisition of rival establishments. Internal growth has generally been encouraged, whereas acquisition of competing concerns has often been thought deleterious to the economy.[14] Certainly that is the view expressed in Section 7 of the Clayton Act. If, however, it would be dangerous to curb internal growth[15] — because to do so might discourage greater production and innovation — then it may be equally hazardous to prevent growth via the acquisition route.[16] In short, growth may be considerably more important than the means of its accomplishment, even if competition is reduced in the short run. In that connection,

---

Smith, 179 Miss. 323, 175 So. 206, 209 (1937); United States v. United Shoe Machinery Corp., 110 F. Supp. 295, 309, 311 (D. Mass. 1953), aff'd per curiam, 347 U.S. 521 (1954); Atty. Gen. Nat. Com. Rep. 123.

[13] In 1874 the first John D. Rockefeller was the low-cost refiner of petroleum. He could have run his competitors out of business but did not do so. Instead, he showed them his books revealing the lower cost of production and then let them into the Standard Oil combination on a favorable basis. 1 Nevins, Study in Power 209 (1953). Selling out, of course, is not the only alternative to liquidation. In 1926 the Celluloid Corporation faced failure. Then a new management took over control of the business and in one year turned a deficit of $700,000 into a profit of almost equal magnitude. Celluloid Corporation, 8 Fortune No. 4, pp. 144, 145 (1933).

[14] Standard Oil Co. of New Jersey v. United States, 221 U.S. 1, 32, 45 (1911); United States v. Columbia Steel Co., 334 U.S. 495, 532 (1948); United States v. American Can Co., 230 Fed. 859, 861, 902, 234 Fed. 1019 (D. Md. 1916), appeal dismissed, 256 U.S. 706 (1921); see United States v. United States Steel Corp., 251 U.S. 417, 460-461 (1920). In United States v. Great Lakes Towing Co., 208 Fed. 733 (N.D. Ohio, 1913), 217 Fed. 656 (N.D. Ohio, 1914), it was said: "The fact that the policy of the Towing Company's promoters was to buy out competitors, rather than to buy new tugs, and by competition compel the loss to other tug owners of their property, does not tend to negative an intent to create a monopoly . . . A wicked purpose to wreck the property and business of those then engaged in towing is not essential to a violation of the statute." 208 Fed. 742-743.

[15] See Appendix B.

[16] United States v. Aluminum Co. of America, 44 F. Supp. 97, 142-143 (S.D.N.Y. 1941), rev'd, 148 F.2d 416 (2d Cir. 1945). Celler Committee II, ser. III, No. 3, at 1855. Many instances can be cited in which corporations enjoying outstanding growth records have increased their business by the acquisition of other firms or by both the acquisition of other firms and internal expansion. Air Reduction, 8 Fortune No. 1, pp. 24, 108 (1933); Cochran, History of the Pabst Brewing Company 60 (1948); Thompson, Since Spindletop 48-49 (Gulf Oil Corp. 1951); Borg-Warner Corp., Ann. Rep. 1952, 12 (Chicago, 1953); McGraw Electric Co., Ann. Rep. 1949, 4-5 (Elgin, 1950); Du Pont II, 10 Fortune No. 6, p. 80 (1934); Mathers, Scott Paper Company 8-9 (Smith, Barney & Co. 1953). A good deal may depend upon how difficult it is to raise new capital from investors. Compare Bowman, Toward Less Monopoly, 101 U. Pa. L. Rev. 577, 582, 610-611 (1953).

note that internal growth as well as exterior acquisitions may constitute a bar to entry by other firms if a sufficient portion of the field is occupied.[17] Furthermore, market frictions of considerable magnitude may be avoided by external consolidation. The technology utilized by the acquired firm may be cheaper to buy outright than to acquire through years of study.[18] Similarly, tangible assets may sometimes be purchased, owing to market frictions, at less than their reproduction costs.[19] Time, too, may be saved by merger.[20]

Considerations such as those outlined above led the Attorney General's Committee to conclude that mergers were a neutral factor and should not be penalized as such:

> . . . mergers are a common form of growth; they may lessen, increase, or have no effect upon competition. A merger as such involves no necessary connotations of coercion, dominance, or lack of effective competitive pressure. In addition, mergers may ease from the market companies which have failed in the competitive struggle and thus prevent potential bankruptcies. Finally, they may spur operating economies by spreading overhead costs or enabling improved technology or management.[21]

As we have suggested above, there may properly arise from any merger or consolidation a presumption of an abuse. Such a presumption may be defeated by showing a lack of any monopoly power upon the part of either the acquiring or the consolidated concern. Moreover, if questions of indivisibility are raised, a court may well hesitate to impose legal sanctions upon the defendant. Much also may depend upon a showing of growth upon the part of the constituent companies and in that connection the court

17 Thus, in United States v. Aluminum Co. of America, 148 F.2d 416 (2d Cir. 1945), it was said at page 429: ". . . so far as concerns the public interest, it can make no difference whether an existing competition is put an end to, or whether prospective competition is prevented."

18 Such an economy may be realized, for example, when a firm diversifies into a new field in which it has had no prior experience. E.g., Gibb, The Whitesmiths of Taunton 120-121 (1943). Compare Chapter 6 infra.

19 E.g., Cross, From Land, Sea and Test Tube 38-39 (Archer-Daniels-Midland Co. 1954).

20 Kaplan, The Criterion of Relative Size in the Sanctioning of Mergers, Current Business Studies No. 21, pp. 29, 38 (Society of Business Advisory Professions, 1954); Philco Corp., Ann. Rep. 1948, 10 (Philadelphia, 1949); Greyhound Bus, 10 Fortune No. 2, pp. 34, 110 (1934). Perhaps for such reasons Professor Kales refused to distinguish growth by acquisition from growth by construction. Kales, Contracts and Combinations in Restraint of Trade §§66, 128 (1918).

21 Atty. Gen. Nat. Com. Rep. 124-125. The Committee went on to say at page 127: "An acquisition which substantially reduces the incentive of sellers or potential sellers to enter new markets and to improve their products or services, widen their distribution, lower their prices, or pass cost savings on to customers may substantially lessen competition."

may have to choose between long-run and short-term considerations.[22] In such circumstances intent will no doubt play a considerable role in making the final determination. The court may not be able to decide where indivisibility and similar factors "justify" the consolidation. It may, however, believe that the parties themselves know whether indivisibility is the motive force behind the merger. Accordingly, the motives of the parties, if they can be ascertained, may prove crucial to judicial conclusions.

§2.27. **High profits.** Occasionally it has been suggested that a rich return on investment should constitute evidence of monopolization and perhaps itself be considered an abuse. In a recent case, for example, the "exhorbitant" and "excessive" profits of the defendant were referred to by the trial court, which said that they "can in no way be justified." Later in the same opinion, the profits of the defendant were referred to as "inordinate." [1]

High profits would not seem to constitute the normal type of abuse: no competitor is directly injured by the earnings of the defendant.[2] On the other hand, one might suppose offhand that high profits could constitute a test of the existence of monopoly which might be useful under the structure theory of the law. It is, of course, elementary economic doctrine that a monopolist will reap a higher rate of return than one who is engaged in purely competitive business. Unfortunately, there are many reasons why one cannot test the existence of monopoly by the rate of return achieved by the defendant. In the first place, the mere measure-

---

[22] Note that the flexible approach suggested in the text (as opposed to a rigid reading of §7 of the Clayton Act) introduces a considerable element of uncertainty into the law. Cf. Markham, Survey of the Evidence and Findings on Mergers, in Business Concentration and Price Policy 141-182 (Stigler ed. 1955).

§2.27. [1] Hughes Tool Co. v. Ford, 114 F. Supp. 525, 541, 544, 551 (E.D. Okla. 1953), rev'd, 215 F.2d 924 (10th Cir. 1954), cert. denied, 348 U.S. 927, 965 (1955). Compare Standard Oil Co. of New Jersey v. United States, 221 U.S. 1, 43 (1911); United States v. Pullman Co., 50 F. Supp. 123, 134 (E.D. Pa. 1943), aff'd per curiam, 330 U.S. 806 (1947); Levi, The Antitrust Laws and Monopoly, 14 U. Chi. L. Rev. 153, 154 (1947). Note the views expressed in United States v. United Shoe Machinery Co., 222 Fed. 349 (D. Mass. 1915), aff'd, 247 U.S. 32 (1918). In that case it was said at page 370: "Nothing shown by the evidence warrants the conclusion that profits unreasonably out of proportion to the extremely large cost at which the business has been developed and is maintained, the great investment of capital it has required, and the enterprise, inventive skill, and business ability devoted to it, have been realized." See also United States v. E. I. Du Pont de Nemours & Co., 118 F. Supp. 41 (D. Del. 1953), aff'd, 351 U.S. 377, 404 (1956).

Several other abuses might be named. It has been suggested, for example, that management use of proxies to retain corporate control and the payment of bonuses to corporate officers both constitute predatory business practices. O'Mahoney Committee I, at 540-541.

[2] Compare §2.10 supra, outlining the abuses inherent in low profits (price discrimination). Cf. §4.10 infra.

ment of that return involves complex problems which have proven increasingly baffling in the public utility field. Again, those high profits might be attributable to some element of indivisibility, such as the ownership of the single molybdenum mine in the United States. High profits may also be attributable solely to innovation or innovation combined with time lags. For such reasons the Attorney General's Committee concluded that the rate of profit was not logically relevant to the existence of monopoly but said that evidence thereof threw some light on the possibilities of entry and power over price.[3] However that may be, it is difficult to conceive of high profits alone as constituting an abuse, since they may reflect neither any direct injury to rivals nor the existence of monopoly power in the legal sense.[4]

§2.28. **Requisite degree of control.** It is of the essence of the abuse test that the defendant enjoy some degree of monopoly power. Under that view of the law, those without monopoly power cannot violate the statutes; even those with monopoly power violate the statutes only when they misbehave and "abuse" their strength. Some kind of "platform" is therefore a necessary ingredient of the crime of monopolization.[1] As stated by a leader of the antitrust bar:

> Dominance in the market . . . while an important element in an alleged violation of Section 1 or of Section 3 of the Clayton Act is not the same as monopolization. Undoubtedly, one who is guilty of monopolization has a dominant market position, but the reverse may not be true. Dominance sufficient to support a Section 1 charge of restraint of trade or a Section 3 charge of a tying arrangement may fall far short of that control requisite to a Section 2 case.[2]

[3] Atty. Gen. Nat. Com. Rep. 48, (3).

[4] Whatever may be thought of high profits as an abuse, one can scarcely claim them to represent an attempt to monopolize, because the time sequence would thereby be reversed.

§2.28. [1] Lorain Journal Co. v. United States, 342 U.S. 143, 154 (1951); Times-Picayune Publishing Co. v. United States, 345 U.S. 594, 608-609 (1953); Kansas City Star Co. v. United States, 240 F.2d 643, 658 (8th Cir. 1957); United States v. International Harvester Co., 214 Fed. 987, 1000 (D. Minn. 1914), *appeal dismissed*, 248 U.S. 587 (1918), *supplemental petition*, 10 F.2d 827 (1926), *aff'd*, 274 U.S. 693 (1927); see Windsor Theatre Co. v. Walbrook Amusement Co., 94 F. Supp. 388, 396 (D. Md. 1950), *aff'd*, 189 F.2d 797 (4th Cir. 1951); Machlup, The Political Economy of Monopoly 99, 137 (1952).

[2] Johnston, Monopolize or Attempt to Monopolize, Proceedings A.B.A., Section of Antitrust Law, 72, 79 (Aug. 26, 1953). Compare G. & P. Amusement Co. v. Regent Theater, 107 F. Supp. 453 (N.D. Ohio, 1952); Levi, A Two Level Anti-Monopoly Law, 47 Nw. U.L. Rev. 567 (1952); Machlup, The Political Economy of Monopoly 470 (1952). The Attorney General's Committee decided: ". . . predatory competition . . . can usually only be waged where a considerable degree of market power already exists, or where an attempt is being made to use a long purse in

This rule may serve to explain, for instance, why the tort of un-fair competition has never been held an abuse within the mean-ing of Section 2 of the Sherman Act: the usual defendant in an unfair competition case does not have the requisite strength in the market place.[3]

Establishing the requisite degree of monopoly power in the defendant would appear to involve all the difficulties inherent in the structure test of monopoly. In some instances, however, that proof might be shortened if the abuses themselves demonstrated the existence of such market strength. Price discrimination, for example, cannot be practiced without some element of monopoly in the seller — whether sufficient to establish a "platform" under the abuse test, however, may be doubtful. Again, if an intent to injure a competitor can be established by unequivocal means (as by the admission of the defendant), then perhaps the courts are justified in presuming the ability to act: the defendant can scarcely deny his capacity once his assertion of intention is ade-quately established. Apart from such situations, however, proof of the necessary degree of monopoly, as stated above, appears to require compliance with the structure theory discussed below.[4]

§2.29. **Necessity of intent.** It has usually been assumed that proof of specific intent is a necessary ingredient to prove the ex-

---

order to destroy or coerce rivals." Atty. Gen. Nat. Com. Rep. 328. In Dirlam and Kahn, Fair Competition (1954), it was said at page 54: "It does not follow that an intent (as the psychologists might use the term) to suppress competition is or should be either a sufficient or in all cases a necessary basis for condemnation. Intent unaccompanied by overt action cannot enter into judgment in the present life. It must be accompanied, first, by the power (actual or imminent) to restrain or exclude and, second, by some evidence that the power has been or, barring interference, will be exercised. Thus, in Sherman Act cases the courts will usually appraise the power of the defendants, to help determine the character and probable results of their actions. But where the objectionable nature of the act is clear, they ordinarily make no 'systematic economic assessment of market power' . . ." The authors of the foregoing language appear to accept the view stated in the text unless an "objectionable" act can be proven against the defendant. Query as to what is "objectionable." Note that a different rule seems to obtain under §1 of the Sherman Act. United States v. Socony-Vacuum Oil Corp., 310 U.S. 150, 220, 225n (1940). A similar possibility exists under the Clayton Act and the Federal Trade Commission Act. E.g., Hodson, The Manufacturer's Right to His Dealer's Loyalty, Symposium, N.Y. State Bar Assn., Section on Antitrust Law, 186, 199 (CCH, 1953). Note, however, the views expressed in Atty. Gen. Nat. Com. Rep. 12, a.

3 See §2.22, supra.

It is, of course, possible that mere wealth, as opposed to a monopoly position, could constitute the necessary "platform" under the abuse theory. To date, how-ever, the courts do not appear to have taken account of that possibility.

4 See Chapter 3. For some inexplicable reason the courts do not appear to have discussed the problem set forth in the text. In most cases the existence of some degree of monopoly power has probably been obvious. E.g., United States v. American Tobacco Co., 221 U.S. 106 (1911). Cf. United States v. E. I. Du Pont de Nemours & Co., 118 F. Supp. 41 (D. Del. 1953), aff'd, 351 U.S. 377, 395 (1956).

istence of the crime of monopolization under the abuse test. Important decisions support that view in a fairly explicit manner.[1] Several of them, however, appear merely to assume that intent must be demonstrated and there are some recent decisions looking in the opposite direction. Thus, in a 1952 case it was said:

> . . . price differentiation . . . becomes illegal only when it is tainted by the purpose of unreasonably restraining trade . . . or attempting to destroy competition or a competitor, thus substantially lessening competition, or when it is so unreasonable as to be condemned as a means of competition.[2]

Such language suggests that no "purpose" need be demonstrated when the conduct is "so unreasonable as to be condemned as a means of competition." Perhaps, however, such decisions are really based upon the structure theory of monopoly.[3]

It is, of course, true that some of the abuses outlined above speak for themselves: res ipsa loquitur. If, for example, it is proven that the defendant set a torch to his rival's factory, the requisite intent to injure competition flows from the mere proof

§2.29. [1] Standard Oil Co. of New Jersey v. United States, 221 U.S. 1, 76 (1911); United States v. Aluminum Co. of America, 148 F.2d 416, 432 (2d Cir. 1945); United States v. Columbia Steel Co., 334 U.S. 495, 527 (1948); United States v. Aluminum Co. of America, 91 F. Supp. 333, 347 (S.D.N.Y. 1950); United States v. General Electric Co., 82 F. Supp. 753, 815 (D.N.J. 1949). Other cases are collected in §§2.10 et seq. *supra*. Compare United States v. Socony Vacuum Oil Corp., 310 U.S. 150, 226n (1940).

No one appears ever to have doubted that a specific intent must be proven when the offense charged is an attempt to monopolize. Eastman Kodak Co. v. Southern Photo Materials Co., 295 Fed. 98 (5th Cir. 1923), *aff'd*, 273 U.S. 359, 375 (1927); United States v. General Electric Co., 80 F. Supp. 989, 1016 (S.D.N.Y. 1948). Such is the general rule with respect to criminal attempts. Thus in Sayre, Criminal Attempts, 41 Harv. L. Rev. 821 (1928), it was said at page 841: ". . . there can be no conviction for a criminal attempt without proof of a specific intent to effect some consequence which constitutes a crime . . ." And in Keedy, Criminal Attempts at Common Law, 102 U. Pa. L. Rev. 464 (1954), it was said at page 466: "The first requisite of a criminal attempt is the intent to commit a specific crime . . . While the completed crime of the murder of *A* may be committed without the intent to murder *A,* and even without the intent to murder any person, there can be no attempt to murder *A* unless there exists the intent to murder *A*."

[2] Balian Ice Cream Co. v. Arden Farms Co., 104 F. Supp. 796, 807 (S.D. Cal. 1952), *aff'd*, 231 F.2d 356 (9th Cir. 1955), *cert. denied*, 350 U.S. 991 (1956). To the same effect see Schine Chain Theatres, Inc. v. United States, 334 U.S. 110, 120 (1948); United States v. Griffith, 334 U.S. 100, 107-108 (1948). In United States v. United Shoe Machinery Corp., 110 F. Supp. 295 (D. Mass. 1953), *aff'd per curiam*, 347 U.S. 521 (1954), the trial court said at page 346: "Defendant intended to engage in the leasing practices and pricing policies which maintained its market power. That is all the intent which the law requires when both the complaint and the judgment rest on a charge of 'monopolizing,' not merely 'attempting to monopolize.' Defendant having willed the means, has willed the end." Note also the dissenting opinion in United States v. Columbia Steel Co., 334 U.S. 495, 539 (1948).

[3] The difficulty with the explanation offered in the text is, of course, that under the structure theory, intent is logically irrelevant. See §3.18 *infra*.

of the act. Similarly, where it is proven that a defendant bought up the plants of rival firms and then dismantled them, the necessity of establishing any separate intent on his part can almost be dispensed with.[4] As a leading authority has said:

> The dangerous probability that monopolization will result connotes at least that potential power to bring about monopoly is present and that some steps have been taken to effectuate that result. It is from these overt acts, indeed, that the specific intent to monopolize is found, since defendants do not generally proclaim their intention of violating the law.[5]

Other acts, however, are equivocal in character: from them there flows no sure inference of malevolence. A firm may, for example, slash its prices to "ruinous" levels; but such an act is as consistent with a desperate effort to avert bankruptcy as it is with a predatory design upon rival firms.[6] Or, to put another case, the seller may be seeking to explore the possibilities of expanding output and profits through reduction of prices.[7] As we shall see, there is room for the complaint that intent is difficult to establish. To dispense with it, however, might require more elaborate proof of other circumstances and conditions, for the underlying justification for requiring a showing of intent is that the defendant knows his business better than anyone else; knowing and understanding the economic situation, his intent reveals much that courts might not otherwise realize. For similar reasons, even under the structure theory of monopoly, the courts are apt to require some showing of "general intent." [8]

§2.30. **Establishing intent.** The intent required to establish the crime of monopolization is "specific" and not "general." There is, of course, ample room for disagreement as to the precise

---

4 United States v. American Tobacco Co., 221 U.S. 106, 181 (1911); United States v. Eastman Kodak Co., 226 Fed. 62, 75-76 (W.D.N.Y. 1915), *decree*, 230 Fed. 522 (W.D.N.Y. 1916), *appeal dismissed*, 255 U.S. 578 (1921). Admissions upon the part of the defendant may, of course, establish the necessary intent. E.g., Boggs v. Duncan-Schell Furniture Co., 163 Iowa 106, 143 N.W. 482 (1913).

5 Johnston, Monopolize or Attempt to Monopolize, Proceedings A.B.A., Section of Antitrust Laws, 72, 77 (Aug. 26, 1953).

6 Compare Gibb, The Saco-Lowell Shops 289 (1950) with Campbell and Hatton, Herbert H. Dow, Pioneer in Creative Chemistry 59 (1951).

7 Dodge v. Ford Motor Co., 204 Mich. 459, 170 N.W. 668, 670, 676, 683 (1919). Compare State ex Information Major v. International Harvester Co., 237 Mo. 369, 141 S.W. 672, 679 (1911), *aff'd*, 234 U.S. 199 (1914); Ben Hur Coal Co. v. Wells, 242 F.2d 481, 486 (10th Cir. 1957) (discussion based upon §3 of Robinson-Patman Act). Another example may be found in a situation where a defendant has bought a competing business to compose patent infringement claims. United States v. United Shoe Machinery Co., 247 U.S. 32, 52 (1918). See Kahn, Standards for Antitrust Policy, 67 Harv. L. Rev. 28, 52 (1953).

8 See §3.18 *infra*.

content of "specific intent."[1]   As in the cases of attempts to monopolize, however, it can probably be said that the specific intent required must relate to the crime attempted; it cannot merely relate to some other crime.   Thus an intent to drive recklessly is not a sufficiently specific intent to support an indictment for attempted murder even though death results from the reckless driving.   A leading authority has said that what must be specific is the crime which is intended.[2]   Limitations of language, however, will probably always leave room for debate as to the specific intent in any monopolization case.

In some instances, it will be easy to establish the existence of the requisite specific intent.   We have noted above[3] that some of the abuses consist of acts which speak for themselves.   In other instances, defendants may be foolish enough to admit in so many words their intent to destroy a rival [4] or to express the same admissions in the form of threats.[5]   The fact that a defendant has chosen to cloak his activities in secrecy may also be taken as some admission of unlawful purpose.[6]

§2.30. [1] E.g., United States v. United Shoe Machinery Corp., 110 F. Supp. 295, 346 (D. Mass. 1953), aff'd per curiam, 347 U.S. 521 (1954). Compare Pope, Vertical Forestalling Under the Antitrust Laws, 19 U. Chi. L. Rev. 583, 604 (1952).

[2] Sayre, Criminal Attempts, 41 Harv. L. Rev. 821, 842 (1928); Keedy, Criminal Attempts at Common Law, 102 U. Pa. L. Rev. 464 (1954).

[3] §2.29 supra. In Dirlam and Kahn, Fair Competition 50 (1954) it was said: "The quest for an explanatory intent does not involve psychoanalysis. The question is not: 'Why did A really do what he did?' but simply: 'What was A really doing? Was he competing or was he suppressing competition?' . . . The attempt is simply to provide a logical ordering and interpretation of the objective record, out of which there may emerge a reasonable, summary description and appraisal of a course of action, in order to ascertain whether it falls within the acts condemned by law." It is not clear whether the test suggested in the foregoing quotation would do away with the requirement of intent and, if so, what would be substituted therefor. Much business conduct is equivocal in character. If we are to penalize "misbehavior" (as the abuse theory requires) the test of intent is difficult to avoid.

[4] United States v. Corn Products Refining Co., 234 Fed. 964, 984-985 (S.D.N.Y. 1916). In United States v. Pullman Co., 50 F. Supp. 123, 126 (E.D. Pa. 1943), aff'd per curiam, 330 U.S. 806 (1947), the trial court relied upon declarations of intent to monopolize uttered long before the enactment of the statute upon which the proceeding was based. Query whether the latter decision is sound.

[5] Boggs v. Duncan-Schell Furniture Co., 163 Iowa 106, 143 N.W. 482 (1913). Compare Schine Chain Theatres, Inc. v. United States, 334 U.S. 110, 119 (1948).

[6] United States v. Corn Products Refining Co., 234 Fed. 964, 982 (S.D.N.Y. 1916); State ex Information Hadley v. Standard Oil Co., 218 Mo. 1, 116 S.W. 902, 990, 1025, 1041 (1909), aff'd, 224 U.S. 270 (1912); see United States v. United Shoe Machinery Co., 247 U.S. 32, 43 (1918). The foregoing cases involved espionage upon the activities of a rival (with a view to cutting prices only to the rival's customers) and the organization of "bogus independents." The latter practice involved the setting up of a supposedly independent business entity which would compete vigorously with the rival firm in an effort to drive it out of business without cutting prices on the defendant's own brands of merchandise.

Undoubtedly, it is tempting to expand the category of res ipsa loquitur. Thus some courts have intimated that price-cutting could speak for itself and that proof of that act would be sufficient to establish the requisite intent.[7] As indicated above, however, there may be explanations for price reduction wholly apart from an attempt to monopolize. The price reduction may, for example, reflect merely an effort to increase volume and eliminate excess capacity;[8] thus to say that price reduction evidences unlawful intent when goods are sold below "cost" or at prices not yielding a "fair" profit[9] merely opens the door to interminable investigation.[10] Again, some courts have thought they could ascertain intent from a "deliberate, calculated purchase for control" in acquisition cases.[11] The difficulty, of course, is that defendants have urged that there were "legitimate business purposes" behind their acts and have sometimes persuaded the courts to accept their arguments.[12]

[7] United States v. United States Steel Corp., 223 Fed. 55, 77 (D.N.J. 1915), aff'd, 251 U.S. 417 (1920); United States v. Corn Products Refining Co., 234 Fed. 964, 983 (S.D.N.Y. 1916); State v. Atlantic Ice & Coal Co., 210 N.C. 742, 188 S.E. 412, 419 (1936). In United States v. United Shoe Machinery Corp., 110 F. Supp. 295, 329 (D. Mass. 1953), aff'd per curiam, 347 U.S. 521 (1954), the trial court appears to have held that reducing prices merely to meet competition was both an abuse and evidence of wrongful intent. But compare Fleetway, Inc. v. Public Service Transport Co., 72 F.2d 761, 763 (3d Cir. 1934).

[8] When Andrew Carnegie was in command of the steel mills which he later sold to form part of the United States Steel Corporation, he operated at full capacity regardless of demand conditions, reducing prices in order to secure orders and putting competitors out of business in the process. After the consolidation of those mills into the United States Steel Corporation, the policy was changed and the corporation maintained prices and operated at less than capacity during the period of slack demand. United States v. United States Steel Corp., 223 Fed. 55, 92-93 (D.N.J. 1915), aff'd, 251 U.S. 417 (1920). Perhaps, however, price reductions aimed at an increase in volume and the elimination of excess capacity are illegal. United States v. New York Great Atlantic & Pacific Tea Co., 173 F.2d 79 (7th Cir. 1949); United States v. Corn Products Refining Co., 234 Fed. 964, 988 (S.D.N.Y. 1916); State v. Atlantic Ice & Coal Co., 210 N.C. 742, 188 S.E. 412, 421 (1936).

[9] United States v. Corn Products Refining Co., 234 Fed. 964, 991 (S.D.N.Y. 1916); United States v. United Shoe Machinery Corp., 110 F. Supp. 295, 326 (D. Mass. 1953), aff'd per curiam, 347 U.S. 521 (1954); Balian Ice Cream Co. v. Arden Farms Co., 104 F. Supp. 796, 807 (S.D. Cal. 1952), aff'd, 231 F.2d 356 (9th Cir. 1955), cert. denied, 350 U.S. 991 (1956). It may, of course, make considerable difference if the defendant can establish that the price-cutting has been carried on over a lengthy period of time. Compare United States v. Corn Products Refining Co., supra, at 1013; Handler, Unfair Competition, 21 Iowa L. Rev. 175, 181 (1936).

[10] See §4.10 infra.

[11] United States v. Reading Co., 253 U.S. 26, 57 (1920); American Tobacco Co. v. United States, 147 F.2d 93, 111 (6th Cir. 1944), aff'd, 328 U.S. 781 (1946); United States v. Yellow Cab Co., 332 U.S. 218, 227-228 (1947); United States v. General Electric Co., 80 F. Supp. 989, 1010 (S.D.N.Y. 1948). Compare Standard Oil Co. of New Jersey v. United States, 221 U.S. 1, 75 (1911). Even prior acquisitions may be examined to determine the intent of a merger currently under review. United States v. Columbia Steel Co., 334 U.S. 495, 532 (1948).

[12] United States v. Standard Oil Co., 47 F.2d 288, 310-311 (E.D. Mo. 1931); United States v. Columbia Steel Co., 334 U.S. 495, 533 (1948); Match Corp. v. Acme Match

An acute observer has suggested the analogy of the difference between a race and a fight. He said:

> It is possible to distinguish between a competitive race and a competitive fight. If the large concern can run away from its competitors by reason of greater efficiency, no policy involved in the Sherman Act is violated by its successful issue from the race, but if the large competitor chooses to take advantage of its greater weight to spike or slug its competitor, the government should intervene as a referee and rule it from the track. . . .[13]

This analogy may prove suggestive in some cases. Yet the possibility will always remain that the defendant has sought to run faster by obtaining some additional means of propulsion which then becomes unavailable to his rival.[14] In short, it is not at all clear that intent can be determined in every case of alleged monopolization.[15]

Corp., 285 Ill. App. 197, 205, 1 N.E.2d 867 (1936). The last-cited case involved an output and requirements contract. Note the language in Patterson v. United States, 222 Fed. 599 (6th Cir. 1915), cert. denied, 238 U.S. 635 (1915), where the court said at page 625: "It is never to be lost sight of that actually doing business, no matter how large, is not monopolizing. It is excluding from the opportunity of doing business that is . . ." Compare United States v. Aluminum Co. of America, 44 F. Supp. 97, 149 (S.D.N.Y. 1941), rev'd, 148 F.2d 416 (2d Cir. 1945); Standard Oil Co. of New Jersey v. United States, 221 U.S. 1, 73, 76 (1911). The courts have sometimes considered the defendants' declining proportion of the relevant market a factor bearing on intent to monopolize. United States v. Columbia Steel Co. supra; Balian Ice Cream Co. v. Arden Farms Co., 104 F. Supp. 796, 807 (S.D. Cal. 1952), aff'd, 231 F.2d 356 (9th Cir. 1955), cert. denied, 350 U.S. 991 (1956). It is not clear, however, why that factor is relevant. Existence of a general depression, on the other hand, may readily be recognized as material. United States v. Aluminum Co. of America, supra, at 222; American Tobacco Co. v. United States, 328 U.S. 781, 805 (1946); TNEC Hearings, pt. 19, at 10,490, 10,535. Note also the legality of a covenant not to compete ancillary to the conveyance of a going business. 2 Restatement of Contracts §516(a). Here the need to protect the business sold from the "imperfection" of market confusion is so well recognized as necessarily to negative an intent to monopolize.

[13] McLaughlin, Legal Control of Competitive Methods, 21 Iowa L. Rev. 274, 280 (1936). Compare United States v. Yellow Cab Co., 332 U.S. 218, 227-228 (1947); Standard Oil Co. of New Jersey v. United States, 221 U.S. 1, 45, 76 (1911). In Standard Oil Co. v. Doyle, 118 Ky. 662, 82 S.W. 271 (1904), it was said at page 273: "Undoubtedly one man may by fair methods compete with a rival until by sheer force of competition, by underselling or outbidding him, his own business is built up to the detriment and ruin of his rival. The damage in such case is in the eye of the law damnum absque injuria. But a different case is presented where one seeks not only to build up his own business at the expense of a rival's, but to impair, and if possible, destroy, that rival's business by the use of unlawful means by saying and doing that which he has no lawful right to say and do, in so far as it works loss and damage to his rival."

[14] Compare United States v. Crescent Amusement Co., 323 U.S. 173, 183 (1944); United States v. United Shoe Machinery Corp., 110 F. Supp. 295, 326 (D. Mass. 1953), aff'd per curiam, 347 U.S. 521 (1954).

[15] Pope, The Reason for the Continued Uncertainty of the Sherman Act, 7 Ill. L. Rev. 201, 206, 211 (1912).

§2.31. Critique of the abuse theory. The case for the abuse theory rests upon a belief that the market is self-correcting[1] in the long run if "predatory practices" are eliminated. Put another way, it is often asserted that monopoly power cannot be maintained without resort to rough tactics. Accordingly, prohibition of abuses which eliminate rivals without regard to their efficiency would appear to accomplish the ends sought by antitrust legislation.[2] Moreover, the abuse theory has the merit of avoiding some of the many stumbling blocks inherent in the structure test.[3] It is not necessary to ascertain whether entry is easy or difficult and the element of indivisibility can largely be disregarded. Furthermore, the abuse doctrine does not curb growth and innovation and it leaves businessmen with an incentive to expand production and undertake new ventures.[4]

---

§2.31.   [1] See §2.4 *supra.*

[2] United States v. Corn Products Refining Co., 234 Fed. 964, 1012 (S.D.N.Y. 1916); Machlup, The Economics of Sellers' Competition 531 (1952); Machlup, The Political Economy of Monopoly 175-176 (1952); Kahn, Standards for Antitrust Policy, 67 Harv. L. Rev. 28, 50, 53-54 (1953); Atty. Gen. Nat. Com. Rep. 327, (4). Empirical support for the abuse doctrine is found in McKie, The Decline of Monopoly in the Metal Container Industry, 45 Proceedings Am. Econ. Assn. 499 (1955). The thesis there advanced is that the courts, by compelling the American Can and Continental Can to abandon their practice of leasing closing machinery, had effectively eliminated monopoly in the can-making business. Just how this result was obtained is not explained. Possibly the companies had a monopoly element in the machinery before the court entered its order. Forced liquidation of the machinery business may have broken that monopoly and prevented its transfer into the can-making field.

[3] See Chapter 3.

[4] The considerations sketched in the text were well stated in Johnston, Monopolize or Attempt to Monopolize, Proceedings A.B.A., Section of Antitrust Law, 72 (Aug. 26, 1953). It was there said at page 74: "The dictum of Judge Learned Hand in the *Aluminum* case that ninety per cent constitutes a monopoly, sixty or sixty-four per cent is doubtful, and thirty-three per cent is not enough, is not helpful. The extent of defendant's power may, it is true, be determined in some cases by a consideration of the elements of size, established reputation of the product produced, distribution facilities and other like factors. In other cases, however, and these are by far the more numerous, monopoly power is determined by an evaluation of what the defendant has actually done to evidence that power. It is in the consideration of the actual exercise of power — the business conduct of the defendant, in short, that the application of the Rule of Reason becomes important. Convenient as it would be to have a Rule of Thumb by which we could automatically determine the existence of monopoly power by measuring a defendant's percentage of production or of sales within the industry, the generality of the term 'monopolization' precludes any such arbitrary classification. We must still resort to the laborious process of balancing all the factors and minutely examining the defendant's conduct to determine whether the requisite power to control prices . . . exists." Compare Kales, Contracts and Combinations in Restraint of Trade §89 (1918). As we shall see, factors such as indivisibility and innovation prevent full application of the structure theory of monopoly under the antitrust laws. Unless, therefore, some new theory can be found and adopted, it is likely that the abuse doctrine will continue to be applied in situations wherein structure or other theory is inadequate.

It is also easy to see the defects in the abuse theory. In actual practice, it is difficult to find criteria by which to distinguish vigorous competition from predatory practices.[5] As noted above, the requisite factor of intent may often prove elusive.[6] As a consequence, abuses are defined loosely. The emotional character of the abuse test permits an easy decline into the troughs of "soft" competition and protectionism.[7] As a result, almost any business practice can constitute an abuse; indeed, simply outstripping a rival may cause a firm to be condemned.[8]

Even more serious a defect lies in the fact that the abuse theory does nothing to rid the economy of monopoly itself;[9] it can only rely on self-correction in the market place to achieve that result. For such reasons many economists have emphasized the structure test. The abuse theory leads directly to a distinction between "good" and "bad" trusts.[10] That, in turn, like many provisions of the Clayton Act, suggests regulation rather than competition.[11]

5 Machlup, The Political Economy of Monopoly 101 (1952); Edwards, Public Policy and Business Size, 24 J. Business 280, 286-287 (1951); Kahn, A Legal and Economic Appraisal of the "New" Sherman and Clayton Acts, 63 Yale L.J. 293, 297 (1954). Note also that to the extent the abuse theory depends upon the structure theory to determine whether a practice has an adverse effect upon competition, it is admittedly incomplete in itself and subject to all the infirmities of the structure doctrine.

6 Professor Bowman has pointed out that businessmen are constantly attempting to achieve some degree of monopoly power by differentiating their product and otherwise. It follows that the requirement of specific intent is unworkable. Bowman, Toward Less Monopoly, 101 U. Pa. L. Rev. 577, 612 (1953).

7 Compare United States v. United Shoe Machinery Corp., 110 F. Supp. 295, 329 (D. Mass. 1953), aff'd per curiam, 347 U.S. 521 (1954); State v. Atlantic Ice & Coal Co., 210 N.C. 742, 188 S.E. 412, 421 (1936). On the other hand, it has been recognized recently that "It is of the essence of competition that it must, of necessity, injure others." Balian Ice Cream Co. v. Arden Farms Co., 104 F. Supp. 796, 801 (S.D. Cal. 1952), aff'd, 231 F.2d 356 (9th Cir. 1955), cert. denied, 350 U.S. 991 (1956).

8 United States v. Aluminum Co. of America, 44 F. Supp. 97, 148 (S.D.N.Y. 1941), rev'd, 148 F.2d 416 (2d Cir. 1945); United States v. New York Great Atlantic & Pacific Tea Co., 173 F.2d 79, 82-83 (7th Cir. 1949); United States v. United Shoe Machinery Corp., 110 F. Supp. 295, 331 (D. Mass. 1953), aff'd per curiam, 347 U.S. 521 (1954). In the cited cases the courts appear to have penalized firms which were active in seeking out and investigating new processes, carrying on technological research and attempting to buy at lower prices. When abuses are so loosely defined, it is, of course, easy to enforce the antitrust laws in a partisan manner. As Dean Levi has said, "The truth is, of course, that in most monopoly cases, if the court has a mind to do so, it can find abuses." Levi, The Antitrust Laws and Monopoly, 14 U. Chi. L. Rev. 153, 158 (1947).

9 Id. at 160.

10 Kales, Contracts and Combinations in Restraint of Trade, c. 5 (1918), but compare United States v. E. I. Du Pont de Nemours & Co., 118 F. Supp. 41 (D. Del. 1953), aff'd, 351 U.S. 377 (1956).

11 Pope, The Legal Aspect of Monopoly, 20 Harv. L. Rev. 167, 191 (1907); Levi, A Two Level Anti-Monopoly Law, 47 Nw. U.L. Rev. 567, 571 (1952). Cf. Vito, Monopoly and Competition in Italy, in Chamberlin, ed., Monopoly and Competition and Their Regulation 43-60 (International Economic Assn. 1954).

Under the abuse theory, the public utility type regulation involved constitutes governmental intervention, however paradoxical that may seem.[12]   At the same time, the regulation is incomplete and often permits the exploitation of monopoly power in avenues not reached by the concept of abuses.[13]   It is not surprising, therefore, that many observers have found the abuse theory wanting and have suggested alternative tests of legality.

[12] The regulation involved in the abuse theory may itself discourage efforts to curb market imperfections and thus do more harm than good.   See, e.g., §2.24 *supra*.   Note also that the abuse theory can be used to prohibit business arrangements which in and of themselves appear to be innocuous.   United States v. Pullman Co., 50 F. Supp. 123, 132, 134 (E.D. Pa. 1943), *aff'd per curiam*, 330 U.S. 806 (1947).

[13] Thus, in United States v. General Motors Corp., 121 F.2d 376 (7th Cir. 1941), *cert. denied*, 314 U.S. 618 (1941), relief was granted against the tying of automobiles and their financing.   If the defendant had genuine monopoly power, however, it remained completely free to raise the prices of its automobiles to any level it chose.

Horizontal Size: The Structure Theory

§3.1. Nature of the structure theory. As we have seen, the abuse theory of monopoly distinguishes the good monopolist from the bad; it punishes only such monopolists as exercise their powers in "predatory" fashion. Under the structure theory behavior is irrelevant: the law proscribes monopoly itself and not merely monopolization; it reaches the fact of market power rather than the manner of its exercise. The term "structure" is derived from the fact that the theory involves analysis of the composition of a market for a specific product in a given geographic area, including computation of the number of sellers and the like. In short, the test involves finding the defendant's "share of the market." [1]

Economists, it may be fair to say, have generally emphasized the structure theory. The abuse doctrine is the creation of lawyers and has received less support in economic circles. While the shortcomings of the structure theory are now widely recognized among economists, it furnishes at least a starting point for most economic analysis.

Structure theory has long dominated economic thinking. Nevertheless, it achieved more explicit recognition with the development of the theory of monopolistic competition shortly after the depression started in 1930. Prior to that time, most economists had contrasted complete monopoly on the one hand with complete competition on the other. Monopoly was the control of a commodity within a single firm. Competition was envisaged as what we now call "pure" competition, meaning that there were so many sellers in the market that no one of them could affect the price which he received for his product. As early as 1838, however, the French economist Cournot had perceived that there were degrees of market power between the polar extremes of monopoly and competition.[2] Shortly after World War I, Pro-

---

§3.1. [1] It may be superfluous to point out that this chapter, like Chapter 2, is concerned with the issue of "horizontal" size. It does not discuss the "shape" of a business enterprise. Questions of "shape" are discussed in Chapters 5, 6, and 7.

[2] Machlup, The Economics of Sellers' Competition 348, 368 (1952); Schumpeter, History of Economic Analysis 150-155, 189, 305, 959-960 (1954).

fessor Viner pointed out that few markets were "purely" competitive; that products were "differentiated" in order to avoid pure
price competition and that there were many gradations between
pure competition and pure monopoly in actual markets.[3]   A few
years later, Professor Sraffa developed the theme, arguing that
monopoly and not free competition was the more appropriate
assumption in market theory.[4]   With publication of works by
Professor Chamberlin and Mrs. Robinson about 1933, the theory
of monopolistic competition jumped to full-blown status.[5]   Those
economists offered an organized approach to the middle ground
between monopoly and competition, emancipating the analysis of
markets from the inadequate categories of competition and single-
firm monopoly.   Their views rapidly achieved widespread acceptance, and almost at once the concepts of duopoly, oligopoly
and the purposeful differentiation of products became accredited
categories in market analysis.   The theory brought the vast phenomenon of merchandising and advertising within the scope of
theoretical discussion.[6]   Today, therefore, it is common to speak
of "pure" competition, meaning that there are so many producers

[3] Viner, Price Policies: The Determination of Market Price, in Business Administration 343, 345 (Marshall ed. 1921).

[4] Sraffa, The Laws of Returns Under Competitive Conditions, 36 Econ. J. 535
(1926); Galbraith, Monopoly and the Concentration of Economic Power, in Ellis,
ed., A Survey of Contemporary Economics 99, 100 (American Economic Assn. 1949).
Professor Sraffa said at page 542: "These two points in which the theory of
competition differs radically from the actual state of things which is most general
are: first, the idea that the competing producer cannot deliberately affect the
market prices, and that he may therefore regard it as constant whatever the
quantity of goods which he individually may throw on the market; second, the
idea that each competing producer necessarily produces normally in circumstances
of individual increasing cost." Professor Galbraith wrote at pages 99-100: "Subject
to qualifications, the tendency at the time Mr. Sraffa's article appeared was to
recognize the limiting case of monopoly, but to assume, in general, a rule of
competition. Competition was not assumed to be perfect. Those already in the
business might variously obstruct the entry of newcomers. Or entry might be
rendered difficult by the prestige associated with trade-marks and trade names.
Imperfect knowledge of opportunities might interfere. Decreasing costs were
deemed an especially serious handicap for the newcomer, who because he was new,
was likely to be small. If large scale and accompanying requirements in capital and
organization brought substantial economies, the small newcomer was faced with an
organic handicap. Nevertheless, these barriers, though widely recognized, were con-
ventionally assumed to be of secondary effect. They were frictions that muddled and
at times diverted but did not check the great underlying current which was toward
a competitive equilibrium. . . . Sraffa attacked the assumption that the 'frictions'
were in fact a secondary and fugitive phenomenon. He argued they were stable
and indeed cumulative and yielded a solution consistent not with a competitive,
but a monopolistic equilibrium . . ."

[5] Chamberlin, The Theory of Monopolistic Competition (1933); Robinson, What
Is Perfect Competition? 49 Q.J. Econ. 104 (1934); Robinson, The Economics of
Imperfect Competition (1936).

[6] Brems, Product Equilibrium Under Monopolistic Competition 160-161 (1951);
Galbraith, Monopoly and the Concentration of Economic Power, in Ellis, ed., A
Survey of Contemporary Economics 99, 101 (American Economic Assn. 1949). Pro-

of a single homogeneous commodity that no member of the group produces more than a negligible fraction of the total output and therefore cannot affect prices. All other situations are deemed to contain at least some elements of monopoly. "Perfect" competition, on the other hand, refers to a situation in which market "imperfections" are nonexistent: inertia, indivisibility, immobility and ignorance do not prevent the rapid allocation of resources to their most productive uses.[7]

For some time lawyers had been vaguely aware that economists were studying the monopoly problem. Announcement of the doctrine of monopolistic competition, however, brought the views of economists forcibly to the attention of the bar.[8] The chief implication of the new development, of course, was that monopolistic results could be obtained even if there were a few sellers in the market. Accordingly, "oligopoly" (few sellers) should be broken up to achieve the benefits of competition.[9] It had earlier

---

fessor Galbraith wrote at page 101: ". . . Professor Chamberlin's theory of monopolistic competition — of competition between numerous sellers differentiated by location, personality, or physical or psychic differences in their product — brought the vast phenomenon of merchandising and advertising within the scope of theoretical analysis. . . . Without much doubt the dominant market of modern capitalism is not one made up of many sellers offering others uniform or differentiated products. Rather it is a market of few sellers, i.e., oligopoly. Apart from consumers' goods the counterpart of few buyers associated with many or few sellers is also a common phenomenon. Where sellers are few the product is automatically identified with its vendor and hence there is always a measure of differentiation — the elasticity of substitution between products of a few sellers can never be quite perfect. But the ruling characteristic is the fewness of the sellers." An example of the "differentiation" upon which Professor Chamberlin laid so much stress is found in Cannon Mills, 8 Fortune No. 5, pp. 50, 134 (1933). But compare Markham, Competition in the Rayon Industry 68-69 (1952). The concept of differentiation is not wholly clear; consider, for example, the effort of authors to produce novels which will appeal to readers because they present new situations or new characters and the like. Compare Metro-Goldwyn-Mayer, 6 Fortune No. 6, p. 50 (1932).

Since 1933 many economists have developed the themes stated by Professor Chamberlin and Mrs. Robinson. E.g., Triffin, Monopolistic Competition and General Equilibrium Theory (1940); Fellner, Competition Among the Few (1949); Chamberlin, Product Heterogeneity and Public Policy, 40 Proceedings Am. Econ. Assn. 85 (1950); Robinson, Imperfect Competition Revisited, 63 Econ. J. 579 (1953); Chamberlin, ed., Monopoly and Competition and Their Regulation (International Economic Assn. 1954). Many other studies could be cited; indeed, the whole economic literature on this subject has stemmed from the developments outlined in the text.

[7] Wilcox, Competition and Monopoly in American Industry 3 (TNEC Monograph No. 21, 1940); Bishop, Elasticities, Cross-Elasticities, and Market Relationships, 42 Am. Econ. Rev. 779, 780 (1952); Appendix A infra.

[8] Fly, Observations on the Anti-Trust Laws, Economic Theory and the Sugar Institute Decisions, 45 Yale L.J. 1339, 1341 et seq. (1936); Galbraith, Monopoly and the Concentration of Economic Power, in Ellis, ed., A Survey of Contemporary Economics 99, 116 (American Economic Assn. 1949).

[9] Burns, The Decline of Competition 522 et seq. (1936); Rostow, The New Sherman Act, 14 U. Chi. L. Rev. 567, 589 (1947); Kahn, Standards for Antitrust Policy, 67 Harv. L. Rev. 28, 34 (1953).

been decided that any agreement among rivals to fix prices was illegal and the new economic doctrines indicated that oligopoly automatically resulted in similar price-fixing.[10]   Thus the stage was set for adoption of the structure test by the law and, indeed, for a stringent variation thereof founded on the theory of monopolistic competition.[11]

§3.2.   **Acceptance of the structure theory.**   While it has been fashionable to say that the older decisions relied exclusively upon the abuse theory, many indications can be found that the structure test was not wholly overlooked.   Indeed, many decisions through the decades appear to rely on both theories.   In the older decisions the courts often spoke of "monopoly" (rather than "monopolization") as being the offense prohibited both at common law and under the statutes.   In one case involving a combination of competitors to fix prices the Supreme Court referred to the "rule against monopolies." [1]   In another older decision, the court said:

> . . . the averment of the answer is positive and direct that the plaintiff has acquired and maintained a monopoly of interstate trade in shoe machinery, and the offer of proof in this regard was co-extensive with the averment.   This brings the case within the words of §2 of the anti-trust act, which subjects to a penalty "every person who shall monopolize . . . any part of the trade or commerce among the several states." [2]

10 Hale, Agreements Among Competitors, 33 Minn. L. Rev. 331, 354 (1949); Harbeson, A New Phase of the Antitrust Law, 45 Mich. L. Rev. 977, 987-988 (1947).

11 It is now generally believed that economic formulas require adaptation before they can be applied to antitrust litigation.   Thus a leading economist wrote: "The theory of monopolistic competition does not, as some appear to suppose, furnish any conclusions from which a concrete program of public policy can be directly derived."   Wallace, Industrial Markets and Public Policy, in Public Policy 59, 65 (Friedrich and Mason ed. 1940).   Failure to heed such admonitions may have resulted in a measure of distrust of economic theory upon the part of the bar. Note, for example, the elaborate qualification of economic considerations found in Atty. Gen. Nat. Com. Rep. 315 et seq.

§3.2.   1 United States v. Addyston Pipe & Steel Co., 175 U.S. 211, 237 (1899).

2 United Shoe Machinery Co. v. La Chapelle, 212 Mass. 467, 99 N.E. 289, 290 (1912).   In United States v. Swift & Co., 286 U.S. 106 (1932), it was said at page 116: "Mere size . . . is not an offense . . . unless magnified to the point at which it amounts to a monopoly . . . but size carries with it an opportunity for abuse that is not to be ignored when the opportunity is proved to have been utilized in the past."   In State ex Information Major v. International Harvester Co., 237 Mo. 369, 141 S.W. 672 (1911), it was said at page 677: "The statute we are now considering is not designed to limit the amount of wealth one may lawfully acquire, therefore not designed to limit the influence that wealth may exert but it is designed to forbid the acquisition of power for the purpose of influencing the market by combinations of interests that otherwise would compete. . . .   The law regards such a power acquired by such a combination as dangerous to the rights of the people and forbids its acquisition."   In Lynch v. Magnavox Co., 94 F.2d 883 (9th Cir. 1938), it was said at page 888: "We believe no offense is pleaded within the words of section 2. . . .   The word 'monopolize,' as there used, apparently means

Moreover, some of the earlier decisions seem to be explicable mainly upon the structure theory.[3]   Among those decisions may be the early *Corn Products* case, in which Judge Learned Hand wrote:

> The opinions of the Supreme Court certainly seem to indicate that it is the power and not its exercise which is the test.[4]

Prior to 1945, however, it was probably true that the abuse test commanded the allegiance of most courts,[5] although as early as 1943 one court was able to say:

> Monopoly being clearly established any number of judicial statements can be found to the effect that instances of its baleful practices need not be shown to prove that the statute is violated. Benevolent monopoly is no less a monopoly because it is benevolent.[6]

The grand impetus for the structure theory, however, arose from Judge Learned Hand's decision in the *Aluminum* case in 1945.[7] Many observers took that decision as the turning point in the

the acquisition of power to fix prices, limit production, or deteriorate quality . . ." In Foster v. Shubert Holding Co., 316 Mass. 470, 55 N.E.2d 772 (1944), it was said at page 774: "The modern concept of a monopoly is a combination or organization which has acquired a position of such dominating influence in a particular branch of trade or commerce that it has a tendency to suppress competition, to regulate supply and to fix prices, all to the detriment of the public, in respect of some commodity which the people must have in order to satisfy an essential need of ordinary living."   See also United States v. Quaker Oats Co., 232 Fed. 499, 500 (N.D. Ill. 1916); Distilling & Cattle Feeding Co. v. People ex rel. Moloney, 156 Ill. 448, 465-466, 491, 41 N.E. 188 (1895).   Compare Bishop v. American Preservers' Co., 157 Ill. 284, 41 N.E. 765 (1895).   Even the congressional debates on the measure now known as the Sherman Act contain hints of such a view.   Walker, History of the Sherman Law 25 (1910).

[3] United States v. Reading Co., 253 U.S. 26, 57 (1920); Northern Securities Co. v. United States, 193 U.S. 197 (1904).

[4] United States v. Corn Products Refining Co., 234 Fed. 964, 1012 (S.D.N.Y. 1916). See also United States v. Quaker Oats Co., 232 Fed. 499, 502 (N.D. Ill. 1916); Kales, Contracts and Combinations in Restraint of Trade §128 (1918).   The decision in the 1911 Tobacco case is commonly thought to rest heavily upon the existence of abuses.   The opinions, however, reveal little evidence of rough tactics aside from some local price-cutting.   Indeed, the court remarked that the record was remarkably free of evidence of such tactics.   United States v. American Tobacco Co., 164 Fed. 700, 720 (S.D.N.Y. 1908), aff'd, 221 U.S. 106, 182, 184 (1911).

[5] In United States v. Pullman Co., 50 F. Supp. 123, 125 (E.D. Pa. 1943), aff'd per curiam, 330 U.S. 806 (1947), the Attorney General did not contend that the defendant violated the statute merely because it was the sole supplier of sleeping-car service to railways in the United States but based his complaint on the allegation of a plan to monopolize which had been carried out many years before.   Note also the dissenting opinion of Mr. Justice Day in United States v. United States Steel Corp., 251 U.S. 417, 460, 464 (1920); Langdell, The Northern Securities case, 16 Harv. L. Rev. 539, 546-547 (1903).

[6] United States v. Pullman Co., 50 F. Supp. 123, 134 (E.D. Pa. 1943), aff'd per curiam, 330 U.S. 806 (1947).

[7] United States v. Aluminum Co. of America, 148 F.2d 416 (2d Cir. 1945).

change from the abuse theory to that more nearly in accord with economic doctrine.[8] A year later, in the *Tobacco* case, the Supreme Court went out of its way to praise Judge Learned Hand's decision, and then said:

> The authorities support the view that the material consideration in determining whether a monopoly exists is not that prices are raised and that competition actually is excluded but that power exists to raise prices or to exclude competition when it is desired to do so.[9]

About two years later the same court declared:

> Monopoly power is not condemned by the Act only when it was unlawfully obtained. The mere existence of the power to monopolize, together with the purpose or intent to do so, constitutes an evil at which the Act is aimed.[10]

Lower courts took up the refrain and one stated several years later:

> The Sherman Act condemns the power which makes pricing abuses possible as well as the abuse itself.[11]

[8] United States v. Aluminum Co. of America, 91 F. Supp. 333, 340-341 (S.D.N.Y. 1950); Levi, The Antitrust Laws and Monopoly, 14 U. Chi. L. Rev. 153, 175 (1947); Rostow, The New Sherman Act, id. 567, 576, 585 (1947); Rostow, Monopoly Under the Sherman Act: Power or Purpose? 43 Ill. L. Rev. 745, 746, 762 (1949); Levi, A Two Level Anti-Monopoly Law, 47 Nw. U.L. Rev. 567, 568 (1952).

[9] American Tobacco Co. v. United States, 328 U.S. 781, 811 (1946). In the same opinion it was said at page 810: "Neither proof of exertion of the power to exclude nor proof of actual exclusion of existing or potential competitors is essential to sustain a charge of monopolization under the Sherman Act." The intermediate court had gone at least part of the way in forecasting the Supreme Court's views. 147 F.2d 93, 110 (6th Cir. 1944). The views expressed in the text are consistent with those set forth in Timberg, Some Justification for Divestiture, 19 Geo. Wash. L. Rev. 132, 135 (1950).

[10] Schine Chain Theatres, Inc. v. United States, 334 U.S. 110, 130 (1948). *Accord:* United States v. Griffith, 334 U.S. 100, 107n (1948); United States v. Paramount Pictures, Inc., 334 U.S. 131, 173 (1948); United States v. Line Material Co., 333 U.S. 287, 305 (1948). The views of the Attorney General were presented shortly thereafter in the following terms:

". . . when bigness achieves a point that it does have . . . monopoly power, the power to control prices and production without paying any attention to normal competitive factors, then we think that a monopoly has been achieved.

"Bigness and monopoly are not synonymous, in my opinion, but when you achieve a monopoly or monopoly power, then I think, that the forces of the antitrust laws come into play." Celler Committee I, pt. 1, at 365.

While the foregoing quotation does clearly indicate that the Attorney General had adopted the structure theory, it leaves much to be desired as an indication of when that theory will be called into play.

[11] Gamco, Inc. v. Providence Fruit & Produce Building, Inc., 194 F.2d 484, 487 (1st Cir. 1952), *cert. denied,* 344 U.S. 817 (1952). *Accord:* United States v. General Electric Co., 82 F. Supp. 753, 893, 899 (D.N.J. 1949); United States v. American Can Co., 87 F. Supp. 18, 32 (N.D. Cal. 1949); Lawlor v. National Screen Service Corp., 99 F. Supp. 180, 185 (E.D. Pa. 1951).

If doubt remained, it appeared to be put to rest by the 1953 decision involving the United Shoe Machinery Company. After surveying the various possible tests of illegality, the court held that the defendant's 75 per cent of the defined market and various practices brought it within the scope of Section 2 of the Sherman Act.[12] In the opinion it was said:

> . . . the Sherman Act is now construed . . . to forbid the continuance of effective market control based in part upon such practices. Those courts hold that market control is inherently evil and constitutes a violation of §2 unless economically inevitable, or specifically authorized and regulated by law.[13]

Similarly, it appears that the Attorney General's Committee accepted the views expressed in the *Shoe Machinery* decision and hence adopted the structure theory of monopoly,[14] at least in part.

Doubts nevertheless do remain. In the first place, the important *Columbia Steel* decision,[15] handed down after the *Aluminum* and *Tobacco* cases, is difficult to reconcile with the structure theory.[16] In the second place, even those decisions which purport

---

[12] United States v. United Shoe Machinery Corp., 110 F. Supp. 295, 343, 345 (D. Mass. 1953), *aff'd per curiam*, 347 U.S. 521 (1954).

[13] 110 F. Supp. at 345. See Handler, Monopolies, Mergers and Markets 12 (Fed. Bar Assn., Nov. 9, 1954). Compare Johnston, Monopolize or Attempt to Monopolize, Proceedings A.B.A., Section of Antitrust Law, 72, 80-81 (Aug. 26, 1953). See also United States v. E. I. Du Pont de Nemours & Co., 118 F. Supp. 41 (D. Del. 1953), *aff'd*, 351 U.S. 377, 395 (1956); the Supreme Court said at page 389: ". . . it came to be recognized . . . that acts bringing the evils of authorized monopoly — unduly diminishing competition and enhancing prices — were undesirable . . . and were declared illegal by §2. . . . Our cases determine that a party has monopoly power if it has, over 'any part of the trade or commerce among the several States,' a power of controlling prices or unreasonably restricting competition"; at page 393, "Whatever the market may be, we hold that control of price or competition establishes the existence of monopoly power under §2. Section 2 requires the application of a reasonable approach in determining the existence of monopoly power just as surely as did §1. This of course does not mean that there can be a reasonable monopoly."

[14] Atty. Gen. Nat. Com. Rep. 43, a, (1). The Committee's report appears to reject the abuse theory, the performance theory, the countervailing power theory and several others, at least by implication.

[15] United States v. Columbia Steel Co., 334 U.S. 495 (1948). Note also the equivocal language in Kansas City Star Co. v. United States, 240 F.2d 643, 660 (8th Cir. 1957).

[16] Professor Handler's views on the Columbia Steel case are found in Celler Committee I, pt. 1, at 537 et seq. Compare Rostow, Monopoly Under the Sherman Act: Power or Purpose? 43 Ill. L. Rev. 745, 787 et seq. (1949), with Johnston and Stevens, Monopoly or Monopolization — A Reply to Professor Rostow, 44 Ill. L. Rev. 269, 274 et seq. (1949), and Johnston, Monopolize or Attempt to Monopolize, Proceedings A.B.A., Section of Antitrust Law, 72, 76 (Aug. 26, 1953). Note also that the language in the opinion in American Tobacco Co. v. United States, 328 U.S. 781 (1946), is not wholly without equivocation. Thus the Court said at page 796: "The marked dominance enjoyed by each of these three, in roughly equal proportions, is emphasized by the fact that the smallest of them at all times showed

to be based upon the structure doctrine also speak of "practices" which may be difficult to distinguish from abuses.[17] In the third place, those same decisions purport to require a showing of "general intent" upon the part of the defendant. (As we shall see, logic makes a finding of intention irrelevant under the structure theory.)[18] In short, while the structure theory may have been incorporated into the law, it was somewhat altered in the process.

§3.3. **Defining the commodity.** Inherent in the structure theory is the problem of defining the affected commodity, sometimes called the process of identifying the relevant market. As we have seen, the structure theory depends on the concept of market shares; and a defendant can scarcely be judged until an answer can be found for the question: market for what?[1] Thus, if we are speaking of a steel company, we may say that it enjoys

---

over twice the production of the largest outsider. Without adverse criticism of it, comparative size on this great scale inevitably increased the power of these three to dominate all phases of their industry. 'Size carries with it an opportunity for abuse that is not to be ignored when the opportunity is proved to have been utilized in the past.'" In the foregoing quotation the phrase "without adverse criticism of it" is difficult to reconcile with unswerving adoption of the structure theory. Note also the following language from the opinion in G. & P. Amusement Co. v. Regent Theater, 107 F. Supp. 453 (N.D. Ohio, 1952), wherein it was said at page 459: "Perhaps the most vital element of the plaintiff's case is the alleged monopoly buying power of Cooperative. It was conceded that under the facts here presented, without a showing that such monopolistic power actually exists, proof of conspiracy, either vertical or horizontal, has failed. While it is true that Cooperative represented a considerable number of exhibitors who comprised the local film market, that fact does not, in and of itself, establish that Cooperative actually possessed the trade restraining potential attributed to it. . . . There is nothing inherently unlawful in the acquisition and retention of a great volume of purchasing power. It is only when that power is used in such a manner as to further an unlawful restraint of trade that the wielder of the power runs afoul of the Sherman Act." Compare Mason, The Current Status of the Monopoly Problem in the United States, 62 Harv. L. Rev. 1265, 1275-1276 (1949).

17 See §3.19 *infra*. Compare United States v. Aluminum Co. of America, 148 F.2d 416, 429 (2d Cir. 1945).

18 See §3.18 *infra*. In United States v. Griffith, 334 U.S. 100, 106, 107, 108 (1948), the Supreme Court played with the structure theory in a tantalizing manner. Moving forward and back between the mere existence of monopoly power and some "general intent" or purpose to exercise that power, the Court danced a neat minuet of apparent contradiction which leaves the law in an uncertain state. Compare Johnston, Monopolize or Attempt to Monopolize, Proceedings A.B.A., Section of Antitrust Law, 72, 74 (Aug. 26, 1953).

§3.3. 1 Wilcox, Competition and Monopoly in American Industry 9-10 (TNEC Monograph No. 21, 1940); Markham, An Alternative Approach to the Concept of Workable Competition, 40 Am. Econ. Rev. 349, 350 (1950). In current British legislation, a presumption of monopoly is made to arise if one third of the supply of "all the goods of that description" is found in a single hand. Monopolies and Restrictive Practices (Inquiry and Control) Act, 1948, 11 & 12 Geo. VI, c. 66. The problem of defining the commodity is, of course, closely linked to the problem of defining the geographic market. See §3.6 *infra*. For it is permissible to regard physically identical goods as different commodities if they are located far apart. Machlup, The Political Economy of Monopoly 8 (1952).

x per cent of the market for all steel products or that it makes 46 per cent of all *rolled* steel products.[2] It is not statutory language which requires the court to define the commodity in question: it is the basic concept of monopoly in the structure theory itself.[3]

§3.4. **Legal approaches to the definition of the commodity.** In the reported decisions we find a wide variety of means by which the courts have defined the relevant commodity or industry. In some decisions the courts seem to have defined the commodity in terms of the boundaries of the defendant's own business[1] — a

[2] United States v. United States Steel Corp., 223 Fed. 55, 65 (D.N.J. 1915), *aff'd,* 251 U.S. 417 (1920); United States v. Columbia Steel Co., 334 U.S. 495, 500, 512, 529 (1948). Infinite possibilities of classification exist and many of them are actually found in the decisions. E.g., United States v. Aluminum Co. of America, 148 F.2d 416, 423-424 (2d Cir. 1945); United States v. Paramount Pictures, Inc., 334 U.S. 131, 172 (1948). See §3.4 *infra.*

[3] Atty. Gen. Nat. Com. Rep. 44, (2), disapproving United States v. Yellow Cab Co., 332 U.S. 218, 225-226 (1947); United States v. E. I. Du Pont de Nemours & Co., 118 F. Supp. 41 (D. Del. 1953), *aff'd,* 351 U.S. 377, 380, 392 (1956). Compare United States v. Paramount Pictures, Inc., 334 U.S. 131, 173 (1948); Indiana Farmer's Guide Co. v. Prairie Farmer Co., 293 U.S. 268, 279 (1934); Peto v. Howell, 101 F.2d 353, 358 (7th Cir. 1939); Syracuse Broadcasting Corp. v. Newhouse, 236 F.2d 522, 526 (2d Cir. 1956); Mackey v. Sears, Roebuck & Co., 237 F.2d 869, 873 (7th Cir. 1956). In United States v. E. I. Du Pont de Nemours & Co., *supra,* the Supreme Court said at pages 380-381: "The ultimate consideration . . . is whether the defendants control the price and competition in the market for such part of trade or commerce as they are charged with monopolizing. Every manufacturer is the sole producer of the particular commodity it makes but its control in the above sense of the relevant market depends upon the availability of alternative commodities for buyers: *i.e.,* whether there is a cross-elasticity of demand between cellophane and the other wrappings. This interchangeability is largely gauged by the purchase of competing products for similar uses considering the price, characteristics and adaptability of the competing commodities." Similar problems are encountered in the administration of price-fixing schemes. Levinson, The Minimum Product Standard, in Eckert, ed., Problems in Price Control: Pricing Standards 91, 101 (OPA, 1947); McMillan, Adjustment of Abnormally Low Prices Under the General Maximum Price Regulation, id. at 421, 429; Dickerson, The Industry Earnings Standard, id. at 27, 70; Abramson, Price Freezing Under the Office of Price Administration, 32 Am. Econ. Rev. 760, 762-763 (1942). Comparable problems arise in deciding how far (to what additional commodities) trade-mark protection should be extended. Schechter, Fog and Fiction in Trade-Mark Protection, 36 Colum. L. Rev. 60, 84 (1936); Oates, Relief in Equity Against Unfair Trade Practices of Non-Competitors, 25 Ill. L. Rev. 643, 650 (1931); 3 Restatement of Torts §730.

§3.4. [1] United States v. General Motors Corp., 121 F.2d 376, 398, 402 (7th Cir. 1941), *cert. denied,* 314 U.S. 618 (1941); Oxford Varnish Corp. v. Ault & Wiborg Corp., 83 F.2d 764, 766 (6th Cir. 1936); United States v. General Electric Co., 82 F. Supp. 753, 816 (D.N.J. 1949); United States v. United Shoe Machinery Corp., 110 F. Supp. 295, 303 (D. Mass. 1953), *aff'd per curiam,* 347 U.S. 521 (1954). In the last-named case, the district court appeared first to define the relevant commodities so as to exclude dry thread sewing machines. Later, however, it found that manufacturers of dry thread sewing machines were forcing the defendant to reduce its prices and thereby causing a price discrimination among the defendants' customers. 110 F. Supp. 329, 303. Without adverting to this particularly astounding aspect of its decision, the court defended its general position on defining a commodity,

procedure which may, of course, have drastic consequences under the structure theory. If the commodities produced by the defendant itself, however homogeneous or diversified, are taken for the definition of the relevant commodity or market, it amounts to a denial that any "substitutes" can affect the defendant's position.[2] From time to time, too, it has been suggested that a trademark, no matter how broadly or narrowly applied, might appropriately measure the relevant commodity.[3] But the courts have generally rejected both the foregoing tests.[4]

as follows, at page 303: "To define a market in terms of what the most important producer offers does not involve circular reasoning. For the problem of defining a market turns on discovering patterns of trade which are followed in practice."

[2] In Gamco, Inc. v. Providence Fruit & Produce Building, Inc., 194 F.2d 484 (1st Cir. 1952), cert. denied, 344 U.S. 817 (1952), the defendant owned and operated a building used by dealers in fruits and vegetables. The plaintiff complained of a refusal to lease space to it within the building. The defendant denied that it had a monopoly, saying that the plaintiff could obtain space elsewhere. On the subject of defining the relevant commodity, the lower court said at page 487: "Defendants contend, however, that a discriminatory policy in regard to the lessees in the Produce Building can never amount to monopoly because other alternative selling sites are available. The short answer to this is that a monopolized resource seldom lacks substitutes; alternatives will not excuse monopolization." Rigorous application of the views expressed in the foregoing quotation could, of course, lead to a finding that almost every business enterprise violates the law.

[3] Goodyear Tire & Rubber Co. v. FTC, 101 F.2d 620 (6th Cir. 1939), cert. denied, 308 U.S. 557 (1939); Eastern Wine Corp. v. Winslow-Warren, Ltd., 137 F.2d 955, 957-958 (2d Cir. 1943), cert. denied, 320 U.S. 758 (1943); Standard Brands, Inc. v. Smidler, 151 F.2d 34, 37 (2d Cir. 1945). If a seller deliberately "differentiates" his product by adopting a trade-mark and advertising, there is at least a superficial argument to be made in favor of finding the relevant commodity in terms of such a trade-mark. Thus, in United States v. Quaker Oats Co., 232 Fed. 499 (N.D. Ill. 1916), Alschuler, J., dissenting, said at page 507: "If these companies have exploited their respective brands so successfully that the public by the hundreds of thousands have been induced to believe that they possess superior merit, and thereby the companies respectively have established this vast package trade in these goods, if then in some way they combine . . . for the advantage thereby accruing, and in such manner they unduly restrict trade and promote monopoly in these products, they ought not, in defense of such transaction, be heard to say that, if the public do not like it, they may get goods of other brands or go without any brand at all." Note also the evidence adduced in the Investment Bankers case, United States v. Morgan, 118 F. Supp. 621, 793 (S.D.N.Y. 1953). The testimony offered therein indicated that pure price competition was difficult to achieve in investment banking because the issuer of securities relies heavily upon the prestige of the investment banker. Again, one investment banker is reluctant to solicit business of an issuer when some rival has handled such business in the past, because he may fear to lose prestige by an unsuccessful solicitation. In other words, the services offered by the investment banker are unique in character.

[4] Atty. Gen. Nat. Com. Rep. 43, (a); Trust Co. of Georgia v. State, 109 Ga. 736, 35 S.E. 323, 329 (1900), and other cases cited below in this section. Compare Whitwell v. Continental Tobacco Co., 125 Fed. 454, 462 (8th Cir. 1903). In Northern Securities Co. v. United States, 193 U.S. 197 (1904), Mr. Justice Holmes dissenting, said at page 406: "According to popular speech, every concern monopolizes whatever business it does . . . Of course, the statute does not forbid that. It does not mean that all business must cease." As to the use of trade-marks to define relevant commodities, consult United States v. Quaker Oats Co., 232 Fed. 499, 502-503 (N.D. Ill.

A series of tests relate to the physical composition of the products involved. To some courts the raw materials used in the fabrication of otherwise competitive products may serve to distinguish the commodities concerned. Thus, in the well-known *Klearflax* case[5] the rugs manufactured by the defendant were distinguished from all other rugs (to say nothing of all floor coverings) because the defendant was the only manufacturer who used linen as a raw material instead of wool, cotton, synthetic fibers and the like. In the *Aluminum* litigation,[6] the question of finding the relevant commodity was raised in all three courts and the results are not wholly harmonious, some courts placing dependence upon the raw material test and others rejecting it. The method or process of manufacture or service has sometimes appeared persuasive to courts. Thus they have indicated that "seamless" pipe is not generally competitive with "lap-weld" pipe,[7] but that

---

1916); Great Atlantic & Pacific Tea Co. v. Cream of Wheat Co., 227 Fed. 46, 48 (2d Cir. 1915); Arthur v. Kraft-Phenix Cheese Corp., 26 F. Supp. 824, 828-829 (D. Md. 1938); Miller Motors, Inc. v. Ford Motor Co., 149 F. Supp. 790, 806 (M.D.N.C. 1957).

[5] United States v. Klearflax Linen Looms, Inc., 63 F. Supp. 32 (D. Minn. 1945). *Accord:* United States v. American Can Co., 87 F. Supp. 18, 21 (N.D. Cal. 1949); McKie, The Decline of Monopoly in the Metal Container Industry, 45 Proceedings Am. Econ. Assn. 499, 500 (1955). Compare United States v. Corn Products Refining Co., 234 Fed. 964, 975-976 (S.D.N.Y. 1916); Appalachian Coals, Inc. v. United States, 288 U.S. 344, 361-362 (1933); Southern Electric Securities Co. v. State, 91 Miss. 195, 44 So. 785, 789 (1907); Perma-Maid, Inc. v. FTC, 121 F.2d 282 (6th Cir. 1941); United States v. E. I. Du Pont de Nemours & Co., 118 F. Supp. 41 (D. Del. 1953), *aff'd,* 351 U.S. 377 (1956); American Crystal Sugar Co. v. Cuban-American Co., 152 F. Supp. 387, 398-399 (S.D.N.Y. 1957).

[6] United States v. Aluminum Co. of America, 44 F. Supp. 97 (S.D.N.Y. 1941), *rev'd,* 148 F.2d 416 (2d Cir. 1945), 91 F. Supp. 333 (S.D.N.Y. 1950). In the original opinion of the trial court it was said at page 305: "Paragraph 38 of the bill declares that steel, nickel, tin, zinc, copper and lead are the 'chief industrial competitors' of aluminum. Numerous witnesses . . . established that there are many metals and materials (those named in the bill, as well as others) which, in a variety of fields, are constantly seeking to displace aluminum; likewise that, in many fields, aluminum is constantly struggling to displace those metals and materials." In the Court of Appeals, however, the principal question discussed with respect to the definition of the commodity was whether virgin aluminum and scrap aluminum should be considered a single commodity. 148 F.2d at 423 et seq. No account was taken of other metals. On remand, however, the trial court re-examined both the question of including scrap aluminum in the commodity and the question of whether to take account of the competition afforded by other metals. 91 F. Supp. at 357-358, 416.

[7] United States v. United States Steel Corp., 223 Fed. 55, 143 (D.N.J. 1915), *aff'd,* 251 U.S. 417 (1920). *Accord:* United States v. Besser Mfg. Co., 96 F. Supp. 304, 306 et seq. (E.D. Mich. 1951), *aff'd,* 343 U.S. 444 (1952); Hughes Tool Co. v. Ford, 114 F. Supp. 525, 533-534 (E.D. Okla. 1953), *rev'd,* 215 F.2d 924 (10th Cir. 1954), *cert. denied,* 348 U.S. 927, 965 (1955); Kobe, Inc. v. Dempsey Pump Co., 198 F.2d 416, 422-423 (10th Cir. 1952), *cert. denied,* 344 U.S. 837 (1952); United States v. United Shoe Machinery Corp., 110 F. Supp. 295, 303 (D. Mass. 1953), *aff'd per curiam,* 347 U.S. 521 (1954); United States v. Pullman Co., 50 F. Supp. 123, 135 (E.D. Pa. 1943), *aff'd per curiam,* 330 U.S. 806 (1947); Foundry Services, Inc. v. Beneflux Corp., 110 F. Supp. 857, 860 (S.D.N.Y. 1953), *rev'd on other grounds,* 206 F.2d 214 (2d Cir.

a wick-type fluid fuel cigar lighter and a butane gas lighter constitute one commodity.[8] Two interesting decisions involved advertising. In the first case, it was held by clear implication that
the operator of a radio station was competing with a newspaper
publisher.[9] In the second, decided only a short while later, the
defendant published two newspapers. The defendant contended
that the commodity in question embraced advertising in the radio,
television, magazine, billboard and other media. The plaintiff
contended that only newspapers should be considered and that all
other media should be excluded from the relevant commodity.
A footnote to that opinion interestingly refers to purely economic
concepts:

> For every product, substitutes exist. But a relevant market cannot
> meaningly encompass that infinite range. The circle must be
> drawn narrowly to exclude any other product to which, within
> reasonable variations and price, only a limited number of buyers
> will turn; in technical terms, products whose "cross-elasticities of
> demand" are small.[10]

In other litigation, sizes, styles, types, colors and other distinctive
features achieved in manufacture have been held distinguishing.[11]

1953); United States v. International Business Machines Corp., 13 F. Supp. 11, 14
(S.D.N.Y. 1935), aff'd, 298 U.S. 131 (1936); McWhirter v. Monroe Calculating
Machine Co., 76 F. Supp. 456, 460-461 (W.D. Mo. 1948). Note also the complaint in
United States v. Servel, Inc., No. 11036, E.D. Pa., CCH Trade Reg. Serv. ¶¶61,271
(1950), 67,665 (1954). In Hughes Tool Co. v. Ford, supra, the trial court said at
page 536: "In order to have a violation of the antitrust statutes it is not essential
that the article or commodity involved be completely free from alternatives or
substitutes, inasmuch as almost every article has competition in some degree from
other available articles. . . ." In Northern Securities Co. v. United States, 193
U.S. 197 (1904), Mr. Justice Brewer, concurring, wrote at page 363: ". . . under
present conditions a single railroad is, if not a legal, largely a practical, monopoly,
and the arrangement by which the control of these two competing roads was merged
in a single corporation broadens and extends such monopoly."

[8] Ronson Patents Corp. v. Sparklets Devices, Inc., 112 F. Supp. 696, 684-685 (E.D.
Mo. 1953); Southern Electric Securities Co. v. State, 91 Miss. 195, 44 So. 785, 789
(1907). In several cases the courts have refused to distinguish handicraft methods
from advanced machine production procedure. United States v. United Shoe
Machinery Co., 222 Fed. 349, 407 (D. Mass. 1915), aff'd, 247 U.S. 32 (1918); Moody
& Waters Co. v. Case-Moody Pie Corp., 354 Ill. 82, 84, 89, 187 N.E. 813 (1933);
United States v. Besser Mfg. Co., 96 F. Supp. 304, 306 et seq. (E.D. Mich. 1951),
aff'd, 343 U.S. 444 (1952).

[9] Lorain Journal Co. v. United States, 342 U.S. 143 (1951). Note, however, that
the Court first speaks of the defendant's monopoly of the newspaper field and then
of an attempt to monopolize the whole field of mass dissemination of news. Id.
at 149-150. Query whether the definition of the commodity was not shifted in the
course of the opinion. Compare Kansas City Star Co. v. United States, 240 F.2d 643,
659-660 (8th Cir. 1957); Veatch v. Wagner, 109 F. Supp. 537 (D. Alaska, 1953).

[10] Times-Picayune Publishing Co. v. United States, 345 U.S. 594, 612n (1953).
Note the position taken in the dissenting opinion at 628.

[11] United States v. Standard Oil Co., 47 F.2d 288, 306 (E.D. Mo. 1931); United
States v. Columbia Steel Co., 334 U.S. 495, 511, 515, 530-531 (1948); Lipson v.
Socony-Vacuum Corp., 87 F.2d 265, 269 (1st Cir. 1937), cert. dismissed, 301 U.S. 711

Thus it was found in one case that all domestically made motion pictures should be treated as one commodity except for "Westerns." [12] In another instance, shoes of a style appealing to city "slickers" were held different commodities from those sold to country "hicks." [13] Gradations in quality appeal to some courts

(1937); Oxford Varnish Corp. v. Ault & Wiborg Corp., Inc., 83 F.2d 764, 766 (6th Cir. 1936); Eastman Kodak Co. v. FTC, 158 F.2d 592 (2d Cir. 1946), cert. denied, 330 U.S. 828 (1947); United States v. General Instrument Corp., 87 F. Supp. 157, 190 (D.N.J. 1949); Lawlor v. National Screen Co., 99 F. Supp. 180, 184 (E.D. Pa. 1951); V. Vivadou, Inc. v. FTC, 54 F.2d 273, 276 (2d Cir. 1931). Compare Tag Manufacturers' Institute v. FTC, 174 F.2d 452, 453n (1st Cir. 1949); Alexander's Department Stores v. Ohrbach's, Inc., 266 App. Div. 535, 42 N.Y.S.2d 703, 706 (1st Dept. 1943); Note, Elimination of Competition Between Merging Corporations, 96 U. of Pa. L. Rev. 591, 593 (1948). Note the comparable problems in the law of unfair competition. E.g., G. P. Kent & Sons, Ltd. v. P. Lorillard Co., 114 F. Supp. 621 (S.D.N.Y. 1953); Callmann, The Law of Unfair Competition and Trade-Marks §5.2(b) (1945). Comparable problems have arisen in the interpretation of commodity definitions in tariff schedules. Many cases are collected in the annotations to §1 of the Tariff Act of 1930, 46 Stat. 590, 19 U.S.C.A. §1001. Other cases have arisen under §201 of that statute (19 U.S.C.A. §1201).

Among the cases which have refused to draw the distinction suggested in the text are United States v. Bausch & Lomb Co., 45 F. Supp. 387, 391 (S.D.N.Y. 1942), aff'd, 321 U.S. 707 (1944); Russellville Canning Co. v. American Can Co., 87 F. Supp. 484, 499 (W.D. Ark. 1949), rev'd, 191 F.2d 38 (6th Cir. 1951); Fargo Glass & Paint Co. v. Globe American Co., 201 F.2d 534 (7th Cir. 1953), cert. denied, 345 U.S. 942 (1953); Philadelphia Record Co. v. Curtis-Martin Newspapers, Inc., 305 Pa. 372, 157 Atl. 796, 797 (1931); United States v. E. I. Du Pont de Nemours & Co., 118 F. Supp. 41 (D. Del. 1953), aff'd, 351 U.S. 377 (1956); O'Halloran v. American Sea Green Slate Co., 207 Fed. 187, 188, 193-194 (N.D.N.Y. 1913); Signode Steel Strapping Co. v. FTC, 132 F.2d 48 (4th Cir. 1942); Timken Roller Bearing v. United States, 341 U.S. 593 (1951), aff'g, 83 F. Supp. 284, 289, 307 (N.D. Ohio, 1949).

[12] United States v. Paramount Pictures, Inc., 85 F. Supp. 881, 894 (S.D.N.Y. 1949), aff'd per curiam, 339 U.S. 974 (1950). At an earlier stage in the same proceedings the Supreme Court had distinguished "first-run" theaters from all others and even divided that category into ownership of "first-run" theaters in the ninety-two largest cities of the United States. 334 U.S. 131, 172-173 (1948). Accord: William Goldman Theatres, Inc. v. Loew's, Inc., 150 F.2d 738, 744 (3d Cir. 1945). See Rostow, Monopoly Under the Sherman Act, 43 Ill. L. Rev. 745, 768 (1949). The much litigated issue of "clearance" in the motion picture industry is really another aspect of defining the commodity. "Clearance" is a device whereby "fresh" films are made available at higher rentals because the public is willing to pay more for fresh than stale films. Compare Windsor Theatre Co. v. Walbrook Amusement Co., 94 F. Supp. 388, 390 (D. Md. 1915), aff'd, 189 F.2d 797 (4th Cir. 1951).

[13] International Shoe Co. v. FTC, 280 U.S. 291, 296 (1930).

The decisions show a particularly high degree of confusion when the products involved are related. Note, for example, the conflicting views with respect to the definition of the relevant commodity presented by the following three cases all involving the same defendant: United States v. Winslow, 227 U.S. 202, 217 (1913); United Shoe Machinery Co. v. La Chapelle, 212 Mass. 467, 99 N.E. 289, 291-292 (1912); United States v. United Shoe Machinery Corp., 110 F. Supp. 295, 302, 305 (D. Mass. 1952), aff'd per curiam, 347 U.S. 521 (1954). The methods employed by the court in the recent decision were the subject of adverse criticism in Keyes, The Shoe Machinery Case and the Problem of the Good Trust, 68 Q.J. Econ. 287, 292-293 (1954). They are defended in Kaysen, Market Definition in Anti-Trust Law Proceedings, Current Business Studies No. 18, pp. 18, 20 (Society of Business Advisory Professions, 1954), partly on the ground that the defendant offered no other delineation of the market. Compare State v. Central of Georgia Railway, 109 Ga. 716, 35 S.E. 37, 41-42 (1900).

as distinctive of separate commodities.[14]   In the recent *Tobacco*
litigation, for example, the Supreme Court computed the defendants' control of the market for cigarettes by excluding the
ten-cent grade from the relevant commodity.[15]   In some instances,
courts have made the definition turn upon the fact that different
uses or applications were to be made of products otherwise identical.[16]

The courts have sometimes said that the "substitute" product

[14] United States v. Corn Products Refining Co., 234 Fed. 964, 1003 (S.D.N.Y. 1916);
Cummings v. Union Bluestone Co., 164 N.Y. 401, 58 N.E. 525 (1900); Eastman Kodak
Co. v. FTC, 158 F.2d 592, 594 (2d Cir. 1946), *cert. denied,* 330 U.S. 828 (1947); United
States v. International Boxing Club, 150 F. Supp. 397, 407, 420 (S.D.N.Y. 1957).   But
compare Bigelow v. Calumet & Hecla Mining Co., 167 Fed. 704, 716 et seq., 719
(C.C.W.D. Mich. 1908); Vanadium-Alloys Steel Co., 18 F.T.C. 194, 201 (1934).   Note
the experience under §2 of the Clayton Act.   Austin, Price Discrimination and
Related Problems under the Robinson-Patman Act 39 (A.L.I. 1950).

[15] American Tobacco Co. v. United States, 328 U.S. 781, 796 (1946).   Note, however, that the Court found (at 803) that the defendants had bought up cheaper
grades of leaf tobacco in order to injure makers of ten-cent brands.   The latter
finding would appear to indicate the existence of competition between the two
quality grades and therefore to be inconsistent with the definition of the commodity adopted by the Court.   The Attorney General of Wisconsin, in 43 Ops.
Wis. Atty. Gen. 27, CCH Trade Reg. Serv. ¶67,830 (1954), found different grades
of bread to be different commodities for purposes of a statute prohibiting pricing
below cost.   As in the cigarette situation, a difference in quality was determined by
the existence of a price differential.

In United States v. General Electric Co., 82 F. Supp. 753, 803, 817 (D.N.J. 1939),
the court appears to have taken the component parts of finished products as
separate commodities for antitrust purposes.   In Fargo Glass & Paint Co. v. Globe
American Co., 201 F.2d 534, 537 (7th Cir. 1953), *cert. denied,* 345 U.S. 942 (1953),
the court disregarded the fact that the household gas ranges there considered were
equipped with an automatic device for shutting off the oven and with an automatic clock control.   It considered the ranges merely another type of gas stove.   To
find the relevant commodity, however, it excluded other types of household ranges
(electric, kerosene) as well as stoves made for restaurant and other purposes.   In
Package Closure Corp. v. Sealright Co., 141 F.2d 972, 979 (2d Cir. 1944), the
court held that milk bottle hoods alone were not the same commodity as milk
bottle caps and hoods in combination within the meaning of §2 of the Clayton Act.

[16] United States v. American Can Co., 230 Fed. 859, 899-900, 234 Fed. 1019 (D.
Md. 1916), *appeal dismissed,* 256 U.S. 703 (1921); Re Pressed Steel Car Corp., 16
F. Supp. 329, 338-339 (W.D. Pa. 1936).   Compare United States v. Yellow Cab Co.,
80 F. Supp. 936 (N.D. Ill. 1948), *aff'd,* 338 U.S. 338 (1949); United States v. E. I.
Du Pont de Nemours & Co., 188 Fed. 127, 129 (C.C.D. Del. 1911).   It is, of
course, true that almost all commodities, especially those near the "raw material"
category, have multiple uses.   If, however, the commodity in question can be
interchanged for several uses without substantial expense, it is difficult to understand upon what rational basis the fact of different uses or applications can be
made controlling.   A surprising standard was adopted in United States v. E. I. Du
Pont de Nemours & Co., 353 U.S. 586, 593 et seq. (1957).   That case, founded on §7
of the Clayton Act, involved sales of paints and fabrics by Du Pont to General
Motors.   The relevant commodity was not taken as all the finishes and fabrics
(suitable for automotive use) sold by Du Pont; neither was it the amount of those
products sold to the automobile industry as a whole.   Instead, only sales to General
Motors were considered, enabling the Court to find that GM bought a large proportion from Du Pont!

must not sell for a substantially greater price or it cannot be included in the same commodity with the product manufactured by the defendant. Thus, in the *Corn Products* case Judge Hand refused to consider starch made by a method not employed by the defendant as constituting a part of the relevant commodity;[17] and in another case "ground" fish were distinguished from salmon, mackerel and halibut purely on a basis of price.[18] Whether to include imports has sometimes proven bothersome,[19] and the courts occasionally also have had to cope with the problem of time. In one case, for example, a defendant accused of cornering the United States corn crop was tested by a definition of the commodity which involved only some seven million-odd bushels then in warehouses or en route to such supply points. The evidence showed, however, that there were more than two billion bushels of corn in the United States, the additional amount being on farms, with much of it destined to stay there as hog feed. Obviously, high prices would have fetched a good part of that corn into the "visible, commercially available" supply within a matter of days, but the court chose the narrower definition of the commodity.[20] Perhaps astounded and bewildered by the various tests enumerated above, some observers have suggested that defendants should be permitted to classify products within commodity categories themselves; in other words, that the defendant's own conduct constitutes the most reliable gauge for the definition of a commodity.[21]

Recently the United States Supreme Court faced the problem

[17] United States v. Corn Products Refining Co., 234 Fed. 964, 975 (S.D.N.Y. 1917).

[18] United States v. New England Fish Exchange, 258 Fed. 732, 741 (D. Mass. 1919), 292 Fed. 511 (D. Mass. 1923). *Accord:* Gamco, Inc. v. Providence Fruit & Produce Building, Inc., 194 F.2d 484, 487 (1st Cir. 1952), *cert. denied,* 344 U.S. at 817 (1952); Times-Picayune Publishing Co. v. United States, 345 U.S. 594, 612n (1953); Atty. Gen. Nat. Com. Rep. 48, (3); Kaysen, Market Definition in Anti-Trust Law Proceedings, Current Business Studies No. 18, p. 18 (Society of Business Advisory Professions, 1954). In the Gamco case the price differential was merely assumed and not proven. It is believed, however, that the case really rests upon factors of indivisibility.

[19] United States v. Aluminum Co. of America, 148 F.2d 416, 426 (2d Cir. 1945). Compare Samuel v. Oliver, 130 Ill. 73, 22 N.E. 499 (1889).

[20] Peto v. Howell, 101 F.2d 353, 361 (7th Cir. 1939). Compare Samuel v. Oliver, 130 Ill. 73, 22 N.E. 499 (1889). Note also the suggestion that the innovator in a business field may be penalized because no one has yet produced as good an oil drilling bit. Hughes Tool Co. v. Ford, 114 F. Supp. 525 (E.D. Okla. 1953), *rev'd,* 215 F. 2d 924 (10th Cir. 1954), *cert. denied,* 348 U.S. 927, 965 (1955). Further discussion of the factor of time will be found in §3.5 *infra.*

[21] Hughes Tool Co. v. Ford, 114 F. Supp. 525, 534 (E.D. Okla. 1953), *rev'd,* 215 F.2d 924 (10th Cir. 1954), *cert. denied,* 348 U.S. 927, 965 (1955); Atty. Gen. Nat. Com. Rep. 44, (2). Compare United States v. Besser Mfg. Co., 96 F. Supp. 304, 312 (E.D. Mich. 1951), *aff'd,* 343 U.S. 444 (1952).

of defining the commodity involved in the *Cellophane* case.[22] It held that the relevant market there consisted of all flexible wrapping materials and not merely plain and moistureproof cellophane. Expressly relying upon economic concepts, the Court discussed at length whether waxed paper, glassine, Pliofilm and other products should be included in the relevant commodity. Perhaps the most illuminating portions of the opinion are:

> As the producers of a standardized product bring about significant differentiations of quality, design, or packaging in the product that permit differences of use, competition becomes to a greater or less degree incomplete and the producer's power over price and competition greater over his article and its use, according to the differentiation he is able to create and maintain. A retail seller may have in one sense a monopoly on certain trade because of location, as an isolated country store or filling station, or because no one else makes a product of just the quality or attractiveness of his product. . . . Thus one can theorize that we have monopolistic competition in every nonstandardized commodity with each manufacturer having power over the price and production of his own product. However, this power that, let us say, automobile or soft-drink manufacturers have over their trade-marked products is not the power that makes an illegal monopoly. Illegal power must be appraised in terms of the competitive market for the product.
>
> Determination of the competitive market for commodities depends on how different from one another are the offered commodities in character or use, how far buyers will go to substitute one commodity for another. For example, one can think of building materials as in commodity competition but one could hardly say that brick competed with steel or wood or cement or stone in the meaning of Sherman Act litigation; the products are too different. . . . On the other hand, there are certain differences in the formulae for soft drinks but one can hardly say that each one is an illegal monopoly.
>
> Because most products have possible substitutes, we cannot . . . give that "infinite range" to the definition of substitutes. Nor is it a proper definition of the Sherman Act to require that products be fungible to be considered in the relevant market.
>
> In considering what is the relevant market for determining the control of prices and competition, no more definite rule can be declared than that commodities reasonably interchangeable by consumers for the same purposes make up that "part of the trade or commerce," monopolization of which may be illegal.
>
> Industrial activities cannot be confined to trim categories.

---

22 United States v. E. I. Du Pont de Nemours & Co., 118 F. Supp. 41 (D. Del. 1953), *aff'd,* 351 U.S. 377 (1956).

Illegal monopolies under §2 may well exist over limited products in narrow fields where competition is eliminated. . . . In determining the market under the Sherman Act, it is the use or uses to which the commodity is put that control. The selling price between commodities with similar uses and different characteristics may vary, so that the cheaper product can drive out the more expensive. Or, the superior quality of higher priced articles may make dominant the more desirable.[23]

Finally, after many such broad statements, the Court pointed to evidence that customers had switched back and forth among various flexible packaging materials, saying:

An element for consideration as to cross-elasticity of demand between products is the responsiveness of the sales of one product to price changes of the other. If a slight decrease in the price of cellophane causes a considerable number of customers of other flexible wrappings to switch to cellophane, it would be an indication that a high cross-elasticity of demand exists between them; that the products compete in the same market.[24]

A vigorous dissenting opinion pointed to the defendant's execution of an agreement in 1923 giving it exclusive North American rights to manufacture cellophane.[25]

§3.5.   Analysis of defining the commodity.   Many of the foregoing decisions seem unrealistic — indeed, fantastic — in the face of widespread actual competition between commodities prepared from different raw materials by different methods and costing varying prices. A competent student of the rayon industry, for example, found that rayon should not be considered a separate commodity because it was part of a larger market for fibers in

[23] United States v. E. I. Du Pont de Nemours & Co., 351 U.S. 377, 392-393 (1956).
[24] Id. at 399-400.

[25] The point is, of course, that the defendant must have regarded cellophane as a unique commodity in 1923, since it obtained no similar exclusive rights with respect to other wrapping materials. Dynamic considerations apart, the foregoing point appears to be valid and might well be considered in future cases. If the conclusion of the majority was right, it seems strange that it was necessary to say so much in support of it. Nevertheless, as is indicated in the next section, the majority relied upon sound economic analysis, even if such analysis be difficult to apply.

One sentence in the opinion is worthy of particular note: "Illegal monopolies under §2 may well exist over limited products in narrow fields where competition is eliminated." Id. at 395. Does that statement mean that the commodity should be defined more narrowly when abuses are involved? Dissenting opinion at page 418 et seq. Note the suggestion that a different standard may be applied to the definition of the commodity under §7 of the Clayton Act. Bicks, Mergers and Acquisitions, 11 A.B.A., Sections of Antitrust Law, Report 20, 29-30 (1957). It is not apparent why the standard should differ under the two acts, although different end results may be reached in the light of variations in legislative purpose.

general.[1] In the *Aluminum* case, the Attorney General admitted that copper cable was "highly competitive with aluminum cable." [2] Hardwood flooring has rapidly lost markets to substitutes such as asphalt tile, vinyl tile and cement.[3] Between 1946 and 1954 straight whiskeys climbed from 12.3 to 40 per cent of the whiskey market while blends slipped from 87.7 to 60 per cent, indicating a relationship between the two.[4] Price in terms of dollars is obviously irrelevant. Customers for refrigerants are not interested in the cost per pound of carbon dioxide as opposed to water ice, but with the cost in terms of refrigeration.[5] Definitions of "industries" are similarly written on water.[6] The decisions referred to

§3.5. [1] Markham, Competition in the Rayon Industry 2 (1952); TNEC Hearings, pt. 1, at 143; Celanese, 8 Fortune No. 4, pp. 50, 54 (1933).

[2] United States v. Aluminum Co. of America, 44 F. Supp. 97, 222 (S.D.N.Y. 1941), rev'd, 148 F.2d 416 (2d Cir. 1945); Celler Committee I, pt. 2B, at 812-813, 815-816, 818-819; Robertson, On the Changing Apparatus of Competition, 44 Proceedings Am. Econ. Assn. 51, 54 (1954); Nolle, Wire Mills, 35 Barron's No. 21, p. 13 (1955).

[3] Hammer, Hardwood Headache, 34 id., No. 42, p. 11 (1954). Compare Chute, Marketing Burned-Clay Products 285 (1939).

[4] Corrado, Straights and Blends, 35 Barron's No. 8, p. 11 (1955). Other examples are found in Burlington Mills, 40 Fortune No. 1, pp. 82, 109 (1949); TNEC Hearings, pt. 20, at 10,867; Management by Morgan, 9 Fortune No. 3, pp. 82, 141 (1934); Du Pont II: The Corporation, 10 id., No. 6, pp. 80, 167 (1934). But compare Just About All About Cellophane, 5 id. No. 2, pp. 74, 101-102 (1932); Sterling Drug, Inc., Ann. Rep. 1952, 5 (New York City, 1953): "In most of our foreign markets, sales were adversely affected by the extraordinary increase in the general cost of living."

[5] United States v. E. I. Du Pont de Nemours & Co., 118 F. Supp. 41 (D. Del. 1953), aff'd, 351 U.S. 377, 400-401 (1956); Dry Ice, 6 Fortune No. 1, pp. 74, 80 (1932); Hobby, Bottles or Cans, 34 Barron's No. 42, p. 7 (1954).

[6] An authoritative review of the problem of defining "an industry" by Professor Willard Thorp will be found in the TNEC Hearings, pt. 1, at 118-119. As Professor Thorp pointed out, tremendous differences in numbers can be achieved by the system of classification used. Thus a census group comprising stone, clay and glass products included 4500 companies. If, however, only manufacturers of glass blocks were listed, the number would be reduced to two. Another illustration is found in the rubber industry. It is commonly said that there are four large producers but the output of the companies is uneven. Goodyear specializes in transportation. Others make tires but Goodrich produces some 32,000 items including footwear, golf balls, fountain pen sacs, life belts, dog collars, press rolls and the like, and tires constitute only 55 per cent of its output. United States Rubber also makes about 30,000 rubber items and "several dozen" non-rubber products. Four Giants, 2 Fortune No. 3, pp. 85, 100 (1930); U.S. Rubber's Two-Way Stretch, Business Week No. 1006, pp. 83, 84 (1948). Diversification thus makes "industry" boundaries overlapping and meaningless. Processors of dairy products have diversified into other grocery lines; steel producers have become important manufacturers of chemicals. The Borden Co., Ann. Rep. 1952, 19 (New York City, 1953); U.S. Steel: Into Chemicals?, Business Week No. 971, p. 30 (1948). Compare Celler Committee I, pt. 1, at 575. Corporations not only diversify their products but may be able to switch existing productive capacity from one field to another in the short run. American Viscose Corp., Ann. Rep. 1952, 13 (Philadelphia, 1953) (company changed from making rayon for women's clothes into rayon for tire yarn). Conklin and Goldstein, Census Principles of Industry and Product Classification, in Business Concentration and Price Policy 15 (Stigler ed. 1955). On the other hand, it is

with respect to defining the relevant market in cases involving newspaper publishers show how arbitrary the courts have been. If the publisher of the Lorain Journal [7] felt the competition of the operator of a radio station, it is amazing that the publisher of the Times-Picayune[8] was judged by a standard which excluded radio, television, magazine, billboard and similar advertising media.

Economic theory is equally devastating in its analysis of the legal principles applied in most of the definitions of commodity cases referred to above.[9] The raw materials used and methods of manufacture utilized in the making of a product bear no logical relationship to the question of substitutability.[10] A buyer is in-

---

undoubtedly true that businessmen frequently speak of themselves as belonging to an industry. E.g., Container Corporation of America, Ann. Rep. 1953, 12 (Chicago, 1954).

[7] Lorain Journal Co. v. United States, 342 U.S. 143 (1951).

[8] Times-Picayune Publishing Co. v. United States, 345 U.S. 594 (1953); United States v. E. I. Du Pont de Nemours & Co., 118 F. Supp. 41 (D. Del. 1953), aff'd, 351 U.S. 377, 393 (1956) (illustrations of relevant commodity seem arbitrary; in fact, brick and stone may be close substitutes in building).

[9] Thorp and Crowder, The Structure of Industry ix (TNEC Monograph No. 27, 1941). Compare Robinson, The Economics of Imperfect Competition 4 et seq. (1933); McLean and Haigh, How Business Corporations Grow, 32 Harv. Bus. Rev. No. 6, pp. 81 et seq. (1954); Enke, Resource Malocation Within Firms, 63 Q.J. Econ. 572, 576 (1949); Robinson, The Industry and the Market, Econ. J. 66, 360-361 (1956). In the theory of monopolistic competition, oligopolistic producers are said to "differentiate" their products so as to obtain a degree of monopoly power over the markets thus separated. Indeed, some economists have gone so far as to characterize the motion picture industry as one in which "extreme product differentiation" is found. Dirlam and Kahn, Fair Competition 163 (1954). Motion pictures are an extreme example because, of course, few patrons desire to see the same film an infinite number of times. A better example might be found in the sale of tooth paste, wherein one manufacturer will claim that he has added a unique element, such as chlorophyl, to his formula. Such differentiation invites the intriguing possibility of defining the commodity in terms of the differentiated product. Thus each defendant's own sales (brands) would constitute the relevant commodity for purposes of defining monopoly and each defendant would ipso facto become a monopolist in violation of §2 of the Sherman Act. While the element of retribution involved in such a program might have some attraction for those who resent the extravagant claims of hucksters, it would fly in the face of economic reality. Compare United States v. E. I. Du Pont de Nemours & Co., 118 F. Supp. 41 (D. Del. 1953), aff'd, 351 U.S. 377, 392-393 (1956). Furthermore, to define the relevant commodity in terms of the defendant's own production opens the door to collision with indivisibility. See §3.13 infra. The fact that the defendant produces a specific number of commodities and no others indicates the possibility that such a degree of diversification involves economies of scale.

[10] In June, 1953, a seminar on the antitrust laws was conducted at the University of Chicago Law School. During that meeting a respected economist offered as a definition of an industry (for antitrust purposes) the slaughter of hogs (eliminating other animals usually associated with the meat-packing business). The trouble with this definition is that products made from pigs (gloves, bacon, football covers and the like) are sold in diverse markets in which the degree of competition may vary widely without relation to the number of slaughterers of hogs. Gloves, for example, can be made of skins other than the skin of the pig, and even of cloth woven from

terested in what the product will do for him; he does not care —
except in terms of performance — whether his sound recorder
utilizes a wire or a tape, whether his hosiery be made of silk or
nylon.   Still less relevant is the notion that price in terms of
dollars alone controls substitutability.   One who desires a needle
for his phonograph may be offered a sapphire product at $5 or a
diamond needle at $15.   If the diamond wears four times as long,
the fact that the price ratio is three to one should not prevent the
products from being defined as the same commodity for purposes
of determining the existence of monopoly.   Much competition
takes place at varying or uniform prices and is reflected in quality,
service and other factors.[11]   Again, it is erroneous to apply pure
engineering principles to determine whether one product can

a variety of fibers.   Judge Learned Hand's refusal to consider scrap aluminum in
the definition of the commodity in the aluminum litigation met with the disapproval of Dean Mason, who pointed out that for many uses virgin and scrap
aluminum were interchangeable.   Mason, The Current Status of the Monopoly
Problem in the United States, 62 Harv. L. Rev. 1265, 1273-1274 (1949).

[11] Compare Atty. Gen. Nat. Com. Rep. 48, (3); Stigler, The Theory of Price 55
(rev. ed. 1952); Robertson, On the Changing Apparatus of Competition, 44 Proceedings Am. Econ. Assn. 51 et seq. (1954).   Despite adherence to quoted prices
for long periods of time, there are numerous devices for varying actual prices, such
as granting discounts, credit facilities, personal service, improvements in quality,
increased selling effort and the like. Rothschild, Price Theory and Oligopoly, 57
Econ. J. 299, 312 (1947); Stackelberg, The Theory of the Market Economy 206
(Peacock trans. 1952); Nelson and Keim, Price Behavior and Business Policy, c. 3
(TNEC Monograph No. 1, 1940); Gibb, The Whitesmiths of Taunton 174 (1943);
Gulf Oil Corp., Ann. Rep. 1953, 23 (Pittsburgh, 1954); TNEC Hearings, pt. 19, at
10,532 et seq.; Container Corporation of America, Ann. Rep. 1953, 3 (Chicago,
1954).   Sales of gasoline to filling station operators are often made on a basis which
includes improvement of the station through the installation of driveways, paint-
ing of the structure, installation of lights, pumps and the like.   Cassady, Price
Making and Price Behavior in the Petroleum Industry 226 (Petroleum Monograph
Series No. 1, 1954).   An interesting example is found in the sale of rayon: when
demand slackened, producers did not shave the public prices but instead misbranded the yarn and sold it at the lower price pertaining to the lesser quality
thus indicated. Markham, Competition in the Rayon Industry 76 (1952).   Note,
too, the phenomenon of "price-lining" whereby a soft drink is always sold for five
cents and a woman's dress is always available at $2.98 despite changes in quality
from time to time.   Machlup, The Economics of Sellers' Competition 466-467
(1952); Brems, Product Equilibrium Under Monopolistic Competition 92 (1951);
Nelson and Keim, Price Behavior and Business Policy 103 (TNEC Monograph
No. 1, 1940); Chamberlin, The Product as an Economic Variable, 67 Q.J. Econ. 1,
6 (1953).   Note also the fear that quality will deteriorate when prices are fixed
either by monopolistic or governmental intervention.   Standard Oil Co. of New
Jersey v. United States, 221 U.S. 1, 52 (1911); Dickerson, The "Freeze" Method of
Establishing Ceiling Prices, in Franck and Quint, eds., Problems in Price Control:
Pricing Techniques 31, 42 (OPA, 1947).

One reading the opinion in the Investment Banking case senses that price competition may well be impossible in that field because the issuer of securities relies
so heavily upon the standing and prestige of the investment banker.   United States
v. Morgan, 118 F. Supp. 621, 793 (S.D.N.Y. 1953).

actually be substituted for another. An engineer might determine that an aluminum frying pan was substitutable for one made of stainless steel. Such a test would be considerably better than one based purely upon a distinction between the raw materials utilized in the manufacture of the products.[12] It would, however, ignore the fact that consumers often make decisions upon grounds which others regard as irrational. Thus to apply pure engineering principles to the problem constitutes a rejection of the basic doctrine of consumer sovereignty.[13]

To cope with the problem of defining commodities, economists have developed the concept of cross-elasticity of demand. This concept is simply a formalized method of taking account of substitutability as it operates under conditions of consumer sovereignty. It compares the quantities of the various products concerned, which consumers are willing to take, at different prices.[14] This analysis has widespread support among economists[15] but admittedly is difficult (if not impossible) to apply to specific situations. Measurement of demand alone is difficult enough; that of cross-elasticity is considerably greater. Thus a leading economist recently wrote: "There is little chance of obtaining the informa-

[12] Note, The Market: A Concept in Anti-Trust, 54 Colum. L. Rev. 580, 586 et seq. (1954).

[13] Elliott, Beauty Contest, 35 Barron's No. 35, p. 3 (1955). It is true that the recent "leveling-up" in income in the United States has resulted in a greater uniformity of taste than theretofore prevailed. Burck and Parker, The Changing American Market, 48 Fortune No. 1, pp. 98, 102 (1953). It is also true that consumer "sovereignty" may merely reflect ignorance and other imperfections. Chamberlin, The Product as an Economic Variable, 67 Q.J. Econ. 1, 4 (1953). On the other hand, the authoritarian effort of the OPA to compel the allocation of yarn into cheap, heavy underwear which consumers were supposed to "need" instead of into better grades of that commodity ended in dismal disaster. Caplan, Price Policy and Production Control; in Textiles and Apparel: OPA and WPB, in Caplan, ed., Problems in Price Control: Changing Production Patterns 7, 37 (OPA, 1947). If, however, buyers are industrial processors who have skilled laboratories to test materials and consequently are quality- and cost-conscious, the engineering tests may be considerably more relevant. United States v. E. I. Du Pont de Nemours & Co., 118 F. Supp. 41, (D. Del. 1953), aff'd, 351 U.S. 377 (1956). The trial court's definition of the commodity involved in the last-cited case is the subject of adverse criticism in Stocking and Mueller, The Cellophane Case and the New Competition, 45 Am. Econ. Rev. 29 (1955). It is not, however, clear upon what criteria and what evidence the authors would have determined the relevant commodity in that suit.

[14] Robinson, The Impossibility of Competition, in Chamberlin, ed., Monopoly and Competition and Their Regulation 245 (International Economic Assn. 1954).

[15] It must be admitted, however, that the concept of cross-elasticity is not crystal clear and that disputes exist among economists as to how it should be formulated. E.g., Chamberlin, Measuring the Degree of Monopoly and Competition, id. at 255, 264-265; Harrod, Economic Essays 114 (1952); Bishop, Elasticities, Cross-Elasticities and Market Relationships, 42 Am. Econ. Rev. 779, 782 (1952); Bishop, Reply, 43 id. 916 (1953); Hieser, Elasticities, Cross-Elasticities and Market Relationships, 45 id. 373 (1955); Papandreou and Wheeler, Competition and Its Regulation 21 (1954).

tion needed for actual estimates of . . . elasticities. The cross-elasticities are particularly hopeless unknowns." [16]

Furthermore, the definition of the commodity must take account of "dynamic" influences in our economy. It must reflect, for instance, that "creative destruction" involved when some wholly new method or product destroys the sales of an established commodity.[17] Take, for example, the case of an electric household iron. In static analysis, a question might arise as to whether a small household mangle should be included in the same commodity because it performs roughly the same service for the housewife. It is scarcely conceivable, however, that static analysis would take account of the introduction of new fibers which can be woven into fabrics needing no ironing at all. Since demand relates to an instant of time, some means must be found to recognize time-consuming factors of growth and innovation.[18]

[16] Machlup, The Political Economy of Monopoly 9 (1952); Hood, Empirical Studies of Demand, 21 Can. J. Econ. & Pol. Sci. 309-327 (1955); Hawkins, Methods of Estimating Demand, 21 J. Marketing 428 (1957).

[17] Schumpeter, Capitalism, Socialism and Democracy 85 (3d ed. 1950); Roos, Dynamic Economics (The Principia Press, Inc. 1934). Other authorities on the subject are collected in Appendix B infra. Compare United States v. Corn Products Refining Co., 234 Fed. 964, 975 (S.D.N.Y. 1916).

[18] In Peto v. Howell, 101 F.2d 353, 361 (7th Cir. 1939), the factor of time appears to have been wholly disregarded. In that case, the commodity was defined in terms which excluded large quantities of corn which apparently could have been shipped into the relevant geographic market within a matter of days or possibly hours. Accord: Samuel v. Oliver, 130 Ill. 73, 22 N.E. 499 (1889).
In dynamic theory great emphasis is placed upon the encouragement of innovation. Commodities, therefore, should be defined in the light of long-term considerations and not merely as of some instant of time. On the other hand, it may be impossible to distinguish innovation from mere product differentiation. E.g., Celanese, 8 Fortune No. 4, pp. 50, 51 (1933). Differentiation, of course, is that method of avoiding the rigors of pure competition stressed in the theory of monopolistic competition. It is generally considered to lead to higher prices and to a poorer allocation of resources. Chamberlin, The Theory of Monopolistic Competition, c. 5 (1933); Bishop, Elasticities, Cross-Elasticities and Market Relationships, 42 Am. Econ. Rev. 779, 780 (1952). An example may exist in the field of marketing sugar. American Sugar Refining, 7 Fortune No. 2, pp. 59, 65 (1933). But compare Nicols, The Development of Monopolistic Competition and the Monopoly Problem, 31 Rev. Econ. & Stat. 118, 120-121 (1949); Clark, Competition: Static Models and Dynamic Aspects, 45 Proceedings Am. Econ. Assn. 450, 452-453 (1955). On the other hand, to denounce all differentiation is to deny consumer sovereignty because, in some degree at least, buyers prefer a variety of products. Human beings have different tastes, and product heterogeneity is the necessary corollary to sovereignty. Chamberlin, Product Heterogeneity and Public Policy, 40 id. at 85, 86 (1950); Machlup, The Political Economy of Monopoly 54 (1952); Wallace, Monopolistic Competition and Public Policy, in Hoover and Dean, eds., Readings in the Social Control of Industry 263, 269 (American Economic Assn. 1942). Undoubtedly much differentiation reflects consumer ignorance and other market imperfections. Consult Appendix A infra. Consumer reliance upon trade-marks may, however, constitute the only feasible means of distinguishing quality goods in some fields. E.g., International Silver, 7 Fortune No. 4, pp. 70, 74, 90 (1933). Such situations support the views of trade-mark enthusiasts such as Rogers, The Lanham Act and

In the face of such considerations there is no disguising the fact that the legal tests applied in most of the reported decisions are basically irrational, arbitrary and hopelessly confused. It is also clear that economic theory offers little in the way of a scientific method upon which the law could be reconstructed. In such circumstances, the difficulties involved in defining commodities have been granted widespread recognition.[19] It is often said that "industry" categories are meaningless. Thus Professor Chamberlin stated:

---

the Social Function of Trade-Marks, 14 Law & Contemp. Prob. 173, 176, 180 (1949). But compare Clark, Social Control of Business 158 (1926); Chamberlin, The Theory of Monopolistic Competition, App. E (1933). Query whether such considerations underlay the decision in Fashion Originators' Guild of America v. FTC, 312 U.S. 457, 467 (1941). Compare Adam Smith on 7th Avenue, 39 Fortune No. 1, pp. 73, 75, 78 (1949).

Innovation is closely connected with that competition in quality which is now recognized widely as an acceptable substitute for the price competition emphasized in neoclassic theory. E.g., Brems, Product Equilibrium under Monopolistic Competition 243 (1951).

Standardization of commodities would, of course, increase that homogeneity which is essential to "pure" competition and make far easier the task of defining the relevant commodity in antitrust proceedings. It is no mere accident, however, that standardization has often been employed as a device in aid of price control, public and private. Caplan, Price Policy and Production Controls in Textiles and Apparel: OPA and WPB, in Caplan, ed., Problems in Price Controls: Changing Production Patterns 7, 32 (OPA, 1947); Russell, Processed Foods Rationing, in Studies in Food Rationing 71, 73 (Russell and Fantin ed. 1947); Singer, The German War Economy, 52 Econ. J. 377, 380 (1942); Marshall, Cottonseed — Joint Products and Pyramidal Control, in Price and Price Policies 201, 202 (Hamilton ed. 1938); Hale, Agreements Among Competitors, 33 Minn. L. Rev. 331, 362 et seq. (1949). Compare Pacific States Box & Basket Co. v. White, 296 U.S. 176, 181, 183 (1935). Note also the discussion of standardization in Appendix A infra.

Even in neoclassic theory, however, elimination of all consumer ignorance and other causes of product heterogeneity and differentiation might not be considered an unmixed blessing. Adelman, Effective Competition and the Anti-Trust Laws, 61 Harv. L. Rev. 1289, 1299-1300 (1948); Brems, Product Equilibrium under Monopolistic Competition 244-245 (1951); compare Triffin, Monopolistic Competition and General Equilibrium Theory 140 (1940).

[19] Machlup, The Political Economy of Monopoly 7 (1952); Wright, Toward Coherent Anti-Trust, 35 Va. L. Rev. 665, 690 (1949); Keyes, The Shoe Machinery Case and the Problem of the Good Trust, 68 Q.J. Econ. 287, 294 (1954). But compare Kaysen, Market Definition in Anti-Trust Law Proceedings, Current Business Studies No. 18, pp. 18, 19 (Society of Business Advisory Professions, 1954); Rostow, Monopoly Under the Sherman Act, 43 Ill. L. Rev. 745, 777 (1949); Stocking and Mueller, The Cellophane Case and the New Competition, 45 Am. Econ. Rev. 29, 55 et seq. (1955). Despite the fact that it appears to be impossible to define commodities under the structure theory of monopoly, the most respected economists and courts continue to speak as if such definition were possible and meaningful. E.g., Machlup, The Political Economy of Monopoly 107n (1952); United States v. Paramount Pictures, Inc., 85 F. Supp. 881, 894 (S.D.N.Y. 1949), aff'd per curiam, 339 U.S. 974 (1950). But compare Mason, The Current Status of the Monopoly Problem in the United States, 62 Harv. L. Rev. 1265, 1274 (1949); United States v. Aluminum Co. of America, 148 F.2d 416, 425-426 (2d Cir. 1945); United States v. E. I. Du Pont de Nemours & Co., 118 F. Supp. 41 (D. Del. 1953), aff'd, 351 U.S. 377 (1956); Celler Committee I, pt. 1, at 352, 355.

"Industry" or "commodity" boundaries are a snare and a delusion — in the highest degree arbitrarily drawn, and, wherever drawn, establishing at once wholly false implications both as to competition of substitutes within their limits . . . and as to the possibility of ruling on the presence or absence of oligopolistic forces by the simple device of counting the number of producers included. . . .[20]

Bewildered by such statements from authoritative economists, lawyers can do little more than hope for the possibility that informed judgment in particular cases may bear some earmarks of rationality. Negatively, of course, the courts can avoid reliance upon the fallacious distinctions which have sometimes been employed in monopoly litigation. On the constructive side, perhaps all they can do is to take account of the factors bearing upon a rational definition of the commodity and make the best guess they can upon the basis of the evidence before them.[21] On this subject, the Attorney General's Committee wrote:

[20] Chamberlin, Product Heterogeneity and Public Policy, 40 Proceedings Am. Econ. Assn. 85, 86-87 (1950). *Accord:* Machlup, The Political Economy of Monopoly 486 (1952); Triffin, Monopolistic Competition and General Equilibrium Theory 79, 86, 88 (1940); Edwards, Maintaining Competition: Requisites of a Governmental Policy 124-125 (1949); Chamberlin, The Product as an Economic Variable, 67 Q.J. Econ. 1, 8-9 (1953); Papandreou, Market Structure and Monopoly Power, 39 Am. Econ. Rev. 887, 896 (1949). It has been pointed out that either substitutability or complementarity may form the basis for the grouping of an industry. Thus the "construction industry" might include both bricks and bathtubs on the latter basis. Machlup, The Economics of Sellers' Competition 215 (1952). Compare Robinson, Imperfect Competition Re-visited, 63 Econ. J. 579, 580 (1953). But compare id. at 580; Triffin, Monopolistic Competition and General Equilibrium Theory 88 (1940); Machlup, The Economics of Sellers' Competition 214-215 (1952). It has been argued that product differences, like price differences, are eliminated by competition itself (i.e., their success in attracting buyers). Nicols, The Development of Monopolistic Competition and the Monopoly Problem, 31 Rev. Econ. & Stat. 118, 123 (1949); but compare Chamberlin, Some Final Comments, id. at 123, 124 et seq. Note the interesting comment upon interindustry competition in Robertson, On the Changing Apparatus of Competition, 44 Proceedings Am. Econ. Assn. 51, 58 (1954).

[21] Evidence of actual switching of customers from one product to another may be helpful. United States v. E. I. Du Pont de Nemours & Co., 118 F. Supp. 41 (D. Del. 1953), *aff'd,* 351 U.S. 377 (1956); Business Concentration and Price Policy 4, 5 (Stigler ed. 1955). Leaving the matter to administrative discretion would not appear to be helpful: it merely shifts the burden of making the decision to other shoulders. But compare Great Britain, Monopolies and Restrictive Practices (Inquiry and Control) Act, 1948, 11 & 12 Geo. VI, c. 66, ss. 3(3), 20(3); Celler Committee I, pt. 1, at 522. Another possibility is that of self-classification. Evidence of membership in trade associations and the like may indicate how businessmen have grouped themselves with regard to their competitors. Thus, in Machlup, The Economics of Sellers' Competition (1952) it was said at page 217: "The very fact that a number of firms, operators or practitioners act as groups, bringing political pressures to obtain protection against newcomers, indicates that they recognize a common boundary line." United States v. E. I. Du Pont de Nemours & Co., 118 F. Supp. 41 (D. Del. 1953), *aff'd,* 351 U.S. 377, 418 et seq. (1956) (note argument re agreement whereby defendant obtained exclusive North American rights to cello-

To ascertain whether a firm or group of firms acting in concert has monopoly power, "the market" should include all firms whose production has so immediate and substantial an effect on the prices and production of the firms in question that the actions of the one group cannot be explained without direct and constant reference to the other. . . . Where the products of different industries compete directly as alternatives for the same use, the market for that class of products should include the rival goods supplied by different industries. One should combine into one market two or more products . . . if an appreciable fall in the price of one product . . . will promptly lead to a relatively large diversion of purchasers from the other product . . .[22]

Little exception can be taken to the foregoing statement except to inquire whether it is meaningful and useful.[23]

§3.6. **Defining the geographic market.** As we have seen, the structure theory requires a definition of the commodity which is the subject of monopoly. It also demands a definition of the geographic area affected. The necessity of delimiting the territory within which the alleged monopoly exists has been recognized again and again in the decisions.[1] Indeed, it is implicit in British cases of the late eighteenth century.[2] One conspicuous exception in which a modern court said and held that there was no need to define the geographic area in holding a defendant

---

phane. Suggestion is that parties thus admitted that cellophane was a commodity for which there were no revelant "substitutes," for otherwise agreement would have been ineffective. Superficially attractive, this argument overlooks dynamic aspects of situation). A good deal may also depend upon whether the court believes that the antitrust laws are designed to afford relief in the short run or only in the long term. Eventually, it may be possible to use atomic energy to propel automobiles. In the short and intermediate period, however, that substitute for gasoline will probably not be available.

[22] Atty. Gen. Nat. Com. Rep. 322, a. See also id. at 48, (3). Note that the problem of defining the commodity has a converse relationship under §7 of the Clayton Act. If a narrow definition is taken for purposes of §2 of the Sherman Act, then mergers otherwise illegal might be lawful under §7 of the Clayton Act and vice versa. The problem of defining the commodity is also directly related to the problem of diversification discussed in Chapter 6.

[23] Compare Fashion Originators' Guild v. FTC, 312 U.S. 457 (1941), in which private efforts to curb style piracy were thwarted. To the extent that the pirates made the garments more alike they were promoting standardization. Hence the decision may in some small measure tend to promote the homogeneity of the products.

§3.6. [1] United States v. E. I. Du Pont de Nemours & Co., 118 F. Supp. 41 (D. Del. 1953), aff'd, 351 U.S. 377, 395 (1956); United States v. Columbia Steel Co., 334 U.S. 495, 501-502, 519-520 (1948); United States v. Standard Oil Co., 47 F.2d 288, 305, 307 (E.D. Mo. 1931); Atty. Gen. Nat. Com. Rep. 44, (2). Other cases cited in this section support the statement in the text.

[2] Dana, "Monopoly" under the National Anti-Trust Act, 7 Harv. L. Rev. 338, 347 (1894).

guilty of violating Section 2 of the Sherman Act [3] cannot be supported and presumably will not be followed.[4]

Although the authorities make it abundantly plain that monopoly can only exist within some specified territory, there is little discussion in the cases as to how the boundaries of that area are to be fixed. While the courts have devoted some attention to the problem of defining the affected commodity, they often discuss the territorial issue without reference to principles. In many cases the courts appear to have simply assumed, without discussion, that the relevant territory is that in which the defendant makes sales.[5] As a result, such small areas have been selected as a single building,[6] a portion of a city[7] or the whole of a city[8] — all, however, without analysis of the reasons underlying such delimitation. Political boundary lines have also been used in cases finding the relevant territory to be state-wide[9] or nation-wide in character[10] — again, however, with practically no discussion of the reasons therefor.

[3] United States v. National City Lines, Inc., 186 F.2d 562, 566-567 (7th Cir. 1951), *cert. denied*, 341 U.S. 916 (1951). The case is the subject of adverse criticism in Johnston, Monopolize or Attempt to Monopolize, Proceedings A.B.A., Section of Antitrust Law, 72, 78 (Aug. 26, 1953). Query what standard was employed in United States v. Nationwide Trailer Rental System, CCH Trade Reg. Serv. ¶68.101 (D. Kan. 1955), *aff'd per curiam*, — U.S. — (1957).

[4] E.g., Transamerica Corp. v. Board of Governors of the Federal Reserve System, 206 F.2d 163, 169 (3d Cir. 1953), *cert. denied*, 346 U.S. 901 (1953). But compare Note, Section 7 Is Applicable to Bank Holding Companies, 67 Harv. L. Rev. 529, 531 (1954); Kilgore Committee, pt. 2, at 482 et seq.; Barnes, Mergers, in Rahl, ed., Conference on Antitrust Laws 57, 64 (Northwestern University, 1955).

[5] E.g., Gamco, Inc. v. Providence Fruit & Produce Building, Inc., 194 F.2d 484 (1st Cir. 1952), *cert. denied*, 344 U.S. 817 (1952); United States v. Columbia Steel Co., 334 U.S. 495, 501-502, 511, 519-520 (1948).

[6] Gamco, Inc. v. Providence Fruit & Produce Building, Inc., 194 F.2d 484 (1st Cir. 1952), *cert. denied*, 344 U.S. 817 (1952).

[7] William Goldman Theatres, Inc. v. Loew's, Inc., 150 F.2d 738, 744 (3d Cir. 1945); Chicago Gas Light & Coke Co. v. People's Gas Light & Coke Co., 121 Ill. 530, 13 N.E. 169 (1887); People v. American Ice Co., 135 App. Div. 180, 120 N.Y. Supp. 41, 443, 457 (1st Dept. 1909), *aff'd per curiam*, 140 App. Div. 912, 125 N.Y. Supp. 1136 (1910). Cases involving geographic delimitation of exclusive sales areas are collected in Hale, Control over Distribution, 14 Miss. L.J. 170, 181 (1942).

[8] United States v. Terminal Railroad Assn. of St. Louis, 224 U.S. 383 (1912); State ex rel. Sager v. Polar Ice Co., 259 Mo. 578, 169 S.W. 126, 128-129 (1914); Love v. Kozy Theatre Co., 193 Ky. 336, 236 S.W. 243 (1922); Burrows v. Interborough Metropolitan Co., 156 Fed. 389, 392, 396 (C.C.S.D.N.Y. 1907); More v. Bennett, 140 Ill. 69, 29 N.E. 888 (1892); Southern Electric Securities Co. v. State, 91 Miss. 195, 44 So. 785, 789 (1907); Adler, Monopolizing at Common Law and Under Section 2 of the Sherman Act, 31 Harv. L. Rev. 246, 253, 261 (1917). In United States v. Griffith, 334 U.S. 100, 106 (1948), it was said that one who operates a single theater in a town has a monopoly in a popular sense but does not violate §2 of the Sherman Act unless he has acquired or maintained his strategic position or has sought to expand it by restraints cognizable under §1.

[9] Georgia Fruit Exchange v. Turnipseed, 9 Ala. App. 123, 62 So. 542, 548 (1913).

[10] United States v. Aluminum Co. of America, 148 F.2d 416 (2d Cir. 1945); United

A few decisions reflect judicial awareness of the problem. In some instances, for example, the relevant market has been defined as that within which some particular crop, such as cotton or sugar beets, is grown, and political boundary lines have been disregarded.[11] For obvious reasons defendants have sometimes argued that a nation-wide delimitation was alone permissible.[12] Under the decisions, however, it is clear that much smaller areas may be selected.[13]

Considerable confusion exists as to whether and to what extent foreign areas may be included within the geographic market under the structure test of monopoly. In at least two cases the courts have apparently considered that the entire world constituted the relevant area.[14] Perhaps worried by jurisdictional problems, other judges have ventured less far and some have even hesitated to take account of imports into the United States.[15] Another trouble-

---

States v. General Electric Co., 82 F. Supp. 753, 817 (D.N.J. 1949). Note the internal inconsistencies in Baush Machine Tool Co. v. Aluminum Co. of America, 72 F.2d 236, 240-241 (2d Cir. 1934). Compare United States v. General Electric Co., 115 F. Supp. 835, 876 (D.N.J. 1953); Brownell v. Ketcham Wire & Manufacturing Co., 211 F.2d 121, 129 (9th Cir. 1954); Foundry Services, Inc. v. Beneflux Corp., 110 F. Supp. 857, 861 (S.D.N.Y. 1953), rev'd on other grounds, 206 F.2d 214 (2d Cir. 1953).

[11] Shawnee Compress Co. v. Anderson, 209 U.S. 423, 434 (1908); Mandeville Island Farms, Inc. v. American Crystal Sugar Co., 334 U.S. 219 (1948); Moody & Waters Co. v. Case-Moody Pie Corp., 354 Ill. 82, 84, 187 N.E. 813 (1935); United States v. E. I. Du Pont de Nemours & Co., 118 F. Supp. 41 (D. Del. 1953), aff'd, 351 U.S. 377, 392-393 (1956). Compare United States v. Lehigh Valley Railroad Co., 254 U.S. 255 (1920); Pearsall v. Great Northern Railway Co., 161 U.S. 646, 677 (1896). A rational effort to cope with the problem will be found in American Crystal Sugar Co. v. Cuban-American Co., 152 F. Supp. 387, 398 (S.D.N.Y. 1957).

[12] Indiana Farmers' Guide Co. v. Prairie Farmer Co., 293 U.S. 268, 279 (1934).

[13] Transamerica Corp. v. Board of Governors of the Federal Reserve System, 206 F.2d 163, 169 (3d Cir. 1953), cert. denied, 346 U.S. 901 (1953); Arnot v. Pittston & Elmira Coal Co., 68 N.Y. 558, 564 (1876); Chicago, Wilmington & Vermillion Coal Co. v. People, 114 Ill. App. 75, 112 (1904), aff'd, 214 Ill. 421, 73 N.E. 770 (1905). Compare United States v. Addyston Pipe Co., 85 Fed. 271, 291-292 (6th Cir. 1938), aff'd, 175 U.S. 211 (1899); United States v. United States Gypsum Co., 340 U.S. 76, 90 (1950); Northern Securities Co. v. United States, 193 U.S. 197, 327 (1904). In the last-cited case Mr. Justice Holmes, dissenting, said at pages 406-407: "A single railroad down a narrow valley or through a mountain gorge monopolizes all of the railroad transportation through that valley or gorge. Indeed every railroad monopolizes, in a popular sense, the trade of some area. Yet I suppose no one would say that the statute forbids a combination of men into a corporation to build and run a railroad between the States." A small area might properly be found the proper geographical territory in an antitrust case if it contains the center of trading in the relevant commodity. Compare Peto v. Howell, 101 F.2d 353, 362 (7th Cir. 1939).

[14] Geddes v. Anaconda Copper Mining Co., 254 U.S. 590, 594-595 (1921); Meredith v. New Jersey Zinc Co., 55 N.J. Eq. 211, 37 Atl. 539, 542 (1897), aff'd, 56 N.J. Eq. 454, 41 Atl. 1116 (1897).

[15] United States v. Aluminum Co. of America, 148 F.2d 416, 424-425, 426 (2d Cir. 1945). Compare American Tobacco Co. v. United States, 328 U.S. 781, 799 (1946). In the latter case, the Court seems to have disregarded exports, although the statement in the opinion seems not wholly consistent within itself.

some question is raised when the defendant operates in noncontiguous geographic areas. Thus, in the *Yellow Cab* case the defendant was accused of monopolizing the business of supplying taxicabs in four separate cities of the United States. The cases appear to hold that it is proper to define the geographic market in terms of such noncontiguous areas and there is some suggestion that the cumulative effect of such a combination is greater than the sum of its parts.[16]

§3.7. Defining the geographic market: Analysis. As indicated above, the cases are unquestionably sound in holding that the geographic market must be delimited before the existence of monopoly can be determined. In the nature of things, we cannot conceive of a monopolist apart from his territorial setting. This requirement flows from the very concept of monopoly in the structure theory;[1] it does not rest upon the language of Section 2 of the Sherman Act. In that section the Congress referred to "any part of the trade or commerce among the several states . . ." That language, of course, is important in determining whether federal power may be exercised over activities claimed to be local in character. It does not, however, form the basis for the fundamental requisite that the geographic market be defined.[2]

It is not difficult to understand why the courts have been so reticent in spelling out the principles upon which they have delimited the geographic areas in monopoly cases. There are two ways of looking at the problem in economic theory. The first viewpoint considers space as a part of the problem of mobility. Distance between two otherwise identical commodities is regarded as an imperfection (immobility).[3] Lack of information as to the existence of commodities in other places is a closely allied imper-

---

[16] United States v. Yellow Cab Co., 332 U.S. 218, 225 (1947); United States v. Paramount Pictures, Inc., 334 U.S. 131, 157-158 (1948), 85 F. Supp. 881, 894 (S.D.N.Y. 1949), *aff'd per curiam*, 339 U.S. 974 (1950); United States v. Great Lakes Towing Co., 208 Fed. 733, 740, 743 (N.D. Ohio, 1913). Compare United States v. Union Pacific Railroad Co., 226 U.S. 61 (1912); Southern Electric Securities Co. v. State, 91 Miss. 195, 44 So. 785, 788 (1907). In United States v. Great Lakes Towing Company, *supra*, the court said at page 743: "It is not necessary to a violation of the federal statutes that a complete monopoly of all towing on the Great Lakes be effected. . . . A monopoly in 14 ports is as offensive against the act as a monopoly in 50 ports . . ."

§3.7. [1] Sraffa, The Laws of Returns Under Competitive Conditions, 36 Econ. J. 535, 544 (1926); Machlup, The Political Economy of Monopoly 482 (1952); Kaplan, The Influence of Size of Firms on the Functioning of the Economy, 40 Proceedings Am. Econ. Assn. 74, 83 (1950); Hotelling, Stability in Competition, 39 Econ. J. 41, 44 (1929). Compare Stigler, The Theory of Price 55 (rev. ed. 1952).

[2] E.g., Mandeville Island Farms, Inc. v. American Crystal Sugar Co., 334 U.S. 219, 236 (1948); Atty. Gen. Nat. Com. Rep. 44, (2).

[3] Marshall, Principles of Economics 324-325 (8th ed. 1922); Stackelberg, The Theory of the Market Economy 206 (Peacock trans. 1952); Knight, Risk, Uncertainty and Profits 79 (1921); Hotelling, Stability in Competition, 39 Econ. J. 41,

fection (ignorance).[4] Thus it is possible to view the whole geographical problem as a "friction" leading to "imperfect" competition. One difficulty with this view is that it gives us no clues whatever to the rational delimitation of territory in a monopoly case.[5] The economists, of course, are not concerned (as are lawyers) with political boundaries. Hence, it is clear under the "imperfection" view that a municipal, state or even a national boundary line is without significance for the purpose of defining a monopoly under the structure test. Beyond that, the "imperfection" view furnishes little assistance to the courts.

Another way of looking at the geographic problem is to conceive of two otherwise identical commodities at different locations as being distinguishable items. That is, two identical bags of cement are treated as if they were separate commodities when one is located in Buffalo and the other in Philadelphia. Then analysis runs in terms of cross-elasticity of demand, the item at the distant point being considered a substitute commodity and the territorial market defined in the same manner as that prescribed for the definition of the commodity itself.[6] Such substitutability

44 (1929); Robinson, What Is Perfect Competition? 49 Q.J. Econ. 104, 112 (1934); Lovasy, International Trade under Imperfect Competition, 55 id. 567, 583 (1941); Copeland, Competing Products and Monopolistic Competition, id. 1, 29 (1940); Garver and Hansen, Principles of Economics 61 (3d ed. 1947).

[4] Ibid. Note that mobility refers to the buyer as well as the seller. There may be but one motion picture theater in a town but sometimes the townsfolks travel to the neighboring city. Note also that immobility in the form of high transport costs and the like can "protect" rivals from competition. Smithies, Optimum Location in Spatial Competition, 49 J. Pol. Econ. 423, 434 (1941).

In considering the definition of the geographic territory we should also take account of the important role of potential competition. If entry into the market is easy, the existing geographic separation may not afford the shelter from competition mentioned above. See §3.12 infra. Again, the element of indivisibility is to be considered; one motion picture theater in a town, one grocery in a shopping center and one railroad in a valley all reflect factors of indivisibility. See §3.13 infra. Note also the role of dispersion: the competition which an alleged monopolist faces depends upon the ability of his rivals to penetrate his own territory. See Chapter 7. Compare Chamberlin, Monopolistic or Imperfect Competition, 51 Q.J. Econ. 557, 562-563 (1937).

[5] Economists have devoted considerable attention to determining how business firms will choose locations in relationship to each other and to markets. Hotelling, Stability in Competition 39 Econ. J. 41 (1929); Lerner and Singer, Some Notes on Duopoly and Spatial Competition, 45 J. Pol. Econ. 145, 151 (1937); Smithies, Optimum Location and Spatial Competition, 49 id. 423 (1941); Weintraub, Price Theory 272 (1949); Chamberlin, Monopolistic or Imperfect Competition, 51 Q.J. Econ. 557 (1937); Brems, Product Equilibrium under Monopolistic Competition 10-11 (1951); Copeland, Competing Products and Monopolistic Competition, 55 Q.J. Econ. 1, 29 (1940). It does not appear, however, that the theories developed with respect to the problem of how competitors will choose locations with respect to each other can be applied directly to the problems here under consideration.

[6] In Lerner and Singer, Some Notes on Duopoly and Spatial Competition, 45 J. Pol. Econ. 145 (1937), the following comment appears at page 145: "Considerable interest has been shown of late both in the problem of space as applied to the market and in the problem of the definition of a commodity. This is because both

or cross-elasticity reflects, of course, transport costs, the mobility of buyers and all the factors, emotional and rational, underlying the demand curve. Transport costs in turn are relative, being influenced not only by the means of carriage available, the natural obstacles of the terrain and the like but also by the ratio between the mass of the commodity and its value. A diamond in New York may easily be a substitute for a similar gem in St. Louis; a ton of ice in Milwaukee may not be a substitute for an equivalent weight of frozen water in Madison. The concept of cross-elasticity does not indicate, however, the geographical limits to be applied in any particular monopoly case. Just as in the problem of defining the commodity itself, cross-elasticity is a theoretical, rather than a practical tool.

Designating the area within which the defendant sells as the proper geographical scope of the alleged monopoly is erroneous in that it takes no account of the fringe areas adjacent thereto. The very existence of competition may be the force which restricts the area within which the defendant can make sales. Lack of such competition might permit the defendant to expand into an adjacent territory.[7] Obviously, therefore, the area within which the defendant has been able to make sales is simply irrelevant to the basic problem. Similarly, it is difficult to find any justification for reliance upon municipal, county or state boundary lines. Indeed, from an economic point of view, national boundary lines may be of little consequence, although the presence of currency and tariff barriers should not be overlooked. The language of Section 2 of the Sherman Act suggests that the commerce to be monopolized must be that among the several states or with foreign nations. Imports and exports can clearly be considered [8] but the language may not permit inclusion of foreign soil in the sales area defined for purposes of the structure

---

of these problems are really the same problem. Not only is it often convenient to deal with spatial problems by calling similar things at different places different things, but it has been found very fruitful to discuss differences in the qualities of the commodities as if they were differences in location." Compare Enke, Space and Value, 56 Q.J. Econ. 627, 637 (1942); Isard, Location Theory and Trade Theory, 68 id. 305-320 (1954).

[7] Note also that if the defendant actually enjoys a monopoly and is selling at monopolistic prices, the trading area within which he can make sales will probably be restricted in size.

[8] Machlup, The Political Economy of Monopoly 485-486 (1952). The error involved in refusing to take account of imports is made obvious by consideration of the jeweled watch industry. Here Swiss importations have driven most United States manufacturers from the field. To define the geographic market for jeweled watches without taking account of those imports would fly in the face of the realities of the market place. But compare United States v. Aluminum Co. of America, 148 F.2d 416 (2d Cir. 1945).

test. Undoubtedly, the artificial character of the international boundary from an economic point of view may give rise to anomalous results when the defendant is selling both at home and abroad.

There appears to be no reason why a number of territories separated by distance, as in the *Yellow Cab* case, should not be combined for purposes of testing compliance with Section 2 of the Sherman Act. Such a combination, however, should be regarded as simply the inclusion of several counts in one complaint; in other words, nothing is added to the sum of the several parts by the accumulation of different territories.[9]

In most cases, the courts must simply make the best guess they can as to the substitutability of commodities located at a distance, and it is not unlikely that the recorded decisions reflect with some accuracy the "trading areas" recognized in various lines of commerce.[10] A judge may not be able to tell precisely how far a housewife will travel to buy groceries. He can, however, determine that a mile is not an impossibility, whereas a hundred miles (mail order apart) would clearly be extravagant.

§3.8. **Permissible size.** Once the product has been defined and the geographic market determined under the structure test of monopoly, a court must decide whether the defendant is of monopolistic size. Clearly that size cannot be reckoned in terms of dollar sales or by reference to the number of the defendant's employees and the like. While a company's total assets, its total sales and the number of persons it employs may indicate its wealth, they bear no rational relationship to the definition of monopoly. As Professor Edwards said,

> . . . ceilings [based on assets or employment] . . . are not practicable. The significance of a given absolute size differs from case to case with variations in technology. . . .
>
> No uniform limit upon size would be equally appropriate to a glove manufacturer, a steel maker, a food chain, and a building contractor. . . .[1]

[9] Unless the areas involved contain recognized trading centers (organized exchanges) where transactions occur affecting prices in much larger areas.

[10] Waite and Cassady, The Consumer and the Economic Order 234 (1939). Goods may, of course, be shipped on order from distant points. If, however, no extra charge is made for delivery, price discrimination may creep into the picture. Weintraub, Price Theory 284-285 (1949).

§3.8. [1] Edwards, Maintaining Competition: Requisites of a Governmental Policy 120-121 (1949). Mr. Justice Brandeis recognized the validity of the argument set forth in the text. Kales, Contracts and Combinations in Restraint of Trade §80 (1918). But compare Kaplan, Small Business: Its Place and Problems 10 et seq. (Committee for Economic Development, 1948).

For such reasons, it has long been apparent that permissible size must be determined in relation to the relevant commodity and geographic markets.[2] Thus arises the "share of the market" concept and the use of percentages to determine legality.

Despite the fact that courts rely heavily upon the "share of the market" test, it is difficult to determine what proportions of market control are legal, since the approved percentages have varied so widely from case to case. It may be reasonably clear that a concentration of more than 80 per cent in single hands would violate Section 2 of the Sherman Act.[3] On the other hand, a per-

[2] Occasionally a court will rely upon absolute figures. Thus, in Schine Chain Theatres, Inc. v. United States, 334 U.S. 110, 118 (1948), the defendants were found to enjoy "monopoly power" by owning 148 theaters in 76 towns, 60 of those towns being without other theaters. There was, however, no showing of how many rival theaters existed in the remaining towns. Compare Storer Broadcasting Co. v. United States, 220 F.2d 204 (D.C. Cir. 1955), rev'd, 351 U.S. 192, 209 (1956).

It is true that several proposals have been made to cope with the problem ot monopoly by placing an arbitrary limit upon the size of the corporation. E.g., Raymond, The Limitist (1947). There have been other proposals of a quasi-absolute type. Thus it has been suggested that corporate size be reduced by requiring directors to own a minimum proportion of a company's stock. Celler Committee I, pt. 2A, at 521. Such proposals actually relate to the problem of wealth and are discussed in Chapter 8.

[3] It has always been clear that a monopoly need not be "complete" in order to achieve illegality. Thus, in United States v. E. C. Knight Co., 156 U.S. 1 (1895), the Court said at page 16: ". . . all the authorities agree that in order to vitiate a contract or combination it is not essential that its results should be a complete monopoly; it is sufficient if it really tends to that end and to deprive the public of the advantages which flow from free competition." See Dana, "Monopoly" Under the National Anti-Trust Act, 7 Harv. L. Rev. 338, 350 (1894). In the table below we have listed in the left-hand column the percentage of market control held to be illegal and the citation of the case in the right-hand column.

100%	United States v. Griffith, 334 U.S. 100 (1948)
97%	Peto v. Howell, 101 F.2d 353 (7th Cir. 1939)
95%	United States v. American Tobacco Co., 221 U. S. 106, 157 (1911)
95%	Distilling & Cattle Feeding Co. v. People ex rel. Moloney, 156 Ill. 448, 465, 41 N. E. 188 (1895)
90-95%	United Shoe Machinery Co. v. La Chapelle, 212 Mass. 467, 99 N.E. 289, 291 (1912)
86%	Harding v. American Glucose Co., 182 Ill. 551, 55 N.E. 577 (1899)
85%	State ex rel. Attorney General v. International Harvester Co., 81 Kan. 610, 106 Pac. 1053, 1054-1055 (1910).
80-90%	State ex Information Major v. International Harvester Co., 237 Mo. 369, 141 S.W. 672, 673, 677, 678 (1911), aff'd, 234 U.S. 199 (1914)
82%	United States v. General Electric Co., 82 F. Supp. 753, 893 (D.N.J. 1949)
75-80%	United States v. Eastman Kodak Co., 226 Fed. 62, 79 (W.D.N.Y. 1915), appeal dismissed, 255 U.S. 578 (1921).

centage as low as 33 is probably immune.[4] As to the many decisions involving the intervening shares, some courts have held them illegal, while others have considered them legal. Reconcilia-

73%	United States v. Paramount Pictures, Inc., 85 F. Supp. 881, 894 (S.D.N.Y. 1949), aff'd per curiam, 339 U.S. 974 (1950)
69%	United States v. Besser Mfg. Co., 96 F. Supp. 304, 307 (E.D. Mich. 1951), aff'd, 343 U.S. 444 (1952)
68-90%	American Tobacco Co. v. United States, 328 U.S. 781, 795 (1946)
64%	United States v. E. I. Du Pont de Nemours & Co., 188 Fed. 127, 145, 154 (C.C.D. Del. 1911)
58%	United States v. New England Fish Exchange, 258 Fed. 732, 750-751 (D. Mass. 1919), 292 Fed. 511 (1923)
40-50%	State ex rel. Sager v. Polar Ice Co., 259 Mo. 578, 169 S.W. 126, 134 (1914)
25%	United States v. New York Great Atlantic & Pacific Tea Co., 173 F.2d 79, 88 (7th Cir. 1949)
20%	United States v. Lehigh Valley Railroad Co., 254 U.S. 255, 270 (1920)
10%	American Handle Co. v. Standard Handle Co., 2 Tenn. Ch. App. 676, 59 S.W. 709, 798 (1900)
.5%	United States v. Klearflax Looms Inc., 63 F. Supp. 32 (D. Minn. 1945).

See also United States v. E. I. Du Pont de Nemours & Co., 118 F. Supp. 41 (D. Del. 1953), aff'd, 351 U.S. 377, 391-392 (1956) (query: Does court here indicate that control of 75 per cent of relevant market is monopolizing within §2? Or is it taking account of Du Pont's patents on moistureproof cellophane under which the sole domestic rival is licensed?). Several of the foregoing decisions involve combinations among competitors rather than single entity situations. Note also that percentages as low as .5 and as high as 24 have been applied under various sections of the Clayton Act. E.g., Oxford Varnish Corp. v. Ault & Wiborg Corp., 83 F.2d 764 (6th Cir. 1936); Arrow-Hart & Hegeman Electric Co. v. FTC, 65 F.2d 336, 340 (2d Cir. 1933), rev'd, 291 U.S. 587 (1934). Under recent British legislation 33 per cent is the touchstone but concentration to that degree merely sets an investigation in process. Monopolies and Restrictive Practices (Inquiry and Control) Act, 1948, 11 & 12 George VI, c. 66; Meier, A Critique of the New British Monopoly Act, 48 Mich. L. Rev. 329, 332 (1950); Harbury and Raskind, The British Approach to Monopoly Control, 67 Q.J. Econ. 380, 382 (1953).

[4] The table below lists various percentages held to be lawful in the proceedings listed in the right-hand column.

75%	Oakdale Manufacturing Co. v. Garst, 18 R.I. 484, 28 Atl. 973, 974 (1894)
64%	Moody & Waters Co. v. Case-Moody Pie Corp., 354 Ill. 82, 90, 187 N.E. 813 (1933)
50%	United States v. General Electric Co., 115 F. Supp. 835, 868-870 (D.N.J. 1953)
40%	Times-Picayune Publishing Co. v. United States, 345 U.S. 594, 612 (1953)
33%	United States v. Aluminum Co. of America, 148 F.2d 416, 424 (2d Cir. 1945)

tion appears to be impossible. Nevertheless, great interest attaches to the question of whether oligopoly (few sellers) is unlawful under the law as it stands today. This question, of course, is simply another way of asking what percentage of market sales is permissible. Under the static doctrines of monopolistic competition, the effects of oligopoly are considered to be similar, if not identical, to those of monopoly itself.[5] The late Professor Simons, an ardent and eloquent champion of the competitive system, suggested that 5 per cent of the relevant market was an acceptable upper limit on the theory that, when market shares are larger, competitors refuse to reduce prices because they realize that others will follow suit.[6] If an agreement among competitors to fix prices is illegal[7] and if oligopoly conditions produce similar

33%	United States v. Columbia Steel Co., 334 U.S. 495, 533 (1948)
30%	Miller Motors, Inc. v. Ford Motor Co., 149 F. Supp. 790, 810 (M.D.N.C. 1957)
26-28%	Bender v. Hearst Corp., 152 F. Supp. 569, 578 (D. Conn. 1957)
25%	United States v. National Lead Co., 332 U.S. 319, 352-353 (1947)
24.6%	United States v. Standard Oil Co., 47 F.2d 288, 312-313 (E.D. Mo. 1931)
24%	United States v. Columbia Steel Co., 334 U.S. 495, 524, 529 (1948).

Under other statutes the percentages of 7.2 and 1.96 have been approved. United States v. Republic Steel Corp., 11 F. Supp. 117, 124 (N.D. Ohio, 1935); Fargo Glass & Paint Co. v. Globe American Co., 201 F.2d 534, 537, 540 (7th Cir. 1953), *cert. denied*, 345 U.S. 942 (1953). Note the hazy discussion of this subject in Atty. Gen. Nat. Com. Rep. 48, (3).

5 Sraffa, The Laws of Returns Under Competitive Conditions, 36 Econ. J. 535, 549 (1926); Machlup, The Economics of Sellers' Competition 145 (1952). In Fellner, Competition Among the Few (1949) it was said at page 41: "Pure competition and Chamberlinian monopolistic competition in the 'large group' require that no firm be large enough in relation to the market to be able to affect the value of the relevant market variables to the extent that any other firm could be influenced by the defect. In such 'atomistic' circumstances concerted action without outside aid is usually impossible. Each firm knows that whether another firm violates an agreement or quasi-agreement does not depend on whether it violates, and this means that each firm has an interest in violating. Consequently, collusion usually is impossible. This is subject to the qualification that in even very large communities the esprit de corps is such in certain respects as to preclude the violation on a major scale of certain unwritten rules which serve the joint interest."

6 Simons, Economic Policy for a Free Society 59 (1948); Rostow, The New Sherman Act, 14 U. Chi. L. Rev. 567, 576-577 (1947); Rostow, Monopoly Under the Sherman Act; Power or Purpose? 43 Ill. L. Rev. 745, 783 et seq. (1949); Rothschild, Price Theory and Oligopoly, 57 Econ. J. 299, 308 (1947); Abramovitz, An Approach to Price Theory for a Changing Economy 17 (1939); Bain, Conditions of Entry and the Emergence of Monopoly, in Chamberlin, ed., Monopoly and Competition and Their Regulation 215, 232 (International Economic Assn. 1954). Professor Bain suggested that "industries" in which eight firms do 70 per cent or more of the business are monopolistic. Id. at 216-217. Further discussion will be found in §3.10 *infra*.

7 Kiefer-Stewart Co. v. Joseph E. Seagram & Sons, 340 U.S. 211 (1951).

results, then it should follow that oligopoly is unlawful.[8] There are decisions which can be interpreted to support that view: the 1946 opinion of the United States Supreme Court in the *Tobacco* case is often relied upon by those who believe that oligopoly is itself unlawful.[9] Other observers, relying upon both earlier and later decisions,[10] have reached opposite conclusions.[11] Accordingly, it is extremely difficult to say whether oligopoly is lawful today; its legality may depend upon other factors to be discussed below.

When sellers are few and one is considerably larger than its rivals, a situation of "price leadership" may arise. Doctrines of monopolistic competition suggest that dominant firm price leadership is a form of monopoly pricing marked by heavy promotional expenditures, relatively high prices and excess capacity.[12] In the famous *Harvester* case, the Supreme Court of the United States specifically said that there was nothing unlawful in the fact that the smaller rivals in the farm implement business followed

---

[8] Compare Lorain Journal Co. v. United States, 342 U.S. 143, 154 (1951).

[9] American Tobacco Co. v. United States, 328 U.S. 781, 789, 795-796, 809-810 (1946); United States v. Lehigh Valley Railroad Co., 254 U.S. 255, 270 (1920); Northern Securities Co. v. United States, 193 U.S. 197 (1904). In United States v. American Can Co., 230 Fed. 859, 234 Fed. 1019 (D. Md. 1916), *appeal dismissed*, 256 U.S. 706 (1921), the trial court said: "One who sells only one-half of the cans that are sold does not, of course, possess a monopoly in the same sense as he would if he sold all or nearly all of them. Yet he may have more power over the industry than it is well for any one concern to possess." 230 Fed. at 901. See Levi, The Antitrust Laws and Monopoly, 14 U. Chi. L. Rev. 153, 178 (1947); but compare Oppenheim, A New Look at Antitrust Enforcement Trends, Symposium, N.Y. State Bar Assn., Section on Antitrust Law, 69, 72 (CCH, 1950).

[10] United States v. E. I. Du Pont de Nemours & Co., 118 F. Supp. 41 (D. Del. 1953), *aff'd*, 351 U.S. 377, 392-393 (1956); United States v. Aluminum Co. of America, 148 F.2d 416, 424 (2d Cir. 1945); United States v. National Lead Co., 332 U.S. 319, 352-353 (1947); United States v. Columbia Steel Co., 334 U.S. 495 (1948); United States v. Morgan, 118 F. Supp. 621, 737 (S.D.N.Y. 1953).

[11] Johnston and Stevens, Monopoly or Monopolization — A Reply to Professor Rostow, 44 Ill. L. Rev. 269, 282 et seq., 290 (1949); Harbeson, A New Phase of the Antitrust Law, 45 Mich. L. Rev. 977, 985 (1947); Note, The Sherman Act and Close Combinations, 43 Ill. L. Rev. 523, 529. Compare Hale, Trust Dissolution, 40 Colum. L. Rev. 615, 619-620 (1940).

[12] Steindl, Small and Big Business 9-10 (Oxford Institute of Statistics Monograph No. 1, 1945); Robinson, Imperfect Competition Revisited, 63 Econ. J. 579, 588 (1953); Oxenfeldt, Industrial Pricing and Market Practices 301 (1951). In Markham, Competition in the Rayon Industry (1952) it was said at page 106: "When a firm occupies the position of a partial monopolist, the remaining firms in the industry have no choice but to accept its price, whether the partial monopolist attempts to maximize his short-run profits or pursue some other line of action. No price other than the price set by the partial monopolist is contemplated by the competitive sector of the industry. Dominant firm price leadership, then, is patently a form of monopoly pricing." Compare Edwards, Public Policy and Business Size, 24 J. Business 280, 290 (1951). Additional discussion of price leadership will be found in §3.10 *infra*.

the prices set by the defendant corporation.[13] Now and again lower courts have intimated that a different rule might be applied.[14] Until the Supreme Court speaks again,[15] however, it will be difficult to establish that price leadership in and of itself is illegal under the Sherman Act.

§3.9. **More than one and less than two.** To apply the structure theory, we must first identify the numbers to count. A distinction between the singular and the plural is fundamental to our antitrust laws. Most of the statutes deal separately with group and individual actions. Thus Section 1 of the Sherman Act refers to a combination, contract or conspiracy in restraint of trade: application to more than one defendant is plainly implied. Section 2, on the other hand, is largely framed in terms of the activities or status of a single firm (except for the conspiracy clause discussed below).

By definition only one can monopolize and yet we find several cases in which Section 2 of the Sherman Act has been applied to groups composed of trade rivals. One of the most explicit statements on the subject appeared in a case involving producers and distributors of motion pictures:

> In respect to monopoly power, we think it existed in this case. As we have shown, the defendants were all working together. There was a horizontal conspiracy. . . . In these circumstances, the defendants must be viewed collectively rather than independently as to the power which they exercised over the market by their theatre holdings. . . .[1]

[13] United States v. International Harvester Co., 274 U.S. 693, 707, 709 (1927), citing United States v. United States Steel Corp., 251 U.S. 417, 448 (1920); Burns, The Decline of Competition 20 (1936).

[14] Gamco, Inc. v. Providence Fruit & Produce Building, Inc., 194 F.2d 484, 486 (1st Cir. 1952), *cert. denied*, 344 U.S. 817 (1952); Hughes Tool Co. v. Ford, 114 F. Supp. 525, 540 (E.D. Okla. 1953), *rev'd*, 215 F.2d 924 (10th Cir. 1954), *cert. denied*, 348 U.S. 927, 965 (1955).

[15] Compare Times-Picayune Publishing Co. v. United States, 345 U.S. 594 (1953). In that case it was said at page 612 n.33: ". . . obviously, if a producer controlling an even lesser share than here is ringed by numerous smaller satellites together accounting for the rest, his mastery of the market is greater than were he facing fierce rivalry of other large sellers."

§3.9. [1] United States v. Paramount Pictures, Inc., 85 F. Supp. 881, 894 (S.D.N.Y. 1949), *aff'd per curiam*, 339 U.S. 974 (1950). *Accord:* United States v. MacAndrews & Forbes Co., 149 Fed. 823, 836 (C.C.S.D.N.Y. 1906), *writ dismissed*, 212 U.S. 585 (1908); United States v. United States Gypsum Co., 340 U.S. 76, 80 (1950); United States v. National Lead Co., 332 U.S. 319, 354 (1947); United States v. General Electric Co., 82 F. Supp. 753, 770, 799, 891 (D.N.J. 1949); Kansas City Star Co. v. United States, 240 F.2d 643, 664 (8th Cir. 1957). The Attorney General's Committee did not approve the foregoing decisions, a fact of some possible significance. But compare Atty. Gen. Nat. Com. Rep. 242, 4.

Possibly the application of Section 2 of the Sherman Act to group activities results from the doctrine that monopolization within the purview of Section 2 is a species of restraint of trade prohibited by Section 1 of the statute.[2]   To speak of monopolization by more than one person can, however, only lead to confusion.   The statute draws a reasonably clear distinction between single firms and groups,[3] and as we shall see, there may be sound reasons for distinguishing the prohibitions applied to individuals from those designed to limit group activity.[4]   A single trader, no matter how large, may set his own prices; if a group of rivals agrees upon prices they commit a per se offense.

One exception to the foregoing view is, however, written into the Sherman Act itself.   For Section 2 sets forth three separate offenses.   One is monopolization, another is attempt to monopolize and the third is directed at a person who shall "combine or conspire with any other person or persons, to monopolize."   Accordingly, it has been held that defendants may conspire to monopolize in violation of Section 2.[5]   The interesting question is whether there is a distinction between the conspiracy prohibited by Section 1 of the Sherman Act and that which falls within the purview of Section 2.   The Supreme Court has told us that

. . . §§1 and 2 of the Sherman Act require proof of conspiracies which are reciprocally distinguishable from and independent of each other although the objects of the conspiracies may partially overlap.[6]

And in one well-known case a jury returned a verdict finding the defendants not guilty of a conspiracy under Section 1 but con-

[2] Standard Oil Co. of New Jersey v. United States, 221 U.S. 1, 61 (1911); United States v. Socony Vacuum Oil Co., 310 U.S. 150, 226n (1940); United States v. Pullman Co., 50 F. Supp. 123, 135 (E.D. Pa. 1943), aff'd per curiam, 330 U.S. 806 (1947); United States v. Whiting, 212 Fed. 466, 478 (D. Mass. 1914); William Goldman Theatres, Inc. v. Loew's, Inc., 150 F.2d 738, 740 (3d Cir. 1945); Shapiro v. King, 125 F.2d 890 (8th Cir. 1942).   In the last case it was said at page 892: "It is true that a monopoly in the interstate trade of a particular article or business may, naturally and ordinarily, result in a restraint of that trade but this is not so necessarily true as to make a monopoly always a restraint."

[3] United States v. Paramount Pictures, Inc., 66 F. Supp. 323, 354 (S.D.N.Y. 1946), rev'd, 334 U.S. 131 (1948).   Compare Holmes, J., dissenting in Northern Securities Co. v. United States, 193 U.S. 197, 404 (1904).   When competitors join in an agreement to fix prices they thereby admit the fact that they have power to fix prices, because otherwise the agreement is meaningless.   No similar deduction can be made under §2 of the Sherman Act if there is a single entity as party defendant. Compare United States v. United States Steel Corp., 251 U.S. 417, 444-445 (1920).

[4] As set forth in §3.13 infra, the factor of indivisibility may play a large role in proceedings under §2 of the Sherman Act and yet not affect the behavior of independent rival firms.   But compare Edwards, Maintaining Competition 91 (1949).

[5] E.g., United States v. General Electric Co., 82 F. Supp. 753, 902 (D.N.J. 1949).

[6] American Tobacco Co. v. United States, 328 U.S. 781, 788 (1946).

victing the defendants under Section 2. This surprising result was sustained in the Court of Appeals, which said:

> . . . the same acts and course of conduct may constitute separate violations of §§1 and 2 of the Sherman Act. . . .[7]

Despite the foregoing assurances, it is difficult to find any difference between the conspiracies embodied in the two different sections of the statute. Many cases refer to them apparently interchangeably[8] and no reason for a distinction appears to have been expressed in judicial opinions.[9] It seems likely that the conspiracy clause in Section 2 was inserted as something of a catchall in an effort to make sure that no loophole was left in the statute. It follows that its application should be restricted to situations (which apparently have not yet arisen) wherein Section 1 would not be applicable.

Another situation in which a prohibition against monopoly may be directed at a plurality of defendants is found when the group combines to form a single entity. Section 2 of the Sherman Act, for example, has been applied in several such instances of consolidation of former rivals.[10] This phenomenon, of course,

---

[7] United States v. National City Lines, Inc., 186 F.2d 562, 569 (7th Cir. 1951), *cert. denied,* 341 U.S. 916 (1951). See Shapiro v. King, 125 F.2d 890, 892 (8th Cir. 1942).

[8] E.g., Swift & Co. v. United States, 196 U.S. 375, 395 (1905); American Tobacco Co. v. United States, 328 U.S. 781, 782, 788 (1946); United States v. Yellow Cab Co., 332 U.S. 218, 220 (1947); United States v. Crescent Amusement Co., 323 U.S. 173, 176 (1944); United States v. Griffith, 334 U.S. 100, 109 (1948); Forgett v. Scharf, 181 F.2d 754 (3d Cir. 1950), *cert. denied,* 340 U.S. 825 (1950). See Nash v. United States, 229 U.S. 373, 374 (1913); Lynch v. Magnavox Co., 94 F.2d 883, 888 (9th Cir. 1938); United States v. Morgan, 118 F. Supp. 621, 628 (S.D.N.Y. 1933).

[9] It is true that monopolization under §2 is different from a restraint of trade under §1; hence it might appear that conspiracy to monopolize would be different from a conspiracy in restraint of trade. As stated in the text, however, the difference is believed to be merely verbal. Compare United States v. National City Lines, 186 F.2d 562, 571 (7th Cir. 1951), *cert. denied,* 341 U.S. 916 (1951); United States v. Griffith, 334 U.S. 100, 106-107 (1948); McConnell v. Camors-McConnell Co., 152 Fed. 321 (5th Cir. 1907); Atty. Gen. Nat. Com. Rep. 30, (1). In United States v. National Retail Lumber Dealers Assn., 40 F. Supp. 448 (D. Colo. 1941), it was said at page 456: "The essential characteristic of monopoly is the wrongful exclusion of competitors from the field. A conspiracy to monopolize is a conspiracy to get control of the industry in which the defendant is engaged, by means which prevent others from engaging in fair competition with them." How does this definition differ from that of a conspiracy to restrain trade?

[10] Northern Securities Co. v. United States, 193 U.S. 197, 209, 327 (1904); United States v. MacAndrews & Forbes Co., 149 Fed. 823 (C.C.S.D.N.Y. 1906), *writ dismissed,* 212 U.S. 585 (1908); United States v. E. I. Du Pont de Nemours & Co., 188 Fed. 127, 152 (C.C.D. Del. 1911); Patterson v. United States, 222 Fed. 599, 620 (6th Cir. 1915), *cert. denied,* 238 U.S. 635, (1915); United States v. Minnesota Mining & Manufacturing Co., 92 F. Supp. 947, 958 (D. Mass. 1915). For a discussion of the acquisition of rival firms as monopolization, see §2.25 *supra.* In Northern Securities Co. v.

reflects the factor of time: before the amalgamation Section 1 of the Sherman Act is applicable to the combination, and afterwards, Section 2 should control. Decisions, however, should not depend upon the chance that the wrong section has been relied upon.[11] Accordingly, we may have to tolerate application of Section 2 of the Sherman Act to situations in which rival firms merely plan to join forces.

Conversely, statutes such as Section 1 of the Sherman Act should be applicable only to a plurality of defendants. It is true that an attempt to monopolize, within the meaning of Section 2 of the Sherman Act, may constitute a restraint of trade under Section 1,[12] just as violations of Section 1 may constitute abuses within the meaning of Section 2.[13] Nevertheless, it is desirable to distinguish individual from group action. For it has often been noted that standards applied under Section 1 of the Sherman Act have differed from those prevailing under Section 2. Most notable is the rule that price-fixing is illegal per se when indulged in by a group

---

United States, 193 U.S. 197 (1904), Mr. Justice Holmes, dissenting, said at page 410: ". . . a contract with a stranger to the defendant's business [is] . . . a true contract in restraint of trade. To suppress competition in that way is one thing, to suppress it by fusion is another."

[11] Thus, in State ex Information Crow v. Continental Tobacco Co., 177 Mo. 1, 75 S.W. 737, 747 (1903), a statute similar to §1 of the Sherman Act was held not applicable to a combination of competitors carrying on their former businesses in a newly organized corporation. But in State ex Information Major v. International Harvester Co., 237 Mo. 369, 141 S.W. 672, 677 (1911), aff'd, 234 U.S. 199 (1914), a combination into corporate form was reached under the same statute. The common law has long recognized the close connection between combination and monopoly. Thus it has been said that the primary object of a "pool" or "trust" is to secure monopoly and that the term "monopoly" embraces any combination to control prices to the detriment of the public. Chicago, Wilmington & Vermillion Coal Co. v. People, 114 Ill. App. 75, 112 (1904), aff'd, 214 Ill. 421, 73 N.E. 770 (1905); Georgia Fruit Exchange v. Turnipseed, 9 Ala. App. 123, 62 So. 542, 545-546 (1913).

[12] Standard Oil Co. of New Jersey v. United States, 221 U.S. 1, 61 (1911); United States v. Columbia Steel Co., 334 U.S. 495, 521-522 (1948); United States v. General Instrument Corp., 87 F. Supp. 157, 196 (D.N.J. 1949); see §9.2 infra. As to the Federal Trade Commission Act, compare, e.g., Fashion Originators' Guild v. FTC, 312 U.S. 457 (1941). The decisions speaking of "foreclosure" with respect to requirements contracts and the like (§2.12 supra) illustrate the delicate boundary lines between §§1 and 2 of the Sherman Act. Such "foreclosure" can be looked upon as "coercion" on the part of one of the parties. It can also be regarded as an agreement between the parties. Apart from the statute there is also a shadowy line between the law of monopoly and the law of conspiracy. 11 Am. Jur. 577, 581.

[13] In United States v. Griffith, 334 U.S. 100 (1948), it was said at page 106: ". . . those things which are condemned by §2 are in large measure merely the end products of conduct which violates §1. . . . But that is not always true. Section 1 covers contracts, combinations, or conspiracies in restraint of trade. Section 2 is not restricted to conspiracies or combinations to monopolize but also makes it a crime for any person to monopolize any part of interstate or foreign trade or commerce. . . ." See §2.9 supra. Compare United States v. Pullman Co., 50 F. Supp. 123, 135 (E.D. Pa. 1943), aff'd per curiam, 330 U.S. 806 (1947).

of rival firms.[14]   Note also that the power to fix prices may not be a necessary element of a case under Section 1 of the Sherman Act,[15] while it clearly must be proven if monopolization is alleged. The rationale of the distinction is not crystal clear, yet it undoubtedly reflects the factors of indivisibility, commodity definition and growth which make so difficult a determination of the existence of monopoly.   Some, at least, of those problems appear less acute when a plurality of defendants is involved [16] and the distinction between Sections 1 and 2 of the Sherman Act thus constitutes a rough rule of thumb reflecting underlying economic differences.[17]

Just as there has been a tendency to find that a group could constitute a monopoly, so there is a line of authority which permits anticombination statutes to be applied to single firms.   The rule, which has an ancient lineage, is that a corporation may conspire with its own officers or subsidiary corporations in violation of the antitrust laws.[18]   It is known as the "intracorporate conspiracy" rule.[19]   It takes the multiplicity of legal entities as a proper foundation for the finding of a combination or conspiracy, despite the fact that the economic entity is sole.   This divergence between law and the realities of the market place has been frowned upon

14 United States v. Socony-Vacuum Oil Co., 310 U.S. 150, 224, 228 (1940); Harbeson, A New Phase of the Antitrust Law, 45 Mich. L. Rev. 977, 978 et seq. (1947).   But compare Handler, Monopolies, Mergers and Markets 12 (Fed. Bar. Assn. Nov. 9, 1954).

15 Compare Atty. Gen. Nat. Com. Rep. 12, 2, a, with United States v. Socony-Vacuum Oil Co., 310 U.S. 150, 224n (1940); Pocahontas Coke Co. v. Powhatan Co., 60 W. Va. 508, 56 S.E. 264, 273 (1907).

16 By definition, the problem of indivisibility does not arise in combination cases. Note also that the definition of the commodity may be less difficult because the parties, by their conduct, may indicate a realistic definition of the articles involved. Again, application of §1 of the Sherman Act rarely results in curbing the growth of enterprise except in instances where cooperative research or similar activities are involved.   But compare Appendix A, page 429 et seq.

17 But compare Levi, The Antitrust Laws and Monopoly, 14 U. Chi. L. Rev. 153, 173 (1947); Handler, A Study of the Construction and Enforcement of the Federal Antitrust Laws 85 (TNEC Monograph No. 38, 1941); Kefauver, The Supreme Court and Congress v. Monopoly, 20 Tenn. L. Rev. 254, 258 (1948).

18 Kiefer-Stewart Co. v. Joseph E. Seagram & Sons, 340 U.S. 211, 215 (1951); United States v. General Motors Corp., 26 F. Supp. 353 (N.D. Ind. 1939), aff'd, 121 F.2d 376 (7th Cir. 1941), cert. denied, 314 U.S. 618 (1941); State ex Information Hadley v. Standard Oil Co., 218 Mo. 1, 116 S.W. 902 (1909), aff'd, 224 U.S. 270 (1912); Standard Oil Co. of New Jersey v. United States, 221 U.S. 1, 45 (1911); Dunshee v. Standard Oil Co., 152 Iowa 618, 132 N.W. 371 (1911); Schine Chain Theatres, Inc. v. United States, 334 U.S. 110, 118 (1948); Lorain Journal Co. v. United States, 342 U.S. 143, 145 (1951); Sanib Corp. v. United Fruit Co., 135 F. Supp. 764, 766 (S.D.N.Y. 1955); Rahl, Conspiracy and the Antitrust Laws, 44 Ill. L. Rev. 745, 763 et seq. (1950); Comment, Intra-Enterprise Conspiracy Under the Sherman Act, 63 Yale L.J. 373 (1954).

19 In many cases the rule is not given a name or even discussed. E.g., United States v. Pullman Co., 50 F. Supp. 123 (E.D. Pa. 1943), aff'd per curiam, 330 U.S. 806 (1947).

by the Attorney General's Committee[20] and should not further be utilized by the courts.

Another problem with respect to numbers is found in the modern doctrine of "conscious parallelism." This doctrine would do away with the necessity of proving a conspiracy. If identical action by rival firms could be established, it would dispense with any showing of an agreement among them.[21]   Thus, in effect, a group would be treated as one person but the law of Section 1 would nevertheless apply.   This view has been urged on the grounds that old-fashioned limitations[22] on the application of the law of conspiracy are not adapted to modern conditions; and further, that oligopoly can only be attacked under Section 1 of the Sherman Act by the pleading of a conspiracy, since the courts have proven so reluctant to apply Section 2 of the Sherman Act thereto.[23]   In recent years, however, the courts have moved away from

[20] Atty. Gen. Nat. Com. Rep. 36, (2); Nelson Radio & Supply Co. v. Motorola, Inc., 200 F.2d 911 (5th Cir. 1952), cert. denied, 345 U.S. 925 (1953); Mackey v. Sears, Roebuck & Co., 237 F.2d 869, 873 (7th Cir. 1956); Whitely v. Foremost Dairies, Inc., 151 F. Supp. 914, 923 (W.D. Ark. 1957); Sprunk, Intra-Enterprise Conspiracy, 9 A.B.A., Antitrust Section Report 20, 24-25 (1956); McQuade, Conspiracy, Multi-corporate Enterprises and Section 1 of the Sherman Act, 41 Va. L. Rev. 183, 215 (1955); Brennan, The Sherman Act and Multi-Corporate Single Traders, 100 U. Pa. L. Rev. 1006 (1952). A majority of the Attorney General's Committee was willing to apply the intraenterprise conspiracy rule in the event that the defendant planned to drive a competitor out of business; the minority dissented from that position, presumably on the grounds that any such activity would constitute an attempt to monopolize and hence could be reached as such. Possibly a distinction can be drawn between a conspiracy between a corporation and its officers, and a corporation and subsidiary corporations. Every corporation must have officers: it cannot function without them. Subsidiary corporations, however, are not always necessary. On the other hand, large diversified corporations with quasi-autonomous divisions may sometimes be treated as if they constituted more than a single entity for economic purposes. Penrose, Limits to the Growth and Size of Firms, 45 Proceedings Am. Econ. Assn. 531, 542 (1955).

[21] American Tobacco Co. v. United States, 328 U.S. 781, 800, 809 (1946); FTC v. Cement Institute, 333 U.S. 683, 716 (1948); Schine Chain Theatres, Inc. v. United States, 334 U.S. 110, 115 (1948); United States v. Paramount Pictures, Inc., 334 U.S. 131, 142 (1948); United States v. General Motors Corp., 121 F.2d 376, 404-405 (7th Cir. 1941), cert. denied, 314 U.S. 618 (1941); Triangle Conduit Co. v. FTC, 168 F.2d 175, 181 (7th Cir. 1948), aff'd per curiam, 336 U.S. 956 (1949); C-O-TWO Fire Equipment Co. v. United States, 197 F.2d 489, 494, 497 (9th Cir. 1952), cert. denied, 344 U.S. 892 (1952). Half-hearted disavowals are recorded in National Lead Co. v. FTC, 227 F.2d 825, 834 (7th Cir. 1955), aff'd, 352 U.S. 419 (1957); Morton Salt Co. v. United States, 235 F.2d 573, 577 (10th Cir. 1956). Compare Krulewitch v. United States, 336 U.S. 440, 445 (1949). Consult Kittelle and Lamb, The Implied Conspiracy Doctrine and Delivered Pricing, 15 Law & Contemp. Prob. 227 (1950); Oppenheim, Federal Antitrust Legislation, 50 Mich. L. Rev. 1139, 1165 (1952); Note, Conscious Parallelism — Fact or Fancy? 3 Stan. L. Rev. 679 (1951).

[22] E.g., United States v. United States Steel Corp., 223 Fed. 55, 154 (D.N.J. 1915), aff'd, 251 U.S. 417 (1920).

[23] Rahl, Conspiracy and the Antitrust Laws, 44 Ill. L. Rev. 745, 753, 756 (1950); Rostow, The New Sherman Act, 14 U. Chi. L. Rev. 567, 581 (1947); McConnell, The Treble Damage Action, [1950] U. of Ill. L. Forum 659, 661; Conant, Consciously Parallel Action in Restraint of Trade, 38 Minn. L. Rev. 797, 822 (1954). In this

the doctrine of conscious parallelism[24] and in 1954 the Supreme Court itself denied that proof of conspiracy was no longer necessary, saying:

> . . . this Court has never held that proof of parallel business behavior conclusively establishes agreement or, phrased differently that such behavior itself constitutes a Sherman Act offense. Circumstantial evidence of consciously parallel behavior may have made heavy inroads into the traditional judicial attitude toward conspiracy; but "conscious parallelism" has not yet read conspiracy out of the Sherman Act entirely. . . .[25]

Circumstantial evidence, of course, has always been sufficient for proof of a conspiracy: it has never been necessary to adduce direct evidence of an agreement among the defendants.[26] Precisely how much evidence must be adduced in a conspiracy case following the recent pronouncement of the Supreme Court is difficult to ascertain. That problem, however, lies outside the boundaries of this book.[27]

---

situation, the prescriptions of law and economics may diverge. To the economist monopoly and oligopoly may be equivalents. A lawyer, in considering the enforcement of a criminal statute, may not be able to accept the economist's views.

24 Pevely Dairy Co. v. United States, 178 F.2d 363, 369-370 (8th Cir. 1949), *cert. denied,* 339 U.S. 942 (1950); United States v. E. I. Du Pont de Nemours & Co., 118 F. Supp. 41 (D. Del. 1953), *aff'd,* 351 U.S. 377 (1956); United States v. Morgan, 118 F. Supp. 621 (S.D.N.Y. 1953). In the last case it was said at page 634: ". . . it is supposed by some that the requirement of combination is a mere empty phrase to which one must at least do lip service, but which may easily be got around by finding agreement, combination or conspiracy when in truth and in fact no agreement . . . exists, provided the result obtained seems desirable and in the public interest. This is not the law. . . ."

25 Theatre Enterprises, Inc. v. Paramount Corp., 346 U.S. 537, 541 (1954); Interborough News Co. v. Curtis Publishing Co., 127 F. Supp. 286 (S.D.N.Y. 1954), *aff'd,* 225 F.2d 289, 301 (2d Cir. 1955); United States v. Twentieth Century Fox Film Corp., 137 F. Supp. 78, 85 et seq. (S.D. Cal. 1956); Atty. Gen. Nat. Com. Rep. 36, (2); Handler, Contract, Combination or Conspiracy, Proceedings A.B.A., Section of Antitrust Law, 38, 42-43, 45 (Aug. 26, 1953); Johnston and Stevens, Monopoly or Monopolization, 44 Ill. L. Rev. 269, 292 (1949). Compare Kotteakos v. United States, 328 U.S. 750, 754-755, 766-767 (1946).

26 Handler, Contract, Combination or Conspiracy, Proceedings A.B.A., Section of Antitrust Law, 38, 41 (Aug. 26, 1953).

27 Professor Handler has written:

"The evidentiary implications of conscious parallelism present different problems . . . there are circumstances where uniformity of action has a direct bearing upon the ultimate fact.

"The weight, if any, to be given to the evidence of uniformity will depend upon the circumstances. There is enormous difference between persistent, undeviating price uniformity in respect to non-fungible products, characterized by differences of structure, quality or brands, and the inevitable uniformity that must occur where fungible articles are sold to informed purchasers. . . ." Id. at 44.

Professor Conant has urged that the notion of conspiracy be abandoned, but that the plaintiffs be allowed to recover on a pleading that parallel action is in itself a restraint of trade. Conant, Consciously Parallel Action in Restraint of Trade, 38 Minn. L. Rev. 797, 824-825 (1954).

§3.10. **Oligopoly: Analysis.** As stated above, there are two ways of approaching the problem of fixing upon a legal share of any given market. One is to indicate the percentage which any one firm may enjoy. The other is to inquire whether markets characterized by few sellers (oligopoly) are lawful. The latter way amounts to the same thing as the former because market shares are comparatively large in oligopolistic industries. Whether such large market shares are deleterious, however, has been the subject of vigorous dispute.

As formulated by Professor Chamberlin and his followers, the theory of monopolistic competition finds oligopoly almost as objectionable as monopoly itself.[1] In the opinion of Professor Stigler, one of the most acute economists of the day, oligopoly should not be condoned:

> . . . indeed, the one important weakness in the Sherman Act as it is sometimes interpreted is the belief that oligopoly affords a satisfactory form of organization of our economy. This belief is apparently held, as it was certainly fostered, by one of the greatest contemporary judges, Learned Hand, the authority of the famous dictum that control by one firm of 64 per cent of an industry may not be monopoly and that 33 percent surely is not. It is true, no doubt, that oligopoly is a weaker form of monopolization than the single firm, but it is not so weak a form that it can be left to its own devices. If this view — which is almost universally held by modern economists — is correct, then our chief task in the field of antitrust policy is to demonstrate beyond judicial doubt, the social undesirability of permitting oligopoly by merger (or by other methods) in large American industries.[2]

When sellers are few, each is aware that any action he takes may induce a reaction upon the part of his rivals. If, for example, he reduces his prices, the rivals will do likewise and no permanent gain will result for any of them.[3] As one economist put it,

> A duopolist should always think twice before he makes up his mind to change his parameters of action. Price reduction may seem

§3.10. [1] Chamberlin, The Theory of Monopolistic Competition, c. 3 (6th ed. 1948). But compare Chamberlin, Product Heterogeneity and Public Policy, 40 Proceedings Am. Econ. Assn. 85 (1950).

[2] Stigler, Monopoly and Oligopoly by Merger, 40 id. 23, 32-33 (1950). But compare Rosenbluth, Measures of Concentration, in Business Concentration and Price Policy 57 (Stigler ed. 1955).

[3] Kaysen, A Dynamic Aspect of the Monopoly Problem, 31 Rev. Econ. & Stat. 109, 112 (1949); Rothschild, Price Theory and Oligopoly, 57 Econ. J. 299, 306 (1947). Empirical evidence in support of the view stated in the text will be found in United States v. United States Steel Corp., 223 Fed. 55, 154 (D.N.J. 1915), aff'd, 251 U.S. 417 (1920); Markham, Competition in the Rayon Industry 100 (1952); Burns, The Decline of Competition 229 (1936); American Sugar Refining, 7 Fortune No. 2, pp. 59, 62 (1933).

profitable for a fortnight, but when the rival has followed suit, both may be worse off. When imitated by the rival an innovation may be of little use. To make up one's mind usually requires a lot of thinking of how one is going to ward off the evils to be expected for the more remote future. One has to find out before he makes up his mind to stir up the rival. If he does not know, he had better refrain from stirring him up.[4]

A consequence of this doctrine is that prices will be "administered" in character, often as a result of collusion — express or tacit [5] — although prices may not be raised to the point where entry becomes attractive to new firms.[6] Competition in price disappears; selling expenses, particularly advertising charges, increase and the product is "differentiated" by each seller. Thus he hopes to gain an advantage by fooling customers into thinking his output is of higher quality than that of the rival firms.[7] Only a slight

[4] Brems, Product Equilibrium Under Monopolistic Competition 232 (1951). See also id. at 203-204, 219, 221; Abramovitz, Monopolistic Selling in a Changing Economy, 52 Q.J. Econ. 191, 205 (1938); Birch, A Revised Classification of Forms of Competition, 20 Can. J. Econ. & Pol. Sci. 157, 162 (1954).

[5] Morgenstern, Oligopoly, Monopolistic Competition and the Theory of Games, 38 Am. Econ. Rev. 10, 14-15 (1948); Stackelberg, The Theory of the Market Economy 202-203 (Peacock trans. 1952). Empirical evidence supporting the views stated in the text will be found in Markham, Competition in the Rayon Industry 69-70, 108, 118, 140-141 (1952); Scoville, Revolution in Glassmaking 223-224, 301-302 (1948); Cochran, History of the Pabst Brewing Co. 64-65 (1948); TNEC Hearings, pt. 18, at 10,300, 10,321; pt. 19, at 10,566-10,568, 10,573, 10,601, 10,621, 10,623, 10,629-10,630; pt. 20, at 10,868; pt. 27, at 14,250, 14,281, 14,308 et seq. But compare pt. 20, at 10,807, 10,812, 10,816. Something may depend upon the level of pricing. Thus price concessions may sometimes be made at the ultimate consumer level more easily than at the retail level because a retailer might pass on a part of the concession and spoil the market for other retailers. Cassady, Price Making and Price Behavior in the Petroleum Industry 227n (Petroleum Monograph Series No. 1, 1954).

[6] Rothschild, Price Theory and Oligopoly, 57 Econ. J. 229, 310 (1947); Stigler, Notes on the Theory of Duopoly, 48 J. Pol. Econ. 521, 533 (1940). Compare Henderson, The Theory of Duopoly, 68 Q.J. Econ. 565, 573 (1954).

[7] E.g., Brems, Product Equilibrium Under Monopolistic Competition 9 (1951); Fellner, Competition Among the Few 292-293 (1949); Chamberlin, Monopolistic Competition and the Productivity Theory of Distribution, in Fellner and Haley, eds., Readings in the Theory of Income Distribution 143 et seq., 151-152 (The Blakiston Co. 1949). Empirical evidence can be found to support the views expressed in the text. E.g., Reynolds, The Canadian Baking Industry, 52 Q.J. Econ. 659, 673, 676 (1938); Nicholls, Price Policies in the Cigarette Industry, c. 7 (1951); Colgate-Palmolive-Peet, 13 Fortune No. 4, pp. 120, 138 (1936). On the other hand, it has more recently been recognized that competition in quality may be as important as competition in price. E.g., Chamberlin, The Product as an Economic Variable, 67 Q.J. Econ. 1, 13, 24 (1953). An example of such competition is found in the sale of industrial supplies wherein technical services are often rendered by manufacturers to customers. E.g. E. I. du Pont de Nemours & Co., Du Pont: The Autobiography of an American Enterprise 133 (1952). Competition in service and even in advertising has been recognized in the courts. United States v. Union Pacific R.R., 226 U.S. 61, 87 (1912); United States v. Quaker Oats Co., 232 Fed. 499, 503 (N.D. Ill. 1916). See §3.15 infra.

variation is necessary to take account of the situation in which one of the firms is much larger than the others. In such an instance of "price leadership" the neoclassic analysis indicates that the "leader" will "hold an umbrella" over the smaller firms.

The rationale behind the partial monopolist type of price leadership is as follows: in an industry composed of one large producer and a number of small ones, the large producer sets a price on the basis of the visualized demand schedule for the commodity, after allowing for the quantities that will be supplied at all possible prices by the small producers. The required conditions are that the dominant firm sell a sufficiently large proportion of the commodity, that the small firms individually ignore any effect they may have on price, and that the dominant firm must behave passively — it sets a price and sells the remainder after the small producers have sold all they wish at the prevailing price.[8]

With the passage of time, however, many economists have come to the view that the price levels which will be reached in an oligopolistic situation are indeterminate in character. The analysis offered by Professor Chamberlin in 1933 is now often viewed as incomplete and inconclusive.[9] Thus Professor Galbraith, writing some fifteen years later, said:

In dealing with small numbers or oligopoly, Professor Chamberlin, who went farthest with the problem on a general theoretical level, did little more than resurrect the engaging but largely irrelevant novelties of Cournot and Edgeworth. . . . One certain fact

[8] Markham, Competition in the Rayon Industry 101 (1952). Compare Machlup, The Political Economy of Monopoly 476 (1952). Note, however, the following comment from a leading economist: "Perhaps price leadership should be regarded as a kind of convenient institution, like the monarchy in a feudal society. For when each firm knows that all will follow the leader's signals they are saved from a perplexing choice between raising prices (when cost has risen), debasing quality or submitting to a loss of profit, so that all have an interest in preserving a tradition of 'loyalty' to the price leader." Robinson, Imperfect Competition Revisited, 63 Econ. J. 579, 588 (1953). Empirical evidence can be found to support the statements in the text. E.g., United States v. American Can Co., 230 Fed. 859, 892 (D. Md. 1916), appeal dismissed, 256 U.S. 706 (1921); Markham, Competition in the Rayon Industry 297-298, 104-105 (1952). But compare Cassady, Price Making and Price Behavior in the Petroleum Industry 118-119 (Petroleum Monograph Series No. 1, 1954); Celler Committee I, pt. 2A, at 371; Learned, Pricing of Gasoline, 26 Harv. Bus. Rev. No. 6, pp. 723, 754 (1948).

[9] Chamberlin, The Product as an Economic Variable, 67 Q.J. Econ. 1, 13, 24 (1953); Machlup, The Economics of Sellers' Competition 415 (1952); Nicols, Rehabilitation of Pure Competition, 62 Q.J. Econ. 31, 63 (1947); Wallace, Industrial Markets and Public Policy, in Public Policy 59, 80 (Friedrich and Mason ed. 1940); Oxenfeldt, Industrial Pricing and Market Practices 274, 267-268 (1951); Lewis, Some Observations on Duopoly Theory, 38 Proceedings Am. Econ. Assn. 1, 9 (1948). Professor Fellner has attributed part of the difficulties to the problem of measuring the results in a world filled with "imperfections." Fellner, Elasticities, Cross-Elasticities and Market Relationships, 43 Am. Econ. Rev. 898, 904 (1953).

about oligopoly (and its counterpart on the buyer's side of the market) is that the entire market solution can be altered unilaterally by any single participant. This is at once the simplest and the most critical distinction between oligopoly and pure competition. It also means that the methodological device by which the competitive market has been analyzed, i.e. laying down general assumptions about the group response of numerous individuals to common stimuli, is inadmissible. Rather the assumptions must be sufficiently comprehensive to cover the behavior of each participant in the market. . . . Edgeworth and Cournot and, in that tradition, Chamberlin, merely derived the market solution that followed from two or three out of a near infinity of possible behavior combinations. It follows that they were not offering a theory of duopoly or oligopoly but displaying a few examples. Little progress has been made to an analysis of oligopoly by this route and little could be expected.[10]

Stressing psychological factors[11] in addition to the possibility that oligopolists will make mistakes and the like,[12] economists have proceeded to spell out a wide variety of possible situations, for each of which a different solution is offered.[13] The qualifications on the older theories stem from unwillingness of rivals to pool resources and to agree on interfirm compensations, particularly in the presence of differences between cost curves of the various

[10] Galbraith, Monopoly and the Concentration of Economic Power, in Ellis, ed., A Survey of Contemporary Economics 99, 101-102 (American Economic Assn. 1949). Compare Rothschild, Price Theory and Oligopoly, 57 Econ. J. 299, 303 (1947); Kaysen, A Dynamic Aspect of the Monopoly Problem, 31 Rev. Econ. & Stat. 109, 112 (1949). An attempt to reformulate the behavior of oligopolists is found in Fellner, Competition Among the Few (1949), wherein it was said at page 35: "Economic behavior under fewness is imperfectly co-ordinated; it remains competitive in a limited sense. The competitive element stays significant; it applies mainly to the dynamic aspects of the problem which are connected with ingenuity and inventiveness and on the discounting of which it is difficult to reach agreement."

[11] Wright, Capitalism 160-161 (1951); Katona, Psychological Analysis of Business Decisions and Expectations, 36 Am. Econ. Rev. 44, 48, 51 (1946). Professor Katona wrote at page 53: ". . . it follows from psychological findings that when expectations do change, they are likely to change at about the same time and in the same direction for many business men . . . the need for re-orientation in one's thinking is usually dependent upon general economic, social and political events which many business men experience at the same time. Uniformity or similarity of new decisions need not, therefore, reflect automatic or imitative responses, but may be the result of many individuals reacting to the same change in the setting." But compare Katz, Psychoanalysis and Law, 5 U. Chi. Law School Record No. 2, 13 (1956).

[12] Wright, Some Pitfalls of Economic Theory as a Guide to the Law of Competition, 37 Va. L. Rev. 1083, 1088 (1951); Abramovitz, Monopolistic Selling in a Changing Economy, 52 Q.J. Econ. 191, 195 (1938).

[13] Machlup, The Economics of Sellers' Competition, cc. 12-15 (1952); Birch, A Revised Classification of Forms of Competition, 20 Can. J. Econ. & Pol. Sci. 157, 158 (1954); Joseph, Review of Monopolistic Competition and General Equilibrium Theory by Robert Triffin, 52 Econ. J. 356, 357 (1942); Fellner, Competition Among the Few 19, 47, 78 et seq., 86 et seq., 180 et seq. (1949).

firms or of product differentiation and the like.[14]   In addition to such theoretical objections to the older doctrine that oligopoly is substantially identical with monopoly, considerable empirical evidence can be mustered to suggest that oligopoly is not incompatible with active price competition.[15]

Because it has seemed so difficult to find acceptable solutions to problems involving oligopoly situations, the attention of economists has been drawn to the newly developed mathematical "theory of games."   That theory, which has claimed wide adaptability to military, diplomatic, business and other situations, deals with games of strategy where the outcome depends primarily on the behavior of the players, although frequently chance factors also intervene as they do anywhere.[16]   Some economists have thought that the theory offered explanations for the conduct of

[14] Id. at 198-199; Bain, Conditions of Entry and the Emergence of Monopoly, in Chamberlin, ed., Monopoly and Competition and Their Regulation 215, 218-219 (International Economic Assn. 1954); Oxenfeldt, Industrial Pricing and Market Practices 286 (1951); Abramovitz, Monopolistic Selling in a Changing Economy, 52 Q.J. Econ. 191, 196 (1938).   It has been suggested that the behavior of an oligopolist depends a good deal upon the long-run trend of demand.   Kaysen, A Dynamic Aspect of the Monopoly Problem, 31 Rev. Econ. & Stat. 109, 112 (1949). There has also been a re-examination of the distinction between selling costs (advertising) and production costs.   Brems, Product Equilibrium Under Monopolistic Competition 236 (1951); Gordon, Comment, 45 Proceedings Am. Econ. Assn. 483, 486-487 (1955).

[15] Kaplan, Big Enterprise in a Competitive System 102-103 (Brookings Institution, 1954); Four Giants, 2 Fortune No. 3, pp. 85, 102 (1930); Mason, Price and Production Policies of Large-Scale Enterprise, 29 Proceedings Am. Econ. Assn. 61, 71 (1939); Wilcox, Competition and Monopoly in American Industry 48, 51 (TNEC Monograph No. 21, 1940); Nicholls, Price Policies in the Cigarette Industry 78-79, 82, 125 (1951); Markham, Competition in the Rayon Industry 73, 200 (1952); Cassady, Price Making and Price Behavior in the Petroleum Industry 265 (Petroleum Monograph Series No. 1, 1954); Learned, Pricing of Gasoline, 26 Harv. Bus. Rev. No. 6, p. 723 (1948); United States v. United States Steel Corp., 223 Fed. 55, 86 (D.N.J. 1915), aff'd, 231 U.S. 417 (1920); E. B. Muller & Co. v. FTC, 142 F.2d 511, 516 (6th Cir. 1944); U.S. Leather, 11 Fortune No. 2, pp. 56, 100 (1935); Celanese, 8 id. No. 4, pp. 50, 143 (1933); Mr. Ford Doesn't Care, 8 id. No. 6, pp. 62, 122 (1933); Crane Co., Ann. Rep. 1952, 2 (Chicago, 1953); Kilgore Committee, pt. 2, at 543; Roosevelt Committee, pt. III, at 1028, 1039, 1089, 1105, 1107, 1118, 1137 (testimony of filling station operators complaining against oil refiners is to effect that refiners attempted to reduce retail price, engaged in price competition; whereas (far more numerous) retailers were getting together to fix prices); Earley, Marginal Policies of "Excellently Managed" Companies, 46 Am. Econ. Rev. 44, 56 (1956); Senate Select Committee on Small Business, Sixth Ann. Rep., Sen. Rep. No. 1368, 84th Cong., 2d Sess. 6 (1956).   There is, of course, evidence to support the theory that oligopoly has the effect of monopoly.   See note 3 supra.   One interesting suggestion is that in making decisions with respect to prices, businessmen are less influenced by marginal revenue and cost than by changes in the rate of inventory turnover.   Eiteman, Price Determination: Business Practice v. Economic Theory 49 (Bureau of Business Research Report No. 16, University of Michigan, Jan. 1949).

[16] Morgenstern, Oligopoly, Monopolistic Competition and the Theory of Games, 38 Am. Econ. Rev. 10, 12-13 (1948); Marschak, Neumann's and Morgenstern's New Approach to Static Economics, 54 J. Pol. Econ. 97 (1946); Hurwicz, The Theory of Economic Behavior, 35 Am. Econ. Rev. 909 (1945); Nicholls, Price Policies in the Cigarette Industry 190 (1951).

buyers and sellers in markets with few participants. In a nut-shell, the theory suggests:

> The rational player thus does not try to maximize his gain but takes the alternative course of accepting a limitation on the maximum in the form of an "optimum." In declining the "best" possible outcome, he likewise avoids the worst possible outcome. Taking a range of possible high and low gains (or losses), he knows the worst. But to prevent his opponent from finding him out and forcing him to accept the worst, he resorts to chance moves that give him a known probable average outcome. There is no way for his opponent to crack this strategy. For the one who follows it knows where he will come out regardless of what his opponent does.[17]

Another important feature of the theory is that the players in any game involving more than two persons will seek to form coalitions with other players; indeed, the essential thing about such a game is that there is absolutely nothing for a player to do but to look for a partner.[18] Upon the whole, however, economists have not found the "theory of games" an acceptable substitute for more conventional analysis of oligopoly situations. Various errors in its economic application have been pointed out,[19] and there is no record of any court having utilized the theory in an antitrust case. But it offers considerable promise of greater utility after further development.

It now appears to be widely admitted that criteria for the distinction between polypoly and oligopoly cannot be found objectively in numbers but rest in subjective attitudes incapable of precise measurement. Several years ago Professor Galbraith summarized the subject as follows:

> The time has come for a brief word of summary. Quite clearly the last fifteen years have been marked by an active effort to resolve the problems presented by large-scale or monopolistic enterprise and to devise a public policy appropriate to their existence. It is apparent that, although the increment of knowledge has been considerable, both tasks have been attended by considerable frustration. The analytical task would appear to have failed because oligopoly, by all evidence of the ruling market form in the modern economy, has not yielded to the kit of tools long employed for

17 McDonald, Strategy in Poker, Business and War 64-65 (1950). See also id. at 85, 101.

18 Id. at 75; Williams, The Compleat Strategyst (Rand Corp. 1954); Brems, Product Equilibrium Under Monopolistic Competition 183 (1951).

19 E.g., id. at 172-173, 184 et seq., 188. Compare Fellner, Competition Among the Few 15 et seq. (1949); Early, The Growth and Breadth of Theoretical Economics, in Economy Theory in Review 11-22, 20-21 (Early et al., Bloomington, Ind. 1949); Henderson, The Theory of Duopoly, 68 Q.J. Econ. 565, 567 (1954).

analysis of the competitive market. In the competitive market, the inability of the individual to affect the solution makes it possible to eliminate the vagaries of individual behavior from among the market data. It was possible to proceed, therefore, with a relatively simple set of assumptions. It is of the essence of the oligopoly solution that any individual can affect the solution. This analysis, therefore, had to take on a wholly unmanageable burden of assumptions as to how each participant in the market would behave. The whole exercise, as a result, bogged down.[20]

While some economists take a more optimistic view of the problem,[21] we can scarcely say that the case for the illegality of oligopoly is so well established as to provide a firm foundation for recommendations to courts and legislatures.[22]

§3.11. **Elasticity of demand.** One difficulty with the structure theory of horizontal monopoly lies in its failure to take account of the slope of the demand curve for the commodity in question. It is well established that if demand for the commodity is highly elastic, there can be no such thing as the exercise of monopoly power with respect thereto.[1] Elasticity of demand roughly distinguishes "necessities" from "luxuries." A monopolist might well be able to raise the price of salt above free-market levels, whereas a single seller of air-conditioned automobiles would not necessarily be able to do so: a small increase in price might result in a disproportionate loss of volume. The effect of high elasticity of demand is closely connected with the problem of defining the relevant commodity outlined above; actually, high elasticity of demand means simply that consumers prefer to spend their money elsewhere if prices go up.[2]

[20] Galbraith, Monopoly and the Concentration of Economic Power, in Ellis, ed., A Survey of Contemporary Economics 99, 127 (American Economic Assn. 1949). Compare Fellner, Competition Among the Few 179-180, 282-283 (1949).

[21] Bain, Workable Competition in Oligopoly, 40 Proceedings Am. Econ. Assn. 35, 39 (1950); Joseph, Review of Monopolistic Competition and General Equilibrium Theory by Robert Triffin, 52 Econ. J. 356, 359 (1942); Cassady, Price Making and Price Behavior in the Petroleum Industry 340-341 (Petroleum Monograph Series No. 1, 1954).

[22] In recent economic thinking considerable stress is laid upon the distinction between business moves which can be imitated by rivals at once (so as to eliminate the advantages thereof) and those which the initiator may enjoy for a period of time. Atty. Gen. Nat. Com. Rep. 329, (6); Brems, Product Equilibrium Under Monopolistic Competition 235, 244 (1951).

§3.11. [1] Sraffa, The Laws of Returns Under Competitive Conditions, 36 Econ. J. 535, 545 (1926); Knight, The Economic Organization 76 (1951); Chamberlin, Measuring the Degree of Monopoly and Competition in Chamberlin, ed., Monopoly and Competition and Their Regulation 255, 261 (International Economic Assn. 1954); Zimmerman, The Propensity to Monopolize 4, 41 (1952).

[2] Machlup, The Political Economy of Monopoly 487 (1952); Hawkins, Methods of Estimating Demand, 21 J. Marketing 428 (1957).

There is little in the reported decisions to indicate that courts have ever taken cognizance of the effect of elasticity of demand in antitrust cases. The decisions deal with commodities such as steel and cement[3] on the one hand, and motion pictures and tobacco[4] on the other, without ever suggesting that different considerations might apply to them. It is true that elasticity of demand probably cannot be measured with accuracy.[5] At the same time, in any given antitrust proceeding, it probably would be possible for the court to make an informed guess as to how much elasticity existed for the commodity in question.[6]

§3.12. Ease of entry. Under the structure theory courts must also take cognizance of the supply side of the equation. If entry into competition is sufficiently easy, monopoly power cannot be said to exist, no matter how few sellers there may be.[1] Even under "static" economic theory, ease of entry will keep prices at competitive levels because of the factor of self-correction:[2] high profits derived from high prices attract new firms into the field. Thus, even if there is but a single seller of a defined commodity in a specific geographic market, there is no reason for government to control or dissolve it if entry into the field is sufficiently easy. Indeed, it has been said that barriers to entrance into competition may constitute the best measure of market control.[3] There is even empirical evidence supporting that view.[4]

Somewhat surprisingly,[5] we find the courts have frequently taken cognizance of ease of entry as a factor in antitrust cases. Again and again they have held that a situation, apparently monopolistic in character, was not violative of public policy when entry into

---

3 E.g., United States v. United States Steel Corp., 251 U.S. 417 (1920); FTC v. Cement Institute, 333 U.S. 683 (1948).

4 E.g., United States v. Paramount Pictures, Inc., 334 U.S. 131 (1948); United States v. American Tobacco Co., 221 U.S. 106 (1911). But compare Foster v. Shubert Holding Co., 316 Mass. 470, 55 N.E.2d 772, 775 (1944); State v. Craft, 168 N.C. 208, 83 S.E. 772, 773, 775 (1914).

5 See §3.5 *supra*.

6 Compare Cassady, Price Making and Price Behavior in the Petroleum Industry 20-21 (Petroleum Monograph Series No. 1, 1954); TNEC Hearings, pt. 20, at 10,817.

§3.12. 1 Mason, The Current Status of the Monopoly Problem in the United States, 62 Harv. L. Rev. 1265, 1274 (1949); Oxenfeldt, Industrial Pricing and Market Practices 279 (1951). Compare Conant, Consciously Parallel Action in Restraint of Trade, 38 Minn. L. Rev. 797, 799 (1954); Trifffin, Monopolistic Competition and General Equilibrium Theory 136 (1940); Bishop, Elasticities, Cross-Elasticities and Market Relationships, 42 Am. Econ. Rev. 779, 801 (1952).

2 See §2.4 *supra;* Walton, U.S. Gypsum, 34 Barron's No. 8, p. 23 (1954).

3 Keyes, The Shoe Machinery Case and the Problem of the Good Trust, 68 Q.J. Econ. 287, 300 (1954).

4 E.g., 2 Nevins, Study in Power 67, 113 (1953); International Shoe, 7 Fortune No. 3, pp. 71, 73, 86 (1933). Other instances are collected in §2.26 *supra*.

5 Compare §3.11 *supra*.

competition was easy.[6]   In fact, only a few years ago the United States Supreme Court said:

> We agree . . . that potential competition from producers of presently non-competitive articles . . . may be taken into consideration in weighing the effect of any acquisition of assets on restraint of trade.[7]

"Ease of entry" is a shorthand expression condensing many complicated factors. The phrase is usually taken to refer to high capital requirements, patent protection or the ownership of unique resources.[8] It will be seen, however, that those three factors may well be but one.[9] All are closely related to the concept of indivisibility.[10] Sometimes it is said that entry is sufficiently easy when the long-run average cost curve for a new firm is not materially higher than for an established firm.[11] That statement, however, may fail to take account of investor information or ignorance[12] (as the case may be) and does not tell us much about the

---

6 United States v. Quaker Oats Co., 232 Fed. 499, 503 (N.D. Ill. 1916); United States v. American Can Co., 230 Fed. 859, 900, 234 Fed. 1019, 1021 (D. Md. 1916), *appeal dismissed*, 256 U.S. 706 (1921); Commonwealth v. North Shore Ice Co., 220 Mass. 55, 107 N.E. 402, 403 (1914); Harding v. American Glucose Co., 182 Ill. 551, 55 N.E. 577 (1899); Oakdale Manufacturing Co. v. Garst, 18 R.I. 484, 28 Atl. 973, 974 (1894); Moody & Waters Co. v. Case-Moody Pie Corp., 354 Ill. 82, 89, 187 N.E. 813 (1933); Morehead City Seafood Co. v. Way, 169 N.C. 679, 86 S.E. 603 (1915); American Crystal Sugar Co. v. Cuban-American Co., 152 F. Supp. 387, 400 (S.D.N.Y. 1957).

7 United States v. Columbia Steel Co., 334 U.S. 495, 528 (1948). To the same effect see United States v. Aluminum Co. of America, 44 F. Supp. 97, 146 (S.D.N.Y. 1941), *rev'd*, 148 F.2d 416 (2d Cir. 1945); United States v. General Electric Co., 82 F. Supp. 753, 893 (D.N.J. 1949). Compare United States v. New England Fish Exchange, 258 Fed. 732, 751 (D. Mass. 1919).

8 United States v. Aluminum Co. of America, 91 F. Supp. 333, 400-401 (S.D.N.Y. 1950); FTC, Monopolistic Practices and Small Businesses, Report to the Subcommittee on Monopoly, Senate Select Committee on Small Business 85 (Feb. 21, 1952); Bain, Economies of Scale, Concentration and the Condition of Entry in Twenty Manufacturing Industries, 44 Am. Econ. Rev. 15, 16 (1954).

9 The suggestion is that patent protection or unique resources are always available at some price; hence that capital requirements constitute the core of the entry problem.

10 Machlup, The Economics of Sellers' Competition 232-233 (1952).

11 Bowman, Toward Less Monopoly, 101 U. Pa. L. Rev. 577, 635 (1953). Compare Bain, Economies of Scale, Concentration and the Condition of Entry in Twenty Manufacturing Industries, 44 Am. Econ. Rev. 15, 16 (1954); Hennipman, Monopoly: Impediment or Stimulus to Economic Progress, in Chamberlin, ed., Monopoly and Competition and Their Regulation 421, 438 (International Economic Assn. 1954). It has been suggested that entry may be easier when existing firms in the same industry are engaged in rapid expansion, and particularly, when they are increasing the number of plants. Howrey, Economic Evidence in Antitrust Cases, 19 J. Marketing 119, 123 (1954). Both theory and empirical evidence are reviewed in Bain, Barriers to New Competition, c. 3 (1956).

12 Capital requirements, no matter how large, can be met if investors are adequately informed. Absent requisite information, the level of the average cost curve in the long run may not be a sufficient index of ease of entry. In this connection

important factor of time.[13] Indeed, it has been suggested that the measurement of ease of entry into an industry may be even more difficult than the measurement of prices and costs within a single firm.[14] In view of its obvious importance under the structure theory, however, the courts cannot disregard ease of entry and it seems likely that they can make an informed guess on that subject in any given antitrust case.

§3.13.   **Indivisibility.**   Those market imperfections which render it disadvantageous to split an antitrust defendant into multiple firms pass under the heading of "indivisibility."   They encompass primarily economies of scale, derived, of course, largely from specialization of labor.   They are related to the fact of space, reflecting locations containing unique resources or advantages.[1] Important also is the concept of sharing risks: partnerships, corporations and other forms of business enterprise exist largely to permit a group to undertake ventures which one would not dare carry on alone.[2] Indivisibility, the necessity for large-scale operations in order to achieve efficiency, is closely related to ease of entry but the two concepts are not identical.[3] Indivisibility wears many guises; in production, financing and distribution of goods and services its effects are manifold and frequently not easy to identify.[4]

Economists have long recognized that indivisibility constitutes

---

note that potential investors are not all inventors starving in lonely garrets. General Motors Corporation found it desirable to enter the field of building railway locomotives and the results of its venture indicated that it had ample capital and technology to achieve success. Such considerations lead to questions of diversification. See Chapter 6. Compare Atty. Gen. Nat. Com. Rep. 48, (3). Note the acute study of Hines, Effectiveness of "Entry" by Already Established Firms, 71 Q.J. Econ. 132 (1957).

[13] Stigler, Monopoly and Oligopoly by Merger, 40 Proceedings Am. Econ. Assn. 23, 25 (1950). Compare United States v. Corn Products Refining Co., 234 Fed. 964, 1012 (S.D.N.Y. 1916).

[14] Machlup, The Political Economy of Monopoly 527 (1952); United Shoe Machinery, 8 Fortune No. 3, p. 34 (1933). It is possible that a degree of monopoly power at one level in the economy may make entry easier at another. Thus shoe manufacturers have sometimes complained that the nondiscriminatory leasing policy of United Shoe Machinery Company made entry into shoemaking too easy.

§3.13. [1] Stigler, The Division of Labor Is Limited by the Extent of the Market, 59 J. Pol. Econ. 185, 188 (1951); Hower, History of Macy's of New York 149 (1943).

[2] United States v. Morgan, 118 F. Supp. 621, 682 et seq. (S.D.N.Y. 1953); Knight, Risk, Uncertainty and Profits (1921); Gordon, Short Period Price Determination, 38 Am. Econ. Rev. 265, 270 (1948). The very existence of the corporation as a legal entity reflects in large measure factors of indivisibility. Compare Chapter 8.

[3] Indivisibility may, as set forth above (§3.12) make entry more difficult. It need not do so, however, if the market is free of "frictions"; that is, if investors are fully informed.

[4] Indivisibility may, for example, play a role in the legality of restrictive covenants not to compete ancillary to the conveyance of a going business. 2 Restatement of Contracts §516(a).

an obstacle to the enforcement of antitrust policy under the structure theory. If economies of scale are involved, it may simply prove too costly to break up the defendant in order to achieve that number of sellers in the market place demanded by the structure theory.[5] Indeed, there is reason to believe that dissolution of the existing firms in such circumstances would prove but a temporary measure and that eventually the greater efficiency of the larger firms would drive the smaller ones from the field again.[6]

Legislatures and courts have likewise recognized indivisibility as an important factor in the monopoly problem. The distinction between Sections 1 and 2 of the Sherman Act,[7] for example, is based largely upon an understanding that different rules must apply when economies of scale can be achieved in a single enterprise. The fact that the federal antitrust law accepts state-created corporations as single persons constitutes a further recognition of indivisibility.[8] Even more fundamentally, the concept of a public utility enjoying a "natural" monopoly and subject to regulation by the state, reflects a belief that competition is impossible when economies of scale are important.[9] Similarly, in many antitrust cases, the courts have taken account of the factor of

[5] Clark, The Conditions of Economic Progress ix (1951); Clark, Monopolistic Tendencies, Their Character and Consequences, 18 Proceedings Acad. Pol. Sci. 124, 130 (1939); Bowman, Toward Less Monopoly, 101 U. Pa. L. Rev. 577, 641 (1953); Robinson, The Impossibility of Competition, in Chamberlin, ed., Monopoly and Competition and Their Regulation 245, 246, 248 (International Economic Assn. 1954); Robinson, Imperfect Competition Revisited, 63 Econ. J. 579, 592 (1953); Kales, Contracts and Combinations in Restraint of Trade §59 (1918). Compare Triffin, Monopolistic Competition and General Equilibrium Theory 136 (1940); Schneider, Real Economies of Integration, in Chamberlin, ed., Monopoly and Competition and Their Regulation 203, 205 (International Economic Assn. 1954).

[6] As indicated in the text, indivisibility is closely related to the question of appropriate remedies under the antitrust laws. See §10.4 infra. It may also be related to the problem of diversification (Chapter 6). Compare Cassady, Price Making and Price Behavior in the Petroleum Industry 43 (Petroleum Monograph Series No. 1, 1954); Hammer, Bottle of Pop, 36 Barron's No. 36, pp. 11, 13 (1956). Vertical integration may also be involved. E.g., Stigler, The Division of Labor Is Limited by the Extent of the Market, 59 J. Pol. Econ. 185, 192 (1951). Compare Chapter 5.

[7] See §3.9 supra.

[8] Thus it has been said: ". . . it does not follow that every combination in trade, even though such a combination may have the effect to diminish the number of competitors in business, is therefore illegal. Such a rule would produce greater public injury than that which it would seek to cure. It would be impracticable. It would forbid partnerships and sales by those engaged in a common business. It would cut off consolidations to secure the advantages of united capital and economy of administration. . . ." Oakdale Manufacturing Co. v. Garst, 18 R.I. 484, 28 Atl. 973, 974 (1894).

[9] E.g., Interocean Publishing Co. v. Associated Press, 184 Ill. 438, 449, 56 N.E. 822 (1900).

indivisibility both in adjudicating violation of the statutes[10] and in devising remedies thereunder.[11]   In only a handful of ill-considered cases have the courts refused to do so.[12]

Some observers minimize the role of indivisibility in the enforcement of the antitrust laws. They find that many firms are above optimal size: too large to be efficient.[13] Studies of consolidations in various periods have been said to support such views,[14] and additional empirical evidence has been adduced to the same effect.[15] A recent investigation conducted by Professor Bain, for

[10] United States v. E. I. Du Pont de Nemours & Co., 118 F. Supp. 41, (D. Del. 1953), aff'd, 351 U.S. 377, 386 (1956) (considerable size often essential for efficient operation in research, manufacture and distribution); United States v. Addyston Pipe Co., 85 Fed. 271, 280, 287 (6th Cir. 1898), aff'd, 175 U.S. 211 (1899); United States v. American Can Co., 230 Fed. 859, 883 (D. Md. 1916), appeal dismissed, 256 U.S. 706 (1921); United States v. United Shoe Machinery Co., 247 U.S. 32, 47 (1918); United States v. United States Steel Corp., 223 Fed. 55, 114, 117, 132 (D.N.J. 1915), aff'd, 251 U.S. 417, 443 (1920); Indiana Farmer's Guide Co. v. Prairie Farmer Co., 88 F.2d 979, 983 (7th Cir. 1937); cert. denied, 301 U.S. 696 (1937); United States v. Pullman Co., 50 F. Supp. 123, 131 (E.D. Pa. 1943), aff'd per curiam, 330 U.S. 806 (1947); Times-Picayune Publishing Co. v. United States, 345 U.S. 594, 623 (1953); United States v. Morgan, 118 F. Supp. 621, 623, 637, 640 (S.D.N.Y. 1953); Commonwealth v. North Shore Ice Co., 220 Mass. 55, 107 N.E. 402, 403 (1914). See Holmes, J., dissenting in Northern Securities Co. v. United States, 193 U.S. 197, 407-408 (1904).

[11] United States v. National Lead Co., 332 U.S. 319, 353 (1947); United States v. Aluminum Co. of America, 91 F. Supp. 333, 416 et seq. (S.D.N.Y. 1950). Compare United States v. Terminal Railroad Assn., 224 U.S. 383 (1912).

[12] Chicago Gas Light & Coke Co. v. Peoples Gas Co., 121 Ill. 530, 544, 13 N.E. 169 (1887); People ex rel. Peabody v. Chicago Gas Trust Co., 130 Ill. 268, 292, 293, 22 N.E. 798 (1889); United States v. New York Great Atlantic & Pacific Tea Co., 173 F.2d 79, 87 (7th Cir. 1949). Note also the railroad cases. E.g., United States v. Trans-Missouri Freight Assn., 166 U.S. 290 (1897), discussed in Hale and Hale, Monopoly and Mobilization, 47 Nw. U.L. Rev. 606, 642-643 (1952). Compare Gamco, Inc. v. Providence Fruit & Produce Building, Inc., 194 F.2d 484, 487 (1st Cir. 1952), cert. denied, 344 U.S. 817 (1952). In Kansas City Star Co. v. United States, 240 F.2d 643, 661 (8th Cir. 1957), it was held proper to exclude testimony offered with respect to the reasons for the failure of the defendant's rival. Since these reasons may well have reflected indivisibility, the decision is dubious.

[13] Wilcox, Competition and Monopoly in American Industry 310, 314 (TNEC Monograph No. 21, 1940); Edwards, Geographic Price Formulas and the Concentration of Economic Power, 37 Geo. L.J. 135, 137 (1949); Bain, Conditions of Entry and the Emergence of Monopoly, in Chamberlin, ed., Monopoly and Competition and Their Regulation 215, 238 (International Economic Assn. 1954); Schneider, Real Economies of Integration and Large-Scale Production, id. at 203, 210; Burns, The Decline of Competition 9 (1936); Kales, Contracts and Combinations in Restraint of Trade §75n (1918); Celler Committee I, pt. 1, at 394; pt. 2A, at 162; Glover, The Attack on Big Business 19-29 (1954).

[14] National Industrial Conference Board, Mergers in Industry 40-41, 170-171 (1929); Bernheim, ed., How Profitable Is Big Business? 112 et seq. (Twentieth Century Fund, 1937); Faulkner, The Decline of Laissez Faire 169 (1951); Cross, From Land, Sea and Test Tube 14-15, 39 (Archer-Daniels-Midland Co. 1954); U.S. Leather, 11 Fortune No. 2, pp. 56, 98 (1935).

[15] Fellner, Competition Among the Few 297 (1949); Lewis, Monopoly and the Law, 6 Mod. L. Rev. 97, 103 (1943); Blair, Technology and Size, 38 Proceedings Am. Econ. Assn. 121, 126, 141, 150 (1949); Prittie, Farben's Offspring, 35 Baron's No. 26,

example, lends support to the view that industrial efficiency does not generally require firms larger than the structure theory of monopoly would indicate.[16] Other students have attributed considerable importance to economies of scale, finding that in several industries the structural ideal of many sellers could not be realized without serious loss of productivity.[17] Considerable empirical evidence can also be cited to support that view.[18] The housing

---

pp. 9, 20 (1955); Celler Committee I, pt. 2A, at 243, 288, 366; United States v. Aluminum Co. of America, 44 F. Supp. 97, 254 (S.D.N.Y. 1941), rev'd, 148 F.2d 416 (2d Cir. 1945); Cochran, History of the Pabst Brewing Company 98 (1948); U.S. Steel, 13 Fortune No. 3, pp. 59, 169 (1936). National Biscuit Company distributes its crackers directly to retailers because the crackers are perishable. The company tried tacking dog food and other products onto that distribution system but later abandoned the project because it proved too costly. It now distributes dog food and cereals through wholesalers. Higbee, National Biscuit, 35 Barron's No. 14, pp. 23, 24 (1955). A recent annual report lists three lines of business which had been sold: a distillery in Panama, a winery in California and a well-known soda-water-producing business. National Distillers' Products Corp., 29th Ann. Rep. 10-11 (New York City, 1953). Apparently those side lines were not "indivisible." Some large corporations find that it is necessary to simulate smallness in order to induce a favorable attitude upon the part of employees. Such simulation is accomplished through elaborate bonus plans and the like, sometimes payable in stock of the employer. E.g., General Motors Corp., 44th Ann. Rep. 49 (New York City, 1953).

[16] Bain, Economies of Scale, Concentration, and the Condition of Entry in Twenty Manufacturing Industries, 44 Am. Econ. Rev. 15, 25, 28 (1954). Professor Bain's calculations may be open to objection on methodological grounds. They may, for example, fail to define the commodity studied with sufficient precision. See §3.5 supra. On April 26, 1954, Professor George J. Stigler of Columbia University delivered a public lecture at the University of Chicago, in which he reported empirical studies with respect to economies of scale in the steel industry. He found a wide range of sizes through which private costs were roughly identical.

[17] Harbeson, A New Phase of the Antitrust Law, 45 Mich. L. Rev. 977, 990 (1947); Edwards, Maintaining Competition 112 (1949); Burns, The Decline of Competition 8-9 (1936); Steindl, Small and Big Business 11 (Oxford Institute of Statistics Monograph No. 1, 1945); Osborn, Efficiency and Profitability in Relation to Size, 29 Harv. Bus. Rev. No. 2, pp. 82, 92 (1951); Mason, Price and Production Policies of Large-Scale Enterprise, 29 Proceedings Am. Econ. Assn. 61, 62-63 (1939); Clark, The Orientation of Antitrust Policy, 40 id. at 93, 96 (1950); National Industrial Conference Board, Mergers in Industry 171-172 (1929); McLean and Haigh, How Business Corporations Grow, 32 Harv. Bus. Rev. No. 6, pp. 81 et seq., 90-92 (1954). In six of the twenty industries studied by Professor Bain he found that optimal size plants would supply 10 to 25 per cent of the market. Bain, Economies of Scale, Concentration, and the Condition of Entry in Twenty Manufacturing Industries, 44 Am. Econ. Rev. 15, 28 (1954). Compare Goetz-Girey, Monopoly and Competition in France, in Chamberlin, ed., Monopoly and Competition and Their Regulation 21-29 (International Economic Assn. 1954); Easterbrook, State Control and Free Enterprise in Their Impact on Economic Growth, in The Progress of Underdeveloped Areas 60, 66-67 (Hoselitz ed. 1952). In Chorak v. R.K.O. Radio Pictures, Inc., 196 F. 2d 225, 228 (9th Cir. 1952), cert. denied, 344 U.S. 887, 910 (1952), it was said that motion picture producers could not simultaneously release prints to all exhibitors; hence some degree of "clearance" was inevitable.

[18] Hower, History of Macy's of New York 228 (1943); Markham, Competition in the Rayon Industry 20-21, 42 et seq., 101 (1952); Mintz, Auto Independents, 35 Barron's No. 16, p. 11 (1955); 2 Nevins, Study in Power 73 (1953); Adelman, Dirlam and Kahn on the A & P Case, 61 J. Pol. Econ. 436, 440 (1953).

industry is pointed to as one in which the scale of operations has been below levels called for by efficiency,[19] and some interesting illustrations of large firms going into joint ventures with their rivals suggest that even our biggest corporations find it advisable to share risks with others when developing new sources of raw materials or transportation facilities connected therewith.[20] The ability of small firms to carry on technological research has been questioned,[21] and there is evidence to suggest that the size of industrial plants has been on the increase in recent decades.[22] Size of plant is, of course, wholly different from size of firm and there have been suggestions to the effect that plant size alone should be considered.[23] On the other hand, some observers find economies in multiplant enterprises[24] and Professor Wright has referred to the "single plant" argument with respect to efficiency as "narrowly static." [25] Many empirical studies have attempted

[19] Hale, Housing, 39 Ky. L.J. 255, 422 (1951); Bain, Advantages of the Large Firm, 20 J. Marketing 336, 340 (1956) (apparently some economies of scale in distribution when product differentiated).

[20] United States Steel Corp., 52nd Ann. Rep. 8 (New York City, 1954); Republic Steel Corp., Ann. Rep. 1953, 8 (Cleveland, 1954); Armco Steel Corp., 53rd Ann. Rep. 18-19 (Middletown, 1954); Link-Belt Co., Ann. Rep. 1953, 3 (Chicago, 1954); Scott Paper Co., Ann. Rep. 1952, 16 (Chester, 1953); Tidewater Associated Oil Co., Ann. Rep. 1948, 8 (New York City, 1949); Ohio Oil Co., 66th Ann. Rep. 13 (Findlay, 1954), Ann. Rep. 1952, 12, 14 (1953); Texas Co. Ann. Rep. 1953, 23, 25 (New York City, 1954); Sinclair Oil Corp., Ann. Rep. 1952, 8 (New York City, 1953); Phillips Petroleum Co., Ann. Rep. 1949, 12 (Bartlesville, 1950); Thompson, Since Spindletop 50 (Gulf Oil Corp. 1951); Gulf Oil Corp., Ann. Rep. 1953, 13, 19 (Pittsburgh, 1954); Answer of Texas Company ¶¶10, 11, 12, 22, 23, United States v. Standard Oil Co., No. 86-27, S.D.N.Y. (1953).

[21] See Appendix B. Compare Celler Committee I, pt. 4A, at 230.

[22] Thorp and Crowder, The Structure of Industry 3-4, 24 (TNEC Monograph No. 27, 1941); United States Steel Corp., Business . . . Big and Small . . . Built America 59 (1950).

[23] Edwards, Maintaining Competition 110, 114, 120 (1949); Blair, Does Large-Scale Enterprise Result in Lower Costs? 38 Proceedings Am. Econ. Assn. 121, 145 et seq. (1948); Bowman, Toward Less Monopoly, 101 U. Pa. L. Rev. 577, 611 (1953); Bain, Economies of Scale, Concentration and the Conditions of Entry in Twenty Manufacturing Industries, 44 Am. Econ. Rev. 15, 29, 32, 38 (1954). Compare Machlup, The Political Economy of Monopoly 52 (1952).

[24] Markham, Competition in the Rayon Industry 316 (1952); Steindl, Small and Big Business 14 (Oxford Institute of Statistics Monograph No. 1, 1945). Many factors affect economies of scale; e.g., the cost of flotation of securities may be excessive in single plant firms. It is said, for example, that as a practical matter it is impossible to raise less than $5 million in capital markets. House Select Committee on Small Business, Review of Small Business, H.R. Rep. No. 2513, 82d Cong., 2d Sess. 61 (1952). Another example: a pharmaceutical manufacturer publishes several technical books and journals for the medical profession. Among the books one is in an eighth edition and has run through 234,000 copies; another is a comprehensive reference work on chemicals and drugs, of which 60,000 copies were sold in the sixth edition alone. Merck & Co., Inc., Report to Stockholders 14 (Feb. 26, 1953). Query whether a single plant firm could hope to engage in such activities (and query whether such activities are desirable).

[25] Wright, Toward Coherent Anti-Trust, 35 Va. L. Rev. 665, 684 (1949). Presumably, Professor Wright had in mind the fact that at any given time a specific

to relate profitability and size.   Other investigations have focused upon costs.[26]   Unfortunately, most of the published works are open to serious objections upon technical grounds.[27]   So difficult are the statistical problems involved that Professor Stigler concluded that the only way to determine the optimal size of a firm is to ascertain whether concerns of various sizes are able to survive in the industry.[28]   Even the test of survivorship, however, may be open to the objection that it takes no account of dynamic factors[29] and, still more, is indifferent to the existence of "umbrella-holding" or other impurities in the market place.[30]   Accordingly, most

---

plant may be either larger or smaller than efficiency requires.   But compare Bain, Advantages of the Large Firm, 20 J. Marketing 336-337, 339 (1956).   Many plants erected in the last century, for example, while still in use, might be considered inefficient in scale at the present time.   To determine economies of scale by size of existing plants, therefore, would be a dubious procedure.

[26] FTC, Bakery Combines and Profits (1927); FTC, Competition and Profits in Bread and Flour (1928); FTC, Copper (1919); FTC, War-Time Profits and Costs of the Steel Industry (1925); FTC, War-Time Costs and Profits of Southern Pine Lumber Companies (1922); Epstein, Industrial Profits in United States (1934); Crum, Corporate Size and Earning Power (1939).

[27] Dean, Statistical Determination of Costs, 7 University of Chicago Studies in Business Administration, c. 3 (1936); Stigler, The Extent and Bases of Monopoly, 32 Am. Econ. Rev., Supp. No. 2, pp. 1, 9 et seq. (1942); Blair, The Relation Between Size and Efficiency in Business, 24 Rev. Econ. Stat. 125, 135 (1942); Kaplan, Small Business: Its Place and Problems 78-79, 87, 100-101 (Committee for Economic Development 1948); Wilcox, Competition and Monopoly in American Industry 311 (TNEC Monograph No. 21, 1940); Edwards, Maintaining Competition 108-109, 119n (1949); Wallace, Industrial Markets and Public Policy, in Public Policy 59, 102-103 (Friedrich and Mason ed. 1940); Osborn, Efficiency and Profitability in Relation to Size, 29 Harv. Bus. Rev. No. 2, pp. 82, 92 (1951); Bain, Economies of Scale, Concentration and the Condition of Entry in Twenty Manufacturing Industries, 44 Am. Econ. Rev. 15, 35, 38 (1954); Buchanan, The Economics of Corporate Enterprise 303 (1940).   Compare Rostow, A Reply, 57 J. Pol. Econ. 60, 65-66 (1949).   Compare §2.2 *supra*.   Additional empirical studies are referred to in the critical articles just cited.

[28] Stigler, Monopoly and Oligopoly by Merger, 40 Proceedings Am. Econ. Assn. 23, 26 (1950); Schneider, Real Economies of Integration and Large-Scale Production, in Chamberlin, ed., Monopoly and Competition and Their Regulation 203, 213 (International Economic Assn. 1954); Faulkner, The Decline of Laissez Faire 156 (1951); Smith, Survey of the Empirical Evidence on Economies of Scale, in Business Concentration and Price Policy 213 (Stigler ed. 1955).

[29] Clark, Competition: Static Models and Dynamic Aspects, 45 Proceedings Am. Econ. Assn. 450, 458 (1955); FTC, Monopolistic Practices and Small Business, Report to the Subcommittee on Monopoly, Senate Select Committee on Small Business 15 (Feb. 21, 1952).

[30] Buchanan, The Economics of Corporate Enterprise 303 (1940); Bain, Advantages of the Large Firm, 20 J. Marketing 336, 341 (1956).   Studies of "survivorship" depend ultimately upon the theory of self-correction of the market set forth in §2.4 *supra*.   The notion is that unless the firms are of approximately optimal size, the self-correcting factors in the market will eliminate them.   The difficulty is, however, that it does not take account of factors other than indivisibility.   Recently, for example, there has been a sharp increase in the number of sulphur producers in North America: the two existing domestic producers were joined by two more, and three new producers entered the market from Mexico.   On the other hand, the number of household washing-machine manufacturers has been de-

observers conclude that the available information about the cost of enterprises of different sizes is too scattered and its comparability too uncertain to justify conclusions about relative efficiency.[31] Of course, it does not require statistical genius to note the factor of indivisibility in some simple situations: one cannot have less than one single railroad track between X and Y, and the economies to be gained by its full utilization are reasonably obvious.

In antitrust litigation, the existence of indivisibiity may be either difficult or easy to prove. Even if the court feels reasonably certain that indivisibility prevents full application of the structure theory of monopoly, it must still decide whether the higher efficiency thus attained is worth its cost to society in terms of the existence of monopoly power.[32] Most courts have been reluctant to break up enterprises when such dissolution would reduce efficiency.[33] The Attorney General's Committee took the position that firm size could be justified even if sellers were few in the presence of indivisibility.[34] The inevitable corollary of public utility type regulation,[35] however, gives one pause:[36] po-

---

creasing rapidly. In six years, the ten largest firms increased their hold on the market from 60 to 80 per cent. Durrance, Spark in Brimstone, 35 Barron's No. 10, p. 3 (1955); Loehwing, Through the Wringer, 35 id. No. 28, p. 5 (1955). LaTourette, Shake-out in Appliances, 36 Barron's No. 27, p. 11 (1956); Gavin, End of the Drought? 36 Barron's No. 16, pp. 11, 12 (1956). We do not know to what extent factors of indivisibility have caused such changes.

[31] Chamberlin, Proportionality, Divisibility and Economies of Scale, 62 Q.J. Econ. 229, 257 (1948); Adelman, Effective Competition and the Antitrust Law, 61 Harv. L. Rev. 1289, 1291-1292 (1948); Bain, Advantages of the Large Firm, 20 J. Marketing 336, 337 (1956). The matter is considerably more complicated than a mere test of engineering design. In consumer durable goods, for example, it may be necessary to create a whole chain of dealers with service facilities before distribution can be effected successfully. Again, first-rate managerial talent may be so scarce as to affect the optimal size of the firm. Machlup, The Political Economy of Monopoly 125 (1952); Mason, Schumpeter on Monopoly and the Large Firm, in Schumpeter, Social Scientist 89, 92 (Harris ed. 1951). But compare Bain, Relation of Profit Rate to Industry Concentration, 65 Q.J. Econ. 293 (1951).

[32] Fellner, Competition Among the Few 292 (1949); Patinkin, Multiple-Plant Firms, Cartels, and Imperfect Competition, 61 Q.J. Econ. 173, 184 (1947). Compare Robinson, The Impossibility of Competition in Chamberlin, ed., Monopoly and Competition and Their Regulation 245, 254 (International Economic Assn. 1954).

[33] See note 11 *supra*.

[34] Atty. Gen. Nat. Com. Rep. 56, (5).

[35] United States v. Associated Press, 326 U.S. 1 (1945).

[36] In United States v. Associated Press, 52 F. Supp. 362 (S.D.N.Y. 1943), *aff'd*, 326 U.S. 1 (1945), Judge Swan wrote a dissenting opinion. He said at page 377: "In the case of a business which was not recognized as a public calling at common law, I believe it is sound policy to leave to the legislature to determine whether the public welfare requires that all applicants be served without discrimination. This is particularly true where the duty to serve all comers does not depend upon the mere nature of the occupation, but upon the fact that a particular business has reached such a state of size and efficiency as to give the persons whom it serves some competitive advantage over applicants whom it declines to serve . . . ."

litical forces will insist upon such intervention if market power is permitted to exist.

§3.14. **Other imperfections.** When lawyers speak of "practical" considerations preventing full application of the structure theory of monopoly, they often refer to indivisibility and other market imperfections.[1] Those other imperfections, embracing immobility, ignorance and inertia, have seldom been recognized in antitrust cases.[2] It is not easy to visualize situations in which they would directly be involved in an action founded upon Section 2 of the Sherman Act. Those imperfections might, however, play a role in Section 2 proceedings seeking to break up a chain store or some other mass merchandiser. In many instances, the large-volume merchant performs considerable services for consumers which help them overcome their ignorance of the quality of commodities offered in the market.[3] In essence, this is the alternative afforded consumers to buy "private brand" merchandise, often at substantial discounts from prices of the same goods bearing the manufacturer's trade-mark.[4] Ignorance upon the part of investors may also play a significant role, particularly in connection with the problem of ease of entry. If capital requirements are high, entry may nevertheless be easy, provided investors have full information as to the opportunities for profit involved.[5] It follows that if entry is difficult because investors lack such information,

---

§3.14. [1] See Appendix A. Compare Sraffa, The Laws of Returns Under Competitive Conditions, 36 Econ. J. 535, 542 (1926).

[2] Compare Gamco, Inc. v. Providence Fruit & Produce Building, Inc., 194 F.2d 484, 487 (1st Cir. 1952), cert. denied, 344 U.S. 817 (1952); Bender v. Hearst Corp., 152 F. Supp. 569, 577-578 (D. Conn. 1957).

[3] See Appendix A, pages 430-431; J. C. Penney Co., Ann. Rep. 1953, 3, 8 (New York City, 1954). Compare Stigler, The Division of Labor Is Limited by the Extent of the Market, 59 J. Pol. Econ. 185, 187 (1951); TNEC Hearings, pt. 19, at 10,570, 10,752, 10,754, 10,674. Note the multitude of imperfections affecting a decision to license a patent rather than develop the product for sole exploitation by the patentee. Wayne Pump, 16 Fortune No. 2, pp. 79, 120 (1937).

[4] Dirlam and Kahn, Antitrust Law and the Big Buyer, 60 J. Pol. Econ. 118, 128 (1952).

[5] Lombardini, Monopoly and Rigidities in the Economic System, in Chamberlin, ed., Monopoly and Competition and Their Regulation 398, 415 (International Economic Assn., 1954); Wallace, Market Control in the Aluminum Industry 29 (1937). Compare American Bank Note, 7 Fortune No. 5, pp. 44, 113 (1933). See §3.12 supra. An economist wrote recently: "It is not too much to say that without the invention and public acceptance of the limited liability share and the development of efficient securities exchanges, the extensive financing of large-scale firms and, therefore, the effective use of modern technology, would have proven impossible." Abramovitz, Economics of Growth, in 2 Haley, ed., Survey of Contemporary Economics 132, 165 (American Economic Assn. 1952). Note also the role of time lags. We rely upon entry into competition to eliminate monopoly; if there are "frictions" impeding such entry, considerable time lags must be expected. Machlup, The Economics of Sellers' Competition 220 (1952).

the remedy may lie in education of the investors rather than in enforcement of the antitrust laws.[6]

§3.15. Dynamic considerations: Innovators and survivors. Unfortunately, the structure test for monopoly is founded in static doctrines; it takes little account of dynamic forces in the market place and tends to overlook growth and change.[1] A good illustration is found in decisions involving "corners" in organized markets. Those decisions relate to the defendant's share of a specific commodity at a given moment in time. No account is taken of additional supplies which could reach the market — even within a matter of hours.[2] As Professor Wright has pointed out, the factor of time should enter into the adjudication of monopoly just as do the definitions of geographic markets and commodities.[3] The innovator who produces new goods or utilizes new methods of production should not be penalized as a monopolist,

---

[6] We have been warned: "We must be careful, however, as to just how much we dismiss as 'friction' and what conclusions of policy we draw from it. 'Friction' can include almost anything — for example, the fact that we live in a particular space-time system and cannot all be at the same place at once. What is needed is a distinction — never very precise — between friction and removable friction. While price flexibility, better knowledge, better organization of the market and the like could conceivably make possible the absorption of a larger flow of current investment, the writer does not believe that any market economy within the realm of possibility could ever be so smoothly organized as to be capable of absorbing any rate of saving-investment which could be thrown into it." Wright, The Economics of Disturbance 53 (1946). See also United States v. Morgan, 118 F. Supp. 621, 793 (S.D.N.Y. 1953) (reluctance of investment banker to solicit business of an issuer when some rival is a member of the board of directors, etc., probably is related to prestige, and solicitation of unsuccessful type might cost prestige and that is part of the commodity the banker has to offer).

§3.15. [1] Mason, Schumpeter on Monopoly and the Large Firm, in Schumpeter, Social Scientist 89, 94 (Harris ed. 1951); Hennipman, Monopoly: Impediment or Stimulus to Economic Progress, in Chamberlin, ed., Monopoly and Competition and Their Regulation 421, 456 (International Economic Assn. 1954); see also Appendix B *infra*.

[2] Wright v. Cudahy, 168 Ill. 86, 91-92, 48 N.E. 39 (1897); Peto v. Howell, 101 F.2d 353, 361 (7th Cir. 1939); United States v. Corn Products Refining Co., 234 Fed. 964, 1012 (S.D.N.Y. 1916). But compare United States v. E. I. Du Pont de Nemours & Co., 118 F. Supp. 41 (D. Del. 1953), aff'd, 351 U.S. 377, 418 et seq. (1956). Perhaps the cases cited really stand for the proposition that no interference with the operation of an organized exchange can be tolerated; in other words, they relate to "imperfections" rather than to "impurities." In other decisions, the courts have been willing to take account of the passage of time. They have noted, for example, that over a period of years competitors have enlarged their share of relevant markets. United States v. United States Steel Corp., 223 Fed. 55, 67 (D.N.J. 1915), aff'd, 251 U.S. 417 (1920); United States v. International Harvester Co., 274 U.S. 693, 709 (1927); United States v. Aluminum Co. of America, 91 F. Supp. 333, 355 (S.D.N.Y. 1950).

[3] Wright, Capitalism 178 (1951); Business Concentration and Price Policy 5-6, 92 (Stigler ed. 1955).

even though others have as yet failed to catch up with him.[4]   It is true that the innovator will continue to have an advantage over his rivals for a considerable period of time.[5]   Trade-mark identification may extend that period.[6]   Such an advantage, however, should not be regarded as an infringement of the antitrust laws.[7]

For the most part, the courts have enunciated views consistent with dynamic doctrine.   They have usually refused to penalize an innovator.   Once the Supreme Court of the United States said:

> . . . certainly improvement of business and its efficiency can be striven for without offense to the law.[8]

In a comparatively recent decision, it was stated:

> The present cases are not comparable to cases where the parties, for example, merely have made a new discovery or an original entry into a field and unexpectedly or unavoidably have found themselves enjoying a monopoly coupled with power and intent to maintain it.[9]

And not long ago a district court found occasion to declare:

---

[4] Schumpeter, Capitalism, Socialism and Democracy 102 (3d ed. 1950); Nourse and Drury, Industrial Price Policies and Economic Progress 270 (Brookings Institution, 1938); Maclaurin, The Process of Technological Innovation, 40 Am. Econ. Rev. 90, 92 (1950); Handler, Monopolies, Mergers and Markets 4 (Fed. Bar Assn., Nov. 9, 1954); Hicks, Value and Capital 124 (1939).   But compare Kreps and Wright, Measurement of the Social Performance of Business 35 (TNEC Monograph No. 7, 1940); Allen, Monopoly and Competition in the United Kingdom, in Chamberlin, ed., Monopoly and Competition and Their Regulation 88, 102 (International Economic Assn. 1954).

[5] There is, in other words, a normal time lag favoring the innovator.   United States v. Aluminum Co. of America, 91 F. Supp. 333, 379-380 (S.D.N.Y. 1950); Chase, Danger at the A. O. Smith Corporation, 2 Fortune No. 5, pp. 62, 102 (1930); Six in the Money, 40 id. No. 2, pp. 68, 71 (1949); Appendix A infra, pages 413-414.

[6] Thus in The Borden Company Annual Report, 1952 (New York City, 1953), the following statement appeared at page 16: "The success of STARLAC has attracted many competitors into the market.   But STARLAC, the first and only consumer brand in national distribution, remains first in consumer favor."

[7] Machlup, The Economics of Sellers' Competition 549 (1952); Smith, Effective Competition, 26 N.Y.U.L. Rev. 405, 414 (1951).   In United States v. United Shoe Machinery Co., 222 Fed. 349 (D. Mass. 1915), aff'd, 247 U.S. 32 (1918), the following statement appeared in the opinion of the trial court at page 414: "During the period of monopoly he may establish a good will which will give him after the expiration of his patents a formidable advantage in competition over imitative manufacturers.   Frequently this good will and the development of his business may be such as to practically and lawfully exclude competition after the expiration of his patents. . . ."

[8] United States v. United Shoe Machinery Co., 247 U.S. 32, 53 (1918).

[9] American Tobacco Co. v. United States, 328 U.S. 781, 786 (1946).

Being the first in an untried and doubtful risky field is neither inherently evil nor prohibited, even when the pioneer venture is crowned with success.[10]

Similar views were expressed by the Attorney General's Committee.[11] The only important decision looking in the other direction is the 1945 opinion of Judge Learned Hand in the *Alcoa* case.[12] Even there, it was admitted that the origin of the monopoly might be critical in determining its legality,[13] a suggestion which may explain the "corner" cases mentioned above.[14] A difficult question, of course, arises when the innovation remains uncopied during a considerable period of time.[15] In the absence of artificial restraints upon entry into competition, however, it would be difficult to formulate any precise length of time at the end of which the monopoly should become unlawful.[16]

It follows that competition in quality may be just as legal as

[10] United States v. Inter-Island Navigation Co., 87 F. Supp. 1010, 1021 (D. Hawaii, 1950). See also Timken Roller Bearing Co. v. United States, 341 U.S. 593, 604 (1951); National Biscuit Co. v. FTC, 299 Fed. 733, 739 (2d Cir. 1924); United States v. E. I. Du Pont de Nemours & Co., 118 F. Supp. 41 (D. Del. 1953), aff'd, 351 U.S. 377 (1956); Commonwealth v. North Shore Ice Co., 220 Mass. 55, 107 N.E. 402, 404 (1914). Compare Excelsior Motor Manufacturing Co. v. Sound Equipment, Inc., 73 F.2d 725, 728 (7th Cir. 1934).

[11] Atty. Gen. Nat. Com. Rep. 56, (5). Such a view appears to be in accord with the legislative history. Walker, History of the Sherman Law 33, 58 (1910).

[12] United States v. Aluminum Co. of America, 148 F.2d 416 (2d Cir. 1945). But compare the opinion below, 44 F. Supp. 97, 183 (S.D.N.Y. 1941), and on remand, 91 F. Supp. 333, 401 (S.D.N.Y. 1950). Note the disturbing statement in Pearsall v. Great Northern Railway Co., 161 U.S. 646, 676-677 (1896), indicating that the greater speed and cheapness of the service performed by railways made them monopolists. Different considerations may be applicable to group activities and the courts have applied the statute rigorously to them. United States v. Patton, 226 U.S. 525 (1913); Hartford-Empire Co. v. United States, 323 U.S. 386, 400, 406 (1945), clarified, 324 U.S. 570 (1945); Slaughter v. Thacker Coal & Coke Co., 55 W. Va. 642, 47 S.E. 247, 249 (1904). In the last-cited case, however, the dissenting opinion argued that the statute should not be applied to a group of firms attempting to invade a new market through a joint agency.

[13] United States v. Aluminum Co. of America, 148 F.2d 416 (2d Cir. 1945), where it was said at page 429: "Nevertheless, it is unquestionably true that from the very outset the courts have at least kept in reserve the possibility that the origin of a monopoly may be critical in determining its legality; and for this they had warrant in some of the congressional debates which accompanied the passage of the Act."

[14] *Supra* this section.

[15] Compare Stocking and Mueller, The Cellophane Case and the New Competition, 45 Am. Econ. Rev. 29, 63 (1955). Possibly there is a helpful analogy in the judge-made rule that interests in property must vest within lives in being and twenty-one years. Gray, The Rule Against Perpetuities §201 (4th ed., Roland Gray, 1942). Transplanting of that rule into the antitrust law would, however, involve many difficulties.

[16] Wright, Toward Coherent Anti-Trust, 35 Va. L. Rev. 665, 690 (1949). Compare Ellis, Monetary Policy and Investment, 30 Am. Econ. Rev. (Proceedings) 27, 33 (1940); Bernstein, Profit Theory — Where Do We Go from Here? 67 Q.J. Econ. 407, 412 (1953).

competition in price. Under the neoclassic theories of monopolistic competition, so basically static in character, little account is
taken of the benefits of competition apart from those reflected
in price reductions. Since an improvement in quality is, however,
an innovation, it follows that such competition may be just as
beneficial as that effected by reducing prices.[17] The courts have
recognized that factor, one of them saying:

> . . . the section does not cover every monopolizing by the acts
> of individuals. A monopolizing by efficiency is producing and
> marketing a better and cheaper article than any one else is not
> within it. . . .[18]

Similarly, the survivor of a group of competitors is not per se a
monopolist within the meaning of the antitrust laws. Such survivorship may be derived from a variety of causes,[19] and in the
absence of abuses, the courts do not hold it unlawful.[20] Indeed,
even in the *Aluminum* decision itself, Judge Hand declared:

> . . . persons may unwittingly find themselves in possession of a
> monopoly, automatically so to say: that is, without having in-
> tended either to put an end to existing competition, or to prevent
> competition from arising when none had existed. . . . Since the
> Act makes "monopolizing" a crime . . . it would be not only un-
> fair, but presumably contrary to the intent of Congress, to include
> such instances. . . . there may be changes in taste or in cost
> which drive out all but one purveyor. . . . In such cases a strong
> argument can be made that, although the result may expose the
> public to the evils of monopoly, the Act does not mean to con-
> demn the resultant of those very forces which it is its prime object

[17] Brems, Product Equilibrium Under Monopolistic Competition 33, 95, 234, 244
(1951); Abbott, Vertical Equilibrium Under Pure Quantity Competition, 43 Am.
Econ. Rev. 826, 833, 844 (1953). Note also the possibility of product deterioration.
Chamberlin, The Product as an Economic Variable, 67 Q.J. Econ. 1, 23 (1953).

[18] Patterson v. United States, 222 Fed. 599, 619 (6th Cir. 1915), *cert. denied*, 238
U.S. 635 (1915). *Accord:* United States v. Union Pacific Railroad Co., 226 U.S.
61, 87 (1912); United States v. Winslow, 195 Fed. 578, 594 (D. Mass. 1912), *aff'd*,
227 U.S. 202 (1913); Hughes Tool Co. v. Cole, 113 F. Supp. 519, 523 (W.D. Okla.
1953), *aff'd*, 215 F.2d 924 (10th Cir. 1954), *cert. denied*, 348 U.S. 927, 965 (1955).

[19] Johnston and Stevens, Monopoly or Monopolization, 44 Ill. L. Rev. 269, 282
(1949). One of the principal causes of survivorship is a decline in demand.
Robinson, Imperfect Competition Revisited, 63 Econ. J. 579, 592 (1953). An example is found in Steel Rails, 8 Fortune No. 6, pp. 42, 44-45 (1933). Indivisibility
may be a cause of survivorship in that the smaller firms find themselves unable to
compete. Celler Committee I, pt. 6A, at 772. In other words, innovation itself,
by lowering costs or increasing the economic size of the firm, may be responsible
for survivorship. Examples are found in Champion Paper, 6 Fortune No. 4, pp.
62, 64, 94, 96 (1932), and Dow Chemical, 3 id. No. 4, p. 58 (1931).

[20] United States v. Pullman Co., 50 F. Supp. 123, 126-127 (E.D. Pa. 1943), *aff'd*
per curiam, 330 U.S. 806 (1947). Compare Times-Picayune Publishing Co. v. United
States, 345 U.S. 594, 626 (1953).

to foster. . . . The successful competitor, having been urged to compete, must not be turned upon when he wins.[21]

§3.16. Dynamic considerations: Limitations upon growth.

The collision between dynamic economic theory and the structure test of monopoly is not confined to the introduction of new commodities. It also extends to the growth of firms producing existing goods. Growth may be curbed under the structure test because after a considerable size (share of the market) has been attained, the statutes may make it criminal[1] to expand further.[2] Dynamic economic doctrines take a wholly different view of the matter. As stated by Professor Wright,

> The differences which the introduction of the growth factor make in the theoretical model are not mere differences of degree. They profoundly alter the whole logic of the situation. There is hardly a single statement which standard economic theory is usually interpreted to make regarding the relative effects of different kinds of competition, which cannot be contradicted upon reference to the functioning of the real growing and changing world.[3]

There is nothing revolutionary in such assertions. Lawyers have long argued that we cannot encourage rivals to compete and then penalize the winner.[4] Instinctively, they have known what the economists now tell us:

[21] United States v. Aluminum Co. of America, 148 F.2d 416, 429-430 (2d Cir. 1945). Compare the opinion below, 44 F. Supp. 97, 154 (S.D.N.Y. 1941).

§3.16. [1] Sections 1 and 2 of the Sherman Act both provide criminal penalties. There can be only civil relief, however, under the Clayton Act and the Federal Trade Commission Act. The subject of remedies is discussed in Chapter 10.

[2] Neoclassic theory also takes account of various imperfections which justify monopoly. Thus, if indivisibility is present, the structure theory does not necessarily penalize further growth but subjects it to regulation. See §3.13 supra.

[3] Wright, Some Pitfalls of Economic Theory as a Guide to the Law of Competition, 37 Va. L. Rev. 1083, 1084 (1951). Accord: Schumpeter, Capitalism, Socialism and Democracy 91 (3d ed. 1950); Mason, Schumpeter on Monopoly and the Large Firm, in Schumpeter: Social Scientist 89, 91 (Harris ed. 1951). In Markham, Competition in the Rayon Industry (1952), a careful student observed at page 205: ". . . to impose limitations upon the size of firms or the percent of total output each firm may control in an industry may conceivably result in more firms and hence, a closer approximation of the industry, structurally, to purely competitive conditions. If, on the other hand, however, the imposition of such limitations could be expected to retard or eliminate technological development and the introduction of new products, or result in losses in economies of scale, the social costs of the more competitive structural features might well prove to be prohibitive." Compare Johnston and Stevens, Monopoly or Monopolization, 44 Ill. L. Rev. 269, 289-290 (1949); Smith, Effective Competition 26 N.Y.U.L. Rev. 405, 406 (1951).

[4] Pope, The Legal Aspect of Monopoly, 20 Harv. L. Rev. 167, 188 (1907); Dana, "Monopoly" Under the National Anti-Trust Act, 7 Harv. L. Rev. 338, 353 (1894). Compare Clark, The Orientation of Antitrust Policy, 40 Proceedings Am. Econ. Assn. 93, 96-97 (1950); Levi, The Antitrust Laws and Monopoly, 14 U. Chi. L. Rev. 153, 156 (1947).

The chief cause of monopoly (in a broad sense) is obviously competition. Firms are constantly striving to expand, and some must be more successful than others. It is easier to defend a position once gained than to conquer it, so that the most successful firms grow the most rapidly.[5]

Courts have long recognized the validity of the foregoing considerations. Years ago the minority shareholders of the Ford Motor Company complained that Henry Ford's policy of retaining earnings, expanding his plants and reducing prices tended toward the creation of a monopoly, but the courts refused to agree with them.[6] And long ago a district court said:

There is no limit under the American law to which a business may not independently grow . . .[7]

[5] Robinson, Imperfect Competition Revisited, 63 Econ. J. 579, 592 (1953). Compare Bowman, Toward Less Monopoly, 101 U. Pa. L. Rev. 577, 584 (1953). For reasons set forth in the preceding sections it is difficult enough to measure monopoly power under neoclassic theories. The addition of dynamic considerations to the static doctrines of neoclassic economies renders the problem practically insuperable. Take, for example, the phenomenon known as "building ahead of demand." In neoclassic theory, the first producer in the field seeks to preserve the advantage arising from his priority; he does so by taking advantage of indivisibility. In other words, he expands ahead of demand so that economies of scale are realized in his plant which would not be available to a newcomer (with lesser amounts of capital). As a result the newcomer's plant would always be unprofitable. United States v. Aluminum Co. of America, 148 F.2d 416 (2d Cir. 1949); Machlup, The Economics of Sellers' Competition 234-235 (1952). In dynamic theory a different view is taken of the matter. Excess capacity no longer appears in such a sinister role. Thus one economist wrote:
". . . a perfectly competitive economy is comparatively free from waste. . . . But this does not tell us anything about how its account looks under the conditions set by the process of creative destruction.
". . . much of what without reference to those conditions would appear to be unrelieved waste ceases to qualify as such when duly related to them. The type of excess capacity, for example, that owes its existence to the practice of 'building ahead of demand' or to the practice of providing capacity for the cyclical peaks of demand would in a regime of perfect competition be much reduced." Schumpeter, Capitalism, Socialism and Democracy 105 (3d ed. 1950).
The decision in the Aluminum case apparently did not bother the leading producer of magnesium in the United States, which in 1953 proceeded to erect the world's largest magnesium rolling mill at Madison, Illinois. Dow Chemical Co., Ann. Rep. 1953, 11 (Midland, 1953). And in the report of a leading oil company it was said: "While production in Canada is still restricted by a lack of adequate transportation and markets, Gulf continues to develop its extensive holdings in anticipation of future requirements. Its reserves of both oil and gas were materially increased during 1952." Gulf Oil Corp., 1952 Ann. Rep. 10 (Pittsburgh, 1953).
[6] Dodge v. Ford Motor Co., 204 Mich. 459, 170 N.W. 668, 673, 681 (1919).
[7] United States v. International Harvester Co., 214 Fed. 987, 1000 (D. Minn. 1914), appeal dismissed, 248 U.S. 587 (1918), supplemental petition, 10 F.2d 827 (1926), aff'd, 274 U.S. 693 (1927). Another district court said: "The fact that the United Shoe Company has acquired so large a percentage of the business of the country to which it devoted itself comes so largely from the use of extraordinarily competent methods as to shut out from the eyes of the impartial investigator suggestions of other methods." United States v. United Shoe Machinery Co., 222 Fed. 349, 357 (D. Mass. 1915), aff'd, 247 U.S. 32 (1918).

One of the reasons advanced by the United States Supreme Court for refusing to break up the United States Steel Corporation was that to do so would penalize competition itself by prohibiting growth.[8] While such a statement may be reminiscent of the abuse test rather than of the structure test of monopoly, it is worth noting that only a few years ago the same court declared:

> . . . no direction has appeared of a public policy that forbids, *per se,* an expansion of facilities of an existing company to meet the needs of new markets of a community. . . .[9]

Even more pointed is the recent comment in the investment banking case:

> If what is complained of is merely that, as a result of successful competitive effort, the seventeen defendant firms have too large a slice of the business, "more than their fair share" as it were, whatever that may mean, then the avenue of approach would seem to be to the Congress for new legislation. . . .[10]

[8] United States v. United States Steel Corp., 251 U.S. 417, 450 (1920). Another court wrote: "Success in business is ordinarily success in competition, and such success is a usual incentive to business effort, and is, of itself, commendable. It is only when this lessening is with an unlawful purpose or by any unlawful means, or when it proceeds to the point where it is or is threatening to become a menace to the public, that it is declared unlawful. At that point the public protects itself. The point of danger is reached when monopoly is threatened." United States v. Standard Oil Co., 47 F.2d 288, 297 (E.D. Mo. 1931). Note the ambiguous position taken by the court in the foregoing quotation, which seems to adopt the abuse test and then switches to the structure theory while still under the influence of phrases from dynamic doctrine.

[9] United States v. Columbia Steel Co., 334 U.S. 495, 526 (1948). In the same opinion, the Court wrote at page 532: "No objection was interposed when United States Steel indicated that it proposed to spend $25,000,000 to erect a cold reduction mill at Pittsburg, and it is doubtful whether objections could be raised if United States Steel proposed to build instead of to buy from a competitor of fabricating facilities similar to those possessed by Consolidated." In United States v. Inter-Island Navigation Co., 87 F. Supp. 1010 (D. Hawaii, 1950), a steamship line was accused of having violated the Sherman Act by establishing an air carrier subsidiary along the same routes. The court held that the defendant had not violated the statute, saying at pages 1016-1017:

"There is nothing in the statute to prevent a corporation from entering a virgin field, and, through a subsidiary or otherwise, engaging in a pioneer enterprise . . .

"The antitrust laws were enacted to promote and not to retard the economic growth of the nation.

"In a word, the Sherman Act is not an instrument of stagnation."

The court continued at page 1021:

". . . adequate capital and a long-time establishment in business are not proscribed by the Sherman Act. Just as it is not an instrument of stagnation, the Act does not penalize business efficiency, unless it be accompanied by some unlawful act."

Compare Windsor Theatre Co. v. Walbrook Amusement Co., 94 F. Supp. 388, 393 (D. Md. 1950), aff'd, 189 F.2d 797 (4th Cir. 1951).

[10] United States v. Morgan, 118 F. Supp. 621, 737 (S.D.N.Y. 1953). Compare United States v. National Lead Co., 332 U.S. 319, 352-353 (1947); United States v.

It was no mere coincidence that the decision so often referred to as adopting the structure test also suggested that growth should be curbed.   The lower court trying the *Alcoa* case found no reasonable basis for allegations that the defendant had bought up water-power sites in order to avoid competition.   It found a dominant motive for the acquisition of the property in the necessity of providing for future expansion.[11]   In reversing, Judge Learned Hand wrote this now famous language:

> The only question is whether it [Alcoa] falls within the exception established in favor of those who do not seek, but cannot avoid, control of a market.   It seems to us that that question scarcely survives its statement.   It was not inevitable that it should always anticipate increases in the demand for ingot and be prepared to supply them.   Nothing compelled it to keep doubling and redoubling its capacity before others entered the field.   It insists that it never excluded competitors; but we can think of no more effective exclusion than progressively to embrace each new opportunity as it opened, and to face every newcomer with new capacity already geared into a great organization. . . .[12]

It is doubtful whether the foregoing views would again be applied by the courts.   One indication of judicial disapproval of curbs upon growth is found in decisions refusing to break up the research laboratories of large firms.[13]   Since growth is often the re-

---

E. I. Du Pont de Nemours & Co., 118 F. Supp. 41 (D. Del. 1953), *aff'd,* 351 U.S. 377 (1956).

[11] United States v. Aluminum Co. of America, 44 F. Supp. 97, 125, 144, 248 (S.D.N.Y. 1941).

[12] United States v. Aluminum Co. of America, 148 F.2d 416, 431 (2d Cir. 1945). In Hughes Tool Co. v. Ford, 114 F. Supp. 525 (E.D. Okla. 1953), *rev'd,* 215 F.2d 924 (10th Cir. 1954), *cert. denied,* 348 U.S. 927, 965 (1955), the trial court wrote at page 544: "The plaintiff's absolute domination of the roller rock bit industry has been achieved and maintained by intensive engineering research, an aggressive patent policy coupled with widespread patent litigation, an abusive use of the 'lease' agreement, an invasive sales policy and an embracing of each opportunity for expansion with such readiness as to discourage competition."   Compare United States v. New York Great Atlantic & Pacific Tea Co., 173 F.2d 79 (7th Cir. 1949). Note, however, the position of the Attorney General's Committee: "This statement [in the Aluminum Company opinion] . . . is sometimes misconstrued to suggest that 'monopoly' may become 'monopolization' merely by being active, enterprising, and dynamic.   This construction implies that the safest course for large companies is passive stagnation, with a gradual loss of market share — a business policy directly at odds with anti-trust aims.   Such is not the teaching of *Alcoa.* . . .   The *Alcoa* case is not to be interpreted as penalizing enterprise. . . ."   Atty. Gen. Nat. Com. Rep. 60.

[13] United States v. Aluminum Co. of America, 91 F. Supp. 333, 392, 416, 417 (S.D.N.Y. 1950).   Compare United States v. Line Material Co., 333 U.S. 287, 310 (1948).   But see United States v. United Shoe Machinery Co., 110 F. Supp. 295, 329, 330, 345 (D. Mass. 1953), *aff'd per curiam,* 347 U.S. 521 (1954); Hughes Tool Co. v. Ford, 114 F. Supp. 525, 552 (E.D. Okla. 1953), *rev'd,* 215 F.2d 924 (10th Cir. 1954), *cert. denied,* 348 U.S. 927, 965 (1955).   In TNEC, Final Rep. of Exec. Secy. 138,

sult of products or processes discovered in research efforts, the decisions seem to reflect an anxiety not to disturb such growth. Unfortunately, however, some empirical evidence indicates that the antitrust laws have curbed growth, possibly by suggesting the greater safety of diversification as an outlet for the energies of large firms.[14]

In static economic doctrine self-correction of the market place is a recognized phenomenon. High profits attract new firms into the industry; price competition results; profits come down and a competitive equilibrium is established.[15] Under dynamic doctrine, however, the very concept of long-run monopoly scarcely exists.[16] The Schumpeterian notion of "creative destruction," whereby innovations bombard earlier positions of market power out of existence, imputes great additional strength to the forces of self-correction.[17] Those forces have long been recognized by

---

the complaint was registered that technological research was carried on largely by big firms and that it therefore accentuated an existing concentration of economic power.

[14] United States v. United States Steel Co., 223 Fed. 55, 149 (D.N.J. 1915), aff'd, 251 U.S. 417 (1920); Brief for Appellant, p. 97, United States v. International Harvester Co., 248 U.S. 587 (1918). This masterful brief, written in 1914, sets forth that International Harvester was originally a combination of competing companies but that after its organization (during the ten years before suit was filed) it lost ground in the sale of harvesting equipment and that its increases in business had been accomplished by diversification in the manufacture of plows, harrows, and so forth, and through increased foreign trade. The brief, with a few modern citations, could be presented to any court today without substantial revision. Additional evidence is found in Hoover, Some Institutional Factors in Business Investment Decisions, 44 Proceedings Am. Econ. Assn. 201, 212 (1954); Wright, Capitalism 192 (1951); Bleiberg, Amazing Shortage, 34 Barron's No. 30, pp. 3, 16 (1954); Henle, Milk Processors, 35 id. No. 8, p. 13 (1955). Note the reference to maintenance of a leading manufacturer's "historical competitive position" in General Motors Corp., Forty-First Ann. Rep. 10 (New York City, 1950), Forty-Fourth Ann. Rep. 8 (1953); Allis-Chalmers Manufacturing Co., Ann. Rep. 1948, 14 (Milwaukee, 1949). In another annual report it was said: "Canco's formula of growing by creating new markets — rather than depending on a larger share of existing markets — has played a major role in the company's growth . . ." American Can Co., 1952 Ann. Rep. 16 (New York City, 1953). But in another report it was said: "Diamond is the unquestioned leader in the manufacture and sale of matches of all types. The expansion into other fields does not affect the company's policy to protect and promote this leadership." Diamond Match Co., Ann. Rep. 1948, 5 (New York City, 1949).

[15] Appendix B infra, page 469. Examples of self-correction in action will be found in Glenn, Room Coolers, 35 Barron's No. 18, p. 11 (1955); National Biscuit, 14 Fortune No. 2, p. 64 (1936). Other material on this subject is collected in Appendix B infra. Compare Business Concentration and Price Policy 3 (Stigler ed. 1955).

[16] Schumpeter, Capitalism, Socialism and Democracy 84, 99 (3d ed. 1950); Hildebrand, Monopolization and the Decline of Investment Opportunities, 33 Am. Econ. Rev. 591, 592 (1943); Mason, Schumpeter on Monopoly and the Large Firm, in Schumpeter: Social Scientist 89, 93 (Harris ed. 1951).

[17] Effect of innovations in advertising media (radio, television and the like) upon the revenues and profits of newspapers appears to have been recognized in Times-

the courts.   In 1911 the Supreme Court of the United States wrote:

> It is remarkable that nowhere at common law can there be found a prohibition against the creation of monopoly by the individual. This would seem to manifest, either consciously or intuitively, a profound conception as to the inevitable operation of economic forces and the equipoise or balance in favor of the protection of the rights of individuals which resulted. . . .[18]

Under either the static or the dynamic view, therefore, there is always a possibility that the market will correct itself before results can be obtained from the notoriously sluggish and expensive procedures of the antitrust laws.[19]   Thus, in any given situation, application of the statutes to a temporary monopolist may depend upon considerations of cost: Will the expense involved be outweighed by the results achieved during the limited time in which the defendant would otherwise retain his monopoly powers?

Dynamic factors of innovation and growth render the structure test of monopoly a tool of dubious value.   As we have seen, the courts will not adhere to static structure notions when innovation and growth are established.[20]   As indicated above, it might be possible to set a limited time during which innovation and growth might be left undisturbed by the antitrust laws.[21]   To fix upon such a period of time, however, would necessarily require judicial legislation of a somewhat arbitrary character.   Despite the precedent of the rule against perpetuities,[22] therefore, it is difficult to

---

Picayune Publishing Co. v. United States, 345 U.S. 594, 603 (1953).   A dramatic account of the role of innovation in the automobile industry and its effect upon leadership therein is found in Mr. Ford Doesn't Care, 8 Fortune No. 6, pp. 62, 66, 68 (1933).   Many other examples are collected in Appendix B *infra*.

[18] Standard Oil Co. of New Jersey v. United States, 221 U.S. 1, 55 (1911).

[19] But compare Bowman, Toward Less Monopoly, 101 U. Pa. L. Rev. 577, 622 (1953), wherein it was said: "That they contain the seeds of their own eventual destruction is not to say that they are necessarily desirable while they last.   The same may be said about similar market control exercised by the single firm.   Nothing in the above quoted passage by Professor Schumpeter would seem to be inconsistent with attempting to achieve the most effective competition in both the short and long run."

[20] But compare Steindl, Maturity and Stagnation in American Capitalism 45, 51 (1952), indicating that innovation leads to an increased rate of profit and hence to a greater or "absolute" concentration.   Survivorship may be equally important. Thus it has been said: "If we want healthy growth of the economy, we must allow healthy growth of business concerns.   The question then becomes: what is healthy growth, and what limits are there to it, if any?" Adelman, Business Size and Public Policy, 24 J. Business 269, 274 (1951).

[21] Compare United States v. Aluminum Co. of America, 148 F.2d 416, 422 (2d Cir. 1945).

[22] Gray, The Rule Against Perpetuities §169 (4th ed., Roland Gray, 1942).

understand how the structure test of monopoly could be so amended.

§3.17. **Dynamic considerations: Effects upon behavior.** As stated above,[1] we know little about the actual behavior of oligopolists. They may or may not raise prices to monopolistic levels. Even in static analysis, the results of having only a few sellers in a given market are indeterminate. If account is taken of dynamic considerations, it is even more difficult to predict what oligopolists will do. The threat of new methods of production and the hazard that existing products will be supplanted by innovations provide a stimulus to make businessmen behave as if conditions of pure competition existed, even though the opposite is true.[2] They may come to value the very existence of their firms more highly than short-run profits.[3] Security, often thought of in terms of the retention of customers, may become a controlling consideration.[4]

§3.17. [1] §3.10 *supra*. Compare Gordon, Short Period Price Determination, 38 Am. Econ. Rev. 265, 266 (1948).

[2] Schumpeter, Capitalism, Socialism and Democracy 85, 102 (3d ed. 1950); Abramovitz, Monopolistic Selling in a Changing Economy, 52 Q.J. Econ. 191, 194, 198 (1938). A careful student recently wrote: "In acting like a competitor, the member of an oligopoly industry realizes that the lack of numbers in competitors in the particular product at a particular time is compensated for by the changing sequence of competitors over time. . . . The acceptance of long-run demand and cost analysis by the big firm compels it as a matter of self-interest to effect a distribution of market benefits equivalent to those that might accrue from transaction to transaction under atomized competition." Kaplan, Big Enterprise in a Competitive System 167 (Brookings Institution, 1954).

[3] Kaysen, A Dynamic Aspect of the Monopoly Problem, 31 Rev. Econ. & Stat. 109, 110 (1949). In Robinson, Imperfect Competition Revisited, 63 Econ. J. 579, 582 (1953), a leading economist wrote: ". . . the most valid simple generalization is that the aim of the entrepreneur is for the firm first to survive, and secondly, to grow. To this end he must pursue profit, but he must avoid action which, though profitable in the present, will damage his future position. . . ." In Rostow, The Process of Economic Growth 32 (1952) it was said: "The conventional assumption in economic theory that entrepreneurs will seek to maximize profit does not adequately take into account the possibility that the responsible lenders and entrepreneurial groups may well differ in the premium attached to profit as against risk, as against the disruption to existing routines, as against the sheer effort and energy required to take the required innovational steps, as against the damage innovation in one firm might do to other firms in the industry, and so forth." In Rothschild, Price Theory and Oligopoly, 57 Econ. J. 299, 309 (1947), it was said: "This impasse can only be overcome, and oligopolistic price theory can only be developed, if we recognize that under this market situation the security motive must be given the same pride of place as has been occupied by the profit maximization principle for such a long time." Compare Bernstein, Profit Theory — Where Do We Go from Here? 67 Q.J. Econ. 407, 415 (1953); Brems, Product Equilibrium Under Monopolistic Competition 116, 136 (1951); Fellner, Competition Among the Few 142, 183 (1949); Gordon, Short Period Price Determination, 38 Am. Econ. Rev. 265, 269, 271 (1948); Clark, Social Control of Business 157 (1926); Gossett, Corporate Citizenship 187 (Washington and Lee University, 1957).

[4] United States v. Aluminum Co. of America, 91 F. Supp. 333, 384, 356 (S.D.N.Y. 1950); Celler Committee I, pt. 1, at 53. Some sellers appear to believe that it is highly desirable to give their customers the impression that their prices are stable, perhaps thereby reducing the elasticity of demand of the customers. Hart, Antic-

Prices which might be raised are often held below free-market levels,[5] and in dynamic theory such practices are neither necessarily presumptive of the existence of monopoly power[6] nor designed to deter others from entering into competition.[7]   Many examples of business conduct falling within the pattern just outlined can be found in economic history.[8]

---

ipations, Business Planning and the Cycle, 51 Q.J. Econ. 273, 285 (1937); American Viscose Corp., Ann. Rep. 1948, 13 (Philadelphia, 1949).

[5] Robinson, Imperfect Competition Revisited, 63 Econ. J. 579, 589 (1953); Nourse and Drury, Industrial Price Policies and Economic Progress 269 (Brookings Institution, 1938); Zimmerman, The Propensity to Monopolize 1 (1952); Wright, Some Pitfalls of Economic Theory as a Guide to the Law of Competition, 37 Va. L. Rev. 1083, 1086-1087 (1951); Gordon, Short Period Price Determination, 38 Am. Econ. Rev. 265, 277 (1948).

[6] Robinson, The Economics of Imperfect Competition, 248 (1933); Evans, The Entrepreneur and Economic Theory, 39 Am. Econ. Rev. Proceedings 336, 344 (1949); Fellner, Competition Among the Few 11 (1949); Brems, Product Equilibrium Under Monopolistic Competition 182, 238 (1951); Abramovitz, Monopolistic Selling in a Changing Economy, 52 Q.J. Econ. 191, 196, 203, 206 (1938).   But compare Markham, Competition in the Rayon Industry 102-103 (1952); Weintraub, Revised Doctrines of Competition, 45 Proceedings Am. Econ. Assn. 463, 465 (1955).

[7] It is, of course, entirely possible that pricing policies are adopted at least in part to discourage entry by others.   Harrod, Economic Essays 146, 156 (1952); Bain, Conditions of Entry and the Emergence of Monopoly, in Chamberlin, ed., Monopoly and Competition and Their Regulation 215, 231 (International Economic Assn. 1954).   Compare Just About All About Cellophane, 5 Fortune No. 2, pp. 74, 101 (1932).   Note also that long-run pricing policies may lead to those rigidities so often attacked by economists.   Rothschild, Price Theory and Oligopoly 57 Econ. J. 299, 309 (1947).   Compare Galbraith, Monopoly Power and Price Rigidities, 50 Q.J. Econ. 456 (1936).

[8] United States v. Aluminum Co. of America, 44 F. Supp. 97, 302 (S.D.N.Y. 1941), rev'd, 148 F.2d 416 (2d Cir. 1945); Celler Committee I, pt. 1, at 451.   In MPH Manufacturing Co. v. Inland Steel Co., No. 54C1516, N.D. Ill. (1955), Clarence B. Randall, Chairman of the Board of the Inland Steel Company, testified on deposition at page 96:

"We . . . try to get the best price that we can   . . .   In trying to get the best price that you can you aren't reaching for the last dollar now, you are considering the future relationship with that particular customer.   During the scarcity period we could often have secured higher prices than we did. . . .

". . . But, in fixing a price at the time of sale, you get the best that you can and still maintain a relationship of confidence and good will with the customer. You want him to stay with you for a long time and you can forgo an immediate easy profit if by doing so you win good will for the company that would help you in the future when the going gets tough."

Similarly, before the Celler Committee, the president of a large chemical concern testified:

". . . the matter of good will weighs very heavily.

"For example, a lot of things can happen in a seller's market that would result in greater profit, let us say, to the supplier.

"We try not to take advantage of those situations, not because we are interested in turning down an honest dollar, but because we look to the long term.   Now, for example, suppose as a seller we are inclined to cast out some small consumer. That might be immediately advantageous to us; but for the long run it would be highly disadvantageous to us because of the loss of good will."   Celler Committee I, pt. 2A, at 558.

Other examples will be found in Hower, The History of an Advertising Agency

If dynamic forces in the market place compel oligopolists to behave as if conditions of pure competition existed, enforcement of the antitrust laws against such defendants would appear to be unnecessary. To date, the courts do not appear to have passed upon many cases in which such considerations were brought to their attention.[9] If, however, a thorough effort were made to apply Section 2 of the Sherman Act to defendants selling in markets wherein rivals were few, it is likely that the courts would be called upon to take account of dynamic factors in evaluating the necessity for judicial action.

§3.18. **Intent under the structure test.** Under the structure theory of monopoly the requirement of intent upon the part of the defendants is not altogether dispensed with.[1] The courts continue to speak of intent but do so in language indicating that no "specific" intent is required; a mere "general" intent suffices to establish an infringement of the statute. Thus, in the *Aluminum* case Judge Learned Hand said:

---

25 (1939); Cassady, Price Making and Price Behavior in the Petroleum Industry 48-49, 52, 217 n.28 (Petroleum Monograph Series No. 1, 1954); Learned, Pricing of Gasoline, 26 Harv. Bus. Rev. No. 6, pp. 723, 753, 756 (1948); National Biscuit Co., Ann. Rep. 1948, 5 (New York City, 1949); Brems, Product Equilibrium Under Monopolistic Competition 4 (1951); Celler Committee I, pt. 6A, at 823, 838, 944-945; Thompson, Address to Shareholders 3 (International Nickel Co. of Canada Ltd., Toronto, April 25, 1951); International Nickel, 10 Fortune No. 2, pp. 64, 102 (1934). The policy of a leading manufacturer of steel has been described as follows: "United States Steel's commercial policy is to sell products of its manufacture at *competitive prices*. Its objective is to realize at all times a profit on the products which it sells. It is constantly guided by the long-range philosophy that the lower the price of steel, the more the needs and desires of the consuming public will be satisfied and the demand for steel stimulated . . ." United States Steel Corp., Business . . . Big and Small . . . Built America 70-71 (1950). But another steel producer with remarkably low costs testified that he did not attempt to cut prices to a point where he would take all the business from his competitors that he could handle because that policy might not be desirable over the long term. Furthermore, he said each firm had a stake in the health of the industry as a whole, referring to financing, relations with employees and with the public. TNEC Hearings, pt. 19, at 10,679. Note also the possibility that a seller of branded goods will keep prices low so that its merchandise will continue moving into consumers' hands. Otherwise, unbranded goods may be purchased with the resultant loss of familiarity of established trade-marks. General Foods, 10 Fortune No. 4, pp. 68, 126 (1934).

9 The courts have consistently refused to condone agreements among competitors with respect to prices, even though the prices fixed were low and reasonable or maximum and not minimum. United States v. Trenton Potteries Co., 273 U.S. 392, 396 et seq. (1927); Kiefer-Stewart Co. v. Joseph E. Seagram & Son, 340 U.S. 211 (1951). Henry Ford, however, was permitted by the courts to reduce his prices aggressively, even though he was not able to fill all the orders received at the low figures quoted. Dodge v. Ford Motor Co., 204 Mich. 459, 170 N.W. 668, 670, 676, 683 (1919).

§3.18. 1 In Atty. Gen. Nat. Com. Rep. 55, (4), the requirement of intent is called an element of "deliberateness."

In order to fall within §2, the monopolist must have both the power to monopolize and the intent to monopolize. To read the passage as demanding any "specific" intent, makes nonsense of it, for no monopolist monopolizes unconscious of what he is doing.[2]

A few years later the Supreme Court itself said:

> . . . "specific intent" is not necessary to establish a "purpose or intent" to create a monopoly. . . . The requisite "purpose or intent" is present if monopoly results as a necessary consequence of what is done.[3]

Such decisions were reflected in the report of the Attorney General's Committee, which stated:

> Monopolizing under Section 2 consists of monopoly in the economic sense — that is, power to fix prices or to exclude competition — plus a carefully limited ingredient of purpose to use or preserve such power.[4]

As indicated, the intent required to violate Section 2 of the Sherman Act is minimal in character. In the language of the Supreme Court of the United States,

> It is, however, not always necessary to find a specific intent to restrain trade or to build a monopoly in order to find that the anti-trust laws have been violated. It is sufficient that a restraint

[2] United States v. Aluminum Co. of America, 148 F.2d 416, 432 (2d. Cir. 1945). In view of the uncertainty as to what constitutes monopolization (which question constitutes the entire subject of this book), it may be difficult to accept the proposition advanced in the quotation from Judge Learned Hand's opinion.

[3] United States v. Paramount Pictures, Inc., 334 U.S. 131, 173 (1948). In another case decided at the same term the Court said: "It is, however, not always necessary to find a specific intent to restrain trade or to build a monopoly in order to find that the anti-trust laws have been violated. It is sufficient that a restraint of trade or monopoly results as the consequence of a defendant's conduct or business arrangements. . . . To require a greater showing would cripple the Act. . . . Specific intent in the sense in which the common law used the term is necessary only where the acts fall short of the results condemned by the Act." United States v. Griffith, 334 U.S. 100, 105 (1948). Many lower court decisions reflect the foregoing views. E.g., United States v. General Instrument Corp., 87 F. Supp. 157, 193 (D.N.J. 1949). Note the similar position taken in the early case of United States v. Quaker Oats Co., 232 Fed. 499, 503-504 (N.D. Ill. 1916). See Rostow, Monopoly Under the Sherman Act, 43 Ill. L. Rev. 745, 762 (1949).

[4] Atty. Gen. Nat. Com. Rep. 43, a. See also Kahn, A Legal and Economic Appraisal of the "New" Sherman and Clayton Acts, 63 Yale L.J. 293, 305 et seq. (1954). It must be admitted, however, that application of the above views is not wholly uniform. In several decisions, the courts appear to have both demanded proof of intent and said that it could be dispensed with, almost in the same breath. E.g., United States v. Columbia Steel Co., 334 U.S. 495, 524-525 (1948); United States v. Richfield Oil Corp., 99 F. Supp. 280, 286-287, 292 (S.D. Cal. 1951), aff'd per curiam, 343 U.S. 922 (1952).

of trade or monopoly results as the consequence of the defendant's conduct or business arrangements. . . .[5]

In other opinions the courts have indicated that the necessary intent may be inferred from the fact of market power. For example, it has been said:

As to the intent or the purpose of monopolies, it is not necessary that the proof include specific intent in a criminal sense. If there is a unification and concentration of power and control over a commodity, this in itself may make a prima facie case of intent and purpose to exercise illegal restraints and to monopolize. It is sufficient to satisfy this requirement if the consequence of a defendant's conduct or business arrangements results in a monopoly. . . .[6]

Such language has suggested to some observers that the requirement of general intent is merely perfunctory in character.[7] Thus the antitrust laws may be likened to those modern statutes which have been held to impose criminal liability wholly without reference to intent.[8]

[5] United States v. Griffith, 334 U.S. 100, 105 (1948). As indicated in the preceding footnote, it is not always clear whether the courts insist upon any showing of intent under the structure theory. In the Griffith case, for example, the quotation in the text suggests that all showing of intent can be dispensed with. On the next page of the opinion (106), however, the discussion of the status of the proprietor of the sole movie theater in a town sounds as if some intent were required of him before he would be guilty of the crime of monopolization. On the following page (107) the court said: ". . . §2 of the Act is aimed, *inter alia,* at the acquisition or retention of effective market control. . . . Hence the existence of power 'to exclude competition when it is desired to do so' is itself a violation of §2, provided it is coupled with the purpose of intent to exercise that power . . ." After thus saying that intent is necessary under structure theory, the opinion is concluded by saying that the defendant will be presumed to have intended the consequences of his conduct (at 108). Many lawyers will find it difficult to follow such reasoning.

[6] Kobe, Inc. v. Dempsey Pump Co., 198 F.2d 416, 423 (10th Cir. 1952), *cert. denied,* 344 U.S. 837 (1952). In Lawlor v. National Screen Co., 99 F. Supp. 180 (E.D. Pa. 1951), the court said at page 185: "No specific intent to monopolize is necessary; the only relevant intent is the intent to enter into the business arrangements which give rise to the power. By entering into exclusive agreements with the eight producer-distributor defendants . . . National Screen has acquired the power to exclude competition and demonstrated its intent to exercise that power. Hence, it would appear that National Screen is in violation of §2 of the Sherman Act." Similarly, in United States v. General Electric Co., 80 F. Supp. 989 (S.D.N.Y. 1948), the court said at page 1016: ". . . there can be actual monopolization without any purpose or intent to create a monopoly, as long as 'monopoly results as a necessary consequence of what was done' . . ."

[7] Johnston and Stevens, Monopoly or Monopolization, 44 Ill. L. Rev. 269, 286 (1949).

[8] Remington and Helstad, The Mental Element in Crime — A Legislative Problem, [1952] Wis. L. Rev. 644, 648, 664, 670; Morisette v. United States, 342 U.S. 246, 251-252, 253-254 (1952). In the case last cited the Court said at page 260: "Neither this Court nor, so far as we are aware, any other has undertaken to delineate a precise line or set forth comprehensive criteria for distinguishing between crimes that require a mental element and crimes that do not. We attempt no closed definition, for the law on the subject is neither settled nor static."

It is scarcely surprising that the requirement of general intent appears to have so little content. For under the structure theory, by definition, no intent whatever need be shown: it is simply a question of the "share of the market" which the defendant enjoys. As stated by one court,

> . . . if there is a monopoly in fact . . . then the intent is wholly immaterial. It would be the fact of monopoly that would be determinative, and not the purposes or intent of the people creating the monopoly. . . .[9]

Under the structure theory the law does not penalize the acts of the defendant: it attacks the defendant's market position as such. A position is not dependent upon intent, as may be acts under the abuse theory.[10] Every enterprise has the purpose and intent to exercise the power it enjoys, or otherwise it is not making full use of its resources for the benefit of its shareholders.[11] We can only conclude, therefore, that the concept of general intent under the structure theory constitutes a crude safety valve. It permits the escape of defendants whom the structure theory, construed strictly, would find to be monopolists but who are affected by

[9] United States v. Quaker Oats Co., 232 Fed. 499, 500 (N.D. Ill. 1916).

[10] Rostow, Monopoly Under the Sherman Act, 43 Ill. L. Rev. 745, 771-772, 776 (1949). Another distinguished authority on the antitrust laws referred, during a session of a subcommittee of the Attorney General's National Committee to Study the Antitrust Laws, to the requirement of general intent as "garbage."

[11] In American Tobacco Co. v. United States, 328 U.S. 781 (1946), the Court said at page 809: "A correct interpretation of the statute . . . makes it the crime of monopolizing, under §2 of the Sherman Act, for parties, as in these cases, to combine or conspire to acquire or maintain the power to exclude competitors from any part of the trade or commerce among the several states . . . provided they also have such a power that they are able, as a group, to exclude actual or potential competition from the field and provided that they have the intent and purpose to exercise that power." As stated in the text, it is difficult to understand how a business enterprise can lack the intent and purpose to exercise whatever power it has in one way or another. Professor Timberg attempted to explain the quoted language from the Tobacco case as follows: ". . . the distinction . . . between 'power' and the 'exercise of power' seems on the surface to strain reality. Like Judge Hand in the *Alcoa* case, I have difficulty visualizing the static power of an industrial complex dissociated from the dynamic exercise of that power. . . . What the *American Tobacco* case, however, is saying is that monopoly not only restrains or suppresses action on the part of existing competitors, but inhibits persons from becoming competitors in the first instance." Timberg, Some Justifications for Divestiture, 19 Geo. Wash. L. Rev. 132, 134 (1950). Query whether the foregoing explanation is satisfactory. Furthermore, evidence of a purpose or intent to exercise power can only be shown by reference to conduct. Hence such conduct itself becomes the test of legality and, as stated in the text, the structure theory of monopoly comes perilously close to the old "abuse" doctrine. Professor Handler has suggested that more recent cases treat the doctrine of general intent as closely allied to objective effects of restraints upon competition. Handler, Recent Antitrust Developments, 9 Record 171, 178 (April, 1954). If intent is to be measured by the effects of horizontal size (assuming that such effects can be ascertained) the whole requirement of intent may be abandoned.

those factors of ease of entry, slope of the demand curve, indivisibility, innovation and growth, which we have outlined in the preceding sections. The requirement of general intent, therefore, is a catchall designed to avoid the impositions of sanctions where such sanctions are either unnecessary or undesirable. The innovator, for example, who has placed a new product upon the market and who has yet to face competition from a seller of identical goods, is not adjudged a violator of the Sherman Act because he lacks the requisite general intent to monopolize.[12]

Obviously, the test of general intent leaves much to be desired. In some of the decisions, it appears to have no content at all; so that the mere doing of business by any firm enjoying a disproportionate share of the market constitutes a violation of the Sherman Act. In other cases, it takes account of indivisibility, ease of entry, growth and similar factors mentioned above. It does so, however, in a crude fashion, compressing many varied concepts into a phrase of limited connotation. It offers nothing by way of a measure of those factors, such as a means of determining whether entry is sufficiently easy so that application of the antitrust law should be considered unnecessary.[13] And in operation it is apt to rest upon establishment of practices which are difficult to distinguish from the abuses familiar in the older decisions.

§3.19.   Abuses under the structure theory.   As we have noted, proof of misconduct upon the part of the defendant is a necessity under the abuse theory of monopoly.[1] Surprisingly, a similar requirement appears to obtain under the structure theory. The misconduct there involved is more often referred to as a "practice" but the requirement nevertheless appears to exist. Thus, in a Supreme Court opinion it was said:

> In the popular sense there is a monopoly if one person owns the only theatre in a town. That usually does not, however, constitute a violation of the Sherman Act. But . . . even such an ownership is vulnerable in a suit by the United States under the Sherman Act if the property was acquired, or its strategic position maintained, as a result of practices which constitute unreasonable restraints of trade.[2]

[12] Rostow, Monopoly Under the Sherman Act, 43 Ill. L. Rev. 745, 770 (1949). Compare Atty. Gen. Nat. Com. Rep. 43, a.

[13] But compare Kahn, Standards of Antitrust Policy, 67 Harv. L. Rev. 28, 31-32 (1953).

§3.19.   [1] Indeed, misconduct is the essence of the abuse theory. See §2.6 *supra.*

[2] United States v. Paramount Pictures, Inc., 334 U.S. 131, 171 (1948). Compare United States v. Griffith, 334 U.S. 100, 108 (1948); United States v. E. I. Du Pont de Nemours & Co., 118 F. Supp. 41 (D. Del. 1953), aff'd, 351 U.S. 377, 390-391 (1956); Atty. Gen. Nat. Com. Rep. 56, (5). On this subject compare American Tobacco Co., v. United States, 328 U.S. 781, 807 (1946), with United States v. Corn Products Refining Co., 234 Fed. 964, 1012 (S.D.N.Y. 1916).

In the recent litigation involving the United Shoe Machinery Company the court made much of such practices. Among those mentioned were the acquisition of rival firms and buying up of patents. Particular stress was laid upon the practice of leasing (as opposed to selling) the shoe machinery produced by the defendant.[3] Since the decisions referred to appear to have been decided under the structure theory, it follows that the existence of wrongful practices is material in a determination of monopolization under that view of the law. It is not easy to characterize the practices which must be established under the structure theory. The courts often speak of such practices as "exclusionary" in character. Thus, in the *United Shoe Machinery* case the trial court wrote:

> . . . it is a violation of §2 for one having effective control of the market to use, or plan to use, any exclusionary practice, even though it is not a technical restraint of trade. . . .[4]

Of course, the result of "exclusion" of a rival may simply mean that the defendant has competed successfully and thus has acquired a large share of the relevant market.[5] The condemned practices

[3] United States v. United Shoe Machinery Corp., 110 F. Supp. 295, 312, 313, 345 (D. Mass. 1953), *aff'd per curiam,* 347 U.S. 521 (1934). Compare United States v. Columbia Steel Co., 334 U.S. 495, 533 (1948).

[4] United States v. United Shoe Machinery Corp., 110 F. Supp. 295, 342 (D. Mass. 1953), *aff'd per curiam,* 347 U.S. 521 (1954). In United States v. Paramount Pictures, Inc., 85 F. Supp. 881 (S.D.N.Y. 1949), *aff'd per curiam,* 339 U.S. 974 (1950), the district court said at page 894: ". . . there was not only the power to exclude which might be exercised at will but an actual exclusion approximating in the aggregate 70% of the first-run theatre market in the 92 largest cities." In United States v. Griffith, 334 U.S. 100 (1948), the Court said at page 108: "Large-scale buying is not, of course, unlawful *per se.* It may yield price or other lawful advantages to the buyer. It may not, however, be used to monopolize or attempt to monopolize interstate trade or commerce. . . . Nor . . . may it be used to stifle competition by denying competitors thus favorably situated access to the market." In Gamco, Inc. v. Providence Fruit & Produce Building, Inc., 194 F.2d 484 (1st Cir. 1952), *cert. denied,* 344 U.S. 817 (1952), the court said at page 486: ". . . abuses of price fixing and price leadership have been traditional criteria of illegality under the Act. . . . But there are other indicia of monopoly power, of which exclusion of competitors from the market is one . . ." Compare United States v. Aluminum Co. of America, 148 F.2d 416, 429 (2d Cir. 1945). It is not too easy to understand exactly how the "exclusion" of rival firms is distinguished from the mere horizontal size of the defendant. In the language quoted from United States v. Griffith, for example, the Court appears to say that mere horizontal size is not unlawful but that it is unlawful if competitors are denied access to the market: i.e., if competitors are small. Since the horizontal size of the defendant itself suggests that rival firms will be small, the nature of the exclusionary practices is difficult to state. Again, the statement in the Shoe Machinery case (110 F. Supp. 295, 312) that acquisition of rival firms can constitute evidence of "market power" is far from clear.

[5] In State v. Black, 5 N.J. Misc. 639, 138 Atl. 513 (1927), the court said at page 513: "It is alleged that the conspiracy contemplates the impoverishment and ruin of competitors, but this adds nothing to the allegation of intent to monopolize, for every attempt to monopolize must necessarily be taken to contemplate and

may, however, involve something more than the mere doing of business.

Just as in the case of the requirement of general intent, it is clear that the existence of abuses or exclusionary practices is logically unnecessary and irrelevant under the structure theory of monopoly. By its very nature the structure theory takes no account of the defendant's conduct. To do so introduces an element of the abuse theory which the structure test seeks to avoid.[6] Reliance upon abuses or practices is related to the safety valve of general intent discussed above. If some requirement of intent is necessary to avoid an application of the antitrust laws which would crush growth and curb innovation, it follows that there must be some means of proving such intent. Objective conduct is the only satisfactory means of establishing intent of any kind. It follows that the defendant must be proven guilty of some act beyond the making of a mere f.o.b. cash sale without service, warranty and the like.[7] If, for example, he leases rather than sells the commodities which he produces, it can be found that he has done so with a "general" intent to "exclude" his rivals.[8] Such an interpretation of the antitrust laws, of course, opens the door to decisions of a strongly protectionist character — decisions which may be harmful to consumers and which may promote a poor allocation of resources throughout the economy as a whole.[9] So long, however, as there is some requirement of intent it seems inevitable that certain practices should be taken as evidence of wrongful motive even under the structure theory.

§3.20. **Critique of the structure theory.** At the outset the structure theory of monopoly is more attractive than the abuse theory. It avoids difficult questions of the application of that test and at the same time strikes at the heart of monopoly power rather than at its manifestations. It is designed to avoid the necessity of regulation inherent in the abuse theory by eliminating

---

involve, in order to maintain the monopoly, the destruction of the business of competitors, if not in presenti then in futuro. . . ." Note that vertical integration is frequently referred to as "exclusionary" in nature. See Chapter 5.

[6] Rostow, Monopoly Under the Sherman Act, 43 Ill. L. Rev. 745, 772 (1949). On the other hand, proof of a genuine "abuse" might constitute an a fortiori violation of §2 of the Sherman Act under the structure theory.

[7] Mere raising or lowering of prices, however, does not appear to constitute a forbidden practice even though the effects thereof on competitors may be approximately the same. United States v. Griffith, 334 U.S. 100, 108 (1948); United States v. Pullman Co., 64 F. Supp. 108 (E.D. Pa. 1946), aff'd per curiam, 330 U.S. 806 (1947).

[8] United States v. United Shoe Machinery Corp., 110 F. Supp. 295, 342 (D. Mass. 1953), aff'd per curiam, 347 U.S. 521 (1954). An interesting example of an innovator indulging in "practices" in an effort to insulate itself from imitators is found in Reader's Digest, 14 Fortune No. 5, pp. 121, 131 (1936).

[9] United States v. Griffith, 334 U.S. 100, 107 (1948). Compare Dirlam and Kahn, Antitrust Law and the Big Buyer, 60 J. Pol. Econ. 118, 132 (1952).

the power that would otherwise be subject to control. So unsatisfactory have proven the various efforts at controlling monopoly that the structure theory, which would do away with monopoly, has undoubted attractions.[1]

On the other hand, it is obvious from the foregoing discussion that the structure theory is afflicted with difficulties of the gravest character. When it incorporates a requirement of "general" intent and associated "practices," the theory becomes so vague as to be scarcely meaningful. It leaves the door open to tremendous degrees of judicial discretion which may be exercised in a partisan manner.[2] Theoretically, it avoids the necessity for regulation but in actual practice we find that it controls abuses in much the same way as the earlier test which bore that name. Paradoxically, it has even developed a protectionist tinge.[3] The difficulty, of course, is that the economic foundations upon which the theory of monopolistic competition was erected, and from which the structure theory of monopoly in turn was derived, have been seriously damaged. A recent observer has pointed out in brief compass the shortcomings of the theories of monopolistic competition which achieved general acceptance after 1933:

> . . . the assumption of short-run profit maximization was accepted much too uncritically. There was attributed to entrepreneurs a precision of knowledge with respect to their cost and demand functions which they obviously do not possess; witness Mrs. Robinson's recent acknowledgment . . . that the firm's demand curve is a "mere smudge," to which it is vain to attribute elegant geometrical properties. The concept of the "group" or "industry" was taken much too literally, with the result that the analysis of substitutability relations was unduly circumscribed. And, of course, the whole analysis suffered from being conducted in a static framework.[4]

§3.20. [1] A direct attack upon monopoly under §2 of the Sherman Act appears preferable to the use of §1 of that legislation against fictitious collusion. But compare Rahl, Conspiracy and the Antitrust Laws, 44 Ill. L. Rev. 745 (1950).

[2] Keyes, The Shoe Machinery Case and the Problem of the Good Trust, 68 Q.J. Econ. 287, 293-294 (1954). Even the Attorney General's Committee, which adopted the substance of the structure theory, admitted that the law embodying that doctrine left something to be desired. The Committee reported at page 54: "Measuring monopoly power depends upon a full evaluation of the market and its functioning, to determine whether on balance the defendants' power over the interrelated elements of supply, price and entry are sufficiently great to be classed as monopoly power. While the decisions illuminate the economic theory of the courts in evaluating these facts, they provide no magic formula for simplifying the inquiry." Some lawyers may regard the foregoing statement as more comforting than informative.

[3] E.g., United States v. New York Great Atlantic & Pacific Tea Co., 173 F.2d 79 (7th Cir. 1949).

[4] Gordon, Comment, 45 Proceedings Am. Econ. Assn. 483 (1955); FTC, Corporate Mergers and Acquisitions 175 (1955); Miller, Measures of Monopoly Power, in Business Concentration and Price Policy 119, 130 et seq. (Stigler ed. 1955); Mason, Economic Concentration and the Monopoly Problem 2 (1957).

So discredited has become the "share of the market" test which underlies the structure theory that an economist well known for his hostility to monopoly recently wrote:

> . . . the concentration index can be only one of several other bits of information, highly significant in some instances, less significant in others, and sometimes quite irrelevant.[5]

Indeed, recent re-examination of economic theory has done more than cast doubt upon the structure test of monopoly; it has questioned the wickedness of monopoly itself.[6]

---

[5] Machlup, The Political Economy of Monopoly 487 (1952). Recent statements by founders of the doctrine of monopolistic competition indicate a considerable change in their views. Thus it was recently written: "The upshot of all these arguments is that insofar as products are actually heterogeneous by reason of buyers' demands being dispersed over space and over a wide range of diverse tastes and incomes it is completely artificial to conceive of purely competitive industries at all, and hence quite impossible to compare an actual situation, with its complex of monopoly and competitive elements, with an assumed state in which the monopoly elements were missing. In arguing that this is so, we have been led incidentally to indicate a fundamental position which I have developed much more at length elsewhere — that not only the real world, but also the welfare ideal, is a complex of monopoly and competition." Chamberlin, Measuring the Degree of Monopoly and Competition, in Chamberlin, ed., Monopoly and Competition and Their Regulation 255, 260 (International Economic Assn. 1954). Another leading economist wrote: "Nowadays everyone is willing to admit that the traditional theory of value based on the assumption of perfect competition is highly unrealistic and that competition in practice is very imperfect. I wish to carry the argument a step further and to maintain that there are logical contradictions in the basic conception of competition as an equilibrium state of affairs . . . the fourth difficulty is that with stationary real income for the economy as a whole conditions are often such that normal profits are normally impossible to obtain so long as competition prevails . . ." Robinson, The Impossibility of Competition, id. at 245, 246-247. Mrs. Robinson also recently wrote: "The degree of concentration in an industry, measured by the proportion of its output produced by, say, the three largest firms, or the degree of monopoly in the sense of the closeness of the organization binding the firms, may have little relation to the degree of monopoly in the markets which it serves, and the sense of power to control prices." Robinson, Imperfect Competition Revisited, 63 Econ. J. 579, 580 (1953). Compare Weintraub, Revised Doctrines of Competition, 45 Proceedings Am. Econ. Assn. 463 (1955). Another economist has pointed out that if a defendant has chosen to restrict his output by maintaining his prices, his share of the market will be small so that the market share test inherent in the structure theory does not indicate monopoly. Kaysen, Market Definition in Anti-Trust Law Proceedings, Current Business Studies No. 18, pp. 18, 22 (Society of Business Advisory Professions 1954). Note also the apparent judicial recognition that there is no need for public utility type regulation when actual competition is present, even in a field sometimes believed reserved to the monopoly sphere. United States v. Champlin Refining Co., 341 U.S. 290 (1951). It may also be recalled that Mr. Justice Holmes wrote in a dissenting opinion: "The court below argued as if maintaining competition were the expressed object of the act. The act says nothing about competition. I stick to the exact words used. . . ." Northern Securities Co. v. United States, 193 U.S. 197, 403 (1904).

[6] E.g., Schumpeter, Capitalism, Socialism and Democracy 81-82 (3d ed. 1950); Schumpeter, Science and Ideology, 39 Am. Econ. Rev. 345, 357 (1949); Humphrey, The Nature and Meaning of Rigid Prices, 45 J. Pol. Econ. 651, 659-660 (1937);

The sad, unfortunate truth is, therefore, that the structure theory is simply not adapted to achieve those results which we generally desire from the enforcement of the antitrust laws. Structural concepts of monopoly leave out too many factors to permit their universal application. In fact, the general refusal of courts to penalize innovators and to curb growth casts doubt upon the very adoption of the structure theory.[7] Note also that the structure theory, when it meets a monopoly situation protected by indivisibility,[8] innovation or the like, offers no guide to the appropriate public policy with respect thereto. Undoubtedly, the structure theory served a purpose in opening the economic foundations of the monopoly problem to judicial scrutiny. Possibly there is some scope for its utilization at the present time.[9] Yet the more one examines the deficiencies of the structure theory, the more one comes to admire the simplicity and adaptability of the abuse test, at which so many have sneered so often.[10]

Wright, Toward Coherent Anti-Trust, 35 Va. L. Rev. 665, 669 (1949); 1 Nevins, Study of Power 157-158, 160 (1953). But compare Wright, Capitalism 175 (1951); Adelman, The Large Firm and Its Suppliers, 31 Rev. Econ. & Stat. 113, 114 (1949); Fellner, Competition Among the Few 290 (1949).

[7] Reluctance to adopt the structure theory is reflected in many opinions. E.g., United States v. Eastman Kodak Co., 226 Fed. 62 (W.D.N.Y. 1915), *decree entered,* 230 Fed. 522 (W.D.N.Y. 1916), *appeal dismissed,* 255 U.S. 578 (1921). In that case the lower court said at page 80: "There is no limit in this country to the extent to which a business may grow, and the acquisitions of property in the present case, standing alone, would not be deemed an illegal monopoly; but when such acquisitions are accompanied by an intent to monopolize and restrain interstate trade by an arbitrary use of the power resulting from a large business to eliminate a weaker competitor, then they no doubt come within the meaning of the statute."

[8] Including monopoly situations resulting from governmental intervention.

[9] An economist fully aware of all the difficulties mentioned in the text has nevertheless suggested that a defendant having a share of the market lying between 40 and 50 per cent should be curbed because a larger proportion would constitute an influence impossible of dislodgment. Wright, Capitalism 193 (1951).

[10] It is encouraging that recent judicial decisions show an awareness of the various economic factors outlined in the text. Thus in United States v. Morgan, 118 F. Supp. 621, 687, 689 (S.D.N.Y. 1953), the court found that the resale price maintenance features of securities "syndicates" could be assimilated into the "rule of reason." This suggests recognition that market "imperfections" constitute the bulk of the "rule of reason."

CHAPTER 4

Horizontal Size: Other Theories

§4.1. Performance as a test of antitrust violation. For reasons set forth in the two preceding chapters neither the "abuse" nor the "structure" test of horizontal size has proven satisfactory. After announcement of new doctrines of "monopolistic competition" about 1933, the structure test was given considerable impetus and, as we have seen, at least partially recognized by the courts. Thereafter economists, taking account of difficulties involved in the structure theory, began to veer away from it. The reasons for that change were set forth succinctly by an economist speaking in 1954:

> The pendulum was bound to swing, and a swing in the present direction was, I think, salutary. Abuses were unquestionably committed in the name of the new theories of competition which were unveiled in 1933. Illustrative firm demand curves were sometimes drawn with a slope such as to suggest that in group equilibrium the scale of the firm would be comparable to that of an itinerant peanut stand.[1]

Recognizing the infirmities of both the abuse and structure theories, economists sought other criteria for judging horizontal size. Many of them fastened upon "performance"; they urged that the legality of a business enterprise be determined not by its "share of the market" but by the way in which it "performed." [2] Thus Professor Adelman wrote: "One must look at the way the market actually behaves: the way prices are set and their trend over the years; at profits, and technological progress, and so on." [3]

As suggested in the foregoing quotation, the performance of a business enterprise depends upon its behavior and achievements

---

§4.1. [1] Gordon, Comment, 45 Proceedings Am. Econ. Assn. 483 (1955).

[2] Griffin, An Economic Approach to Antitrust Problems, c. 7 (American Enterprise Assn. 1951); Mason, The Current Status of the Monopoly Problem in the United States, 62 Harv. L. Rev. 1265, 1281 (1949). See Oppenheim, A New Look at Antitrust Enforcement Trends, Symposium N.Y. State Bar Assn., Section on Antitrust Law, 69, 76 (CCH 1950). Compare Stocking and Watkins, Monopoly and Free Enterprise 541 (Twentieth Century Fund, 1951).

[3] Adelman, Business Size and Public Policy, 24 J. Business 269, 273 (1951).

in a number of fields.   One factor frequently mentioned is the price policy of the firm.   The suggestion is, of course, that low prices are indicative of good performance, and frequently this criterion is phrased in terms of passing on cost reductions to consumers.[4]   Efficiency of operation is another factor considered under the heading of "performance."   Here the suggestion is, obviously, that a business enterprise should not be wasteful and that it should achieve low costs of production.[5]   To attain such efficiency, the firm must be "progressive" and hence "progress" is another criterion of performance.   Usually such progress is conceived in terms of technological improvement[6] but the term is capable of a somewhat larger application. "Social responsibility" is another criterion frequently mentioned.   During the depression of the thirties, at least, that term appeared to refer principally to the maintenance of employment: the firm which had large payrolls was considered to be rendering a better performance than the company which

[4] Mason, The Current Status of the Monopoly Problem in the United States, 62 Harv. L. Rev. 1265, 1281-1282 (1949); Kreps and Wright, Measurement of the Social Performance of Business 3 (TNEC Monograph No. 7, 1940).   One economist put the matter this way:

"Does this scheme of pricing, with its corollary scale of operations pass on to consumers the net gain from technological improvement?

". . . This is the ultimate test of sound pricing in an industrial system in which managers do not have prices made for them by a fully competitive market but themselves determine the pitch and intensity of competition and the scale of activity."   Nourse, Price Making in a Democracy 349 (Brookings Institution, 1944).

In Celanese Corp. of America, Ann. Rep. 1948, 9 (New York City, 1949), the following appeared:

"The Company's record over a long period of years has been one of reducing the prices of its products in terms of consumer purchasing power. . . .

"By means of this policy the Company has expanded its initial markets and opened new markets, placing its products within the reach of large masses of people."

As to high prices and resulting high profits, see §2.27 *supra* and §4.10 *infra;* as to price "flexibility," see §4.12 *infra.*

[5] Nourse, Price Making in a Democracy 322-323 (Brookings Institution, 1944); Svennilson, Monopoly, Efficiency and the Structure of Industry, in Chamberlin, ed., Monopoly and Competition and Their Regulation 271-280 (International Economic Assn. 1954).   Note the emphasis upon efficiency in production in recent British legislation.   Harbury and Raskind, The British Approach to Monopoly Control, 67 Q.J. Econ. 380, 382 (1953).   Putting the matter in a slightly different way, the United States Chamber of Commerce has urged that high utilization of capacity should be considered good performance.   Celler Committee I, pt. 2B, at 816-817.

[6] Svennilson, Monopoly, Efficiency and the Structure of Industry, in Chamberlin, ed., Monopoly and Competition and Their Regulation 271, 272 (International Economic Assn. 1954); Griffin, An Economic Approach to Antitrust Problems, c. 7 (American Enterprise Assn. 1951); Wiles, Growth versus Choice, 66 Econ. J. 244-255 (1956).   It is not uncommon for manufacturers to boast that their current models represent constantly expanding progress in research and engineering and the passing on to customers of greater values resulting from technological developments.   E.g., General Motors Corp., 40th Ann. Rep. 12 (New York City, 1949), 44th Ann. Rep. 8 (1953).   Compare Sunlight and Shadow, 5 Fortune No. 5, pp. 51, 114 (1932).

operated with fewer employees. Even today, the number and size of "benefits" afforded employees may be considered under the heading of "social responsibility." [7] More broadly, however, that term may relate to the difference between cost to the firm and total social cost. Unemployment, traumatic injuries to employees and others, emission of noxious fumes, and the like constitute costs to society as a whole which may not be reflected in the individual firm's operating statement;[8] the extent to which those social costs are minimized may measure a firm's social responsibility. Finally, some economists, taking a purely pragmatic approach, would simply examine the conduct of a business in an effort to determine whether any governmental action could influence its conduct for the better.[9]

§4.2. **Application of performance criteria by the courts.** From time to time in antitrust opinions the courts appear to have recognized performance as a test of horizontal size. In one of the older decisions involving the United Shoe Machinery Company, for example, the court noted that customers had been given the benefits of improvements made by the defendant and that new machines had been substituted for old ones without disproportionate charges.[1] Such decisions, however, are few and far between. For the most part, the courts have refused to consider the per-

[7] Kreps and Wright, Measurement of the Social Performance of Business 3 (TNEC Monograph No. 7, 1940). An example may be found in Reader's Digest, 14 Fortune No. 5, pp. 121, 131 (1936). Somewhat related to the above problem are current doubts concerning the assumption that profit maximization is the dominant motive of business managers. Compare Lauterbach, Discussion, 45 Proceedings Am. Econ. Assn. 555, 558 (1955). Some general discussion of social responsibility will be found in Chapter 8 of this book. Examples of such "performance" may be found in the scholarship programs now sponsored by many prominent corporations. The scholarships may be available to children of employees or merely to residents of towns in which factories are located. E.g., Pittsburgh Plate Glass Co., 69th Ann. Rep. 15 (Pittsburgh, 1953); American Can Co., 1952 Ann. Rep. 9 (New York City, 1953); Phelps Dodge Corp., Ann. Rep. 1952, 12 (New York City, 1953). Hospital and medical facilities may be made available both to employees and to their families. E.g., id. at 18.

[8] Rothschild, The Waste of Competition, in Chamberlin, ed., Monopoly and Competition and Their Regulation 301, 308 (International Economic Assn. 1954).

[9] Markham, An Alternative Approach to the Concept of Workable Competition, 40 Am. Econ. Rev. 349, 360-361 (1950). It is worth noting that an attempt to establish performance criteria for competition leads directly to the alternative of government price-fixing. E.g., Rothschild, The Waste of Competition, in Chamberlin, ed., Monopoly and Competition and Their Regulation 301, 314 (International Economic Assn. 1954); Johr, Regulation of Competition, id. at 338, 342, 348.

§4.2. [1] United States v. United Shoe Machinery Co., 247 U.S. 32, 56 (1918). See also United States v. Morgan, 118 F. Supp. 621, 713 (S.D.N.Y. 1953); United States v. E. I. Du Pont de Nemours & Co., 118 F. Supp. 41 (D. Del. 1953), aff'd, 351 U.S. 377 (1956). Compare Board of Trade v. Christie Grain & Stock Co., 198 U.S. 236, 252 (1905).

formance of the defendants when firms seek to rebut evidence of monopoly by showing that their conduct has been "good." Thus the fact that prices have not been raised by the alleged monopolist will not save him from the operation of the Sherman Act.[2]   Particularly in those decisions which seek to apply the structure theory, the courts have indicated that they will not distinguish "good" from "bad" monopolies.[3]   Thus the fact that the defendants have eliminated trade misrepresentations, improved service to customers, and the like will not justify the maintenance of monopoly.[4]   Recently a lower court said:

> . . . the Sherman Act was not designed to compel business men in any industry to compete in any particular way, but rather to break up and dissolve monopolistic or restraining combinations, conspiracies or agreements not to compete.[5]

In accordance with those tenets of the structure theory, the Attorney General's Committee reported:

> The economists' distinction between "effective monopoly" and "effective competition" does not turn on whether the industry in question is progressively managed or technologically advanced, nor on its policies with regard to wages, profits or high- or low-price programs. . . . The ultimate question . . . is whether the pressures of the market situation are such as tend of themselves to

2 United States v. Besser Mfg. Co., 96 F. Supp. 304, 314 (E.D. Mich. 1951), aff'd, 343 U.S. 444 (1952); United States v. National Lead Co., 63 F. Supp. 513 (S.D.N.Y. 1945), aff'd, 332 U.S. 319 (1947); Harding v. American Glucose Co., 182 Ill. 551, 55 N.E. 577 (1899); see Fashion Originators' Guild v. FTC, 312 U.S. 457, 467 (1941). In United States v. National Lead Co., the lower court said at page 525: ". . . during the regime of the combination, the art has rapidly advanced, production has increased enormously and prices have sharply declined . . . it does not follow that the public interest has not been abused. . . . Anyone is free to speculate, whether, in the absence of the arrangement, the stimulus of competition might not have produced far greater strides. . . . The economic theory underlying the Sherman Act is that in the long run, competition is a more effective prod to production . . . than even an enlightened combination." In Harding v. American Glucose Co., supra, the court said at page 619: "The material consideration in the case of such combinations is, as a general thing, not that prices are raised, but that it rests in the power and discretion of the trust or corporation . . . to raise prices at any time, if it sees fit to do so." But compare United States v. American Can Co., 230 Fed. 859, 893-894, 234 Fed. 1019 (D. Md. 1916), appeal dismissed, 256 U.S. 706 (1921); International Harvester Co. v. Kentucky, 234 U.S. 216 (1914).

3 United States v. Aluminum Co. of America, 148 F.2d 416, 427 (2d Cir. 1945). Note, however, that in the same opinion (at 426) the court considered the profits earned by the defendant and found them to represent a return of about 10 per cent on invested capital and decided that such earnings were not unreasonable. See the lower court opinion. 44 F. Supp. 97, 203, 265-266 (S.D.N.Y. 1941).

4 United States v. Great Lakes Towing Co., 208 Fed. 733, 740, 743-744 (N.D. Ohio, 1913), 217 Fed. 656 (N.D. Ohio, 1914).

5 United States v. Morgan, 118 F. Supp. 621, 738 (S.D.N.Y. 1953).

bring about the main beneficial effects which constitute the economic reasons why we try to maintain competition . . .[6]

Thus at the present writing it cannot be said that the performance test has achieved any substantial recognition in the courts.

§4.3. **Critique of the performance test.** Some years ago two proponents of the performance theory argued that the social performance of individual companies was no less measurable than that of entire industries or segments of the economy.[1] Whether that statement is true or not, one can point out difficulties involved in the application of the performance test. In determining whether prices, for example, reflect proper performance, numerous problems are involved.[2] One recent student examined the price of gasoline and compared it with that of many other commodities, including bread, milk, coffee, apples, beef, dog food, lumber and automobiles. The basis of the comparison was sales price per pound. As the author himself said, the results were "not too meaningful."[3] Several years ago observers complained that the price of steel was held below free-market levels by the exercise of some degree of monopoly power. At that very time, however, a congressional committee complained bitterly when steel companies increased their prices and attributed those increases to a lack of competition in the industry.[4] The notion that the performance of a business can be judged by the quantity of goods it produces is open to the objection that the goods may not be wanted by con-

[6] Atty. Gen. Nat. Com. Rep. 322, b. In the same section the committee went on to say: ". . . a monopolistic industry, with dynamic management and active research, might perform better, for example, in the sense of cost reduction, than a fairly competitive branch of industry which is inferior in these characteristics. Our public policy, however, is founded on the economically sound assumption that competition will on the average result in much more progressiveness and efficiency than monopoly."

§4.3. [1] Kreps and Wright, Measurement of the Social Performance of Business 93 (TNEC Monograph No. 7, 1940).

[2] Id. at 47.

[3] Cassady, Price Making and Price Behavior in the Petroleum Industry 320 (Petroleum Monograph Series No. 1, 1954). We fully concur in the author's own comment on his statistics; indeed, we will go so far as to say that they are obviously without meaning.

[4] Bowman, Toward Less Monopoly, 101 U. Pa. L. Rev. 577, 617 (1953); Joint Committee on the Economic Report, December 1949 Steel Price Increases, Sen. Rep. No. 1373, 81st Cong., 2d Sess. 18, 29 (1950). Compare United States v. Trenton Potteries Co., 273 U.S. 392 (1927). Comparison of prices over a period of time involves of course the definition of the commodity, which may have changed radically during the period. The automobile of 1926 was different from that of 1939 and the 1955 automobile is still another commodity. Compare Kreps and Wright, Measurement of the Social Performance of Business 83 (TNEC Monograph No. 7, 1940); Nelson and Keim, Price Behavior and Business Policy 57 (TNEC Monograph No. 1, 1940).

sumers. Similarly, the fact that a firm has a tremendous payroll may simply suggest that it has failed to install modern machinery and is inefficient.[5] Whether a firm actually is progressive in adopting advanced technological techniques, may be extremely difficult to ascertain: who is to say whether a particular innovation is sufficiently proven to warrant the large financial risks involved in its introduction into an assembly line?[6] Observers have pointed out that application of performance tests of horizontal size might result in the imposition of public utility type regulation upon all enterprise: the courts could be left with the task of fixing prices and determining the type of goods to be produced.[7] Putting the matter another way, tests of performance may in some instances constitute the other side of the "abuse" coin. Under the abuse theory, the courts look to the bad behavior of defendants in order to ascertain whether the statutes against monopoly have been violated. Under the performance test, the defendants should establish their good behavior as a defense to allegations of monopoly. Neither procedure is apt to prove wholly satisfactory.[8]

We can only conclude that the courts have been commendably cautious in rejecting the performance test. It is too vague, as presently formulated, for application to criminal and civil cases. As stated by Professor Clark:

> A general judgment may be influenced by appraisal of the performance of the system in the large. But for purposes of specific policy in actual cases, rates of progress and fairness of profits are

[5] Compare Kreps and Wright, Measurement of the Social Performance of Business 3, 7 (TNEC Monograph No. 7, 1940).

[6] Edwards, Public Policy and Business Size, 24 J. Business 280, 288 (1951); Scitovsky, Economic Theory and the Measurement of Concentration, in Business Concentration and Price Policy 101, 109 (Stigler ed. 1955). Measuring efficiency is much more complicated than would be apparent at first glance. Svennilson, Monopoly, Efficiency and the Structure of Industry, in Chamberlin, ed., Monopoly and Competition and Their Regulation 271, 273 (International Economic Assn. 1954). Note the close relationship between performance and those doctrines of dynamic economics examined in Appendix B *infra*. The earning of "excessive" profits is sometimes referred to under the heading of "performance." E.g., Joint Committee on the Economic Report, December 1949 Steel Price Increases, Sen. Rep. No. 1373, 81st Cong., 2d Sess. 9, 29 (1950). As noted in §2.27 *supra*, testing monopoly by profits is a risky affair. Compare Bowman, Toward Less Monopoly, 101 U. Pa. L. Rev. 577, 618-619 (1953). Note also the experience of R. H. Macy & Co.: it was a successful business until it became preoccupied with "community relations" and the like; then its earnings dropped to about 25 per cent of prior levels and investors began to be worried. Durrance, Miracle on 34th Street, 34 Barron's No. 50, pp. 3, 23 (1954).

[7] Rostow, Market Organization and Stabilization Policy, in Income Stabilization for a Developing Economy, c. 10, pp. 439, 511 (Millikan ed. 1954).

[8] Edwards, Public Policy and Business Size, 24 J. Business 280, 287 (1951). But compare Mason, The Current Status of the Monopoly Problem in the United States, 62 Harv. L. Rev. 1265, 1269 (1949).

too uncertain, dependent on too many irrelevant circumstances. . . .[9]

To adopt performance criteria could saddle the judiciary with the tasks of management and might possibly result (under the criterion of "social responsibility") in a feudalism far surpassing the effects of any degree of monopoly heretofore experienced in the United States.[10]

§4.4. **Countervailing power.** In recent years it has been suggested that the problem of market power[1] be dealt with through creation of a "balanced force polity" or the application of "countervailing power." Those two phrases seem substantially synonymous.[2] They envision the creation of a "countervailing" force on the opposite side of the market to offset existing monopoly power. Such a countervailing force may compel the monopolist to share his profits with others and will, it is claimed, produce the effects of competition without the necessity of litigation. Monopoly, in other words, is to be offset with monopsony to arrive at the situation economists term "bi-lateral monopoly."[3]

As a description of large segments of the existing economy, "countervailing power" no doubt constitutes a valid explanation of widespread phenomena. The rise of mass merchandisers, for example, may have been induced by an effort to share monopoly profits in manufacturing and may have resulted in the effects of competition being felt despite the presence of oligopolistic market structures.[4] Certainly much recent legislation is based upon the

---

[9] Clark, Competition: Static Models and Dynamic Aspects, 45 Proceedings Am. Econ. Assn. 450, 456 (1955). See also Oppenheim, Economic Background, 19 Geo. Wash. L. Rev. 120, 128-129 (1950); Kahn, Standards for Antitrust Policy, 67 Harv. L. Rev. 28, 41-42 (1953); Dirlam and Kahn, Fair Competition 37 (1954).

[10] Edwards, Public Policy and Business Size, 24 J. Business 280, 286 (1951).

§4.4. [1] The concept of "countervailing power" applies to oligopoly as well as monopoly; it also applies on the buying side of the market.

[2] Clark, Alternative to Serfdom (1948); Galbraith, American Capitalism 118, 136, 145-146 (1952); Smith, Federal Regulation of Industry, Current Business Studies No. 14, pp. 6, 14 (Society of Business Advisory Professions, 1953). Professor Galbraith would differentiate (at 145-146) between "original" and "countervailing" power. Original power is bad and wicked; countervailing power is desirable.

[3] Stackelberg, The Theory of the Market Economy 182 (Peacock trans. 1952); Fellner, Prices and Wages Under Bilateral Monopoly, 61 Q.J. Econ. 503, 505, 523 (1947).

[4] Galbraith, American Capitalism 121-122, 125 et seq. (1952); U.S. Steel II: Prices, 13 Fortune No. 4, p. 127 (1936); Allen, Monopoly and Competition in the United Kingdom, in Chamberlin, ed., Monopoly and Competition and Their Regulation 88, 92-93 (International Economic Assn. 1954). Others have pointed to situations in which countervailing power did not explain market structures. E.g., Adelman, Review of Galbraith's American Capitalism, 49 Nw. U.L. Rev. 155, 158 (1954).

theory that countervailing power is desirable,[5] and perhaps some such notion has crept into a few antitrust decisions.[6]

The concept of a "balanced force polity" suggests that there is no need to enforce the antitrust laws. Instead of reducing positions of monopoly power, the government should merely create some countervailing force.[7] Unfortunately, however, this simple prescription for curing the ills of the economy does not appear to be sound. "Countervailing power" is itself ambiguous and vague. To a certain extent it overlaps with the older and simpler concept of competition itself. Furthermore, and more important, the results of the application of countervailing power may or may not be favorable. It is not clear, for example, why the person possessing countervailing power will necessarily pass on the fruits thereof (in the form of lower prices or otherwise) to consumers. Moreover, the distinction between those who possess "original" power (a wicked monopoly) and those blessed with "countervailing" power (a beneficent force) may often be difficult to draw.[8] More fundamentally, the suggestion involves the awesome prospect of the growth of larger and larger political pressure blocs which would eventually influence all economic and political decisions. The position of those who fear such a development was well stated in the testimony of Professor Machlup:

> . . . the whole theory of equalizing the bargaining strength of different groups in the markets is fallacious if it means building up the bargaining strength of the weaker instead of reducing the bargaining strength of the stronger. Real competition implies small bargaining strength on the part of everybody. In the name of equalizing the bargaining strength of the weaker party with that of its counterpart, we have built up the power of labor unions to the point where they can terrorize the Nation. If, instead, we had

[5] E.g., National Labor Relations Act. 49 Stat. 449, 29 U.S.C.A. §§151 et seq.

[6] United States v. Republic Steel Corp., 11 F. Supp. 117, 124 (N.D. Ohio, 1935); United States Telephone Co. v. Central Union Co., 202 Fed. 66, 73 (6th Cir. 1913); Home Telephone Co. v. North Manchester Co., 47 Ind. App. 411, 92 N.E. 558, 562 (1910); see United States v. Champlin Refining Co., 341 U.S. 290, 298 et seq. (1951). But compare United States v. Crescent Amusement Co., 323 U.S. 173, 188 (1944).

[7] Galbraith, American Capitalism 155 (1952). Compare Harbury and Raskind, The British Approach to Monopoly Control, 67 Q.J. Econ. 380, 396-397 (1953).

[8] Adelman, Review of Galbraith's American Capitalism, 48 Nw. U.L. Rev. 155, 158 (1954); Levi, 49 id. 150, 153 (1954); Stigler, The Economist Plays with Blocs, 44 Proceedings Am. Econ. Assn. 7 (1954). Whether mass merchandising of groceries has proved a beneficent force is, for example, the subject of heated and sometimes acrimonious debate. E.g., Adelman, The Large Firm and Its Suppliers, 31 Rev. Econ. & Stat. 113 (1949); Dirlam and Kahn, Anti-Trust Law and the Big Buyer, 60 J. Pol. Econ. 118 et seq. (1952); Adelman, Integration and Dissolution of A & P Company, 29 Ind. L.J. 367 (1954).

reduced the power of corporations, we would have secured more industrial peace, a better allocation of national resources, and a larger national product.[9]

In these circumstances we can only conclude that the courts have been wise not to adopt the theory of countervailing power for antitrust purposes.

§4.5. Workable or effective competition. Another effort to avoid the difficulties inherent in the abuse and structure theories of horizontal size is found in doctrines of "workable" and "effective" competition. Under such headings economists have attempted to take account of the various market imperfections and dynamic considerations which render application of the pure structure theory so difficult. Professor Stigler, for example, would define "workable competition" in terms of three criteria: (1) a considerable number of firms in each market area, (2) lack of collusion among those firms, and (3) a long-run average cost curve for new firms not materially higher than that of established firms.[1] Professor Wilcox wrote:

> Competition among sellers, even though imperfect, may be regarded as effective or workable if it offers buyers real alternatives sufficient to enable them, by shifting their purchases from one seller to another, substantially to influence quality, service and price. Competition, to be effective, need not involve the standardization of commodities; it does, however, require the ready substitution of one product for another; it may manifest itself in differences in quality and service as well as in price. Effective competition . . . cannot be expected to obtain in fields where sellers are so few in number, capital requirements so large, and the pressure of fixed charges so strong, that price warfare . . . will lead almost inevitably to collusive understandings. . . .[2]

The United States Chamber of Commerce suggested a four-point test: (1) improvement in products, (2) lower prices for better prod-

---

[9] Celler Committee I, pt. 2A, at 504-505; Hale, Agreements Among Competitors, 33 Minn. L. Rev. 331, 387-388 (1949). Compare Robinson, Imperfect Competition Revisited, 63 Econ. J. 579, 581 (1953); Union Trust Co. v. Kinloch Telephone Co., 258 Ill. 202, 211, 101 N.E. 535 (1913).

§4.5. [1] Stigler, The Extent and Basis of Monopoly, 32 Am. Econ. Rev., Supp. No. 2, pp. 1, 2 et seq. (1942). A review of the economic writing with respect to "workable" competition will be found in Brief for the United States on Liability, pp. 63-67, filed Jan. 29, 1952, in United States v. United Shoe Machinery Corp., 110 F. Supp. 295 (D. Mass. 1953), aff'd per curiam, 347 U.S. 521 (1954).

[2] Wilcox, Competition and Monopoly in American Industry 8 (TNEC Monograph No. 21, 1940). Presumably the word "buyers" in the passage quoted in the text does not refer to individuals but to groups of consumers. To the same effect see Edwards, Maintaining Competition 124 (1949).

ucts, (3) a high volume of output, and (4) near-capacity operations.[3] The Attorney General's Committee contrasted "workable" competition with "pure" and "perfect" competition. If competition is both pure and perfect, the product involved must be purely homogenous; sellers and buyers must both have perfect knowledge of the market; no one seller may produce more than a negligible share of the goods in that market; new firms can enter into competition with the same costs as those experienced by existing firms; and there is perfect mobility for all resources. "Workable" competition sets its sights less high.[4]

As suggested above, one of the prime tests of workability is the

[3] Celler Committee I, pt. 2, at 816-817. Inadequate competition, the chamber stated (at 817), could be identified by disregarding new processes and products; a lack of disposition to work for lower costs and selling prices; maintenance of profits without fighting to maintain volume; and failure to bring unused capacity into use whenever sales revenue can be increased enough to warrant additional cost. Professor Bain prescribed a five-point test for absence of workable competition: profits above normal; the scale of firms seriously outside the optimal range; chronic excess capacity; high competitive selling cost; and a persistent lag in adoption of cost-reducing changes or product improvement. Bain, Workable Competition in Oligopoly, 40 Proceedings Am. Econ. Assn. 35, 37 (1950). Another student wrote: "One *positive* test of whether competition is Effective Competition is whether the business performance in the situation *tends* to serve the public interest in increasing values in goods and services for more people, in proportion to human effort. This means ideally a type of competition where competitors are progressively striving in rivalry with their direct or indirect competitors, and with a constant eye on their potential competitors, endeavoring to expand their markets, to improve products or services offered relative to prices, or conversely to improve prices relatively to goods or services. This is the test of relative efficiency. American manufacturing industry on the broad overall statistical basis has improved output per man hour at a rate of about 2.8% per year as compared to the British (and probably European) rate of somewhere near one half that." Smith, Effective Competition, 26 N.Y.U.L. Rev. 405, 413 (1951).

[4] Atty. Gen. Nat. Com. Rep. 338-339. There it was said: ". . . the concept of workable competition posits a lesser degree of 'perfection' [than pure and perfect competition combined]. Thus perfect competition would require an extremely large number of sellers. Criteria of workable competition . . . could be satisfied by a lesser number of sellers, some of whom may well produce significant fractions of total supply, provided they really compete and do not foreclose entry of new competitors, except by reason of their superiority. Pure and perfect competition would require that all sellers produce goods that were identical and that no buyers have preferences among sellers. The concept of workable competition is consistent with considerable product differentiation and recognizes the existence of buyer preference . . . As to entry, too, perfect competition contemplates complete freedom of entry by new firms, whereas workable competition is compatible with practical barriers to entry, such as considerable capital and even advertising requirements, and a period of higher costs while production is organized and management trained . . . workable competition goes beyond the theory of perfect competition . . . While the theory of perfect competition examines certain implications of the sellers' quest for profit under a limited set of assumptions, the literature of workable competition seeks to identify those aspects of competition which provide market incentives for innovation, including quality innovation as well as cost reduction, and taking directly into account other elements of the market situation which change through time."

number of sellers in the market place. No precise number of sellers, however, is prescribed. The Attorney General's Committee wrote on this subject:

> The basic characteristic of effective competition in the economic sense is that no one seller, and no group of sellers acting in concert, has the power to choose its level of profits by giving less and charging more. . . . In an effectively competitive market, the individual seller cannot control his rivals' offerings, and those offerings set narrow limits on his discretion as to price and production. He must, in the light of his own cost, adjust his offerings to a market scale of prices for offerings of different quality or attractiveness. In the moderately long run, he must accept market prices determined by changes in supply and demand beyond any effect which may be attributable to his own change in price or output. These market conditions inflict penalties on high costs or poor services. . . .[5]

It is clear, however, that there should be no collusion whatever among the sellers. Thus the Attorney General's Committee wrote:

> A primary condition of workable competition in an economic sense is that there be genuine independence on the part of the business units in an industry, so that each firm pursues its own individual advantage. . . . Where there are only a limited number of sellers . . . concerted action can be subtle and informal, and sometimes difficult to detect.[6]

Ease of entry is another important factor. As stated by Professor Ellis,

[5] Atty. Gen. Nat. Com. Rep. 320, (2). Another student put the matter this way: "Workable competition is considered to require, principally, a fairly large number of sellers and buyers, no one of whom occupies a large share of the market, the absence of collusion among either group, and the possibility of market entry by new firms." Mason, The Current Status of the Monopoly Problem in the United States, 62 Harv. L. Rev. 1265, 1268 (1949). Professor Edwards put the matter this way: "The number of firms should be regarded as unduly small when the buyer no longer encounters substantial variations in business policy, whether the uniformity which has become good business practice is due to a single control, to agreement or to mutual forbearance among a few large enterprises. In reasonable precaution against such developments, enterprises should be regarded as too few whenever their number is so small as to entail substantial risk that their policies will not vary. . . ." Edwards, Maintaining Competition 128 (1949). Compare Bowman, Toward Less Monopoly, 101 U. Pa. L. Rev. 577, 631 et seq. (1953).

[6] Atty. Gen. Nat. Com. Rep. 327, (3). Note also the following excerpt from the same report at page 326: "Effective competition may be affected not only by the total number of sellers; their relative size and strength must also be considered. This does not mean that close equality of size among the various firms is essential for workable competition to exist, but only that the rivalry should not depend entirely upon sellers who are so weak or inefficient as to exist by sufferance." Compare Wright, Democracy and Progress 127 (1948).

In any situation we can be sure that the greater the ease of entry into production the closer is the approach to a workably competitive norm.[7]

The Attorney General's Committee wrote:

The cost of entry into the competitive area should not be impracticably high. This does not imply an absolute criterion . . . in terms of a given number of dollars. . . . But it does mean that under prevailing conditions as to the availability of capital, an attempt by existing firms to raise prices considerably above the competitive norm would make it profitable and practicable for new firms or existing borderline firms to invade the field. In economic terms, this means that conditions of cost for a new firm should not be excessively higher, at least after a reasonable period of initial development, than conditions of cost for an existing member of the industry.[8]

Ease of entry, of course, is closely related to that "exclusion" which has often been thought to characterize monopoly. Other students place less emphasis upon market "structure" than upon actual rivalry between firms resulting in choices open to buyers.[9] And Professor Clark recently emphasized the progress of technology:

The essential limits on private discretionary power are presumably satisfied if the discretion of business units does not extend to doing things that obstruct the progress of the "generally available state of the arts" or prevent the public from getting the benefit of it. This is admittedly a not-too-precise standard; and may need some care to avoid tautology, centering in the phrase "generally available." It has a logical kinship with Marshall's "representative firm" and I believe it is not wholly meaningless.[10]

[7] Ellis, Economic Expansion Through Competitive Markets, in Homan and Machlup, eds., Financing American Prosperity 126, 177 (Twentieth Century Fund, 1945).

[8] Atty. Gen. Nat. Com. Rep. 326, (2). *Accord*: Smith, Effective Competition, 26 N.Y.U.L. Rev. 405, 416 (1951); Fellner, Competition Among the Few 294-295 (1949). This of course is the theme developed in §3.12, *supra,* that ease of entry alone may suffice to make a "monopoly" situation tolerable under the structure theory. It has been suggested, however, that competition may be "workable" when entry into the industry is neither excessively easy nor unduly difficult. The thought is that somewhere between those extremes established firms will hold prices low enough to discourage entry and thus maximize long-run return. Bain, Workable Competition in Oligopoly, 40 Proceedings Am. Econ. Assn. 35, 42-43, 46 (1950). Note the close connection between both the abuse and the structure theories inherent in the foregoing requirement of workable competition.

[9] Adelman, Effective Competition and the Anti-Trust Laws, 61 Harv. L. Rev. 1289, 1303 (1948). Note also the thought that effective competition may depend upon the expectation that an innovator can gain in volume of business for a time; that his customers' responses to an inducement may be quicker than his rivals' responses; that the gap may afford an interval during which the innovator may reasonably expect to enjoy an advantage. Atty. Gen. Nat. Com. Rep. 329, (6).

[10] Clark, Competition: Static Models and Dynamic Aspects, 45 Proceedings Am. Econ. Assn. 450, 456 (1955).

Professor Markham, finding the foregoing tests inadequate, suggested a single over-all criterion:

> . . . an industry may be said to be workably competitive if public policy measures can produce no changes in the industry that would obviously make society better off.[11]

§4.6. Workable or effective competition in the courts. Most doctrines of workable and effective competition are too new for the courts to have taken extensive cognizance of them. Several decisions, however, can be cited[1] in support of the proposition that the courts are ready to adopt such yardsticks in judging horizontal size. In fact, some opinions expressly refer to the proposed test by name.[2] Other cases are, to say the least, inconsistent with acceptance of workable competition.[3] As we have seen, the Attorney General's Committee recommended workable competition and there is therefore at least a reasonable prospect that the courts will accord workable competition some scope in future antitrust litigation. Indeed, it could be argued that the legal concept known as the "rule of reason" is simply a lawyer's way of referring to workable or effective competition.[4] Unfortunately, however, the rule of reason, which has claimed the favor of the courts during most

---

[11] Markham, Competition in the Rayon Industry vii (1952); Markham, An Alternative Approach to the Concept of Workable Competition, 40 Am. Econ. Rev. 349, 361 (1950). A different approach is reflected in the following statement: "Monopoly is properly defined as such a degree of important continuing control, however achieved, as to render the purchaser practically without freedom of choice. It is the ability to exploit a trade position without the necessity of maintaining it. The determination of this situation is a matter of opinion." Knauth, Monopoly Reconsidered, 60 Pol. Sci. Q. 563, 576 (1945).

§4.6. [1] United States v. United States Steel Corp., 223 Fed. 55, 67 (D.N.J. 1915), aff'd, 251 U.S. 417 (1920); United States v. Columbia Steel Corp., 334 U.S. 495, 524, 529 (1948). In United States v. Aluminum Co. of America, 91 F. Supp. 333 (S.D.N.Y. 1950), the trial court on remand expressed views almost identical to some formulations of workable competition. The court said at page 347: "In determining the extent of permissible power that is consistent with the anti-trust laws in a particular industry, the following factors are relevant: the number and strength of the firms in the market; their effective size from the standpoint of technological development and from the standpoint of competition with substitute materials and foreign trade; national security interests in the maintenance of strong productive facilities, and maximum scientific research and development; together with the public interest in lowered cost and uninterrupted production."

[2] United States v. E. I. Du Pont de Nemours & Co., 118 F. Supp. 41, 50 (D. Del. 1953), aff'd, 351 U.S. 377, 386 (1956). Note the cases cited supra §3.12 with respect to ease of entry.

[3] United States v. Griffith, 334 U.S. 100 (1948); United States v. United Shoe Machinery Corp., 110 F. Supp. 295, 343 (D. Mass. 1953), aff'd per curiam, 347 U.S. 521 (1954). Compare Kahn, A Legal and Economic Appraisal of the "New" Sherman and Clayton Acts, 63 Yale L.J. 293, 298 (1954).

[4] Oppenheim, Federal Anti-Trust Legislation, 50 Mich. L. Rev. 1139, 1187 (1952); Johnston, Monopolize or Attempt to Monopolize, Proceedings A.B.A., Section of Antitrust Law 72, 78-79 (Aug. 26, 1953).

of the administration of the Sherman Act, has so uncertain a content that we cannot be wholly sure it is the same thing as workable competition.[5]

§4.7. **Critique of workable competition.** As we have suggested, the merits of workable competition lie in its avoidance of difficulties inherent in the structure and abuse tests. Under doctrines of workable competition, it is possible to take account of market imperfections. Again, "workable competition" may recognize dynamic forces in our economy and not stifle innovation and change.[1] Professor Chamberlin, once considered an advocate of "pure competition," said several years ago that no one advocates establishing an economy wholly characterized by purity. He went on to say that some form of workable competition is desired by all.[2] Furthermore, it has been asserted that workable competition is itself workable: that application of the doctrine does not set an impossible task for the courts and that one can distinguish between situations of mild and aggravated monopoly power.[3]

Other students have questioned whether workable competition is actually workable. Professor Stocking referred to six characteristics of workability chosen by Professor Wilcox. He put considerable emphasis on two factors not included in Wilcox's list and placed only incidental reliance on those which did appear therein.[4] Professor Markham examined the concepts of workability set forth by Professors Clark, Stigler and Edwards and propounded his own theory of workability. He was unable, however,

[5] E.g., Smith, Federal Regulation of Industry, Current Business Studies No. 14, pp. 6, 13 (Society of Business Advisory Professions, 1953): "While it is fair to say that the Rule [of Reason] is imprecise, its application in Sherman Act litigation, as directed against enhancement of price or throttling of competition, has given a workable content to antitrust legislation"; United States v. E. I. Du Pont de Nemours & Co., 118 F. Supp. 41 (D. Del. 1953), aff'd, 351 U.S. 377, 386-387 (1956).

§4.7. [1] Hayek, Individualism and Economic Order 92 (1948); Wright, The Economics of Disturbance 89-90 (1946); Clark, Competition and the Objectives of Government Policy, in Chamberlin, ed., Monopoly and Competition and Their Regulation 317, 327, 337 (International Economic Assn. 1954); Rothschild, The Wastes of Competition, id. at 301, 306-307.

[2] Chamberlin, Product Heterogeneity and Public Policy, 40 Proceedings Am. Econ. Assn. 85 (1950). Compare Dirlam and Kahn, Anti-Trust Law and the Big Buyer, 60 J. Pol. Econ. 118, 119 (1952).

[3] Rostow, Market Organization and Stabilization Policy, in Income Stabilization for a Developing Economy, c. 10, pp. 439, 512 (Millikan ed. 1954).

[4] Stocking and Mueller, The Cellophane Case and the New Competition, 45 Am. Econ. Rev. 29, 30-31 (1955). Another student has frowned upon formulations of workable competition arrived at by others. Edwards, Public Policy and Business Size, 24 J. Business 280, 285-286 (1951). Professor Edwards was protesting the necessity of weighing various performance factors, such as technological research, labor policies, conservation policies, and the like, of the defendant under the banner of "workable competition."

to accept any of the others.[5]   Indeed, the concept of workable competition is derived from two probably incompatible sources: the market structure and the performance of the alleged monopolist.   We may translate those sources into the structure test and the abuse test respectively, and thus find that workability is nothing more than a loose amalgamation of those earlier doctrines.   As a consequence, it is often said that the notion of workable competition has a subjective character rendering it impossible of application in judicial proceedings.   It is, in short, only a vague guide to public policy.[6]

We conclude that the notion of workable competition as now formulated is too imprecise to support an interpretation of the antitrust laws.   Consider, for example, whether the following test could be applied in litigation:

> The main implication of a program of workable competition is to decide, on the basis of the specific information available for individual industries, what degree of competition is obtainable by methods of practical policy without substantial loss of technological efficiency . . . and does not presumably create a degree of uncertainty such as would offset the advantages.[7]

A leading lawyer stated the content of the workability test in the following language:

> If business men are expected to understand and do what is wanted, the definition of competition to be followed in any realistic clarification of the Antitrust Laws as applied to imperfect competition should be a practical business standard for judging service to the public.   It should relate to production and other useful performance, emphasizing freedom in the functioning of incentives and

---

[5] Markham, An Alternative Approach to the Concept of Workable Competition, 40 Am. Econ. Rev. 349, 354 et seq. (1950).

[6] Mason, The Current Status of the Monopoly Problem in the United States, 62 Harv. L. Rev. 1265, 1269, 1280 (1949); Stigler, The Extent and Basis of Monopoly, 32 Am. Econ. Rev., Supp. No. 2, pp. 1, 4 (1942); Bain, Workable Competition in Oligopoly, 40 Proceedings Am. Econ. Assn. 35, 36-37 (1950); Markham, An Alternative Approach to the Concept of Workable Competition, 40 Am. Econ. Rev. 349, 361 (1950); Wallace, Industrial Markets and Public Policy, in Public Policy 59, 67 (Friedrich and Mason ed. 1940); Keyes, The Shoe Machinery Case and the Problem of the Good Trust, 68 Q.J. Econ. 287, 298 (1954).

[7] Fellner, Competition Among the Few 289-290 (1949). Note the comment that "it is much easier to organize control over one industry serving many markets than over one market served by the products of several industries." Robinson, Imperfect Competition Revisited, 63 Econ. J. 579, 580 (1953). While not labeled a definition of workable competition, the foregoing statement, with its loose use of words such as "industry" and "market," suggests the type of problems encountered in workable or effective competition formulas.

consumer choice, freedom to enter and compete within the market, and the minimum of exceptions to such freedoms, consistent with the absence of predatory, coercive, unfair or deceptive acts, etc.

It should be presumed that competition is of the good kind when actual performance shows that there is a healthy condition, judged by actual creation of adequate alternatives in goods, services and markets for both buyers and sellers.[8]

Ultimately, lawyers and economists may be able to refine the content of "workable competition" and give that phrase a meaning sufficiently specific for judicial use. We cannot find that it now has any such uniformly accepted connotation.[9]

§4.8. Lerner's formula. Some years ago Professor Lerner proposed a formula whereby one could determine the existence of monopoly power. That formula operates simply by measuring the deviation of prices from marginal costs. Mathematically expressed, it is simply $P - \dfrac{MC}{P}$ wherein P is price and MC is marginal cost.[1] This formula, however, has not (to our knowledge) been so much as mentioned in a single judicial opinion. An active question exists as to whether marginal cost can be calculated accurately enough to apply the formula to specific situations.[2] Marginal cost, of course, is the cost of producing one additional unit of a commodity. Thus, if a factory is turning out a thousand bags of cement a day, marginal cost is found by calculating the additional expense necessary to produce one more bag of cement. While this concept seems, at first glance, to be a simple one, many economists believe that the formula cannot practically be applied to a large number of firms; and it has been said that data for its application would be extremely difficult of ascertainment in the

[8] Smith, Effective Competition, 26 N.Y.U.L. Rev. 405, 412 (1951). Note the emphasis placed upon "performance" in the above quotation. Compare George, The Measurement of Industrial Concentration, 34 Rev. Econ. & Stat. 146, 170 et seq. (1952).

[9] ". . . there are most assuredly no operational criteria capable of being applied concretely to any given industry with any likelihood of reaching an unambiguous appraisal of the workability of competition. . . . The workably competitive industry, like the workable wife or the workable university, is a concept which is unlikely to assist in the study of the subject to which it pertains. . . ." Stigler, Discussion, 66 Proceedings Am. Econ. Assn. 504-505 (1956). Compare Mason, Economic Concentration and the Monopoly Problem 380-381 (1957).

§4.8. [1] Machlup, The Political Economy of Monopoly 510 (1952); Wallace, Industrial Markets and Public Policy, in Public Policy 59, 107 (Friedrich and Mason ed. 1940); Dunlop, Price Flexibility and the Degree of Monopoly, 53 Q.J. Econ. 522, 526-527, 532 (1939).

[2] Machlup, The Political Economy of Monopoly 510, 524 (1952). But compare Machlup, The Economics of Sellers' Competition 25 (1952).

case of plants producing more than one product and hence requiring an allocation of common costs among them.[3]

Some firms cannot recover total costs if they price individual products at marginal cost levels. In decreasing cost industries, wherein indivisibility puts many firms in a position never to experience "diminishing returns," the charging of marginal costs will tend to drive rival concerns out of business.[4] It has been pointed out, too, that the Lerner formula is purely static in character: it takes no account of innovation and change.[5] Other students have indicated that the Lerner formula does not measure the degree of monopoly but merely shows the existence of some degree of monopoly.[6] Furthermore, a gap between marginal cost and price may merely reflect inertia or failure to exercise existing monopoly power. In short, the formula tests the exercise of monopoly power rather than its existence.[7] For such reasons, we do not anticipate adoption of the Lerner formula by the courts.

§4.9. **Analysis of demand as a measure of monopoly.** We have already suggested that the slope of the demand curve may play an important role under the structure test of monopoly. It has often been urged that the test should focus upon demand and abandon all relationship to structure.[1] Theoretically, at least, the elasticity of the individual firm's demand curve indicates its exposure to competition.[2] This concept is usually refined into the notion of "cross-elasticity" of demand, which is sometimes known as the Triffin formula, after a leading student of the subject. Cross-elasticity relates the demand for two products: in other words, it shows in what degree the second product may be "sub-

[3] Machlup, The Political Economy of Monopoly 474-475, 512 (1952); Dunlop, Price Flexibility and the Degree of Monopoly, 53 Q.J. Econ. 522, 526-527 (1939); Gordon, Short Period Price Determination, 38 Am. Econ. Rev. 265, 274 (1948); Miller, Measures of Monopoly Power, in Business Concentration and Price Policy 119, 123 (Stigler ed. 1955); Scitovsky, Economic Theory and the Measurement of Concentration, id. at 101-118.

[4] Compare Tyndall, The Relative Merits of Average Cost Pricing, Marginal Cost Pricing and Price Discrimination, 65 Q.J. Econ. 342 (1951).

[5] Wallace, Industrial Markets and Public Policy, in Public Policy 59, 109 (Friedrich and Mason ed. 1940).

[6] Id. at 107.

[7] Machlup, The Political Economy of Monopoly 511-512, 527 (1952); Bowman, Toward Less Monopoly, 101 U. Pa. L. Rev. 577, 615-616 (1953); compare §3.12 *supra.*

§4.9. [1] Schumpeter, Capitalism, Socialism and Democracy 99 (3d ed. 1950); Bowman, Toward Less Monopoly, 101 U. Pa. L. Rev. 577, 615 (1953). Compare §3.11 *supra.*

[2] E.g., Sraffa, The Laws of Return Under Competitive Conditions, 36 Econ. J. 535, 545 (1926); Mason, Price and Production Policies of Large-Scale Enterprise, 29 Proceedings Am. Econ. Assn. 61, 62 (1939); Zimmerman, The Propensity to Monopolize 26, 47 (1952).

stituted" for the first.   It is the ratio between relative changes in the quantity demanded of the product concerned and the relative changes in the prices of another product.[3]   Other formulas have been developed along the same general lines.   Professor Rothschild has tried to determine the control of the market exercised by a single firm by comparing its demand curve to the demand curve facing the industry as a whole.[4]   Professor Papandreou has added additional features, such as the capacity of one firm to penetrate another's markets.[5]

We find no record of a court ever having utilized any of the foregoing theories.   There are, moreover, weighty objections to their adoption.   In the first place, the statistical derivation of demand is a task of monumental proportions and one which is afflicted with many unsolved difficulties.   According to Professor Mason, it is extremely unlikely that economists will be able by independent investigation to ascertain the shape of an individual firm's demand curve except by a rough sort of deduction from other data.[6]   Mrs. Robinson went so far as to remark:

> In reality, evidently, an individual demand curve (for a particular product produced by a particular firm) is a mere smudge, to which it is vain to attribute elegant geometrical properties.[7]

In the second place, even the theoretical formulas proposed for measuring monopoly via statistical studies of demand have not met with universal approval.   The Triffin formula, for example, has been said not to show the degree of monopoly power.   Professor Machlup commented upon it as follows:

> This so-called Triffin criterion of monopoly . . . fails to furnish any single index of the degree of monopoly.   There is no meaningful way in which the individual cross-elasticities can be aggregated, averaged, or otherwise combined in a numerical value indicative of the monopoly power of any particular firm. . . .   The Triffin criterion obviously holds only for defining the limit, but not for evaluating any intermediate positions.[8]

[3] Triffin, Monopolistic Competition and General Equilibrium Theory 100, 102, 130 (1940); Fellner, Elasticities, Cross-Elasticities and Market Relationships, 43 Am. Econ. Rev. 898, 900-901, 907 (1953); Machlup, The Political Economy of Monopoly 522 (1952).

[4] Id. at 519 et seq.

[5] Papandreou, Market Structure and Monopoly Power, 39 Am. Econ. Rev. 887, 891, 893 (1949); Papandreou and Wheeler, Competition and Its Regulation (1954).   In the latter work (at 138 et seq.) the authors appear to give weight to dynamic factors such as the youth, maturity or age of the industry and the "time horizon scale."

[6] Mason, Price and Production Policies of Large-Scale Enterprise, 29 Proceedings Am. Econ. Assn. 61, 64 (1939); Wallace, Industrial Markets and Public Policy, in Public Policy 59, 65 (Friedrich and Mason ed. 1940).

[7] Robinson, Imperfect Competition Revisited, 63 Econ. J. 579, 585 (1953).

[8] Machlup, The Political Economy of Monopoly 522 (1952).   **Compare** Zimmer-

Meanwhile a lively debate continues in the periodicals as to whether cross-elasticity of demand is a meaningful concept and, if so, how it should be formulated.[9] The Rothschild formula may have some merit; on the other hand, it may not even be theoretically conceivable. In any event it is not considered to be of practical application and the Papandreou formula has been declared hopeless for use in specific situations.[10] Eventually, economists may develop a means of utilizing statistical determination of demand as a tool in antitrust litigation. At this writing, however, that day does not appear to be near.

§4.10. **High profits.** We have outlined, above, some of the tests suggested to determine the legality of horizontal size in lieu of the abuse and structure theories discussed in preceding chapters. In addition to the tests we have mentioned, a number of other considerations might rank as "factors": these considerations would not alone determine the legality of horizontal size but might, in combination with other factors, be considered as evidence of monopoly power. Among such factors is the existence of high profits. The theory is a simple one: high profits reflect high prices and high prices indicate the absence of competition, which in turn reflects the existence of monopoly.[1]

In the reported decisions, the courts have not placed much

---

man, The Propensity to Monopolize 23 (1952). See also Miller, Measures of Monopoly Power, in Business Concentration and Price Policy 119, 125 (Stigler ed. 1955).

[9] Bishop, Elasticities, Cross-Elasticities, and Market Relationships, 42 Am. Econ. Rev. 779 (1952); Chamberlin, Elasticities, Cross-Elasticities and Market Relationships, 43 id. 910 (1953); Bishop, Reply, id. at 916. But compare United States v. E. I. Du Pont de Nemours & Co., 118 F. Supp. 41 (D. Del. 1953), aff'd, 351 U.S. 377 (1956).

[10] Machlup, The Political Economy of Monopoly 519, 522, 524 (1952). Some economists have laid stress upon price flexibility as an index of monopoly; others have suggested a "qualitative analysis of markets." Dunlop, Price Flexibility and the Degree of Monopoly, 53 Q.J. Econ. 522, 527 et seq. (1939); Bain, The Profit Rate as a Measure of Monopoly Power, 55 Q.J. Econ. 271, 272 (1941); Keyes, The Shoe Machinery Case and the Problem of the Good Trust, 68 Q.J. Econ. 287, 300-301 (1954). The problem is, of course, closely related to the measure of "concentration." See §2.2 supra. Compare Miller, Measures of Monopoly Power, in Business Concentration and Price Policy 119 (Stigler ed. 1955); Scitovsky, Economic Theory and the Measurement of Concentration, id. at 101; Rosenbluth, Measures of Concentration, id. at 57, 60-61; Machlup, The Political Economy of Monopoly 475 et seq., 482 et seq., 487, 490 (1952). Note also the concept of "struggle" as opposed to "peace" suggested by Professor Callmann in The Essence of Anti-Trust, 49 Colum. L. Rev. 1100, 1109 (1947).

4.10. [1] Stocking and Mueller, The Cellophane Case and the New Competition, 45 Am. Econ. Rev. 29, 57 (1955); Kahn, A Legal and Economic Appraisal of the "New" Sherman and Clayton Acts, 63 Yale L. J. 293, 302 (1954). Compare Bain, The Profit Rate as a Measure of Monopoly Power, 55 Q.J. Econ. 271, 273 (1941). See §§2.27, 4.1 supra.

weight upon the existence of high profits.[2] On the other hand, they have occasionally examined the profit rates of defendants in antitrust cases, even though they may at the same time disclaim reliance thereon.[3]

Perhaps the most appealing aspect of high profits as a factor in determining the existence of monopoly power is the superficial simplicity of the test. It is not too difficult to assume a "normal" rate of profit from the experience of other firms and other industries. If, therefore, the defendant's rate of profit is substantially higher than such a norm, one may readily conclude that it must enjoy some degree of monopoly power.[4] Unfortunately, the objections to such a simple test are legion. In the first place, the existence of high profits may merely reflect innovation upon the part of the defendant. That objection is closely linked with various market imperfections, such as time lags, whereby additional resources have not yet flowed into the production of the commodity sold by the defendant. If high profits are taken as an index of monopoly power, we may be in danger of destroying the incentives to growth and technological improvement which our economic system should foster.[5] Again, if high profits merely reflect imperfections, such as consumer ignorance,[6] they presumably should be attacked by weapons other than the antitrust laws.

[2] Thus, in United States v. General Electric Co., 82 F. Supp. 753 (D.N.J. 1949), the court said at page 895: "Substantial profits [do] not render it violative of the anti-trust laws. Like size, itself, it can only be given consideration along with myriad other circumstances for the purpose of determining whether in combination they are elements in the generation of that power to monopolize that constitutes violation of the law." But compare United States v. E. I. Du Pont de Nemours & Co., 118 F. Supp. 41 (D. Del. 1953), aff'd, 351 U.S. 377, 385, 404 (1956).

[3] United States v. Aluminum Co. of America, 148 F.2d 416, 426-427 (2d Cir. 1945) (but compare lower court opinion, 44 F. Supp. 97, 287); United States v. United Shoe Machinery Corp., 110 F. Supp. 295, 325 (D. Mass. 1953), aff'd per curiam, 347 U.S. 521 (1954).

[4] Bain, The Profit Rate as a Measure of Monopoly Power, 55 Q.J. Econ. 271, 293 (1941); Zimmerman, The Propensity to Monopolize 51 (1952).

[5] Wright, Capitalism 165 (1951); Papandreou and Wheeler, Competition and Its Regulation 181 (1954); Enke, Profit, in Basic Economics: A Book of Readings 237 et seq., 241 (Gayer, Harriss, Spencer ed. 1951); Gordon, Enterprise, Profits and the Modern Corporation, in Fellner and Haley, eds., Readings in the Theory of Income Distribution 558 et seq., 562-563 (The Blakiston Co. 1949); Reader's Digest, 14 Fortune No. 5, pp. 121, 131 (1936); Appendix B infra. It has recently been suggested that monopoly profits have no important effect upon resource allocation and distribution of income. Villard, The Social Cost of Corporate Monopoly Profits, 72 Pol. Sci. Q. 380 (1957).

[6] Wright, Capitalism 167 (1951); United States v. Bausch & Lomb Co., 45 F. Supp. 387, 389 (S.D.N.Y 1942), aff'd, 321 U.S. 707 (1944). Note also the effect of uncertainty, time lags, overinvestment, high production costs, and the like. Machlup, The Economics of Sellers' Competition 229 (1952); Machlup, The Political Economy of Monopoly 493, 496 (1952); Rostow and Sachs, Entry into the Oil Refining Business, 61 Yale L.J. 856 (1952); Appendix A infra.

Another possibility, of course, is that high profits reflect some form of governmental intervention, such as a protective tariff. Again, the remedy would appear to lie in action outside the antitrust sphere. Another highly important consideration is that profits are not easy of measurement. Offhand, it would seem a simple matter to determine the rate of return on investment in any given concern. Careful study, however, has shown that a determination of the true rate would require so much investigation of the reported figures and adjustment of accounts as to leave an embarrassingly wide leeway to the judgment of the investigator. The difficulty is that the economic concept of profit differs from that used in accounting records, and new accounts would have to be constructed almost from the original transactions.[7]

In these circumstances, we can only conclude that the existence of high profits can hardly be relied upon as a factor indicating the existence of monopoly power. As the Attorney General's Committee observed, the rate of technical progress and the level of profit in a firm or an industry can reflect many forces other than the presence or absence of effective competition.[8] Indeed, as stated above, the use of high profits as a factor in determining the existence of illegal horizontal size might do much to discourage growth and innovation. In addition, it might place business concerns in a dilemma: if they sold at a figure so low that they did not earn a "fair" profit, they might be guilty of an attempt to monopolize; if, on the other hand, they sold at a price yielding an "excessive" profit, they might be guilty of monopolization.[9] This dilemma, of course, assumes the existence of some degree of power over prices but it may nevertheless be realistic if one concedes that it is impossible to eradicate every element of monopoly from the market place and that many imperfections afflict the economy.

[7] Machlup, The Political Economy of Monopoly 490, 494 et seq. (1952); Bowman, Toward Less Monopoly, 101 U. Pa. L. Rev. 577, 619 (1953); Epstein, Industrial Profits in the United States, bk. IV (National Bureau of Economic Research, 1934); Bernheim, How Profitable Is Big Business? 8 et seq. (Twentieth Century Fund, 1937); 2 Nevins, Study in Power 371 (1953); Bain, The Profit Rate as a Measure of Monopoly Power, 55 Q.J. Econ. 271, 289, 291 (1941). Compare Scitovsky, Economic Theory and the Measurement of Concentration, in Business Concentration and Price Policy 101, 109-110 (Stigler ed. 1955). Experience in public utility rate regulation suggests some of the difficulties involved in determining profit rates on a scientific basis. It has also been suggested that ease of entry and absolute size of firm have a relationship to earning power. Steindl, Maturity and Stagnation in American Capitalism 41 (Oxford University Institute of Statistics Monograph No. 4, 1952).

[8] Atty. Gen. Nat. Rep. 322 (b). See also Scitovsky, Economic Theory and the Measurement of Concentration, in Business Concentration and Price Policy 101, 109 (Stigler ed. 1955); Miller, Measures of Monopoly Power, id at 119, 127 et seq.

[9] Compare United States v. Corn Products Refining Co., 234 Fed. 964, 991 (S.D.N.Y. 1916).

§4.11. **Advertising.** During the period when the theory of monopolistic competition evoked widespread enthusiasm among economists, heavy advertising expenditures were often regarded as indicia of monopoly power.[1] In the analysis by Professor Chamberlain, the mere existence of advertising demonstrated a departure from "pure" competition. Large sums are spent to "differentiate" one seller's product from that of his rival, and the selling costs thus incurred caused buyers to become attached to one brand as opposed to another. Hence the advertised brand is partially insulated from the competition of identical goods bearing different trade-marks.[2]

We find only one instance in which the courts have considered the possibility that heavy advertising expenditures might constitute an index of monopoly power. In the second *American Tobacco* case, the Court wrote:

> Such tremendous advertising . . . is . . . a widely published warning that these companies possess and know how to use a powerful offensive and defensive weapon against new competition. New competition dare not enter such a field, unless it be well supported by comparable national advertising.[3]

Clearly the Court regarded heavy advertising expenditures as an exclusionary device, perhaps an abuse or illegal practice, and possibly as evidence of undue horizontal size. Without clarification, however, it would be hazardous to accept the above-quoted language as indicating judicial approval of volume of advertising as a test of illegality under Section 2 of the Sherman Act. Indeed, with the waning of the original theories of monopolistic competi-

---

§4.11. [1] For a discussion of heavy advertising expenditures as an abuse see §2.23 *supra*. A general discussion of the role of advertising will be found in Appendix A *infra*.

[2] Chamberlin, The Theory of Monopolistic Competition, cc. 4, 5, 7 (6th ed. 1948); Rostow, The New Sherman Act, 14 U. Chi. L. Rev. 567, 577 (1947); Machlup, The Political Economy of Monopoly 10 (1952); Dirlam and Kahn, Fair Competition 162 (1954); Bishop, Elasticities, Cross-Elasticities, and Market Relationships, 42 Am. Econ. Rev. 779, 780 (1952); Mason, Price and Production Policies of Large-Scale Enterprise, 29 Proceedings Am. Econ. Assn. 61, 69-70 (1939); Nicols, The Rehabilitation of Pure Competition, 62 Q.J. Econ. 31, 33 (1947). Attempts to apply the above theory to specific situations will be found in Nicholls, Price Policies in the Cigarette Industry 409 (1951); Stocking and Mueller, The Cellophane Case and the New Competition, 45 Am. Econ. Rev. 29, 63 (1955).

Some observers have carried the analysis a step farther and indicated that advertising can actually influence demand. Thus doubt is thrown upon the whole doctrine of consumer sovereignty with far-reaching consequences for a free enterprise system. Rothschild, The Wastes of Competition, in Chamberlin, ed., Monopoly and Competition and Their Regulation 301, 303-304 (International Economic Assn. 1954); Brems, Product Equilibrium under Monopolistic Competition 6-7 (1951); Dirlam and Kahn, Fair Competition 20 (1954).

[3] American Tobacco Co. v. United States, 328 U.S. 781, 797 (1946).

tion, most economists would now hesitate to rely upon such a simple test.[4] In the words of the Attorney General's Committee:

> The effect of product differentiation depends on the market setting in which it is placed. Extreme product differentiation, by tending to insulate the demand for one product against that for rival products, may allow real positions of monopoly to develop. Relatively mild differentiation of products within a market otherwise effectively competitive, however, may be a factor favorable to the intensiveness of competition, including price competition . . . For product differentiation . . . may be a means whereby the seller can take advantage of the time interval the market allows within which he can expect to gain from a competitive move. . . .[5]

And as Professor Edwards has pointed out, it would be impractical, even if desirable, to regulate the amount of sales effort or the exact forms of persuasion which sellers might use.[6]

§4.12. **Pricing policies.** It has often been suggested that the pricing practices of a business entity should constitute a test of its transgression of the antitrust laws. As we have seen, price discrimination is often relied on as evidence of monopoly power. As also noted, however, there are so many different types of and motives for price discrimination that it is unreasonable to pronounce a wholesale condemnation of that practice. In many instances, price discrimination operates to increase or maintain a monopoly position, and it is true that only the monopolist can, in theory, discriminate among his customers. On the other hand, price discrimination may merely represent departures from prevailing prices and hence result in more active competition.[1]

We have also already examined the concept of "price leadership." It has often been urged that when one firm in an industry is found again and again to have led in the the setting of new

---

[4] E.g., Buchanan, Advertising Expenditures, 50 J. Pol. Econ. 537, 556 (1942); Nicols, The Rehabilitation of Pure Competition, 62 Q.J. Econ. 31, 32 (1947).

[5] Atty. Gen. Nat. Com. Rep. 330, (7).

[6] Edwards, Maintaining Competition 194 (1949). Further discussion of advertising will be found in Appendix A *infra*. Compare Tosdal, The Advertising and Selling Process, 209 Annals 62, 70 (1940); Buchanan, Advertising Expenditures, 50 J. Pol. Econ. 537, 556 (1942).

§4.12. [1] Machlup, The Political Economy of Monopoly 163 (1952); Bowman, Toward Less Monopoly, 101 U. Pa. L. Rev. 577, 619-620 (1953); Atty. Gen. Nat. Com. Rep. 333, (10); §2.11 *supra*. Compare United States v. United States Steel Corp. 223 Fed. 55, 79 (D.N.J. 1915), *aff'd*, 251 U.S. 417 (1920); United States v. United Shoe Machinery Corp., 110 F. Supp. 295, 336 (D. Mass. 1953), *aff'd per curiam*, 347 U.S. 521 (1954). Note also the phenomenon known as "clearance" in the motion picture industry, whereby patrons willing to pay more are allowed to see fresh films before they are shown in outlying theaters. E.g., United States v. Paramount Pictures, Inc., 66 F. Supp. 323, 341 (S.D.N.Y. 1946), *rev'd on other grounds*, 334 U.S. 131 (1948).

prices, higher or lower, such a firm enjoys monopoly power.[2] As we have seen, however, price leadership is not a conclusive test of monopoly.[3] Similarly, price uniformity, whether resulting from leadership or otherwise, cannot be considered evidence of a violation of the antitrust laws. Under conditions of both pure and perfect competition, all prices for identical commodities would be uniform at any given time and place. There is, for example, but one price prevailing for the common stock of the General Motors Corporation on the New York Stock Exchange at any given moment in time.[4]

A more promising test is found in the pricing of products below free-market levels. It is, of course, well established that important industrial concerns in the United States have held prices below levels which could have been obtained by the free play of market forces. Thus President Fairless of the United States Steel Corporation testified before a congressional committee:

> . . . I would like to establish that the steel corporation, its subsidiaries, never charged all that they could have charged for any product.
>
> In other words, during that period we had offers for prices far in excess of our announced prices which, of course, we never accepted.[5]

It follows, of course, that a seller who maintains his prices below free-market levels, just as a landlord whose rents are frozen below

---

[2] E.g., Rostow, The New Sherman Act, 14 U. Chi. L. Rev. 567, 577 (1947).

[3] §3.8 *supra;* Celler Committee I, pt. 2A, at 371.

[4] Watkins, Price Discrimination, 12 Encyc. Soc. Sci. 350, 351 (1934).

[5] Celler Committee I, pt. 4A, at 616, 520-521. See also United States v. United States Steel Corp., 223 Fed. 55, 90 (D.N.J. 1915), aff'd, 251 U.S. 417 (1920); TNEC Hearings, pt. 20, at 10,744. But compare id. at 10,750-10,751.

Many other companies have made similar admissions. Thus, in General Motors Corp., 44th Ann. Rep. (New York City, 1953) it was said at page 16: "General Motors is holding the line on passenger car prices despite increased costs." To the same effect see id., 40th Ann. Rep. 7 (1949). In Allis-Chalmers Manufacturing Co., Ann. Rep. 1948 (Milwaukee, 1949) it was said at page 14: "Although all plants set new production records, the demand for most of the Division's products continue to be greater than the supply throughout the year." In Inland Steel Co., Ann. Rep. (Chicago, 1949) it was stated at page 5: "The Company reduced the selling prices of most of its products in the hope that this action would exert an important influence against inflationary forces and aid in the achievement of national price stabilization. However, it soon became apparent that the forces of inflation were beyond the control of any one company, and even any one industry. Wage increases granted . . . made it necessary to increase the selling prices of many of the Company's products . . ." To the same effect see General Electric Co., 57th Ann. Rep. 5 (Schenectady, 1949). Other examples are found in St. Joseph Lead Co., 85th Ann. Rep. 3 (New York City, 1949); United Fruit Co., Ann. Rep. 7 (Boston, 1949); West Virginia Pulp & Paper Co., Ann. Rep. 1948, 3, 16 (New York City, 1948); American Viscose Corp., Ann. Rep. 1950, 4, 21 (Philadelphia, 1951); Eastman Kodak Co., Ann. Rep. 1948, 20 (Rochester, 1949); Celler Committee I, pt. 6A, at 930. Compare Acme Steel Co., Ann. Rep. 1953, 10 (Chicago, 1954).

such figures, must ration the commodities he has produced. In other words, he must allocate his production among the consumers who buy from him. Many corporate reports contain admissions of such allocations. Thus the International Nickel Company of Canada announced:

> Upon relaxation of governmental controls the Company allocated its supply available for civilian use on an equitable basis taking into consideration past patterns of consumption and current conditions.[6]

The number of voluntary admissions of such practices makes it apparent that many important industrial concerns have held prices below free-market levels during times of inflation.

It can and has been argued that such holding of prices below free-market levels evidences the existence of monopoly power. Theoretically, of course, anyone can sell his goods for less than the going price. There is, however, no motive for one engaged in pure competition to do so.[7] A monopolist, on the other hand, may desire to preserve the structure of his industry. By that it is meant that the monopolist may seek to discourage new firms from entering into competition with him. This is sometimes referred to as "far-sighted industrial statesmanship": profits are not made so attractive as to excite the interest of would-be producers of the same commodity.[8] At the same time, there are equally valid explanations of pricing below free-market levels which do not in-

---

[6] International Nickel Co. of Canada, Ltd., Ann. Rep. 1953, 6 (Copper Cliff, 1954). See to the same effect id., Ann. Rep. 1950, 7 (1951). In Phillips Petroleum Co., Ann. Rep. 1949 (Bartlesville, 1950) it was said at page 18: "For a number of years during and after the war, products were in such short supply in relation to the high demand that the sales problem was primarily to allocate available supplies equitably among jobbers, dealers and consumers." In Sylvania Electric Products, Inc., Ann. Rep. 1953 (New York City, 1954) it was said at page 9: "Your Company continued to hold its dominant position as industry's largest producer of photoflash bulbs which were back-ordered and on allocation most of the year." Other examples will be found in Scott Paper Co., 1952 Ann. Rep. 2 (Chester, 1953); Gulf Oil Corp., Ann. Rep. 1948, 19 (Pittsburgh, 1949); Philco Corp., 58th Ann. Rep. 10 (Philadelphia, 1950); General Motors Corp., 40th Ann. Rep. 1948, 7 (New York City, 1949); American Viscose Corp., Ann. Rep. 1948, 4 (Philadelphia, 1949); Eastman Kodak Co., Ann. Rep. 1948, 23 (Rochester, 1949); National Biscuit Co., Ann. Rep. 1948, 6 (New York City, 1949); Caterpillar Tractor Co. (California), Ann. Rep. 1950, 6 (Peoria, 1951); United States Steel Corp., 47th Ann. Rep. 9 (New York City, 1949); Inland Steel Co., Ann. Rep. 1948, 6 (Chicago, 1949); id., Ann. Rep. 1950, 12-13 (1951); Celler Committee I, pt. 4A, at 916.

[7] Thus, in Bowman, Toward Less Monopoly, 101 U. Pa. L. Rev. 577 (1953), it was said at 617: "The presence of voluntary non-price rationing presents one of the least ambiguous kinds of evidence of monopoly power and one which is rather easily spotted."

[8] Machlup, The Economics of Sellers' Competition 344, 539 (1952). Such business conduct of course is only rational where substantial barriers to entry into the industry exist. Compare §2.26 supra.

volve the existence of monopoly power. Take, for example, the warning given to other businessmen by the experience of producers of natural gas. Those producers, in the period following World War II, found themselves faced with both inflation and a greatly increased demand for their product. Accordingly, in the free-market tradition, they permitted prices to rise to levels greatly in excess of those which had prevailed in the preceding period. As a result of their conduct — and their number suggested that none of them had monopoly power — political pressure resulted in the imposition of price controls by governmental agencies.[9] Lessons of that type can scarcely have been lost upon other industries, and even if a seller does not expect governmental intervention, he may well fear adverse "public relations." Again, price stability is often thought of as a desirable device to retain customers into periods of slack demand;[10] it may, in addition, be explained by a desire to expand markets by keeping real prices low and encouraging greater utilization of the product.[11] In any event, the courts appear not to have taken cognizance of the pos-

[9] Phillips Petroleum Co. v. Wisconsin, 347 U.S. 672 (1954). Compare FTC, Monopolistic Practices and Small Business 34, Report to the Subcommittee on Monopoly, Senate Select Committee on Small Business (Feb. 21, 1952); Stocking and Mueller, The Cellophane Case and the New Competition, 45 Am. Econ. Rev. 29, 60 (1955). In the FTC report it was recorded that there were complaints with respect to the "shortage" of newsprint, apparently resulting from holding of prices below free-market levels in fear of governmental intervention.

[10] It has been reported to the authors by persons of prominence in the steel industry that free-market pricing was tried during and after the Korean War by the Great Lakes Steel Division of National Steel Corporation. In other words, Great Lakes raised its prices in order to avoid the necessity of allocating its output. When demand subsided, it was found that the free-market pricing program had created widespread resentment among customers of Great Lakes. Accordingly, in the slight business recession of 1954 it was felt necessary to replace all the top management of Great Lakes Steel Division of National Steel Corporation. To the same effect is Kriesberg, Occupational Controls Among Steel Distributors, 61 Am. J. Sociol. 203, 206 (1955).

[11] See §3.17 *supra* and Appendix B *infra*. An example of such pricing is reported in Celanese Corp. of America, Ann. Rep. 1948, 8-9 (New York City, 1949). These pricing practices can also be explained on the ground that the management of the firm is attempting to feel out demand and to determine its elasticity. Note also the effect of time lags; it is probably not feasible to increase the price of television sets for a month or two while production catches up to a sudden increase in demand. Compare Philco Corp., 58th Ann. Rep. 10 (Philadelphia, 1950). Furthermore, there is always the possibility that business pricing reflects irrelevant factors such as changes in the rate of inventory turnover. Eitman, Price Determination: Business Practice v. Economic Theory 49 (Bureau of Business Research Report No. 16, University of Michigan, Jan. 1949). Note also the bitter political attacks which have been made upon corporations which held prices below free-market levels. It has been said, for example, that such pricing practices represented an attempt to "squeeze" nonintegrated competitors out of business because they could not afford to pay current prices for raw materials and meet low prices for finished goods charged by the vertically integrated rival. Kilgore Committee, pt. 1, at 206.

sibility that holding prices below free-market levels could constitute evidence of monopoly power.[12]

Another possibility is that the existence of price rigidity should be interpreted as evidence of monopoly power. If a defendant can resist a tendency toward lower prices and maintain his own prices at prosperity levels in the face of dwindling demand, monopoly power is suggested as an explanation of the phenomenon.[13] Moreover, one with monopoly power may conceive it to be advantageous not to change prices on a short-term basis.[14] From time to time, evidence is forthcoming of such "rigid" or "sticky" prices.[15] The courts have not yet recognized price rigidity as a test of illegal horizontal size.[16] On the other hand, the legislative history of the Sherman Act indicates that power to raise prices at the expense of consumers was prominent in the minds of the framers of the statute.[17] In addition, numerous cases have mentioned the power to fix prices as an element in determining violation of the statutes.[18] Thus, in an older state decision it was said:

> It is the consensus of the authorities that a monopoly, within the meaning of the anti-trust laws, is created when, as a result of any contract or combination, previously competing businesses are so concentrated into the hands of a single individual or corporation, or of a few individuals or incorporations acting in concert, that they thereby have the power to practically control the prices of commodities, and thus practically suppress competition.[19]

[12] In Commonwealth v. North Shore Ice Co., 220 Mass. 55, 107 N.E. 402 (1914), the court said at page 403 that the fact that prices had not been increased by a combination of sellers of ice was evidence that a monopoly had not been created.

[13] Machlup, The Political Economy of Monopoly 498 (1952); Galbraith, Monopoly Power and Price Rigidities, 50 Q.J. Econ. 456, 458, 460 (1936).

[14] Id. at 466-467. It has been suggested that a demonstration of power to raise prices eliminates the necessity of defining the appropriate geographical market and commodity. Compare §§3.4-3.7 supra (our notes attribute the foregoing suggestion to Professor Rostow but we are now unable to find that statement among his published works). Obviously proof of actual power to raise prices is no simple matter.

[15] E.g., United States v. United States Steel Corp., 223 Fed. 55, 91, 172 (D.N.J. 1915), aff'd, 251 U.S. 417 (1920); TNEC Hearings, pt. 20, at 10,751.

[16] United States v. United States Steel Corp., 251 U.S. 417, 448-449 (1920).

[17] Walker, History of the Sherman Law 4 (1910).

[18] United States v. United States Steel Corp., 251 U.S. 417, 444-445 (1920); United States v. Corn Products Refining Co., 234 Fed. 964, 993 (S.D.N.Y. 1916); American Tobacco Co. v. United States, 328 U.S. 781, 805-806 (1946); United States v. E. I. Du Pont de Nemours & Co., 118 F. Supp. 41 (D. Del. 1953), aff'd, 351 U.S. 377 (1956); State ex Information Barker v. Armour Packing Co., 265 Mo. 121, 176 S.W. 382, 388 (1915); State ex Information Hadley v. Standard Oil Co., 218 Mo. 1, 116 S.W. 902, 1042 (1909), aff'd, 224 U.S. 270 (1912).

[19] State ex Information Hadley v. Standard Oil Co., 218 Mo. at 457, 116 S.W. at 1045. In State v. Black, 5 N.J. Misc. 639, 138 Atl. 513 (1927), the court said at page 514: "The allegation that prices were merely to be enhanced also adds nothing. The characteristic of uncontrolled monopoly is its ability to control and vary prices at will from those which the natural course of supply and demand would establish.

And such power to affect prices is sometimes considered to have been established by proof of price rigidity.[20]

"Sticky" prices do not, however, necessarily indicate the presence of monopoly power. In the first place, we should note that price rigidity is merely a special case of departure of prices from marginal cost: the continuation of an existing price over a period of time when costs change constitutes a variance between marginal cost and price.[21] Such variations, however, have explanations other than the existence of monopoly power. As in the case of the simple test of power to fix prices, we do not know from rigidity alone that horizontal size has reached objectionable levels.[22] Furthermore, even if statistical determination of price flexibility were feasible,[23] rigidity would not be a suitable measure of monopoly power because no account would be taken of varying costs.[24] For such reasons, it would be unfortunate if the courts were to adopt price rigidity as an unvarying test of illegality. As the Attorney General's Committee reported:

> While information of continued price rigidities may be some indication of the existence or absence of incentives to competitive moves, such information cannot of itself be determinative from an economic standpoint of either effective monopoly or effective com-

---

This control, unless in the meanwhile human nature be revolutionized must sooner or later, when favorable opportunity presents, normally result in the enhancement of prices." See Rostow, Monopoly Under the Sherman Act, 43 Ill. L. Rev. 745, 779 (1949).

20 Consider, for example, the following language which appeared in the annual report of a large corporation: "Consumers made what amounted to mass decisions to postpone purchases of home appliances. The consequence was an industry-wide slump. Your operating managers, however, held to their belief that this must prove to be a temporary condition and thus were able to generally limit adjustments in pricing and production . . ." General Electric Co., 61st Ann. Rep. 3 (Schenectady, 1953). Compare American Tobacco Co. v. United States, 328 U.S. 781, 805 (1946).

21 Bowman, Toward Less Monopoly, 101 U. Pa. L. Rev. 577, 618 (1953).

22 Id. at 617; Machlup, The Political Economy of Monopoly 502-503 (1952); Galbraith, Monopoly Power and Price Rigidities, 50 Q.J. Econ. 456, 458, 470 (1936); Heflebower, Full Cost, Cost Changes, and Prices, in Business Concentration and Price Policy 361, 392 (Stigler ed. 1955); compare §§4.8-4.10 supra.

23 Dunlop, Price Flexibility and the "Degree of Monopoly," 53 Q.J. Econ. 522, 523-524 (1939). Similarly it has been said that power to fix prices as a test of monopoly is virtually useless because we cannot tell when a firm has power to fix prices. Mason, Workable Competition v. Workable Monopoly, Symposium, N.Y. State Bar Assn., Section on Antitrust Law 67, 70-71 (CCH, 1951).

24 Machlup, The Political Economy of Monopoly 506 (1952). The relationship between price flexibility and the business cycle has been the subject of extensive exploration by economists. Some of the leading authorities are collected in Rostow, Market Organization and Stabilization Policy, in Income Stabilization for Developing Economy, c. 10, pp. 439, 450 et seq. (Millikan ed. 1954). Particular attention is invited to Fels, The Effects of Price and Wage Flexibility on Cyclical Contraction, 64 Q.J. Econ. 596, 602, 607 (1950); Patinkin, Price Flexibility and Full Employment, 38 Am. Econ. Rev. 543, 556 (1948).

petition. Monopolies may change prices in their own interest, and competitive industries may have periods of stable demand and supply conditions. Price changes, or the absence thereof, must therefore be considered in their market settings in order to evaluate their significance.[25]

It nevertheless remains true that rigid price uniformity over periods of changing supply and demand is not usually compatible with effective competition.[26]

§4.13. **Excess capacity and freedom of entry.** Economists often point to excess productive capacity as indicative of monopoly power.[1] While the courts have not directly accepted such views as a test of the legality of horizontal size, they have adverted to the dismantling of acquired plants and similar activities as evidence of monopolistic intent.[2] As in the case of other economic criteria, however, we find that mere existence of excess capacity does not necessarily reflect an undue degree of horizontal size. In the first place, changes in demand may give rise to capacity to produce products which are "obsolete" in character.[3] Ignorance upon the part of businessmen with respect to both the demand curve facing the individual firm and the availability of raw materials and the like may produce similar results. A vivid example occurred during the administration of President Theodore Roosevelt. President Roosevelt and Gifford Pinchot mistakenly conceived that the supply of timber in the United States was practically exhausted. They therefore started a campaign against waste of lumber and in favor of conservation of timberland resources. Lumber companies and speculators took this political campaign at face value,

---

[25] Atty. Gen. Nat. Com. Rep. 329, (6). See also Business Concentration and Price Policy 13 (Stigler ed. 1955).

[26] Atty. Gen. Nat. Com. Rep. 331, (8). Compare Ruggles, The Nature of Price Flexibility and the Determinants of Relative Price Changes in the Economy, in Business Concentration and Price Policy 441, 495 (Stigler ed. 1955). Price rigidity is a great aid to resale price maintenance. Galbraith, Monopoly Power and Price Rigidities, 50 Q.J. Econ. 456, 468 (1936).

§4.13. [1] E.g., Adelman, Effective Competition and the Antitrust Laws, 61 Harv. L. Rev. 1289, 1298 (1948).

[2] United States v. Corn Products Refining Co., 234 Fed. 964 (S.D.N.Y. 1916); United States v. Eastman Kodak Co., 226 Fed. 62, 70 (W.D.N.Y. 1915), decree, 230 Fed. 522 (W.D.N.Y. 1916), appeal dismissed, 255 U.S. 578 (1921); United States v. American Can Co., 230 Fed. 859, 875, 234 Fed. 1019 (D. Md. 1916), appeal dismissed, 256 U.S. 706 (1921); Love v. Kozy Theatre Co., 193 Ky. 336, 236 S.W. 243, 245 (1922).

[3] Smith, Effective Competition, 26 N.Y.U.L. Rev. 405, 412 (1951). In recent years, for example, consumers in the United States have reduced the starch content of their diet. As a result there has been some tendency to excess capacity in the flour milling industry despite the general growth of population. More extreme examples probably could be found in fields heavily affected by fashion factors. No doubt, for example, there is (or was) excess capacity for the production of bustles after that item of female attire went out of style.

bid up the price of timberlands to an extravagant degree and ended by enjoying considerable excess capacity.[4] Furthermore, as we have noted above, excess capacity may reflect dynamic factors in the growth of the economy.[5] Excess capacity, when demonstrated by the purchasing and dismantling of competitive plants, is rightfully considered evidence of an attempt to monopolize. Yet if caused by factors such as those we have just enumerated, no penalty should be attached to its existence. Furthermore, as pointed out by the Attorney General's Committee, while failure to expand under conditions of strong demand may prevent the existence of excess capacity at some time in the future, it also may suggest the existence of some restrictive agreement in the present.[6]

It is widely agreed that freedom of opportunity to enter into competition is an important characteristic of a free-market economy. Hence the existence of freedom of entry is sometimes urged as an important or perhaps the sole criterion of the legality of an industrial situation.[7] Unfortunately, it is difficult to determine

[4] Bunyan in Broadcloth, 9 Fortune No. 4, pp. 63, 174, 176 (1934). Another example is set forth in I.P. & P., 1 Fortune No. 4, pp. 65, 69-70 (1930). Compare Gordon, Short Period Price Determination, 38 Am. Econ. Rev. 265, 277 (1948); Robinson, Imperfect Competition Revisited, 63 Econ. J. 579, 591 (1953).

[5] §3.16 *supra;* Appendix B *infra.* Additional analysis will be found in Harrod, Economic Essays 152 (1952); Zimmerman, The Propensity to Monopolize 43 (1952). Note also that the excess capacity may be temporary in nature. Thus, in Celanese Corp. of America, Ann. Rep. 1953 (New York City, 1954) it was said at page 7: "We intend to maintain production at a level sufficient to satisfy actual demand. By adjusting production to meet real requirements rather than to operate at existing capacity, the industry may be able to avoid periods of over-production with their consequent price instability and general dislocations." In Chrysler Corp., 29th Ann. Rep. (Detroit, 1954) the management wrote at page 6: "Conditions in the automobile industry are more competitive than they have been since before World War II. In scheduling output of 1954 new cars and trucks, Chrysler Corporation conforms to what it realistically believes its dealers, with sound aggressive merchandising and promotion practices, are in a position to sell." In Socony-Vacuum Oil Co., Inc., Ann. Rep. 1952 (New York City, 1953) it was said at page 3: "Any major industry such as oil cannot serve the public properly unless it is in a position to accommodate itself to sudden changes in demand, and this can be done only if some extra capacity is in hand." Compare National Distillers Products Corp., 29th Ann. Rep. 1952, 7 (New York City, 1953).

[6] Atty. Gen. Nat. Com. Rep. 332, (4). In Clark, Competition: Static Models and Dynamic Aspects, 45 Proceedings Am. Econ. Assn. 450 (1955), it was said at page 453: "Excess capacity tends to be treated by theory as a monopolistic symptom, but in anti-trust cases it may or may not be so treated, depending on circumstances. And businessmen tend to the view that competition does not begin until they have difficulty disposing of capacity output and becomes more severe as excess capacity gets larger."

[7] Thus it has been said: "From the point of view of the prevention of excess returns, a good prima facie case can be made for reliance on a program entirely devoted to the elimination of artificial restrictions on freedom of factor movement, since an unrestricted market sets a defensible long-term limit on the exploitative power of any firm regardless of the closeness or relative size of its competitors." Keyes, The Shoe Machinery Case and the Problem of the Good Trust, 68 Q.J.

whether freedom of entry exists. The mere fact there has been an increase in the number of competitors does not show that more firms would not have entered had entry been easier. The same can be said of the fact that rivals are gaining on the market leader and increasing their share of the industry's output.[8] Furthermore, as pointed out above,[9] freedom of entry is a complicated concept depending upon many "imperfections," such as investor information and the like.

§4.14. **Conclusions with respect to horizontal size.** Our quest for scientific methods of determining the legality of asserted monopoly has been fruitless. The sad truth is that we simply do not have a method of measuring monopoly power. Even the recently developed concept of cross-elasticity of demand is a subject of vigorous dispute, and agreement as to its utility has not been achieved. Professor Chamberlin recently referred to the work of another economist as a convincing demonstration of the complexity and even the treachery of cross-elasticity of demand as a measure of anything.[1] Professor Machlup has written that, as a practical matter, given the information now available, we should admit that no measurement of monopoly at all is possible. He has also said that so many different elements enter into what is called a monopolistic position, and so complex are their combined effects, that a measurement of the exact degree of monopoly is even conceptually impossible.[2] For such reasons the Attorney General's Committee concluded:

Econ. 287, 302 (1954). The Attorney General's Committee said: "From the economic point of view, relative freedom of opportunity for entry of new rivals is a fundamental requisite for effective competition in the long run." Atty. Gen. Nat. Com. Rep. 326 (1955). Compare id. at 328, (5). Compare also §3.12 *supra*.

[8] United States v. Standard Oil Co., 47 F.2d 288, 316 (E.D. Mo. 1931). In United States v. Corn Products Refining Co., 234 Fed. 964, 1014 (S.D.N.Y. 1916), the fact that new firms had entered the field was taken by the court as an indication that the defendant's profits were too high and that therefore the defendant enjoyed monopoly power. Compare §4.10 *supra*.

[9] §3.12 *supra*.

§4.14. [1] Chamberlin, Elasticities, Cross-Elasticities and Market Relationships, 43 Am. Econ. Rev. 910, 911 (1953). Compare Bishop, Elasticities, Cross-Elasticities and Market Relationships, 42 id. 779, 797, 800 (1952); Fellner, Elasticities, Cross-Elasticities and Market Relationships 43 id. 898, 904 (1953).

[2] Machlup, The Political Economy of Monopoly 527 (1952). See also id. at 470, 473. Professor Knauth has denied that there is such a thing as monopoly, saying that what goes by that name is merely a matter of trade advantages of many types and of varying importance and permanence. Knauth, Monopoly Reconsidered, 60 Pol. Sci. Q. 563, 574 (1945). Compare Edwards, Maintaining Competition 125 (1949); Keyes, The Shoe Machinery Case and the Problem of the Good Trust, 68 Q.J. Econ. 287, 297 (1954); Triffin, Monopolistic Competition and General Equilibrium Theory 137 (1940). Some students of the subject have suggested that further analysis must

The number and relative strength of firms necessary to effective competition cannot be compressed into a formula. The answer to the question depends also on other factors, including those hereafter discussed, so that a given number of firms might be compatible with effective competition in one industry and not in another. . . .

For effective competition, in the economic sense, to exist, there should be that degree of self-interested independent rivalry in any given market that exists where there is no one firm or group of firms acting in concert which have effective monopoly power . . .[3]

When such loose formulations constitute the end product of a careful canvass of expert opinion, it is no wonder that others throw up their hands in despair. Professor Machlup has pointed out that monopoly never becomes perceptible except by its causes or its effects.[4] That may lead back to the much-abused "abuse" theory: if monopoly can only be known through its manifestations, then perhaps the older view of the law is deserving of more respect than has usually been accorded it.[5] On the other hand, as pointed out above, making abuses or performance the test of legality brings us perilously close to public utility type regulation.[6] For if conduct (as evidenced by performance or abuses or the lack thereof) is to be the controlling criterion, then courts must in effect undertake detailed control of all business enterprises subject to the antitrust laws.

---

take the economist into the realms of psychology, sociology and political science. Wold, Demand Analysis 127 (1953); Nicholls, Social Biases and Recent Theories of Competition, 58 Q.J. Econ. 1 (1943).

[3] Atty. Gen. Nat. Com. Rep. 325, (1).

[4] "The chief difficulty of our task of measuring 'monopoly' lies in the fact that monopoly never becomes perceptible except by its causes or its effects. It has this in common with many other concepts, such as force, power, strength, potential capacity; none of them is *directly measurable.*" Machlup, The Political Economy of Monopoly 472 (1952). Another observer has written: "The fact is that economics offers no objective measure of the vitality of competition in all its aspects, or any way of balancing its possible attenuation in certain respects or in certain markets against its intensification in other markets or in other respects." Kahn, Standards for Anti-Trust Policy, 67 Harv. L. Rev. 28, 50 (1953).

[5] See §2.31 *supra;* Machlup, The Political Economy of Monopoly 470 (1952). The Attorney General's Committee declared that predatory preclusive tactics should be outlawed to achieve "effective competition." Atty. Gen. Nat. Com. Rep. 327, (4). Such tactics were defined as those that enable the user to eliminate rivals without regard to their efficiency. Long ago another student concluded that we should draw the line between good and bad trusts at the place where excluding purposes or unlawful excluding practices commence. Kales, Contracts and Combinations in Restraint of Trade §92 (1918).

[6] §§2.31, 4.3 *supra.*

CHAPTER 5

Vertical Integration*

§5.1. Vertical integration defined. "Vertical integration" may be defined as the unified control of more than one successive stage in the production or distribution of goods and services. As an economist wrote,

> . . . vertical integration may be described as the functional co-ordination of one or more units in each of the several successive stages of production, so that they are all operated as a single, unified industrial process.[1]

The word "integration" is also used loosely to describe other forms of combination. "Horizontal integration" refers to a union of former competitors; "geographical integration" or "dispersion" refers to the area in which a business operates and to its expansion into new territory; "circuitous integration" or "diversification" describes a concern producing more than one product or service. Thus, if A Company, a manufacturer of clothespins, is consolidated with B Company, a maker of the same product, the result may be described as "horizontal integration."[2] If A Company, formerly having sold its goods only in New England, establishes a factory and distribution facilities in the Middle West, we have an example of "dispersion."[3] If A Company enters upon the manufacture of motion picture film, it has achieved "diversification."[4]

In the nature of things, vertical integration must be a matter of

---

* This chapter appeared under the same title as an article in 49 Columbia Law Review 921 (1949). It has been revised and new authorities have been added. Consult generally Adelman, Integration and Antitrust Policy, 63 Harv. L. Rev. 27 (1949); Spengler, Vertical Integration and Antitrust Policy, 58 J. Pol. Econ. 347 (1950); Rostow and Sachs, Entry into the Oil Refining Business: Vertical Integration Re-examined, 61 Yale L.J. 856 (1952); Bork, Vertical Integration and the Sherman Act, 22 U. Chi. L. Rev. 157 (1954); Note, Vertical Integration in Aluminum, 60 Yale L.J. 294 (1951).

§5.1. [1] Frank, The Significance of Industrial Integration, 33 J. Pol. Econ. 179 (1925). See Wiedenfeld, Combinations, Industrial, 3 Encyc. Soc. Sci. 664 (1934); Dewing, The Financial Policy of Corporations 778 (3d ed. 1934).
[2] See §2.25 *supra.*
[3] See Chapter 7.
[4] See Chapter 6.

degree. A proprietor who conducts a retail pastry shop with a bakery in the rear has a vertically integrated business.[5] Furthermore, there is nothing novel in vertical integration: more than a century ago it was a conspicuous feature of the industrial landscape.[6] Today the degree of vertical integration found in industry varies widely. In automobile manufacture, for example, there is no generally accepted starting point; some firms merely assemble parts, while others reach back toward raw materials in varying degrees. Often the Ford Motor Company has been cited as an example of extreme integration. At River Rouge that company has coke ovens, blast furnaces, steel mills and foundries. Its own ships carry iron ore to its furnaces. At one time the firm cultivated 7400 acres of soya beans from which to make horn buttons. Despite such activities, the Ford automobile is said to be more than 65 per cent purchased from something like 20,000 independent outside suppliers of parts and materials.[7] Trade practices affecting integration change back and forth from time to time.[8] Even within single plants there is a considerable measure of vertical integration, since several successive operations may be performed at one location.[9] In view of such factors it is difficult to determine whether there is any trend toward an increased degree of vertical integration in American industry.[10]

For purposes of the antitrust laws, Professor Burns' definition may serve as well as any. He took as a test of the existence of vertical integration the salability of intermediate products: if goods can be sold at various stages of manufacture or distribution under the control of a single enterprise then vertical integration is present.[11] It should be noted that the definition does not require that the goods actually be offered for sale; it is the possibility of finding a buyer which controls. Under the foregoing test it

[5] Adelman, Effective Competition and the Antitrust Laws, 61 Harv. L. Rev. 1289, 1312 (1948).

[6] Gibb, The Saco-Lowell Shops 13, 17, 21-22 (1950); Hower, History of Macy's of New York 111 (1943).

[7] Mr. Ford Doesn't Care, 8 Fortune No. 6, p. 62 (1933); Kilgore Committee, pt. 2, at 652; Hearings Before House Special Committee on Investigation of American Retail Federation, 74th Cong., 1st Sess., pt. 4, at 2 (1936).

[8] E.g., watches were formerly sold without cases. United States v. Keystone Watch Co., 218 Fed. 502, 513 (E.D. Pa. 1915), *appeal dismissed,* 257 U.S. 664 (1921); Hamilton, Price and Price Policies 57 (1938).

[9] Thorp, The Integration of Industrial Operation 235-236 (Census Monograph III, 1924).

[10] Jewkes, Factors in Industrial Integration, 44 Q.J. Econ. 621, 622 (1930); Stigler, The Division of Labor Is Limited by the Extent of the Market, 59 J. Pol. Econ. 185, 188 et seq. (1951); Adelman, Concept and Statistical Measurement of Vertical Integration, in Business Concentration and Price Policy 281, 303 (Stigler ed. 1955); Barnes, Comment, id. at 322.

[11] Burns, The Decline of Competition 421 (1936).

would seem rare that the term "vertical integration" could be applied to operations within one physically connected plant; but that possibility is not excluded.

Vertical control may be attained by devices other than owner-ship. Exclusive dealing arrangements, for example, may have similar effects.[12] "Fair trade" statutes frequently legalize retail price maintenance and thus give a manufacturer a measure of vertical control.[13] Two other devices may be utilized to achieve some of the same ends. A manufacturer may appoint a dealer as his agent and thus retain control over many aspects of wholesale or retail sales.[14] With something of the same effect a manufacturer may refuse to deal with distributors whose policies are unfavorable to him.[15] Availability of such other devices of vertical control should be borne in mind in considering the legality of vertical integration.

§5.2. A page of history. Until recent times vertical integration was rarely attacked as such.[1] True, its presence was a factor in some of the old trust dissolution cases. In the first *American Tobacco* case,[2] for example, the defendant had bought up some of its sources of supply, including makers of tinfoil (wrappers) and licorice paste (flavor for plug). It also had a chain of retail stores and a system of warehouses in which raw tobacco was aged for three-year periods. In a horizontal dissolution, which split the defendant into three competing concerns, the tin-foil and licorice suppliers were cut loose, the Court saying that their acquisition

---

[12] See §§2.12, 2.13 *supra;* McLaren, Related Problems of "Requirements" Contracts and Acquisitions in Vertical Integration, 45 Ill. L. Rev. 141 (1950). Compare Bascom Launder Corp. v. Telecoin, 204 F.2d 331 (2d Cir. 1953), *cert. denied,* 345 U.S. 994 (1953), with Dictograph Products, Inc. v. FTC, 217 F.2d 821 (2d Cir. 1954), *cert. denied,* 349 U.S. 940 (1955); Atty. Gen. Nat. Com. Rep. 137, B. The specific prohibitions of §3 of the Clayton Act do not, by their own terms, apply to vertical integration.

[13] Fulda, Resale Price Maintenance, 21 U. Chi. L. Rev. 175 (1954); Bowman, The Prerequisites and Effects of Resale Price Maintenance, 22 id. 825 (1955); Note, Operation of Fair-Trade Programs, 69 Harv. L. Rev. 316 (1955).

[14] United States v. General Electric Co., 272 U.S. 476 (1926); apparently not over-ruled in this respect in United States v. Line Material Co., 333 U.S. 287 (1948). See also Standard Oil Company of California v. United States, 337 U.S. 293, 310 (1949).

[15] United States v. Colgate & Co., 250 U.S. 300 (1919); Times-Picayune Publishing Co. v. United States, 345 U.S. 594, 625 (1953); Note, Refusals to Sell and Public Control of Competition, 58 Yale L.J. 1121 (1949).

§5.2. [1] The ancient crimes of forestalling, engrossing and regrating bore some resemblance to vertical integration. In part they were designed to protect the normal operation of local markets, to preserve their "perfection"; they also reflected the ancient prejudice against middlemen and were partly protectionist in character. Adler, Monopolizing at Common Law and under Section Two of the Sherman Act, 31 Harv. L. Rev. 246, 255-256 (1917); Letwin, The English Common Law Concerning Monopolies, 21 U. Chi. L. Rev. 355, 370 (1954).

[2] United States v. American Tobacco Co., 221 U.S. 106 (1911).

had been part of an attempt to monopolize.[3] In the Supreme
Court, the same fate befell the retail stores, although the lower
court, despite the protest of Mr. Brandeis, had found them harmless.[4] Warehouses were left attached in the principal successor
units.[5]

Vertical integration was also a factor in the *Corn Products* case.[6]
In the first place, the defendant, having purchased a candy factory,
had threatened to compete with its own customers, the candy
makers, unless they bought their supplies from the defendant.
That conduct was held part of an attempt to monopolize, and
divestiture of the candy factory was decreed.[7]

In the second place, the defendant was accused of "squeezing"
rival mixers of syrup. Syrup was made from glucose by adding
about 15 per cent of sugar. The defendant was a manufacturer of
both glucose and syrup. It sold glucose to other syrup makers,
allowing them so little spread between the price of glucose (as
charged by the defendant) and the price of syrup (as fixed by the
defendant for its own product, "Karo") that several syrup mixers
abandoned the business. According to the evidence, the defendant,
on its books, charged its own syrup factory less than cost and less
than the open-market price for glucose.[8] Moreover, an intent to
monopolize the syrup-mixing trade was proven.[9] Thus the
"squeeze" was judicially condemned, but the decree did nothing
vertically to separate the defendant into distinct concerns, aside
from cutting off the candy factory.[10]

Nothing in the opinions in the *First Standard Oil* case[11] indicated disapproval of the extensive vertical combination of transportation, refining, and marketing which the defendants con-

3 Id. at 170.

4 In the lower court the opinion expressly found that the acquisition of the retail
stores was not part of a scheme to monopolize. It appeared that the defendants
had a chain of some 400 retail cigar stores out of about 600,000 places where tobacco
was sold in the United States. 164 Fed. 700, 709 (S.D.N.Y. 1908). The court emphasized that a mere investment in retail stores would not amount to a conspiracy
to monopolize commerce. Id. at 710. See generally Hale, Trust Dissolution, 40
Colum. L. Rev. 615, 624 (1940). Cf. Locker v. American Tobacco Co., 218 Fed. 447,
449 (2d Cir. 1914).

5 United States v. American Tobacco Co., 221 U.S. 106, 178 (1911).

6 United States v. Corn Products Refining Co., 234 Fed. 964 (S.D.N.Y. 1916).

7 Id. at 984.

8 Id. at 989-990.

9 Id. at 1007.

10 Id. at 1015 et seq. It is apparent from the opinion (at 984) that the candy
business was separated because of the use to which it had been put. Vertical integration as such was not condemned. But see the differing views of Professor Bork
in Vertical Integration and the Sherman Act, 22 U. Chi. L. Rev. 157, 159 (1954).

11 Standard Oil Co. of New Jersey v. United States, 221 U.S. 1 (1911), *aff'g* 173
Fed. 177 (E.D. Mo. 1909).

trolled. True, the dissolution decree worked a considerable measure of vertical disintegration, but it probably did so more by accident than by design.[12] Twenty years later two of the successor units secured judicial approval of their recombination.[13] One of the firms (Vacuum Oil Company) was chiefly a manufacturer of lubricants. In order to sell its grease to motorists it needed retail outlets in the form of filling stations. Purchase of those stations by other oil companies had allegedly excluded Vacuum from an important part of its market.[14] The other company, Socony, was principally a marketer of light petroleum products, such as gasoline and kerosene. It operated a large chain of filling stations. In approving the merger the court declared:

> The industry, as a whole, is thoroughly into the stage of integrated companies . . . [from production of crude oil through pipeline and tank car transportation to refineries and thence to filling stations] with special emphasis, as to marketing, upon the operation or control of retail automobile outlets. The superior business position of such an integrated company is evident. . . . The whole tendency of the industry is in that direction. It is this situation which is the motivating cause of the merger. [And] . . . it is clear that there are sound business reasons for this merger which are entirely sufficient and are wholly unconnected with any design to create a monopoly.[15]

International Harvester[16] had reached back to operate its own lumber tracts and steel mills. Although conceding that the timber business was not successful,[17] opponents of the combination asserted that ownership of the steel-producing facilities was a great element of strength,[18] giving the company a raw material at cost and thus creating a monopolistic position.[19] Despite such

---

[12] Hale, Trust Dissolution, 40 Colum. L. Rev. 615, 624 (1940); Kales, Contracts and Combinations in Restraint of Trade §127 (1918).

[13] United States v. Standard Oil Co., 47 F.2d 288 (E.D. Mo. 1931).

[14] In four years Vacuum had lost 19.2 per cent of its retail outlets. Id. at 310. There were other complementary aspects of the union, in the nature of integration, which seemed to be persuasive with the court.

[15] Id. at 309 et seq. The court also laid considerable stress on a lack of intent to monopolize. Id. at 317-318.

[16] United States v. International Harvester Co., 214 Fed. 987 (D. Minn. 1914), *appeal dismissed,* 248 U.S. 587 (1918), 10 F.2d 827 (D. Minn. 1926), *aff'd,* 274 U.S. 693 (1927).

[17] Commissioner of Corporations, The International Harvester Company 269-270 (1913).

[18] Ibid. Sales by Wisconsin Steel Corporation, the Harvester subsidiary, to the parent corporation were made at market prices. No interest was charged, however, on loans from International Harvester to Wisconsin Steel.

[19] FTC, Causes of High Prices of Farm Implements 675 (1920). The Commission urged that Wisconsin Steel be separated from the Harvester Company after a horizontal dissolution because the subsidiary would be too large for any one remaining unit. The Trade Commission added that the disposition of the lumber and fiber enterprises was not considered "very important." Id. at 674. More than

suggestions, the courts made no move toward vertical disintegration. The company still operates iron mines in the Mesabi range, ore boats, the steel works at South Chicago, six thousand acres of coal fields in Kentucky, a railway to carry steel to two of its plants, and a five-thousand-acre sisal plantation in Cuba.[20]

In the *Eastman Kodak* case[21] it was shown that the defendant had acquired some fifteen wholesale outlets, apparently in an effort to exclude competing manufacturers from the market. The court found it difficult to avoid the conclusion that the acquisition of the various wholesale companies was for the purpose of suppressing competition and in furtherance of an intention to form an illegal monopoly.[22] Nevertheless, no relief was granted in the form of vertical dissolution, and a later decree expressly permitted the defendant to engage in wholesaling and retailing.[23] Subsequently the defendant was attacked by the Federal Trade Commission by reason of the acquisition of three film-finishing plants,[24] which Kodak allegedly used to threaten its own customers with competition. Acquisition of those plants also received judicial approval.[25]

By 1915, so widely accepted was the legality of vertical integration that the United States Steel Corporation, it would seem, defended its combination on the ground that it was largely vertical rather than horizontal in character.[26] A vertical combination actuated by considerations of efficiency and marketing and not by a desire to create a monopoly in iron ore, the lower court held, was not a violation of the Sherman Act.[27] The Supreme Court approved:

---

a decade later the question of vertical integration was still active and the Commission again suggested the separation of the steel (and lumber) interests. FTC, Agricultural Implement and Machine Industry 158-159 (1938).

[20] International Harvester, 8 Fortune No. 2, pp. 21, 29-30 (1933); Moody's Investors Service, Industrial Manual 248-249 (1955).

[21] United States v. Eastman Kodak Co., 226 Fed. 62 (W.D.N.Y. 1915).

[22] Id. at 75-76. Cf. Eastman Kodak Co. v. Southern Photo Materials Co., 295 Fed. 98 (5th Cir. 1923), aff'd, 273 U.S. 359 (1927).

[23] In the absence of an intent to monopolize. Hale, Trust Dissolution, 40 Colum. L. Rev. 615, 625 (1940).

[24] Eastman Kodak Co. v. FTC, 7 F.2d 994 (2d Cir. 1925), aff'd, 274 U.S. 619 (1927).

[25] The Circuit Court of Appeals expressly approved acquisition by Kodak of the film-finishing plants and the operation thereof. Id. at 996. Judge Manton dissented on the ground that the purchase of the plants, combined with threats to use them, tended to create a monopoly. In the Supreme Court the decision was affirmed on the theory that the Trade Commission had no power to order a divestiture of property once acquired. Justices Stone and Brandeis dissented from that proposition and expressly refused to discuss the issue of vertical integration, contending that the acquisition by Kodak did not constitute bona fide business conduct.

[26] United States v. United States Steel Corp., 223 Fed. 55 (D.N.J. 1915), aff'd, 251 U.S. 417 (1920).

[27] Evidence indicated that integration contributed to efficiency. See 223 Fed. 55, 124-125, 127-128. Moreover, the acquisition of ore properties in the Mesabi range

And we add no comment except, it may be, that they [the judges below] underestimated the influence of the tendency and movement to integration, the appreciation of the necessity or value of the continuity of manufacture from the ore to the finished product. And there was such a tendency; and though it cannot be asserted it had become a necessity, it had certainly become a facility of industrial progress.[28]

Some years before, Mr. Justice Holmes, speaking for the same court, had been even more explicit:

The disintegration aimed at by the statute does not extend to reducing all manufacture to isolated units of the lowest degree. It is as lawful for one corporation to make every part of a steam engine and to put the machine together as it would be for one to make the boilers and another to make the wheels.[29]

§5.3.   More history: Public utilities and others.   In regard to public utilities, it is true, vertical integration has long been less favored.   A quaint Illinois decision condemned grain trading by elevator operators.[1]   It was shown that the operators of the eleva-

---

"did not so increase the ore reserves and the transportation facilities of the corporation as to give it a monopolistic power over the raw materials of the industry." Id. at 164.   The separate opinion of Wooley, J., found no fault with vertical integration.   Id. at 166 et seq.

28 United States v. United States Steel Corp., 251 U.S. 417, 442 (1920).   Even the dissenting opinion seems not to challenge the approval of vertical integration.   Id. at 460-461.   Indeed, the plaintiff appears to have conceded its legality.   Id. at 426. Acquisition of the Tennessee Coal & Iron Co. likewise was viewed favorably.   Id. at 446-447.   Similar views were expressed in Dodge v. Ford Motor Co., 204 Mich. 459, 170 N.W. 668, 670, 671, 681 (1919).

29 United States v. Winslow, 227 U.S. 202, 217-218 (1913) (the remarks were not strictly necessary to the decision).   Cf. Appalachian Coals, Inc. v. United States, 288 U.S. 344, 376-377 (1933); Alexander Milburn Co. v. Union Carbide Corp., 15 F.2d 678 (4th Cir. 1926), cert. denied, 273 U.S. 757 (1927); Locker v. American Tobacco Co., 218 Fed. 447, 449-450 (2d Cir. 1914); Bigelow v. Calumet & Hecla Mining Co., 167 Fed. 704, 720 (C.C.W.D. Mich. 1908); State v. Missouri Pacific Ry., 237 Mo. 338, 141 S.W. 643 (1911).   But compare Johnston v. Townsend, 103 Tex. 122, 124 S.W. 417 (1910); Bork, Vertical Integration and the Sherman Act, 22 U. Chi. L. Rev. 157, 194 (1954) (courts have always held integration suspect).

Earlier history is recorded in Herbruck, Forestalling, Regrating and Engrossing, 27 Mich. L. Rev. 365 (1929); Letwin, The English Common Law Concerning Monopolies, 21 U. Chi. L. Rev. 355 (1954).   Compare Mund, Open Markets 199 et seq., 205 et seq. (1948) (refusals to trade in organized markets).   In some degree statutes against forestalling merely reflect the ancient prejudice against the middleman. Id. at 388.   See Jewkes, Ordeal by Planning 117 et seq. (1948).

It is worthy of note that in its Final Report the Temporary National Economic Committee failed to reach an adverse conclusion with respect to vertical integration.

§5.3.   1 Central Elevator Co. v. People, 174 Ill. 203, 51 N.E. 254 (1898).   Apparently the principal ground of the decision was that the duty of a warehouseman was of a quasi-fiduciary nature and, therefore, inconsistent with his trading on the market in competition with his customers.   It also appeared that the grading of

tors bid a quarter cent higher to obtain wheat, stored it in their own warehouses, and sold it a quarter cent lower than the market.

In 1906 the "commodities clause" applied a similar rule to railroads.[2] A leading student has declared that the clause was "directed against an insidious source of discrimination" and

> . . . primarily against the so-called coal roads which, as owners of mines and transporters of their own product in competition with that of independent operators, frequently made adjustments in rates and service unduly favorable to themselves . . .[3]

Apparently the theory behind the legislation was that the railways charged competing mine operators higher rates than they "charged" themselves, thus reducing the profits of their rivals.[4] The clause played an important role in *United States v. Reading Co.*,[5] in which it appeared that, in addition to a horizontal combination, the defendant had acquired control of extensive coal properties. As a result, the Court found, the railway exercised considerable control over the supply, and hence, the price, of coal in consuming markets. In the opinion of the Court,

> Obviously, this dominating power was not obtained by normal expansion to meet the demands of a business growing as a result of superior and enterprising management, but by deliberate, calculated purchase for control. That such a power, so obtained, regardless of the use made of it, constitutes a menace to and an undue restraint upon interstate commerce within the meaning of the Anti-Trust Act, has been frequently held by this court.[6]

---

grain was not sufficiently precise to prevent some advantage accruing to the elevator operator when he mixed his goods with those of his customers.

[2] Act of June 29, 1906, §1, 34 Stat. 584, 49 U.S.C. §1(8) (1952). The statute reads: "It shall be unlawful for any railroad company to transport . . . any article or commodity, other than timber . . . manufactured, mined, or produced by it . . . or which it may own in whole or in part . . . except such articles or commodities as may be necessary and intended for its use in the conduct of its business as a common carrier." Consult Marshall, The Commodities Clause, 17 J. Pol. Econ. 448 (1909). Similar state legislation is collected in Martin, ed., State Antitrust Laws liii (WPA, 1940).

[3] 1 Sharfman, The Interstate Commerce Commission 42, 43n (1931).

[4] 3-B Sharfman, id. 367n, quoting the Commission.

[5] 253 U.S. 26 (1920).

[6] Id. at 57 et seq. Quaere whether the cases cited by the court fully sustain the assertion in the last-quoted sentence. In the lower court the opinion declared that there was no objection to a miner of coal building and operating his own railway and that therefore the joint ownership of coal mine and railway could not be unlawful. United States v. Reading Co., 226 Fed. 229, 267 (E.D. Pa. 1915). It is believed that the Reading case depends considerably upon both the commodities clause (253 U.S. at 60) and the existence of a horizontal combination. A similar decision was rendered in United States v. Lehigh Valley R.R., 254 U.S. 255 (1920). See also Meeker v. Lehigh Valley R.R., 21 I.C.C. 129, 154 (1911).

Similar legislation has been applied to the airlines[7] and is not unknown even in fields unrelated to the carriage of goods.[8]   Indeed, vertical integration is widely prohibited in the liquor trade, apparently on the theory that the "tied house" of preprohibition days constituted an incentive to intoxication.[9]   And one famous consent decree prohibited a degree of vertical integration in the meat-packing business.   Later the defendants chafed under their voluntary bonds and sought freedom to sell meats at retail on the ground that conditions had changed.   Authority to do so was denied them, Mr. Justice Cardozo saying:

> The court below annulled the restraint upon sales of groceries by wholesale, but retained the prohibition in respect of sale by retail both for groceries and for meats.   The one prohibition equally with the other was directed against abuse of power by the individual units after the monopoly was over; and the death of the monopoly, the breaking up of the combination, if an adequate reason for terminating one of them, is an adequate reason for terminating both.[10]

In the main, however, the decision was procedural; the Court refused to disturb the consent decree.[11]

With the foregoing modest exceptions, courts, legislators and economists until recently appeared to approve vertical integration. Lawyers generally understood that form of combination to be lawful as such.   Businessmen employed the device widely where it appeared to add to efficiency of operations.   Vertical integration has indeed become a widespread phenomenon and studies have shown that it may play a role in reducing costs and increasing

[7] Civil Aeronautics Act of 1938, §409, 52 Stat. 1001, 49 U.S.C.A. §489.   An earlier provision of like import appeared in §7 of the Act of June 12, 1934, 48 Stat. 933.

[8] In Crescent Cotton Oil Co. v. Mississippi, 257 U.S. 129 (1921), the Court sustained a state statute prohibiting a corporation manufacturing cottonseed oil from operating its own cotton gin.   Other legislation, much of it obviously designed with protectionist aims, is collected in Cook, Legislative Restrictions on Marketing Integration, 8 Law & Contemp. Prob. 273, 286 et seq. (1941).

[9] E.g., Ill. Rev. Stat., c. 43, §121 (1955); Federal Alcohol Administration Act §5(b), 49 Stat. 981 (1935), 27 U.S.C.A. §205.   See de Ganahl, Trade Practice and Price Control in the Alcoholic Beverage Industry, 7 Law & Contemp. Prob. 665, 667 (1940); Note, A Comparative Survey of Post-repeal Liquor Legislation, 83 U. Pa. L. Rev. 510, 518 (1935); Martin, ed., State Liquor Legislation 20, 22 (WPA, 1941).   Why vertical integration should promote intemperance remains obscure.   Perhaps the true explanation of the legislation lies in its protectionist character.   It has been said, for example, that the wholesaler is inefficient and unnecessary (for the most part) in the liquor trade.   Hamilton, Price and Price Policies 418-419, 422 (1938).

[10] United States v. Swift & Co., 286 U.S. 106, 117 (1932).

[11] Id. at 119.   Previously the Federal Trade Commission had attacked ownership of branch houses and private car routes as a "bulwark of monopoly."   Burns, The Decline of Competition 427 (1936).

stability.[12] Furthermore, a degree of vertical integration may tend to thwart horizontal price-fixing schemes.[13]

§5.4. **Onslaught upon integration: Sleeping cars.** In recent decades vertical integration has been a target of attack in many industries. In the *Pullman* case[1] a principal complaint against the defendant was that it both operated sleeping cars and manufactured them. Indeed, it insisted upon using cars of its own make, refusing to purchase those manufactured by others. It had contracts with almost all railroads, requiring the latter to take Pullman service exclusively. Thus the competing manufacturers (or would-be manufacturers) of sleeping cars had no market. It was held that the manufacturing and operating ends of the business should be separated and a decree to that effect was entered.

§5.5. **Onslaught upon integration: Petroleum.** In the oil industry, control of the pipelines has long stirred accusations of monopoly.[1] Many years ago a federal statute was enacted which had the effect of making most interstate lines common carriers.[2]

More recently a consent decree was entered regulating the dividends which may be paid by pipeline subsidiaries of integrated oil companies.[3] In that case, the Attorney General asserted that vertical integration in the oil industry was "inherently monopolistic," and offered to "prove" that pipeline rates were excessive because "profits" therefrom were used to cover deficits in other branches of the oil business.[4] Professor Rostow flatly stated that the control of pipelines was the source of monopoly power in oil:

> The essential instrument of economic power in the oil industry is integration, and particularly the ownership by the major companies of transportation facilities. . . . Integration . . . is the

[12] E.g., McLean and Haigh, How Business Corporations Grow, 32 Harv. Bus. Rev. No. 6, pp. 81, 82 (1954).

[13] Roosevelt Committee, pt. III, at 1108; Scitovsky, Economic Theory and the Measurement of Concentration, in Business Concentration and Price Policy 101-118, 106 (Stigler ed. 1955).

§5.4. [1] United States v. Pullman Co., 50 F. Supp. 123 (E.D. Pa. 1943). Opinions regarding relief to be afforded are reported in 53 F. Supp. 908 (E.D. Pa. 1944), 64 F. Supp. 108 (E.D. Pa. 1946), aff'd per curiam, 330 U.S. 806 (1947). It has been asserted, however, that the decision did not actually involve vertical integration. Bork, Vertical Integration and the Sherman Act, 22 U. Chi. L. Rev. 157, 173 (1954).

§5.5. [1] Burns, The Decline of Competition 427 (1936); Pipe Line Cases, 234 U.S. 548, 559 (1914).

[2] Act of June 29, 1906, 34 Stat. 584, 49 U.S.C. §1(1)(b).

[3] United States v. Atlantic Refining Co., Civ. 14,060, D.D.C. (1941), described in Note, Dividends from Oil Pipe Line Subsidiaries under Elkins Act, 9 U. Chi. L. Rev. 503, 504 (1942).

[4] Black, Oil Pipe Line Divorcement by Litigation, 25 Cornell L.Q. 510, 525, 527 (1940). Compare Whitesel, Recent Federal Regulation of the Petroleum Pipe Line, 32 id. 337, 349 (1947).

basic means of achieving and maintaining monopolistic control over price . . .[5]

Other attacks have been more specific. One allegation is that pipelines permit the integrated oil companies to transport crude oil to a centrally located refinery.[6] Such a refinery, it is said, has an advantage over one located near the crude oil field in that it will remain useful after nearby wells run dry.[7]

Another complaint is that the integrated concerns squeeze the independent refiner. It is said that the price of crude oil is raised and that the price of gasoline is lowered to such a degree that the independent refiner cannot operate.[8] Putting the matter another way, it is said that the integrated firms charge excessive rates for transporting oil by pipeline, again squeezing the refiner who owns no such facilities.[9] In full flower the theory is that the major oil concerns operate their refining and marketing departments at a loss and make profits only on producing and transportation.[10]

And it is true that there has been some slight support in the past within the oil industry itself for the notion that portions of the business are run at a loss.[11] Of course, the end product of the

[5] Rostow, A National Policy for the Oil Industry 57 et seq., 117 (1948). Neither data nor doctrine was cited in support of those assertions. But compare Rahl, Book Review, 43 Ill. L. Rev. 421 (1948). In United States v. Richfield Oil Corp., 99 F. Supp. 280 (S.D. Cal. 1951), aff'd per curiam, 343 U.S. 922 (1952), the lower court said at page 292 that it was unlawful for a refiner of petroleum to build filling stations in which its products would be sold on an exclusive basis by lessees. Compare Hamilton, Price and Price Policies 150 (1938).

[6] Cook, Control of the Petroleum Industry by Major Oil Companies 20 (TNEC Monograph No. 39, 1941). It followed, the author asserted, that control of the pipelines permitted integrated firms to set the price of crude oil to suit their own convenience. Id. at 25.

[7] Note, Public Control of Petroleum Pipe Lines, 51 Yale L.J. 1338, 1340 (1942). No mention was made of the comparative cost of shipping crude oil and refined products or of the relative efficiency of locating refineries in oil fields as opposed to marketing areas.

[8] Cook, Control of the Petroleum Industry by Major Oil Companies 32-33 (TNEC Monograph No. 39, 1941); Celler Committee I, pt. 1, at 349; Edwards, Maintaining Competition 98, 171 (1949). But cf. McLean and Haigh, The Growth of Integrated Oil Companies 659 (1954) (empirical investigation reaching different result).

[9] Note, Public Control of Petroleum Pipe Lines, 51 Yale L.J. 1338, 1341 (1942).

[10] Cook, Control of the Petroleum Industry by Major Oil Companies 22 (TNEC Monograph No. 39, 1941). In the same study it was said at page 6: "As a result of integration it is possible to lose money in one division and show a profit at the end of the year on the entire activities. . . . The marketing division is usually operated at a loss, but it does make a dependable outlet and extension of other divisions possible. Likewise, a rigid price structure can be maintained." It is not clear why the statement in the last sentence quoted flows from the preceding discussion. Cf. Edwards, Maintaining Competition 98, 171-172 (1949).

[11] It is said that until 1931, Gulf Oil Company regarded its refineries purely as a means of disposing of its profitable crude oil production. Drake, who became president of Gulf in that year, resolved to make refining and retailing profitable: "Gulf was in four businesses: why not make four profits?" Gulf Oil, 14 Fortune No. 4, pp. 79, 142, 144 (1937).

foregoing theory is that independent refiners and marketers are squeezed into a profitless position.

§5.6. **Onslaught upon integration: Aluminum.**   A squeeze of independent rollers of sheet aluminum has been a persistent charge against the Aluminum Company of America (Alcoa).   That firm was long the sole domestic producer of virgin aluminum ingot.   According to the allegation, it set such a high price on the ingot and such a low price on the sheet aluminum rolled by itself that independent rollers were squeezed out of business.   Baush Machine Tool Company, an independent roller, sued Alcoa on that theory.   At one point the plaintiff seemed to have convinced the United States Court of Appeals for the Second Circuit that the squeeze existed and was unlawful.[1]

Not until the Attorney General filed his grand action against Alcoa, however, was the matter really determined.[2]   In that case it was alleged that until 1932, when complaints of Baush and others reached the Department of Justice, Alcoa's margin between the prices of its ingot and its sheet were not sufficient to cover the costs of rolling the ingot into sheet form.   After 1933, the spread was increased.   The court regarded the squeeze with disfavor.   In the language of Judge Learned Hand,

> That is was unlawful to set the price of "sheet" so low and hold the price of ingot so high, seems to us unquestionable, provided, as we have held, that on this record the price of ingot must be regarded as higher than a "fair price."   True, this was only a consequence of "Alcoa's" control over the price of ingot, and perhaps it ought not to be considered as a separate wrong . . .[3]

In reaching that conclusion, the court accepted Alcoa's cost of rolling ingot into sheet, taken from its own books, with only a trifling dispute as to "unabsorbed burden." [4]   Thus the court did not face the necessity of computing those costs for itself.

§5.6. [1] Baush Machine Tool Co. v. Aluminum Co. of America, 72 F.2d 236, 242 (2d Cir. 1934), *cert. denied*, 293 U.S. 589 (1934). The defendant had prevailed in the lower court. The Court of Appeals reversed because the trial judge had excluded many types of evidence allegedly indicating monopolization by the defendant. In the opinion the court indicated acceptance of the "squeeze" theory.

[2] United States v. Aluminum Co. of America, 44 F. Supp. 97 (S.D.N.Y. 1941), *rev'd*, 148 F.2d 416 (2d Cir. 1945).

[3] 148 F.2d 416, 438 (2d Cir. 1945). Cf. Celler Committee I, pt. 1, at 326.

[4] In the lower court Judge Gaffey had approved the exclusion of the "unabsorbed burden" in ascertaining the cost of particular commodities. Judge Learned Hand, in the appellate tribunal, thought otherwise, but the difference was not sufficiently great to cause a change in the conclusions reached as to squeeze. 148 F.2d 416, 436. It appeared that unabsorbed burden constituted the cost of maintaining unused plant.

Apparently the defendants' exhibit No. 1748 was the source of the cost data used in computing squeeze. There is nothing to indicate that the defendants pressed the

Although acts made possible by vertical integration were condemned in the *Aluminum* case, the court refused to disapprove integration itself. In the opinion Judge Hand expressly announced that Alcoa's acquisition of the whole or parts of fabricators of aluminum ingot was neither unlawful nor relevant to the action.[5] And the remedy finally afforded the plaintiff did not involve disruption of the defendant's vertical structure.[6]

§5.7. Onslaught upon integration: Chain stores. Squeeze was likewise the theme of the Attorney General's attack upon the Great Atlantic & Pacific Tea Company.[1] His argument was that the retail stores of that grocery chain are operated at a loss, being "subsidized" by profits realized at the chain's headquarters. Such profits were derived from advertising allowances granted by suppliers and from the chain's own manufacturing operations. That contention was accepted by the district court; Judge Lindley followed the plaintiff's argument and concluded that losses of the retail stores were covered by "allocations" of profits derived at "headquarters." [2]

Two other complaints against the A & P bear on its vertical integration. In the first place, the chain was said to have threatened its suppliers with manufacturing its own groceries at a loss and, in some cases, to have done so. In that way it obtained goods at favorable prices[3] and could therefore resell to the consumer more cheaply than its nonintegrated rivals. In the second place, a subsidiary of the A & P, the Atlantic Commission Company (Acco), was organized to buy produce directly from the grower.

---

issue of cost allocation in detail. They did attack the plaintiff's contention that excessive profits had been realized on ingot-making, saying that there had been a failure to allocate sufficient capital to that project. Brief for Aluminum Company, pp. 498-499 (2d Cir.). Cf. Celler Committee I, pt. 1, at 335.

[5] 148 F.2d 416, 435-436. Compare Aluminum Co. of America, 3 F.T.C. 302 (1921), *aff'd sub nom.* Aluminum Co. of America v. FTC, 284 Fed. 401 (3d Cir. 1922), in which the same defendant had been compelled to divest itself of stock in a competing rolling mill under the provisions of §7 of the Clayton Act. It is interesting to note that Judge Gaffey, who heard the evidence in the principal case found that the failure of the Baush Machine Tool Co. to compete successfully was due to its inferior equipment, insufficient capital, high cost of production, inadequate sales effort and limitation of output to a restricted line of commodities. 44 F. Supp. 97, 207-208.

[6] United States v. Aluminum Co. of America, 91 F. Supp. 333 (S.D.N.Y. 1950). Note that the two new producers of ingot in the United States were then found to be just as integrated vertically as the defendant. Id. at 536.

§5.7. [1] United States v. New York Great Atlantic & Pacific Tea Co., 173 F.2d 79 (7th Cir. 1949), *aff'g* 67 F. Supp. 626 (E.D. Ill. 1946).

[2] 67 F. Supp. 626, 630-631, 638, 640-641, 664. Cf. Celler Committee I, pt. 1, at 313.

[3] Note, Chain Store Integration as Restraint of Trade under the Sherman Act, 15 U. Chi. L. Rev. 392, 396 (1948). A more sophisticated statement of the same theory appears in Edwards, The Place of Economics in the Course on Trade Regulation, 1 J. Legal Ed. 1, 10 (1948).

Again, the A & P was accused of obtaining its supplies below "cost" and hence of violating the Sherman Act.[4]

§5.8. Onslaught upon integration: Taxicabs. In the *Yellow Cab* case,[1] Checker (CCM), a manufacturer of taxicabs, gained control over concerns operating cabs for hire in Chicago, Pittsburgh, Minneapolis and New York City. In Chicago it obtained 86 per cent of the cabs on the streets; in Pittsburgh, 100 per cent; in Minneapolis, 58 per cent; and in New York, only 15 per cent. As in the *Pullman* case,[2] the contention of the Solicitor General was that by conspiracy between CCM and its subsidiaries, other manufacturers of taxicabs were excluded from large portions of the market for those vehicles.[3] That theory was adopted by the Supreme Court, which declared:

> By excluding all cab manufacturers other than CCM from that part of the market represented by the cab operating companies under their control, the appellees effectively limit the outlets through which cabs may be sold in interstate commerce. Limitations of that nature have been condemned time and again. . . . In addition, by preventing the cab operating companies under their control from purchasing cabs from manufacturers other than CCM, the appellees deny those companies the opportunity to purchase cabs in a free, competitive market. The Sherman Act has never been thought to sanction such a conspiracy to restrain the free purchase of goods. . . .[4]

[4] 67. F. Supp. 626, 655-656. Some other activities of Acco, such as organizing committees of growers of produce seeking to channel all their production to itself, seem to have verged on attempts to monopolize. Id. at 658 et seq. The lower court's opinion laid much stress upon the activities of Acco. See Note, Chain Stores under the Sherman Act, 47 Colo. L. Rev. 786, 788 (1947); Pope, Vertical Forestalling under the Antitrust Laws, 19 U. Chi. L. Rev. 583, 587-588 (1952); Celler Committee I, pt. 1, at 219. But compare Adelman, The A & P Case: A Study in Applied Economic Theory, 63 Q.J. Econ. 238, 255 et seq. (1949) (vigorous challenge to Attorney General's position). A subsequent civil suit was settled by consent decree. United States v. New York Great Atlantic & Pacific Tea Co., CCH Trade Reg. Serv. ¶67,658 (S.D.N.Y. 1954). By the terms of that decree the defendant was required to dissolve Acco, but not, apparently, to dispose of the business formerly carried on by that subsidiary.

§5.8. [1] United States v. Yellow Cab Co., 332 U.S. 218 (1947). Subsequent proceedings are reported in 80 F. Supp. 936 (N.D. Ill. 1948), aff'd, 338 U.S. 338 (1949). The original opinion in the United States Supreme Court was followed in United States v. National City Lines, 186 F.2d 562 (7th Cir. 1951), cert. denied, 341 U.S. 916 (1951).

[2] §5.4 supra.

[3] Brief for United States, p. 28. The notion that such industrial giants as General Motors had been "excluded" was the subject of some incredulity in a later opinion in the case. 338 U.S. 338, 340.

[4] 332 U.S. 218, 226. Quaere whether the Court's assertion that "limitations of that character have been condemned again and again" was sustained by the authorities there cited. Note the comment in Adelman, Integration and Antitrust Policy, 63 Harv. L. Rev. 27, 143 (1949), to the effect that the language of the opinion indicated all vertical integration to be illegal per se.

It should be noted that the Court also adopted the Solicitor General's theory that two parts of a vertically integrated concern may conspire with each other in violation of Section 1 of the Sherman Act. That conclusion led the tribunal to make a comment which comes near to being a condemnation of vertical integration:

> The fact that these restraints occur in a setting described by the appellees as a vertically integrated enterprise does not necessarily remove the ban of the Sherman Act. The test of illegality under the Act is the presence or absence of an unreasonable restraint on interstate commerce. Such a restraint may result as readily from a conspiracy among those who are affiliated or integrated under common ownership as from a conspiracy among those who are otherwise independent.[5]

§5.9. **Onslaught upon integration: Motion pictures.** Exclusion from the market has also been the battle cry against the vertically integrated firms in the motion picture industry. Originally the industry was divided into separate branches of production, distribution, and exhibition. Producers then started to invade the field of distribution. In 1917 the exhibitors countered by organizing distributing and producing facilities under the name of First National Pictures. Thereupon the producers bought up theaters in order to preserve outlets for their films.[1]

Over the years several states have attempted to prevent producers from controlling theaters[2] but their efforts have borne no fruit.[3] Some time ago the Attorney General proceeded under the Sherman Act against the vertically integrated concerns. Dissatisfied with the terms of a consent decree entered in 1940,[4] he

[5] 332 U.S. 218, 227. In the subsequent proceedings (note 1 *supra*) the plaintiff's case failed for want of evidence. Mr. Justice Black, however, dissented vigorously. 338 U.S. 338, 343. It has been suggested that the second Yellow Cab opinion established that vertical integration combined with unlawful horizontal monopoly cannot be proven illegal unless there is a showing of a specific intent to do more than monopolize the market between the integrating units. Pope, Vertical Forestalling under the Antitrust Laws, 19 U. Chi. L. Rev. 583, 592 (1952). Sed quaere.

§5.9. [1] Evans, Bertrand and Blanchard, The Motion Picture Industry 5-6 (TNEC Monograph No. 43, 1941); Note, Enforced Independence for Motion Picture Exhibitors, 48 Yale L.J. 339 (1938). See also Brief for Paramount Pictures, Inc., p. 113, United States v. Paramount Pictures, Inc., 334 U.S. 131 (1948).

[2] E.g., North Dakota, Act of March 15, 1937, Laws 1937, c. 165, §3. The statute was sustained in Paramount Pictures v. Langer, 23 F. Supp. 890 (N.D. 1938), *rev'd as moot*, 306 U.S. 619 (1938) (statute repealed). The trial court sustained the statute despite a finding (at 900) that the producers enjoyed no (horizontal) monopoly in the state.

[3] Note, Enforced Independence for Motion Picture Exhibitors, 48 Yale L.J. 339, 340n (1938).

[4] A description of the decree will be found in United States v. Paramount Pictures, Inc., 63 F. Supp. 323, 331 (S.D.N.Y. 1946).

subsequently brought the case to trial and prevailed in the lower court.[5] On appeal the decree was generally affirmed, but the matter was remanded for further consideration as to the form of relief to be granted.[6]

One aspect of the complaint against integrated motion picture companies was that the films of independent producers were denied a showing. What proportion of the theaters of the United States was controlled by the defendants can be stated in various ways. Overall, the five major producers controlled only 17 per cent of the theaters, but that 17 per cent produced 45 per cent of the revenues.[7] Of the metropolitan "first-run" theaters, the defendants were alleged to control 80 per cent, and it was found that 70 per cent of the first-run houses in the ninety-two cities with populations in excess of 100,000 were so affiliated.[8] Couple such facts with the popular impression that a film cannot succeed unless it receives a favorable reception in a first-run theater, and there is a basis for the argument that independent producers were excluded from the market. Thus the Solicitor General's position before the Supreme Court was:

Any manufacturer has a right to use his own product in his own outlets, so long as he does not use the advantage resulting from integration to restrain unreasonably the competition of others or monopolize. But no manufacturer . . . has the right deliberately to acquire control of a particular market for his produce when the purpose or necessary effect is to exclude others from an important segment of the market.[9]

[5] Id. Findings of fact and conclusions of law reported in 70 F. Supp. 53 (S.D. N.Y. 1947).

[6] United States v. Paramount Pictures, Inc., 334 U.S. 131 (1948).

[7] Id. at 173-174.

[8] Evans, Bertrand and Blanchard, The Motion Picture Industry 11, 53, 167 (TNEC Monograph No. 43, 1941). Cf. Famous Players-Lasky Corp., 11 F.T.C. 187 (1927), rev'd sub nom. FTC v. Paramount Famous-Lasky Corp., 57 F.2d 152 (2d Cir. 1932). The Trade Commission found that the defendant producers had conspired to monopolize the whole motion picture industry. They bought large theaters to secure favorable "first runs" for their pictures in an effort to dominate the entire motion picture industry. Id. at 206. They threatened to build theaters in an effort to coerce independent exhibitors. Id. at 210. The group of theaters which they controlled grew from 50 to 368. Among other practices which the Trade Commission condemned was that of "block booking" or leasing film only in "packages." The Commission's order to cease and desist prohibited the defendants from coercing individual theaters as well as other types of conduct. On appeal only the prohibition against block booking was considered. In the view of the Circuit Court, block booking did not have the effect denounced by §3 of the Clayton Act. In Minnesota, exhibitors sponsored a statute which made block booking, with certain modifications from the system then in force, compulsory. See Note, Operation of the Consent Decree in the Motion Picture Industry, 51 Yale L.J. 1175, 1179 (1942).

[9] Brief for plaintiff, p. 103, United States v. Paramount Pictures, Inc., 334 U.S. 131 (1948). In the brief filed upon behalf of the Society of Independent Motion

The other facet of the complaint that vertical integration excluded competitors from markets was an argument that owners of independent theaters could not obtain films.[10] Apparently that was the motivating force behind state legislation aimed at divorcement of theater holdings. Since theaters are expensive and cannot be built without an assured supply of films,[11] we arrive back at the argument that independent producers have no market for their pictures because no one can build theaters in which to show them.

The issue of appropriate relief also raised questions concerning the legality of vertical integration. It had been said that integration was the root of all monopoly in motion pictures.[12] Professor Rostow had declared: "Entry into the industry would be impossibly handicapped and not really competitive, so long as the existing majors continue to own or to control access to the best theaters. . . ."[13] Accordingly, the bill filed in the latest governmental proceedings specifically charged that the vertical integration of the major defendants violated Sections 1 and 2 of the Sherman Act.[14] In his brief before the Supreme Court the Solicitor General flatly asserted that vertical integration, as such, violates the antitrust laws.[15] Accordingly, the plaintiff was seeking a decree that the integrated motion picture companies be shorn of their theater holdings. The 1940 consent decree forbade further

---

Picture Producers (at 16 et seq.) the argument was carried a step farther. It was urged that ownership of theaters permitted integrated firms to force their films into those houses and thus to obtain a substantial return on any picture, however poor.

[10] Compare West Coast Theatres, Inc., 12 F.T.C. 383 (1929); West Coast Theatres, Inc., 12 F.T.C. 436 (1929); Paramount Pictures, Inc. v. Langer, 23 F. Supp. 890, 898-899 (S.D.N.D. 1938), *rev'd as moot*, 306 U.S. 619 (1938).

[11] Evans, Bertrand and Blanchard, The Motion Picture Industry 55 (TNEC Monograph No. 43, 1941).

[12] Id. at 13, 55. Cf. Note, The Sherman Act and the Motion Picture Industry, 13 U. Chi. L. Rev. 346, 356-357 (1946).

[13] Rostow, The New Sherman Act, 14 id. 567, 599 (1947).

[14] United States v. Paramount Pictures, Inc., 334 U.S. 131, 141 (1948).

[15] Brief for United States, pp. 90 et seq., 334 U.S. 131. It was asserted that vertical integration violated both §§1 and 2 of the Sherman Act. The defendants, of course, denied that assertion. In the Brief for Paramount Pictures, Inc., p. 115, the Reading and Lehigh Valley cases were distinguished on the ground that in those cases an intent to monopolize was readily apparent. In the Brief for Loew's, Inc., p. 47, the same cases were distinguished on the ground that there the control of the market was much greater, running up to 95 per cent of the coal fields along the defendants' right of way. An interesting discussion is found in the Brief for Warner Brothers, p. 65. There it is said that Warner Brothers pioneered the talking motion picture. Finding that independent theater owners were unwilling to purchase the expensive equipment necessary to project sound films, Warner Brothers were compelled to operate their own theaters in order to provide for their pictures. Cf. Appendix B *infra*.

acquisition of motion picture houses.[16] In the contested proceedings, however, the lower court refused to decree divestiture. It
preferred a scheme of competitive bidding for films and thought
that cutting off the theaters would take the defendants out of the
market, replacing them (as exhibitors) with less experienced
persons.[17]

It should also be noted that the complaint charged the defendants with a horizontal conspiracy to maintain prices, allegations which were sustained by the trial court. The Supreme Court
left those findings undisturbed. Thus the combination which
faced the Supreme Court had width as well as depth.[18] Whatever
the effect of that fact may have been — and argument can be presented in either direction — the Court refused to follow the Soloci-
tor General's suggestion that it declare vertical integration unlawful as such. According to the opinion, vertical integration is
judged in the light of the intent with which it is created and of
the power thus accruing to its sponsors. The conclusion reached
was that vertical integration is unlawful if it is a "calculated
scheme to gain control over an appreciable segment of the market
and to restrain . . . competition . . ." or if "a power to exclude
competition is coupled with a purpose or intent to do so." [19] On
remand the trial court was, of course, bound by the views expressed by the Supreme Court. It proceeded to examine certain
aspects of vertical integration pursuant to directions from the
higher tribunal. It found that the horizontal conspiracy to fix
prices had been powerfully aided by vertical integration and that
the theater holdings of the producers played a vital part in effecting violations of the Sherman Act.[20] On that subject, the court
said:

> We do not suggest that every vertically integrated company which
> engages in restraints of trade or conspiracies will thereby render
> its vertical integration illegal. The test is whether there is a close
> relationship between the vertical integration and the illegal prac-
> tices. . . .[21]

[16] Note, Legislation by Consent in the Motion Picture Industry, 50 Yale L.J.
854, 868 (1941).

[17] United States v. Paramount Pictures, Inc., 66 F. Supp. 323, 353 (S.D.N.Y. 1946).

[18] But cf. Judge Augustus N. Hand's opinion in the court below at page 354:
"The five major defendants cannot be treated collectively so as to establish claims
of general monopolization in exhibition. They can only be restrained from the
unlawful practices in fixing minimum prices, obtaining unreasonable clearances,
block-booking, and other things we have criticized." Cf. §3.9 *supra*.

[19] United States v. Paramount Pictures, Inc., 334 U.S. 131, 174 (1948). Can both
tests be assimilated in the category of an attempt to monopolize? See §9.2 *infra*.

[20] United States v. Paramount Pictures, Inc., 85 F. Supp. 881, 887, 893-894 (S.D.
N.Y. 1949).

[21] Id. at 893.

In the motion picture decision the court apparently was influenced by the fact that no producer made enough films to supply its own theaters. Accordingly the defendant producers were not only rivals but also customers and suppliers of each other. This fact apparently led the court to conclude that vertical integration had assisted in the maintenance of the horizontal conspiracy; hence separation of the business carried on as exhibitors from that operated as producers and distributors was decreed.[22]

§5.10. **Onslaught upon integration: Steel.** A decision concerning the steel industry also bore upon exclusion from the market.[1] Processing of steel may be divided into two divisions, rolling and fabricating. Rolled products include plates, pipe, sheet, and bars. The United States Steel Corporation, through its subsidiaries, engaged in such rolling. Fabrication itself is divided into two categories, structural and plate fabrication. United States Steel engaged in the first type of fabrication, manufacturing such things as bridges, frames for buildings, and the like. Consolidated Steel Company was a fabricator of structural steel and also of plate steel (tanks, large pipe). United States Steel did not engage in the fabrication of plate. United States Steel was vertically integrated, producing rolled steel at several plants, among which was one at Geneva, Utah, acquired with the approval of the Attorney General in 1946. Consolidated was not an integrated concern.

In the period 1937-1946, U.S. Steel rolled a third of all steel products produced in the United States, and had rolling mills in Utah and California. Consolidated engaged in structural fabrication at Los Angeles, California, and at Orange, Texas, and plate fabrication in both California and Arizona. In its fabrication, Consolidated used about .5 per cent of the annual production of rolled steel in the United States. In its marketing area, it utilized about 3 per cent. If plates and shapes (among other types of rolled steel) alone were considered, Consolidated required about 13 per cent of the rolled steel sold in its trading area. Benjamin Fairless, president of U.S. Steel, testified that his company wanted

---

[22] Id. at 895-896. See McLaren, Related Problems of "Requirements" Contracts and Acquisitions in Vertical Integration under the Anti-trust Laws, 45 Ill. L. Rev. 141, 158 (1950); Bork, Vertical Integration and the Sherman Act, 22 U. Chi. L. Rev. 157, 191 (1954).

§5.10. [1] United States v. Columbia Steel Co., 334 U.S. 495 (1948). The case is discussed in Note, Vertical Integration Under the Sherman Act, 33 Minn. L. Rev. 398, 399 et seq. (1949), and Note, The Columbia Steel Case: New Light on Old Antitrust Problems, 58 Yale L.J. 764 (1949). Informative testimony will be found in TNEC Hearings, pt. 20, at 10,744, 10,769, 10,834, 10,865.

to acquire Consolidated's plant in order to assure a market for the plates and shapes rolled at Geneva.[2]

Again the Solicitor General urged that vertical integration be declared unlawful as such. In presenting that contention, he placed much reliance upon the *Yellow Cab* case,[3] but the Court refused to sustain him. It denied that the *Yellow Cab* decision was susceptible of such a construction and attempted to distinguish it on both the pleadings and the facts. Then the opinion said:

> Exclusive dealings for rolled steel between Consolidated and United States Steel, brought about by vertical integration or otherwise, are not illegal, at any rate until the effect of such control is to unreasonably restrict the opportunities of competitors to market their products.[4]

After referring to the *Paramount* decision, handed down after argument of the steel case, the Court went on:

> It seems clear to us that vertical integration, as such and without more, cannot be held violative of the Sherman Act. It is an indefinite term without explicit meaning. Even in the iron industry, where could a line be drawn — at the end of mining the ore, the production of the pig-iron or steel ingots, when the rolling mill operation is completed, fabrication on order or at some stage of manufacture into standard merchandise? . . . Technological advances may easily require a basic industry plant to expand its processes into semi-finished or finished goods so as to produce desired articles in greater volume and with less expense.[5]

Following the reasoning thus laid down, the Court could not find the acquisition unlawful. Since Consolidated bought only 3 per cent of the rolled steel used in the marketing area, the purchase "does not unreasonably restrict the opportunities of the competitor producers of rolled steel to market their product." [6] Mr. Justice Douglas' dissenting opinion was disappointing in its failure to

---

[2] 334 U.S. 495, 506. In the plaintiff's petition for rehearing (at 4) much was made of the above admission. The acquisition of Consolidated was characterized as a deliberate, calculated purchase for control and hence within the rule laid down in the Yellow Cab case. If acquisition of Consolidated was necessary in order to provide a market for plates and shapes rolled at Geneva, the desirability of buying the latter plant in the first place appears dubious. Perhaps Geneva was too far away from the coastal area to meet the competition of rolling mills in California and yet had (indivisible) capacity requiring sales in that territory.

[3] Brief for plaintiff, p. 33, 334 U.S. 495, 519.

[4] Id. at 524.

[5] Id. at 525-526.

[6] Id. at 527. The truth of the matter would seem to be that the court retreated considerably from the position taken in the Yellow Cab case.

analyze the problem fully. He merely denied that the restriction was reasonable.[7]

§5.11. **General complaints against integration.** Recent years have heard many general attacks upon vertical integration. Henry Simons would have permitted it only "so far as clearly compatible with the maintenance of real competition."[1] Professor Corwin D. Edwards stated his position in a much more sophisticated manner but still spoke of a vertically integrated concern having "the power to squeeze" its rivals.[2] The woes of independent tire dealers have been blamed upon the retail outlets of tire manufacturers by a committee of the United States Senate.[3] That same committee later cautioned concerns building military aircraft for the federal government to subcontract the making of component parts (and not to enter upon their manufacture themselves so as to prevent independent firms doing that work).[4] In the eyes of the Federal Trade Commission, integration is undesirable because it enables big producers to reach back and gobble up supplies, thus cutting off small rivals from raw materials. As late as 1955, the Commission was still speaking of vertical integration in terms of permitting a squeeze on nonintegrated rivals.[5]

[7] Id. at 538. The dissenting opinion, however, does focus on the issue of vertical integration. Its argument is a simple one of exclusion from the market. Just where the decision leaves the law is difficult to say. See Note, Vertical Forestalling under the Antitrust Laws, 19 U. Chi. L. Rev. 583, 593 (1952). After the above text had been set in type there was decided the case of United States v. E. I. Du Pont de Nemours & Co., 353 U.S. 586 (1957). The decision held unlawful the stock ownership of the Du Pont Company in General Motors Corporation. While the Court carefully avoided utilizing the Sherman Act, it reversed thirty-five years' interpretation of §7 of the Clayton Act and held it applicable to vertical integration. Perhaps the opinion presages a revival of the Yellow Cab doctrine. Most lawyers will prefer the dissent of Mr. Justice Burton.

§5.11. [1] Simons, A Positive Program for Laissez-Faire 20-21 (1934). Cf. Raymond, The Limitist 120 (1947). Note application of the "foreclosure" theory in United States v. National City Lines, 186 F.2d 562, 567 (7th Cir. 1951), cert. denied, 341 U.S. 916 (1951). In patent law recent decisions suggest that any "extension" of the patent grant is unlawful. Note, Patent Abuses and Antitrust, 64 Harv. L. Rev. 626, 629 (1951). Conceivably such cases could affect vertical integration. In some situations the Robinson-Patman Act may curb vertical integration. Adelman, Integration and Antitrust Policy, 63 Harv. L. Rev. 27, 138 (1949).

[2] Edwards, Maintaining Competition 98, 130 (1949).

[3] Senate Select Committee on Small Business, 5th Ann. Rep., Sen. Rep. No. 129, 84th Cong., 1st Sess. 55 (1955).

[4] Id., 6th Ann. Rep., Sen. Rep. No. 1368, 84th Cong., 2d Sess. 43 (1946).

[5] FTC, The Present Trend of Corporate Mergers and Acquisitions 12 (1947); FTC, Corporate Mergers and Acquisitions 112 (1955). Testimony with respect to "squeeze" in the steel industry will be found in Celler Committee I, pt. 4A, at 345, 533, 615.

Professor Miller has pointed out the connection between vertical integration and indivisibility ("natural" monopoly at one level). Miller, Unfair Competition 211 (1941). It has been asserted that vertical integration is the same as horizontal price-fixing, the conclusion, of course, being that it should be unlawful as such. See

A shrewder observation was that of Professor Chamberlin. He found that vertical integration was a catching fever: if one enterprise engaged in it, its rivals were compelled to do likewise. Supporting such a conclusion is the vertical integration in the motion picture business, which was motivated by defensive reasons. Such compulsory parallel integration, Chamberlin thought, leads to waste:

> The result is much duplication of distributive machinery, and higher margins of profit which attract more people into the field and bring still more waste, always subtly concealed by the fact that the average profit for business man or business unit is held down by the increase in numbers.[6]

§5.12. Buying at "cost." We turn now to analysis of the several complaints made against vertical integration. One of the most persistent grounds of attack is that a firm vertically integrated earns "double profits." But even today, when all profits are under fire, the allegation is usually stated in slightly more subtle fashion. And frequently the opposite argument is made. Thus, in the *A & P* case the Attorney General contended that the grocery chain's possession of a subsidiary engaged in the buying of produce, part of which was sold to the parent, enabled A & P to obtain merchandise at "cost." In the same case the defendant was charged with threatening its suppliers with competition and, by directly engaging in manufacturing, obtaining additional goods at "cost." Again, the concern was alleged to have operated its retail stores at a "loss," subsidizing them from "profits" realized at "headquarters." The major oil companies are accused of operating their refining and distributing system at a "loss," thus effecting sales of their crude oil below "cost." [1]

Slight reflection will suffice to bring out the manifest error in such assertions. An integrated firm, by definition, demands a

---

Note, Chain-Store Integration as Restraint of Trade Under the Sherman Act, 15 U. Chi. L. Rev. 392, 393 (1948). Mr. Berge has gone all the way in insisting that vertical integration should be illegal per se. Berge, Problems of Enforcement and Interpretation of the Sherman Act, 38 Am. Econ. Rev. 172, 177 et seq. (1948). His argument relies heavily upon International Salt Co. v. United States, 332 U.S. 392 (1947). Cf. Stigler, The Extent and Bases of Monopoly, 32 Am. Econ. Rev., Supp. No. 2, pp. 1, 22 (1942). See also Watkins, Discussion, 38 Am. Econ. Rev. 204, 207-208 (1948).

[6] Chamberlin, The Theory of Monopolistic Competition 123 (3d ed. 1938).

§5.12. [1] Cook, Control of the Petroleum Industry by Major Oil Companies 22 (TNEC Monograph No. 39, 1941). Compare the assertion that a vertically integrated motion picture firm can thrust its films, however poor, upon its own theaters and thus compete unfairly. Brief for Association of Independent Motion Picture Producers, pp. 16 et seq., United States v. Paramount Pictures, Inc., 334 U.S. 131 (1948).

larger investment than its nonintegrated rival. If it is to secure a return on that additional investment, its profits must be larger. It can obtain raw materials at "cost" from its vertically integrated source of supply only by the sacrifice of return on its investment in that source. It can distribute its products at "cost" through profitless retail stores only if it is willing to forgo interest on the money invested in the retail enterprise.[2] If a vertically integrated firm does thus secure its supplies or sell its products at "cost," it dilutes its return upon the investment in the principal part of its business. An amusing illustration of the notion that vertical integration develops double profits turned up in the *Aluminum* case. There, it will be recalled, Alcoa was accused of operating its rolling mills at a loss in order to squeeze independent operators of such mills. At the trial a manufacturer of utensils made of rolled sheet aluminum complained that one of *his* competitors, another utensils manufacturer, had a competitive advantage (which accounted for his higher profits) because he rolled his own sheet! [3]

As applied to public utilities, however, the production-at-cost theory contains a measure of truth. For the prices of public utilities are regulated, and vertical integration may constitute an attempt to escape regulation. It offers an avenue for effective exploitation of a concern's monopoly position. To prevent such exploitation is the legitimate purpose of the "commodities clause." [4] But if a public utility enterprise uses vertical integration to avoid

2 Dennison, Vertical Integration and the Iron and Steel Industry, 49 Econ. J. 244, 246 et seq. (1939); Wallace, Market Control in the Aluminum Industry 392 (1937); Adelman, Effective Competition and the Antitrust Laws, 61 Harv. L. Rev. 1289, 1313n (1948); Burns, The Decline of Competition 443 (1936). Ownership of raw materials (iron ore mines) by a manufacturer may or may not be profitable, depending a good deal upon the stage of the business cycle. United States Steel Corp., Business . . . Big and Small . . . Built America 22 (1950).

3 United States v. Aluminum Co. of America, 44 F. Supp. 97, 213 (S.D.N.Y. 1941).

4 Compare 1 Sharfman, The Interstate Commerce Commission 42-43 (1931). Unfortunately Professor Sharfman carried his analysis of the problem no further than a declaration that the commodities clause was directed at "an insidious source of discrimination" and that without it the railroads published rates "unduly favorable unto themselves." Those charged with the regulation of public utilities have long been cognizant of the possibility of evasion presented by vertical integration, e.g., Illinois, Act of July 8, 1933, Laws 1933, p. 841, Rev. Stat. c. 111⅔, §8a(3) (1955). Compare United States v. Yellow Cab Co., 332 U.S. 218 (1947). See Edwards, Maintaining Competition 98 (1949); Adelman, Integration and the Outlook for the Future, Symposium N.Y. State Bar Assn., Section on Antitrust Law 135, 149 (CCH, 1951); Porter, Federal Regulation of Private Carriers, 64 Harv. L. Rev. 896 (1951); Steel Rails, 8 Fortune No. 6, pp. 42, 46 (1933). Some of the problems of interventionist controls arise out of the existence of vertical integration. E.g., Armstrong, The Problem of Finished Piece Goods Margins, in Caplan, ed. Problems in Price Control: Changing Production Patterns 128, 130 (OPA, 1947); Ritz, Wartime Subsidies, in Franck, ed., Problems in Price Control, pt. II, 93, 152 (OPA, 1947).

rate regulation, integration should not be condemned generally. If, for example, the American Telephone & Telegraph Company inflates its rate base through high cost purchases from its subsidiary, Western Electric Company (on which issue no opinion is expressed), it does not follow that integration is an instrument of iniquity.[5]

§5.13. "Squeeze." Complaints that the nonintegrated firm is squeezed depend upon the production-at-cost theory. When the Attorney General accused Alcoa of squeezing independent rollers of aluminum, he meant that Alcoa rolled sheet at a "loss" covered by the profits of its ingot-making division. Or, in the alternative, that Alcoa obtained its ingot below "cost."[1] And when critics charge the large oil companies with squeezing their independent one-stage competitors, they mean that higher profits in production and transportation are used to cover deficits in refining and distribution.[2] For the reasons just advanced, the squeeze contention must fail. In the long run, a vertically integrated enterprise cannot afford to forgo profits on a part of its operations. And the existence of vertical integration is by no means incompatible with vigorous competition. For example, a study of the Sun Oil Company, a fully integrated concern, showed that it engaged its rivals in vigorous

[5] United States v. Western Electric Co., CCH, Trade Reg. Serv. (9th ed.) ¶61,186 (D.N.J. 1949), consent decree, id. ¶68,246 (1956) (consent decree did not disturb vertical integration). Other illustrations of vertical integration in the public utility field will be found in Celler Committee I, pt. 1, at 544; pt. 4A, at 253-254, 862. Many of the complaints to the effect that vertical integration forecloses a rival from a source of raw material reflect "shortages" — high levels of demand and allocation of such raw materials under conditions of some horizontal monopoly. Id., pt. 4A, at 305; FTC, Monopolistic Practices and Small Business, Report to the Subcommittee on Monopoly, Senate Select Committee on Small Business 22, 29 (Feb. 21, 1952). Compare Edwards, Antimonopoly Policy during Rearmament, 42 Proceedings Am. Econ. Assn. 404 (1952). Additional examples of the effects of intervention upon integration will be found in Harris and others, eds., Problems in Price Control: Stabilization Subsidies 22-23 (OPA, 1947); Fantin and Madigan, Livestock Slaughter Control, in Studies in Food Rationing 315, 329 (1947).

§5.13. [1] Wallace, Market Control in the Aluminum Industry 381 et seq. (1937). Wallace appeared to conclude (at 487) that vertical integration was harmful. His data (at 390, 395), however, do not seem to present convincing evidence of squeezing with intent to monopolize. Compare The Aluminum Company of America, 10 Fortune No. 3, pp. 46, 102 et seq. (1934). Complaints of "squeeze" against a vertically integrated firm in the steel industry will be found in TNEC Hearings, pt. 19 at 10,501; pt. 20, at 10,865.

[2] Cook, Control of the Petroleum Industry by Major Oil Companies 32-33 (TNEC Monograph No. 39, 1941); Note, Public Control of Petroleum Pipe Lines, 51 Yale L.J. 1335, 1341 (1942). Compare Farish and Pew, Review and Criticism of Monograph No. 39, 42 (TNEC Monograph No. 39-A, 1941) (price squeeze explained on ground that market prices changed at various levels without full coordination). See also Sun Oil, 23 Fortune No. 2, pp. 51, 52 (1941). A comment on the steel industry will be found in Celler Committee I, pt. 4A, at 721.

competition. Against that firm the charge of making profits on pipelines to support unprofitable refineries "does not carry much weight." The study concluded:

> The concept of free enterprise to the Pews [the Pew family controls Sun Oil] does not imply the close ownership of a corporation; it does imply competition. It implies more hard-hitting functional enterprises like Sun, which are big enough to create lowered cost, small enough to be manageable, daring enough to open up new technological frontiers.[3]

Genuine horizontal monopoly at some stage of production may permit squeeze. Thus, if Alcoa squeezed the independent rollers, its ability to do so arose from the fact that it was the sole domestic producer of virgin aluminum. Vertical integration did not make the squeeze possible, for if there had been other producers of ingot, then the competing rollers could presumably have secured that raw material at a more favorable price.

It is nevertheless true that a vertically integrated firm may utilize squeeze in an attempt to monopolize. If, during the short run, it is willing to forgo a normal return upon its investment, it may sell below cost, thus hurting its competitors. But a nonintegrated firm may do likewise. Although some type of integration may be helpful in providing a cushion of profit to sustain the price-cutter during his foray, local price-cutting to drive a competitor out of business is not a phenomenon limited to vertically integrated firms.[4]

A more sophisticated explanation of squeeze may be found in price discrimination. Thus Alcoa, the sole domestic producer of aluminum ingot, may have been in a position to maximize profits by discriminating among its customers. Those who bought aluminum ingot for casting could not, perhaps, pay the maximum price charged those who rolled the ingot into sheet.[5] Just as a railroad

3 Sun Oil, 23 Fortune No. 2, pp. 51, 119 (1941). Compare Rostow, A National Policy for the Oil Industry 65 (1948). But see Thompson, Since Spindletop 54 (Gulf Oil Corp. 1951) (apparent admission that some portions of business "subsidized" others).

4 Adelman, Effective Competition and the Antitrust Laws, 61 Harv. L. Rev. 1289, 1314 (1948). Compare United States v. Corn Products Refining Co., 234 Fed. 964, 1008 (S.D.N.Y. 1916). Undoubtedly Corn Products' use of its candy factory to club its customers into submission was an attempt to monopolize apart from the concept of vertical integration. Note also that local price-cutting to injure competition has long been recognized as an attempt to monopolize. E.g., Standard Oil Co. of New Jersey v. United States, 221 U.S. 1 (1911); and see §9.2 infra.

5 Professor Wallace starts with the proposition that there was some monopoly element in Alcoa's rolling of sheet. He said: "Explanation of the hesitancy of independent enterprise to enter this field must be found in a distaste for dependence upon monopoly for ingot supply and in the power of integrated monopoly over the ingot-sheet price differential, with both of which elements the tariff has

charges the shipper of diamonds more than the shipper of coal per ton mile, so Alcoa may have maximized profits by dividing its customers into classes.[6] And its own rolling department, of course, would fall into a favored class. Again, vertical integration was not behind the squeeze. It was Alcoa's position as the sole domestic producer of ingot which enabled it to differentiate among the users of its products.

§5.14. **Common cost.** Let us analyze the squeeze contention further. The argument is that Alcoa either rolled sheet below "cost" or else obtained ingot (from itself) below "cost." If ingot were sold in a free market, that market price might be taken as the cost of raw material to Alcoa as a roller of sheet. In the absence of such a free market, we must somehow fix the "cost" of the ingot to Alcoa,[1] and in so doing we run head on into the problem of common costs. Common cost problems have plagued attempts to prove "double profits" and "squeeze" in the oil industry. In an integrated company, assignment of costs to specific operations presents problems of infinite complexity. A storage tank, for example, may sometimes be used as a facility in the process of refining petroleum and at other times to hold refined products in the marketing stage.[2] Again, when several products result from a single process it is obvious that some allocation of expense must be made in order to arrive at the cost of making each one of them. In refining crude oil, for example, the expenses of the refinery must be divided among the products of gasoline, kerosene, diesel oil, lubricants and the like.[3]

Many methods are used to allocate joint costs. Sometimes the two products are made to bear costs of production in proportion to their weight or bulk.[4] Upon other occasions market values of

---

been intimately connected." Wallace, Market Control in the Aluminum Industry 374-375 (1937). He did not find, however, any clear explanation of the price squeeze: "The whole of the evidence seems to allow either the interpretation that the declining price differential was partly due to a desire to take business away from the independents or that it is explainable on other grounds entirely, but does not indicate that discouragement of competition was the chief motive." Id. at 390. In this connection note that Alcoa was already rolling 75 per cent of the sheet produced in the United States. Id. at 376, 380.

[6] Id. at 390-391.

§5.14. [1] Wallace, Market Control in the Aluminum Industry 463-464 (1937). Compare Brief for Defendants, pp. 459, 524, United States v. Aluminum Co. of America, 148 F.2d 416 (2d Cir. 1945). The case also raised an active question as to whether virgin aluminum ingot competed with scrap aluminum; i.e., whether there actually was a free market for aluminum ingot.

[2] TNEC Hearings, pt. 17-A, at 10,038. See McLean and Haigh, The Growth of Integrated Oil Companies 504-505 (1954).

[3] Canning, Cost Accounting, 4 Encyc. Soc. Sci. 475, 477 (1931).

[4] TNEC Hearings, pt. 17-A, at 10,092.

the various commodities are used to allocate joint costs.[5] It is easy to demonstrate that such methods are arbitrary and can result in fantastic computations.[6] In his classroom Professor Viner commonly used an illustration in which a ton of slag (radium by-product) was sold for a pittance. If, however, allocation of costs was made upon the basis of weight, the result would be the production of radium for almost nothing.

From a theoretical point of view it is possible to allocate joint costs properly if the entrepreneur is able to vary the output of the several products.[7] A dispute continues among economists as to whether it is always possible to vary the portion of the various products resulting from joint methods.[8] Granting that such variation is possible, then familiar marginal principles permit a theoretical allocation of costs.[9] On the other hand, there is little to indicate that such a computation is practical in an actual business situation. Similar considerations affect the allocation of overhead costs.

During World War II the OPA often faced the problem of allocating overhead costs. Apparently the only solution reached was to "pass the buck" to the manufacturers. Sometimes a business concern was required to use its customary methods of allocation; in other instances the OPA seems to have permitted any method to be used. Apparently the government officers involved were unable or unwilling to state upon what basis, if any, they had proceeded.[10]

In the face of such problems it is difficult to understand how critics can assert with so much confidence that part of a vertically integrated enterprise is carried on at a loss. If the oil companies refine crude oil into gasoline and other products without profit, the theoretical analysis and statistical facts necessary to prove that assertion appear to be lacking.[11] In individual instances it might

---

[5] Id. at 10,056.

[6] Kreps, Joint Costs in the Chemical Industry, 44 Q.J. Econ. 416, 420 (1930).

[7] Conference on Price Research, Committee on Price Determination, Cost Behavior and Price Policy 179 (1943).

[8] Id. at 176.

[9] Viner, Cost, 4 Encyc. Soc. Sci. 466, 473 (1931). Compare Cady, Entrepreneurial Costs and Price, c. 8 (1942).

[10] Franck and Quint, Problems in Price Control: Pricing Techniques 85 (OPA, 1947); Peel, Survey of Rubber Tire and Tube Manufacturers 1 (OPA Economic Data Series No. 10, 1947); Peel, Survey of Shirt, Shorts and Pajama Manufacturers 3n (OPA Economic Data Series No. 5, 1947). Compare Adelman, Integration and Antitrust Policy, 63 Harv. L. Rev. 27, 35-36 (1949).

[11] It is perhaps true, however, that the more vertically integrated an enterprise, the smaller in general is the proportion of common costs. Conference on Price Research, Committee on Price Determination, Cost Behavior and Price Policy 174 (1943).

be possible to allocate joint and overhead costs by comparison with single-stage firms. Thus, if the A Company is purely a roller of sheet aluminum and produces about the same quantity as its integrated rival does, its overhead costs per ton might provide at least a clue to proper allocation. In the reported decisions, however, it does not appear that such comparisons have been made.

If squeeze can be shown solely on the basis of direct costs — without, that is, any allocation of common costs — then the problem of common cost division can, of course, be avoided. On the other hand, the government's contentions in the *A & P* case constituted an attempt to reallocate direct costs and revenues. No one would have paid "advertising allowances" to the A & P "headquarters" if A & P had not run a chain of retail stores! Such an allocation is pure fantasy.[12]

Squeeze, as suggested above, may be a symptom of price discrimination. Thus the whole problem of vertical integration may resolve itself into a question of the effect of charging others more for a product than one charges oneself. Professor Wallace's careful analysis of the aluminum industry suggested that Alcoa's desire to expand the market for aluminum products generally had been the cause of the squeeze felt by other rollers of sheet. Only by taking profits on ingots sold for rolling, as opposed to other uses (casting), could Alcoa effectively expand its production.[13] It followed that avoidance of the squeeze could only be achieved through monopolization of the rolling process as well as the refining.[14] A monopolist will always attempt to discriminate among his customers. It is difficult, however, to reach any conclusion as to the effects of such discrimination.[15] And in the absence of ideal competition, elimination of such differences would seem to convert all industry into the class of public utilities.

§5.15. Exclusion from the market. As we have noted above, it is often charged that the vertically integrated concern excludes its rivals from a market. At times the argument stresses access to raw materials. Thus the major packers were not allowed to enter

[12] Adelman, The A & P Case: A Study in Applied Economic Theory, 63 Q.J. Econ. 238, 244 (1949).

[13] Wallace, Market Control in the Aluminum Industry 392 (1937). Note the potential effect upon growth and innovation. See Appendix B *infra*. A company which had developed a new type of outdoor sign acquired several firms engaged in the erection of roadside advertising to push acceptance of its product. Minnesota Mining & Manufacturing Co., Ann. Rep. 1948, 7 (St. Paul, 1949), 1952 Ann. Rep. 18 (1953).

[14] Wallace, Market Control in the Aluminum Industry 380 (1937). A hint that Professor Wallace's analysis was correct is found in Brief for Defendants, p. 405, United States v. Aluminum Co. of America, 148 F.2d 416 (2d Cir. 1945).

[15] E.g., Robinson, The Economics of Imperfect Competition 179 et seq. 206 (1933). But compare Wallace, Market Control in the Aluminum Industry 393-394 (1937).

the retail meat market business on the theory that existing
butchers might thereby be cut off from supplies.[1] Pullman was
not to operate sleeping cars because the railroads could not then
buy such vehicles from Budd.[2] Exhibition was to be separated
from production and distribution in the motion picture industry
because independent theaters otherwise secure only the stale and
unpopular films.[3]

In other cases exclusion from the market refers to opportunities
to make sales. One of the complaints against the old Standard Oil
Company was that it impeded its rivals' access to the consuming
public.[4] Today ownership of pipelines is said to prevent the
independent oil producer and refiner from marketing his wares.[5]
In the 1948 steel case the Solicitor General argued that acquisition of Consolidated by U.S. Steel deprived other rollers of steel
of a market.[6] Ownership of theaters by the integrated motion
picture companies was said to deny essential exhibition facilities
to independent producers.[7]

To exclude a competitor from a market is, of course, tanta-
mount to an attempt to monopolize. It is therefore a violation of
the antitrust laws.[8] But that does not indicate that vertical integration, as such, is unlawful.

Denial of access to raw materials, it will be observed, is a
boomtime phenomenon. In the period following World War II,
many raw materials, particularly steel, were difficult to obtain.
But in depressions, raw materials are abundant and cheap. There
was no shortage of steel, wheat or copper in 1933. Only a monop-

§5.15. [1] United States v. Swift & Co., 286 U.S. 106 (1931). See Burns, The Decline of Competition 429 (1936) (decision protectionist in character). Compare
United States v. Lehigh Valley R.R., 254 U.S. 255, 269 (1920); Eastman Kodak Co.
v. Southern Photo Materials Co., 273 U.S. 359 (1927). A classic example of an attempt to injure competitors by buying up their sources of raw materials is reported in 1 Nevins, Study in Power 226 (1953).

[2] United States v. Pullman Co., 50 F. Supp. 123 (E.D. Pa. 1943).

[3] Evans, Bertrand and Blanchard, The Motion Picture Industry 55 (TNEC Monograph No. 43, 1941). Compare United States v. General Electric Co., 82 F. Supp.
753, 803, 817 (D.N.J. 1949); FTC, The Present Trend of Corporate Mergers and
Acquisitions 12 (1947); Mund, The Right to Buy, Report to Senate Committee on
Small Business, Sen. Doc. No. 32, 85th Cong., 1st Sess. 87, 89-90 (1957).

[4] Burns, The Decline of Competition 439 (1936); Kales, Contracts and Combinations in Restraint of Trade §126 (1918).

[5] Rostow, A National Policy for the Oil Industry 57-58 (1948).

[6] Plaintiff's Brief for Rehearing, p. 4, United States v. Columbia Steel Corp., 334
U.S. 495 (1948). Note also the dissenting opinion of Douglas, J., at 537; Celler
Committee I, pt. 4A, at 310-311.

[7] Evans, Bertrand and Blanchard, The Motion Picture Industry 55 (TNEC Monograph No. 43, 1941). Compare United States v. National City Lines, 186 F.2d 562
(7th Cir. 1951), cert. denied, 341 U.S. 916 (1951); Anaconda Copper, 14 Fortune No.
6, pp. 83, 94 (1936); Celler Committee I, pt. 1, at 445; pt. 2A, at 309, 342.

[8] Compare United States v. Associated Press, 326 U.S. 1 (1945); Hastings Mfg. Co.
v. FTC, 153 F.2d 253 (6th Cir. 1946); Carter Carburetor Corp. v. FTC, 112 F.2d 722
(8th Cir. 1940).

oly of inconceivable force could damn the flood of raw materials which becomes available in times of slack business.

By the same token, denial of access to retail outlets is a phenomenon of depression. When consumers are buying heavily, there is no problem in disposing of well-made goods. As the saying goes, it is a "seller's market," and no competent producer experiences difficulty in marketing his wares.

Now both situations, boom and depression, cannot exist at one time. If one does exist, the other cannot. As applied to the motion picture industry, either independent producers can find no theaters in which to show their films, *or* independent theater owners can obtain no films to present in their houses. Both situations cannot obtain at once! And under less extreme conditions, it would seem that normal forces of competition would open up markets in either direction. Unless and until there is monopoly at some horizontal level in the line of integration, firms should, by definition, enjoy access both to raw materials and consumers.

It is true that there are genuine instances of exclusion from markets. Independent theater owners did experience difficulty in obtaining good films.[9] But the blame did not lie with vertical integration. It was the "horizontal" combination of producers and distributors, each dependent in part upon the other for bookings in theaters, which excluded the independent. Eliminate the combination and you end the exclusion. Even harsh observers of the film and oil industries have confessed that dissolution of integrated firms will not alone achieve full competition.[10] And certainly nothing is gained by the fiction that a vertically integrated firm conspires with its subsidiaries to exclude others from the market.[11]

[9] What's Playing at the Grove? 38 Fortune No. 2, p. 95 (1948).

[10] Note, The Sherman Act and the Motion Picture Industry, 13 U. Chi. L. Rev. 346, 358-359 (1946); Evans, Bertrand and Blanchard, The Motion Picture Industry 56 (TNEC Monograph No. 43, 1941); Note, Public Control of Petroleum Pipe Lines, 51 Yale L.J. 1338, 1355-1356 (1942); Dirlam and Kahn, Fair Competition 158 (1954). Compare Kilgore Committee, pt. 6, at 2537, 2542. Decline in the role of "independent" oil refiners has been attributed to factors other than vertical integration of the "majors" in a careful study. McLean and Haigh, The Growth of Integrated Oil Companies 556 (1954). Note also that when dissolution of integration has been decreed, the courts have sometimes added injunctive provisions suggesting that the dissolution alone was not wholly effective. E.g., United States v. Pullman Co., 64 F. Supp. 108, 113 (E.D. Pa. 1946), *aff'd per curiam*, 330 U.S. 806 (1947). See generally Spengler, Vertical Integration and Antitrust Policy, 58 J. Pol. Econ. 347, 351-356 (1950); Cross, Vertical Integration in the Oil Industry, 31 Harv. Bus. Rev. No. 4, pp. 69, 70 (1953); Whitney, Vertical Disintegration in the Motion Picture Industry, 45 Proceedings Am. Econ. Assn. 491, 498 (1955). In the last-cited study, however, the author concludes generally that vertical disintegration is desirable.

[11] Watkins, Discussion, 38 Am. Econ. Rev. 204, 206-207 (1948). Compare McQuade, Conspiracy, Multicorporate Enterprises and Section 1 of the Sherman Act, 41 Va. L. Rev. 183 (1955); Hale, The Sherman Act, in Conference on the Antitrust Laws and the Attorney General's Committee Report 33, 35 (Rahl ed. 1955).

§5.16.   Integration as an abuse.   If vertical integration as such does not produce double profits and excludes no one from the market, its enemies fall back on the contention that it leads to abuses. Thus Professor Levi said that the lower court's decision in the *A & P* case was easily rested on the abuses proven against that firm.[1] Others, while recognizing the economies of vertical integration and refusing to condemn it as such, contended that this type of integration might lead to abuses and should be prohibited when misused for undesirable market control.[2]

Abuses are close to attempts to monopolize.[3] Thus, in the *A & P* case the efforts of A & P's subsidiary, Acco, to obtain control of all the vegetable produce of large areas was termed an "abuse." In the old oil company cases the typical abuse was local price-cutting to injure competition.[4]   Both of the foregoing activities are clear-cut examples of attempts to monopolize on a horizontal level. In other words, integration is a purely incidental factor.[5]   An attempt to monopolize does suggest, however, that the would-be monopolist enjoys other resources from which he may (temporarily) finance his efforts.   Thus the great chain of A & P stores furnished funds with which to support Acco's venture in the produce business.   But such resources are not necessarily derived from vertical integration. Undistributed profits of a horizontal concern could just as easily be employed for such a purpose. If shareholders are willing to forgo dividends, a fund may be created with which to

§5.16. [1] Levi, The Antitrust Laws and Monopoly, 14 U. Chi. L. Rev. 153, 180 (1947).

[2] E.g., Adelman, Effective Competition and the Antitrust Laws, 61 Harv. L. Rev. 1289, 1317, 1321 (1948).

[3] See §2.9 supra, §§9.1, 9.2 infra; United States v. General Electric Co., 82 F. Supp. 753, 799 (D.N.J. 1949).   It is often urged that vertical integration permits the exercise of "leverage": i.e., that monopoly power at one level may thus be spread over into another. E.g., Rostow and Sachs, Entry into the Oil Refining Business, 61 Yale L.J. 856, 877 (1952); Dirlam and Kahn, Fair Competition 147 (1954); Celler Committee I, pt. 4A, at 844.   Such a contention may be supported by the fact that horizontal monopoly power appears to have been present (in some degree) in most of the cases condemning vertical integration. See §§5.4-5.11 supra. Thus vertical integration is likened to the use of a "tying" clause. See §2.17 supra. It follows that it is subject to similar analysis. See §2.19 supra. On the other hand, vertical integration is not precisely similar to tying, since the customer may have no economic use for the end product as transformed from raw material by the integrated firm. Compare Levi, A Two Level Anti-Monopoly Law, 47 Nw. U.L. Rev. 567, 585 (1952).

[4] Standard Oil Co. of New Jersey v. United States, 221 U.S. 1 (1911); compare 1 Nevins, Study in Power 224 (1953).

[5] Levi, The Antitrust Laws and Monopoly, 14 U. Chi. L. Rev. 153, 179 (1947).   Examination of empirical evidence led a later observer to a different conclusion. Whitney, Vertical Disintegration in the Motion Picture Industry, 45 Proceedings Am. Econ. Assn. 491, 498 (1955).   One cannot help wondering whether the data collected by Professor Whitney was influenced by other factors, such as the increased popularity of television, drive-in theaters, and the like.

club competitors out of existence. Perhaps that was the essence of the old-fashioned trust.

If vertical integration is to be judged by its abuses, we shall bog down in moral muddlement. For if an abuse is an attempt to monopolize, that attempt requires an intent to monopolize.[6] Intent, may, of course, be inferred from conduct. History is helpful. Internal growth looks proper; the acquisition of an outside concern, already in operation, is suspicious.[7] On the other hand, purchase of a going concern may be more economical than erection of a new plant. In times of shortage a manufacturer of automobiles might well find it more expedient to purchase an existing steel mill to assure himself supplies of raw material than to build anew at inflated costs. We must determine the purposes of conduct. In other words, to judge vertical integration by its abuses leads us back to Professor Kales' distinction between good and bad trusts: ". . . there might be good and bad trusts. The bad trusts would be those which had the power and the purpose . . . to exclude others by illegal and unfair methods of competition. The others would be good trusts." [8] And if we are to distinguish the good from the bad by the existence of a purpose to exclude others by illegal and unfair methods of competition, we do not need to consider integration at all. By all means, let us apply the Sherman Act vigorously to every attempt to monopolize. But let us call an attempt to monopolize by its proper name. By doing so we shall relieve vertical integration, as such, of a stigma it does not merit. For if vertical integration always and inevitably leads to attempts to use existing resources as a base for predatory attacks at the horizontal level, the evidence thereof has yet to be presented.

§5.17. **Effects on entry.** What may be sound is the contention that vertical integration compels universal vertical integration where competition contains monopolistic elements. We have noted the defensive character of the integration which developed

---

[6] See §9.3 *infra;* United States v. Quaker Oats Co., 232 Fed. 499, 500 (N.D. Ill. 1916), *appeal dismissed,* 253 U.S. 499 (1920). Compare United States v. Paramount Pictures, Inc., 334 U.S. 131, 173-174 (1948); West Coast Theaters, Inc., 12 F.T.C. 383 (1929).

[7] United States v. Reading Co., 253 U.S. 26, 57-58 (1920); §§2.25, 2.26 *supra.*

[8] Kales, Contracts and Combinations in Restraint of Trade §62 (1918). A leading student of the subject wrote: "Since integration which results in a lower cost for doing certain operations as a group, rather than separately, can destroy the non-integrated rivals even more quickly than flagrant or quiescent monopoly power, destruction of the actual or potential competitors of an integrated firm may result either from suppressing competition or from actively practicing it. In order to judge the merits of any integration, therefore, we must place it in some wider competitive context." Adelman, Integration and the Outlook For the Future, Symposium N.Y. State Bar Assn., Section on Antitrust Law, 135, 137 (CCH, 1951). Evidence in support of such views will be found in Celler Committee I, pt. 4A, at 956.

in the motion picture industry.[1] Similarly, the evidence in the oil merger case showed that the firm without retail outlets was losing ground rapidly.[2] Although sometimes integration is an offensive move, more frequently it is employed as a defensive weapon.[3] Now if it is true that the vertical integration of one enterprise leads to adoption of a similar structure upon the part of its competitors, it follows that entry into the business may become more difficult. A new firm must possess a fully integrated structure like its rivals.[4] By definition, such an integrated organization is more expensive to finance. Thus the normal forces of competition may be hampered.

§5.18. **Efficiency.** Compelled vertical integration may also result in needless expansion at certain levels. Such overexpansion would necessarily raise costs and, hence, prices.[1] Perhaps the oil industry furnishes an example. Prior to the depression of 1930, the large oil companies fell over each other in a rush to integrate. In particular, they built and acquired filling stations. As a result, by 1932 there was one gasoline pump for every seventy-two cars, whereas one for every four hundred might have sufficed.[2] Downward vertical integration (to the consumer) permits the effective exploitation of branded goods and such trade-marks *may* contain an element of monopoly.[3] It would thus appear that, when mo-

---

§5.17.　[1] §5.9 *supra*, note 1.

[2] United States v. Standard Oil Co., 47 F.2d 288, 303 (E.D. Mo. 1931). Another illustration will be found in Gibb, The Whitesmiths of Taunton 223 (1943). But compare Consolidated Cows, 9 Fortune No. 5, p. 77 (1934).

[3] Jewkes, Factors in Industrial Integration, 44 Q.J. Econ. 621, 629-630 (1930). Compare Note, Chain Store Integration as Restraint of Trade, 15 U. Chi. L. Rev. 392, 397 (1948). Evidence sustaining the assertion in the text will be found in Celler Committee I, pt. 2A, at 309, 310; pt. 4A, at 224, 323-324; Thompson, Since Spindletop 18 (Gulf Oil Corp. 1951).

[4] Rostow, The New Sherman Act, 14 U. Chi. L. Rev. 567, 599-600 (1947). Note the effect of indivisibility: if the extended (new) part of the business is subject to extensive economies of scale, the capital costs of integration will be higher and entry presumably more difficult. See §§3.12, 3.13 *supra*, and Appendix A *infra*. But compare Bork, Vertical Integration and the Sherman Act, 22 U. Chi. L. Rev. 157, 195 (1954).

§5.18.　[1] Chamberlin, The Theory of Monopolistic Competition, 123 (3d ed. 1938).

[2] Gasoline, 6 Fortune No. 4, pp. 32, 34, 103-104 (1932). There is, of course, no way to establish that four hundred cars per pump is the optimum number; furthermore, the phenomenon described in the text may have been affected by the depression, during which persons otherwise unemployed opened filling stations for a livelihood.

[3] E.g., LaTouraine Coffee Co. v. Lorraine Coffee Co., 157 F.2d 115, 118 (2d Cir. 1946), *cert. denied*, 329 U.S. 771 (1946). This elusive question is discussed in some detail in Appendix A. It has also been suggested that vertical integration, like resale price maintenance, may be related to horizontal price-fixing. Celler Committee I, pt. 4A, at 320. Resale price maintenance, however, is contractual and can be compared to vertical integration only as a horizontal price-fixing agreement to a horizontal merger. In resale price maintenance, the risks of integration are avoided.

nopoly elements are already present in an industry, vertical integration may have an effect of some undetermined magnitude in raising costs of distribution.[4]

Other diseconomies may appear in vertical integration. Various steps in production may require different horizontal sizes for efficiency. In other words, as Professor Dewing observed, the lack of balance in production at successive stages of an integrated industry is actually uneconomical from a practical standpoint.[5] And once production is out of balance, management is faced with the novel and difficult task of disposing of unwanted surpluses. A different business problem is presented to which existing management may not prove equal.[6] Statistical studies have sometimes shown that nonintegrated firms were more efficient than their integrated rivals.[7]

On the other hand, there are potential economies in vertical integration. It is recognized that sales expense between units in the line of vertical integration is eliminated.[8] Assurance of a

[4] It has been urged that if monopoly exists at one level, vertical integration will maximize profits in the short run. Schneider, Real Economies of Integration, in Chamberlin, ed., Monopoly and Competition and Their Regulation 203, 212 (International Economic Assn. 1954). This is similar to the "leverage" theory mentioned *supra* §5.16, note 3.

[5] Dewing, The Financial Policy of Corporations 778 (3d ed. 1934). Compare Wallace, Market Control in the Aluminum Industry 177-178 (1937); Burns, The Decline of Competition 779 (1936); Dennison, Vertical Integration and the Iron and Steel Industry, 49 Econ. J. 244, 251 (1939).

[6] Dewing, The Financial Policy of Corporations 780 (3d ed. 1934). Instances wherein integration appears to have been a dubious venture are found in Celanese Corp. of America, Ann. Rep. 1953, 8 (New York City, 1954); S. S. Kresge Co., 39th Ann. Rep. 17 (Detroit, 1951); TNEC Hearings, pt. 19, at 10,664.

[7] FTC, War-Time Profits and Costs of the Steel Industry 32 (1925); FTC, Relative Efficiency of Large, Medium-Sized and Small Business 93 (TNEC Monograph No. 13, 1941). A vivid example is found in the history of the yeast business. One yeast producer developed a famous system of making deliveries in its own wagons directly to grocers. Subsequently, however, it was found that distribution could be accomplished more efficiently through standard wholesalers, and the delivery routes were abandoned. Standard Brands, Inc., Ann. Rep. 1948, 4 (New York City 1949). Striking examples will also be found in Williamson, Winchester: The Gun That Won the West 348, 352 (1952); Gibb, The Whitesmiths of Taunton 317, 320 (1943). See also Cross, Vertical Integration in the Oil Industry, 31 Harv. Bus. Rev. No. 4, pp. 69, 72-73 (1953); Celler Committee I, pt. 1, at 414; pt. 2A, at 551; pt. 4A, at 952; Dow Chemical, 3 Fortune No. 4, pp. 58, 61 (1931) (this firm's policy, however, has subsequently changed; see TNEC Hearings, pt. 20, at 10,744).

[8] Burns, The Decline of Competition 431 (1936); Nourse and Drury, Industrial Price Policies and Economic Progress 77-78 (1938); Farish and Pew, Review and Criticism of Monograph No. 39, 13 (TNEC Monograph No. 39-A, 1941); Meyers, Modern Economic Problems 183 et seq. (2d ed. 1948); McLean and Haigh, The Growth of Integrated Oil Companies 504 (1954); Greyhound Bus, 10 Fortune No. 2, pp. 34, 110 (1934). As Professor Adelman has pointed out, this is another way of saying that indivisibility has affected the structure of industry. Adelman, Integration and the Outlook For the Future, Symposium N.Y. State Bar Assn., Section on Antitrust Law, 135, 137 (CCH, 1951). Compare Appendix A *infra*.

steady flow of supplies may effect efficiency in production.[9] Professor Wallace's study of the aluminum industry concluded that such factors were "undoubtedly of substantial importance." [10] It is sometimes said that vertical integration smooths out the shocks of the business cycle, but that claim is poorly substantiated.[11] Another criticism of vertical integration, which may have some merit, is that planning and control replace buying and selling in the market. Such planning can encourage the use of obsolete methods and materials. It removes a wayside check on the efficiency of operations. As Professor Burns said,

> Vertical integration, however, diminishes the effectiveness of the market as a stimulus to the improvement of methods of production. Where little integration occurs the efficiency of producers is checked at a great many points along the chain of operations from the production of raw material to that of finished product; costs of production are separated for each stage and the market facilitates the frequent comparison of costs and utilities.[12]

On the other hand, there is a tendency for vertical integration to

9 Frank, The Significance of Industrial Integration, 33 J. Pol. Econ. 179, 183-184 (1925); Burns, The Decline of Competition 423-424 (1936); Flugge, Possibilities and Problems of Integration in the Automobile Industry, 37 J. Pol. Econ. 150, 154 (1929); Adelman, The A & P Case, 63 Q.J. Econ. 247 (1949); Celler Committee I, pt. 4A, at 102, 222, 229, 240, 417, 813. Impressive evidence is available from the field of house construction. Colean, American Housing 100, 142-143, 150, 330-331 (Twentieth Century Fund, 1944); Stone and Denton, Toward More Housing 38-39, 66-67, 139-140 (TNEC Monograph No. 8, 1940); Edwards, Legal Requirements that Building Contractors Be Licensed, 12 Law & Contemp. Prob. 76, 93 (1947). But compare Edwards, Maintaining Competition 98, 130 (1949). Muddy thinking with respect to vertical integration is not confined to legal circles. E.g., Hallanan, Statement, at Annual Meeting of Stockholders, Plymouth Oil Co., Pittsburgh, pp. 2-3 (May 17, 1949).

10 Wallace, Market Control in the Aluminum Industry 178-179, 182 (1937); see also Wiedenfeld, Combinations, Industrial, 3 Encyc. Soc. Sci. 664, 669 (1934); United States v. Keystone Watch Case Co., 218 Fed. 502, 508 (E.D. Pa. 1915), appeal dismissed, 257 U.S. 664 (1921); Celler Committee I, pt. 2A, at 312; McLean and Haigh, The Growth of Integrated Oil Companies 326 (1954); Phillips, An Evaluation of Large-Scale Retailing with Emphasis on the Chain Store, 8 Law & Contemp. Prob. 348, 349 (1941); United States v. United States Steel Corp., 223 Fed. 55, 122 (D.N.J. 1915), aff'd, 251 U.S. 417 (1920); Hower, The History of an Advertising Agency 54-55 (1939); Spengler, Vertical Integration and Antitrust Policy, 58 J. Pol. Econ. 347, 350-351 (1950).

11 Dennison, Vertical Integration and the Iron and Steel Industry, 49 Econ. J. 244, 255-256 (1939); Jewkes, Factors in Industrial Integration, 44 Q.J. Econ. 621, 631 (1930). Compare Lorie, Book Review, 45 Am. Econ. Rev. 447 (1955); McLean and Haigh, The Growth of Integrated Oil Companies 180 (1954); Diamond Match Co., Ann. Rep. 1948, 6 (New York City, 1949).

12 Burns, The Decline of Competition 431-432 (1936). In Celanese Corp. of America, Ann. Rep. 1953, 5 (New York City, 1954) the complaint is registered that vertical integration injured the textile industry by making it unresponsive to changes in styling demand (reason not clear). Note also the possibility that vertical integration might conceal monopoly profits from public scrutiny.

make prices along the line of integration more flexible. A manufacturer reducing his price is assured of consumer response because the eliminated distributor cannot continue to maintain the higher charge to the consumer.[13]

§5.19. **Promotion of competition.** Integration may work in both directions. Vertical integration by one firm may undermine the monopoly position of another. International Harvester is said to have started making its own steel because it could realize such large savings thereby. By doing so, of course, it tended to break the horizontal power of the steel companies.[1] In Germany the cartels struggled constantly with vertical integration. Members of those combinations, in order to reap the benefits of reduced production by others without sacrificing their own operations, indulged in vertical integration. Thus they effectively confused the problem of production control.[2] It is therefore apparent that even the strongest aspect of the contention that vertical integration spells exclusion from markets is subject to considerable qualification.

§5.20. **Vertical integration: Conclusions.** The chief complaints against vertical integration, it is believed, have been shown to be groundless. A vertically integrated concern does not earn double profits; it does not secure its raw materials at cost; nor can it sell its goods without adequate compensation. A vertically integrated concern does not, of itself, exclude its nonintegrated competitors from markets. As suggested above, the cases in

---

13 Burns, The Decline of Competition 433-434 (1936); Bowman, Toward Less Monopoly, 101 U. Pa. L. Rev. 577, 636 (1953). Compare Kaplan, Big Enterprise in a Competitive System 224 (Brookings Institution, 1954).

Note also that vertical integration may play a prominent role in innovation. See Appendix B *infra*. A familiar example is found in situations where manufacturers of new materials find others unable or unwilling to fabricate them into finished products. E.g., Wallace, Market Control in the Aluminum Industry 9 et seq., 349-350 (1937); Aluminum Company of America, 10 Fortune No. 3, pp. 46, 50 (1934); Gibb, The Saco-Lowell Shops 39 (1950); Minnesota Mining in Motion, 39 Fortune No. 3, pp. 93, 172 (1949); Hobby, Bottled Gas, 35 Barron's No. 1, p. 15 (1955). But note the surprising statement in United States v. Richfield Oil Corp., 99 F. Supp. 280, 292 (S.D. Cal. 1951), *aff'd per curiam*, 343 U.S. 922 (1952), to the effect that vertical integration should not be permitted despite its promotion of innovation. But compare United States v. Columbia Steel Corp., 334 U.S. 495, 526 (1948). Perhaps the presence of such "imperfections" as ignorance of fabricators and consumers had something to do with the decision of a prominent manufacturer to package its own products for direct distribution to users, changing a long-standing policy. Monsanto Chemical Co., 51st Ann. Rep. 19 (St. Louis, 1953); compare note 7 *supra*.

§5.19. 1 Burns, The Decline of Competition 421-422 (1936); Stigler, The Division of Labor Is Limited, 59 J. Pol. Econ. 185, 190-191 (1951); Williamson, Winchester: The Gun That Won the West 110, 154, 205 (1952); State v. Central of Georgia Railway, 109 Ga. 716, 35 S.E. 37, 43 (1900); U.S. Leather, 11 Fortune No. 2, pp. 56, 96 et seq. (1935).

2 Wiedenfeld, Combinations, Industrial, 3 Encyc. Soc. Sci. 664, 667 (1934).

which vertically integrated concerns have apparently excluded competitors from markets may be explained by the existence of a horizontal monopoly at some point along the line of vertical integration. Alcoa could not have squeezed the independent rollers of sheet aluminum had it not occupied a monopolistic position in the production of aluminum ingot.[1] Even the most active enemies of integration have admitted that horizontal size is the real foe.[2] Those who attack vertical integration as such make the same mistake as the framers of the Clayton Act; they would prohibit the exhibition of monopoly power but not monopoly itself. And perhaps it is significant that, despite the Attorney General's vehement attack upon integration as such, few antitrust actions have been brought in those industries in which integration is most often found.[3]

Experience does suggest that vertical integration hampers entry into impurely competitive industry. And it may raise costs. But integration is not to blame; rather, impurities in the industry itself are responsible for the failure of the normal forces of competition to manifest themselves. Certainly those forces can be effective. Millers do not raise their own grain. Competitive forces assure them an abundant supply.

If monopolistic factors are already present, vertical integration, admittedly, does contain unfavorable elements. As stated above, it may make entry into a market more difficult and it may raise costs. In any event it constitutes an extension of "planning" without the control of a free market. It is doubtful, however, whether such factors, standing alone, should cause vertical integration to be condemned. In a particular case, these facts might assume sufficient importance to warrant dissolution, but as a general proposition their importance would scarcely seem sufficient to justify destruction of vertical integration everywhere.

It is true that much of the foregoing argument is based upon

§5.20. [1] Burns, The Decline of Competition 444 (1936).

[2] Rostow, The New Sherman Act, 14 U. Chi. L. Rev. 567, 599-600 (1947); Black, Oil Pipe Line Divorcement by Litigation and Legislation, 25 Cornell L.Q. 510, 523-524 (1940).

[3] It has been said that vertical integration is most highly developed in forest products, textiles, paper products, and iron and steel. Thorp and Crowder, The Structure of Industry 197 (TNEC Monograph No. 27, 1941) (query how this conclusion was reached). Three of the four areas thus indicated have been free from antitrust attack on grounds touched upon in this chapter. Compare Champion Paper, 39 Fortune No. 1, p. 80 (1949); House Select Committee on Small Business, Subcommittee on Monopoly, United States vs. Economic Concentration and Monopoly 37 (Staff Report pursuant to H.R. Res. No. 64, 79th Cong., 2d Sess. 1947). Indeed, the Attorney General recently instituted an action against an association, alleging that it was seeking to prevent vertical integration of advertising services into manufacturing establishments. Kilgore Committee, pt. 1, at 30.

long-run considerations. In the short term, vertical integration may effectively foreclose markets.[4] Over the short term the man who enjoys retail custom has a commanding position. It takes some capital and effort to establish a new store. Prices may respond slowly to changes in supply. As every lawyer knows, there is a difference between being ready, able and willing to serve clients and enjoying a profitable practice. Thus the manufacturer likes a measure of downward (toward the consumer) vertical integration to assure a market for his products. The time necessary to acquire an important clientele cannot be wholly overlooked. On the other hand, the length of antitrust litigation makes it questionable whether short-term considerations should be controlling.[5] If a lawsuit to dissolve vertical integration takes a decade, the normal forces of the free market may already have corrected the situation. Indeed, some such condition appears to have existed in the aluminum industry.[6]

Public utilities may attempt to use vertical integration as a means of obtaining forbidden profits on their basic monopolies. Perhaps we may thus explain the apparent anomaly that public utilities are subject to the antitrust laws at all.[7] But whether vertical integration includes a monopoly stage in the public utility field is immaterial. If a bottleneck in the line of integration permits monopoly to flourish, we should attempt to crush or control that monopoly. If the monopoly falls into the public utility category, presumably it should be regulated. And if it is said that regulation of public utilities has been a failure, it would seem time to find an alternative to that procedure.

Finally, the fact that vertical integration is so difficult of definition — so largely a matter of degree — would probably preclude effective action against it. Even if we assume that vertical integration is monopolistic in character, therefore, it would be difficult to frame a program to eliminate it. As the Supreme Court pointed out in the 1948 steel case, the concept of integration is too vague for judicial control.[8]

4 Burns, The Decline of Competition 439 (1936).

5 United States v. National City Lines, 334 U.S. 573, 590 (1948); Hamilton and Till, Antitrust in Action §2 (TNEC Monograph No. 16, 1941); see concurring opinion of Commissioner Mason in Grocery Distributors' Assn. of Northern California, 44 F.T.C. 1200, 1217 (1948).

6 United States v. District Court, 334 U.S. 258, 261-262 (1948).

7 Hale and Hale, Monopoly and Mobilization, 47 Nw. U.L. Rev. 606, 642 (1952).

8 United States v. Columbia Steel Corp., 334 U.S. 495, 525 (1948); Celler Committee I, pt. 1, at 135-136, 544.

CHAPTER 6

Diversification: Impact of Monopoly
Policy upon Multiproduct Firms*

§6.1. Definitions. Production or distribution of more than one commodity, commonly called "diversification," is a widespread phenomenon in modern industry. Degrees of diversification vary widely. A manufacturer may produce two sizes of the same screw driver;[1] another may offer photographic film in both color and black and white.[2] Some firms spread across an entire industry;[3] others lap over into adjacent fields.[4] In some instances

---

* This chapter appeared in article form under the same title in 98 University of Pennsylvania Law Review 320 (1950). It has been revised slightly and brought up to date. Compare generally Adelman, Integration and Antitrust Policy, 63 Harv. L. Rev. 27 (1949); Edwards, Conglomerate Bigness as a Source of Power, in Business Concentration and Price Policy 331 (Stigler ed. 1955). Professor Edwards presents the strongest arguments available against diversification and his views are somewhat dissimilar from those expressed herein. But compare Chapter 8 *infra*.

§6.1. [1] Conant, One or Many Lines? 20 Barron's No. 28, p. 7 (1940).

[2] Richmond, Profits Out of Pictures, 61 Mag. of Wall Street 24 (Oct. 23, 1937). A tobacco company makes six brands of cigarettes, nine brands of smoking tobacco and nine brands of chewing tobacco. Liggett & Myers Tobacco Co., Ann. Rep. for 1948, 12 (New York City, 1949). A prominent insurance company has two principal lines of business. Under the heading of "bonding business" it lists fidelity bonds, bankers' bonds, fiduciary bonds, public official bonds, court bonds, forgery bonds and contract bonds. Under the heading of "casualty insurance" it lists workmen's compensation, automobile liability, automobile theft, general liability, burglary, accident and health, boiler and machinery, glass and water damage. Maryland Casualty Co., Ann. Rep. for 1948, 19 (Baltimore, 1949).

[3] A rubber manufacturer produced tires and tubes, footwear, raincoats, hose, belting, motor mountings, foam latex rubber, baby pants, gloves and toys. U.S. Rubber's Two-Way Stretch, Business Week No. 1006, p. 83 (1948). (Subsequently the same firm diversified into the production of plastics, Lastex yarn, radiant heating panels, textiles, laundry starch and chemicals. Id. at 84.)

[4] A 32-page booklet entitled "Products and Processes" was enclosed with Union Carbide and Carbon Corp., 1948 Ann. Rep. (New York City, 1949). It listed the products of the company in five general groups as follows: (1) alloys and metals, (2) chemicals, (3) electrodes, carbons and batteries, (4) industrial gases and carbide, and (5) plastics. The products themselves were too numerous to count. E. I. du Pont de Nemours & Company operates through ten departments plus a Mexican subsidiary, four controlled companies and four subsidiaries engaged in foreign trade. Each manufacturing department has a long list of products. E. I. du Pont de Nemours & Co., Ann. Rep. 1948, 48 et seq. (Wilmington, 1949). In addition,

the commodities produced are wholly dissimilar; a prominent company has two subsidiaries, one building railway cars and the other erecting oil refineries.[5] Investment trusts carry diversification farther. While some focus upon a specific industry[6] and others provide management for any type of enterprise,[7] the majority are intentionally diversified over the whole field of commerce. This chapter examines the relationship between diversification and the problem of monopoly.

Multiproduct firms are one of several types giving rise to monopoly problems. Vertical integration, the combination of successive stages of production or distribution in a single concern, is another.[8] The term "horizontal integration" usually refers to a union of former competitors making the same product. Diversifiction is sometimes called "distribution" or "circuitous"[9] or "conglomerate" or "lateral"[10] integration. Its existence in trade is roughly as common as vertical integration.[11] But to date its bearing upon monopoly has received less attention.

§6.2. **A page of history.** Diversification is a recent phenomenon. Early corporate charters were granted for narrow purposes, and in the eighteenth century, companies seem to have had only one general mission. Thus a concern was organized as an insurance company, a bank, a toll bridge company or a turnpike company.[1] A few firms were granted authority to undertake differ-

---

it owns ten million shares of the common stock of General Motors Corporation, constituting 22.7 per cent of the outstanding common stock. Id. at 19. Compare American Home Products Corp., Ann. Rep. 1948, 23 et seq. (New York City, 1949); General Electric Co., Ann. Rep. 1948, 23 et seq. (Schenectady, 1949); General Motors, 18 Fortune No. 6, pp. 41, 44 et seq. 170 et seq. (1938).

5 Pullman, Inc., Ann. Rep. 1948, 7 et seq. (Chicago, 1949).

6 Chemical Fund, Inc., Ann. Rep. 1948, 4, 6, 13 (New York City, 1949). Insurance companies are similar to investment trusts. Maryland Casualty Co., Ann. Rep. 1948, 10 et seq. (Baltimore, 1949).

7 Happy AGWI, 39 Fortune No. 2, p. 16 (1949); Financial Fun After Fifty, 15 Modern Industry No. 4, 67 (1948).

8 See Chapter 5. Compare Canadian Pacific Railway, 11 Fortune No. 3, pp. 42, 144 (1930) (railroad's investments in hotels, coal mining ventures, etc., made chiefly to create traffic).

9 Hale, Trust Dissolution, 40 Colum. L. Rev. 615, 626 (1940).

10 Buchanan, The Economics of Corporate Enterprise 309 (1940). For definition, compare Triffin, Monopolistic Competition and General Equilibrium Theory 94-95 (1940).

11 Thorp and Crowder, The Structure of Industry 168 (TNEC Monograph No. 27, 1941). Unfortunately the census data from which the foregoing conclusions were reached is not sufficiently precise to permit fine distinctions between the various types of integration. Id. at 597.

§6.2. 1 2 Davis, Essays in the Earlier History of American Corporations 22 et seq. (1917). A railroad chartered to operate from X to Y cannot divert its capital from the objects contemplated and extend its lines to Z. Pearce v. Madison & Indianapolis R.R., 62 U.S. 441, 443 (1858); compare Banet v. Alton R.R., 13 Ill. 504 (1851).

ent objects, but usually in such obvious combinations as operating both a bridge and a toll road or both a bridge and a canal.[2] In general, legislatures were chary of granting, and the companies hesitant to ask, combinations of diverse powers.[3]

Because the system of special acts had led to abuses and scandals, in the latter part of the nineteenth century many states turned away from the practice of granting special charters to corporations. The first to do so was New Jersey, which amended its constitution in 1875 to forbid the further granting of such privileges.[4] Other states quickly followed. The reaction against abuses incidental to special charters, joined with the feeling that there should be full equality of opportunity to incorporate, encouraged the adoption of general incorporation acts.[5] Today almost every state grants corporate charters under general statutes whereby the issuance of the authority becomes a ministerial act.[6] It follows that the persons forming a corporation may choose the powers it shall enjoy. As a consequence, corporate charters now generally contain broadly diversified authority.[7]

In the last century several allied developments helped clear the way for diversified enterprise. New legislation made amendment of corporate charters far easier. Common law and statutory rules requiring unanimous consent of shareholders were abrogated.[8] Today it is the general practice to permit broad amendments with few formalities.[9]

Relaxation of the formerly rigorous doctrine of ultra vires has had a similar effect. Until recent times the corporate charter was the strict measure of a company's powers. Any action beyond its confines was unlawful,[10] and the corporation itself could plead its

---

[2] 2 Davis, Essays in the Earlier History of American Corporations 318 (1917).

[3] Id. at 319. Compare Ramsey v. Tod, 95 Tex. 614, 69 S.W. 133 (1902); Williams v. Citizens' Enterprise Co., 25 Ind. App. 351, 57 N.E. 581 (1900). But compare Marion Bond Co. v. Mexican Coffee Co., 160 Ind. 558, 65 N.E. 748 (1902).

[4] 2 Davis, Essays in the Earlier History of American Corporations 205 (1917).

[5] Dodd and Baker, Cases on Business Associations 20 (1940). See also Rutledge, Significant Trends in Modern Incorporation Statutes, 22 Wash. U.L.Q. 305, 306 (1937).

[6] Id. at 313 et seq.

[7] Re Humphrey Advertising Co., 177 Fed. 187, 188 (7th Cir. 1910).

[8] Dodd, Statutory Developments in Business Corporation Law, 50 Harv. L. Rev. 27, 33, 37 (1936).

[9] See Rutledge, Significant Trends in Modern Incorporation Statutes, 22 Wash. U.L.Q. 305, 324 et seq. (1937).

[10] Morawetz, Private Corporations 23 (1882). In People ex rel. Peabody v. Chicago Gas Trust Co., 130 Ill. 268, 283, 22 N.E. 798, 799 (1889), it was said: "Corporations can only exercise such powers as may be conferred by the legislative body creating them, either in express terms or by necessary implication . . ." Only slight deviations were permitted under the doctrine. Brown v. Winnisimet Co., 11 Allen 326, 333 (Mass. 1865); 6 Fletcher, Cyclopedia of the Law of Private Corporations §2535 (1931).

own lack of capacity in order to defeat the obligation of contracts entered into in good faith. Gross injustice was often the result. In the first third of the present century a revulsion from the doctrine[11] resulted in legislative action. In most jurisdictions today only the state or the shareholders may assert that corporate acts are ultra vires.[12]

One further aspect of state incorporation statutes deserves mention. When one concern holds stock in another, diversification may result just as readily as in the case of a corporation empowered to embark upon several different branches of endeavor. Until modern times corporations were not allowed to hold stock of other corporations.[13] About the same time that special charters were replaced by articles of incorporation under general acts, the states began to permit corporations to hold stock,[14] until today the law in almost every state permits it.[15] It is true that there are some limitations in the permissive statutes. For example, the former Illinois law allowed one corporation to hold stock in another so long as the acquisition did not substantially lessen competition or tend to create a monopoly.[16] It was clear, however, that the limitation in question was designed to prevent horizontal integration and not diversification. Thus an express provision declared:

> This section shall not apply to corporations purchasing . . . stock solely for investment . . . nor shall anything contained in this section prevent a corporation from causing the formation of a subsidiary corporation or from owning stock in such a corporation,

[11] Hale, A Field for Corporate Law Revision — Collateral Attack, 11 Ill. L. Rev. 1, 2 et seq. (1916). Ease of amendment had removed the substance of even the state's objection to ultra vires acts. Carpenter, Should the Doctrine of Ultra Vires Be Discarded? 33 Yale L.J. 49, 64 (1923).

[12] E.g. Illinois Business Corporation Act, 1933, §8, Ill. Rev. Stat., c. 32, §157.8 (1957). Compare Rutledge, Significant Trends in Modern Incorporation Statutes, 22 Wash. U.L.Q. 305, 310 (1937). Ultra vires was a doctrine designed primarily to protect the dissenting shareholders. Brice, Ultra Vires 78n (Green ed. 1880). Diversification was not regarded as dangerous to the state. Thompson, The Doctrine of Ultra Vires in Relation to Private Corporations, 28 Am. L. Rev. 376, 396 et seq. (1894); Carpenter, Should the Doctrine of Ultra Vires Be Discarded? 33 Yale L.J. 49, 64 (1923).

[13] See, e.g., Hall v. Woods, 325 Ill. 114, 130, 156 N.E. 258, 264 (1927). Accord: Golden v. Cervenka, 278 Ill. 409, 440, 116 N.E. 273, 286 (1917). See Hale, The Law of Private Corporations in Illinois 7 (1916); Hale, Holding Companies in Illinois Law, 7 Ill. L. Rev. 529, 535 (1913); 6 Fletcher, Cyclopedia of Law of Private Corporations §2825 (1931).

[14] Keasbey, New Jersey and the Great Corporations, 13 Harv. L. Rev. 198, 207 (1899); Rutledge, Significant Trends in Modern Incorporation Statutes, 22 Wash. U.L.Q. 305, 307 (1937).

[15] E.g., Roth v. Ahrensfeld, 300 Ill. App. 312, 321, 21 N.E.2d 21, 25 (1939), aff'd, 373 Ill. 550, 27 N.E.2d 445 (1940). Compare dissenting opinion in Louis K. Liggett Co. v. Lee, 288 U.S. 517, 554 et seq. (1933).

[16] Illinois General Corporation Act, 1919, §7, Ill. Rev. Stat., c. 32, §§1 et seq. (1931).

for the actual carrying on of its immediate lawful business or the natural and legitimate branches or extensions thereof. . . .[17]

It is worth noting that Section 7 of the Clayton Act, after which the quoted statute was modeled, itself permitted the formation of subsidiary corporations for the same purposes.[18]

Thus, within the field of the "private" law of corporations — that branch of the law dealing with corporate powers and the relationship of the component parts of the association — diversification is now readily achieved.   Indeed, it is unquestioned that diversified business may be conducted in corporate form.

§6.3. **Assumed legality of diversification in the past.**   Our problem is the relationship between diversification and the law of monopoly, which includes the common law of the several states, state legislation and the familiar federal antitrust acts.   Although such law long ago parted company with the "private" law of corporations, monopoly policy in the past has not frowned upon diversification.

Perhaps the leading case is *United States v. Winslow*,[1] the first major decision affecting the United Shoe Machinery Company. It was there proven that the defendants had combined three previously existing concerns.   The first of these firms was the producer of 60 per cent of the lasting machines used in the manufacture of shoes, while the second made 80 per cent of the welt sewing machines and outsole stitching machines.   The third produced 70 per cent of the heeling machines and 80 per cent of all metallic fastening machines.   All the machines in question were protected by patent rights.   The combined concern refused to sell machines but leased them to shoe manufacturers on condition that each lessee use all the machines produced by the com-

---

[17] Ibid.

[18] 15 U.S.C. §18 (1946), where it is provided that nothing therein shall prevent a corporation from "causing the formation of subsidiary corporations for the actual carrying-on of their immediate lawful business, or the natural and legitimate branches or extensions thereof . . ." Limitations remain in selected fields. National Bank Act, 18 Stat. 123 (1874), as amended, 12 U.S.C.A. §24 (1946). National banking associations are also prohibited from underwriting the issuance of securities. Ibid. Utilities often are denied the privilege of holding stock. Mass. Ann. Laws, c. 156, §5. See Steckler v. Pennroad Corp., 44 F. Supp. 800, 803 (E.D. Pa. 1942); Public Utility Holding Company Act of 1935, 49 Stat. 817, 15 U.S.C.A. §79i. The Investment Company Act of 1940, 54 Stat. 800, 15 U.S.C. §80a-5(b)(1), defines a "diversified company" as one with no more than 5 per cent of its assets invested in the securities of a single issuer. But, in general, the holding of stock is now condoned. Bonbright and Means, The Holding Company 64 (1932).

§6.3. [1] 195 Fed. 578 (D. Mass. 1912), *aff'd*, 227 U.S. 202 (1913). Argument for the defendant stressed the fact that the combination did not involve previously competing firms. Compare **United Shoe Machinery Co. v. La Chapelle**, 212 Mass. 467, 478, 99 N.E. 289, 291 (1912).

bination. It was held that the defendants had not violated the Sherman Act. Mr. Justice Holmes, laying stress upon the lack of competition between the three component firms in the combination, said:

> As . . . they did not compete with one another, it is hard to see why the collective business should be any worse than its component parts. It is said that from 70 to 80 per cent of all the shoe machinery business was put into a single hand . . . Taking it as true we can see no greater objection to one corporation manufacturing 70% of three non-competing groups of patented machines collectively used for making a single product than to three corporations making the same proportion of one group each. The disintegration aimed at by the statute does not extend to reducing all manufacture to isolated units of the lowest degree.[2]

In many ways the *Winslow* case is a perfect authority for the proposition that diversification is lawful. Since each machine was protected by patents, the combination could lawfully enjoy a high percentage of the output of that particular commodity. Yet the fact that such high percentages of total production were attained for each of the several commodities makes the case a stronger authority for the proposition that diversification does not infringe the statute. Subsequently, of course, the tying clauses involved in the leases of the shoe machinery company were declared unlawful under the specific prohibitions of Section 3 of the Clayton Act.[3]

Another important decision is *Alexander Milburn & Co. v. Union Carbide & Carbon Corp.*[4] This was an action for triple damages under Section 7 of the Sherman Act. The plaintiff alleged that the defendants, Union Carbide and Carbon Corporation and its subsidiary corporations, constituted a combination in restraint of trade, which caused the plaintiff to suffer damages. One subsidiary was a maker of calcium carbide. Another, the Prest-O-Lite Company, converted calcium carbide into acetylene gas. Oxweld Acetylene Company produced apparatus for welding with acetylene gas. Oxweld Railroad Service Company used the foregoing products to weld railroad equipment in various locations. It was held that the combination was not unlawful. In the course of his opinion Judge Parker said:

2 United States v. Winslow, 227 U.S. 202, 217 (1913). A similar result was reached in the lower court in 195 Fed. 578 (D. Mass. 1912). *Accord:* United States v. United Shoe Machinery Co., 247 U.S. 32 (1918); United States v. Inter-Island Navigation Co., 87 F. Supp. 1010 (D. Hawaii, 1950). In the latter case the court held that the defendant, which engaged in the haulage of freight and passengers by surface ship, might enter into the business of carrying them also by airplane over same routes.
3 38 Stat. 731 (1914), 15 U.S.C.A. §14; United Shoe Machinery Corp. v. United States, 258 U.S. 451 (1922).
4 15 F.2d 678 (4th Cir. 1926), *cert. denied,* 273 U.S. 757 (1927).

Of course plaintiff has shown a combination existing on the part of these defendants; but it has not shown a combination in restraint of trade. Their business . . . is not competing but complementary. . . .

. . . As there is no competition between their products, the unity of control secured by the stock ownership of Union Carbide and Carbon Corp. cannot be said to stifle competition between the companies themselves. The combination results not in suppression of competition, but in greater efficiency on the part of the constituent companies, and although as pointed out by plaintiff this unified control results in bringing larger resources under one management, mere size does not constitute a violation of the Act . . . nor is it violated merely by reason of the fact that there is brought under control companies engaged in non-competing branches of the industry.[5]

A third decision approving diversification is found in the sequel to the famous *Standard Oil* case.[6] In 1931 application was made to the court which had decreed dissolution of the old Standard Oil Company for permission to merge the Standard Oil Company of New York with the Vacuum Oil Company. The former, commonly known as Socony, was chiefly engaged in the marketing of gasoline and kerosene. Vacuum was principally a refiner of high quality lubricants. The court approved the merger of these two successor concerns, with the result that both vertical integration and diversification were extended. One of the reasons given for the approval was that there was little real competition between the two concerns. Each produced different products. Accordingly, the court said: "It is clear that there are sound business reasons for this merger which are entirely sufficient and are wholly unconnected with any design to create a monopoly." [7]

Thus it is seen that despite vast enlargement of corporate pow-

---

[5] 15 F.2d at 682 et seq. As to the old trust dissolution cases, it is said in Hale, Trust Dissolution, 40 Colum. L. Rev. 615, 625 (1940): "There was only a slight amount of circuitous dissolution in the oil case and while the snuff and cigar companies were cut loose in the tobacco decree, the three large successor units were 'full line' companies. All of the successor units in the powder case were 'full line' producers and later the decree was modified to permit one of them to purchase the assets of a non-competing concern. Explicit disapproval of circuitous integration (involving cameras and films) was voiced in the photographic equipment case, but the decree as finally framed abandoned the notion."

In United States v. International Harvester Co., 248 U.S. 587 (1918), apparently no effort was made to disturb the defendant's production of several types of farm implements. It was only ordered to dispose of certain brands thereof (decree not reported).

[6] United States v. Standard Oil Co., 47 F.2d 288 (E.D. Mo. 1931).

[7] Id. at 310 et seq. Compare National Industrial Conference Board, Mergers and the Law 89 (1929); Automatic Radio Co. v. Hazeltine Research, Inc., 176 F.2d 799, 805 (1st Cir. 1949), aff'd, 339 U.S. 827 (1950) (mere accumulation of patents is not unlawful per se).

ers under "liberalized" state statutes, there have been few suggestions in the past that diversification was or should be unlawful.[8]
Possibly Professor Handler may be taken to have hinted that
United States v. Reading Co.[9] casts doubts upon diversification,[10]
and it is true that some remarks of Mr. Justice Cardozo can be
given similar interpretation.[11] Not until 1941, however, did any
court in effect disapprove of diversification as opposed to our
antimonopoly policy.

§6.4. **Attacks upon diversification.** Now storm clouds are
gathering. In 1936, Professor Burns expressed considerable mis-
givings in regard to diversification. He found that it might have
consequences similar to non-price competition from which consumers might benefit little. Buyers might be confused by the
spread of one brand name over several unrelated products[1] and

8 But see dissent in Eckman v. Chicago, Burlington & Quincy R.R. Co., 169 Ill.
312, 324, 48 N.E. 496, 500 (1897). A similar objection was raised in the eighteenth
century: 1 Davis, Essays in the Earlier History of American Corporations 388, 429
(1917). For a modern version of the same vague fears, see Arnold, The Bottlenecks
of Business 24 et seq. (1940). Compare the statutes of mortmain, 1 Blackstone,
Commentaries on the Laws of England* 479 (Cooley's 3d. 1884); 2 Davis, Essays in
the Earlier History of American Corporations 317 (1917); Hale, A Field for Corporate Law Revision — Collateral Attack, 11 Ill. L. Rev. 1, 8 (1916); National Home
Building Assn. v. Home Savings Bank, 181 Ill. 35, 41, 54 N.E. 619, 620 (1899).

9 253 U.S. 26 (1920). A bill was filed to dissolve intercorporate relations under
§§1 and 2 of the Sherman Act and the commodities clause, 34 Stat. 585 (1906), 49
U.S.C.A. §1(8). A holding company had been formed to own a coal company and
a railway company operating in and serving the Schuylkill anthracite field, which is
the largest of three fields in Pennsylvania. Subsequently, the combination bought
an interest in Central Railway Company of New Jersey, one of six carriers serving
the Wyoming anthracite field and itself an owner of a coal company. It was held
that the combination must be dissolved, emphasis being laid upon the combination of competing railway companies and coal companies (whether the concerns
actually competed may be another question).

10 Handler, Industrial Mergers and the Anti-Trust Laws, 32 Colum. L. Rev. 179,
230 (1932), where it was said: "The conclusion is inescapable that the union of the
Reading and the Central interests did not stifle competition in the industry at
large; at best it merely eliminated competition between two of the largest factors.
No one can read the court's opinion without feeling that what is being forbidden
is the combination of giant companies doing a substantial part of the business in
their fields."

11 United States v. Swift & Co., 286 U.S. 106, 116 (1932). Compare United States
v. Corn Products Refining Co., 234 Fed. 964 (S.D.N.Y. 1916), in which Judge
Learned Hand held diversification questionable where the defendant made profits in
lines less affected by competition and therewith supported price-cutting attempts to
monopolize. It is worth noting that diversification has sometimes been approved
by legislation. Thus the legislation administered by the ICC comprises the commodities clause and a converse (Freight Forwarders Act, 56 Stat. 284, 49 U.S.C.
§§1001 et seq.) applicable to shippers engaging in business as freight forwarders
but does not apply to motor or water carriers; this omission was intentional. Celler
Committee I, pt. 4A, at 850.

§6.4. 1 In Burns, The Decline of Competition 453 (1936) it is said: ". . . in so
far as one product tends, or is deliberately used, to 'sell' another, the buyer is

the application of profits to wholly new ventures might invite monopolistic results.[2]

In 1941 there was decided the *General Motors* case,[3] in which the court found that General Motors and one of its subsidiaries, which conducted a business in the financing of automobiles, had violated the Sherman Act. The theory was that the two corporations had conspired to compel dealers to use the finance service. The word "diversification" was not mentioned but an implication of disapproval was clearly present.

More recently the Attorney General objected vigorously to a lower court decree permitting railroad companies to purchase the sleeping-car business of the Pullman Company.[4] He argued that such an arrangement would make it impossible for anyone else to offer sleeping-car service.

In 1949 an important study of monopoly was published by Professor Edwards. His program for maintaining a free, com-

---

confused in his distribution of expenditure; products sold under the same brand name are not necessarily equally desirable."

2 Ibid.

3 United States v. General Motors Corp., 121 F.2d 376 (7th Cir. 1941), *cert. denied,* 314 U.S. 618 (1941). In that year, too, Illinois enacted an amazing statute prohibiting sales outside the regular course of trade. Illinois Rev. Stat., c. 121½, §204 (1957). See Cook, Legislative Restrictions, 8 Law & Contemp. Prob. 273, 275 (1941); Note, Legislative Monopolies Achieved by Small Business, 48 Yale L.J. 848 (1939).

4 United States v. Pullman Co., *aff'd per curiam,* 330 U.S. 806 (1947). On appeal, the question was whether the railroads should be permitted to own the Pullman Company and thus to furnish sleeping-car service as well as coach service to their passengers. In that connection the brief of the United States declared at page 28: "It is apparent on its face that the rail plan vests in the commonly owned Pullman Company a complete monopoly of the market in the operation and servicing of sleeping cars . . . under the rail plan it would be impossible for anyone else to get into the sleeping car business."

In United States v. United Shoe Machinery Corp., 110 F. Supp. 295 (D. Mass. 1953), *aff'd per curiam,* 347 U.S. 521 (1954), it was said at pages 335-336: "United's success in the shanks and clicking die fields, and in some other fields where United has not half the market but does have more than any competitor, is often traceable to United's market power in the shoe machinery market, its own long line of supplies, its competitor's short lines, the satisfactory quality of United's products, customer confidence in United, and customer inertia." The case appears to hold that diversification, with probable savings in distribution cost and customer convenience, constitutes an attempt or an abuse; or that the quality of the defendant's products and customer inertia are factors rendering diversification an attempt or an abuse. The opinion (at 340-341) also seems to say that a diversified defendant's offering of supplies incidental to use of leased machinery is promoted by the fact that the defendant is a convenient supplier, and that this situation constitutes a practice exclusionary in economic effect (and, therefore, that diversification is illegal, and all cost reduction in distribution invalid?); again (at 343), that the defendant's "long line," with no important competition at some points, was a factor permitting price discrimination (and hence, an abuse); also (at 344), that the defendant had been aided in retaining control of the shoe machinery market by its activities in selling to shoe factories supplies which it and others manufactured. *Accord:* United States v. General Electric Co., 82 F. Supp. 753, 902 (D.N.J. 1949), *intervention denied,* 95 F. Supp. 165 (D.N.J. 1950), *decree,* 115 F. Supp. 835 (D.N.J. 1953).

petitive economic system included the elimination of "bigness." His strictures against size were not limited to "horizontal" integration: they specifically included diversified firms. He asserted that such concerns could play one market off against another and disregard short-term costs in manipulating resources from one field to another.[5]

Later that same year the Attorney General filed a complaint against the Du Pont Company and others.[6] There he alleged that common control of Du Pont, General Motors and United States Rubber resulted in an agreement among those three corporations to trade with each other to the exclusion of outside suppliers. Again the charge was couched in the familiar form of "conspiracy." But the complaint also (perhaps somewhat inconsistently) alleged common control. Hence adverse implications for diversification were inescapable.

A few weeks thereafter a member of the Congress in charge of a monopoly investigation stated that he was opposed to "conglomerate operations." And he denounced the use of profits earned in one industry to diversify into another.[7] Thus the stage is set for an explicit assault upon diversification as such.

§6.5. **Origins of diversification and its relation to efficiency.** Before we examine specific complaints against diversification, it may be well to set forth a general outline of its origins.[1] Con-

---

[5] Edwards, Maintaining Competition: Requisites of a Governmental Policy 106 (1949). In Edwards, Issues in the Monopoly Problem, in Chamberlin, ed., Monopoly and Competition 188 (International Economics Assn. 1954), the same author wrote at page 192: "A large enterprise, particularly, is likely to look upon its various commodities and markets as specialized aspects of one strategic plan. Producing various commodities for sale in many markets, the large enterprise may plan to make profits on some and lose money on others, and, as to still others, may neither know nor greatly care whether it gains or loses from their sale. Neither convenience goods nor loss leaders nor fighting brands can be understood by an analysis confined to the markets for these particular commodities. Much of the strategy of a large enterprise may consist in deciding what existing markets to enter or abandon and what new markets or commodities to create. Moreover, the great strategy of using markets to establish and maintain an overall business position is supplemented by (or perhaps supplements) the non-market aspects of the strategy of position, such as litigation, basic research, political and public relations activities, and the formation of comprehensive commercial and financial alliances."

[6] United States v. E. I. Du Pont de Nemours & Co., 126 F. Supp. 27, 235 (N.D. Ill. 1954), rev'd, 353 U.S. 586 (1957). Compare United States v. Lorain Journal Co., 342 U.S. 143 (1951).

[7] Celler, Breaking Up Big Business, U.S. News & World Report 28, 31 (Sept. 23, 1949); Celler Committee I, pt. 1, at 438; pt. 2A at 304-305, 307-308; pt. 2B, at 1210. On the Senate side of the Congress, Senator Kefauver has expressed antagonism to a diversified wealthy firm growing rapidly. Kilgore Committee, pt. 2, at 836. Senator O'Mahoney expressed distaste for diversification of the Borden Company from the dairy field into coffee and chemicals. Id. at 912.

§6.5. [1] Some general but not too acute discussion of the causes of diversification is found in Whitmore, Shaping 1937 Policies to Side-Step Competition, 6 Am. Business No. 11, p. 11 (1936); The Profits of Diversification, Business Week No. 404, pp. 35, 36 (1937).

siderations which cause businessmen to diversify may play a two-fold role in analysis of diversification's effects. They suggest the different forms in which the multiproduct firm appears. They also throw light on the efficiency which diversification achieves, for often an entrepreneur adds a new product in order to reduce costs. The scale of such economies may be difficult to estimate. We can, however, take account of their nature and proceed to suggest their effect upon the economy as a whole.

§6.6. **Origins of diversification and its relation to efficiency: Fuller use of existing facilities.** If a concern finds a new use for the raw material presently required in its business, diversification may be the result. Thus a maker of glass containers used the same basic material to branch out into the manufacture of glass brick for buildings, glass insulation and glass filters.[1] By-products are another cause of diversification. Thorp and Crowder found that in forty-seven out of fifty of the largest firms, at least half of their products each accounted for less than half of 1 per cent of those firms' gross sales.[2] In other words, minor by-products are important numerically. It follows that they may assume a large quantitative role. Thus a recent annual report says:

> In the early part of the century Diamond acquired extensive holdings of timber lands to provide reserves for the manufacture of wood matches.
>
> Research and experience have demonstrated that the most efficient match production can be achieved by careful selection of match lumber . . . with the rest being sawed for building purposes. . . .[3]

§6.6. [1] The Profits of Diversification, Business Week No. 404, pp. 35, 40 (1937). Basic identity of materials led Dow Chemical Company into the magnesium alloy business. Id. at 41. Similarly, Eastman Kodak Company went into the plastics. Barnes, What's in a Name? 80 Mag. of Wall Street 30, 32 (Apr. 12, 1947). Exhaustion of the soil led a fruit grower into the production of other crops. United Fruit Co., Ann. Rep. 1948, 8, 21 (Boston, 1949). It should also be noted that the same company owns the "Great White Fleet" of merchant vessels, 25,000 cattle, 17,000 horses, sugar mills, and railroads. Barnes, id. at 32; Thorp and Crowder, The Structure of Industry 657 (TNEC Monograph No. 27, 1941). The Glidden Company, formerly a maker of paint, studied its raw material, linseed oil; then it developed the production of edible oils. Barnes, id. at 30 et seq.

[2] Thorp and Crowder, The Structure of Industry 602 (TNEC Monograph No. 27, 1941). As defined in the census reports, by-products are not important from a revenue standpoint. Id. at 609. "Joint" products are much more frequent than "by-products." Id. at 170. But the definition of by-product requires it to be made in a separate plant. Id. at 174 et seq.

[3] Diamond Match Co., Ann. Rep. 1948, 5 (New York City, 1949). With every ton of ore extracted primarily for its nickel content, ninety-five pounds of copper are refined as opposed to forty-seven pounds of nickel. Gold, silver, and platinum are also recovered. International Nickel, 10 Fortune No. 2, pp. 64, 68 (1934). A concern extracting natural gas from the ground derived 16.7 per cent of its sales from the vending of gasoline. Natural Gas Pipe Line Co. of America, Ann. Rep. 1948, 10 (Chicago, 1949).

An existing product may be converted to another purpose, thereby enabling a producer to reach new markets. A photographic concern, for example, now makes a device called "Recordak," a specialized camera for use as a business machine.[4] Changes in the basic product have placed its maker in another industry.

Existing technology may be applied to produce new devices. Thus a dental manufacturing company entered the field of producing flexible shafting for use upon automobiles, airplanes and other vehicles:

> Experience in making flexible tubing for the dentist proved valuable when industrial demand sprang up for similar products, to which the company wisely and rather easily adjusted its schedules.[5]

Observers who find even the broad "chemical industry" narrower than the field of endeavor of Union Carbide and Carbon Corporation have been unable to discover a central theme for that concern's operations. But one writer saw that the development of existing technology accounted for the concern's wide diversification.[6]

A desire for fuller use of existing tools and personnel may give rise to diversification. At the end of World War I a powder company had a large plant with excess capacity. Gradually it found uses for its factories and tools in the production of soluble cotton for the lacquer, photographic, coated fabric and plastic indus-

---

[4] Richmond, Profits Out of Pictures, 61 Mag. of Wall Street 24, 25 (Oct. 23, 1937). A machine used by farmers to spray crops was developed into a fog fire fighter and also into a car-wash machine. Food Machinery Corp., A Saga in Diversity, Business Week No. 971, pp. 88, 92 (1948). Compare The Profits of Diversification, id. No. 404, pp. 35, 41 (1937).

[5] Barnes, What's in a Name? 80 Mag. of Wall Street 30, 31 (Apr. 12, 1947). See also Weldon, Coming Competitive Clash, 79 id. 127, 168 (Nov. 9, 1946); The Profits of Diversification, Business Week No. 404, pp. 35, 39 (1937); Jordan, Profits from Diversification, 59 Mag. of Wall Street 300, 301 (Dec. 19, 1936); Minnesota Mining in Motion, 39 Fortune No. 3, pp. 93, 162 (1949); American Smelting & Refining Co., Ann. Rep. 1948, 16 et seq. (New York City, 1949). Similarly, Pittsburgh Plate Glass Co., 69th Ann. Rep. (Pittsburgh, 1953) stated at page 8: ". . . the Company began production of fiberglass. . . . Entry into this field still further diversifies the Company's products and presents an added opportunity for the effective utilization of a great wealth of glass production experience."

[6] In Union Carbide I: The Corporation, 23 Fortune No. 6, p. 61 (1941), it was said at page 66: "To define exactly what the nature of that business is has baffled almost everyone who has tried it, including Union Carbide itself. It ranges through hundreds of seemingly unrelated products. . . . It is merely bewildering . . . to look at this business as a series of products or simply an expression of the American financial will to organize. . . . Carbide is neither a 'products' company nor a creation of Wall Street, but primarily a process company built upon a few basic techniques . . ."

tries.[7]   A Wisconsin firm makes an assortment of products which seem to bear little relationship to each other.   Among them are tanks for transport and storage; dump-truck bodies of various types; oil- and gas-fired home-heating systems; farm and industrial dehydration plants; milk bottle washers; and road-making machinery.   It is nevertheless claimed that all of the products are built with pre-existing tools.[8]   Even services made available to corporations upon a permanent basis form a foundation for diversification.   A large concern may have departments specializing in accounting, finance, law, advertising and the like.   The existence of such services may suggest the desirability of diversification.[9]

Vertical integration may lead to entry into new fields.   A tire maker had a textile division to produce the cord and fabric needed in its casings.   When it converted from cotton to rayon tire cord, it was left with excess textile capacity.   Now it makes a branded dishcloth in a part of the textile mills formerly producing tire cord.[10]   The United Fruit Company started its radio business purely as a service to the company's operations in the harvesting and shipment of bananas.   It now offers, through its subsidiary, Tropical Radio Telegraph Company, a general communications service to the public.[11]   United States Steel Corporation originally got into the cement business in order to afford an outlet for its slag.[12]   Diversification is greatly encouraged by

[7] Clifford, Diversified Outlets Contribute to Strong Position, 61 Mag. of Wall Street 164 (Nov. 20, 1937); Thorp and Crowder, The Structure of Industry 653 (TNEC Monograph No. 27, 1941).

[8] Local Needs Influence Product Planning, Business Week No. 989, pp. 44 et seq. (1948).   Compare The Profits of Diversification, id. No. 404, pp. 35, 39 (1937).

[9] Armstrong, Top Management Policies that Speed Healthy Sales Growth, 54 Sales Management No. 9, p. 35 (1945).

[10] U.S. Rubber's Two-way Stretch, Business Week No. 1006, pp. 83, 88 (1948).

[11] United Fruit Co., Ann. Rep. 1948, 22 (Boston, 1949).   The Fruit Company's fleet of vessels now carries passengers as well as the company's own freight.   Id. at 23.   White Castle System, Inc., an operator of hamburger dispensaries, entered the production of a prefabricated steel building which it made primarily for its own use.   It also made paper caps for its employees.   Now both products are sold to others.   The Profits of Diversification, Business Week No. 404, pp. 35, 40 (1937).   Bethlehem builds ships, some of which carry ore from its own mines to its own steel mills.   Bethlehem Steel Corp., Ann. Rep. 1948, 6, 20 (Wilmington, 1949).   Use of diversification and vertical integration on a complementary basis is illustrated in Diamond Match Co., Ann Rep. 1948, 5 (New York City, 1949).

[12] U.S. Steel: I, 13 Fortune No. 3, pp. 59, 184 (1936).   Vertical integration by the major automobile manufacturers deprived some of the accessory producers of their markets.   They therefore turned to other fields.   Applegate, Earning Power of Motor Accessory Industry Upheld by Wide Diversification, 54 Annalist 531 (1939).   Vertical integration may also cause diversification when the acquired firm has a sideline.   Thorp and Crowder, The Structure of Industry 655 (TNEC Monograph No. 27, 1941).   Foreclosure of mortgages and similar operations may likewise result in diversification.   Id. at 657.

operational changes in a vertically integrated business which result in the abandonment of a raw material. Thereafter it must be sold to some outsider or processed in a different manner.[13]

§6.7. **Origins of diversification and its relation to efficiency: Sales promotion.** As we have seen, diversification may result from attempts to make use of existing facilities. Entrepreneurs may also go into new lines of business in order to improve sales of their original products. Complementary merchandise is often produced with such purposes in mind. Thus it has been said: "The Eastman Kodak Company makes cameras and, incidentally, money on them. But it makes them mainly as a sideline that photography may grow in popularity and usefulness and thereby widen the demand for film." [1]

Public utilities engage in the sale of appliances which will utilize their principal products.[2] In some instances a manufacturer desires to preserve the good will in the machinery he has sold by supplying articles for use with it.[3] In the *General Motors* case[4] the automobile manufacturer sought to justify its entry into the business of financing the sale of cars by showing that the "unethical" practices of other financers would hurt its good will. Indeed, it succeeded in showing that it had originally entered the financing business almost wholly for the convenience of its customers. At that date there were scant facilities for the sale of automobiles on time.[5]

Sometimes the manufacturer wants to round out his line be-

---

13 Id. at 656.

§6.7. 1 Richmond, Profits Out of Pictures, 61 Mag. of Wall Street 24 (Oct. 23, 1937). Compare Alexander Milburn Co. v. Union Carbide & Carbon Corp., 15 F.2d 678 (4th Cir. 1926), *cert. denied,* 273 U.S. 757 (1927). American Can Company developed machinery to seal cans in order to stimulate their use. Now it sells such machinery to canners. American Can Co., Ann. Rep. 1948, 246 (New York City, 1949). A manufacturer of sprayers went into the insecticide business in order to provide a product which could be used with its original item. Food Machinery Corp.: A Saga in Diversity, Business Week No. 971, pp. 88, 93 (1948).

2 About 8.65 per cent of a utility's gross receipts were obtained from the sale of appliances and about 12 per cent from the sale of by-products. Peoples Gas Light & Coke Co., 1948 Ann. Rep. 31 (Chicago, 1949).

3 Thorp and Crowder, The Structure of Industry 652 (TNEC Monograph No. 27, 1941).

4 United States v. General Motors Corp., 121 F.2d 376 (7th Cir. 1941), *cert. denied,* 314 U.S. 618 (1941).

5 121 F.2d at 386. As to another industry it has been said: ". . . it has been recognized that, with a return to more normal conditions, the volume of time sales would increase. . . . The Company must always be prepared to supplement existing agencies in this financing to whatever extent may be required to obtain desirable business. One method under consideration is the establishment of a subsidiary finance company to assist in carrying out this function." International Harvester Co., 1948 Ann. Rep. 6 (Chicago, 1949).

cause the business policy of carrying a full line meets the convenience of distributors or consumers. If important customers demand varied items, a manufacturer or distributor may supply them.[6] Since most of the big buyers of steel require a variety of steel products, steel companies for years have set up their sales offices and trained their salesmen to sell the whole line of products.[7]

In other instances, additions to the sales line have been motivated by a desire to economize. In other words, sales costs are heavy and it is believed that they may successfully be spread over a larger number of products to result in lower unit costs. Thus a glass company entered upon the manufacture of paint: "The production of these [paint] items on a large scale has been logical because paint stores generally feature glass as well, thus encouraging distribution of the dual line." [8] In almost the converse situation a small firm may merge with a larger one in order to secure the advantages of an existing system of distribution.[9] Of course

[6] Thorp and Crowder, The Structure of Industry 651, 656 (TNEC Monograph No. 27, 1941). A reason for diversification was a necessity to produce a full line. Gibb, The Whitesmiths of Taunton: A History of Reed & Barton 1824-1943, 118 (1943); Gibb, The Saco-Lowell Shops: Textile Machinery Building in New England, 1813-1949, 405 (1950) (explanation of merger of Saco and Pettee was that it enabled the combination to offer an almost complete line of cotton textile machinery.)

[7] U.S. Steel: I, 13 Fortune No. 3, pp. 59, 184 (1936). As to the car washer made out of an insecticide sprayer, it has been said: "Food Machinery also converted the basic sprayer into an efficient car washer. Selling it, though, wasn't so easy. Salesmen reported they needed a broader line of automotive service equipment . . . so the engineering department developed an auto wheel aligner and a wheel balancer. Now all three items enjoy brisk demand." Food Machinery Corp.: A Saga in Diversity, Business Week No. 971, pp. 88, 92 (1948). A similar instance is recounted in Thompson, Since Spindletop 69 (Gulf Oil Corp. 1951).

[8] Barnes, What's in a Name? 80 Mag. of Wall Street 30, 31 (Apr. 12, 1947). Compare Kelley, Chain Store Merchandizing Ideas Helped This Little Business Grow, 55 Sales Management No. 3, pp. 103, 164 (1945), wherein it was said: "At first glance, it might seem that Testor Chemical Co. has expanded in a haphazard way. But upon analysis, it becomes evident that the expansion has been along these lines: (1) as a result of intensive research into allied fields; (2) into fields in which sales outlets have already been well established."

A manufacturer of candies added soft drinks, muffin mix, potato chips and other foods because it was already distributing its wares to grocers. Schnering, Facts Behind the Curtiss Candy Program of Line Expansion, 52 id. No. 22, pp. 24, 25-26 (1943). One of the advantages of a department store was that variety attracted customers; also expenses would be spread over a variety of wares and thus perhaps lowered. Hower, History of Macy's of New York, 1858-1919, 102 (1943); Kilgore Committee, pt. 6, at 2716.

[9] Philco Corporation, Letter to Stockholders (Mar. 14, 1949), wherein the acquisition by Philco of the assets of Electromaster, Inc. was described as follows: "This transaction was a good one from the point of view of both companies. To the Electromaster shareholders, it gave broader diversification through representation in a number of different fields and the strength of the Philco distributor-dealer organization. The acquisition of Electromaster enabled Philco to enter the electric range field with an accepted product, modern plant facilities and a highly efficient

diversification in order to round out a sales line and to reduce selling costs may be overdone. A firm with three separate brands of the same item would seem to have carried the notion into mere conglomeration for its own sake.[10] Indeed, there are hints that the attainment of prestige has had something to do with rounding out the line.[11]

Exploitation of the value of trade-marks leads to sales diversification. An interesting illustration is that of the Rieser Company, Inc., a concern engaged in the manufacture of "Venida" hair nets. During the period 1922-1930, bobbed hair replaced earlier styles and the sales of hair nets declined drastically. The company thereupon entered into the production of hair pins and allied products, such as shampoos, applying its trade-mark to those new items. Diversification worked so well that it later extended its line to include cleansing tissues.[12] An officer of the concern said: "Our purpose was to make a double play on our trade mark. Identified with an established trade name, we felt that these two products would benefit from an immediate acceptance." [13] Apparently makers of women's dresses are now entering the perfume and cosmetic field. Manufacturers have decided to take advantage of their names in the way it has been done in France.[14]

§6.8. Origins of diversification and its relation to efficiency: Research and security. There are, of course, instances in which diversification is a positive policy: it seeks additional profit rather than negative elimination of waste. Many corporations, for ex-

---

organization. To our former line of products . . . we have now added electric ranges, a field which offers very attractive opportunities for growth and development."

A big firm may also acquire a smaller one to market some one product. Food Machinery Corp.: A Saga in Diversity, Business Week No. 971, pp. 88, 93 (1948).

[10] Ekco Products Co., Ann. Rep. 1948, 6 (Chicago, 1949). But Ekco's lines may reflect differing quality standards.

[11] Food Machinery Corp.: A Saga in Diversity, Business Week No. 971, pp. 88, 92 (1948).

[12] Rieser, When Hair Nets Flopped, 170 Printer's Ink No. 4, pp. 56, 57 (1935).

[13] Id. at 57. Concerning the venture of a miller in the home appliance field, it has been said: "General Mills went into the appliance field partly because of Maurice H. Graham, 59-year-old inventor of the Toastmaster, whom it had retained in 1943. His first idea: Capitalize on Betty Crocker's famous name. The upshot came in 1946: The Betty Crocker Tru-Heat Iron." Diversification Pays Off, Business Week No. 965, pp. 66, 74 (1948). A survey showed that General Mills' trade-mark was known to 91 per cent of all housewives. Id. at 76.

[14] In some instances, trade-marks have been broadcast over unrelated products. Fairbanks, Morse Steps Out, Business Week No. 242, p. 10 (1934) (maker of scales added windmills, gas engines, pumps, radios, washing machines, refrigerators). Compare the case in which a company starts to produce its old product from a wholly new raw material. Texas Gulf Sulphur Co., Ann. Rep. 1948, 3 (New York City, 1949).

ample, carry on a continuous program of industrial research. In studying one problem, they often hit on variations which can be applied to create new products.[1] So intensive is the industrial research carried on by some corporations that diversification flows in an unending stream. One company sold nine million dollars' worth of products in 1948, all of which had been developed in its own laboratories within the two previous years.[2] In 1937, 58 per cent of the net income of a prominent chemical manufacturer was derived from the sale of products developed in its own laboratories since 1919.[3] Diversification results from research because by-products are frequently more important than the items sought. And since research is a deliberate policy, it must also be considered that diversification it causes is deliberate in character.[4]

Growth and innovation might be seriously retarded were diversification to be curbed by law. A firm producing a standard product may be able to move quickly into production of a new variant; to "create" demand for an existing commodity fabrication into new forms may be required.[5] An example is found in

§6.8. [1] Thorp and Crowder, The Structure of Industry 648 (TNEC Monograph No. 27, 1941); Abbott Laboratories, Ann. Rep. 1948, 3 (North Chicago, 1949); Butters, Lintner and Cary, Effects of Taxation: Corporate Mergers 225 (1951). Technological research with one specific objective never attained that goal but turned up many other useful products. Anonymous, Carbide & Carbon Chemicals, 24 Fortune No. 3, pp. 57, 65 (1941).

[2] Minnesota Mining & Manufacturing Co., Ann. Rep. 1948, 10 (St. Paul, 1949); Celler Committee I, pt. 2B, at 837; TNEC, Final Report of Exec. Secy. 230.

[3] Devlin, Making Diversification Pay, 63 Mag. of Wall Street 88 (Nov. 5, 1938); Celanese Corp. of America, Ann. Rep. 1948, 18 (New York City, 1949).

[4] General Mills, Inc., 20th Ann. Rep. 34 (Minneapolis, 1948), wherein it was said: "The research philosophy of General Mills is summed up in the words of James F. Bell: 'You can influence research environmentally, but you cannot lead it. You must follow where research leads.'"

In General Mills' Horizons 9 (Feb. 1949), it was said: "We see no good reason for limiting ourselves to food products. Our research explores possibilities in many fields . . . Research led us into the chemical field where we are now extracting and processing oils. We believe that diversification will assist us in building a stronger and better company." Compare Celler Committee I, pt. 2A, at 553 (diversification necessary to utilization of research).

In Socony-Vacuum Oil Co., 1949 Ann. Rep. 13 (New York City, 1950), it was said: "Our research is directed primarily toward finding ways to improve the quality of our products and reduce the cost of producing and processing crude oil. In doing that work our scientists and engineers frequently make important discoveries in fields other than petroleum . . . Our researchers were looking for something else, when they discovered the process we use in making thiophene . . ." Compare Corn Products Refining Co., 43d Ann. Rep. 8 (New York City, 1950).

[5] If a corporation is to remain in business in a moving world, it must diversify as new products replace old. Adelman, Business Size and Public Policy, 24 J. Bus. 269, 276 (1951). Compare Richmond, Profits Out of Pictures, 61 Mag. of Wall Street 24 (Oct. 23, 1937); Alexander Milburn Co. v. Union Carbide & Carbon Corp., 15 F.2d 679 (4th Cir. 1926), cert. denied, 273 U.S. 757 (1927). American Can Com-

the sale of appliances by electric utilities companies: pushing the acceptance of food freezers, room coolers, and the like is a "load-building" activity resulting in greater demand for current.[6] Finally, if firms must grow to remain healthy, and if horizontal enlargement would violate the Sherman Act, diversification may be a necessary outlet for corporate energies.[7] A dynamic view of the economic process, in other words, suggests that diversification should be permitted.[8]

Deliberate adoption of diversification also occurs when a company is concerned lest a substitute product may capture its market. When can companies started to market special cans for beer, a prominent maker of glass beer bottles jumped into the business of making tin containers.[9] As Professor Burns said, integration into substitute products starts with a desire to reduce risks. The firm is impelled to enter into the production of goods and services likely to displace its existing products.[10] And to a certain extent the production of substitutes is akin to the broadening of trademarks to cover new products.

§6.9. **Origins of diversification and its relation to efficiency: Stabilization.** Perhaps more important is the effort to stabilize business. Diversification has long been urged as a means of avoiding both seasonal and cyclical slumps in sales. To avoid the seasonal character of the ice trade, a prominent corporation went

---

pany developed machinery to seal cans in order to stimulate their use. Now it sells such machinery to canners. American Can Co., Ann. Rep. 1948, 246 (New York City, 1949). A manufacturer of sprayers went into the insecticide business in order to provide a product which could be used with its original item. Food Machinery Corp.: A Saga in Diversity, Business Week No. 971, pp. 88, 93 (1948).

Diversification may be necessary to the introduction of new products. Gibb, The Saco-Lowell Shops: Textile Machinery Building in New England 1813-1949, 90 (1950). But compare id. at 291. Similarly, research may lead a firm into new lines of business.

[6] Diversification of a public utility into sale of appliances for load building is a prime example of promotion of growth via "shape" change. Standard Oil Co. of New Jersey, 1947 Ann. Rep. 15 (New York City, 1948) (in introducing liquid petroleum gas to Brazil, also distributed stoves and water heaters under its own trademark). Growth is intimately related to diversification because often additional facilities do not duplicate those now in existence and new products become possible. Celler Committee I, pt. 4A, at 475. Note id. at 580, where a steel company in the cement business as an outlet for slag then combined steel and cement for a new product, reinforced concrete.

[7] Diversification may be a means of continuing growth without violating the Sherman Act. E. I. du Pont de Nemours & Co., 1952 Ann. Rep. 7 (Wilmington, 1953); Gibb, The Saco-Lowell Shops: Textile Machinery Building in New England 1813-1940, 63 (1950).

[8] See Appendix B.

[9] The Profits of Diversification, Business Week No. 404, pp. 35, 40 (1937). Compare Consumers' Gas Trust Co. v. Quinby, 137 Fed. 882, 896 et seq. (7th Cir. 1905); Republic Steel Corp., 1953 Ann. Rep. 10 (Cleveland, 1954).

[10] Burns, The Decline of Competition 454 (1936).

into the business of selling coal and oil.[1]   A manufacturer of Christmas tree lights, sold only in the holiday season, expanded its output so as to produce stoves, refrigerators, freezers, kitchen cabinets, automobile lamps and explosives.[2]   Efforts to bridge gaps of the business cycle are perhaps even more important as a cause of diversification than efforts to avoid seasonal slumps. Many of the depression troubles of a prominent maker of electrical equipment were blamed upon its concentration in producers' goods.   It was suggested that the concern diversify so as to make radios, refrigerators and other items sold directly to ultimate consumers.[3]

Imperceptibly, a desire to stabilize may become an urge to allocate resources into greener pastures.   As the demand for cigars declined, a tobacco manufacturer went into the wine business.[4] When air conditioning was first introduced, many existing concerns, including two automobile manufacturers,[5] hastened to enter the new field.   A desire to get in on the ground floor of a new industry[6] and the urge to avoid rigorously competitive markets

---

§6.9.   [1] City Ice Diversifies, Business Week No. 872, p. 73 (1946); Donaven, We Are Stabilizing Employment, 92 Factory Management and Maintenance 480, 481 (1934). Resort to diversification weathered depression. Hower, History of Macy's of New York, 1858-1919, 103-104 (1943).

[2] Santa Claus Diversifies, Business Week, No. 904, pp. 56, 60 (1946); The Profits of Diversification, id. No. 404, pp. 35, 39 (May 29, 1937); Gates, Diversity of Output the Key to Recovery, 55 Mag. of Wall Street 328, 329 (1935).   Other examples are found in Diversification Smooths Cycle of National Acme, 29 Barron's No. 12, pp. 35, 135 (1949); Gillette Begins to Diversify, Business Week No. 958, p. 44 (1948).   On the other hand, Thorp and Crowder found the trend toward diversification stronger during the period 1920-1933 than during the period 1933-1939.   The Structure of Industry 660 (TNEC Monograph No. 27, 1941).   They also pointed out that the cause of diversification does not necessarily indicate why a firm selects a particular new product.   Id. at 646.   See also Ex-Cello-O-Corp., Ann. Rep. 4 (Detroit, 1942).

[3] Efforts are frequently made to depart from the production of highly cyclical producers' goods into the making of consumers' goods.   Baird, Wider Line of Products Pulls Evans Out of the Red, 34 Sales Management No. 135, p. 135 (1934) (concern making product to load automobiles on railway cars turned to manufacture of separators for automobile batteries, etc.); The Profits of Diversification, Business Week No. 404, pp. 35, 38 (1937); Stern, Borg-Warner Makes Diversification Pay, 58 Mag. of Wall Street 408, 409 (July 18, 1936); Cost-cutting Aids Bell & Howell's Net, 30 Barron's No. 20, p. 17 (1950) (office machines to offset luxury movie cameras). Compare Celler Committee I, pt. 2A, at 683 (security quest cause of size); id., pt. 2B, at 824-825, 835.   Note the comment: "The advantages of diversification of products were vividly apparent, however, during 1952 . . . while sales in many markets were off, other products achieved record-breaking sales during the year."   Monsanto Chemical Co., 52d Ann. Rep. 15 (St. Louis, 1954).

[4] The Profits of Diversification, Business Week No. 404, pp. 35, 37 (1937).   Price competition of imports led Elgin Watch to also offer men's jewelry, emblems for autos, horn buttons, and so forth.   Elgin National Watch Co., 88th Ann. Rep. 2, 11 (Elgin, 1953).

[5] The Profits of Diversification, Business Week No. 404, pp. 35, 37 (1937).

[6] Id. at 37.

are both factors to be considered.[7] An important maker of radio sets went into the refrigerator and air-conditioning business because profit margins on its existing production were low.[8]

§6.10. **Origins of diversification and its relation to efficiency: Multiple causes for diversification.** It must be plain that more than one of the foregoing factors may be a simultaneous cause for diversification. For example, a prominent maker of matches also makes and sells toothpicks, paper towels and other paper products. They are made out of the same raw material as matches and are sold through the same channels.[1] An amusing case which rings almost all the changes upon the asserted virtues of diversification is that of Globe Union, Inc., formerly a maker of batteries for farm, automobile and radio use. Its expansion into new lines of production was explained in the following terms:

It was decided to seek additional lines which would tend to level out production and steadily employ our . . . equipment. Because [facilities were available] . . . we took on the manufacture of spark plugs. Spark plugs are distributed through the same channels as automotive batteries and the demand is fairly constant. With punch-press and screw machine equipment available, we further diversified by adding roller skates, the sale of which is in seasonal peaks opposite from battery peaks. Development of roller skates led to making a beginner's ice skate and later a roller scooter set (all of which fit into toy and sporting goods markets). Our automotive lines require manufacture of other items, such as battery test equipment, spark plug testing and cleaning equipment and spark plug gap gages.[2]

[7] Minnesota Mining in Motion, 39 Fortune No. 3, pp. 93, 162 (1949).

[8] Philco Diversifies, Business Week No. 498, p. 23 (1949); Diversification Pays Off, id., No. 965, pp. 66, 68 (1948). It is said that General Mills makes a low margin of profit on flour milling and is attempting to improve its position by diversification into packaging machines, vitamin concentrates, household appliances, refineries for soybean oil, fatty acids, farm feeds, and so forth. Id. at 66 et seq. A revealing statement is that of the American Brake Shoe Co.: "Over a period of years, we have been following the policy in our foundry divisions of adapting a substantial part of their capacity to the production of more specialized and complex products. This has been done to achieve a more balanced output between the standard foundry items and special products." American Brake Shoe Co., Ann. Rep. 1948, 15 (New York City, 1949).

6.10. [1] Diamond Match Co., Ann. Rep. 1948, 5 (New York City, 1949). In December, 1948, the McGraw Electric Company acquired two other concerns. It was stated in McGraw Electric Co., 1948 Ann. Rep. 2 (Elgin, 1949): "This acquisition had a double objective. The first was to diversify our company's position and amplify its scope of operation. The second was to avoid current excessive building and equipment costs for major plant expansion by acquiring profitable going concerns . . . both badly needed to round out our company's line of small electrical appliances. . . ."

[2] The Profits of Diversification, Business Week No. 404, pp. 35, 38 (1937). See also Wesson Oil, 20 Fortune No. 3, pp. 67, 69 (1939) (multiple reasons for diversification:

§6.11. **Origins of diversification and its relation to efficiency: Effect of political forces; Involuntary diversification.** Some diversification results from forces beyond the control of corporate management. Indeed, there are causes of diversification which are noneconomic in character. Take, for example, the effect of war. Many corporations expanded their plants in order to take war contracts. After hostilities ceased, the entrepreneurs sought uses for the additional plant.[1] In the period following World War II many makers of aircraft expanded into new lines of products. One, for example, despite the unfavorable experiences of its competitors, branched out into the refrigerator business.[2] Machine tool manufacturers also have been compelled to find uses for excess capacity born of war necessity.[3] Once war has caused the creation of excess capacity, the resultant diversification is simply a question of making that fuller use of facilities suggested above. Political considerations may also suggest the desirability of engaging in new enterprises using raw materials produced by large voting blocs.[4]

§6.12. **Origins of diversification and its relation to efficiency: Impact of taxation.** Another important political cause of diversification is found in the federal tax structure. At the present

---

fuller utilization of distribution outlets, getting rid of surplus by-products, etc.); Food Machinery Corp., 35 Fortune No. 4, pp. 114, 117 (1947).

§6.11. 1 Munitions Makers Venture into New Lines to Use War Plants and Experience, 25 Barron's No. 28, p. 1 (1945). A builder of battleships went into the automobile and radio business. Ibid.
2 Hellman, Bell Aircraft Would Take on New Lines, 29 Barron's No. 16, p. 41 (1949). Compare Weldon, Coming Competitive Clash, 79 Mag. of Wall Street 127 (Nov. 9, 1946). Pressed Steel Car Company, a railway equipment manufacturer, expanded into the production of household appliances, air conditioning, and refrigerators. Munitions Makers Venture into New Lines to Use War Plants and Experience, 25 Barron's No. 28, p. 1 (1945).
3 Warner & Swasey Co., 1948 Ann. Rep. 3 (Cleveland, 1949): ". . . we have been undertaking the conversion of a part of our operations to the manufacture of products other than machine tools. This is in line with our long-range program for the utilization of added plant and equipment acquired during the war." General Mills expanded its machine shop in wartime and now makes machinery for printers, canmaking equipment, and the like. Barnes, What's in a Name? 80 Mag. of Wall Street 30 (Apr. 12, 1947).
4 General Mills, Inc., 16th Ann. Rep. 4 (Minneapolis, 1944). "Several important new products will come in a relatively new field, that of the non-food use of agricultural products. Finding new industrial uses for farm products is an avowed research project for General Mills. . . . Extension of activities into the non-food uses of agricultural products bears promise of future benefit to the company. It will also help to create a more stable market for the farmer, give him a greater return for his investment of capital and labor, and help to maintain his buying and producing power." Elliott, Greener Pastures, 36 Barron's No. 3, p. 22 (1956) (big dairies, finding profits squeezed by government raising cost of raw milk and public agitation over higher prices for drinking milk, are diversifying into other food and chemical products).

time the combination of normal taxes and surtaxes results in a 52 per cent direct levy upon corporate earnings.[1] At the same time rates on individual incomes are steeply graduated. An individual is taxed at the rate of 20 per cent on his first $2000 of taxable income. On the next $2000 the rate is 22 per cent, and it increases with each additional $2000 (or larger amount in the higher brackets). For example, it is 34 per cent between $8000 and $10,000, and 50 per cent between $16,000 and $18,000; at $44,000 the personal tax rate reaches 72 per cent.[2] Computation shows that the effective rate of total tax on dividends in the lowest bracket is about 61.5 per cent. If the shareholder already has income of $8000, a similar computation shows the effective rate of tax to be about 68.2 per cent. With income over $16,000, the effective rate rises to 76 per cent, and when the shareholder already has $44,000 of income, his dividend is taxed at 86.5 per cent. Even if the earnings of the corporation can somehow be transmuted into capital gains of a long-term variety, the shareholder will still pay 25 per cent of his dividends out in tax.[3]

Another tax factor which may bear on the popularity of diversification is the limitation upon deductions for capital losses.[4] A going concern may be able to absorb a considerable expenditure for developing new products against its current gross receipts. If an individual subscribes to stock in a new venture, he will receive only $1000 of tax benefit against ordinary income in the event of total loss.

Stiff penalties are attached to the accumulation of corporate earnings beyond the needs of the business.[5] It can hardly be imagined, however, that the tremendous burdens imposed on shareholders in the declaration of dividends are overlooked. If the corporation can reinvest the earnings with any profitability whatsoever, the result will almost inevitably be advantageous to the shareholders.

Such taxation encourages debt financing. When taxes are steeply progressive, return from investment becomes less impor-

§6.12. [1] Int. Rev. Code of 1954, §11. Corporate income under $25,000 is taxed at a 30 per cent rate.

[2] Id. §1. But compare §34.

[3] Id. §1201.

[4] Id. §§165(f), 1211(b).

[5] Id. §531; U.S. Treas. Reg. 111, §29.102-3 (1943), provides: "An accumulation of earnings or profits . . . is unreasonable if it is not required for the purposes of the business. . . . The business of a corporation is not merely that which it has previously carried on, but includes in general any line of business which it may undertake. However, a radical change of business when a considerable surplus has been accumulated may afford evidence of a purpose to avoid the surtax . . ."

tant. Investors prefer to avoid risks and seek the shelter of bonds, particularly those which are tax-exempt. And it is worth noting that the Internal Revenue Code does not discourage the formation of subsidiary corporations. Eighty-five per cent of the dividends received by one corporation from a domestic corporation subject to tax are credits to the taxpaying stockholder.[6]

§6.13. **Benefits of diversification.** In the foregoing survey an attempt has been made to discover the origins of diversification. In many instances it would seem that additional products had been added mainly to reduce costs. In other cases a more positive effort to create additional earnings can be discerned as a motivating force. Involuntary diversification may be caused by political factors, among which the impact of federal taxation is perhaps the most important.

Some of the forms of diversification thus adopted are clearly beneficial to the economy as a whole. In the first place, certain efficiencies undoubtedly result from the production or distribution of several products.[1] Such full utilization of raw materials as is encompassed in the production of by-products seems almost certain to avoid waste.[2] Similarly, distribution of several products through the same channels has afforded enough customer convenience to assure the success of mail order houses and department stores. Some types of diversification resulting from vertical integration may cause substantial savings, and if we were to forbid the use of existing technology in new ways, we should prevent firms from making full use of their real assets (despite the fact that the balance sheet does not show them). Even apart from economies within a plant, diversification may be efficient. Thus use of similar tools to produce commodities varied by the season may cut costs,[3] and it is also possible that the element of

---

[6] Int. Rev. Code of 1954, §243.

§6.13. [1] Thorp and Crowder, The Structure of Industry 178 TNEC Monograph No. 27, 1941). Even within a single plant, diversification may produce economy. Id. at 663. But compare United States v. United Shoe Machinery Corp., 110 F. Supp. 295 (D. Mass. 1953), aff'd per curiam, 347 U.S. 521 (1954).

[2] Compare Attorney General v. Pere Marquette Ry. Co., 263 Mich. 431, 248 N.W. 860 (1933) (surplus property may be used without violation of doctrine of ultra vires). As for the necessity of diversification to create new products, compare Conant, One or Many Lines? 20 Barron's No. 28, p. 7 (1940), where it is said: "There must be fairly constant input into a business against the ravages of fading-out demand. . . . We cannot get all set on our favorite product and sink or swim on that alone. Sooner or later it may get water-logged and fail to keep us afloat. We cannot hope always to find intimately related lines in which to expand. We may have to seek new trade entirely . . ."

[3] Thorp and Crowder, The Structure of Industry 664 (TNEC Monograph No. 27, 1941).

transportation charges will create a similar effect.[4] As we have seen, some firms are spreading services over a large number of products. Legal, financial and marketing services may be allocated to a number of different commodities in an effort to reduce overhead costs.[5] Of course all the foregoing considerations scarcely apply to concerns producing wholly unrelated products.[6]

[4] If freight costs are high, diversification may be a wise move, even though specialization within the plant would otherwise be more desirable. Diversification Can Result in Greater Production and Better Market Coverage, 105 Brick & Clay Record No. 1, p. 18 (1944).

[5] In the period 1935-1945, American Home Products Corporation added twenty-seven formerly independent concerns to its assets. Each former concern enjoyed considerable independence. As to various services, however, it was said: ". . . all subsidiaries, while exercising a wide degree of autonomy, share in and may draw upon a vast pool of marketing experiences, and top-flight talent to expedite any program or assist with any problem. Greater benefits through research and economies in production and distribution are thus realized . . ." Armstrong, Top Management Policies that Speed Healthy Sales Growth, 54 Sales Management No. 9, p. 35 (1945). An interesting statement of a similar situation involving Continental Industries is found in Strength in Unity: Continental Industries Is Uniting Well-Established Small Business, Business Week No. 788, p. 66 (1944). A review of appliance manufacturers indicates that small firms find it difficult to compete with large diversified firms. LaTourette, Shake-out in Appliances, 36 Barron's No. 27, p. 11 (1956).

[6] Eureka Williams, 36 Fortune No. 6, p. 108 (1947). Compare Daly, Cotton and Woolen Mills in Big Merger, 115 Manufacturer's Record No. 10, p. 69 (1946) (assertion that merger of cotton, woolen and rayon mills was expected to effect operating economies). A specialized machine maker resisted temptation to beat bad times by diversifying. Gibb, The Saco-Lowell Shops: Textile Machinery Building in New England, 1813-1949, 368 (1950). The firm sold a narrow line of machines. Id. at 356-357. Compare LaTourette, Dresser Industries, 34 Barron's No. 30, p. 15 (1954) (company absorbed half-dozen odd businesses unrelated to company's field, and profits declined). A gun company took on an extensive line of hardware and sporting goods, and finally failed on a line of mechanical refrigerators. Williamson, Winchester: The Gun That Won the West 359 (1952). In Texas Co., Ann. Rep. 1953, 15 (New York City, 1954), it was reported that $17 million was lost in a futile effort to produce liquid fuel from natural gas. Diversification is not always profitable: some big business remains single-line. Celler Committee I, pt. 4A, at 827. Diversification may be costly in that it prevents specialization upon a single product. Machlup, The Economics of Sellers' Competition 331 (1952). Management of widely differing businesses is difficult, and may lead to failure when there is no business reason for diversification. Foulke, Diversification in Business Activity 31 et seq. (Dun & Bradstreet, Inc., 1956). And spreading of common costs may give rise to difficulties. Burns, The Decline of Competition 450 (1936). Compare the controversy concerning the allocation of costs within the Tennessee Valley Authority. By allocating a large part of the capital expense to flood control, navigation, and so forth, it is possible to reduce the "cost" of electricity to a low level. Roberts, Certain Aspects of Power Irrigation and Flood Control Projects, Task Force Report to Commission on Organization of the Executive Branch of the Government 15 et seq. (1949). But compare Acheson and others dissenting in Hoover (Ch.), Commission on Organization of Executive Branch of Government, Reorganization of Federal Business Enterprise 106 et seq. (1949) (denial of assertion that costs should be allocated upon economic basis). See §6.24 infra. The lack of efficiency which may inhere in diversification was well expressed by the following lines from the Wall Street Journal of January 28, 1958 reprinted with the permission of the publisher:

One school of thought favors the spreading of risks. Andrew Carnegie, on the other hand, was quoted as urging businessmen to put all their eggs in one basket and to watch the basket. Those two divergent theories may be compared to the views that experience is the most important factor in business success[7] and its opposite, the belief that intelligence, industry and judgment will produce favorable results in any field. It is difficult to suggest any test of efficiency in the varying degrees of diversification. Every change is likely to increase some costs as it decreases others. In other words, efficiency is a question of balance, which can only be ascertained, if at all, from a study of practical effects. It is sometimes said that the United States Steel Corporation is so large that it is inefficient. As evidence of such inefficiency, it is shown that the company has progressively lost part of its market to smaller rivals. Such a concern faces a difficult problem when it is tempted to expand into a new field of endeavor.[8]

CORPORATE DESTINY

A baffled president viewed the sky,
Then shouted forth this clarion cry —
"Huge profits are such easy pie
Our only need — diversify!"

Where once they knitted only socks,
They soon made crocks and frocks and clocks;
Another group made only soaps,
But now it's nails and shooks and ropes.

Instead of grinding grain to flour,
The mill makes motors with horse power!
They all have broadened selling scopes —
No standing still, like silly dopes.

But company dreams have faded far,
And now they see another star.
Alas, for them, it shines too late —
Its well-known name is Concentrate!

— PAUL HINKHOUSE

[7] The late J. O. McKinsey, an efficiency expert called to the chairmanship of Marshall Field and Company, was quoted as favoring concentration of that firm's endeavors within narrow limits. Acting upon that theory, the company sold another department store which it operated, and reduced its wholesale business. Field Sells a Store, Business Week No. 404, p. 34 (1937); Celler Committee I, pt. 2A, at 652, 680.

[8] U.S. Steel: I, 13 Fortune No. 3, p. 59 (1936); U.S. Steel: Into Chemicals? Business Week No. 971, p. 30 (1948). It is often said that a specialized concern can operate more efficiently than its diversified competitor. "Many large companies attained their greatest growth, in other words became big, when they were one-line businesses . . . Bigness gave them greater diversity and strength, but it also gave them disadvantages which they did not have when they were small. The company with a small line of products can throw all its resources into making that line profitable. It has nothing else to worry about. Often the large company has to scatter its

Another important benefit of diversification is that it increases competition. Entry of the Chrysler Corporation into the air-conditioning business must have stiffened competition in that industry more than the creation of a new firm would have done.[9] Professor Edwards took account of this favorable aspect of diversification.[10] As Thorp and Crowder said, "mobility is increased," that is, resources are rapidly shifted to more economic uses.[11] And they found that half of the companies studied which diversified into new products created new facilities to do so: there was not merely a change of ownership resulting in aggrandizement of an existing concern.[12]

It seems likely that diversification adds to the stability of individual firms. Avoidance of seasonal patterns of business, for example, would seem to reduce risks of failure. Similarly, the circumventing of cyclical fluctuation must tend to preserve existing concerns from the grasp of bankruptcy.[13] There is, of course, a

---

efforts over so many activities that on the average only some of these activities result in a profit. Other activities pile up losses that partly or entirely offset the profits being made in some divisions." Murphy, The Simple Business Is Best, 20 Barron's No. 2, p. 7 (1940). In the last analysis the problem is undoubtedly one of balance.

[9] Thorp and Crowder, The Structure of Industry 668 et seq. (TNEC Monograph No. 27, 1941); Hines, Effectiveness of "Entry" by Already Established Firms, 71 Q.J. Econ. 132 (1957); Ways to Skin a Cat, Business Week No. 273, p. 12 (1934). Drastic "overproduction" and price-cutting followed competition in sales of penicillin and other antibiotics by ethical drug firms, patent medicine makers and diversified firms. Parke, Davis & Co., 86th Ann. Rep. 3 (Detroit, 1953). Growth of a new instant coffee line brought sharp competition from old ground coffee companies who entered the instant field. Borden Co., 1952 Ann. Rep. 16 (New York City, 1953).

[10] Edwards, An Appraisal of the Antitrust Laws, 36 Proceedings Am. Econ. Assn. 172, 187 n.1 (1946). An interesting statement has been made concerning the introduction of the insecticide DDT: "Many [chemical] firms hastened to make the remarkable insecticide DDT when it first appeared on the market. It wasn't long before supplies were more than adequate and the price came down. Only a few big firms with favorable costs . . . fared well in the final accounting." Self, Soft Spots and Competition Appear in Chemical Sales, 29 Barron's No. 17, p. 9 (1949). Compare Conant, The International Harvester Co. 189 (1913).

[11] Thorp and Crowder, The Structure of Industry 669 (TNEC Monograph No. 27, 1941). Sometimes exclusive dealing arrangements are defended upon the grounds that they are necessary to give a dealer an incentive to buck an established monopoly. See the statement of Senator Walsh, 51 Cong. Rec. 14,097, 14,098 (1914).

[12] Thorp and Crowder, The Structure of Industry 661 (TNEC Monograph No. 27, 1941).

[13] Burns, The Decline of Competition 450 (1936): Stabilizing the Brass Business, 40 Fortune No. 1, p. 70 (1949); Bowen, Big Chemical Companies Outwit Business Decline, 29 Barron's No. 46, p. 11 (1949). As to cyclical changes, compare the following statement: "When a specialized enterprise is caught with a product for which the demand is disappearing, its demise is apt to lead to a definite break in employment both of men and machines. In the case of the large multi-product enterprise, on the other hand, there is more likelihood, though no certainty, that the transition can be carried out in an orderly way with a maximum of salvage." Thorp and Crowder, The Structure of Industry 665 (TNEC Monograph No. 27, 1941).

tremendous variation in the cyclical patterns of different industries. For example, the 1932 production of steel rails was only 14.7 per cent of the 1929 figure, but in 1932 the tobacco companies produced about 93 per cent of the cigarettes they had rolled in 1929.[14] A concern with a foot in each industry, therefore, would seem to be less vulnerable to cyclical hazards than one wholly concentrated in the less stable business.

To the extent that each firm is more stable it would seem likely that employment would fluctuate less. And if machines and inventories are not dumped on markets at distress sales, prices generally would be less likely to swing between extreme positions. Thus it can be argued that stabilization of individual firms results in stabilization of the economy as a whole. The fact that underdeveloped areas of the world are constantly striving toward diversified production lends credence to that conclusion.[15]

Professor Dewing, on the other hand, was more than skeptical of industrial consolidations as a means of warding off depressions. Dewing, The Financial Policy of Corporations 765 (3d ed. 1934). He said: "And, as in the earlier periods of the eighteen nineties, the professional economists acquiesced in the presumption that combinations were a means of suppressing competition, so now the contemporary theoretical students see in the continued merging of corporations a groping after stability. But one set of phrases cannot be substituted for another in the hope of discovering a new truth . . . nor can we presume that a stability arising from the presumption that the larger the unit of production or distribution, the greater its vitality, has any lasting reality as an abiding economic truth. Economic laws are made of more robust stuff." As an abstract ideal, bankruptcy may suggest desirable fluidity but in the absence of perfect competition, the losses inherent in bankruptcy are probably real. In addition, there are court costs and delays which can hardly contribute to increased production. It is interesting to note that the courts have usually been wary of giving the mortgagee his pound of flesh. Even in the most obvious cases, the courts have not always squeezed the holders of common stock in corporate reorganizations. See Dodd, The Los Angeles Lumber Products Company Case and Its Implications, 53 Harv. L. Rev. 713, 734 et seq. (1940). Apparently there is a feeling that the business cycle swings away from "fair" values.

The Gillette Company, which purchased the Toni hair-waving business in order to diversify its activities and thus avoid cyclical changes, reported a decline in its over-all profits owing to slack sales of Toni products and not to lack of profits in the original razor blade business. Gillette Ready to Ship New Product, Boston Traveler, May 19, 1949, p. 40, col. 5.

Compare New Products Broaden Goodrich Earnings Base, 30 Barron's No. 19, p. 15 (1950) (benefits of ability to shift emphasis from producers' to consumers' goods with cycle).

[14] Chicago Daily News, Almanac 115, 266 (1931); 366, 679 (1934). Of course diversification reduces high earnings in boom times as much as it protects corporate existence during depressions. That fact is recognized by industry. Thus it has been said: "General American will continue to build toward making its business more and more depression-resistant, sacrificing where necessary, quick profits to gain that end. The leasing business, the backbone of your Company's stable earnings, is expanding on a sound basis. In addition, our diversification in manufacturing makes possible for us sharply increased earnings. That should result in periods of good business activity." General American Transportation Corp., Ann. Rep. for 1947, 3 (Chicago, 1948). The question might well be asked why firms do not hoard cash during boom times instead of diversifying into new products.

[15] Hutcheson, Problems of the Underdeveloped Countries II, 24 Foreign Pol.

§6.14. Attacks and analysis. Having outlined the causes and benefits of diversification, we shall now appraise the complaints against diversification set forth below — complaints which relate to the existence of alleged monopoly. The charges set forth do not, however, include every conceivable argument against the multi-product firm: only the more important grounds of attack are considered. After each follows an analysis of its validity.

§6.15. Tying clauses. One of the chief complaints against diversification is that it leads to the "tying" of one product to another. (Sometimes the phrase "full line forcing" is used instead of "tying.") It is alleged that the diversified manufacturer pre-empts the dealers' shelves. The maker of a single product, even if it is better or cheaper, cannot secure a market.[1]

In the pre-war assault upon General Motors,[2] the theory that diversification leads to tying was not advanced in those terms. But such a theory was implied. In that case it appeared that General Motors, a manufacturer of automobiles, had several wholly owned subsidiaries. Among them were General Motors Sales Corporation (GMSC) and General Motors Acceptance Corporation (GMAC). GMSC was merely an agent for the parent in making the original sales of cars to dealers. GMAC extended credit both to dealers buying from GMSC and to ultimate consumers buying from dealers. Some 375 independent finance companies competed with GMAC. A system of making payment for automobiles on the part of the dealers was so arranged as to favor GMAC: an officer of GMSC held agency powers from each dealer so that he might execute appropriate notes to GMAC. As applied to sales from dealers to consumers, the evidence showed that dealers who failed to use the GMAC service were in danger of losing their "franchises." In other words, General Motors would not sell automobiles unless the dealers compelled consumers to purchase through GMAC. Oddly enough, however, it was found that only 75 per cent of the dealers were utilizing the GMAC service.

Nowhere in the Attorney General's brief nor in the opinion is it suggested that the mere combination of making motor cars and extending credit to purchasers thereof violated the Sherman Act. Apparently the lack of prior authority caused avoidance of that position. Instead, the whole case was predicated on the theory

Reps. No. 9, p. 98 (1948). Note also that farmers are constantly urged to diversify their crops so as to reduce dependence upon a single commodity.

§6.15. 1 Raymond, The Limitist 35 (1947). Compare Edwards, Maintaining Competition: Requisites of a Governmental Policy 104 (1949).
2 United States v. General Motors Corp., 121 F.2d 376 (7th Cir. 1941), *cert. denied,* 314 U.S. 618 (1941).

that General Motors "coerced" the dealers into using GMAC financing. Thus the court said:

> When the evidence is boiled down, it is seen at once that the appellants agreed among themselves not to do business with any dealer who would not purchase the retail and wholesale service from GMAC. . . . In the usual case the recalcitrant dealer had become firmly established in his community and was operating a profitable business, when he was given the ultimatum either to use GMAC or to liquidate his business.[3]

> Although every dealer is an independent business man, the supervision and control exercised by GMAC and GMSC over his business operations is almost as complete as if the dealer were an agent in all respects. Every dealer also acquires a substantial investment in buildings, cars, parts and accessories, and builds up good will in his community. Consequently a cancelled dealership leaves the appellants with one less retail outlet which can be replaced readily, but leaves the disenfranchised dealer without a business and burdened with his substantial investment in the liquidation of which he is likely to sustain a heavy loss.[4]

Conspiracy between GMC and its two subsidiaries was the foundation of the case, although some stress was laid upon the power of General Motors as an important producer of automobiles:

> Not only is market control present in the instant case, but a peculiarly pernicious form of it is exhibited.

> This becomes apparent at once when it is observed that GMC occupies a dominant position in the automobile industry. . . .[5]

The court concluded:

> The necessary and inevitable effect of the coercive conduct tended to produce two distinct restraints of trade, namely a restraint on the commerce in General Motors cars and a restraint on the commerce in instruments of credit.[6]

As every lawyer knows, the practice of tying is prohibited by Section 3 of the Clayton Act.[7] And recently the decisions have

[3] 121 F.2d at 399.

[4] Id. at 398.

[5] Id. at 403. In United States v. United Shoe Machinery Corp., 110 F. Supp. 295 (D. Mass. 1953), aff'd per curiam, 347 U.S. 521 (1954), it was said at page 346: "The most important fact with respect to United's manufacturing and distributive activities in these supply markets is that they are a consequence of United's power in the shoe machinery market and to some extent buttress that power." It was also said that an enterprise which, by monopolizing one field, secures dominant market power in another violates §2 of the Sherman Act. Ibid.

[6] 121 F.2d at 399. For further history of the automobile finance cases, see Ford Motor Co. v. United States, 335 U.S. 303, 306, 312 (1948).

[7] 38 Stat. 731 (1914), 15 U.S.C. §14. The authorities up to 1940 are collected in Hale, Control over Distribution, 14 Miss. L.J. 170, 177 et seq. (1942).

tended to apply the terms of that prohibition stringently.[8] They have suggested that foreclosure from any "substantial market" would bring Section 3 of the Clayton Act into play.[9] Possibly the "substantial market" may consist only of the defendant's own sales. When a patentee has attempted to tie an unpatented item to his patented product, the arrangement has been treated with special severity. Ever since the *Motion Picture Patents* case[10] a patentee has been held powerless to compel his licensee to purchase unpatented supplies for use in the patented machine. In fact recent decisions have gone to the extreme of refusing to enforce any rights in a patent if a tying clause is used in connection therewith.[11]

§6.16. Analysis of tying. It has been suggested — although possibly only indirectly — that diversification results in the tying of one product to another. In other words, it is urged that tying clauses are an inevitable concomitant of diversification. Certainly, full line forcing and similar practices may result from diversification,[1] and, of course, cannot exist without it. An officer of a prominent farm equipment manufacturer was once quoted as saying that his company's policy did not favor full line forcing. He admitted, however, that his salesmen had to be dis-

---

[8] Oxford Varnish Corp. v. Ault & Wiborg Corp., 83 F.2d 764 (6th Cir. 1936).

[9] Note, Tying Restrictions: Changing Standards of Legality, 48 Colum. L. Rev. 733, 740 (1948); §2.17 *supra*.

[10] Motion Picture Patents Co. v. Universal Film Mfg. Co., 243 U.S. 502 (1917).

[11] Note, Tying Restrictions: Changing Standards of Legality, 48 Colum. L. Rev. 733, 739 (1948). But compare FTC v. Gratz, 253 U.S. 421, 427 (1920), where it was said: "The words 'unfair method of competition' . . . are clearly inapplicable to practices never heretofore regarded as opposed to good morals because characterized by deception, bad faith, fraud or oppression, or as against public policy because of their dangerous tendency unduly to hinder competition or create monopoly." Arguments against the tying of one product to another are found in United Shoe Machinery Corp. v. United States, 258 U.S. 451, 457 (1922); Dissent by Mr. Justice Brandeis in FTC v. Gratz, 253 U.S. 421, 440 (1920); Stevens, Unfair Competition 75 (1917); Remarks by Senator Reed, 51 Cong. Rec. 14,091, 14,097 (1914); Stockhausen, The Commercial and Anti-trust Aspects of Term Requirements Contracts, 23 N.Y.U.L.Q. Rev. 412, 421 (1948); Lewis, Motion Pictures, 11 Encyc. Soc. Sci. 58, 62 (1933); Sen. Rep. No. 698, 63d Cong., 2d Sess. 6 et seq. (1914). There is, of course, an active question as to what constitutes a tied contract as opposed to a combination sale. Note, Tying Restrictions: Changing Standards of Legality, 48 Colum. L. Rev. 733, 742 (1948). Similarly the distinction between tying clauses and full line forcing is vague. Compare Davies, Trust Laws and Unfair Competition 322 (1915). Diversification is closely related to the definition of the commodity (§3.3 *supra*). In the last Shoe Machinery case (United States v. United Shoe Machinery Corp., 110 F. Supp. 295 (D. Mass. 1953), *aff'd per curiam*, 347 U.S. 521 (1954)), for example, the court took the view that all shoe machinery constituted the relevant commodity, whereas in previous litigation each machine had been taken separately and the defendant regarded as diversified (United States v. Winslow, 195 Fed. 578 (D. Mass. 1912), *aff'd*, 227 U.S. 202 (1913)); §2.19 *supra*.

§6.16. [1] Conant, The International Harvester Company 308 (1913).

suaded from the practice.[2]   And there is something to be said
for the view that sellers will take every advantage they can and
hence will tie one product to another whenever that is possible.
Perhaps Professor Levi had such a thought in mind when he suggested that integration would always lead to abuses.[3]

On the other hand, there is considerable weakness in any argument that diversification inevitably leads to tying.   In the first
place, the process of rounding out the line is not the same as full
line forcing.   The former is undertaken on behalf of the customer.   Thus, in the postscript to the *Standard Oil* decision
whereby Socony was permitted to merge with Vacuum, the
court declared: "The struggle for this trade made the pleasure of
that customer worthwhile, and such pleasure and convenience
soon directed that he be able to procure oil at the same place and
time that he bought gasoline. . . ."[4]   In other words, the consumer requests the manufacturer to round out the line for the
former's convenience.   Full line forcing, on the other hand, is
usually described as a program to compel a distributor to take
merchandise he does not want.   Surely there is some inconsistency
between the repeated stress laid upon full line forcing and the
fact that rounding out the line is frequently undertaken at the
insistence of the dealer.[5]   Although this analysis may not apply

2 Ibid.

3 Levi, The Antitrust Laws and Monopoly, 14 U. Chi. L. Rev. 153, 180 (1947).
Compare Alexander Milburn Co. v. Union Carbide & Carbon Corp., 15 F.2d 678
(4th Cir. 1926), *cert. denied*, 273 U.S. 757 (1927), with United States v. General
Motors Corp., 121 F.2d 376 (7th Cir. 1941), *cert. denied*, 314 U.S. 618 (1941). If coercion is the natural and inevitable consequence of diversification, it would be
difficult to reconcile the two foregoing decisions.

4 United States v. Standard Oil Co., 47 F.2d 288, 300 (E.D. Mo. 1931).   In a recent case it was noted that the defendant's "roadmen" [servicemen] were available
for all sorts of counsel and cooperation for the various technical shoemaking and
shoe factory problems.   United States v. United Shoe Machinery Corp., 110 F. Supp.
295, 322 (D. Mass. 1953), *aff'd per curiam*, 347 U.S. 521 (1954).   The opinion went
on: "All these supplies are technically closely related to machines.   The principal
cause of United's success in marketing them is United's market power with
respect to shoe machinery.   Having roughly an 85 per cent share of the shoe
machinery market, and, as a result of lease system having regular contacts with
shoe factories, United is readily able to market over 80 per cent of the supplies in
these fields because they so intimately affect the functioning of the machines.
Customers already know United, have current business relations with it, trust it
generally, believe it able to specify, select or manufacture suitable supplies, and are
aware that because of the lease provisions United is, as it were, a partner interested
in the effective functioning of the machines.   Moreover, there is an element of
customer inertia favoring United . . ."   110 F. Supp. at 336.   Note id. 336 at 337
(economies of scale in distribution).   But compare id. at 336 (unlawful to take
advantage of customer's inertia or convenience to sell him additional goods).

5 Possibly rounding out the line may be overemphasized.   Thus it has been
said: ". . . it may be necessary to sell some articles at a loss in order to offer a
'complete line' to the customer so that he will buy other articles on which a satis-

equally to all dealers and may be adversely affected by the passage of time, it would nevertheless seem that rounding out the line would, to a degree, cancel out the argument based upon full line forcing.

In the second place, it will be remembered that rounding out the line is by no means the only reason for diversification. Take, for example, the case of complementary goods. A complementary product may be used as part of a tying scheme.[6] On the other hand, it is often provided for the convenience of the customer. It may be a trade necessity arising out of a time lag. When the motive is the convenience of the customer, it scarcely seems possible that tying can be objectionable. A similar argument can be applied to General Motors as a financier of the sale of its automobiles.[7] A railroad which builds a resort hotel along its lines so as to attract passenger traffic can scarcely be said to have created an objectionable monopoly.[8]

A more important factor arises out of the fact that diversification does not always lead to sales in the same market. Thorp and Crowder broke their analysis of diversification down into three principal categories. These categories were divergent functions, convergent functions and unrelated functions. Under divergent functions they listed joint products, by-products and like processes. Under convergent functions they listed complementary products, auxiliary products and goods made to sell in like markets.[9] In other words, they distinguished diversification arising out of economies in production from diversification aimed at the process of distribution. When functions are "divergent," the products end up in different markets. When functions are "convergent," goods made from varying materials are sold through the same channels. It must be plain that there can be no tying of products when the diversification is of the divergent type. Compare, for example, the *First Shoe Machinery* case[10] with the situation of the International Harvester Company at a more recent date. All of the products of the United Shoe Ma-

---

factory profit is earned . . . It is sometimes necessary to follow this plan, but sales departments are likely to over-emphasize the necessity." McKinsey, Business Administration 138 (1924).

[6] Thorp and Crowder, The Structure of Industry 652 (TNEC Monograph No. 27, 1941).

[7] United States v. General Motors Corp., 121 F.2d 376 (7th Cir. 1941), *cert. denied*, 314 U.S. 618 (1941).

[8] Jacksonville Railway v. Hooper, 160 U.S. 514, 523 (1896).

[9] Thorp and Crowder, The Structure of Industry 146 (TNEC Monograph No. 27, 1941). The definitions of these authors should be examined with care. Id. at 147, 149.

[10] United States v. Winslow, 227 U.S. 202 (1913).

chinery Company were sold to shoemakers. Thus it was possible to require the customers to take all or none of the manufacturer's products. International Harvester Company sells its trucks chiefly to industry. Its agricultural implements are sold principally to farmers.[11] The Harvester Company can scarcely be accused of tying the sales of motor trucks to its farm implement business.

Another important factor relates to the existence of some element of monopoly in the principal product to which the ancillary commodity is tied. In the absence of such an element the two items cannot be tied together.[12] On the New York Stock Exchange, for example, a seller cannot insist that a buyer take a hundred shares of Standard Oil when he purchases a hundred shares of Dow Chemical stock.

In some instances diversification may result in the tying of one commodity to another. The conditions for such tying are (1) that the seller is not rounding out his line in a bona fide manner; (2) that the diversified product is sold in the same market; (3) that there is no genuine need for a complementary article; and (4) that the seller has some monopoly power. In the light of the foregoing limitations, it would seem difficult to prove that diversification inevitably results in tying.

Tying clauses otherwise objectionable may be justified when they are merely designed to protect the good will of the seller.

11 International Harvester I: Supremacy, 8 Fortune No. 2, p. 21 (1933). Query whether there is a relationship between tying clauses and the stabilization of industry.

The theory, embodied in §3 of the Clayton Act, that tying is monopolistic in nature, has often been disputed. According to one school of thought, buyers retain complete freedom of choice; they can either take the combination of principal and ancillary (tied) goods or leave them. United States v. United Shoe Machinery Co., 247 U.S. 32, 66 (1918); Whitwell v. Continental Tobacco Co., 125 Fed. 454, 461 (8th Cir. 1903); FTC v. Paramount Famous-Lasky Corp., 57 F.2d 152, 156 (2d Cir. 1932); United Shoe Machinery Co. v. Brunet, [1909] A.C. 330, 343. Compare Stevens, Unfair Competition 75 (1917); Hale, Trust Dissolution, 40 Colum. L. Rev. 615, 625 (1940). Another argument, chiefly applicable to patents, is comparable to the freedom-of-choice theory. It may be called the "unlimited condition" theory. Mr. Justice Holmes, dissenting in Motion Picture Patents Co. v. Universal Film Mfg. Co., 243 U.S. 502, 519 (1917); Kales, Contracts to Keep Up the Price on Resale and to Buy or Use Other Articles in Connection with Those Sold, 3 Cornell L.Q. 89, 97 (1918). Compare Supplemental Brief for Plaintiff, p. 19, United States v. General Motors Corp., 26 F. Supp. 353 (N.D. Ind. 1939), aff'd, 121 F.2d 376 (7th Cir. 1941), cert. denied, 314 U.S. 618 (1941). Such arguments imply the absence of monopoly in the principal product. FTC v. Gratz, 253 U.S. 421, 428 (1920); Whitwell v. Continental Tobacco Co., 125 Fed. 454, 460 (8th Cir. 1903); FTC v. Paramount Famous-Lasky Corp., 57 F.2d 152, 157 (2d Cir. 1932). And conversely, that there is monopoly in the principal product: United States v. General Motors Corp., 121 F.2d 376, 400 (7th Cir. 1941), cert. denied, 314 U.S. 618 (1941). See §2.19 supra.

12 Miller, Unfair Competition 194, 199 (1941); see Standard Oil Co. of California v. United States, 337 U.S. 293, 306 (1949).

Another decision[13] involving the General Motors Corporation held that that concern could require its dealers not to use rival replacement parts in repairing automobiles. In the opinion of the court the restriction was justified by General Motors' legitimate desire to maintain good will in its vehicles. It is nevertheless plain that protection of good will does not justify the use of tying clauses when other lawful means would accomplish the same purpose.[14] Accordingly, in the *General Motors* case involving the tying of the automobiles to GMAC financing, the court found that other methods would have protected the defendant's good will. In the opinion it was said:

> The appellants justify their coercive course of business on the ground that the GMAC service is superior to that of its competitors, and because they fear that unregulated dealers' financing would promote such evils as packing, excessive repossessions and cut-throat methods of competition. . . .
>
> The evidence shows that the coercive conduct in question was not intended to discriminate against an inferior or unreliable finance service. Rather its entire force and effect was directed against any use of any independent finance service. . . .
>
> No doubt it is proper for GMC and GMSC to promote manufacturer's goodwill and to protect the manufacturer against inefficient and unscrupulous dealers. . . . But there is a limit to how far a manufacturer may go to control the whole process of distribution. The jury found that the appellants had gone too far with their control plans, and we are inclined to approve and to indorse the jury finding.[15]

Even in those instances in which diversification does result in tying, therefore, the result is not necessarily objectionable. The

13 Pick Mfg. Co. v. General Motors Corp., 80 F.2d 641 (7th Cir. 1935), *aff'd per curiam*, 299 U.S. 3 (1936).

14 International Business Machines Corp. v. United States, 298 U.S. 131, 138 et seq. (1936).

15 United States v. General Motors Corp., 121 F.2d 376, 400 (7th Cir. 1941), *cert. denied*, 314 U.S. 618 (1941). The court continued:

". . . we should think that the appellants would have been able to find a way to punish unscrupulous dealers without penalizing the others at the same time.

"If in fact unregulated dealers' financing leads to widespread abuses in the retail sale of automobiles, a need indeed would arise for regulation and control in order to protect the public interest. It is doubtful whether regulation in this respect should be entrusted to the dominant manufacturers . . . If in truth some outside control of dealers' financing is necessary, it should originate with the legislators . . ."

Even the Attorney General admitted that the maintenance of good will justified some control over the finance companies. That admission took the form of an attempt to create a regulatory code for the independent financiers. Birnbaum, The Auto-Finance Consent Decree, 24 Wash. U.L.Q. 525, 547 et seq. (1939).

bona fide protection of good will is an approved justification for tying clauses.

§6.17. **Price-cutting.** A second complaint against diversification is that it leads to price-cutting. The seller of more than one product may take a loss upon a single item and continue a profitable business by maintaining high prices on his other products. In trade parlance, this is the familiar "loss leader" practice.[1] In the older antitrust cases a similar practice was characterized as the use of "fighting brands." In those days a manufacturer, attempting to ruin his competitor, would package his goods in a container similar to those of the rival and sell the "fighting brand" far below cost.[2]

Upon several occasions it has been argued that diversification leads to ruinous price-cutting. Mr. Justice Cardozo's reluctance to permit the large meat packers to enter the grocery business was based upon such fears. He laid stress upon the immense size of the packers, saying that the consent decree imposed upon them had been designed to prevent the use of that size to "drive their rivals to the wall."[3] Professor Burns demonstrated that profits from one branch of a business could be used to attempt monopoly in another.[4] Similar fears of diversification were voiced by Professor Edwards:

> . . . an enterprise that sells a wide variety of commodities may select as its victim a concern that specializes in the sale of one or a few of these commodities, and may with impunity undertake a similar program of price cutting limited to the items sold by the specialized concern. In its crudest form such an attack may be pushed so far as to destroy one concern after another and thus to enlarge the attacking enterprise. Less crudely, however, the power to make such localized attacks may be used as a disciplinary device to induce the small concerns to adopt policies that the larger and more diversified enterprise regards as satisfactory. In

§6.17. [1] Edwards, Maintaining Competition: Requisites of a Governmental Policy 20, 101 (1949); Celler Committee I, pt. 1, at 220; pt. 2A, at 342; pt. 2A, at 383. The complaint of an independent single-line fabricator against a diversified fabricator was that the latter can make up losses on one product by gains on others. Id., pt. 4A, at 334.

[2] Davies, Trust Laws and Unfair Competition 313 (1915). The practice of using "fighting brands" is only a result of diversification if each brand be considered a separate commodity. Otherwise, it falls into the category of horizontal integration.

[3] United States v. Swift & Co., 286 U.S. 106, 116, 117 (1932). Partly in recognition of this point of view, the Congress enacted the commodities clause of the Interstate Commerce Act, Feb. 4, 1887, as amended, June 29, 1906, 34 Stat. 585, 49 U.S.C.A. §1(8). Compare 1 Scharfman, The Interstate Commerce Commission 42 (1931). Similar legislation has been enacted in several states. Martin, ed., State Antitrust Laws liii (WPA, 1940).

[4] Burns, The Decline of Competition 451 (1936).

this form the program is unlikely to require many instances of localized price cutting or to require that these cuts be very deep or very long sustained. The mere power to undertake such a program is sufficient to lend authority to the large enterprise and to persuade the small one that a conciliatory policy is wise.[5]

§6.18. **Analysis of price-cutting.** If the maker of two products cuts the price of one of them below cost, using profits from the other to maintain his general position, he may be attempting to monopolize the first product. His ability to do so depends upon several conditions. First, he must have enough monopoly in the second product to earn high profits, for without high profits he cannot subsidize his attempt to monopolize the first commodity. In the second place, he must enjoy a reasonable prospect of successfully monopolizing the first item. Unless he has such a prospect of potential success, he will be making a poor investment. Again, as a price-cutter he must be prepared to fend off retaliatory action by competitors.[1] And if the cut prices are subsequently raised in an effort to capitalize upon monopoly achieved, new firms may be attracted into the industry.[2]

A would-be monopolist can finance his effort to control a market from many sources. Subscribed capital may be used to keep an enterprise solvent during a price-cutting foray. Earnings may be hoarded for such a purpose. A company with little working capital may be able to raise cash by means of loans secured by a mortgage. Or it may resort to the recently popular practice of selling its plant and leasing it back from the grantee.[3] There are, in other words, many methods by which funds can be obtained to support an attempt to monopolize. Profits from diversified operations constitute but one means of accomplishing that result. Professor Edwards admitted as much.[4] Unless, therefore, we are

[5] Edwards, Maintaining Competition: Requisites of a Governmental Policy 159 (1949).

§6.18. [1] Edwards, Maintaining Competition: Requisites of a Governmental Policy 20 et seq. (1949).

[2] Burns, The Decline of Competition 452 (1936). Compare Edwards, Maintaining Competition: Requisites of a Governmental Policy 95 (1949), where it is said: "Alternately the need for internal congruity in the policies adopted for different products, channels of distribution, and classes of customers may induce the monopoly to refrain from pressing its advantage in dealing with buyers whose bargaining position is unusually weak; and differences in the products, markets, and distributive channels of a few large enterprises may make collusion relatively difficult. Thus the complex monopoly may be either harsher or milder than the simple one."

[3] Cary, Corporate Financing Through the Sale and Leaseback of Property, 62 Harv. L. Rev. 1 (1948).

[4] Edwards, Maintaining Competition: Requisites of a Governmental Policy 169 (1949). Compare Stevens, Unfair Competition 43 et seq. (1917). Note that in the use of "fighting brands" as described by Stevens, a seller may be competing with

prepared to block all other avenues of raising cash to finance a price-cutting venture, it is doubtful whether diversification should be condemned on that ground.

Possibly price-cutting may constitute discrimination of a monopoly type.[5] And diversification may furnish the foundation for such price-cutting. It certainly does not follow that diversification inevitably leads to such conduct: there is nothing to indicate that price-cutting necessarily or even probably flows from the existence of diversification. And one can scarcely argue that diversification causes both price-cutting and tied sales concurrently. For in a tied sale, the ancillary product is sold at a price above free-market levels, while price-cutting implies a sale below such figures. In other words, tied sales and price-cutting cannot exist together in the same circumstances: either the sale is tied or the price is cut, but both practices cannot exist at once. Thus no one should assert that diversification causes both price-cutting and tying, unless he refers to different times or places.

Another consideration results from the fact that sales of complementary goods may be made upon a tied basis without an attempt to monopolize.[6] An aspect of this issue was raised in the well-known *Gasoline Pump* case.[7] There leading oil companies leased gasoline pumps to operators of filling stations at nominal rentals, the operators agreeing not to sell rival gasoline from the leased pumps. Since the agreement permitted the service station operator to deal in rival gasoline from other pumps, the courts

---

himself as well as with his rivals. It should also be observed that the fighting brands theory requires an acceptance of the doctrine that each brand is a separate commodity before it affects diversification. Compare also United States v. Quaker Oats Co., 232 Fed. 499 (N.D. Ill. 1916). On the other hand a diversified producer will find that some of his products must meet stiffer competition than others. As a result, those products will earn a smaller proportion of profit. E.g., Kilgore Committee, pt. 6, at 2829. Hence, in some degree diversification may be regarded as a cause of a measure of price discrimination; or is competition the cause?

[5] Stevens, Unfair Competition 51 (1917). Compare Robinson, The Economics of Imperfect Competition, c. 15 (1936). When a firm produces via diversification, analysis of competitive effects demands the incorporation of the price discrimination theory, that is, the diversified firm realizes larger profit on some items than on others. Robinson, Imperfect Competition Revisited, 63 Econ. J. 579, (1953).

[6] Thorp and Crowder, The Structure of Industry 667 (TNEC Monograph No. 27, 1941).

[7] FTC v. Sinclair Refining Co., 261 U.S. 463, 476 (1923). There Mr. Justice McReynolds declared: "The suggestion that the assailed practice is unfair because of its effect upon the sale of pumps by their makers is sterile and requires no serious discussion." He also said at page 475: "The powers of the Commission are limited by the statutes. It has no general authority to compel competitors to a common level, to interfere with ordinary business methods or to proscribe arbitrary standards for those engaged in the conflict for advantage called competition . . . it is essential that those who adventure their time, skill and capital should have large freedom of action in the conduct of their own affairs."

held that violation of neither the Federal Trade Commission Act[8] nor the Clayton Act had been proven. The Trade Commission had urged an injury both to other marketers of gasoline who were not in a position to supply pumps at nominal rentals and to makers of pumps who lost business through the practice. But the courts dismissed those suggestions in summary fashion. Possibly the case would not be followed today, but to the extent that it was soundly decided, it is authority for the view that diversification resulting in the provision of complementary goods below cost is not necessarily the same thing as price-cutting with an intent to monopolize: the practice may constitute a mere convenience to the consumer. In essence, it is only an extension of credit. And every firm which extends credit is partly in the banking business[9] and is thus cutting the price of credit below banker's rates. Theoretically we might prohibit the extension of credit by sellers of other commodities. Concentration of all such transactions in commercial banks might focus lending in a desirable manner.[10] But the course of trade for centuries indicates that the extension of credit by sellers is a practical necessity. Indeed, there is support for the contention of General Motors[11] that its extension of credit through GMAC was necessary to effect satisfactory sales. A prominent farm implement company has adopted a similar program.[12]

To the extent that price-cutting does constitute an attempt to monopolize, it would seem desirable to deal with it under the specific terms of Section 2 of the Sherman Act.[13] Cutting the price of a particular product with intent to monopolize is surely comparable to the old-fashioned local price-cutting upon a geo-

8 38 Stat. 717 (1914), 15 U.S.C. §41.

9 Hautrey, Credit, 4 Encyc. Soc. Sci. 545, 548 (1931).

10 Under 62 Stat. 1291, c. 836 (1948), 12 U.S.C. §248n, the Federal Reserve Board was authorized to control consumer credit until June 30, 1949. Section 1 of the act refers to Exec. Order No. 8843 (1941), which was the basis of the original Regulation W. As revised, Regulation W, 12 C.F.R. §222 (1948), regulated down payments and the interval of subsequent payments in time sales (§222.3). If all lending transactions were concentrated in commercial banks, it would not be necessary to adopt such elaborate controls over sellers generally. The complaint has been registered that General Motors' easy finance terms sell more automobiles than people "ought" to buy. Arnold, The Bottlenecks of Business 24 (1940).

11 United States v. General Motors Corp., 121 F.2d 376, 406 (7th Cir. 1941). On the other hand, a control of credit may be accomplished better through regulations of the type in question than through an attempt to press the antitrust laws into such prohibitions.

12 International Harvester Co., Ann. Rep. 1948, 6 (Chicago, 1949).

13 28 Stat. 209 (1890), 15 U.S.C. §2. An interesting solution of the loss leader practice would be to require a seller below "cost" to sell his entire stocks to anyone (including, especially, rival sellers). Kemp, An Appraisal of Loss Leader Selling, 21 Can. J. Econ. & Pol. Sci. 245 (1955).

graphical basis. Such a territorial discrimination is clearly a violation of the Sherman Act;[14] Professor Levi has called it a typical "abuse" falling within the prohibitions of that statute.[15] Neither reliance on other statutes[16] nor general condemnation of diversification seems necessary.

§6.19. **Price-cutting by public utilities.** If a business is subject to the fixing of its prices by public authority, diversification (and tying clauses) may have a more serious effect. It is commonplace for fixed-price industries to indulge in outside activities. Many public utility companies sell electric or gas appliances and at least one prominent utility company has a large stake in the production of oil.[1] If such a business is regulated, diversification may become the basis for a scheme to avoid the effect of government control. Vertical integration may have a similar effect. Thus it has been charged that a prominent public utility corporation has inflated its rate base by the purchase of supplies and materials from a wholly owned subsidiary at exorbitant prices.[2] A good example of the use of diversification to avoid the effect of government control is found in the liquor business under OPA controls. By government action, the price of whiskey was fixed at a low figure in relation to market values. Accordingly, distributors refused to sell whiskey unless rum, gin and other products less in demand were also purchased. The effect of such tying arrangements was to move a considerable quantity of the less desired products at prices above the market with accompanying profit to the dealers, thus enabling them to partially avoid the price control.[3]

More frequently fixed-price businesses are accused of price-cutting in the sale of ancillary products. Putting the matter another way, diversification may permit a public utility to juggle its cost

---

[14] Standard Oil Co. of New Jersey v. United States, 221 U.S. 1 (1911).

[15] Levi, The Antitrust Laws and Monopoly, 14 U. Chi. L. Rev. 153, 158 (1947). But compare Package Closure Corp. v. Sealright Co., Inc., 141 F.2d 972, 977 (2d Cir. 1944).

[16] Compare §2 of the Clayton Act, 38 Stat. 703 (1914), 15 U.S.C. §13.

§6.19. [1] Southern California Edison Co., Ann. Rep. 1948, 6 (Los Angeles, 1949) (nearly one fourth of net profit derived from oil production). Compare Commonwealth ex rel. Baldridge v. Philadelphia Electric Co., 18 Pa. Corp. Rep. 243 (1929), aff'd, 300 Pa. 577, 151 Atl. 344 (1930) (corporation chartered to supply light, heat and power may properly engage in sale of appliances).

[2] Complaint in United States v. Western Electric Co., No. 17-49, D.N.J. (1949).

[3] Coffin-Redington Co. v. Porter, 156 F.2d 113 (9th Cir. 1946); New York Times, Jan. 30, 1945, p. 13, col. 6. Compare Union Pacific Coal Co. v. United States, 173 Fed. 737 (8th Cir. 1909). As emphasized in §5.12 supra, public utilities may diversify and use tying clauses, and so forth, to avoid (public authority) price-fixing measures.

figures. Since a utility is guaranteed a limited return upon its public utility business, it may try to allocate the cost of diversified operations to the controlled enterprise and thereby justify rate increases.[4] It will be noted that the foregoing practice is substantially the reverse of that usually found in the diversification-tying clause situations. There the tied commodity is sold above market price; but erroneous cost accounting will result in the sale of the by-products of the utility below market price. This fact is the source of much complaint from independent dealers who compete with the public utility companies in the sale of electric and gas appliances. They assert that losses incurred in the sale of refrigerators, stoves and the like are recouped by higher rates for utility service.[5]

That the sales of appliances may actually be made below cost is evident from the following statement:

> The crux of the matter is whether or not a utility shall be privileged to sell appliances below cost and recoup losses by capitalizing them or by charging them to operating expenses. The public utilities emphasize the promotional aspect, namely, that appliances and service are complementary goods, and that from the standpoint of the consumer, the demand is a joint one . . . The utilities have urged that the merchandising department is properly a promotional department, and as such should not be required to be self-supporting. The argument that appliance losses are recovered through rates for service is answered by pointing to the decreased costs and lower rates which result from the expansion of business made possible by cheap appliances. . . .[6]

Pressure from independent merchants has resulted in the adoption in some states of statutes prohibiting the sale of appliances by public utilities.[7]

Considerations of the foregoing character have suggested that public utility companies should be forbidden to diversify. Professor Barnes urged that the utility should be under a heavy burden of proof to justify entry into businesses other than its principal public service.[8] And Professor Edwards was even more insistent upon a separation of controlled from uncontrolled busi-

4 Barnes, The Economics of Public Utility Regulation 627 (1942).

5 Behling, Competition and Monopoly in Public Utility Industries 50 (Illinois Studies in the Social Sciences, Vol. 23, No. 1, 1938); Note, Section 11(b), 59 Yale L.J. 1088, 1096-1097 (1950).

6 Behling, Competition and Monopoly in Public Utility Industries 51 (Illinois Studies in the Social Sciences, Vol. 23, No. 1, 1938).

7 Id. at 50. Expenditures incurred in such sidelines may be disregarded in fixing rates. People's Gas Co. v. Slattery, 373 Ill. 31, 65, 25 N.E. 2d 482, 499 (1940).

8 Barnes, The Economics of Public Utility Regulation 277 et seq. (1942).

ness.[9] Perhaps there is no satisfactory basis upon which to fix the prices of public utility concerns. But if regulation is to be attempted, it may be necessary to prevent diversification into free markets.

§6.20. **Exclusion from markets.** In the *Du Pont* case[1] a principal allegation of the complaint is that suppliers are excluded from markets. According to the Attorney General, the Du Pont Company, General Motors Corporation and the United States Rubber Company enjoy common control by members of the Du Pont family. That control is so exercised — or a conspiracy among the three corporations has similarly arranged — that the firms trade among themselves whenever possible. General Motors, for example, buys its tires from U.S. Rubber and its paint from Du Pont. Thus independent tiremakers and paint manufacturers are excluded from the General Motors market.[2]

In large measure the question is one of vertical integration. Assuming that the three corporations are under the alleged common control, they may be regarded as a single, highly diversified firm: there is actually but one enterprise, engaged in many different businesses. To the extent that the different departments of the one concern have occasion to buy supplies from each other, diversification will give rise to the alleged vices of vertical integration.[3] Thus, it is said, markets may be foreclosed and competition reduced.

In the long run, the alleged exclusion of tiremakers other than U.S. Rubber from the General Motors market suggests that Gen-

---

[9] Edwards, An Appraisal of the Antitrust Laws, 36 Proceedings Am. Econ. Assn. 172, 262 (1946). In Bonbright and Means, The Holding Company 199 (1932), the authors declared: "Whether or not this [Cities Service Company type] interrelation between utility companies and unregulated business companies is desirable from a public point of view is more than doubtful. The greatest danger lies in the menace to the credit of the public utilities when these essential and non-competitive enterprises are financially affiliated with highly speculative businesses like oil production."

Several statutes attempt to reach such problems: e.g., Illinois Public Utility Act, Ill. Rev. Stat. c. 111⅔, §§1 et seq., 12, 27(g) (1957); Civil Aeronautics Act of 1938, 52 Stat. 973, 49 U.S.C.A. §§401 et seq. Section 408 appears to prohibit both control of an air carrier by another type of common carrier and control of an aircraft manufacturer by an air carrier (subject to approval of the CAB). United States v. Inter-Island Co., 87 F. Supp. 1010 (D. Hawaii, 1950); 2 Sharfman, The Interstate Commerce Commission 21 (1931). Compare United States v. Western Electric Co., No. 17-49, D.N.J., consent decree entered Jan. 24, 1956, CCH Trade Reg. Serv. ¶68,246.

§6.20. [1] United States v. E. I. Du Pont de Nemours & Co., 126 F. Supp. 27, 235 (N.D. Ill. 1954), rev'd, 353 U.S. 586 (1957). Compare People ex rel. Moloney v. Pullman's Palace Car Co., 175 Ill. 125, 153, 51 N.E. 664 (1898).

[2] Complaint §§20, 21, 22, 24, 30(b)(1), 30(b)(2), United States v. E. I. Du Pont de Nemours & Co., 126 F. Supp. 27, 235 (N.D. Ill. 1954), rev'd, 353 U.S. 586 (1957).

[3] See §5.15 *supra*.

eral Motors is paying more for its casings than independent suppliers ask. For if the rival rubber firms do not meet U.S. Rubber's price, it is difficult to understand upon what ground it is thought that they should obtain General Motors' business.

But what motive have the Du Ponts in causing General Motors to pay more than market prices for tires? Can they grow rich by selling to themselves at fancy figures? And if General Motors actually did pay more than market prices for tires, paint and a host of other products, it is difficult to understand how it could compete successfully with rival automobile manufacturers.

In the complaint against the Du Ponts it is alleged both that U.S. Rubber made unwarranted profits out of its sales to General Motors and that the latter obtained its tires at lower cost than its competitors, thus enhancing its size and power.[4] It would seem to follow that U.S. Rubber produced tires at lower cost than its competitors. Otherwise the statement would contradict itself. And if U.S. Rubber produced more efficiently, its rivals would stand in a poor position to complain of its success.

Perhaps the foregoing analysis rests upon assumptions of pure and perfect competition. Under conditions of pure competition, "selling costs," which exist in markets characterized by a degree of imperfect competition, would disappear.[5] The complaint against the Du Ponts states that General Motors was "giving," and had "arbitrarily granted," a substantial percentage of its business to U.S. Rubber.[6] Such language implies a market of rigid or "sticky" prices, possibly made so by reason of the effects of Section 2 of the Clayton Act.[7] Apart from the alleged combination, it suggests the absence of pure competition.

Sales among three companies under common control would reduce selling costs, thus enabling each concern to secure an advantage over its competitors. That advantage would be de-

---

[4] Complaint §§132, 133, United States v. E. I. Du Pont de Nemours & Co., 126 F. Supp. 27, 235 (N.D. Ill. 1954), rev'd, 353 U.S. 586 (1957). It is alleged in the complaint (§30(c)) that the defendants conspired to prevent diversification by General Motors into the chemical industry. At the same time it is alleged that the defendants agreed to divide the fields of activity among the three corporations (§65). It is difficult to understand how defendants can be both sued as a combination and also charged with division of territory. If a defendant constituted a single unit in violation of §2 of the Sherman Act, he could hardly conspire with himself in violation of §1. Compare The Sherman Act and the Enforcement of Competition, Discussion, 38 Am. Econ. Rev. 204, 206 (1948) (remarks by Mr. Watkins).

[5] Chamberlin, The Theory of Monopolistic Competition 126 (1938).

[6] Complaint §123, United States v. E. I. Du Pont de Nemours & Co., 126 F. Supp. 27, 235 (N.D. Ill. 1954), rev'd, 353 U.S. 586 (1957).

[7] Burling and Sheldon, Price Competition as Affected by the Robinson-Patman Act, 1 Wash. & Lee L. Rev. 31, 34 (1939); Goodyear Tire & Rubber Co. v. FTC, 92 F.2d 677 (6th Cir. 1937).

rived from the elimination of an element of monopoly — conditions of imperfect competition. It is doubtful whether public policy should favor the dissolution of the combination: an attack upon the monopolistic elements in the markets which made the combination profitable might achieve the same immediate results, if any, and also farther reaching benefits.[8]

§6.21. **Control of substitutes.** Another complaint against diversification is that it leads to the control of substitutes and hence to monopoly. Since diversification is required to carry a firm into the sale of substitute products, any argument against the control of substitutes may be considered an argument against a form of diversification. Thus it has been said:

> A business unit which enters upon the production of a substitute for its original product frequently does so to protect its investment in plant and good will. There is little inducement to such a concern to compete vigorously with itself.[1]

Particular attention has been paid to the entry of newspaper publishers into the field of radio broadcasting. In 1941 the Federal Communications Commission issued an order directing an investigation into applications for broadcasting licenses by persons publishing newspapers.[2] After much opposition had developed, the Commission finally dismissed the investigation and refused to adopt a general rule on the subject. In doing so, however, it voiced serious doubts as to the desirability of permitting newspaper publishers to operate radio broadcasting stations:

> . . . the Commission recognizes the serious problem involved in the broader field of the control of the media of mass communications and the importance of avoiding monopoly of the avenues of communicating fact and opinion to the public. All the Commissioners agree to the general principle that diversification of control of such media is desirable. . . . The Commission does not feel that it should deny a license merely because the applicant is engaged or interested in a particular type of business. However,

---

[8] It may be easier to obtain protective legislation to shelter an existing group in the economy than to open the door to the entry of a new group, simply because the existing participants in a trade have an established position and thus find it easier to round up votes. Palamountain, The Politics of Distribution (1955).

§6.21. [1] Hale, Trust Dissolution, 40 Colum. L. Rev. 615, 626 (1940). In that connection it has also been said: "The protection afforded by competition does not consist merely in the ability to play one trader off against another within a single market. It consists also in the ability to turn to substitute goods and to satisfy one's needs from the products of different industries." Edwards, Maintaining Competition: Requisites of a Governmental Policy 266 (1949).
[2] 8 F.C.C. 589 (1941).

it does not intend in granting licenses in the public interest to permit concentration of control in the hands of the few to the exclusion of the many . . .[3]

Similar views have been expressed by individual commissioners in cases involving specific applications. Thus Commissioner Fly said that a broadcast license should not be granted when the applicant controlled the only newspaper in the area.[4]

In the realm of public utilities, statutes have specifically prohibited certain types of diversification. Thus the Public Utilities Holding Company Act of 1935 provides that no holding company is to acquire the stock of both electric and gas utilities in the same area when state law prohibits such action.[5] A comparable limitation is found in the Communications Act of 1934.[6]

Control of substitutes, except for that achieved by patent control, can result only from diversification. Without the adding of additional commodities to the seller's line, he can scarcely be said to control substitutes for his basic commodity. On the other hand, it has never been contended that diversification necessarily leads to the control of substitutes. Indeed, the control of substitutes can only occur when diversification is narrowly limited. If diversification extends beyond one industry, it is unlikely that it will include a substitute product. Professor Burns declared that it was difficult to find actual examples of diversification motivated by a desire to control substitutes.[7]

As in the case of tying clauses, control of substitutes depends upon an element of monopoly in the sale of the original product. If a seller of butter enters the oleomargarine business, then, in order to create a wasteful effect, he must either monopolize the butter market or monopolize the oleomargarine market. Unless he accomplishes one of the two foregoing results, he will not have caused harm.[8] Such considerations lead to the conclusion that the mere fact of diversification into the field of substitute prod-

---

3 9 Fed. Reg. 702, 703 (1944). See also Conrad, Economic Aspects of Radio Regulation, 34 Va. L. Rev. 283, 291 (1948).

4 Barnes & Weiland, 8 F.C.C. 46, 54 (1940). Query whether a distinction should be drawn between the problem of substitute control in the field of radio broadcasting and elsewhere, in that radio stations broadcast news. (Is monopoly of the dissemination of news worse than other alleged monopolies?)

5 49 Stat. 817 (1935), 15 U.S.C. §79i.

6 48 Stat. 1087 (1934), 47 U.S.C.A. §314 (Supp. 1948). Complaints are heard from time to time that railroads have tried to monopolize transportation by air and motor carriers; regulatory commissions, responsive to demands of competitors, have largely prevented entry into such fields by the railroad companies. Celler Committee I, pt. 4A, at 277.

7 Burns, The Decline of Competition 454 (1936). Professor Burns also declared that substitute integration is not always easy to identify. Id. at 453.

8 Id. at 455.

ucts is not a cause of monopoly conditions. Thus Professor Burns said:

> The opportunity for postponing the introduction of new products or the utilization of new methods depends upon the degree of imperfection of the market. If new substitute products are made but sold at a high price with the object of maintaining the sales of older types, new non-integrated firms with no losses arising from obsolescence may enter the market. Moreover, if the new product is introduced by non-integrated firms, integrated firms whose sales are likely to be reduced may . . . fight for survival by entering the new field of production and may even hasten the decline of prices there.[9]

There are several statutory prohibitions against diversification into substitutes, but these relate chiefly to public utilities companies.[10] Since almost every public utility company enjoys some degree of horizontal monopoly, the statutes may be justified, but any prohibition upon trade in general might have unfortunate effects. In these times of a rapidly changing economy, business may have to run fast in order to stand still.[11] In other words, it may not be a question of diversification, but of the production of new products to take the place of old ones. Finally, an attempt to prevent diversification into substitute goods would involve serious administrative difficulties. In the last analysis, substitution is a question of degree, since almost every service or product competes against every other. It has often been remarked, for example, that consumers have preferred to buy new automobiles rather than to improve their housing conditions. To prevent diversification into substitutes, therefore, might well mean the prevention of diversification altogether.

§6.22. **Continuity of corporate existence.** An important effect of diversification is that it permits continuity of corporate exist-

---

[9] Id. at 456.

[10] Interstate Commerce Act, 24 Stat. 380 (1887), as amended, 49 U.S.C.A. §5; New York Public Service Law §70. But compare Stahlman v. FCC, 126 F.2d 124, 127 (D.C. Cir. 1942), wherein it was said: "If in this case it had been made to appear, as counsel for appellant insist, that the Commission's investigation [pursuant to order No. 79 of March 20, 1941] was solely for the purpose of the consideration or adoption of a hard and fast rule or policy, as the result of which newspaper owners may be placed in a proscribed class and thus made ineligible to apply for or receive broadcast licenses, we should be obliged to declare that such an investigation would be wholly outside of and beyond any of the powers with which Congress has clothed the Commission. For we have previously held that there is nothing in the Act which either prevents or prejudices the right of a newspaper, as such, to apply for and receive a license to operate a radio broadcast station."

[11] Devlin, Making Diversification Pay, 63 Mag. of Wall Street 88 (Nov. 5, 1938), where it is said: "The ability of a company successfully to develop new products and create new markets is the hallmark of corporate vitality and industrial leadership. . . ."

ence. Even though the product originally made has become obsolete and unsalable, the company may continue as prosperous as before. An interesting example is found in a recent annual report:

> Your company was originally started to manufacture husking pins and other hand husking equipment. As time went on the glove and mitten line was added and far outgrew the original products in volume of business. With the improvement of corn husking machines, demand for hand corn huskers dwindled to such small proportions that it was deemed advisable to dispose of this part of our business.[1]

Those who believe in the importance of new firms as promoters of competition[2] will, of course, find in diversification a cause of monopolistic conditions. They have seen many new fields of industry pre-empted by existing firms.[3] In other words, diversification prevents a corporation from declining or dying with its product. It perpetuates investments and management powers.

Mere perpetuation of corporate existence does not seem objectionable. While diversification may reduce the number of wholly new firms, the important question is whether that effect is undesirable. A going concern may be in a position to compete more avidly than a newcomer. Certainly the complaint that diversification leads to price-cutting suggests such a result. From the standpoint of costs, as suggested above, there may be considerable savings in the diversified, as opposed to the wholly new, enterprise. There is some efficiency in avoiding the closing up and reopening of a business venture. In other words, continuity of operation, however diversified, may in itself result in the saving of costs. But more important, an existing concern has facilities in the nature of purchasing agents, employment officers, accountants and the like, all of whom would have to be recruited anew for a separate venture. Although the new activity undoubtedly in-

§6.22. 1 Boss Manufacturing Co., 1948 Ann. Rep. 2 (Kewanee, 1949). Another firm said: ". . . new products . . . give promise of helping balance the scale for products which have felt the effect of retarded demand." Dow Chemical Co., 52d Ann. Rep. 1 (Midland, 1949). Similarly, a producer chose to add gold, oil, titanium, aluminum and phosphate products to its copper line to avoid frictions incident to liquidation and the starting of new firms. Kennecott Copper Corp., 39th Ann. Rep. (New York City, 1954). An enterprise which depended on diversification to survive is described in Celler Committee I, pt. 4A, at 954. An example of rediversifying is found in the Saco-Lowell Shops: that firm divested itself of producing machines other than for cotton textiles, and then, to meet hard times after 1896, returned to the field of multitype machine producer. Gibb, The Saco-Lowell Shops: Textile Machinery Building in New England 1813-1949, 291 (1950).

2 Oxenfeldt, New Firms and Free Enterprise 17 et seq. (1943). Celler Committee I, pt. 2B, at 933.

3 Oxenfeldt, New Firms and Free Enterprise 45 (1943).

creases the costs of maintaining such services, it probably does so at a less than proportional rate.

§6.23. **Avoidance of market appraisal of new ventures.** It may be urged that diversification avoids the test of the market place. Funds obtained from corporate earnings and applied to new ventures bypass the rigorous tests applied by investment bankers to wholly new ventures. If a single man dominates a corporation, his judgment alone may be responsible for entry into a new line of business. No concurrence from the investing public is necessary.

It is true that diversification into new lines may be accomplished without the floating of securities in the investment market. Of course, the question relates as much to horizontal or vertical integration as it does to diversification. And it must be noted that the complaint cannot be made as to capital raised from normal investment sources: at most, the argument relates to the reinvestment of earnings. A clever observer has noted that a company which is in a position to direct its earnings into new facilities would also be favorably situated to attract new capital from investors.[1] In other words, private investment of earnings in diversified lines is not objectionable because the same result could be reached through the flotation of additional securities.

Retention and reinvestment of earnings does tend to increase total investment. If earnings were all distributed to stockholders in the form of dividends, they would, as indicated above, be heavily penalized by taxation. Again, at least some of the shareholders would use those earnings for current consumption rather than save them for capital purposes.[2] Thus the whole practice of reinvesting earnings runs into the familiar controversy in regard to "oversaving" and "underinvestment." Although the oversaving theory was once popular,[3] it is difficult to understand how general standards of living can be raised without additional investment of capital.

§6.24. **Subsidies to ancillary products.** A similar argument is that inefficiently made products are subsidized through diversification. A firm may remain profitable despite the fact that one of its products is made in a wasteful manner.[1] If this is so, it vio-

§6.23.   1 Buchanan, The Economics of Corporate Enterprise 256 (1940). See also Sweezy, Socialism 221 et seq. (1949) (attempt to prove that socialist economy will not necessarily result in faulty allocation of resources).

2 Buchanan, The Economics of Corporate Enterprise 257 (1940).

3 Simons, Economic Policy for a Free Society 185 (1948).

§6.24.   1 Thorp and Crowder, The Structure of Industry 666 (TNEC Monograph No. 27, 1941). Compare Complaint §§30(b)(4), 30(b)(5), 30(b)(6) in United States v. E. I. Du Pont de Nemours & Co., 126 F. Supp. 27, 235 (N.D. Ill. 1954), rev'd, 353

lates one of the canons of competition laid down by Professor Edwards:

> Traders must be responsive to incentives of profit and loss; that is, they must not be so large, so diversified, so devoted to political rather than commercial purposes, so subsidized, or otherwise so unconcerned with results in a particular market that their policies are not affected by ordinary commercial incentives arising out of that market.[2]

It will be noted that the complaint just mentioned is not wholly different from that of price-cutting. In both instances the product is sold below its true cost. In price-cutting, however, there is a deliberate effort to injure a competitor.

Diversification does of course raise problems of cost accounting. When diversification is of the divergent type, it will almost certainly give rise to joint costs. Convergent diversification may also result in joint costs, and even if the products are wholly unrelated, it will still be necessary to allocate certain overhead costs, such as executives' salaries and specialized services, among the several products.

Many methods are used to allocate joint costs. Sometimes the two products are made to bear costs of production in proportion to their weight or bulk.[3] Upon other occasions, market values of the various commodities are used to allocate joint costs.[4] It is easy to demonstrate that such methods are arbitrary and can result in fantastic computation.[5] Professor Viner commonly used an illustration in which a gram of radium was extracted from twenty tons of ore. The radium, of course, was of great value but the slag (by-product) was sold for a pittance. If, however, the allocation of costs were made upon the basis of weight, the result would be the production of radium for almost nothing.

From a theoretical point of view, it is possible to allocate joint costs properly if the entrepreneur is able to vary the output of the

---

U.S. 586 (1957); TNEC Hearings, pt. 19, at 10,672, 1939 (steel mill official testified that some products were profitable and others not). Compare Eckert, ed., Problems in Price Control: Pricing Standards 317, 339, 344 (OPA, 1947); Franck, The Changing Character of Product Price Adjustments, in Eckert, ed., Problems in Price Control: Pricing Standards 175, 193, 204, 225 (OPA 1957); Director of Price Stabilization CPR 22, Manufacturer's General Ceiling Price Regulation SR 2, 16 Fed. Reg. 11,809 (Nov. 21, 1951).

[2] Edwards, Maintaining Competition: Requisites of a Governmental Policy 9 (1949).

[3] TNEC Hearings, pt. 17-A, at 10,092.

[4] Id. at 10,056. This method also is faulty. Kreps, Joint Costs in the Chemical Industry, 44 Q.J. Econ. 416, 420 et seq. (1930).

[5] Canning, Cost Accounting, 4 Encyc. Soc. Sci. 475, 477 (1931).

several products.[6]   A dispute continues among economists as to whether it is always possible to vary the proportion of the various products produced by joint methods.[7]   Granting that such variation is possible, then familiar marginal principles permit a theoretical allocation of costs.[8]   On the other hand, there is little to indicate that such a computation is practical in an actual business situation.[9]

Similar considerations affect the allocation of overhead costs. Again, several methods of effecting such allocation are used by cost accountants.   Only upon marginal principles, however, would it be possible to effect an accurate computation.[10]   And the difficulties involved in any such attempt have led a number of economists to the conclusion that overhead costs cannot be apportioned properly.[11]

It is thus apparent that diversification may so cloud a concern's cost structure as to result in the shelter of inefficiently made products; a given commodity may be subsidized without the knowledge of its producer.   Admitting that such sheltering can occur, it must be noted that the only means of avoiding the cost allocation problems outlined above would be to prohibit all variations in manufacture and distribution.   In other words, a manufacturer would be permitted to make only one model, size or style of a commodity.   A distributor could vend but a single item.   Only then would all common costs be eliminated.   While it might not

6 Conference on Price Research, Committee on Price Determination, Cost Behavior and Price Policy 179 (1943).   In Kreps, Joint Costs in the Chemical Industry, 44 Q.J. Econ. 416, 427 (1930), it is said: "Neither accountants nor economists have been able to devise a method which will yield [joint] cost figures that do not contain a large element of arbitrariness."

7 Conference on Price Research, Committee on Price Determination, Cost Behavior and Price Policy 176 (1943); Kreps, Joint Costs in the Chemical Industry, 44 Q.J. Econ. 416, 452 (1930).

8 Viner, Cost, 4 Encyc. Soc. Sci. 466, 473 (1931).

9 Conference on Price Research, Committee on Price Determination, Cost Behavior and Price Policy 177 et seq. (1943); Price and Price Policies 201 (Hamilton ed. 1938); Clark, The Possibility of a Scientific Electrical Rate System, 27 Proceedings Am. Econ. Assn. 243, 246 (1937) (problem of cost of electric current consumed versus cost of poles and wires); Dickerson, The Industry Earnings Standard, in Eckert, ed., Problems in Price Control: Pricing Standards 27, 70, 75 (OPA, 1947) (allocation of overheard costs and profits varies widely among manufacturers even within the same industry); Brems, Product Equilibrium under Monopolistic Competition 115 (1951) (neither useful nor possible to allocate costs among products of multiproduct firm using same dealers and facilities).   But compare Early, Recent Developments in Cost Accounting and "Marginal Analysis," 63 J. Pol. Econ. 227 (1955).

10 Conference on Price Research, Committee on Price Determination, Cost Behavior and Price Policy 181, 183 (1943).

11 Garver and Hansen, Principles of Economics 114 (3d ed. 1947).   Compare Gillespie-Rogers-Pyatt Co. v. Bowles, 144 F.2d 361, 365 (Em. App. 1944).

be impossible so to confine manufacturers, it would obviously be inefficient to compel distributors thus to narrow the goods they sell. Such a program would close every department store.

§6.25. **Price rigidity.** Diversification is also said to permit the maintenance of prices. Even though demand for a single item is slack and output must be restricted, a diversified producer need not reduce the price of that particular product. When firms are turning out more than one product, the profits from one part of their output may be used to compensate for the losses arising from restriction of other parts of the output. That is, a firm may want to maintain prices for fear of "spoiling" the future market by price reductions. The judgment of the managers might be that, viewed over a long period, the loss should be incurred in the expectation that the situation would be temporary and that future profits would be greater by virtue of their not having spoiled the market by price reductions. The restriction may be financed in many ways. Use of profits from other parts of the output is one possibility.[1]

Price rigidity differs from the sheltering of an inefficiently made product in that it suggests that the commodity is priced too high rather than too low. But it does involve the problems of common costs outlined above. In addition, if a firm diversifies so as to avoid seasonal or cyclical trends, it may thus be enabled to support its price structures. A maker of Christmas tree ornaments who diversifies into the knitting of bathing suits may regularize his receipts in such a manner as to avoid the necessity of reducing the price of his primary product in periods of low seasonal demand.[2] This is obviously a contradiction of the argument, previously discussed,[3] that diversification leads to price-cutting. Prices cannot be both too rigid and too fluid at the same time and place. Thus to some degree the argument that diversification leads to price rigidity is balanced by the allegation that it leads to sales below cost. And there is little in available literature to indicate that diversification is an important cause of price rigidity.

§6.26. **Excessive selling costs; Increased capital requirements.** It is further urged that diversification compels competitors to diversify also. When one producer starts selling a "full line," all

---

§6.25. [1] Thorp and Crowder, The Structure of Industry 668 (TNEC Monograph No. 27, 1941).

[2] Time is an important factor. A merchant does not cut the price of a commodity because a single day's sales are poor. He lets his other goods carry the commodity for some period of time.

[3] See §6.17 *supra*.

others must do likewise in order to remain in the market.[1] The effect then may be to increase the amount of capital required to enter the industry. A new enterpriser may find that he is unable to get dealers to handle his new and better product unless he can introduce a complete line and the advertising services to go with it. This increase in capital requirements automatically reduces the number of persons who are able to start new enterprises.[2] And it is urged that such a raising of capital requirements is inherently wasteful.[3]

The complaint that diversification leads to excessive selling costs is related to the argument against the spreading of trademarks. For the value of a trade-mark results from advertising, and vigorous attacks are constantly leveled at merchandising expenditures.[4] In modern economic thinking sales expenses are suspect.[5] As to divergent diversification, however, no such argument can be made because the products are not sold together. We may therefore test the thesis that divergent diversification is efficient, whereas convergent diversification is wasteful.[6] The argument would run that the latter type of diversification related only to sales and that selling expenses are uneconomic. On the other hand, it has been said that divergent diversification is not necessarily efficient. It may cause plant expansion beyond the optimum scale.[7] Again, convergent diversification may contain

§6.26. [1] Thorp and Crowder, The Structure of Industry 652 (TNEC Monograph No. 27, 1941).

[2] Raymond, The Limitist 36 (1947); Celler Committee I, pt. 2B, at 932.

[3] Chamberlin, The Theory of Monopolistic Competition 123 (3d ed. 1938).

[4] Simons, Economic Policy for a Free Society 71 (1948). Compare National Industrial Conference Board, Mergers and the Law 88 (1929), where it is said: ". . . most manufacturers are constrained to build up their own sales forces and to maintain their own advertising campaigns. This practice has resulted in excessive duplication of selling effort and an enormous waste in advertising outlays. Not infrequently a whole line of similar products may be advertised just as effectively, and with no greater cost, than a single product in the line. The same situation applies to the maintenance of selling agencies, distributing warehouses and like facilities."

[5] Chamberlin, The Theory of Monopolistic Competition 120 et seq. (3d ed. 1938). Professor Chamberlin said at page 123: "Cost of production includes all expenses which must be met in order to provide the commodity or service, transport it to the buyer, and put it into his hands ready to satisfy his wants. Cost of selling includes all outlays made in order to secure a demand, or a market, for the product. The former costs create utilities in order that demands may be satisfied; the latter create and shift the demands themselves."

[6] Compare People ex rel. Tiffany & Co. v. Campbell, 144 N.Y. 166, 38 N.E. 990 (1894); Richmond Guano Co. v. Farmer's Ginnery Co., 126 Fed. 712 (4th Cir. 1903); Burk v. Mead, 159 Ind. 252, 64 N.E. 880 (1902) (doctrine of ultra vires applied to convergent diversification).

[7] Thorp and Crowder, The Structure of Industry 664 (TNEC Monograph No. 27, 1941).

elements of efficiency. As we have seen,[8] the practice of "rounding out the line" is indulged in for the benefit of the distributor. Thus a manufacturer practicing convergent diversification may partially replace a wholesaler.[9] To the extent that he does so, he may be able to function at a reduced cost and thus to increase efficiency. Professor Burns suggested that integration of this type may secure technical economics of production.[10]

In these circumstances it is difficult to arrive at any conclusion regarding the alleged inefficiency of convergent diversification. Perhaps market forces can be counted upon to effect satisfactory adjustments.[11]

§6.27. **Conclusions.** In the larger sense, most of the alleged vices of diversification should be blamed upon the lack of pure[1] and perfect competition. Diversification is only the surface cause of many economic faults whose roots lie in a degree of horizontal monopoly. Competitive imperfections account for much of the remainder: lack of organized markets,[2] buyers' inadequate knowledge, absence of standardized commodities and, above all, the factor of time prevent goods from moving as rapidly and prices as freely as required for maximum utilization of resources.[3]

[8] §6.7 *supra.*

[9] Id. at 670.

[10] Burns, The Decline of Competition 446 (1936). See also National Industrial Conference Board, Mergers and the Law 89 (1929). Diversification may raise barriers to entry into competition; but if such integration involves significant economies, it may really be a question of indivisibility.

[11] One of the outstanding examples of convergent diversification is Standard Brands, Inc. Its delivery service for Fleischmann's Yeast was used as the nucleus of a system of distributing all types of groceries. Recently, however, the company has abandoned the use of its own delivery system. Standard Brands, Inc., 1948 Ann. Rep. 4 (New York City, 1949). Apparently an oil company has similarly abandoned the sale of sporting goods through filling stations. Phillips Petroleum Co., 1948 Ann. Rep. 18 (Bartlesville, 1949).

When a trade-mark is applied to a new commodity, the question whether its alleged monopoly effect is thereby increased is a difficult one. Professor Burns said in The Decline of Competition 447-448 (1936): ". . . emphasis upon brand names being an inevitable accompaniment of advertising, attempts to increase the return per unit of advertising expenditure sometimes lead to the use of a brand name for a variety of products. The advertising of each product tends, not only to promote the sales of that product, but also to make the brand name under which it is sold more familiar, and to promote the sales of other products of the same name."

6.27. [1] Chamberlin, The Theory of Monopolistic Competition 6 (3d ed. 1938).

[2] Compare Hale, Agreements Among Competitors, 33 Minn. L. Rev. 331, 356 (1949).

[3] In United States v. General Motors Corp., 121 F.2d 376, 398 (7th Cir. 1941), *cert. denied*, 314 U.S. 618 (1941), the court declared that a dealer would suffer a loss if his "franchise" was canceled. No doubt market imperfections account for such truth as may be contained in that statement.

Coupled with a degree of horizontal monopoly, diversification may serve as a basis for undesirable conduct. It may, for instance, supply reserve funds for a price-cutting foray. Or it may permit an attempt to monopolize a substitute product, thus adding additional force to a horizontal monopoly power. But this study suggests that diversification is not monopolistic per se.[4] The mere fact that a firm produces or distributes more than one commodity should not constitute an infringement of the antitrust laws. Professor Edwards can be taken to have almost admitted as much.[5] And even if diversification contained a considerable element of monopoly, its efficiency and stabilizing effect might compel us to accept it in considerable degree. In addition, the administrative difficulties in its prevention might well prove insuperable.[6]

Diversification may lead to tremendous size without horizontal monopoly. A concern may acquire large resources and remain without undue strength in any one market. This, of course, is the old problem of wealth. Today the crushing burden of taxation can be counted upon to rapidly dissipate the fortunes of natural persons. There remain the corporations, which gather the savings of millions into managed focus. The Supreme Court has said that mere size is not an offense.[7] But Professors Simons and Edwards argued that a vast concentration of financial power, even in the absence of monopoly, offends the public interest.[8] In one old decision it was quaintly said:

[4] It is interesting to note that the Du Pont Company, officially charged with violation of the Sherman Act, seems to have been less prosperous than two of its less diversified competitors. According to Fitch Individual Stock Bulletins, Du Pont profits in 1939 were $7.66 per share. In that year Dow Chemical Co. earned $.94 a share and Monsanto Chemical Co. $1.34 a share. Du Pont's 1948 report shows profits of $13.12 a share; Fitch shows Dow's 1948 profit at $3.72 a share; and Monsanto's 1948 report shows its profit for that year $3.95 a share. In other words, Du Pont's profits rose 71½ per cent, while Dow increased its profits 296 per cent and Monsanto 195 per cent.

[5] Edwards, Maintaining Competition: Requisites of a Governmental Policy 130 (1949). Compare id. at 100.

[6] In the General Motors case the company could, so far as extension of credit to dealers alone was concerned, have merely permitted delayed payment on its own books. Certainly there is little authority to suggest that such a practice is unlawful. Again, the question of where protection of good will is justified raises difficult problems. But see United States v. General Motors Corp., 121 F.2d 376, 407 (7th Cir. 1941), wherein the court says that motive is immaterial; Celler Committee I, pt. 1, at 135-136.

[7] United States v. United States Steel Corp., 251 U.S. 417, 451 (1920): "The Corporation is undoubtedly of impressive size and it takes an effort of resolution not to be affected by it or to exaggerate its influence. But we must adhere to the law and the law does not make mere size an offence . . . ."

[8] Thus Professor Edwards said: "Bigness gives power whether it is attained in one industry or in many. Great size is common to all giant enterprises whether

All experience has shown that large accumulations of property, in hands likely to keep it intact for a long period, are dangerous to the public weal. Having perpetual succession, any kind of a corporation has peculiar facilities for such accumulation, and most governments have found it necessary to exercise great caution in their grants to corporate powers . . . Freed, as such bodies are, from the sure bound to the schemes of individuals — the grave — they are able to add field to field and power to power, until they become entirely too strong for that society which is made up of those whose plans are limited by a single life.[9]

Obviously there is a relationship between diversification and size: a tiny concern can scarcely produce many items. Thus Thorp and Crowder found that the fifty largest corporations in the United States were active in making 2043 products, that number constituting almost half the number of products distinguished in the 1937 Census of Manufacturers.[10]   Three fourths of the largest concerns made 100 or less products; one made 320 products; and the least diversified made only 6.[11]   There is not, however, any necessary correlation between diversification and size, since an enterprise can grow large in the production or distribution of a single commodity.

Whether wealth alone is objectionable is a subject dealt with in Chapter 8. What should be done about it, if it is, is likewise discussed in the same place. All we can conclude here is that diversification as such is not monopolistic.

---

their strength is based upon monopoly in a single large industry, upon vertical integration, or upon a conglomerate union of activities which are industrially unrelated. The significance of bigness alone is seen most readily in the case of the conglomerate enterprise, in which power due to size is not reinforced by power due to monopoly or to vertical integration." Edwards, Maintaining Competition: Requisites of a Governmental Policy 100 (1949). See also Simons, Economic Policy for a Free Society 95 (1948).

At page 52, Professor Simons said: "Even if the much advertised economies of gigantic financial combinations were real, sound policy would wisely sacrifice these economies to preservation of more economic freedom and equality." And, "We should look toward a situation in which the size of ownership units in every industry is limited by the minimum size of operating plant requisite to efficient, but highly specialized, production — and even more narrowly limited, if ever necessary to the maintenance of freedom and enterprise." Id. at 60. Compare Handler, Unfair Competition, 21 Iowa L. Rev. 175, 208 (1936); Celler Committee I. pt. 2A, at 379; but compare id., pt. 2A, at 545 (large resources needed for research).

[9] Central Railway Co. v. Collins, 40 Ga. 582, 630 (1869). Compare State ex. rel. Steubenville Gas Co. v. Taylor, 55 Ohio St. 61, 65, 44 N.E. 513, 515 (1896).

[10] Thorp and Crowder, The Structure of Industry 586 (TNEC Monograph No. 27, 1941). See also Wells, International Paper: Diversification of Products Is Key to Company's Steady Growth, 30 Barron's No. 23, p. 17 (1950).

[11] Thorp and Crowder, The Structure of Industry 595 (TNEC Monograph No. 27, 1941).

CHAPTER 7

Dispersion: Monopoly and Geographic Integration*

§7.1. Nature of dispersion. Producers and consumers are separated by space. Markets exist only in relationship to geographic areas. Expansion of the territory in which a business enterprise operates may affect its character as a monopoly.[1] It is not surprising, therefore, that many of the questions arising in the enforcement of the antitrust laws originate in the spatial growth of profit-seeking firms.

In this study the concept of geographic expansion is termed "dispersion." Such "territorial integration"[2] is, like vertical integration and diversification, an aspect of the "shape" of an enterprise rather than its size.[3] As we shall see, however, dispersion is intimately related to the more readily recognized problems of "horizontal" size and wealth. And while it is possible to consider monopoly in its several aspects for purposes of analysis, in formulating policy only the whole is significant.

* This chapter originally appeared under the same title as an article in 30 Texas Law Review 423 (1952). It has been revised and new authorities have been added. The Appendix, recording a field study, is omitted from this book.

§7.1. 1 Thus it has been said: ". . . private monopoly power comes into being as a local power — relative to a place. This means that the sales territory in which private monopoly power is exercised in the first instance is a regional area or zone." Mund, Government and Business 113 (1950).

2 Burns, The Decline of Competition 456 (1936). In the public utility field the term "integration" is used in the opposite sense, to connote a compact, nondispersed area served by a single firm. Ritchie, Integration under Section 10(c) of the Public Utility Holding Company Act, 41 Mich. L. Rev. 1, 20 (1942).

3 Whether the geographic factor should be treated as an imperfection of competition or as part of the definition of a commodity is perhaps open to question. Compare Chamberlin, The Theory of Monopolistic Competition 62 (3d ed. 1939); Hale, Trust Dissolution: "Atomizing" Business Units of Monopolistic Size, 40 Colum. L. Rev. 615, 627 (1940). Compare §3.7 *supra*.

Whether local or interstate commerce is involved may make a significant difference in terms of legal results. In this study, however, no attempt is made to estimate the boundaries of the commerce clause of the Federal Constitution. U.S. Const., Art. I, §8. See §1.6 *supra*. Nor are we concerned with the famous basing point controversy, involving systems used by competitors in the quotation of prices and carriage costs, or the method of stating prices adopted by individual firms.

§7.2. **Nature and extent of dispersion.** Geography affects the location of economic activity in many ways: producers seek easy access both to raw materials and markets; factors of climate and population cannot be overlooked.[1] Means of transportation and communication are of particular importance: installation of rail lines opens new territory to economic development, and improvements in highway carriage profoundly alter the pattern of competition.[2]

In the nature of things, dispersion is a loose notion. Markets are not marked by bright boundaries. Penetration of new territory is always a matter of degree.[3] And the means of expansion vary from firm to firm: the mail order house relies on the postal service; chain sellers establish local retail stores; the Fuller Brush Company sends its solicitors to housewives' doors.[4] In other words, enterprises canvass consumers in different degrees of intensity, and the device used for penetration may affect the "depth"[5] of the dispersion achieved.

No data have been found to indicate the amount of dispersion prevalent in our economy, nor do we know whether it is on the increase or decline.[6] In fact, one may well doubt whether statistics of value could be compiled. It is nevertheless clear that many

§7.2. [1] Hoover, The Location of Economic Activity, in The Growth of the American Economy 580 (Williamson ed. 1944); Celler Committee I, pt. 4A, at 109, 640; pt. 6A, at 212, 790; Thompson, Address to Shareholders 16 (International Nickel Co. of Canada, Ltd., Toronto, Apr. 25, 1951) (essential that nickel rolling mills be located near customers so as to assure rapid delivery and response to changing requirements); Standard & Poor, Manual of Issues on the Midwest Stock Exchange 62 (May 17, 1950) (Greif Bros. Cooperage Co. maintains shops adjacent to customers' plants); Chrysler Corp., 1950 Ann. Rep. 5 (Detroit, 1951). Even emotional factors are relevant. Abrahamson,: The Automobile Tire — Forms of Marketing in Combat, in Price and Price Policies 83, 90 (Hamilton ed. 1938); Adams, The Automobile — a Luxury Becomes a Necessity, id. at 30 n.1 (industry moved to area where bankers more optimistic).

Geography may be irrelevant in the absence of competition. Hoover, The Location of Economic Activity 10 (1948). For an analysis of factors influencing the placing of new plants to compete with established factories, consult, e.g., Lerner and Singer, Some Notes on Duopoly and Spatial Competition, 45 J. Pol. Econ. 145, 153 (1937).

[2] Hoover, The Location of Economic Activity, c. 2 (1948); Stocking and Watkins, Monopoly and Free Enterprise 21 (1951); Sears, Roebuck in Rio, 41 Fortune No. 2, pp. 78, 80 (1950) (lack of transportation atomizes Brazil's markets). Compare Nelson, Price Behavior and Business Policy 271 (TNEC Monograph No. 1, 1940).

[3] Burns, The Decline of Competition 456 (1936). Perhaps the extent of dispersion is identical with the size of market area. Compare Hoover, The Location of Economic Activity 222 n.5 (1948); May's Drug Stores, Inc. v. State Tax Commission, 242 Iowa 319, 45 N.W.2d 245, 257 (1950).

[4] See Orangeburg v. Farmer, 181 S.C. 143, 186 S.E. 783 (1936).

[5] "Depth" is defined *infra* notes 16, 17.

[6] Compare Quinn, Human Ecology 348, 350 (1950) with authorities cited *infra* §7.3, note 25.

degrees of dispersion are found on the current business scene.
Despite the growth of chain retailing, there still exist independent storekeepers who do business from a single and often small
stand.[7] Relatively little chains, consisting of five to a hundred
outlets, abound in many areas;[8] at the same time, forty chains in
the food field alone operate more than a hundred stores.[9] Many
sellers offer their wares in two, three, or four adjacent states.[10]
Others do business in broader regions and approach nationwide
distribution.[11] Manufacturers of some size commonly sell in all
of the forty-eight states, even though their plants may not be
distributed in all parts of the country.[12] Retailers have started
to cross international boundaries, and producers frequently des-
patch their products to the ends of the earth.[13] International

[7] Nystrom, Retail Trade, 13 Encyc. Soc. Sci. 346, 352 (1934); Twentieth Century
Fund, Does Distribution Cost Too Much? 140 (1939). Compare §7.12 *infra*, note 5.

[8] Porter v. Cole, 66 F. Supp. 11 (N.D. Tex. 1946), *aff'd*, 157 F.2d 856 (5th
Cir. 1946); Standard & Poor, Manual of Issues on the Midwest Stock Exchange 124
(May 17, 1950) (Northern Illinois Corp. finances automobile, etc. sales in ten small
cities); In re A. H. L. Building Corp., 79 F.2d 823 (7th Cir. 1935) (19 restaurants in
one city); United States v. Spotless Cleaners, 6 F. Supp. 725 (S.D.N.Y. 1934) (32 stores
in one city); Standard & Poor *supra* at 95 (33 retail furniture stores in five states);
Jewel Tea Co., 1950 Ann. Rep. 25 (Barrington, 1951); Standard & Poor, Standard
Listed Stocks 561 (Jan. 2, 1951) (154 retail food stores in environs of Chicago).

[9] Fulda, Food Distribution in United States, 99 U. Pa. L. Rev. 1051, 1055 n.18
(1951). While the chain store idea is an old one, there was an upsurge in the
decade following World War I, at the end of which chains made 21.9 per cent of
the retail sales in the United States. Nystrom, Retail Trade, 13 Encyc. Soc. Sci. 346,
351 (1934). A reduction in the size of newspaper chains has recently been noted, but
they are said to account for 53.8 per cent of all newspaper circulation. Commission on Freedom of the Press, A Free and Responsible Press 42 (1947); compare
Celler Committee I, pt. 6A, at 370.

[10] Standard & Poor, Manual of Issues on the Midwest Stock Exchange 13 (May
17, 1950) (W. H. Barber Co., wholesaler of gasoline and turpentine); Middle South
Utilities, Inc., Prospectus 20 (Nov. 17, 1949); Fitch Investors Service, Thorofare
Markets, Inc. (Aug. 10, 1950) (89 groceries in three states).

[11] National Dairy Products Corp., 1949 Ann. Rep. 28 (New York City, 1950);
Beneficial Industrial Loan Corp., 1948 Ann. Rep. 14 (Wilmington, 1949) (475
"personal" loan offices in thirty-four states and Canada); W. T. Grant Co., 1948
Ann. Rep. 19 (New York City, 1949) (482 stores in thirty-nine states).

[12] Standard & Poor, Manual of Issues on the Midwest Stock Exchange 122, 123,
125 (May 17, 1950) (Whirlpool Corp., Advance Aluminum Castings Corp., Carr-Con-
solidated Biscuit Co.); TNEC Hearings, pt. 19, at 10,583; Pittsburgh Plate Glass Co.,
1950 Ann. Rep. 10 (Pittsburgh, 1951); E. I. du Pont de Nemours & Co., 1948 Ann.
Rep. 50 (Wilmington, 1949).

[13] Fitch Investors Service, Sears, Roebuck & Co. (Oct. 10, 1950); Abbott Laboratories, 1949 Ann. Rep. 24 (North Chicago, 1950) (operates in Australia, Italy, and
intermediate points); Standard Brands, Inc., 1948 Ann. Rep. 13 (New York City,
1949) (plants in Norway and South Africa); Philip Morris & Co., Ltd., 1950 Ann.
Rep. 16 (New York City, 1951) (warehouses and leaf markets in United States;
sources of tobacco supply in Near East shown on map); Electric Bond & Share Co.,
1948 Ann. Rep. 9 (New York City, 1949) (electric service supplied in many states
of Central and South America); Procter & Gamble Co., 1947 Ann. Rep. 12 (Cincinnati, 1948) (subsidiaries in Canada, Cuba, Philippines, etc.).

Harvester distributes its machines directly in nineteen foreign states; and in areas ranging from Sweden to Australia it sells through some five hundred independent jobbers.[14] Westinghouse ships its electrical equipment to every territory free from Soviet domination.[15]

To a large extent the degree of dispersion reflects over-all size: the larger the enterprise, the greater the area in which it does business. The factor of "depth," however, is also significant. By "depth" is meant the ratio of resources employed to area occupied. In the oil industry, for example, we find firms ranging in size and scope from the mighty Esso with its world-wide sources and sales to regional refiners distributing in several states.[16] No doubt there is considerable correlation between total assets and geographic expansion. But there are firms in the trade, with approximately the same resources, which operate in markedly varying territories.[17] Some, therefore, concentrate their activities and penetrate their restricted areas more "deeply."

[14] International Harvester Co., 1948 Ann. Rep. 28 (Chicago), 1950 Ann. Rep. 8, 10, 24.

[15] Westinghouse Abroad, 41 Fortune No. 2, p. 76 (1950). A manufacturer may sell some of his products over a wider area than others. General Mills, Inc., 23d Ann. Rep. 21 (Minneapolis, 1951) (national and regional brands). Governmental units are of varying size. E.g., Morgan, The Small Community: Foundation of Democratic Life 71 (1942). We know little of the spatial mobility of human beings. Quinn, Human Ecology 389 (1950).

[16] Standard Oil Co. of New Jersey, 1949 Ann. Rep. 20 (New York City, 1950), 1950 Ann. Rep. 20 (1951); Lion Oil Co., 1948 Ann. Rep. 10 (El Dorado, Ark., 1949) (markets in central United States from Minnesota to Florida, from Michigan to Louisiana); Derby Oil Co., 1950 Ann. Rep. 8 (Wichita, 1951) (markets in Colorado, Illinois, Iowa, Kansas, Minnesota, Missouri, Nebraska, New Mexico, North Dakota, South Dakota, Texas, Wisconsin). No doubt there are many refiners who sell in considerably smaller areas than Lion and Derby. As to the number of dealers a manufacturer should utilize in a specific area, compare McNair and Hansen, Problems in Marketing 193 (1949); Note, 63 Harv. L. Rev. 1010, 1011 (1950).

[17] The following tabulation has been prepared to illustrate differences in degrees of depth:

Enterprises	1949 Gross Sales	Sales Area
Texas Co.	$1,077,270,000	Entire U.S.A. and some foreign areas.
Gulf Oil Corp.	1,150,094,000	Thirty-seven states east of Mississippi River except Wisconsin and plus Arkansas, Louisiana, and Texas; also parts of several European nations.
Standard Oil Co. of Indiana	1,158,124,000	Middle-western U.S.A.; two western states; part of eastern seaboard.

Note the considerable variation in sales area for companies with approximately the same gross receipts. Sources: Standard & Poor, Standard Corporation Records 1502, 7137 (1951); Moody's Investors Service, Industrial Securities 2811 (1950); Texas Co., 1948 Ann. Rep. 8, 15 (New York City, 1949), 1950 Ann. Rep. 18 (1951); Gulf Oil Corp., 1950 Ann. Rep. 14, 24 (Pittsburgh, 1951); Standard Oil Co. of Indiana, 1948 Ann. Rep. 12 (Chicago, 1949). See also §7.4 infra, notes 3, 4. Of course the firms

§7.3. **Efficiency of dispersion.** Several factors induce companies to disperse their activities. Perhaps most important are the earnings to be realized in new markets as diminishing returns affect the old. Apparently a point of saturation is reached for a single brand in a given territory beyond which additional sales effort fails to yield commensurate returns.[1] The fact that over-all growth is often accompanied by territorial expansion[2] suggests that firms are actively influenced by the factor of diminishing returns.

If the product to be sold demands heavy advertising expenditure, the existence of magazines and radio networks with nationwide coverage may make national distribution economical.[3] Vertical integration back to sources of raw materials leads the steel companies into Venezuela and oil refiners into the Sinai Peninsula.[4]

---

may also differ in the number and size of dealers per square mile covered; that is, the foregoing tabulation is a superficial study of depth.

§7.3. [1] Mr. G. Bowman Kreer of McCann-Erickson, Inc., suggested the foregoing application of the doctrine of diminishing returns. He illustrated his theory by reference to a bottler of a new soft drink who commenced sales within a single city. At some point of sales effort the bottler found that he could capture an increased share of the soft drink market in the single city only by disproportionate effort. Accordingly, he expanded his sales area to include additional towns. Perhaps the facts found in Goldberg Corp. v. Levy, 170 Misc. 292, 9 N.Y.S.2d 304 (Sup. Ct. 1938), also substantiate the foregoing theory. Compare Chapman, Concentration of Banking 306 (1934); Louis K. Liggett Co. v. Lee, 288 U.S. 517, 534 (1933). The small population of Milwaukee was a factor in pushing beer sales throughout the country; big home markets of New York and Philadelphia needed no out-of-town sales effort. Cochran, History of the Pabst Brewing Company 79 (1948).

[2] Gulf Oil Corp., 1950 Ann. Rep. 24 (Pittsburgh, 1951); Abbott Laboratories, 1949 Ann. Rep. 23 (North Chicago, 1950); Beneficial Industrial Loan Corp., 1950 Ann. Rep. 6, 10 (Wilmington, 1951). Another fact suggesting the accuracy of the diminishing returns theory is that firms sometimes attempt to find the total quantitative market for a product by the "market saturation" test. In such a test a small area is selected and huge quantities of advertising are displayed there. The effort is to find the most effective amount of sales effort. Brown, Marketing and Distribution Research 161 (rev. ed. 1949); Cochran, History of the Pabst Brewing Company 31 (1948) (in 1857, Pabst had an office on Randolph Street in Chicago and was already trying to sell on a nationwide market).

[3] Stocking and Watkins, Monopoly and Free Enterprise 73 (1951). Perhaps the Parker Pen Company and the National Pressure Cooker Company afford examples of firms dispersed to take advantage of national magazine and radio advertising. Standard & Poor, Manual of Issues on the Midwest Stock Exchange 118, 130 (May 17, 1950). Geographic dispersion was a factor in about half of the industries studied for savings in nationwide promotion and distribution systems requiring considerable scale. Bain, Advantages of the Large Firm, 20 J. Marketing 336, 344 (1956).

[4] Celler Committee I, pt. 4A, at 217 (millions spent in searching globe for new sources of iron ore); Socony-Vacuum Oil Co., 1948 Ann. Rep. 15 (New York City, 1949); Standard Oil Co. of New Jersey, 1950 Ann. Rep. 16 (New York City, 1951); Gulf Oil Corp., 1950 Ann. Rep. 16 (Pittsburgh, 1951) (Barbados, British Honduras, Canada, Cuba, Denmark, Kuwait, Mozambique, Tunisia, Venezuela). A large mining concern prospected some 24,000 square miles in a recent year and made

Sellers test novel products in limited markets; if success is achieved, wider distribution follows.[5]

Some commodities are used daily by the bulk of the population; almost everyone seasons his food with salt. Buyers of fire engines, on the other hand, are spread thinly over the land and come into the market at irregular intervals. The manufacturing facilities of a firm catering to a few spasmodic consumers may be relatively small, yet to attain productive efficiency the plant may have to become so large as to require a national market. Thus firms making hydraulic jacks and permanent magnets may employ fewer than half a thousand persons and still ship their wares over the entire United States.[6]

Political factors induce dispersion: onerous regulation of busi-

---

detailed surveys of 3215 square miles. International Nickel Co. of Canada, Ltd., 1950 Ann. Rep. 14 (Copper Cliff, 1951). Some large retailers have buyers abroad (F. W. Woolworth Co. v. United States, 115 F.2d 348, 351 (C.C.P.A. 1940)).

[5] National Dairy Products Corp., 1950 Ann. Rep. 6 (New York City, 1951); P. Lorillard Co., 1948 Ann. Rep. 12 (New York City, 1949); International Minerals & Chemical Corp., 39th Ann. Rep. 9 (Chicago, 1948); Scott Paper Co., 1952 Ann. Rep. 2 (Chester, 1953) (new product, paper napkins, tried out in Providence, R. I., and then distributed throughout New England); Bruce's Juices v. American Can Co., 87 F. Supp. 985, 991 (D. Fla. 1949), aff'd, 187 F.2d 919 (5th Cir. 1951); Butters, Lintner, and Cary, Effects of Taxation; Corporate Mergers 97 (1951); McNair and Hansen, Problems in Marketing 665 (1949); Acme Steel Co., 1953 Ann. Rep. 18 (Chicago, 1954) (new product test-marketed in key city areas, found ready for nationwide distribution); American Home Products Corp., 28th Ann. Rep. 9 (New York City, 1954) (new product, mushrooms in brown gravy, tested in selected areas and distribution then extended to other regions). Compare National Biscuit Co., 1949 Ann. Rep. 6 (New York City, 1950) (new type of advertising tried in limited area). A seller who suspects that a price reduction may increase his volume may well experiment in a selected market area. Edwards, Pricing Practices and the Federal Trade Commission 6 (Address before National Council of Farmer Cooperatives, Chicago, Jan. 8, 1951).
Dispersion is related to diversification. A firm producing more than one product, for example, does not necessarily penetrate all its markets with all its products in equal depth. Compare Pittsburgh Plate Glass Co. 1950 Ann. Rep. 16 (Pittsburgh, 1951); E. I. du Pont de Nemours & Co., 1950 Ann. Rep. 48 (Wilmington, 1951); General Motors Corp., 1950 Ann. Rep. 23 (New York City, 1951); Penney's, King of the Soft Goods, 42 Fortune No. 3, p. 101 (1950). The introduction of the can as a container for soft drinks may dramatically affect the pattern of distribution; small local bottlers may give way to nationwide distributors because cans can be shipped farther and canning takes more capital than bottling. Hobby, Bottles or Cans, 34 Barron's No. 42, p. 7 (1954).

[6] E.g., Hein-Warner Co., Indiana Steel Products Co., Seagrave Corp. (see Fitch Investors Service, June 6, 1950). See Standard & Poor, Manual of Issues on the Midwest Stock Exchange 69, 78 (May 17, 1950). This volume contains other interesting examples involving such products as rare earth, four-wheel drive trucks, and the like. Id. at 7, 11, 18, 22, 36, 51, 97. Stigler, The Division of Labor Is Limited by the Extent of the Market, 59 J. Pol. Econ. 185, 192 (1951) (throws onto the table the suggestion that dispersion is possible only for large industries — when industry shrinks it concentrates). Firms producing highly differentiated (styled) products are also said to be unlikely to operate branch plants. Hoover, The Location of Economic Activity 82 (1948).

ness in its original area may make distant pastures look greener.[7] Pressure exerted by labor unions may lead employers to establish new plants in other zones; take, for example, the well-known flight of the textile industry from New England to the South.[8] Again, states, cities, railroads, and electric utility companies attempt to lure manufacturers into their sections.[9]   One great public utility maintains a "Territorial Information Department" designed to sell the idea that its area is second to none as a place in which to work and live.[10]

Other considerations discourage dispersion.   Transportation, a necessity to geographic expansion, is also a limiting factor.   At some degree of distance, shipping costs bulk so large that market penetration becomes impossible.   Heavy and perishable commodities are particularly limited by the expense of carriage costs.[11] Traditionally, beer, ice, and bricks are limited to local markets,[12]

---

[7] Compare 2 Sharfman, The Interstate Commerce Commission 233 (1931) (Shreveport doctrine).

[8] Hoover, The Location of Economic Activity 148 (1948).   Hoover found that when skilled workers are concentrated in a small area producing stylized products for a seasonal or unstable market, they enjoy great bargaining power with employers; hence the industry tends to decentralize to avoid restrictive practices.   Id. at 114. See also Robinson, Collective Bargaining and Market Control in the New York Coat and Suit Industry 210 (1949) (flight to Connecticut, New Jersey, Pennsylvania); Shister, Economics of the Labor Market 129 (1949); TNEC Hearings, pt. 19, at 10,588; Celler Committee I, pt. 6A, at 192.   But compare Schumacher, Location of Industry, 9 Encyc. Soc. Sci. 585, 589 (1933).   Other movements are mentioned in Thorp, The Changing Structure of Industry, in Recent Economic Changes 167, 208, 214 (Hoover ed. 1930).

[9] Hoover, The Location of Economic Activity 146, 227 (1948); Mississippi Code Ann. §9703 (1942); Mississippi Laws 1950, c. 528 (tax exemption); Chicago & North Western Ry., 1950 Ann. Rep. 7 (Chicago, 1951); Cincinnati Gas & Electric Co., 1950 Ann. Rep. 18 (Cincinnati, 1951).   The practice was disapproved in TNEC, Final Rep. of Exec. Secy. 312 (1941).

[10] Freeman, A Year of Growth 11 (Address to Shareholders, Commonwealth Edison Co., May 22, 1951).   Nations sometimes use similar devices to aid their citizens in the penetration of foreign markets.   See F. W. Woolworth Co. v. United States, 115 F.2d 348, 351 (C.C.P.A. 1940) (currency controls).

[11] Crisp, How to Reduce Distribution Costs 29 (1948); Hoover, The Location of Economic Activity, in The Growth of the American Economy 581 (Williamson ed. 1944); TNEC Hearings, pt. 19, at 10,542, 10,552.   Even when it is economical to locate plants near customers, breweries do not spring up in each beer drinker's backyard.   Hoover, The Location of Economic Activity 48 (1948).   Compare Enke, Space and Value, 56 Q.J. Econ. 627, 632 (1942); Note, Section 11(b) of the Holding Company Act, 59 Yale L.J. 1088, 1099 (1950) (SEC limitations upon utilities).   Mere mass does not, however, limit marketing areas: it is the ratio of value to mass that is vital.   Hale, Trust Dissolution, 40 Colum. L. Rev. 615, 629 (1940).

[12] Standard & Poor, Manual of Issues on the Midwest Stock Exchange 17, 56, 68, 76, 163 (May 17, 1950); Standard & Poor, Standard Corporation Records 5844 (1951). An advertising executive reported that immediately after World War II the management of a middle-western brewery attempted national distribution at a "premium" price.   As a result, the company lost money and soon reverted to distribution in three contiguous states where it enjoys profits despite the presence of seventy-five competitors.

and perhaps other commodities are even more narrowly confined.[13]

Markets are not continuous and uniform but discrete and varied.[14] In the tropics the demand for furnaces is slight. Poverty afflicts many areas.[15] Natural barriers, water and mountains, often separate regions.[16] Thus exploitation of remote and thin markets may be inefficient for firms established in richer terrain.[17] Twenty of the 184 trading areas recognized in the grocery trade, for example, do half of all the business. Sales in the remaining 164 may prove considerably more costly.[18]

Finally, political factors limit dispersion as much as they encourage it. Tariffs and their modern counterparts, exchange controls, restrict international movement of goods.[19] Controlled economies in foreign areas are so difficult of entry that exporters

---

[13] Hoover, The Location of Economic Activity 123 (1948). Perishability is a factor having similar effect.

Economies may sometimes be achieved by splitting manufacture into geographically separated processes. Studebaker Corp., 1950 Ann. Rep. 5 (South Bend, 1951) (company constructed assembly plant in eastern area).

There is a body of literature on the pattern in which competitors will locate in order to minimize transport costs. E.g., Lerner and Singer, Some Notes on Duopoly and Spatial Competition, 45 J. Pol. Econ. 145, 183 (1937). Changes in the transportation factor may compel an alteration in the method of achieving market penetration. Bowden and Cassady, Decentralization of Retail Trade in the Metropolitan Market Area, 5 J. Marketing 270, 274 (1941) (decline of "downtown" shopping areas in favor of suburban locations).

[14] Ackley, Spatial Competition in a Discontinuous Market, 56 Q.J. Econ. 212, 213 (1942).

[15] Crisp, How to Reduce Distribution Costs 60, 67, 73 (1948). Accordingly, businessmen use quantitative market research to find the most promising sales areas. Brown, Marketing and Distribution Research 161, 165 (rev. ed. 1949); Heidingsfield and Blankenship, Market and Marketing Analysis, c. 12 (1947); Lawrence, Market Research in the Chemical Industry, 30 Monsanto Magazine No. 1, pp. 22, 23 (1951). A man who operated thirty-six buses with depots in six cities was said not to be a "small business man" by Alaskan standards in O'Hara v. Littlejohn, 69 F. Supp. 274, 277 (D.D.C. 1946).

[16] Hoover, The Location of Economic Activity 124 (1948).

[17] Twentieth Century Fund, Does Distribution Cost Too Much? 192, 318 (1939); Brown, Marketing and Distribution Research 165 (rev. ed. 1949); TNEC, Final Rep. of Exec. Secy. 268 (1941). "Shopping" goods may be concentrated; sellers group themselves together so that buyers may compare rival wares. Hoover, The Location of Economic Activity 60 (1948).

[18] Crisp, How to Reduce Distribution Costs 118 (1948). Compare Cochran, History of the Pabst Brewing Company 76, 77 (1948).

[19] Gulf Oil Corp., 1950 Ann. Rep. 25 (Pittsburgh, 1951); Standard Oil Co. of New Jersey, 1950 Ann. Rep. 17 (New York City, 1951). Dispersion abroad (assembly plants, etc.) is sometimes effected to overcome exchange controls, to avoid political rather than economic barriers. General Motors Corp., 42d Ann. Rep. 21-22 (New York City, 1951).

[20] 14 Dow Diamond No. 2, p. 29 (1951) (Dow Chemical Co.). Compare Celler Committee I, pt. 6A, at 198 (newsprint tariff reduced at instance of consumers so as to bring Canadian products into effective competition with domestic). The advantage of a seller in his nearby area, arising out of transportation costs, has been

must maintain special personnel to study their regulations.[20]
Trade barriers, however, increase incentives to the migration of
enterprise. If tariffs make it impossible to export, many a business will establish a branch plant within the protected region.
Thus the barriers, because they are incomplete, encourage a
deeper dispersion than would otherwise result.[21]

From the foregoing discussion it is apparent that conflicting
factors will bring dispersion into something approaching equilibrium: at some point the benefits and burdens will roughly
balance.[22] As in efforts to define "trading areas," however, the
multiplicity of factors makes it difficult for business managers to
estimate the ideal degree of dispersion at any one time.[23] More
difficult still, the relevant factors are continually changing: adjustment to the optimum amount of dispersion is a dynamic process.
As recently as 1913, for example, practically all brands of cigarettes were promoted on a limited, regional basis. In that year a
venturesome manufacturer launched the "Camel" brand into the
national market and most of its competitors quickly converted
from sectional to country-wide distribution.[24] The relatively
recent growth of the chain stores affords another vivid example
of the dynamic equilibrium of dispersion.[25] Territorial expansion by progressive firms is a commonplace today.[26]

---

likened to a protective tariff. Fetter, The Economic Law of Market Areas, 38 Q.J.
Econ. 520, 522 (1924).

[21] Hoover, The Location of Economic Activity 230 (1948); General Motors Corp.,
1950 Ann. Rep. 20 (New York City, 1951); Caterpillar Tractor Co. (California),
1950 Ann. Rep. 11 (Peoria, 1951); National Biscuit Co., 1950 Ann. Rep. 12 (New
York City, 1951). Compare Celler Committee I, pt. 6A, at 199. Some firms penetrate foreign markets merely by licensing the use of patents and the like. Westinghouse Abroad, 41 Fortune No. 2, p. 76 (1950); Johns-Manville Corp., 1950 Ann.
Rep. 6 (New York City, 1951).

[22] Hoover, The Location of Economic Activity 89 (1948). Organization and
structure are the result of adaptation to conditions and should not be stifled by
prohibitions, as this is an important form of competition. McLean and Haigh,
How Business Corporations Grow, 32 Harv. Bus. Rev. No. 6, pp. 81, 92-93 (1954).

[23] Converse, New Laws of Retail Gravitation, 14 J. Marketing 379, 384 (1949);
President's Research Committee on Social Trends, Recent Social Trends 457 (1933).

[24] R. J. Reynolds Tobacco Co., 1950 Ann. Rep. 13 (Winston-Salem, 1951);
Lawrence, Market Research in the Chemical Industry, 30 Monsanto Magazine No. 1,
pp. 22, 23 (1951).

[25] Palmer, Economic and Social Aspects of Chain Stores, 2 J. Business 272, 273
(1929); Twentieth Century Fund, Does Distribution Cost Too Much? 81 (1939).
There are indications, however, that the chain store movement has passed its peak.
Engle, Chain Store Distribution vs. Independent Wholesaling, 14 J. Marketing 241,
245, 251 (1949); Fulda, Food Distribution in the United States, 99 U. Pa. L. Rev.
1051, 1064 (1951); see United States v. New York Great Atlantic & Pacific Tea Co.,
67 F. Supp. 626, 633 (E.D. Ill. 1946), aff'd, 173 F.2d 79 (7th Cir. 1949).

[26] See the following annual reports: National Dairy Products Corp., 1949 Ann.
Rep. 6 (New York City, 1950); W. T. Grant Co., 1948 Ann. Rep. 7 (New York City,
1949), 1950 Ann. Rep. 5 (1951); S. S. Kresge Co., 1950 Ann. Rep. 15, 19 (Detroit,
1951); National Biscuit Co., 1949 Ann. Rep. 19 (New York City, 1950).

§7.4. Dispersion and wealth.

Obviously, dispersion is related to over-all size. In some industries small, nondispersed firms hold their own or even best their nationwide competitors. A manufacturer cannot compete in the national cigarette market, however, without considerable resources.[1] Growth of business enterprise is often characterized by dispersion. Expanding firms constantly open new warehouses and plants in territory previously untouched: within two years from their introduction by General Mills, "brown 'n' serve" rolls were in commercial production all over the North American continent and had been pushed into Australasia.[2] Dispersion and size, however, are not synonymous. As noted above, the depth of dispersion is important: some firms employ greater resources to serve a limited area than others do in spreading out farther. One enterprise operates ten retail stores in three states; another focuses the business of its fourteen outlets in a single city and environs.[3] A small specialty manufacturer may peddle his wares over the globe and require far fewer resources than the public utility serving but one metropolis.[4]

§7.5. Assumed legality of dispersion.

In the past the desirability of dispersion in general was rarely questioned. Few firms were challenged as violators of the antitrust laws because they had expanded the geographic scope of their activities. Considerable complaint, however, was directed at specific types of dispersion.

For many decades there has been powerful economic and political resistance to the idea of branch banking. Legislation against the establishment of branches was enacted as early as 1808, and by the middle of the nineteenth century many such

---

§7.4. [1] For an example of a firm apparently competing successfully with another about four times as large, see Standard & Poor, Standard Corporation Records 5894, 7037 (1951) (Central Fibre Products Co. and Container Corp. of America). But compare TNEC Hearings, pt. 1, at 114.

[2] General Mills, Inc., 23d Ann. Rep. 7 (Minneapolis, 1951); Abbott Laboratories, 1949 Ann. Rep. 22 (North Chicago, 1950). See also Philip Morris & Co., Ltd., 1950 Ann. Rep. 22 (New York City, 1951); Pittsburgh Plate Glass Co., 1950 Ann. Rep. 15 (Pittsburgh, 1951); Standard Oil Co. of New Jersey, 1948 Ann. Rep. 23 (New York City, 1949); Parke, Davis & Co., 1950 Ann. Rep. 6, 11 (Detroit, 1951); Sears, Roebuck & Co., 1948 Ann. Rep. 3 (Chicago, 1949); Idaho Power Co., Ann. Rep. 4 (Boise, 1945) ("The service area of Idaho Power Company was expanded during the year 1944 by purchase of the West Coast Power Company's electric properties located in the State of Idaho, all of which were adjacent to the Company's system").

[3] National Bellas Hess, Inc., 1949 Ann. Rep. 8 (North Kansas City, 1949); Standard & Poor, Manual of Issues on the Midwest Stock Exchange 57 (May 17, 1950). A firm supplying towel service in 430 communities had smaller capital than a concern distributing building materials in one city and environs. Id. at 34, 40.

[4] An electric utility serving only a single city and environs had total assets of $1,042,000,000 and working capital of $67,000,000. Commonwealth Edison Co., 1948 Ann. Rep. 22 (Chicago, 1949).

statutes were in force.[1] Branch banking is now permissible in less than half the states of the Union.[2] Fear of monopoly may have been a motivating force in the enactment of the legislation curbing the establishment of branches, but protection of depositors appears to have played at least an equal role in the minds of proponents of the statutes.[3]

In more recent years chain stores have constituted the targets of legislators. Taxes graduated in proportion to the number of stores operated by the chain have been imposed in many states. Such taxation exists in at least twenty jurisdictions; and the later statutes are more restrictive of the size of chains than the earlier ones.[4] Whatever the motives of the proponents of such measures,[5] the fact is clear that the operators of chain stores are objects of widespread disapproval.[6]

As noted above, there has been some general resistance to dispersion in the form of protective tariffs and the like. Duties were raised in the 1920's and many new systems invented to impede the flow of commerce. Exchange restrictions, taxes, price-fixing, import quotas, confiscation, and other devices have dammed the flow of international trade.[7] Even within the

§7.5. [1] Henderson, The Position of Foreign Corporations in American Constitutional Law 45 (1918); Willis, Branch Banking, 2 Encyc. Soc. Sci. 679, 680 (1932); President's Research Committee on Social Trends, Recent Social Trends 244 (1933).

[2] See Bank of Italy v. Johnson, 200 Cal. 1, 14, 251 Pac. 784, 788 (1927). An example of a restrictive statute is Illinois Rev. Stat., c. 16½, §9 (1949) (banking); compare Illinois Business Corporation Act, Ill. Rev. Stat., c. 32, §157.102 (1957) (foreign corporations may not transact banking, insurance, etc. business in state). Federal legislation has not done much more than permit national banking associations to establish branches if permissible under state law. 44 Stat. 1228 (1927), as amended, 12 U.S.C.A. §36 (1946) (McFadden Act); 38 Stat. 259 (1913), as amended, 12 U.S.C.A. §321 (Supp. 1950).

[3] Willis, Branch Banking, 2 Encyc. Soc. Sci. 679 (1932); see Bruner v. Citizens' Bank, 134 Ky. 283, 293, 120 S.W. 345, 348, 350 (1909).

[4] Burns, The Decline of Competition 430 (1936); Gould, Legislative Intervention in the Conflict between Orthodox and Direct-Selling Distribution Channels, 8 Law & Contemp. Prob. 318, 324 (1941); Nystrom, Retail Trade, 13 Encyc. Soc. Sci. 346, 349 (1934); Collins, Anti-Chain Store Legislation, 24 Cornell L.Q. 198, 206, 211 (1939); State Board of Tax Commissioners v. Jackson, 283 U.S. 527 (1931); McIntire and Rhyne, Municipal Legislative Barriers to a Free Market, 8 Law & Contemp. Prob. 359, 365 (1941); Feldman, Legislative Opposition to Chain Stores and Its Minimization, 8 id. 334, 338, 342; Roper, 187 Bills: A Digest of Proposals Considered in Congress in Behalf of Small Business 1943-1944, 54 (U.S. Dept. of Commerce, Economic Small Business Series No. 491, 1946); Lee, Protectionism and Chain Store Taxes, in Tax Barriers to Trade 151, 160 (Tax Institute, 1940); Beckman and Nolen, The Chain Store Problem 224, 228 (1938).

[5] Lee, Anti-Chain Store Tax Legislation 68, 79 (1939); Collins, Anti-Chain Store Legislation, 24 Cornell L.Q. 198, 202 (1939).

[6] Compare facts found in State v. Board of Health, 237 Wis. 638, 298 N.W. 183 (1941); Central Lumber Co. v. South Dakota, 226 U.S. 157, 160 (1912).

[7] Heckscher, Protection, 12 Encyc. Soc. Sci. 559, 566 (1934); Sears, Roebuck in Rio, 41 Fortune No. 2, pp. 78, 79 (1950); The Esso Handicap, id. at 73, 75 (1950); Stand-

United States, protectionism has a long history: statutes regulating and taxing peddlers and drummers were enacted in Colonial days; states of the youthful Union were jealous of the "foreign" corporations chartered in adjacent jurisdictions; and the depression of the 1930's brought forth a flood of legislation protecting local traffic in such varied commodities as motor vehicles, butter, nursery stock, and liquor.[8] Peddlers, dignified as "itinerant merchants," are plagued with licensing requirements, and many measures, ostensibly designed to protect public health, are aimed by legislators or administrators at "foreign" competition.[9] Even cabinet members do not blush to advocate measures of a similar import.[10]

A century ago the courts were reluctant to strike down protectionist legislation, and even today many dubious statutes are allowed to stand.[11] On the other hand, the long-term judicial trend is more favorable to dispersion. Rules may appear uncertain and distinctions fine, but the courts are not disposed to permit an all-out "Balkanization" of the United States. Taxes, for example, have been scrutinized with care and those obviously discriminatory against "foreign" producers stricken from the books.[12]

---

ard Oil Co. of New Jersey, 1949 Ann. Rep. 12, 18 (New York City, 1950); Liggett & Myers Tobacco Co., 1950 Ann. Rep. 2 (New York City, 1951).

[8] Collins, Anti-Chain Store Legislation, 24 Cornell L.Q. 198, 200 n.16 (1939); Henderson, The Position of Foreign Corporations in American Constitutional Law 102 (1918); see Commonwealth v. Milton, 12 B. Mon. 212, 222 (Ky. 1851); Truitt, Interstate Trade Barriers in the United States, 8 Law & Contemp. Prob. 209, 212 (1941); TNEC, Final Report of Exec. Secy. 145.

[9] Gould, Legislative Intervention in the Conflict between Orthodox and Direct-Selling Distribution Channels, 8 Law & Contemp. Prob. 318, 320 (1941); Illinois Rev. Stat., c. 121½, §165 (1957) (note §§2, 4, 5 (itinerant merchants by motor vehicle)); McIntire and Rhyne, Municipal Legislative Barriers to a Free Market, 8 Law & Contemp. Prob. 359, 360 (1941); Hoover, The Location of Economic Activity 216 (1948); Illinois Rev. Stat., c. 29, §36 (1957) (preference for state coal). On the administration of the measures, compare TNEC Hearings, pt. 20, at 10,899; Green, Tax Barriers to Trade with Respect to Alcoholic Beverages, in Tax Barriers to Trade 130, 138 (Tax Institute, 1940); Kunstenaar, Internal Marketing Barriers in Europe, 8 Law & Contemp. Prob. 402, 403 (1941) (in Austria seamstresses needed permission of Tailors' Guild to move across street; usually refused).

[10] Celler Committee I, pt. 4A, at 73.

[11] Breard v. Alexandria, 341 U.S. 622 (1951); Parker v. Brown, 317 U.S. 341 (1943); Nebbia v. New York, 291 U.S. 502 (1934); Henderson, The Position of Foreign Corporations in American Constitutional Law 48 (1918); Twentieth Century Fund, Does Distribution Cost Too Much? 254, 279 (1939).

[12] Brown, State Taxation of Interstate Commerce — What Now? 48 Mich. L. Rev. 899, 905, 922 (1950); Lockhart, State Tax Barriers to Interstate Trade, 53 Harv. L. Rev. 1253, 1255, 1260 (1940); French, Municipal Tariffs Under the Guise of Occupation Taxes, 18 Iowa L. Rev. 342, 345 (1933); Dean Milk Co. v. City of Madison, 340 U.S. 349, 354 (1951); Walgreen Co. v. Lenane, 363 Ill. 628, 2 N.E.2d 894 (1936); Note, The Constitution and State Control of Natural Resources, 64 Harv. L. Rev.

Until recent years, therefore, the climate of opinion did not discourage dispersion in general. Statutes forbidding monopoly were not thought to prohibit geographic expansion by business enterprise. Neither specific legislation aimed at branch banking and chain retailing nor general protectionist measures were considered to suggest the advisability of prohibiting dispersion under the terms of the antitrust laws. Indeed, the courts seemed to smile upon the dispersed company.[13]

§7.6. New threats to dispersion. Now storm clouds gather. Agitation against branch banking persists and federal administrative action has been taken against one of the largest state-wide banks.[1] Taxes aimed at chain stores have been enacted less frequently, but other weapons, such as statutes prohibiting sales below "cost," are employed against the same targets.[2] By the Public Utility Holding Company Act of 1935, federal power was exerted to disintegrate the electric "empires of scatteration," and the Securities and Exchange Commission has waged successful war upon the unpopular utility companies.[3] Network broadcasting has incurred the disfavor of the Federal Communications

---

642, 646 (1951); compare 1 Sharfman, The Interstate Commerce Commission 221 (1931) (Shreveport doctrine).

[13] International Shoe Co. v. FTC, 280 U.S. 291, 295 (1930); United States v. American Tobacco Co., 164 Fed. 700, 710 (1908), *modified,* 221 U.S. 106 (1911); United States v. Standard Oil Co., 47 F.2d 288, 305, 312 (E.D. Mo. 1931); In re Pressed Steel Car Co., 16 F. Supp. 329, 339 (W.D. Pa. 1936); Bruner v. Citizens' Bank, 134 Ky. 283, 290, 120 S.W. 345, 347 (1909). Compare the employer-employee cases cited *infra* §7.8, note 7. Note also the recognition of localized monopolies. E.g., Indiana Farmer's Guide Pub. Co. v. Prairie Farmer Pub. Co., 293 U.S. 268, 279 (1934); compare United States v. Pullman Co., 64 F. Supp. 108, 112 (E.D. Pa. 1946), *aff'd per curiam,* 330 U.S. 806 (1947); United States v. Paramount Pictures, Inc., 66 F. Supp. 323, 354 (S.D.N.Y. 1946), *rev'd,* 334 U.S. 131, 171 (1948). See also §7.8 *infra,* note 7.

§7.6. [1] 38 Stat. 259 (1913), as amended, 12 U.S.C.A. §321 (Supp. 1950); Note, Judicial Invalidation of Federal Reserve Policy Against Bank Holding Company Expansion, 57 Yale L.J. 276, 299, 305 (1947); Roper, 187 Bills: A Digest of Proposals Considered in Congress in Behalf of Small Business 1943-1944, 47, 53 (U.S. Dept. of Commerce, Economic Small Business Series No. 491, 1946); Transamerica Corp. v. Board of Governors of the Federal Reserve System, 206 F.2d 163 (3d Cir. 1953), *cert. denied,* 346 U.S. 901 (1953).

[2] Feldman, Legislative Opposition to Chain Stores and Its Minimization, 8 Law & Contemp. Prob. 334, 340 (1941).

[3] 49 Stat. 803 (1935), 15 U.S.C.A. §§79a(b)(4), 79b(a)(29), 79k(b)(1); Note, 59 Yale L.J. 1088, 1095 (1950); Shaw, Public Utility Holding Company Act, 36 Mich. L. Rev. 1360, 1364 (1938); Ritchie, Integration Under Section 10(c) of the Public Utility Holding Company Act, 41 Mich. L. Rev. 1, 16 (1942); FTC, Utility Corporations (Public Utility Holding Companies), Sen. Doc. No. 92, 70th Cong., 1st Sess., pt. 72-A, 871 et seq. (1935) (state commissions cannot regulate big holding company systems effectively because latter have more legal and engineering talent; companies take cases to court and pay unwarranted fees; companies avoid shareholders' double liability; state commissions cannot get at holding company books or, if they do, allocate costs).

Commission, and the Commission's authority has been exerted in favor of contractual arrangements conducive to the maintenance of "local" programs.[4]

Legislatures have joined the crusade against dispersed business. Congress contributed the Robinson-Patman Act,[5] a measure aimed at several targets, but clearly designed to handicap firms of widespread geographic scope. State statutes imitated the federal legislation and added prohibitions against sales below "cost" and the like. Many such laws were obviously drafted in an effort to protect independent local sellers from the competition of their dispersed rivals.[6]

Finally, and most importantly, the Attorney General of the United States decided that the Sherman Act should be employed against dispersed firms. Basic antitrust statutes, as well as supplementary legislation, were hurled into the fray. Although the judiciary declined to outlaw vertical integration, it has not balked at the new attack on dispersion.[7]

The opening blow was struck in *United States v. Crescent Amusement Co.*[8] In that case the defendants had formed a chain of some seventy motion picture theaters scattered over cities and towns in several states. Most of the towns were small and could support but one theater; in only five were there competing houses. The defendants negotiated with the distributors of films for all seventy theaters as a group and, according to the findings of the trial court, attempted to eliminate such competition as they had (in the five towns where there were rival theaters) by threatening the distributors with refusal to exhibit their pictures in the "closed" areas where no competition existed. Evidence was

---

4 FCC, Public Service Responsibility of Broadcast Licensees 36, 55 (1946); see National Broadcasting Co. v. United States, 319 U.S. 190, 197, 207 (1943); Simmons v. FCC, 169 F.2d 670, 671 (D.C. Cir. 1948), *cert. denied*, 335 U.S. 846 (1948); Note, The Impact of the F.C.C.'s Chain Broadcasting Rules, 60 Yale L.J. 78, 86 (1951).

5 49 Stat. 1526 (1936), 15 U.S.C.A. §13. This is an amendment to the Clayton Act.

6 Martin, ed., State Antitrust Laws xlviii, lix, lx (WPA, 1940); see Carroll v. Schwartz, 127 Conn. 126, 129, 14 A.2d 754, 756 (1940); May's Drug Stores, Inc. v. State Tax Commission, 242 Iowa 319, 45 N.W.2d 245, 249 (1951); Kaplan, Small Business: Its Place and Problems 204 (1948). Dispersion within §7 of the Clayton Act is not illegal per se; there must be a showing that increased wealth eventually will reduce competition. Neal, The Clayton Act and the Transamerica Case, 5 Stan. L. Rev. 179 (1953).

7 Hale, Vertical Integration, 49 Colum. L. Rev. 921, 935 (1949); United States v. Columbia Steel Co., 334 U.S. 495 (1948) (court refused to approve Solicitor General's view that performance of successive functions of production or distribution should be considered illegal per se), discussed *supra* §5.10.

8 323 U.S. 173 (1945). Compare Schine Chain Theatres, Inc. v. United States, 334 U.S. 110, 119 (1948), *on remand, consent decree*, CCH Trade Reg. Serv. ¶¶62,447, 67,237 (W.D.N.Y. 1952); United States v. Paramount Pictures, Inc., 85 F. Supp. 881 (S.D.N.Y. 1946), *aff'd per curiam*, 339 U.S. 974 (1950).

offered to show that the defendants were thus enabled to buy out competing exhibitors.[9]   A violation of the Sherman Act was found.   In view of the proven monopolistic intent of the defendants the decision occasioned little surprise.

In his several suits against the New York Great Atlantic & Pacific Tea Company the Attorney General jumped on the anti-chain bandwagon.   That concern, of course, operated thousands of grocery stores, scattered over the United States.   While it was the largest single retail grocer in the nation, it enjoyed only about 7.1 per cent of the trade over the country as a whole.   Thus it scarcely constituted a monopoly.   Much fault was found, however, with the firm's operations, and among the practices attacked was that of selling below "cost" in localized areas.   To date the courts have sustained the complaints,[10] but such results are not wholly surprising in terms of their effect upon dispersion, since local price-cutting has long been suspect.[11]

Another suit against motion picture exhibitors afforded the occasion for a telling blow at dispersion.   In *United States v. Griffith*[12] the defendants operated a motion picture "circuit" in some eighty-five southwestern towns.   It was difficult in most respects to distinguish the facts from those proven in the *Crescent Amusement* case.   In some fifty-three of the eighty-five towns, no competing theaters were operated and, according to the allegation of the complaint, the defendants were able to obtain "first-run" and other privileges from film distributors in bargaining for their entire circuit as a unit.   The significant difference lay in the fact that the trial court found neither a conspiracy in restraint of trade nor an attempt to monopolize:[13] the defendants had not even tried to obtain their special "clearances" and other exclusive rights.   In short, the mere existence of the combination resulted in the securing of advantages over independent local exhibitors.   Again the defendants were found in violation of the Sherman Act.

Dispersion was not condemned by name.   Mr. Justice Douglas,

[9] At favorable prices, presumably.   No complaint would have arisen had the prices been thought high.

[10] United States v. New York Great Atlantic & Pacific Tea Co., 67 F. Supp. 626, 631, 633, 639 (E.D. Ill. 1946), *aff'd*, 173 F.2d 79 (7th Cir. 1949).   Whatever can be said in support of the decision is not expressed in the opinion of the Court of Appeals, a monument to muddlement.   Adelman, The A. & P. Case: A Study in Applied Economic Theory, 63 Q.J. Econ. 238 (1949).

[11] See §7.7 *infra*, notes 4, 5.

[12] 334 U.S. 100 (1948).

[13] Id. at 104.   In examining the President of the Borden Company, which is geographically spread out, Senator O'Mahoney expressed antagonism to dispersion. Kilgore Committee, pt. 2, at 881-883.

in writing the majority opinion, did not announce that thereafter all business enterprise must confine itself to a single area of operation. Chain stores were not explicitly directed to shut up shop. Yet the implications of the decision can scarcely be overlooked by those seeking to ascertain the legal status of dispersion.

The opinion began by stating that an exhibitor operating the sole theater in one town may be a monopolist in the popular sense but not within the meaning of the Sherman Act.[14] If, however, the exhibitor seeks to expand that monopoly, and particularly if he uses his strategic position in the first town to acquire exclusive privileges in a place where he has competitors, he is employing his monopoly power illegally. Existence of a power to exclude competition, if coupled with a purpose to exercise that power, violates Section 2 of the Sherman Act; it is unreasonable per se to exclude competitors from any substantial market:

> . . . the use of monopoly power, however lawfully acquired, to foreclose competition, to gain a competitive advantage, or to destroy a competitor, is unlawful.[15]

And

> The consequence of such a use of monopoly power is that films are licensed on a non-competitive basis in what would otherwise be competitive situations . . . if monopoly power can be used to beget monopoly, the Act becomes a feeble instrument indeed.[16]

In view of the fact that no finding of an attempt to monopolize was made by the trial court, the decision in *United States v. Griffith* casts a heavy cloud over dispersion in any industry and in any degree.[17] True, the decision was applied only to a situation

[14] 334 U.S. 100, 106 (1948).

[15] Id. at 107 (1948). But compare United States v. Columbia Steel Co., 334 U.S. 495, 533 (1948); Gamco v. Providence Bldg., 194 F.2d 484 (1952).

[16] 334 U.S. 100, 108 (quarrel with the logic of the opinion is not material to this discussion) *Accord:* Schine Chain Theatres, Inc. v. United States, 334 U.S. 110, 116 (1948). But compare United States v. Paramount Pictures, Inc., 334 U.S. 131, 171 (1948); Russellville Canning Co. v. American Can Co., 87 F. Supp. 484, 498 (W.D. Ark. 1949), *rev'd,* 191 F.2d 38 (8th Cir. 1951). Mr. Raymond's remedy for "bigness" does not discriminate against dispersion as such but limits an enterprise either to a single location or to a number of employees, the latter provision being inserted for the benefit of the chain stores. Celler Committee I, pt. 4A, at 323. The attractive simplicity of this solution shields its basically arbitrary character. (Mr. Raymond is the author of The Limitist (1947).)

[17] But compare United States v. Columbia Steel, 334 U.S. 495, 526 (1948); Transamerica Corp. v. Board of Governors of the Federal Reserve System, 206 F.2d 163 (3d Cir. 1953), *cert. denied,* 346 U.S. 901 (1953); Windsor Theatre Co. v. Walbrook Amusement Co., 94 F. Supp. 388, 393 (D. Md. 1950), *aff'd,* 189 F.2d 797 (4th Cir. 1951) (view here expressed that owner of two theaters was not liable for outbidding owner of one theater appears at variance with United States v. Griffith, which is cited in the footnote to the opinion. In G. & P. Amusement Co. v. Regent Theater,

in which the defendants enjoyed a local "monopoly" in some
parts of their circuit." Monopoly, however, may be a question of
degree, and many dispersed firms probably find competition
stiffer in some areas than in others.[18] Indeed, it is that fact —
that the vigor of competition varies from place to place — which
gives rise to one of the most serious charges against dispersion;
that it leads to local price-cutting in an attempt to monopolize.

§7.7. **Local price-cutting.** Complaints against dispersion are
variously phrased. Despite the variety of expression used, it is
believed that the gist of the attacks can be condensed under a
handful of headings. Dispersion, it is claimed, leads to local
price-cutting in an attempt to monopolize; it induces the raising
of local prices to secure monopoly profits (geographic price discrimination); it drains away funds; it raises the cost of entering
into competition; and it results in the vice of absentee ownership.
We shall examine these contentions in turn and suggest countervailing considerations.

Local price-cutting is one of the oldest and strongest complaints. In the branch banking dispute, for example, it was
argued that the establishment of local units by metropolitan
bankers would drive the competing, non-chain banks out of existence by ruthless cutting of competitive interest rates.[1] Similar
charges were leveled at the old Standard Oil Company.[2] Use of
bargaining power obtained in monopolistic areas (the "closed"
towns of the Griffith case) is basically the same complaint as local
price-cutting. It differs only in that the defendant is dealing
with suppliers rather than with customers. In both instances the
argument against dispersion is that it furnishes a solid platform
of resources to support the defendant while he attempts to im-

---

107 F. Supp. 453, 460 (N.D. Ohio, 1952), it was said: "The plaintiff seeks to
establish Cooperative's wrongful use of its purchasing power by showing that Mooney
customarily, in bargaining with the distributors, joined together in a single pre-
liminary contract theaters represented by Cooperative in 'closed situations' with
those located in 'open situations.' Thus, it is claimed that Mooney was able to
use the possibility of his refusal to buy in the closed market as a sword above the
heads of the distributors to force them to prefer the Regent or any other theater
which he represented in an open situation. . . . The mere representation by Cooperative of both competitive and noncompetitive clients, in a single negotiation,
does not *per se* violate the mandate of 'picture by picture' and 'theater by theater'
dealing. Nor does failure to employ that formula, under all circumstances, constitute a violation of the Sherman Act . . ."

18 Note, Cow Chows — and Wow! 37 Fortune No. 1, pp. 84, 154 (1948).

§7.7. 1 Chapman, Concentration of Banking 306 (1934).
2 Standard Oil Co. of New Jersey v. United States, 221 U.S. 1, 43, 45, 74 (1911);
Commissioner of Corporations, Petroleum Industry, pt. II, xxxviii, 30 (1907); Davies,
Trust Law and Unfair Competition 311 (1916); Mund, Government and Business
116 (1950).

prove his competitive position in a limited area — his local competitor meanwhile lacking such a foundation.[3]

It has long been law that local price-cutting, adopted in an attempt to monopolize, infringes the Sherman Act[4] as well as supplementary antitrust legislation.[5] Local price-cutting was one of the most important targets of the Robinson-Patman amendments to the Clayton Act.[6] As suggested above, however, many other methods have been employed to protect local sellers from "foreign" competition. Tariffs, chain store taxes, sales below "cost" acts, and the like have been used in various times and places.[7]

There is a widespread feeling that at least the "predatory" type of local price-cutting is now rare.[8] No substantial evidence of territorial expansion motivated largely by intent to injure competition has come to light during the course of this study. On the other hand, from abundant current complaints registered it would not appear that local price-cutting had been wholly abandoned.[9] Such price-cutting as exists may be explained in part on

[3] See United States v. Griffith, 334 U.S. 100, 108 (1948); Rostow, Problems of Size and Integration, Proceedings N.Y. State Bar Assn., Section on Antitrust Law, Third Annual Meeting, 117, 122 (CCH, 1951).

[4] 26 Stat. 209 (1890), 15 U.S.C.A. §1; Kales, Contracts and Combinations in Restraint of Trade §50 (1918); Stocking and Watkins, Monopoly and Free Enterprise 371 (1951). Price-cutting not aimed at the elimination of a competitor does not infringe the basic statute. See §2.10 *supra*, §9.2 *infra*. See United States v. Great Western Sugar Co., 39 F.2d 152, 155 (D. Neb. 1930).

[5] Porto Rican American Tobacco Co. v. American Tobacco Co., 30 F.2d 234 (2d Cir. 1929), *cert. denied*, 279 U.S. 858 (1929); National Nut Co. v. Kelling Nut Co., 61 F. Supp. 76, 81 (N.D. Ill. 1945). But compare Sears, Roebuck & Co. v. FTC, 258 Fed. 307, 312 (7th Cir. 1919); Lovell, Sales Below Cost Prohibitions: Private Price Fixing Under State Law, 57 Yale L.J. 391, 400 n.28 (1948).

[6] 38 Stat. 731 (1914), as amended, 49 Stat. 1526 (1936), 15 U.S.C.A. §13; Adelman, Integration and the Outlook for the Future, Proceedings N.Y. State Bar Assn., Section on Antitrust Law, Third Annual Meeting, 135, 140 (CCH 1951). Bitter complaints have been recorded on the enforcement of the amended act. E.g., Simon, Legal Price Fixing, id. at 83, 94.

[7] Heilperin, The Trade of Nations 77 (1947); compare Celler Committee I, pt. 6A, at 192; Lee, Protectionism and Chain Store Taxes, in Tax Barriers to Trade 151, 158, 160 (Tax Institute, 1940); Edwards, Thurman Arnold and the Anti-trust Laws, 58 Pol. Sci. Q. 338, 349 (1943); Lovell, Sales Below Cost Prohibitions: Private Price Fixing Under State Law, 57 Yale L.J. 391, 394 (1948). Exclusion of foreign corporations was rested on the theory that every corporate charter granted monopoly privileges which could not extend to another jurisdiction. Henderson, The Position of Foreign Corporations in American Constitutional Law 21 (1918); see Paul v. Virginia, 8 Wall. 168, 181 (U.S. 1868).

[8] Oxenfeldt, Industrial Pricing and Market Practices 258 (1951); Edwards, Pricing Practices and the Federal Trade Commission 2 (Address before National Council of Farmer Cooperatives, Chicago, Jan. 8, 1951); Grether, Geographical Price Policies in the Grocery Trade, 1941, 8 J. Marketing 417, 419 (1944); compare Mund, The Development and Incidence of Delivered Pricing in American Industry, 15 Law & Contemp. Prob. 141, 154 (1950).

[9] Stocking and Watkins, Monopoly and Free Enterprise 339 (1951); House Select

grounds of meeting local competition,[10] passing lower costs on to consumers,[11] and the like. Even if data were available on a quantitative basis, however, it would not be easy to arrive at a conclusion as to the importance of the practice. Some firms use local price-cutting as a defensive weapon. That was the attitude, for example, of a chain store executive who said boldly: "Rather than simply cutting prices to meet competition we prefer to shoot specials into the town until the competitor gives up his warfare." [12] Also, A & P officers attempted to explain the price policies of that concern by saying that the grocery chain, in moving into new territory, operated at a temporary loss in order to gain enough volume:[13] they admitted the practice but sought to justify it.

§7.8.   **Analysis of local price-cutting.**   Local price-cutting may remain a valid complaint against dispersion today.   But the other side of the coin presents a wholly different picture.   A dispersed

Committee on Small Business, United States v. Economic Concentration and Monopoly, Staff Report Pursuant to H. Res. No. 64, 79th Cong., 2d Sess. 183 (1947); Moore v. Mead Service Co., 184 F.2d 338, 339 (10th Cir. 1950); Mund, Government and Business 131, 209 (1950); Tooke & Reynolds v. Bastrop Ice & Storage Co., 172 La. 781, 785, 135 So. 239, 240 (1931); E. B. Muller & Co. v. FTC, 142 F.2d 511, 518 (6th Cir. 1944); Clark, The Law and Economics of Basing Points: Appraisal and Proposals, 39 Am. Econ. Rev. 430, 436 (1949); Hearings Before House Special Committee on Investigation of American Retail Federation, Vol. 3, No. 1, p. 70, 74th Cong., 1st Sess. (1935); Central Lumber Co. v. South Dakota, 226 U.S. 157, 161 (1912); United States v. New York Great Atlantic & Pacific Tea Co., 67 F. Supp. 626, 641, 664 (E.D. Ill. 1946), aff'd, 173 F.2d 79, 87 (7th Cir. 1949); FTC, Chain Stores, Sen. Doc. No. 85, 73d Cong., 2d Sess. xv, 27 (1934); Fulda, Food Distribution in the United States, 99 U. Pa. L. Rev. 1051, 1152 (1951); compare FTC, Cooperative Grocery Chains, Sen. Doc. No. 12, 72d Cong., 1st Sess. 106 (1932); Ackley, Spatial Competition in a Discontinuous Market, 56 Q.J. Econ. 212, 229 n.8 (1942); Phillips, An Evaluation of Large-Scale Retailing with Emphasis on the Chain Store, 8 Law & Contemp. Prob. 348, 354 (1941); Till, Gasoline — the Competition of Big Business, in Price and Price Policies 117 (Hamilton ed. 1938); Sears, Roebuck & Co. v. FTC, 258 Fed. 307, 309 (7th Cir. 1919); Celler Committee I, ser. 5, pt. 1, at 33, 243; Wagley v. Colonial Co., 208 Miss. 815, 45 So.2d 717 (1950). A national grocery chain engaged in the "most unjust marketing practice" of using its huge financial resources to oppress small competitors in selected areas while maintaining business as usual in other, less competitive areas. Senate Select Committee on Small Business, 6th Ann. Rep., Sen. Rep. No. 1368, 84th Cong., 2d Sess. 68 (1956).

[10] Hearings Before House Special Committee on Investigation of American Retail Federation, Vol. 3, No. 3, 141, 74th Cong., 1st Sess. (1935); Simon, Price Discrimination to Meet Competition, 1950 U. of Ill. L. Forum 575, 579; Feldman, Legislative Opposition to Chain Stores and Its Minimization, 8 Law & Contemp. Prob. 334, 341 (1941). Independent stores, as well as chains, can indulge in the "loss leader" practice. Compare FTC, Cooperative Grocery Chains, Sen. Doc. No. 12, 72d Cong., 1st Sess. xix (1932).

[11] FTC, Chain Stores, Sen. Doc. No. 85, 73d Cong., 2d Sess. xiii, xiv (1934); see Great Atlantic & Pacific Tea Co. v. Ervin, 23 F. Supp. 70, 78 (D. Minn. 1938).

[12] FTC, Chain Stores, Sen. Doc. No. 85, 73d Cong., 2d Sess. xv (1934).

[13] See United States v. New York Great Atlantic & Pacific Tea Co., 67 F. Supp. 626, 664 (E.D. Ill. 1946), aff'd, 173 F.2d 79 (7th Cir. 1949).

firm entering new territory increases the degree of competition in that area. As we have seen, the decision to undertake such geographic expansion frequently rests upon a belief that conditions are favorable for the reaping of profits in the new region. It follows that, prior to the entry of the dispersed firm, the existing suppliers may well have enjoyed a monopolistic position. Seen in this light, dispersion shifts resources to a more economic use. Many a handicraft monopoly disappeared when the railroads carried the products of factories into remote areas.[1] Recently, Sears, Roebuck & Company opened a retail store in Brazil; within a year the prices of some products had fallen to about half their former level.[2] Branch bankers and chain store proprietors shift money and goods rapidly to areas where demand is most vigorous, thus satisfying local requirements and reducing monopolistic positions.[3] Local sellers are pushed into more efficient practices, and living standards are raised.[4]

§7.8. [1] Stocking and Watkins, Monopoly and Free Enterprise 491 (1951). Stocking and Watkins stated flatly: ". . . effective competition requires continual shifting of productive resources from industry to industry and from region to region in response to changes in market conditions . . ." Id. at 511. In Wilcox, On the Alleged Ubiquity of Oligopoly, 40 Proceedings Am. Econ. Assn. 67, 70 (1950), it was said: "Hard roads and automobiles have brought the local merchant into competition with the supermarket, the wayside stand, the specialty shop, and the department store. And even in the most isolated communities, he must compete with Sears, Roebuck and Montgomery Ward. The consumer makes his contact with oligopoly, if at all, at second hand." Accord: Butters, Lintner, and Cary, Effects of Taxation: Corporate Mergers 20 (1951); McNair, Monopolistic Competition in Retailing in Chain Stores and Legislation 245 (Bloomfield ed. 1939); Hale, Trust Dissolution: "Atomizing" Business Units of Monopolistic Size, 40 Colum. L. Rev. 615, 627 (1940).

[2] Sears, Roebuck in Rio, 41 Fortune No. 2, pp. 78, 155 (1950); Wilcox, On the Alleged Ubiquity of Oligopoly, 40 Proceedings Am. Econ. Assn. 67, 71 (1950) ("the formula for competition is simple: add one part of Sears Roebuck to twenty parts of oligopoly"). Careful observers are agreed that the mass merchandisers have shown no tendency to monopolize trade. Phillips, An Evaluation of Large-scale Retailing with Emphasis on the Chain Store, 8 Law & Contemp. Prob. 348, 356 (1941); Hoffman, Large-scale Organization in the Food Industries 157 (TNEC Monograph No. 35, 1940); The Great A & P, 36 Fortune No. 5, pp. 103, 249 (1947); Wilcox, Competition and Monopoly in American Industry 56 (TNEC Monograph No. 21, 1940); Stocking and Watkins, Monopoly and Free Enterprise 329 (1951). In Abrahamson, The Automobile Tire — Forms of Marketing in Combat, in Price and Price Policies 83, 115 (Hamilton ed. 1938), it was said: "The mail order house and the large retail chain represent the first intelligent attack upon the wastes of distribution and the first systematic attempt to bring economy into the processes of marketing . . . bigness in itself is not of necessity a move into monopoly."

[3] House Committee on Small Business, United States v. Economic Concentration and Monopoly, Staff Report Pursuant to H. Res. 64, 79th Cong., 2d Sess. 405 (1947); Swift & Co., 1950 Year Book 15 (Chicago, 1950); Chapman, Concentration of Banking 297 (1934); Beckman and Nolen, The Chain Store Problem 57 (1938). But compare Chamberlin, The Theory of Monopolistic Competition 197 (6th ed. 1948) (increase in number of sellers will not affect slope of demand curve).

[4] Palmer, Economic and Social Aspects of Chain Stores, 2 J. Business 272, 287 (1929); Kaplan, Small Business: Its Place and Problems 186 (1948); Hoffman, Large-

It has often been recognized that dispersion performs the functions just described. In the decrees dissolving the old tobacco and powder trusts, for example, the courts took pains to assure each successor concern at least one plant in every section of the nation.[5]

Vigorous foes of big business have taken cognizance of this factor.[6] The baneful effects of local monopoly, untouched by penetration of its sheltered market, have been repeatedly recognized by both courts and observers.[7] As indicated above, the

---

scale Organization in the Food Industries 14, 66 (TNEC Monograph No. 35, 1940); The Esso Handicap, 41 Fortune No. 2, pp. 73, 74 (1950); Penney's, King of the Soft Goods, 42 id. No. 3, p. 130 (1950). A vivid illustration of the effects of market penetration by an enterprise of superior skills is found in Tsumeb: Three-year Wonder, 41 id. No. 2, pp. 84, 85 (1950). *Accord.* Phelps, Migration of Industry to South America 305 (1936); Westinghouse Abroad, 41 Fortune No. 2, pp. 76, 114 (1950); Sears, Roebuck in Rio, id. at 78, 152 (local manufacturing encouraged in order to supply Brazilian store). Dispersion is, by definition, antimonopolistic in that it reduces intensity of market coverage in the original area.

[5] Hale, Trust Dissolution, 40 Colum. L. Rev. 615, 620, 627 (1940); compare Mund, Government and Business 183 (1950); United States v. Columbia Steel Co., 334 U.S. 495, 533 (1948). In buying materials the trustees of Illinois state institutions are directed to give preference to those states whose laws do not prohibit the purchase of Illinois commodities for public institutions. Illinois Rev. Stat., c. 29, §40 (1949).

[6] Celler Committee I, pt. 4A, at 261, 779 (Mr. Wiprud, a believer in competition among carriers, nevertheless favored end-to-end consolidation of railroads); Edwards, Economic and Political Aspects of International Cartels, Subcommittee on War Mobilization, Senate Committee on Military Affairs, Sen. Monograph No. 1, p. 19, 78th Cong., 2d Sess. (1944) (semble); Fetter, The Economic Law of Market Areas, 38 Q.J. Econ. 520, 523 (1924) (semble); compare Note, Judicial Invalidation of Federal Reserve Policy Against Bank Holding Company Expansion, 57 Yale L.J. 297, 298 n.8 (1947). Congress did not abolish holding companies completely in the utility field. It recognized that such companies could render valuable services. Note, 59 Yale L.J. 1088, 1111 n.117 (1950). But see Hale, Control Over Distribution, 14 Miss. L.J. 170, 181, 182 (1941) (restricted sales area and exclusive sales area usually lawful).

[7] See Mandeville Island Farms, Inc. v. American Crystal Sugar Co., 334 U.S. 219, 235 (1948); United States v. Yellow Cab. Co., 332 U.S. 218, 225 (1947); United States v. Crescent Amusement Co., 323 U.S. 173 (1944); Indiana Farmer's Guide v. Prairie Farmer Co., 293 U.S. 268, 279 (1934); United States v. Lehigh Valley R.R., 254 U.S. 255, 258, 263 (1920); United States v. Reading Co., 253 U.S. 26 (1920); United States v. Terminal Railroad Assn., 224 U.S. 383 (1912); United States v. Great Western Sugar Co., 39 F.2d 152 (D. Neb. 1930); More v. Bennett, 140 Ill. 69, 29 N.E. 888 (1892); Chicago Gas Light & Coke Co. v. People's Gas Light & Coke Co., 121 Ill. 530, 544, 13 N.E. 169, 174 (1887); Tooke & Reynolds v. Bastrop Ice Co., 172 La. 781, 135 So. 239 (1931); Edwards, Maintaining Competition 111 1949); Levi, The Antitrust Laws and Monopoly, 14 U. Chi. L. Rev. 153, 176 (1947); Celler Committee I, pt. 2A, at 442; Clark, Monopolistic Tendencies, Their Character and Consequences, 18 Proceedings Acad. Pol. Sci. 124, 128 (1939); Veblen, Absentee Ownership 147 (1923). Note the amendment to §7 of the Clayton Act, 64 Stat. 1125 (1950), 15 U.S.C.A. §18 (Supp. 1950) ("in any section of the country"). Compare Rural Electrification Act of 1936, 49 Stat. 1363, 7 U.S.C.A. §901 (1946).

Division of powers between state and federal governments may account for some judicial views looking in the opposite direction. E.g., United States v. Griffith, 334 U.S. 100, 106 (1948).

evils of protectionism are now generally understood. Enactment of the Reciprocal Trade Agreements Act constituted recognition of the burdens placed upon consumers by international tariffs.[8] And many provisions of our Federal Constitution have been utilized to strike down barriers to trade among the several states of the Union.[9]

It is not difficult to puncture the argument that dispersion is bad because it fosters local-price cutting. In the *Griffith* case,[10] for example, the monopoly position enjoyed by the defendants in the "closed" towns (where there was no competition) could have been utilized simply to drive better bargains in such areas. The fact that the defendants chose to exploit their monopoly power in another way — by securing advantageous terms in the "open" towns — seems irrelevant to the legality of their dispersed structure. Thus the objection to dispersion seems founded in that concept of "soft" competition which is said to

In cases involving agreements by employees not to compete with employers after termination of the relationship, the courts have insisted that the area involved be no larger than necessary to protect the promisee. Bausch & Lomb Optical Co. v. Wahlgren, 68 F.2d 660 (7th Cir. 1934); *cert. denied,* 292 U.S. 639 (1934); Interstate Finance Corp. v. Wood, 69 F. Supp. 278 (E.D. Ill. 1946); Roy v. Bolduc, 140 Me. 103, 34 A.2d 479 (1943); Tawney v. Mutual System, Inc., 186 Md. 508, 47 A.2d 372 (1946); 2 Restatement of Contracts §515, Illustrations 5-7, §516 (f).

[8] 48 Stat. 943 (1934), 19 U.S.C.A. §1351 (1946). Comparative costs and division of labor are the fundamental considerations. Heilperin, The Trade of Nations 7, 9, 19 (1947); Stocking and Watkins, Monopoly and Free Enterprise 382 (1951). Refinements of the classic theory are presented in Viner, International Trade, 8 Encyc. Soc. Sci. 200, 203 (1932).

[9] U.S. Const., Art. I, §10 (no state shall lay duty on exports or imports); Henderson, The Position of Foreign Corporations in American Constitutional Law 19, 66, 111 (1918). U.S. Const., Art. IV, §2 (privileges and immunities) and id., Amend. XIV, §1 (privileges and immunities); O'Connell v. Kontojohn, 131 Fla. 783, 179 So. 802 (1938). U.S. Const., Amend. XIV, §1 (denial of due process; equal protection); Hair v. City of Humboldt, 133 Kan. 67, 299 Pac. 268 (1931); City of Elgin v. Winchester, 300 Ill. 214, 133 N.E. 205 (1921); C. D. Kenny Co. v. Town of Brevard, 217 N.C. 269, 7 S.E.2d 542 (1940); Orangeburg v. Farmer, 181 S.C. 143, 186 S.E. 783 (1936); New York Dugan Bros., Inc. v. New York, 169 Misc. 209, 7 N.Y.S.2d 162 (Sup. Ct. 1938); Louis K. Liggett Co. v. Lee, 288 U.S. 517, 534 (1933); compare dissenting opinions in Great Atlantic & Pacific Tea Co. v. Grosjean, 301 U.S. 412, 433 (1937); Campbell Baking Co. v. Harrisonville. 50 F.2d 670, 681 (8th Cir. 1931); see Lee, Protectionism and Chain Store Taxes, in Tax Barriers to Trade 151, 159 (Tax Institute, 1940); Silverman, Bennett, and Lechliter, Control by Licensing Over Entry into the Market, 8 Law & Contemp. Prob. 258 (1941). U.S. Const., Art. I, §8 (power to regulate commerce); Best & Co. v. Maxwell, 311 U.S. 454 (1940); Hale v. Bimco Trading Co., 306 U.S. 375 (1939); Real Silk Mills v. Portland, 268 U.S. 325, 335 (1925); Henderson, The Position of Foreign Corporations in American Constitutional Law 116 (1918); McIntire and Rhyne, Municipal Legislative Barriers to a Free Market, 8 Law & Contemp. Prob. 359, 370, 373 (1941); see generally Truitt, Interstate Trade Barriers in the United States, 8 Law & Contemp. Prob. 209, 214, 220 (1941). *Contra:* Singer Sewing Machine Co. v. Brickell, 233 U.S. 304, 315 (1913); Waters-Pierce Oil Co. v. Texas, 177 U.S. 28 (1900); Jewel Tea Co. v. City of Troy, 80 F.2d 366, 368 (7th Cir. 1935); Campbell Baking Co. v. Harrisonville, 50 F.2d 670 (8th Cir. 1931); Williams v. Bowling Green, 254 Ky. 11, 70 S.W.2d 967 (1934).

[10] United States v. Griffith, 334 U.S. 100 (1948).

characterize the Robinson-Patman amendments: competitors, not consumers, are to be protected by the antitrust laws.[11] Such an attitude leads to a situation in which a firm operating in more than one area faces a dilemma: if it maintains a uniform price everywhere, it does not meet local competition, discriminates against its nearby customers, and must earn monopoly profits somewhere to equalize the losses incurred where competition is strong; if, on the other hand, it varies its prices to meet local conditions, it is guilty of injuring its independent competitors.[12]

It is also true that the benefits of dispersion just outlined are difficult to appraise. For one thing, we have little notion as to the extent of those local monopolies which dispersion counteracts.[13] Again, dispersion is not a requisite to the geographic shifting of resources to their most economic use: independent firms could accomplish the same feat, although perhaps less rapidly.[14]

Local price-cutting with intent to injure a competitor is possible when disparity of size exists. Such size may be reflected in a dispersed organization. As we have seen, however, dispersion is not necessarily correlated with over-all wealth. The larger resources of the dominant firm, rather than its geographic extent, permit it to crush the independent.[15] Limitation upon wealth itself is the logical remedy if it is deemed that disparity of size necessarily leads to elimination of competitors.[16]

§7.9. **Discrimination.** Unless the prices of the dispersed seller are uniform in all areas, he may be attacked, as we have

[11] Id. at 106.

[12] FTC v. A. E. Staley Mfg. Co., 324 U.S. 746 (1945); Corn Products Refining Co. v. FTC, 324 U.S., 726, 737 (1945); Fairmount Creamery Co. v. Minnesota, 274 U.S. 1 (1927); United States v. New York Great Atlantic & Pacific Tea Co., 173 F.2d 79, 87 (7th Cir. 1949); compare Clark, The Law and Economics of Basing Points: Appraisal and Proposals, 39 Am. Econ. Rev. 430, 432 (1949).

[13] TNEC, Final Rep. of Exec. Secy. 10, 16; Edwards, Maintaining Competition 111 (1949); Chandler, Monopolistic Elements in Commercial Banking, 46 J. Pol. Econ. 1, 7 (1938).

[14] One factor affecting the problem is the second tax on corporate earnings levied by Internal Revenue Code of 1954, §§1, 34. Examples of shifting of resources within a firm are found in Armco Steel Corp., 1948 Ann. Rep. 13 (Middletown, 1949); W. T. Grant Co., 1948 Ann. Rep. 7 (New York City, 1949); Celler Committee I, pt. 2B, at 1140. Compare Adelman, The A. & P. Case: A Study in Applied Economic Theory, 63 Q.J. Econ. 238, 247 (1949); House Select Committee on Small Business, United States v. Economic Concentration and Monopoly, Staff Report Pursuant to H. Res. 64, 79th Cong., 2d Sess. 405 (1947); Willis, Branch Banking, 2 Encyc. Soc. Sci. 679 (1932). The complaint against "draining off of funds" (see §7.10 *infra,* note 1) may reflect the ability of dispersed firms to allocate resources more effectively.

[15] Edwards, Geographic Price Formulas and the Concentration of Economic Power, 37 Geo. L.J. 135, 136 (1949); Burns, The Decline of Competition 259 (1936).

Note the relationship between the problem of monopoly and that of the business cycle: protectionism gains adherents during periods of business depression when immediate relief is demanded regardless of long-run consequences.

[16] Chapter 8.

seen, for cutting prices in regions where competition is strong. By the same token he will be accused of raising prices where competition is weak. Such difference in prices is commonly called "price discrimination." It was an important target of Section 2 of the Clayton Act, both before and after its amendment.[1] In the field of regulated industry the practice of charging less for longer hauls than for shorter ones was condemned in the Interstate Commerce Act. As described by Professor Sharfman:

> The long-and-short-haul clause was designed to eliminate the pernicious practice of charging higher rates for shorter than for longer hauls which had become widely prevalent prior to 1887 as a result of unrestrained resort to competitive rate-making. . . .
>
> The legislative purpose was seen to be that of relieving small intermediate communities from existing disabilities in their rivalry with those larger and more favored points where carrier competition had created conspicuous rate advantages; while the competition of carriers was to be retained as a beneficial condition, its destructive manifestations were to be curbed.[2]

Many of the motives behind the enactment of the Public Utility Holding Company Act of 1935 [3] were basically similar to the anti-discrimination sentiments which prompted adoption of the Clayton and Interstate Commerce Acts.

Little direct evidence is available to show the extent of geographic price discrimination in modern markets.[4] Certainly a

§7.9. [1] 38 Stat. 731 (1914), as amended, 15 U.S.C.A. §13 (1946). A comparable complaint is that dispersion leads to nationwide bargaining with labor unions; that such bargaining results in nationally standardized wage rates; and that such standardization handicaps backward industrial areas. Compare Stocking and Watkins, Monopoly and Free Enterprise 409 (1951).

[2] 1 Sharfman, The Interstate Commerce Commission 28 (1931); 3-B id. at 543. The trick of retaining competition and abolishing it at the same time has not been as simple in performance as in intent. 2 id. at 54; 3-B id. at 543, 588. It took the ICC twenty-five years to dispose of the flood of applications for relief from the long- and short-haul clause filed before 1911. 4 id. at 284. When a railway charges more for a short than long haul over the same route, this fact reflects more monopoly power at one point (terminus of short haul) than at the other (terminus of long haul); hence, this is a probable use of dispersed position to meet a competitive situation.

[3] 49 Stat. 803, 15 U.S.C.A. §79a(b) (1946). Thus one of the most frequently professed reasons for the legislation lay in the alleged ability of dispersed firms to evade local price regulation. It was argued that the state commissions could not effectively reach the holding companies and allocate their costs. FTC, Utility Corporations, Sen. Doc. No. 92, 70th Cong., 1st Sess., pt. 72-A, 871 (1935); Senate Committee on Interstate Commerce, Public Utility Act of 1935, Sen. Rep. No. 621, 74th Cong., 1st Sess. 11 (1935); Note, 59 Yale L.J. 1088, 1090, 1092 (1950).

[4] Commissioner of Corporations, Petroleum Industry, pt. II, 452 (1907); Celler Committee I, pt. 4A, at 343; compare Stocking and Watkins, Monopoly and Free Enterprise 181 (1951). Existence of multiple plants is not required for the exer-

single firm cannot be guilty of both cutting and raising prices in the same area at the same time.[5] It is believed, however, that many goods are sold on a nationwide basis at a uniform price, and it is easy to understand that the maker of a branded commodity hesitates to vary his price in precise proportion to transportation costs.[6] Such considerations led Professor Adelman to conclude that a dispersed firm's price structure might well consist of a "honeycomb of discrimination."[7] Thus, while the amount of such discrimination is not calculable, its persistence seems highly likely.

The argument has been advanced that the dispersed firm cuts its prices in some areas and recoups its losses by raising them in others. Here price discrimination is not only evil in itself but encourages local price-cutting. It is easy, however, to dispose of the contention. Such recoupment is possible only in areas where competition is weak. And in those regions the seller will raise his prices to a monopolistic level regardless of losses which may or may not be sustained in other geographic divisions.[8] In other words, local price discrimination merely reflects an absence of competition in the area. Monopoly is the only cause of such high prices.[9]

It is true, as we have seen, that dispersion may both increase and reduce costs. Establishment of numerous branch plants may reduce shipping expenses but at the same time undermine that specialization of labor which is the foundation of mass production's efficiency.[10] Supervisory costs may rise.[11] On the other hand, dispersion effects some reduction in costs. Indeed, unless

---

cise of geographic price discrimination. See FTC v. A. E. Staley Mfg. Co., 324 U.S. 746, 749 (1945).

[5] Compare United States v. New York Great Atlantic & Pacific Tea Co., 67 F. Supp. 626, 641, 671 (E.D. Ill. 1946), aff'd, 173 F.2d 79 (7th Cir. 1949).

[6] Hoover, The Location of Economic Activity 56 (1948); compare Grether, Geographical Price Policies in the Grocery Trade 1941, 8 J. Marketing 417, 419 (1944). Dispersed oligopoly may behave more like monopoly. Clark, The Law and Economics of Basing Points: Appraisal and Proposals, 39 Am. Econ. Rev. 430, 441 (1949).

[7] Adelman, Integration and Antitrust Policy, 63 Harv. L. Rev. 27, 40 (1949).

[8] Id. at 46, 58; Fulda, Food Distribution in the United States, 99 U. Pa. L. Rev. 1051, 1149 (1951); compare Central Lumber Co. v. South Dakota, 226 U.S. 157, 161 (1912).

[9] FTC, Chain Stores, Sen. Doc. No. 85, 73d Cong., 2d Sess. xv 7, 19 (1934); Palmer, Economic and Social Aspects of Chain Stores, 2 J. Business 272, 282 (1929); Penney's, King of the Soft Goods, 42 Fortune No. 3, pp. 101, 104 (1950); Adelman, Integration and Antitrust Policy, 63 Harv. L. Rev. 27, 41 (1949); compare Fairmount Creamery v. Minnesota, 274 U.S. 1, 8 (1927). Complaint has been registered that a multiplant firm has difficulty in setting prices so as not to compete with itself. Mund, The Development and Incidence of Delivered Pricing in American Industry, 15 Law & Contemp. Prob. 141, 145 (1950). The foregoing complaint seems unrealistic. Compare Celler Committee I, pt. 4A, at 525.

[10] Stocking and Watkins, Monopoly and Free Enterprise 72 (1951); Edwards, Maintaining Competition 114 (1949).

a firm is free to enter more distant markets, it may not be able to sell all the goods produced in a plant of efficient size.[12] As indicated above, the economically desirable degree of dispersion can be found only in an equilibrium resulting from the interaction of conflicting costs.[13]

Dispersion is not the cause of objectionable price discrimination. Indeed, the whole concept of price discrimination, insofar as it is unrelated to the absence of competition, may be unsuited to free markets. It is a notion derived from ideas of fairness and applied to regulated public utilities. Incorporation of the concept in the Clayton Act may have been a serious mistake, rendering that statute inconsistent with the basic antitrust law.[14]

§7.10. Draining away of funds. Another complaint upon which we need not tarry long is that the dispersed concern withdraws money from local communities and concentrates deposits in metropolitan centers. Thus credit is restricted in areas where small business needs it and poured into New York, where it cannot be used.[1] Thurman Arnold blamed continuance of the depression upon the drainage of funds from the South and West and into the rich eastern United States.[2]

---

[11] Compare Celler Committee I, pt. 4A, at 418. Dispersion is not inevitably followed by uneconomic nationwide labor bargaining. Id. at 243; Shister, Economics of the Labor Market 158 (1949).

[12] Compare Heilperin, The Trade of Nations 13 (1947); Celler Committee I, pt. 4A, at 503; Note, 59 Yale L.J. 1088, 1100 n.58 (1950).

[13] A multiplant firm can, for example, save shipping costs by routing orders to its nearest factory. Burns, The Decline of Competition 256 (1936); Wilcox, On the Alleged Ubiquity of Oligopoly, 40 Proceedings Am. Econ. Assn. 67, 310 (1950); Stocking and Watkins, Monopoly and Free Enterprise 59 (1951); Celler Committee I, pt. 1, at 515; compare Corn Products Refining Co. v. FTC, 324 U.S. 726 (1945) (dispersion might enable firm to avoid illegal discrimination); Celler Committee I, pt. 6A, at 229. Decentralization may assist the dispersed firm to achieve economies. Hearings Before House Special Committee on Investigation of American Retail Federation, Vol. 3, No. 1, p. 14, 74th Cong., 1st Sess. (1935); Ritchie, Integration Under Section 10(c) of the Public Utility Holding Company Act, 41 Mich. L. Rev. 1, 19 (1942).

[14] Burling and Sheldon, Price Competition as Affected by the Robinson-Patman Act, 1 Wash. & Lee L. Rev. 31, 34 (1939); McAllister, Price Control by Law, 4 Law & Contemp. Prob. 273, 289 (1937); Taft, Basic Concepts of Price Control, 11 Geo. Wash. L. Rev. 191, 202 (1943); Adelman, Integration and Antitrust Policy, 63 Harv. L. Rev. 27, 77 (1949); Simon, Legal Price Fixing, Proceedings N.Y. State Bar Assn., Section on Antitrust Law, Third Annual Meeting 86 (CCH, 1951). Note the acute comment of Professor Clark to the effect that antidiscrimination statutes convert free businesses into public utilities in the area surrounding plants. Clark, The Law and Economics of Basing Points: Appraisal and Proposals, 39 Am. Econ. Rev. 430, 432 (1949); compare Corn Products Refining Co. v. FTC, 324 U.S. 726, 737 (1945). On the other hand, §1(b)(4) of the Public Utility Holding Company Act of 1935, 49 Stat. 803, 15 U.S.C.A. §79 (1946), frowns upon dispersion.

§7.10. [1] See, e.g., Richmond Linen Supply Co. v. Lynchburg, 160 Va. 644, 169 S.E. 554 (1933), aff'd, 291 U.S. 641 (1934); Celler Committee I, pt. 2A, at 453.

[2] Id., pt. 1 at 408.

It is, of course, true that dispersed sellers remove funds from points of sale. Chain stores, for example, after meeting payrolls, rentals, and other local charges, remit the balance of their receipts to company headquarters. There the money is available to pay for merchandise, taxes, overhead, and the like.[3] This process, however, is merely part of an economic shifting of resources. Savings are concentrated in the eastern United States. Insurance companies, collecting premiums there and elsewhere, invest the available proceeds in the Southwest where returns are most promising. Mobility of investment funds reduces differentials in interest rates.[4] And there is evidence indicating that the dispersed firm, whether chain store, branch banking enterprise, or insurance company, reallocates resources more rapidly and effectively than do geographically separated entities.[5] If dispersion drains dollars away from small towns more quickly than other forms of business, then it directs investment funds to their most effective use on a faster schedule. Thus, to the extent that money can be put to better use in some small communities than in large ones, dispersion may well achieve that result faster than transfer through a number of independent business units.[6]

§7.11. **Compelled universal dispersion.** A more substantial charge against dispersion is that geographic expansion by one firm may compel similar action by its competitors. If United States Steel installs a rolling mill on the Pacific coast, Bethlehem may have to follow suit or forgo further sales in that market. Thus a new firm, seeking to enter into competition, may find that it must raise larger capital in order to meet the dispersion of established concerns.[1] Efficient use of advertising media may effect such a degree of dispersion.[2] It appears that the com-

3 See J. C. Penney Co. v. Wisconsin Tax Commission, 233 Wis. 286, 289, 289 N.W. 677, 678 (1940); J. C. Penney Co. v. Wisconsin Tax Commission, 238 Wis. 69, 77, 298 N.W. 186, 190 (1941). But compare Celler Committee I, pt. 2A, at 512 (no actual drain of funds because chain prices lower than non-chain competitors).

4 Id., pt. 2B, at 1140; TNEC, Final Rep. of Exec. Secy. 217; Hoover, The Location of Economic Activity 69 (1948); Chapman, Concentration of Banking 299 (1934); Dallas, Chain Stores — Pro and Con (Public Affairs Committee, Inc. 1940).

5 Willis, Branch Banking, 2 Encyc. Soc. Sci. 679 (1932); compare Lockhart, State Tax Barriers to Interstate Trade, 53 Harv. L. Rev. 1253, 1274 (1940) (shifting of perishable products).

6 Compare Lovell, Sales Below Cost Prohibitions: Private Price Fixing Under State Law, 57 Yale L.J. 391, 396 (1948). To the extent — and it may be important — that corporations retain part of their earnings and do not distribute all to their shareholders, liquid resources may be concentrated in commercial centers. As indicated above, however, they are probably thus more readily available for investment where most productive than they would be if they were paid out to scattered equity owners.

§7.11. 1 Beckman and Nolan, The Chain Store Problem 225 (1938).

2 TNEC Hearings, pt. 1, at 114; Hoover, The Location of Economic Activity 56

munications business may be afflicted with a similar problem arising out of technological requirements.[3] Otherwise, no data appear to be available on the subject.

In passing upon the validity of chain store taxes, courts have often written unsophisticated opinions. It has been urged, for example, that taxes aimed at chain stores are justified because the chain can pay cash and thus secure goods at lower prices, while the independent competitor cannot.[4] It is easy to explode such contentions: the profit-making merchant, large or small, can pay cash. Many of the other alleged advantages of the chains are attributable to their over-all size, rather than to their dispersion, and are therefore shared with other large sellers, such as department stores.[5] Something like the argument here considered, however, may have inarticulately underlain the reasoning of the courts in the *Chain Store Tax* cases.

A countervailing consideration may be found in the stabilizing effects of dispersion. By spreading risks over a wide geographic area the dispersed firm avoids the peaks and valleys of sales and profits experienced in single areas. Crop failures, floods, and other local conditions thus have less impact upon the enterprise.[6] For such reasons branch banking has been urged as a protection

---

(1948); Celler Committee I, pt. 2A, at 313; Burns, The Decline of Competition 457 (1936). In Fox v. Standard Oil Co., 294 U.S. 87, 98 (1935), it was suggested that the mere identical appearance of chain stores has an advertising value which the independent merchant cannot match. In the tire business localized manufacturers have had to sell at concessions from the nationally advertised prices of larger competitors, even though they enjoyed advantages in transportation costs. Abrahamson, The Automobile Tire — Forms of Marketing in Combat, in Price and Price Policies 83, 90, 102 (Hamilton ed. 1938). In the international field, compare Phelps, Migration of Industry to South America 302 (1936); Standard Oil Co. of New Jersey, 1950 Ann. Rep. 11 (New York City, 1951) (direct dealings between big corporation and foreign governments to remove import restrictions).

[3] Commission on Freedom of the Press, A Free and Responsible Press 5, 84, 104 (1947); compare Chapman, Concentration of Banking 306 (1934).

[4] See Fox v. Standard Oil Co., 294 U.S. 87, 98 (1935) (opinion by Cardozo, J.; four Justices dissenting); State Board of Tax Commissioners of Indiana v. Jackson, 283 U.S. 527, 534 (1931) (opinion by Roberts, J.; four Justices dissenting); Great Atlantic & Pacific Tea Co. v. Grosjean, 301 U.S. 412, 419, 421, 426 (1937) (opinion by Roberts, J.; three Justices dissenting, two taking no part).

[5] See Great Atlantic & Pacific Tea Co. v. Kentucky Tax Commission, 278 Ky. 367, 379, 128 S.W.2d 581, 587-588 (1939); Sutherland, J., dissenting in State Board of Tax Commissioners of Indiana v. Jackson, 283 U.S. 527, 546 (1931).

[6] Burns, The Decline of Competition 257 (1936); Beckman and Nolen, The Chain Store Problem 56 (1938); Heilperin, The Trade of Nations 76 (1947); Thorp, The Changing Structure of Industry, in Recent Economic Changes 167, 215 (Hoover ed. 1929). Compare Hoover, The Location of Economic Activity 262, 282 (1948); Morgan, The Small Community: Foundation of Democratic Life 189 (1942). Geographic dispersion, with raw materials available in manufacturing areas, plus product diversification will provide stability despite dangers of war and other political disturbances. Sterling Drug, Inc., 1950 Ann. Rep. 19 (New York City, 1951).

to depositors.[7]   Business managers are aware of the stability which dispersion can achieve,[8] and even socialist planners take the factor into account.[9]

No satisfactory method of weighing the foregoing contentions has been found. On the one hand, it is possible that the effect of dispersion in compelling counterdispersion by competitors has been exaggerated. Certainly we find many instances, as indicated above, in which small, local concerns compete effectively with geographically spread-out firms.[10] The role of national advertising in causing universal dispersion may have been overestimated.[11] It is also true that an increase in capital requirements is characteristic of the age: as mass production techniques replace handicrafts, the stake necessary to enter into competition has been raised enormously. Technology, in other words, may have increased such costs far more than dispersion. Yet the complaint cannot be wholly dismissed. It has at least theoretical validity,

7 Chapman, Concentration of Banking 296 (1934).

8 President's Research Committee on Social Trends, Recent Social Trends 244 (1933); Sterling Drug, Inc., 1950 Ann. Rep. 19 (New York City, 1951) ("Company . . . fortunate in the diversity of its products and of the geographical incidence of their manufacture and sale"); Argus Research Corp., Weekly Staff Report & Market Summary 4 (July 25, 1951) (United Fruit hedged against political difficulties by spreading its plantations among seven different republics); Mutual Life Insurance Co. of New York, 1950 Ann. Rep. 8 (New York City, 1951) ("geographic diversification of both policyholders and investments is a great factor of strength if the homeland is ever subjected to attack").

9 One of the several benefits found by the planners is the ability to shift labor into another industry when seasonal or cyclical factors reduce employment. Sykes, Diversification of Industry, 60 Econ. J. 697, 705, 707 (1950). Thus the author concluded: "The chief positive arguments for industrial diversification may now be stated. The first is the need to counteract the abnormal industrial specialization of certain areas. The central reason is to prevent damage — perhaps serious and irrevocable damage — to the economy of those areas arising from cyclical contractions of demand, or export fluctuation or the decline of a predominant industry." Id. at 707. The approach of the "planners," of course, is wholly on the "welfare" side, laying stress on full employment in all areas and the like. Its coincidence with economic analysis based upon efficient allocation of resources is, however, interesting. Compare Smaller War Plants Corp., Small Business and Civic Welfare, Sen. Doc. No. 135, 79th Cong., 2d Sess. 9 (1946).

There is also some evidence that dispersion makes it more difficult for labor union leaders to stifle competition among employers. Robinson, Collective Bargaining and Market Control in the New York Coat and Suit Industry 130 (1949); Celler Committee I, pt. 4A, at 242.

On the other hand it can be argued that dispersion spreads risks so far that markets no longer keep a taut rein upon business judgment. Burns, The Decline of Competition 459 (1936).

10 President's Research Committee on Recent Social Trends, Recent Social Trends 245 (1929); Celler Committee I, pt. 2A, at 646 (branch banking the trend but local competition persists).

11 Nixon, Principles of Advertising 327, 361 (1937). Mr. G. Bowman Kreer of McCann-Erickson, Inc., expressed the view that national advertising was not a necessity; local display, he believed, was often more effective.

and every barrier to free entry into the market is a handicap to pure competition.[12]

§7.12. **Absentee ownership.** An even more serious group of complaints can be placed under the familiar heading of absentee ownership. It is urged that individual initiative is stifled under a system of dispersed enterprise; that local managers are mere messenger boys, carrying out decisions made in far-off headquarters by officers unfamiliar with local conditions and people; that levels of civic welfare are lower when business is ultimately controlled by distant directors.[1] In recent years the attack has been pressed principally against the chain stores,[2] perhaps because retail selling is a stronghold of very small business.[3]

We know little about the amount of dispersion which now characterizes our economy.[4] Nor is there current information to indicate a trend toward a greater or lesser degree of geographic

[12] Compare Taussig, Tariff History of the United States 5, 7 (8th ed. 1931) (justification for protective tariff in undeveloped states rapidly changing from agriculture to manufactures).

Although the basing point problem is beyond the scope of this study, a few comments on the effects of dispersion on it may be in order. As stated above, methods of quoting prices are not material to the question of dispersion. Nor is any reason apparent why a dispersed firm should more readily enter into a basing point conspiracy; the power to retaliate inherent in dispersion would suggest both that the agreement was unnecessary and that it might prove convenient. Compare Stocking, The Economics of Basing Point Pricing, 15 Law & Contemp. Prob. 159, 163 (1950); Clark, The Law and Economics of Basing Points: Appraisal and Proposals, 39 Am. Econ. Rev. 430, 442 (1949) (effect of uniform f.o.b. mill pricing (by dispersed firms) depends on slope of demand curve). On the other hand, existence of dispersion is fundamental to the whole basing point problem because if each plant sold only in its area of natural advantage and did not attempt to penetrate other areas, no basing point system would have started. A multiplant, dispersed firm both gains and loses more under a basing point system. Edwards, Geographic Price Formulas and the Concentration of Economic Power, 37 Geo. L.J. 135, 137, 141 (1949). Freight absorption may be less painful for the multiplant firm because it can ship from a nearby factory. But the end of the basing point system appears to be causing dispersion in the steel industry. Mullaney, F.T.C. Steel Order Is Held "Academic," N.Y. Times, June 24, 1951, p. 2, col. 3. In any event few would be willing to treat the basing point problem by the drastic remedy of prohibiting dispersion.

§7.12. [1] Ernst, Too Big 176 (1940) (recording views of Mr. Justice Brandeis); Kefauver, The Supreme Court and Congress Versus Monopoly, 20 Tenn. L. Rev. 254, 255 (1948); Chapman, Concentration of Banking 294 (1934); Villard, Editorial Power of the Chains, in The Newspaper and Society, 459, 461 (Bird and Merwin ed. 1942); Note, The Impact of the F.C.C.'s Chain Broadcasting Rules, 60 Yale L.J. 78, 80, 97 (1951); Ritchie, Integration Under Section 10(c) of the Public Utility Holding Company Act, 41 Mich. L. Rev. 1, 18 (1942); Committee on Interstate Commerce, Public Utility Act of 1935, Sen. Rep. No. 621, 74th Cong., 1st Sess. 4 (1935); Note, 59 Yale L.J. 1088, 1104 (1950).

[2] See, e.g., Great Atlantic & Pacific Tea Co. v. Grosjean, 301 U.S. 412 (1937).

[3] Kaplan, Small Business: Its Place and Problems 28 (1948); TNEC, Final Rep. of Exec. Secy. 298.

[4] Compare Quinn, Human Ecology 348, 350 (1950), with authorities cited *supra* §7.3, note 25.

expansion by business enterprises. Therefore, the importance of absentee ownership is difficult to assess. It is common knowledge that in all but the largest cities many stores and factories are owned by firms whose headquarters are located elsewhere. There is some evidence suggesting, however, that in the retail field dispersion has been halted and that perhaps the chain stores are now contracting their geographic scope. In the grocery business, at least, independent merchants, particularly those organized in "voluntary" chains or operating supermarkets, appear able to compete with the regular chains on approximately even terms.[5]

Part of the case against absentee ownership consists of unsupported assertion. It is argued, for example, that absenteeism destroys the "flavor" of community life and depersonalizes local relationships. Managers of branch banks refuse loans secured only by the borrower's character. Local editors of chain newspapers prepare news and editorials without knowledge of community conditions.[6] But careful observers have also reported that the problem is real. Mr. Justice Cardozo, dissenting in one of the *Chain Store Tax* cases, was unwilling to dismiss absentee ownership as a frivolous complaint.[7] Other cautious judges have felt that control from a distance affects the stability and moral fiber of communities.[8] The fact that managers are shifted from town to town has suggested to many minds that such persons cannot logically take a deep interest in the affairs of the place where they happen to work at any given time.[9] American enter-

---

[5] Oakes, Price Differences for Identical Items in Chain, Voluntary Group, and Independent Grocery Stores, 14 J. Marketing 434, 435 (1949); Brunner and Kolb, Rural Social Trends 150 (President's Research Committee on Social Trends, 1933); Beckman and Nolen, The Chain Store Problem 71 (1938); FTC, Cooperative Grocery Chains, Sen. Doc. No. 12, 72d Cong., 1st Sess. 9 (1932); Phillips, An Evaluation of Large-Scale Retailing with Emphasis on the Chain Store, 8 Law & Contemp. Prob. 348, 356 (1941); Kaplan, Small Business: Its Place and Problems 29 (1948); Fulda, Food Distribution in the United States, 99 U. Pa. L. Rev. 1051, 1065 (1951).

[6] Collins, Anti-Chain Store Legislation, 24 Cornell L.Q. 198, 203 (1939); Beckman and Nolen, The Chain Store Problem 237 (1938); Collins, The Branch Banking Question 9 (1926); Chapman, Concentration of Banking 300 (1934); Villard, Editorial Power of the Chains, in The Newspaper and Society 459, 461 (Bird and Merwin ed. 1942). An interesting comment on the status of the sole newspaper in a city is found in Celler Committee I, pt. 6A, at 375.

[7] Louis K. Liggett Co. v. Lee, 288 U.S. 517, 581, 583 (1933).

[8] See Great Atlantic & Pacific Tea Co. v. Kentucky Tax Commission, 278 Ky. 367, 128 S.W.2d 581 (1939); State v. Langley, 53 Wyo. 332, 84 P.2d 767 (1938).

[9] Chapman, Concentration of Banking 309 (1934); Celler Committee I, pt. 2A, at 334; President's Committee on Recent Social Trends, Recent Social Trends 525 (1929); Fulda, Food Distribution in the United States, 99 U. Pa. L. Rev. 1051, 1080 (1951). A recent study suggesting that local managers of diversified businesses are afraid to participate in community affairs, and hence remain detached, is reported in Schulze, The Role of Economic Dominants in Community Power Structure, 23 Am. Soc. Rev. 3, 7-8 (1958).

prises operating abroad have found it expedient to form subsidiary companies, organized under local laws and staffed with
native directors.[10] No doubt they thus hope to avoid the stigma
of far-off control which so often arouses antagonism against absentee owners.[11]

In economic terms the argument against absentee control is
feeble. If the manager of a branch bank makes only secured
loans, whereas conditions are such that unsecured credit is a sound
investment, then the dispersed institution will lose business to a
localized competitor. If the editor of a chain newspaper is so
ignorant of community conditions that he prepares a stupid
journal, presumably he will lose circulation.[12] Dispersion,
moreover, tends to reduce the social and political shadow which
hangs over a one-company town:[13] additional plants and stores
give the area a better balance of power.

In the absence of information from other sources as to the
effects of absentee control, a field study of the subject was carried
out. Again no exact answers were discovered. The results indicate that a problem of absentee ownership exists. They suggest
that steps have been taken to overcome it. How successful those
efforts have been and what importance should be attached to the
situation which remains could not be determined.[14] Nor is it

[10] Celler Committee I, pt. 6A, at 537, 961; compare id., p. 1, at 412; The Canadian
Troubles of U.S. Business, 66 Fortune No. 1, p. 139 (1957).

[11] Id., pt. 4A, at 907 (vitriolic attack upon steel companies which operate iron
mines in Minnesota; said to control very thoughts of citizenry). Compare Kaplan,
Small Business: Its Place and Problems 4 (1948) (satisfactions of self-employment).
It is sometimes said that a dispersed concern will shut down its high-cost plants
in times of slack demand, regardless of local consequences. Compare Standard Oil
Co. of New Jersey, 1949 Ann. Rep. 24 (New York City, 1950) (crude oil taken from
Middle East in preference to Latin America). Similar results would probably fol-
low, however, in the absence of dispersion.

[12] Compare Knight, Absentee Ownership, 1 Encyc. Soc. Sci. 376, 377 (1930); Willis,
Branch Banking, 2 Encyc. Soc. Sci. 679, 680 (1932). It is perhaps a mistake to
assume that all local independent merchants are community-minded. Phillips, An
Evaluation of Large-Scale Retailing with Emphasis on the Chain Store, 8 Law &
Contemp. Prob. 348, 355 (1941).

[13] Compare Edwards, Maintaining Competition 107 (1949). Dispersion is often
urged for reasons of national defense. Celler Committee I, pt. 4A, at 767; Neal,
M-Day Economic Plans Highlighted by H-Bomb, 30 Barron's No. 19, p. 40 (1950);
Morison, Program of the Department of Justice, Proceedings N.Y. State Bar Assn.,
Section on Antitrust Law, Third Annual Meeting 43, 45 (CCH, 1951). The dispersion referred to, however, is not necessarily that of the single firm. And defense
needs continue to be placed in the category of short-run considerations.

[14] Phelps Dodge Corp., 1952 Ann. Rep. 12 (New York City, 1953) ("A scholarship
program related to our operations in Arizona was put into effect in 1949 in cooperation with the University of Arizona and the Arizona State College . . . It is
provided that certain of the scholarships shall be open only to persons resident in
the localities in which the Corporation operates in Arizona . . ."); Safeway Stores,
22 Fortune No. 4, pp. 60, 131 (1940) (fear of local antagonism to chain stores causes

possible to weigh the countervailing factors, making dispersion desirable, which have been mentioned herein.

As we have seen, the problem is political and sociological, rather than economic, in character. At this writing it does not appear likely that we shall soon secure authoritative data of a quantitative type upon which to base conclusions. The mere fact that noneconomic considerations are involved, however, does not mean that the factor of absentee ownership may be overlooked. Nor does it indicate that the antitrust laws cannot be applied to the situation. For in the words of Judge Learned Hand,

> . . . Congress . . . did not condone "good trusts" and condemn "bad" ones; it forbad all. Moreover, in so doing, it was not necessarily actuated by economic motives alone. It is possible, because of its indirect social or moral effect, to prefer a system of small producers, each dependent for his success upon his own skill and character, to one in which the great mass of those engaged must accept the direction of a few.[15]

And, as the illustrious judge suggested, the problem of absentee ownership is related to the large question of corporate wealth.[16]

§7.13. Conclusion. This study has indicated that a few of the complaints against dispersed enterprises are partially justified. It has also suggested that dispersion produces beneficial results of a countervailing tendency. Further analysis, and particularly the collection of additional information concerning actual business situations, could well sharpen the picture here presented. It would probably remain difficult, however, to balance the various factors against each other.

Prohibition of dispersion per se, as suggested by the *Griffith* decision,[1] is nevertheless open to serious question. For one thing, the limitations would be difficult to administer. The setting of boundaries for each economic enterprise might well require a wisdom surpassing human experience; in practice, political considerations might soon gain the upper hand at the expense of the

---

Safeway to encourage local managers to join luncheon clubs, give promptly to local charities, maintain unnecessary balances in neighborhood banks); Pittsburgh Plate Glass Co., 69th Ann. Rep. 3 (Pittsburgh, 1953) ("The Company operates manufacturing plants and distribution units in 245 cities of the country. In each of these communities it strives to be a good citizen and to assume its full share of the costs of local charities and community enterprises"); S. S. Kresge Co., 21 Fortune No. 6, pp. 70, 100 (1940).

15 United States v. Aluminum Co. of America, 148 F.2d 416, 427 (2d Cir. 1945). Compare the imposition of direct controls over prices and production during periods of mobilization.

16 Compare TNEC, Final Rep. of Exec. Secy. 245; Chapter 8 *infra*.

§7.13. 1 United States v. Griffith, 334 U.S. 100 (1948).

consumers' living standards.[2]   Again, such limitations would either divert the activities of existing enterprises into uneconomic channels or stifle their growth.   Unlimited expansion of huge firms may be undesirable, but certainly we should hesitate before restricting the growth of smaller concerns.   Note, too, that fencing each enterprise into a restricted zone would curb those experiments which business managers like to carry out in selected regions.[3]

Dispersion is intimately related to the problem of "horizontal" size.   If we adopted Professor Edwards' suggestion and broke the United States Steel Corporation into three units, one each in Birmingham, Pittsburgh, and Gary,[4] we should effect a corresponding reduction in the proportion of the steel market supplied by that great combination.   And, as we have seen, the complaints against dispersion are often more properly directed against the "pure" size of corporate enterprise.[5]   In other words, the issue is really joined between those who believe that giant aggregations of corporate wealth are necessary to sustain our standard of living and those who concur in the philosophy of Thoreau and Brandeis[6] to the effect that such size is neither necessary nor desirable. Friends of freedom may well insist, however, that enforcement officers consider the phenomenon of dispersion with caution and avoid sham skirmishes with monopoly's manifestations.

[2] See, e.g., Celler Committee I, pt. 1, at 64.
[3] Oxenfeldt, Industrial Pricing and Market Practices 185 (1951).
[4] Edwards, Maintaining Competition 113 (1949).
[5] Compare Stocking and Watkins, Monopoly and Free Enterprise 73 (1951).
[6] Thoreau, Walden (1854); Ernst, Too Big xv (1940); see also Chapter 8 *infra*.

CHAPTER 8

Wealth

§8.1. Pure size contrasted with market power. In earlier chapters we have discussed the "horizontal" size of business firms in relation to the antitrust laws. Such a "horizontal" aspect of the firm — size with respect to a specific product and in a particular geographic market — has long and properly been viewed as the essence of monopoly. It should be carefully distinguished from the absolute or "pure" size of a business enterprise. Absolute or pure size, herein referred to as "wealth," simply means that a concern is large when compared with other business units with which it does not necessarily compete.[1] Wealth, of course, has commanded the attention of students of politics, morals and

§8.1. [1] Wilcox, Competition and Monopoly in American Industry 307 (TNEC Monograph No. 21, 1940). Confusion of wealth with monopoly is frequently encountered in the antitrust laws. E.g., House Select Committee on Small Business, United States v. Economic Concentration and Monopoly, Staff Report Pursuant to H. Res. No. 64, 79th Cong., 2d Sess. (1947). Another writer said some years ago: "Is there any escape from the conclusion that it is the power to aggregate an enormous amount of wealth in one corporate person which is the essential element of an industrial monopoly? . . . It cannot be too often affirmed that a large aggregation of capital and assets under one directory is the essential element of an industrial monopoly — that no corporation can monopolize any branch of profitable industry without enormous wealth." Benjamin, The Illinois Plan for the Prevention and Suppression of Monopolies, 73 Cent. L.J. 131, 132, 134 (1911). There is, however, a connection between monopoly and wealth: the rich competitor can stand the stress of competition longer than his poor rival and thus afford to indulge in attempts to monopolize. That such was the case was recognized in the eighteenth century: "Engrossing was also described to be the getting into one's possession . . . large quantities of corn, or other dead victual, with intent to sell them again. This must of course be injurious to the public, by putting it in the power of one or two rich men to raise the price of provisions at their own discretion." Blackstone, 4 Commentaries on the Laws of England 156 (Cooley's 3d ed. 1884). Only a few years ago an economist wrote: ". . . fluid society demands enough inequality of individual income, individual wealth, and corporate size to furnish adequate incentive. But it cannot permit that income and that size to become so entrenched that there is no possibility of ousting it." Wright, Some Pitfalls of Economic Theory as a Guide to the Law of Competition, 37 Va. L. Rev. 1083, 1094 (1951). The subject is discussed at some length in Edwards, Conglomerate Bigness as a Source of Power, in Business Concentration and Price Policy 331, 352 (Stigler ed. 1955). See also §6.27 *supra*, in which it is suggested that wealth is closely related to the concept of diversification discussed therein.

theology throughout the ages.[2] We cannot here attempt to en-compass all the implications to society arising from the existence of inequalities in the pure size of business firms. We cannot even consider every aspect of the business corporation as a citizen — an entity in the political and sociological scene. What we can ex-amine briefly is the relationship between corporate wealth and antitrust policy.

In recent years studies have indicated that a surprisingly large proportion of the total assets devoted to business purposes in the United States is held by a relatively few corporations. Thus it has been said that the 200 largest corporations own be-tween a fifth and a fourth of the income-producing national wealth.[3] One observer found that the 594 largest corporations held over half of the total assets of all business enterprises.[4] It has also been asserted that in 1933 about 5 per cent of all the cor-porations filing income tax returns showed they held 85.5 per cent of the corporate assets of all filing corporations.[5] Led by

[2] Whittaker, A History of Economic Ideas 58-68, 107-111 (1943). At pages 71-73 it is said: "Early Christian doctrine as revealed in the gospels and epistles holds that riches are an impossible impediment to salvation. To be saved one must sell one's possessions and 'take up the cross and follow Christ.' Preoccupation with what one would eat or how one would be clothed was wrong for God would take care of those who were seeking salvation." See also 1 Blackstone, Commentaries on the Laws of England*479 (Cooley's 3d ed. 1884) (statutes of mortmain); Weber, Law in Economy and Society, c. 12 (Rheinstein ed. 1954); Tilgher, Work: What It Has Meant to Men Through the Ages (Fisher trans. 1930); Smith, Book Review, 45 Am. Econ. Rev. 149 (1955). Thoreau said: "The nation itself, with all its so-called internal improvements, which, by the way, are all external and superficial, is just such an unwieldy and overgrown establishment, cluttered with furniture and tripped up by its own traps, ruined by luxury and heedless expense, by want of calculation and a worthy aim, as the million of households in the land; and the only cure for it, as for them, is in a rigid economy, a stern and more than Spartan simplicity of life and elevation of purpose. It lives too fast. Men think that it is essential that the *Nation* have commerce, and export ice, and talk through a tele-graph, and ride thirty miles an hour, without a doubt, whether *they* do or not; but whether we should live like baboons or like men, is a little uncertain. If we do not get out sleepers, and forge rails, and devote days and nights to the work, but to tinkering upon our *lives* to improve *them*, who will build railroads? And if railroads are not built, how shall we get to heaven in season? But if we stay at home and mind our business, who will want railroads?" . . . "a man is rich in proportion to the number of things which he can afford to let alone."

[3] Adelman, Measurement of Industrial Concentration, 33 Rev. Econ. & Stat. 269, 277 (1951); Hurff, Social Aspects of Enterprise in the Large Corporation 16 (1950). A recent study indicates that the 500 largest industrial firms in the United States em-ployed 44 per cent of industrial labor in 1944 and produced almost half of the in-dustrial output of the nation. Box Score of Business Bigness, 52 Fortune No. 1, p. 96 (1955).

[4] Bernheim, ed., Big Business: Its Growth and Place 54-55 (Twentieth Century Fund, 1937).

[5] O'Mahoney Committee I, pt. 4, at 518. A few basic statistics will be found in Statistical Abstract of the United States 475, 482, 485 (1953). Data have also been collected with reference to the percentage of national employment found in the

Professors Berle and Means, another group of students has loudly proclaimed the existence of a rapid increase in the rate of concentration, asserting that the proportion of national wealth held by the largest firms was greater year by year. Later studies have suggested that there has been little change in the share of the nation's total assets held by the largest firms and it has also been found that there is a rapid turnover in the list of big firms. Thus, of the 100 largest corporations in 1909, only 36 remained on a similar list prepared for the year 1948.[6] Nevertheless, it must be confessed that the figures show a very considerable concentration of industrial and commercial assets in the hands of relatively few organizations. True, the device of stock ownership, with its infinite divisibility, has spread ownership of the large corporations into thousands of hands. A careful estimate made in 1952 showed that some 9.5 per cent of the family units in the United States owned stock in publicly held corporations.[7] On the other hand, control of the assets of the big firms remains vested in management in the first instance and only a potential or residual power is diffused widely among thousands or millions of shareholders.[8]

---

largest corporations. Thus it has been found that only about 500 firms, constituting two tenths of 1 per cent of the total number, employ more than 2500 persons. E.g., House Select Committee on Small Business, Review of Small Business, H.R. Rep. No. 2513, 82d Cong., 2d Sess. 2 (1952); Spiegel, Current Economic Problems 352-353 (The Blakiston Co. 1949).

6 Berle and Means, The Modern Corporation and Private Property 40 (1933); Smaller War Plants Corporation, Economic Concentration and World War II, Sen. Doc. No. 206, 79th Cong., 2d Sess. 6, 19 (1946); FTC, Changes in Concentration in Manufacturing 17 (1954); Levi, The Anti-Trust Laws and Monopoly, 14 U. Chi. L. Rev. 153, 164-165 (1947). But compare soberer studies: Kaplan, Big Enterprise in a Competitive System 73, 127, 141 (Brookings Institution, 1954), and works cited therein; Bernheim, ed., Big Business: Its Growth and Place 101-102 (Twentieth Century Fund, 1937); Spiegel, Current Economic Problems, 350 (The Blakiston Co. 1949); The Fluid 500, 66 Fortune No. 1, 114 (1957) (annual turnover in top 500 industrial firms *may* be as high as 7 per cent; largest firms less profitable than smaller ones in 500). Contrary experience in the United Kingdom is reported in Prais, The Financial Experience of Giant Companies, 67 Econ. J. 249, 262 (1957). Compare Florence, New Measures of the Growth of Firms, id. 244.

7 Kimmel, Share Ownership in the United States 89 et seq. (Brookings Institution, 1952). Of course not all publicly held corporations are big and a few closely held companies have attained considerable size (e.g., Ford Motor Company before stock offered publicly).

8 Berle and Means, The Modern Corporation and Private Property 117-118 (1933); Hurff, Social Aspects of Enterprise in the Large Corporation 22 (1950); Spiegel, Current Economic Problems 380 (The Blakiston Co. 1949); Gordon, Enterprise, Profits and the Modern Corporation, in Fellner and Haley, eds., Readings in the Theory of Income Distribution 558 et seq., 566 (The Blakiston Co. 1949). On the other hand it has been argued that there is a high degree of concentration of stock ownership in the 200 largest corporations, one study finding that 1 per cent of the shareholders owned 60 per cent of the common stock. SEC, The Distribution of Ownership in the 200 largest Non-Financial Corporations 5, 13, 38 (TNEC Mono-

If the individual shareholder now has little voice in the management of giant corporations,[9] the reason is not hard to find. Under the impact of taxation,[10] personal wealth is rapidly disappearing. There appear to be both an absolute and a relative decrease in the size of individual fortunes,[11] and the inequality between natural persons and the great corporations thus probably tends to increase with the passage of years. Hence the wealth of big business is made more conspicuous. Whether based on its conspicuous character or more deeply rooted in theory, there is considerable hostility toward the giants of business enterprise. Only in part does such animosity reflect socialist aspirations: the goal of mitigating inequality has long been shared by those who are in no way ready to give up the institutions of private property and free enterprise.[12] Indeed, the Jeffersonian ideal envisaged a rough equality of incomes and the dream of the American Revolution conceived of many small independent economic units in which political relationships were reduced to a minimum. Big business threatens that dream much as does the concept of the socialist or welfare state.[13]

---

graph No. 29, 1940). Some of the statistical methods used to reach that result appear, however, open to question. Id. at 38. Note also the suggestion that large institutional shareholders, including investment trusts, have a considerable voice in management of big business. Kaplan, Big Enterprise in a Competitive System 179 (Brookings Institution, 1954).

[9] It is common, for example, for giant companies to report that no one stockholder owns as much as 1 per cent of their outstanding shares. E.g., United States Steel Corp., 47th Ann. Rep. 22 (New York City, 1949). In the nineteenth century the situation was often different. E.g. Gibb, The Whitesmiths of Taunton 8-9 (1943).

[10] It is true that division of estates at death and the spending proclivities of succeeding generations may dissipate fortunes. Celler Committee I, pt. 1, at 665; Tree v. Continental Bank, 346 Ill. App. 509, 105 N.E.2d 324 (1953). There is nothing to indicate, however, that those factors were not equally operative in an earlier age. Hence it may be proper to attribute the shrinkage of personal wealth to the tax factor.

[11] Statistical Abstract of the United States 304 (1938); Statistical Abstract of the United States 295-296 (1955).

[12] Blum and Kalven, The Uneasy Case for Progressive Taxation, 19 U. Chi. L. Rev. 417, 489 (1952); Klaw, The Entrepreneurial Ego, 54 Fortune No. 2, pp. 100, 146 (1956) (young presidents of relatively small corporations fear wealthy corporations; GM is too big, they say). Compare Smigel, Public Attitudes toward Stealing as Related to the Size of the Victim Organization, 21 Am. Soc. Rev. 320 (1956).

[13] Brinton, Equality, 5 Encyc. Soc. Sci. 574, 579 (1931); Becker, Jefferson, 8 id. 377 (1932); Bunzel, The General Ideology of American Small Business, 70 Pol. Sci. Q. 87, 90 (1955); 2 Nevins, Study in Power 127-128 (1953); Boulding, The Organizational Revolution 138 (Federal Council of Churches of Christ in America, 1953); Rostow, Market Organization and Stabilization Policy, in Income Stabilization for a Developing Economy 439, 478 (Millikan ed. 1954). A recent public opinion poll shows that big business is favorably regarded for its economic accomplishments but that it is in disfavor from a political point of view. Glover, The Attack on Big Business 108 et seq. (1954). For example, there are frequent allegations that big business controls the machinery of government. Thus it has been said: "In the United States popular

Many of our leading thinkers have expressed doubts as to the widsom of permitting business entities to assume tremendous proportions. William James wrote:

> I am against bigness and greatness in all their forms, and with the invisible molecular moral forces that work from individual to individual, stealing in through the crannies of the world like so many soft rootlets, or like the capillary oozing of water, and yet rending the hardest monuments of man's price, if you give them time. The bigger the unit you deal with, the hollower, the more brutal, the more mendacious is the life displayed. So I am against all big organizations as such, national ones first and foremost. . . .[14]

More specifically addressing himself to the economic world, Mr. Justice Brandeis wrote:

> . . . size alone gives to giant corporations a social significance not attached ordinarily to smaller units of private enterprise. Through size, corporations, once merely an efficient tool employed by individuals in the conduct of private business, have become an institution — an institution which has brought such concentration of economic power that so-called private corporations are sometimes able to dominate the State. The typical business corporation of the last century, owned by a small group of individuals, managed by their owners, and limited in size by their personal wealth, is being supplanted by huge concerns in which the lives of tens or hundreds of thousands of employees and the property of tens or hundreds of thousands of investors are subjected, through the corporate mechanism, to the control of a few men. Ownership has been separated from control; and this separation has removed many of the checks which formerly operated to curb the misuse of wealth and power. And as the ownership of the shares is becoming continually more dispersed, the power which formerly accompanied ownership is becoming increasingly concentrated in the hands of a few. The changes thereby wrought in the lives of the workers, of the owners and of the general public, are so fundamental and far-reaching . . . to compare the evolving "corporate system" with

---

feeling has always regarded wealth as the chief obstacle to equal administration of justice. Much of the bitterness of the anti-trust movement came from the popular belief that corporate wealth in particular possessed unfair advantages in the courts." Id. at 125. Brinton, Equality, 5 Encyc. Soc. Sci. 574, 577 (1931). It is also urged that bigness in business destroys democracy because the employee is a mere servant, not accustomed to making his own decisions, and hence cannot as a citizen play an independent political role or assume responsibility. The individual is reduced to an automaton and authoritarian results are achieved. Even the alleged excessive materialism of the twentieth century has been blamed on big business. Glover, The Attack on Big Business, cc. 5, 6 (1954).

[14] James, Letter to Mrs. Henry Whitman.

the feudal system; . . . to assert that this "master institution of civilized life" is committing it to the rule of plutocracy.[15]

Brandeis is gone but antagonism to giant corporate wealth continues.[16] Small business men, it is said, regard the close relationship of big business to big government and big labor as an "unholy alliance" subversive of American[17] ideals. Perhaps some of the hostility is based upon romantic nostalgia for a rural age of handicraft production and the widespread notion that democracy is more stable when each citizen owns a small amount of property.[18] In part, too, the antagonism reflects ancient prejudices against absentee control and the general distrust of "foreigners" characteristic of many civilizations.[19] There remains a serious

[15] Louis K. Liggett v. Lee, 288 U.S. 517, 565, 580 (1933) (dissenting opinion).

[16] Edwards, Maintaining Competition 106 (1949); Lewis, Monopoly and the Law, 6 Mod. L. Rev. 97, 104 (1943); Gerschenkron, Economic Backwardness in Historical Perspective, in The Progress of Underdeveloped Areas 3, 14 (Hoselitz ed. 1952); Stocking and Watkins, Monopoly and Free Enterprise 554 (Twentieth Century Fund, 1951). Some of the most extreme views of this school will be found in Quinn, Giant Business: Threat to Democracy (1953). On the other hand, the Puritan tradition is not egalitarian. Puritans believed poverty to arise from sloth and encouraged the poor to labor rather than sheltering them with charity. Tawney, Religion and the Rise of Capitalism 216, 224 (Mentor ed. 1947). Furthermore, it has been said: "In the United States the nineteenth century distrust of great corporate and individual wealth has almost disappeared. None but the intellectuals now dislike Henry Ford." Brinton, Equality, 5 Encyc. Soc. Sci. 574, 580 (1931). Compare Whittaker, A History of Economic Ideas pp. 69-71 (1943).

[17] Bunzel, The General Ideology of American Small Business, 70 Pol. Sci. Q. 87, 97, 99, 100 (1955); Hurff, Social Aspects of Enterprise in the Large Corporation 16 (1950). It might be difficult to support some of the above views with empirical evidence. The notion, for example, that labor relations are better in the shops of small employers might be difficult to prove.

[18] Hale, Housing, 34 Ky. L.J. 255, 270, 435 (1951).

[19] See Chapter 7. Evidence of prejudice against absentee ownership is reflected in the following excerpts from corporate reports:

"From the beginning, the Company merchandising branches have been of a definitely local character. These branches are similar to other locally-operated businesses buying merchandise from other suppliers as well as from Company factories. Each branch is staffed with highly qualified local employees who participate in local undertakings and who are active as members of the local community." Pittsburgh Plate Glass Co., 70th Ann. Rep. 13 (Pittsburgh, 1954).

"There is a common impression that executive employees of chain organizations are transferred so frequently that it is not expedient for them to become home owners, and that, as a result, they do not have their roots down in a community to the same degree as other local businessmen. Statistics for the entire Sears executive force are not available, but a recent check of our store managers indicates that two out of three own their own homes. It is evident that they, like the company they represent, have made their investment in the community and want to help it grow and develop." Sears, Roebuck & Co., 1953 Ann. Rep. 19 (Chicago, 1954).

"One of the major responsibilities of Sylvania's plant managers throughout the country is to demonstrate constantly that the local plant is playing its full role as a community citizen. . . .

"This entire program was given greatly increased attention during the past

and deep-rooted feeling, however, that the mere existence of enormous corporate wealth is undesirable and incompatible with our republican institutions.

No doubt there are contradictions in the views of those who have expressed antagonism to corporate wealth. As Professor Knight wrote,

> In a competitive game, it is absurd to speak of equality as an ideal, a fact which much radical discussion overlooks. Some of the criticisms brought against existing society amount to condemning a foot race as unfair because some one has come out ahead.[20]

Nevertheless, our political climate, reflected in prohibitions upon contributions to campaign funds by corporations and otherwise, reflects animosity toward the business giants.[21] Pluralism, the wide sharing of power as a bulwark against tyranny, is often conceived of as in conflict with the existence of huge aggregations of productive capacity. Also involved are the concepts of social mobility and equality of opportunity: many believe that the existence of large firms impedes realization of those ideals.[22]

§8.2. **Effects upon behavior of big business.** We need not look far to observe the impact of the foregoing public sentiments. Large enterprises have been forced into a defensive posture and struggle to improve their public relations. In one corporate report after another, big companies lay stress on the number of their shareholders. They point to the fact that they have more shareholders than employees and that the shareholders occupy every occupational status and economic level in the nation.[1] Often

---

year. . . ." Sylvania Electric Products, Inc., 1953 Ann. Rep. 15 (New York City, 1954).

Other examples will be found in National Dairy Products Corp., 30th Ann. Rep. 8 (New York City, 1954); Tide Water Associated Oil Co., 1948 Ann. Rep. 8 (New York City, 1949).

20 Knight, The Ethics of Competition 61 (1935). Note, however, the argument that gross inequality of income distribution fosters monopoly by making it possible for a few to acquire the training or the capital to enter a field of enterprise and exclude others. Ellis, Monetary Policy and Investment, 30 Proceedings Am. Econ. Assn. 27, 33 (1940).

21 Federal Corrupt Practices Act §10, 2 U.S.C.A. §§251 et seq., 18 U.S.C.A. §610; see United States v. International Union of United Auto Workers, 352 U.S. 567, 570-575 (1957). Discussions with Charles F. Harding, Esquire, indicate that modern anthropology may find wealth as damaging to the social organism as monopoly. Compare Brandeis, J., dissenting in Louis K. Liggett Co. v. Lee, 288 U.S. 517, 574 (1933).

22 Rostow, The New Sherman Act, 14 U. Chi. L. Rev. 567, 569 et seq. (1947); Kaplan, Small Business: Its Place and Problems 3 (Committee for Economic Development, 1948). Compare Mallalieu, The Structure of British Private Industry, 21 Can. J. Econ. & Pol. Sci. 80 (1955).

§8.2. 1 General Motors Corp., 40th Ann. Rep. 16 (New York City, 1949), 42d Ann. Rep. 38 (1951); E. I. du Pont de Nemours & Co., 1948 Ann. Rep. 32 (Wilmington,

their reports point to the small holdings of many owners[2] and
there is also frequent mention of the fact that the big firms both
buy from and sell to a multitude of far smaller enterprises.[3] Apparently fearing that both the public and their employees regard
big firms as bottomless pits of wealth available for distribution
in the form of taxes, wages or otherwise, huge companies publi-
cize the burdens which they are carrying and the contribution
made to employees in the form of tools by their investors.[4] The
medieval prejudice against profits is combatted by corporate
statements to the effect that earnings are actually lower than they
should be[5] and by assertions that far more is distributed to the

1949), 1949 Ann. Rep. 27 (1950), 1950 Ann. Rep. 31 (1951); National Dairy Products
Corp., 30th Ann. Rep. 6 (New York City, 1954); Eastman Kodak Co., 1948 Ann. Rep.
3, 5 (Rochester, 1949); Dow Chemical Co., 1950 Ann. Rep. 17 (Midland, 1950); Phelps
Dodge Corp., 1948 Ann. Rep. 17 (New York City, 1949); Sterling Drug Inc., 1952 Ann.
Rep. 11, 14 (New York City, 1953); American Can Co., 47th Ann. Rep. 12 (New York
City, 1949). In some of the foregoing reports management has been at pains to point
out that educational and other charitable institutions are stockholders.

2 Standard Oil Co. of Indiana, 1952 Ann. Rep. 25 (Chicago, 1953); Standard Oil
Co. of Ohio, 1952 Ann. Rep. 16 (Cleveland, 1953); Greyhound Corp., 1952 Report
to Stockholders 12, 18 (Chicago, Mar. 12, 1953). One large company polled its
shareholders and reported that only 26 per cent of them had incomes in excess of
$10,000 per year. Eight per cent of them had incomes so small that they were
not subject to federal income tax. United States Steel Corp., 52nd Ann. Rep. 23
(New York City, 1954).

3 E.g., Standard Oil Co. of New Jersey, 1948 Ann. Rep. 40 (New York City, 1949).

4 Anonymous, Who Pays for Your Social Security? 3 Enterprise No. 10, p. 3 (1954);
National Biscuit Co., 1950 Ann. Rep. 20 (New York City, 1951); E. I. du Pont de
Nemours & Co., 1949 Ann. Rep. 13, 15 (Wilmington, 1950). In the latter report
aggressive research carried on by the company is given credit for many new products "giving employment to approximately 40,000 workers." In Continental Can Co.,
Inc., 1948 Ann. Rep. 3 (New York City, 1949) it was said: "The average U.S. individual common stockholder owns only 60 shares, worth about $2,650 at book value.

"These are the people who have supplied the major portion of the 187 millions
of dollars worth of plants, tools, materials and working capital for the use of Continental's employees in producing more and better products. . . .

"Failure to recognize the importance of the part that millions of stockholders have
paid in contributing to the welfare of the nation many times has resulted in unwarranted attacks on stockholders as a group and on the corporations which they
own. . . ."

Often large corporations indicate apprehension of political pressure from organized
agricultural interests. E.g., Deere & Co., 1952 Ann. Rep. 7 (Moline, 1953); National
Biscuit Co., 1950 Ann. Rep. 9, 21 (New York City, 1951). Reports such as those cited
refer to the effort of the corporations to produce better tools for farmers and to
increase consumption of farm products. Compare Rothschild, Price Theory and
Oligopoly, 57 Econ. J. 299, 317-318 (1947).

5 United States Steel Corp., 47th Ann. Rep. 4-5 (New York City, 1949), 1949 Ann.
Rep. 23 (1950); Diamond Match Co., 1948 Ann. Rep. 8-9, 13 (New York City, 1949);
Dow Chemical Co., 1950 Ann. Rep. 16 (Midland, 1950); General Electric Co., 57th
Ann. Rep. 4 (Schenectady, 1949); General Motors Corp., 40th Ann. Rep. 23-24 (New
York City, 1949). It has been suggested that big corporations are no longer operated
with a view to the maximization of profit, perhaps as a result of pressures mentioned
in the text. Bernstein, Profit Theory — Where Do We Go From Here? 67 Q.J. Econ.
407, 415 (1953). Prejudice against profits is, of course, ancient and derived partly

employees in the form of wages than is received by the stock-holders as dividends.[6] A large steel company published a claim that 53 per cent of its shareholders had less income than its average worker.[7]

Attitudes such as those described above have permitted politicians to place pressure upon big business. From their point of view, the corporations are vulnerable to demagogic attacks seeking to confiscate the fruits of success from the industrious or fortunate.[8] There is, of course, another way of looking at the problem.[9] In any event, the big firms seek to forestall such "raids" with extensive public reations activities.[10] Usually the matter is not phrased in such a bald fashion by corporate executives, who are more inclined to make a statement such as this:

> U.S. Steel as a national institution seeks to provide the public with detailed information about its affairs and its part in American life. The extent and depth of the public's esteem bear upon the future ability of U.S. Steel effectively to serve the nation in both peace and war.[11]

from the notion that only manual labor is really productive; that the intangible contributions of taking risks, making decisions and mental calculation are unworthy of reward. It is also customary to refer to the large profits of big business wholly without reference to the large investment which has made those earnings possible.

[6] Pittsburgh Plate Glass Co., 70th Ann. Rep. 17 (Pittsburgh, 1954); General Motors Corp., 44th Ann. Rep. 4-5 (New York City, 1953). Sometimes such reports assert that lower-paid workers have been gaining economically on executives and that their wages have increased more than the cost of living. E.g., E. I. du Pont de Nemours & Co., 1950 Ann. Rep. 30 (Wilmington, 1951); Inland Steel Co., 1948 Ann. Rep. 5, 7 (Chicago, 1949). We do not mean to suggest that any of the foregoing facts indicate that big corporations are too large or too small or that their management is "good" or "bad." We merely refer to the corporate reports to indicate the pressures to which big concerns are subject.

[7] United States Steel Corp., 52nd Ann. Rep. 24 (New York City, 1954).

[8] Holton, Remarks 5 (Annual Meeting of Socony-Vacuum Oil Co., April 29, 1954). Compare United States v. Socony-Vacuum Oil Corp., 310 U.S. 150, 241 (1940). An example of political pressure on pricing policies is clearly indicated in United States Steel Corp., 1949 Ann. Rep. 4-5 (New York City, 1950). See also §4.12 *supra*. Pressure from domestic crude oil producers and farmers respectively is reflected in Gulf Oil Corp., 1949 Ann. Rep. 4 (Pittsburgh, 1950); Borden Co., 1952 Ann. Rep. 9 (New York City, 1953). See also note 6 *supra*.

[9] Whether for defensive or offensive reasons big business often finds itself embroiled in attempting to change legislation for its own benefit. An interesting example of unconventional political activity on the part of management of a big corporation is found in Du Pont III: 11 Fortune No. 1, pp. 62, 125 (1935).

[10] E.g., Minnesota Mining & Manufacturing Co., 1948 Ann. Rep. 10-11, 18 (St. Paul, 1949).

[11] United States Steel Corp., 47th Ann. Rep. 21 (New York City, 1949). In United States Steel Corp., 51st Ann. Rep. 20-21 (New York City, 1953), it was said: "The creation of public understanding and, through it, of good-will is the basic objective of any public relations effort. For a number of years U.S. Steel has undertaken in an organized way to inform the American people fully of the important services which the members of its industrial family have performed. In 1952 U.S. Steel continued to use every means at its command to tell its story to the nation."

Another of the industrial giants reported to its shareholders:

> The health and well-being of a corporation today are to an increasing extent affected by the public's attitude toward industry.
> . . .
>
> The interests of the Du Pont Company, a large and conspicuous industrial enterprise, are particularly sensitive to the effects of this influence. Therefore it has been thought advisable to promote a wider understanding of the Company's policies and practices.
> . . .[12]

Such firms also frequently engage in localized public relations, including programs of open-house events and the like, for example:

> . . . for the purpose of conveying to employees and their friends and relatives, in plant cities and towns, a broader knowledge of the Company's policies and operations, its part and that of its people in the industrial system. . . .[13]

Firms also place stress upon "employee economic education."[14]

[12] E. I. du Pont de Nemours & Co., 1950 Ann. Rep. 20-21 (Wilmington, 1951). See also Sinclair Oil Corp., 1952 Ann. Rep. 4 (New York City, 1953). In Weyerhaeuser Timber Co., 1952 Ann. Rep. 13 (Tacoma, 1953) the following statement appeared: "In cooperation with American Forests Products Industries, Inc., the Opinion Research Corporation was commissioned to conduct a national poll to determine public attitudes toward the forest industry. Information so obtained has been helpful to the Company in its public information activities. During the year our color magazine advertisements were published in 90 million copies of national magazines. . . . Work with educators was expanded. . . . The Company is cooperating with other industry members in preparing an acceptable textbook for high schools and colleges. . . ."

[13] American Can Co., 47th Ann. Rep. 13 (New York City, 1949). In United States Steel Corp., 47th Ann Rep. 20 (New York City, 1949) the following statement appeared:

"In 1948 U.S. Steel continued its efforts to encourage the maintenance of good community relations. Among activities in furtherance of this policy were regular 'Open House' for the public at various plants, the increasing participation of officials in civic undertakings, assistance in public health needs in relation to present and prospective operations.

". . . In order to establish mutually satisfactory relationships, U.S. Steel recognizes that it must know the community problems in those areas in which it operates and that it is equally necessary that the public in those localities understand U.S. Steel's policies, products, and production and distribution methods."

Similar statements will be found in Allis-Chalmers Manufacturing Co., 1948 Ann. Rep. 2 (Milwaukee); Chrysler Corp., 29th Ann Rep. 10 (Detroit, 1954); Kennecott Copper Corp., 39th Ann. Rep. 15 (New York City, 1954); Minnesota Mining & Manufacturing Co., 1948 Ann. Rep. 10 (St. Paul, 1949). See also §8.1 *supra,* note 19 and Chapter 7.

[14] In E. I. du Pont de Nemours & Co., 1950 Ann. Rep. 25 (Wilmington, 1951) it was stated: "Considerable expansion was made during 1950 of the training activities for foreman and supervisory employees. . . . These activities included discussion programs aimed at the economic education of hourly as well as supervisory employees. . . . Over 13,000 employees have participated in economic discussion groups at the plants on Company time." To the same effect are statements in

Passing from propaganda to behavior, there are grounds for believing that giant firms are assuming a considerable role in determining how the national income shall be divided. The mere earning and distribution of profits is not a fashionable goal of the largest corporations. As the management of one such firm wrote:

> Not the illusory and superficial index of profit but something much more basic, measures the success of a corporation. The true expression lies in human terms — how well it fulfills its obligation to employee, owner, customer and community. Management's gravest responsibility is to adjust the rights and interests of each in adequate proportion; to keep in delicate balance the rights and interests of all.[15]

Like the ancient lord of the manor, management of the tremendous business enterprise divides the return from its operation among its suppliers, its customers, its employees and its owners. One great corporation reported as follows:

> U.S. Steel continuously strives to conduct its affairs in such a way as to advance the best interests of its stockholders, its employees, and its customers. At all times, it seeks to further the proper functioning of the whole American economy, for only as the nation as a whole prospers can U.S. Steel, as a part of the nation, also prosper.[16]

Kennecott Copper Corp., 39th Ann. Rep. 15 (New York City, 1954); Gulf Oil Corp., 1952 Ann. Rep. 22 (Pittsburgh, 1953).

[15] E. I. du Pont de Nemours & Co., Du Pont: The Autobiography of an American Enterprise 137 (1952). See also Holton, Remarks 5 (Annual Meeting of Socony-Vacuum Oil Co., April 29, 1954). In Standard Oil Co. of New Jersey, 1948 Ann. Rep. 5 (New York City, 1949) the following statement appeared: "As we see it, the basic interest of the stockholder — security for his investment and a fair return — is best served only if the corporation deserves and enjoys public confidence. Such confidence can be based only on recognition by people at large that their interest — the interest of society — is a factor in corporate action. This company, as does every company, needs public confidence." It is interesting to note that an attempt to justify the income tax laid upon corporations rests basically upon the same theory: namely, that corporate enterprises are social and economic entities with their own character and pattern of behavior and not merely a collection of shareholders of varying abilities to pay. Colm, The Corporation and the Corporate Income Tax in the American Economy, 44 Proceedings Am. Econ. Assn. 486, 488 (1954).

[16] United States Steel Corp., 47th Ann. Rep. 21 (New York City, 1949). Somewhat similar statements will be found in National Dairy Products Corp., 1949 Ann. Rep. 4 (New York City, 1950); Continental Can Co., Inc., 1948 Ann. Rep. 2 (New York City, 1949); Allis-Chalmers Manufacturing Company, 1948 Ann. Rep. 4 (Milwaukee); The Borden Co., 1952 Ann. Rep. 4 (New York City, 1953). In General Motors Corp., 41st Ann. Rep. 5 (New York City, 1950) the following statement appeared:
". . . 1949 . . . dollar sales exceeded those of any peacetime year. . . .
"As a result of this performance, material benefits accrued to a large number of individuals as well as to the economy as a whole. Payrolls were the largest in

In thus "dividing up the pie," management acts as an umpire between various conflicting interest groups:

> Your management tries to balance the interests of consumers, stockholders, employees and the general public, for the long-run interest of all. The effects of this policy can be seen in products of improved quality at no higher prices, larger dividends reflecting greater investment in the Company, wage increases above those required to meet the rise in the cost of living, and a reputation for good corporate citizenship. . . .[17]

Apparently some concerns act like a public utility because of the activities of congressional committees and other governmental

---

G.M. history. . . . Profits were higher and dividends paid to common stockholders were substantially increased. . . . With this increase in profits, taxes payable to Federal, state and local governments were greater than for any other year. Thousands of suppliers profited in proportion to their contribution to G.M.'s output for the year. Last, but by no means least, G.M. customers received substantial benefits in the form of improved product values."

So far has the foregoing trend gone that in Endicott Johnson Corp., 1952 Ann. Rep. 14 (Endicott, 1953) the following statement appeared: "Management also recognizes the responsibility of providing a proper and regular return on the investments of the stockholders. . . ." The implication was that dividends have the last claim on corporation earnings.

[17] Standard Oil Co., of Ohio, 1952 Ann. Rep. 3 (Cleveland, 1953). In General Electric Co., 57th Ann. Rep. 3 (Schenectady, 1949) the following statement appeared:

"This annual report . . . is submitted not only to record the Company's 1948 operating results and its financial position . . . but also to show it carried out its responsibilities to society as a whole. . . . Accordingly, the Report contains information which should be of interest to all persons affected by the functioning of General Electric as a corporate enterprise and who benefit most when the company's operations are successful — its stockholders, its employees, its customers, the Government, and the public at large."

In Continental Can Co., Inc., 1948 Ann. Rep. 8-9 (New York City, 1949) the following statement was made:

"The Management recognizes its responsibilities in seeing that those that buy our products, those who invest their time and those who invest their money are treated equitably, each in relation to the other. At the same time, we also recognize our over-all responsibility to the general public, the plant communities and the national welfare.

"Within the economic and social framework applying in 1948, we feel that progress was made in meeting each of these responsibilities. Our customers were supplied with a variety of high quality products in record volume at the lowest possible prices on which the Company made a modest profit. Employees' wages, salaries and extra benefits were maintained at levels equal to and in some cases higher than those generally applying in the industry. Moderately higher dividends were paid to the stockholders. The public received substantial benefits through the Company's contributions to a higher standard of living, stabilized employment and its support of national and community projects."

Similar statements will be found in Gulf Oil Corp., 1953 Ann. Rep. 7 (Pittsburgh, 1954); General Motors Corp., 44th Ann. Rep. 7 (New York City, 1953); National Biscuit Co., 1949 Ann. Rep. 3 et seq. (New York City). Compare Patinkin, Multiple-Plant Firms, Cartels and Imperfect Competition, 61 Q.J. Econ. 173, 193 (1947); Gossett, Corporate Citizenship 178, 187 (Washington and Lee University, 1957).

bodies;[18] others appear to have assumed a quasi-public utility status more or less voluntarily. Thus in 1949, General Motors Corporation reduced prices on its automobiles, allegedly because a cost of living index adjustment had reduced its labor expense.[19] It is worth noting, too, that some of the largest corporations proudly proclaim the tremendous size of their tax contributions to the government's treasury and otherwise emphasize the nation's dependence upon them in peace and war.[20]

In its relationship with its employees, the modern big business

[18] In United States Steel Corp., 1949 Ann. Rep. 4-5 (New York City, 1950), it was reported:

"Near the end of the year U.S. Steel made a general revision in its steel prices. These changes, resulting in an average price increase of $3.82 a ton . . . reflect the increased cost of production resulting primarily from the new insurance and pension programs. . . .

"The Chairman of the Congressional Joint Committee on the Economic Report questioned the propriety of the price increase immediately following their announcement and requested representatives of U.S. Steel to appear before the Committee to explain them. . . ."

The prepared testimony presented before the Joint Committee on the Economic Report was published under the title of U.S. Steel's Policies on Cost, Prices, Plants, Productivity (Washington, Jan. 24, 1950). An actuary testified with the respect to the increased costs arising out of a newly adopted pension plan and the whole attitude of the company reflected the belief that it had to "justify" its prices in terms of higher labor expense. See also Celler Committee I, pt. 4, at 615-616; §4.12 supra.

[19] General Motors Corp., 41st Ann. Rep. 15 (New York City, 1950). In Acme Steel Co., 1948 Ann. Rep. 3 (Chicago, 1949) the following statement appeared: "The demand . . . was so great that price was of little importance and had we elected to do so, we could have received premium prices for nearly every ton sold. We believe that our policy of charging only published market prices will be to our benefit in the future when competition for customer orders will again prevail."

In Continental Can Co., Inc., 1948 Ann. Rep. 5 (New York City, 1949) it was said:

"Every effort is being made to keep prices for the Company's products as low as possible in spite of constantly increasing costs. At the beginning of 1948 prices of metal cans were advanced an average of about 14%. . . .

"Similarly at the beginning of 1949 it was necessary to raise metal can prices a further 10%. . . . After providing for the increased cost of plate, the remaining portion of this latest price increase will offset less than half of the higher cost of wages, salaries, miscellaneous materials, freight and other operating charges. . . ."

Similar statements will be found in American Can Co., 47th Ann. Rep. 4 (New York City, 1949); General Electric Co., 57th Ann. Rep. 5 (Schenectady, 1949); E. I. du Pont de Nemours & Co., 1948 Ann. Rep. 12 (Wilmington, 1949). The closely allied practice of holding prices below free-market levels in boom times and above such levels in slack times apparently existed in the first decade of this century. United States v. United States Steel Corp., 223 Fed. 55, 79, 90 (D.N.J. 1915), aff'd, 251 U.S. 417 (1920). See also §4.12 supra. Economists have noted that political pressures may curb the competition of larger firms, inducing them to moderate their pricing policies and to hold "umbrellas" over smaller rivals. Mason, Price and Production Policies of Large-Scale Enterprise, 29 Proceedings Am. Econ. Assn. 61, 63 (1939); Edwards, Maintaining Competition 104 (1949). Note also the discussion of "social responsibility" supra §4.1.

[20] General Electric Co., 57th Ann. Rep. 3 (Schenectady, 1949); National Biscuit Co., 1948 Ann. Rep. 18 (New York City, 1949); General Motors Corp., 44th Ann. Rep. 9, 32-33 (New York City, 1953).

unit adopts programs reminiscent of feudal or socialist states. Many employers boast that their workers are protected in the event of injury, illness, hospitalization, permanent or total disability and death.[21] Pension plans are a commonplace[22] and one large corporation has gone so far as to provide the services of a "pastor-counselor" to discuss the personal problems of employees on a confidential basis.[23] Training courses, group life insurance, sports, picnics, shows, concerts, dances, arts and crafts, hobbies and monthly magazines are all among the services rendered employees by a modern corporation of considerable size.[24] In 1914, when Henry Ford instituted his profit-sharing system, raising the wages of his men to a minimum of $5 a day, the Ford Motor Company set up a "sociological department." The duties of that department included encouraging the employees to save, to participate in civic activities, to learn English, to own their own homes, to discourage the use of liquor, gambling and the practice of taking in boarders.[25] Nowadays, even the children of employees begin to take on the character of wards of the giant enterprises, for they are frequently favored with scholarships for advanced education.[26]

[21] National Biscuit Co., 1950 Ann. Rep. 19 (New York City, 1951); General Motors Corp., 44th Ann. Rep. 27 (New York City, 1953). An account of the origin of one of the most extensive programs of employee benefits will be found in Life of Owen D. Young, 3 Fortune No. 2, pp. 38, 113 (1931). A few years ago it required two full printed pages to describe the employee benefits now offered by his company. General Electric Co., 57th Ann. Rep. 20-21 (Schenectady, 1949). Compare Oil and Social Change in the Middle East, 176 Economist 14 (July 2, 1955).

[22] In Endicott Johnson Corp., 1952 Ann. Rep. 14 (Endicott, 1953) is was said:
". . . The Company . . . is the second largest producer of shoes in the United States, operating 28 shoe factories . . .

"A major policy of Endicott Johnson, from the inception of the business, has been the recognition of the responsibility of the Company to its workers and the community in which they live. The Company has actively promoted the welfare of its employees. Among the benefits provided are free medical care and hospitalization for the workers and their families, a liberal pension plan, over 3,500 homes built by the Company and sold to them at cost, and extensive parks, playgrounds and recreational facilities. . . ."

[23] R. J. Reynolds Tobacco Co., 1952 Ann. Rep. 9 (Winston-Salem, 1953). The report does not indicate which denomination was thus established within the company walls.

[24] Abbott Laboratories, 1948 Ann. Rep. 26 (North Chicago, 1949); Chas. Pfizer & Co., Inc., 1953 Ann. Rep. 16 (Brooklyn, 1954); The Northern Trust Company, Ann. Rep. 25 (Chicago, 1953). Not long ago it was reported that labor unions were growing weaker in Western Germany because employers were providing so many benefits such as sports fields, convalescent homes, transportation to and from work, anniversary gifts and the like. The unions had protested, saying that the employer programs had insulated the employees from the community. German Unions, 34 Barron's No. 43, p. 5 (1954).

[25] Nevins, Ford: The Times, the Man, the Company 555 (1954).

[26] Standard Oil Co., of Ohio, 1952 Ann. Rep. 17 (Cleveland, 1953); Ohio Oil Co., 66th Ann. Rep. 9 (Findlay, 1954); Lion Oil Co., 30th Ann. Rep. 15 (El Dorado, Ark. 1954); General Electric Co., 57th Ann. Rep. 21 (Schenectady, 1949), 61st Ann. Rep. 25 (1953); Weyerhaeuser Timber Co., 1952 Ann. Rep. 13 (Tacoma, 1953).

Increasingly, too, large corporations take over civic activities formerly reserved to natural persons. They speak of "honoring their social responsibilities"[27] and many of them have created (partly for tax reasons) charitable foundations. Thus an important producer of building materials reported to its stockholders:

> The company also continues its interest in the broader field of philanthropy — hospitals, colleges and technical schools — whose graduates are essential to efficient industrial operations. To make provision for current and future needs of this nature the Company . . . contributed to Pittsburgh Plate Glass Foundation the full amount permitted as a tax deduction.[28]

As indicated, the obligation of the corporate citizen is now understood as running to higher education. Thus the American Brake Shoe Company reported to its shareholders:

> Industry today recognizes to an extent greater than ever before its social responsibilities in the communities where it operates, to colleges and universities, and to the numerous welfare organizations in need of the support of all citizens. . . .[29]

Between 1936 and 1952, donations by corporations (or affiliated foundations) to higher education increased more than tenfold and at the end of the period more than 7 per cent of the cost of operating universities was being met through such gifts.[30] Corporations take part in civic activities too, particularly those of a local character in which the large firm tries to demonstrate that it is a "good citizen" in the community.[31] There is even a hint

---

27 National Lead Co., 62nd Ann. Rep. 14 (New York City, 1954). The report recorded the formation of National Lead Company Foundation with an initial contribution of $1,500,000.

28 Pittsburgh Plate Glass Co., 70th Ann. Rep. 4 (Pittsburgh, 1954). See also Chas. Pfizer & Co., Inc., 1953 Ann. Rep. 18 (Brooklyn, 1954); Sylvania Electric Products Inc., 1953 Ann. Rep. 7 (New York City, 1954); Carrier Corp., 1952 Ann. Rep. 17 (Syracuse, 1953); Republic Steel Corp., 1953 Ann. Rep. 10-11 (Cleveland, 1954); United States Steel Corp., 52nd Ann. Rep. 20 (New York City, 1954); Campbell and Hatton, Herbert H. Dow, Pioneer in Creative Chemistry 118 (1951).

29 American Brake Shoe Co., 1953 Ann. Rep. 13 (New York City, 1954). See also Phelps Dodge Corp., 1953 Ann. Rep. 13 (New York City, 1954); Pittsburgh Plate Glass Co., 69th Ann. Rep. 3, 15 (Pittsburgh, 1953); Sears, Roebuck & Co., 1953 Ann. Rep. 17 (Chicago, 1954); United Fruit Co., 1948 Ann. Rep. 9, 26 (Boston, 1949).

30 Foundations of Learning, 176 Economist 1034 (Sept. 24, 1955).

31 Sears, Roebuck & Co., 1953 Ann. Rep. 14, 16, 18, 19 (Chicago, 1954); F. W. Woolworth Co., Woolworth's First 75 Years 41, 43 (1954); Borg-Warner Corp., 1952 Ann. Rep. 14 (Chicago, 1953); Kennecott Copper Corp. 1952 Ann. Rep. 19-20 (New York City, 1953); Illinois Bell Telephone Co., 1950 Ann. Rep. 24-25 (Chicago, 1951). Compare Pellegrin & Coates, Absentee-owned Corporations and Community Power Structure, 61 Am. J. Soc. 413, 414 (1956) (study of a single southern city suggests that branch managers of national corporations having plants there play large roles in civic affairs).

that the furnishing of mass recreation through television entertainment is now a duty of the giant firms.[32] Since he who pays the piper will ultimately call the tune, there is thus evidence to support the thesis that the management of big business is increasingly dominating the charitable aspects of American life. To the extent that such domination displaces an earlier and more diffused control — and we do not know to what extent philanthropy was formerly vested in a few large donors since stricken down by taxation — such a change would appear to constitute a departure from more democratic methods.

§8.3. **Wealth and the law.** As we have seen, the courts often have said that "mere size" is no offense under the Sherman Act.[1] To the extent that the foregoing statement is meant to apply to that horizontal size which reflects economic notions of monopoly, the assertion may be in error.[2] If, however, the statement is taken as referring to pure size — that is, wealth disassociated from a position in a particular market — then it represents the orthodox understanding of both state and federal antitrust laws. No matter how large a corporation may be in terms of assets, employees, sales, and the like, it is not considered to be in violation of the antimonopoly statutes unless it either engages in "misconduct" or occupies an undue position in specific geographic and commodity markets.[3]

And yet the foregoing statement does not tell the whole story. Courts have long expressed apprehension lest aggregations of corporate wealth distort the political and social balance of the nation. Many years ago a state court said:

A society in which a few men are the employers and the great body are merely employees or servants, is not the most desirable in any republic; and it should be as much the policy of the laws to multiply the numbers engaged in independent pursuits . . . as to cheapen the price to the consumer.[4]

[32] United States Steel Corp., 52nd Ann. Rep. 20-21 (New York City, 1954).

§8.3. [1] See §§2.1, 8.1 *supra.*
[2] See §3.2 *supra.*
[3] United States v. Columbia Steel Co., 334 U.S. 495, 533 (1948); Atty. Gen. Nat. Com. Rep. 43, (a); Celler Committee I, pt. 2B, at 820; Edwards, Maintaining Competition 130-131 (1949). In State ex Information Major v. International Harvester Co., 237 Mo. 369, 141 S.W. 672 (1911), *aff'd,* 234 U.S. 199 (1914), the state's supreme court said at page 677: "Wealth is power, and it may, without violation of law, be exercised to influence the market." Compare Stewart Dry Goods Co. v. Lewis, 294 U.S. 550 (1935).

[4] State ex rel. Attorney General v. Standard Oil Co., 49 Ohio St. 137, 30 N.E. 279, 290 (1892). In one old decision it was quaintly said: "All experience has shown that large accumulations of property, in hands likely to keep it intact for a long period, are dangerous to the public weal. Having perpetual succession, any kind of a

Another state court wrote in the same era:

> . . . it is doubtful if free government can long exist in a country
> where such enormous amounts of money are allowed to be accu-
> mulated in the vaults of corporations. . . . It is always destructive
> of individual rights, and of that free competition which is the life
> of business, and it revives and perpetuates one of the great evils
> which it was the object of the framers of our form of government
> to eradicate and prevent. . . .[5]

The history of the Sherman law itself is not without incidents in
which similar fears have been expressed.[6] In short, the courts
reflect the ancient American prejudice against bigness.

---

corporation has peculiar facilities for such accumulation, and most governments have
found it necessary to exercise great caution in their grants of corporate powers. . . .
Freed, as such bodies are, from the sure bound to the schemes of individuals — the
grave — they are able to add field to field and power to power, until they become
entirely too strong for that society which is made up of those whose plans are
limited by a single life." Central Railway Co. v. Collins, 40 Ga. 582, 629 (1869).
Compare State ex rel. Steubenville Gas Co. v. Taylor, 55 Ohio St. 61, 65, 44 N.E. 513,
515 (1896).

[5] Richardson v. Buhl, 77 Mich. 632, 43 N.W. 1102, 1110 (1889). In State ex Information Crow v. Armour Packing Co., 173 Mo. 356, 73 S.W. 645 (1903), the court
wrote at page 652: "Pools, trusts, and conspiracies to fix or maintain the prices of
the necessaries of life strike at the foundations of government; instill a destructive
poison in the life of the body politic; wither the energies of competitors; blight individual investments in legitimate business; drive small and honest dealers out of
business for themselves, and make them mere 'hewers of wood and drawers of
water' for the trust; raise the cost of living and lower the price of wages; take from
the average American freeman the ability to supply his family with necessary,
adequate and wholesome food; force the boys away from school, and into the various
branches of trade and labor, and the girls into workshops and other avenues of
business, and make them breadwinners while they are yet almost infants because the
head of the house cannot earn enough to feed and clothe his family. The people
are helpless to protect themselves. The powers that be must protect them, or, as
surely as history records the story of republican government in Rome, so surely will
the foundations of our government be shaken, and its perpetuity threatened." In
Woodbury v. McClurg, 78 Miss. 831, 29 So. 514, 515 (1901), the court said, speaking of
a proposed corporation which could acquire the stock of any other concern provided
it did not compete: "That the powers attempted to be lodged in the Laurel Gravel
Company would be illegal, if granted, we cannot doubt. They would make it a
stupendous monster, capable of swallowing into its insatiable maw all the mercantile
and manufacturing institutions of the entire country. . . . We approve . . . the
advice of the attorney general as sound, wholesome and patriotic. . . . Compare
People ex rel. Peabody v. Chicago Gas Trust Co., 130 Ill. 268, 22 N.E. 798 (1889).
Compare also the interesting opinion in Dodge v. Ford Motor Co., 204 Mich. 459,
170 N.W. 668 (1919). In that case the court said (at 684) that a corporation might
provide incidental benefits for employees, such as hospitalization. It could not,
however, be managed, the court said, to provide as much possible employment for
the workers and to provide the largest possible output at lowest possible prices for
the benefit of consumers to the detriment of minority shareholders. Note the conflict between those views and the conduct of many corporate managers set forth
supra §8.2.

[6] Speaking in support of the bill which bore his name, Senator Sherman said:
"Monopolies are fast producing that condition of our people in which the great mass

It should, of course, also be noted that decisions applying the old abuse theory of horizontal size are partly compatible with the proposition that wealth alone is pernicious. Abuses are only possible when the defendant has large economic strength. That strength may be derived as much from wealth as from horizontal size in and of itself. A fat treasury will supply ammunition for a ruinous campaign of local price-cutting just as readily as monopolistic earnings within the affected industry.[7] On top of that, some judicial opinions in the last few years have evidenced bitter hostility to wealth itself. As yet no opinion flatly states that wealth is a proper target of enforcement for Section 2 of the Sherman Act. As early as 1945, however, Judge Learned Hand wrote in the *Aluminum* case:

Many people believe that possession of unchallenged economic power deadens initiative, discourages thrift and depresses energy; that immunity from competition is a narcotic, and rivalry is a stimulant, to industrial progress; that spur of constant stress is necessary to counteract an inevitable disposition to let well enough alone.[8]

---

of them are servitors of those which have this aggregated wealth at their command." Walker, History of the Sherman Law 15 (1910). In Standard Oil Co. of New Jersey v. United States, 221 U.S. 1 (1911), the Court found occasion to comment upon the purpose of the federal legislation at page 50: "The debates show that doubt as to whether there was a common law of the United States which governed the subject in the absence of legislation was among the influences leading to the passage of the act. They conclusively show, however, that the main cause which led to the legislation was the thought that it was required by the economic condition of the times, that is, by the vast accumulation of wealth in the hands of corporations and individuals, the enormous development of corporate organization. . . ." In Pearsall v. Great Northern Railway Co., 161 U.S. 646 (1896), the Court had commented in a more general fashion. In that case it was said at page 677: "There are . . . dangers to the moral sense of the community incident to such great aggregations of wealth, which, though indirect, are even more insidious in their influence. . . ." In Indiana Farmer's Guide Pub. Co. v. Prairie Farmer Pub. Co., 88 F.2d 979 (7th Cir. 1937), *cert. denied*, 301 U.S. 696 (1937), the Circuit Court said at page 982: "The purpose of the Sherman Anti-Trust Act is to secure equality of opportunity and to prohibit abnormal contracts and combinations which tend directly to suppress the conflict for advantage called competition." Note how the language quoted in this and preceding footnotes confuses the issues of monopolies, wealth and fraud.

[7] Compare §2.28 *supra;* Kilgore Committee, pt. 6, at 2655, 2665, 2659 (GM gained business in some instances because it was in a position to extend credit over longer term, etc.); id. at 2632 (rival business manufacturer believed competition hurt because GM was able to influence customers through banks, directors, railroads, etc.).

[8] United States v. Aluminum Co. of America, 148 F.2d 416, 427 (2d Cir. 1945). In the opinion it was said at pages 428-429: "We have been speaking only of the economic reasons which forbid monopoly; but, as we have already implied, there are others, based upon the belief that great industrial consolidations are inherently undesirable, regardless of their economic results. . . . Throughout the history of these statutes it has been constantly assumed that one of their purposes was to perpetuate and preserve, for its own sake and in spite of possible cost, an organization of industry in small units which can effectively compete with each other."

In subsequent litigation against proprietors of chains of motion picture theaters[9] and groceries,[10] the trend has crept into the holdings themselves. Taken as a monopoly matter, the litigation in which the A & P was held to have infringed the antitrust laws seems irrational; for even in isolated markets the defendants' proportion of the grocery business done never exceeded 25 per cent. It follows that the decision can only be explained as a holding that wealth in and of itself is illegal regardless of the absence of monopolistic elements.[11] Similarly, the litigation attacking affiliation between the Du Pont, General Motors and United States Rubber companies,[12] while phrased in terms of vertical integration and "foreclosure," is really an assault upon concentration of wealth and not upon monopoly or its manifestations. The "quantitative substantiality" rule under the Clayton Act represents a similar attitude.[13] We await clarification from the courts. In the meanwhile, it is not safe to assume that Section 2 of the Sherman Act never reaches that "pure" size which we have called herein "wealth"; indeed, there is good reason to believe the contrary may be true.

§8.4. **Comments on corporate wealth.** We start with the proposition that concentration of wealth in the hands of a few large corporations *could* result in the creation of feudal forms in-

[9] United States v. Griffith, 334 U.S. 100 (1948); Schine Chain Theatres, Inc. v. United States, 334 U.S. 110 (1948).

[10] United States v. New York Great Atlantic & Pacific Tea Co., 173 F.2d 79 (7th Cir. 1949).

[11] In the course of the opinion in that case the court nevertheless asserted at page 82: "The Government insists that this case is not an attack upon A & P because of its size or integration and the power that may rightly go with such size and integration, but it is an attack upon the abuse of that power." It is not believed that the decision can be supported upon that ground. Furthermore, the notion that wealth is vulnerable under the Sherman Act is not a new one. See note 6 *supra*. Further, in United States v. American Can Co., 230 Fed. 859, 234 Fed. 1019 (D. Md. 1916), *appeal dismissed,* 256 U.S. 706 (1921), the court said: "If it be true that size and power, apart from the way in which they were acquired, or the purpose with which they are used, do not offend against the law, it is equally true that one of the designs of the framers of the Anti-Trust Act was to prevent the concentration in a few hands of control over great industries. They preferred a social and industrial state in which there should be many independent producers. Size and power are themselves facts some of whose consequences do not depend upon the way in which they were created or in which they are used." 230 Fed. 901.

[12] United States v. E. I. Du Pont de Nemours & Co., 126 F. Supp. 27, 235 (N.D. Ill. 1954), *rev'd,* 353 U.S. 586 (1957). Compare Atty. Gen. Nat. Com. Rep. 43, (a), which appears to take the more orthodox view of the scope of §2 of the Sherman Act.

[13] Standard Oil Co. of California v. United States, 337 U.S. 293 (1949); Lockhart and Sacks, The Relevance of Economic Factors in Determining Whether Exclusive Arrangements Violate Section 3 of the Clayton Act, 65 Harv. L. Rev. 913 (1952); Atty. Gen. Nat. Com. Rep. 137, B. Under the "quantitative substantiality" rule a large volume of business suffices to call §3 of the Clayton Act into play, even though that volume is not proportionally large in the relevant geographic and commodity market. Thus the Clayton Act is applied to wealthy defendants as such.

compatible with the maintenance of democratic institutions.[1] It has not, of course, been proven that the concentration of wealth will produce such effects.[2] Since, however, many leaders of thought have entertained such fears, we may fairly start with an inquiry as to whether corporate wealth or pure size could be curbed without harmful consequences. We can ask, in other words, whether limitations upon pure size would produce undesirable results.

Many of those imbued with the Jeffersonian ideal hesitate to suggest that big business be carved into smaller units, because they fear that thereafter the political and economic power of organized labor would be too great.[3] In prevailing circumstances they adhere to the concept of a "balanced force polity" or, as it is sometimes known, "countervailing power." [4] If, therefore, wealthy firms were to be dissolved, it might well be necessary to

§8.4.   [1] If the goal of government is free exercise of man's talents, it must leave considerable room for leadership; many have such talents, and wealth tends to reduce opportunities for exercise of them. The Fortune Survey XXVII, 21 Fortune No. 2, pp. 10, 14, 20 (1940); Fromm, Man for Himself 20, 246-247 (1947); Glover, The Attack on Big Business 111, 139-189, 323 (1954). It should also be noted that the political pressures upon big business outlined above could result in an uneconomic allocation of resources. We have mentioned above the phenomenon of pricing below free-market levels. Practices of big business could also impede the mobility of employees and cause other frictions to arise in the market place. Siegel, Conditions of American Technological Progress, 44 Proceedings Am. Econ. Assn. 161, 176 (1954).

[2] If man's role is to exercise those talents with which he is endowed, it does not necessarily follow that society must be atomized; not all wish to or can be leaders; some have talents as followers or at some intermediate level of leadership. The Fortune Survey XXVII, 21 Fortune No. 2, pp. 5, 14, 20 (1940); Ward, The American Economy — Attitudes and Opinions 29 (National Council of Churches of Christ, 1955). Perhaps it should be noted that there has recently been some weakening in the egalitarian thinking which characterized so much political action of recent decades. Blum and Kalven, The Uneasy Case for Progressive Taxation, 19 U. Chi. L. Rev. 417, 493 (1952). Compare Katz, Natural Law and Human Nature, 3 U. Chi. L. School Record No. 3, p. 1 (1954). The attempt to equate corporate wealth with materialism and the consequent warping of personal relationships, for example, takes no account of the impersonality of mass merchandising through mail order houses, chain stores, and the like. Compare Glover, The Attack on Big Business, c. 6 (1954). It is also worth nothing that "concentration" is known in fields outside the strictly economic sphere. Some church denominations, for example, "dominate" the religious life of persons in various geographic areas. Some cities contain more people than entire states. Some educational institutions are vastly larger than others. All of these conditions of "concentration" are presumably subject to the same objections as those leveled at corporate wealth.

[3] Note, for example, the combination of economic and political power on the side of organized labor outlined in Youngstown Sheet & Tube Co. v. Sawyer, 343 U.S. 579 (1952); Standard Oil Co. of Indiana, 1952 Ann. Rep. 25 (Chicago, 1953). On the other hand there is something to be said for the proposition that the public would not tolerate the exercise of such mammoth power against small business; and big labor may learn to work in cooperation with big business against the public interest. Hoover, Institutional and Theoretical Implications of Economic Change, 44 Am. Econ. Rev. 1, 13 (1954).

[4] See §4.4 supra; Clark, Alternative to Serfdom, c. 5 (1948). Compare Coker, Pluralism, 12 Encyc. Soc. Sci. 170 (1934).

take action against labor and other economic pressure groups.[5] On the other hand, political expediency suggests that any such program should begin with concentrations in the business sector: otherwise resistance to dissolution would be far too great. Besides, it is worth remembering that, historically at least, some of the big business firms antedate the organization of labor unions and farmers' blocs. The breaking up of giant corporations might therefore have a legitimate prior appeal to the electorate.[6]

Another argument against limitations upon corporate wealth depends upon dynamic economic doctrine. Only the large firm, it is sometimes said, can supply adequate capital to assure technological progress.[7] It is the big firms, so that argument runs, which introduce new processes and new devices. Through their "plow-back" of earnings[8] they accumulate funds which can be readily moved into new fields.[9] The resultant diversification means that resources are more mobile and that growth will take place more rapidly. Such an argument, however, depends upon the imperfection of the capital market. It is only valid to the extent that investors cannot be interested in such new fields without dependence upon established business entities. And it is only partly proper to argue that factors of indivisibility affect the problem of wealth. As we have seen, indivisibility (economies of scale) usually relates to efficiency in the production of some one commodity or group of related commodites.[10] A firm may, by coincidence, be both absolutely and relatively large; that is, it

[5] Kaplan, The Influence of Size of Firms on the Functioning of the Economy, 40 Proceedings Am. Econ. Assn. 74, 83 (1950); Celler Committee I, pt. 2A, at 302-303, 505 (Statements of Mr. Raymond and Professor Machlup).

[6] Id. at 303 (Statement of Representative Celler).

[7] See Appendix B. A wealthy corporation may move rapidly into new situations; its technology and ample capital may bring new or improved products to market sooner. E.g., Kilgore Committee, pt. 6, at 2355. An element of courage is also required. Id. 2437-2438. (Needless to say, judgment is necessary.) There is, however, impressive evidence to the effect that the very largest corporations are not increasing in size as rapidly as those in the middle bracket and that their profits are also lower. Celler Committee I, at 2A, at 604; TNEC Hearings, pt. 19, at 10,664; Kaplan, Small Business: Its Place and Problems 39 (Committee for Economic Development, 1948); Osborn, Efficiency and Profitability in Relation to Size, 29 Harv. Bus. Rev. No. 2, pp. 82, 93 (1951).

[8] Gibb, The Whitesmiths of Taunton 289, 337 (1943). The courts however, have not always looked with favor upon retention of corporate earnings. Dodge v. Ford Motor Co., 204 Mich. 459, 170 N.W. 668, 671, 677, 683-684 (1919). Compare United States v. Aluminum Co. of America, 44 F. Supp. 97, 302 (S.D.N.Y. 1941), rev'd 148 F.2d 416 (2d Cir. 1945).

[9] Gibb, The Saco-Lowell Shops 4 (1950); Hower, History of Macy's of New York 98 (1943); Deere & Co., 1952 Ann. Rep. 9, 11 (Moline, 1953); American Viscose Corp., 1948 Ann. Rep. 5 (Philadelphia, 1949); E. I. du Pont de Nemours & Co., 1952 Ann. Rep. 7 (Wilmington, 1953); Crane Co., 1952 Ann. Rep. 3 (Chicago, 1953).

[10] §3.13 supra.

may be both wealthy and occupy a large proportion of its industry. Such is the case with important railroads and electric generating companies. To the extent that we think in terms of physical production, however, wealth is not necessarily correlated with indivisibility. On the other hand, it is possible that indivisibility can be discovered in the centralized operation of a highly diversified business.[11] Instances can no doubt be found in which management and advisory services are available to an enterprise on the most efficient basis only when its size is great in absolute terms. Again, pure size may actually affect access to capital funds. There is, however, little evidence with respect to the prevalence and magnitude of such indivisibility: we only know it is wound in a tangled skein of imperfections.

Those charged with the onerous duty of maintaining and improving our charitable institutions look gratefully to big corporations as a replacement for the personal wealth of bygone days.[12] Naturally, those responsible for charities welcome statements such as this by a large oil company:

> Corporate citizens have . . . come to accept many of the obligations traditionally imposed only upon the individual citizen. Today, companies concern themselves with employee and community welfare, and with many other activities going beyond a strictly economic concept of business functions.
>
> The management of this company is devoting an increasing share of its attention to the social problems affecting its business. We believe that in this way the continuity of the enterprise may best be assured and its economic health sustained. . . .[13]

Changes in the "private" law of corporations now widely permit business concerns to make donations for charitable purposes. Where statutes are not explicit, courts have made similar adjustments in the law. In one of the best-known decisions a New Jersey court declared:

11 One sometimes has the feeling that observers have focused too heavily upon physical production in assessing the presence of indivisibility and have overlooked distribution as well as other factors mentioned in the text. Compare Spiegel, Current Economic Problems 366 (The Blakiston Co. 1949); id. at 368.

12 See §8.2 *supra*. Early doctors of the church were against luxury; not all were against riches but if one had worldly goods they must be used for charitable purposes. Whittaker, A History of Economic Ideas 73-77 (1943). In medieval times there were different attitudes toward wealth. St. Thomas Aquinas claimed that one should give alms but not to the extent that these gifts imperiled one's standard of living for it was necessary to maintain one's station in life. The Franciscan orders founded in the early thirteenth century followed the early Christian policy of giving up one's wealth and caring for the poor. The concept of charity spread during the Middle Ages and was an important part of life. Id. at 77-79.

13 Standard Oil Co. of New Jersey, 1948 Ann. Rep. 5 (New York City, 1949).

Control of economic wealth has passed largely from individual entrepreneurs to dominating corporations, and calls upon the corporations for reasonable philanthropic donations have come to be made with increased public support. In many instances such contributions have been sustained by the courts within the common law doctrine upon liberal findings that the donations tended reasonably to promote the corporate objectives. . . .

When the wealth of the nation was primarily in the hands of individuals they discharged their responsibilities as citizens by donating freely for charitable purposes. With the transfer of most of the wealth to corporate hands and the imposition of heavy burdens of individual taxation, they have been unable to keep pace with increased philanthropic needs. They have, therefore, with justification, turned to corporations to assume the modern obligations of good citizenship. . . .[14]

Personal income taxes and death duties have created a situation of indivisibility wherein collection of funds for charitable purposes almost demands recourse to big business. As we have seen above, many of the industrial and commercial giants of the business world have responded by supporting scientific, educational, artistic and community charities of one type and another.[15] To the extent that the corporations thus supplant private donors we may expect a more farsighted and pioneering use of funds than would be available from governmental sources.[16] At the same time, we

---

[14] A. P. Smith Mfg. Co. v. Barlow, 13 N.J. 145, 98 A.2d 581, 584, 585-586 (1953), *appeal dismissed per curiam*, 346 U.S. 861 (1953). See also Illinois Business Corporation Act §5(m), as amended, Ill. Rev. Stat., c. 32, §157.5(m) (1957); Cousens, How Far Corporations May Contribute to Charity, 35 Va. L. Rev. 401 (1949).

Whether corporate wealth must be preserved in order to assure a fountainhead for charitable and artistic endeavors may depend greatly upon whether one believes such projects cannot thrive in a wholly egalitarian society. Compare also the concept of corporate "performance" discussed *supra* §4.1.

[15] §8.2 *supra*. See also Chrysler Corp., 29th Ann. Rep. 6 (Detroit, 1954); Holton, Remarks 3-4 (Annual Meeting of Socony-Vacuum Oil Co., April 29, 1954); Sears, Roebuck & Co., 1953 Ann. Rep. 20 (Chicago, 1954). Whether the benefactions of wealth are worth their cost in terms of inequality appears to be beyond measurement. There is, however, some impressive evidence of gains from carefully managed charitable endeavors. E.g., 2 Nevins, Study in Power, cc. 34, 37 (1953). Note too, that there are values beyond mere equality. Thus it has been said: "In a superficial sense social equality has been attained to a degree which has alarmed men who consider individual idiosyncracies the charm of life if not the key to progress." Brinton, Equality, 5 Encyc. Soc. Sci. 574, 580 (1931). On the other hand, there is grave doubt as to whether corporations are strong enough to carry such tremendous burdens, particularly through periods of business depression. Corporate Management, 7 Fortune No. 6, pp. 47, 51 (1933).

[16] In general, innovations in charity (as perhaps in other fields) are found in inverse proportion to the number of donors and the "distance" between them and the administrators of the fund. One spending the money of millions of taxpayers cannot justify the risks of untried ventures. Corporate giving probably represents a middle ground between private and governmental contributions with respect to

cannot ignore the economic and social power inherent in the management of the giant enterprise. The mere authority to select the charity which shall be favored is an important matter.

Again, there are those who see in big business a stabilizing force for the entire economy. All those dependent upon big business — its employees, its distributors, its charitable beneficiaries — find comfort in the thought that a firm of tremendous size will not and perhaps cannot fold its tents and steal silently away when conditions become adverse.[17] Big corporations have been quick to take advantage of such sentiments and their reports are filled with boasts of the number of jobs they have "provided" and the high payrolls they have met.[18] They point, too, to continuity of employment, many having a large proportion of employees who have served ten, twenty-five or more years.[19] Mere horizontal size of a business corporation may contribute somewhat to its own perpetuation or to the stability of the economy as a whole. Wealth, however, can do far more.[20] The enormous diversified enterprise, much like an investment trust, can shift resources rapidly from one field to another. It disposes of unsuccessful ventures in wine-making and plunges into the construction of chemical plants. Ore mining and smelting of copper no longer seem attractive. So it engages in uranium,

---

the efficiency with which the funds are used. There may be other reasons for believing that governmental control of charity would be less desirable than corporate control. Compare Whittaker, A History of Economic Ideas 83-90 (1943); The church itself during the Middle Ages became wealthy and it held on to its property as only a bureaucracy can. There were cases of bishops and others living too well and being too preoccupied with luxury. There was also considerable criticism of this tendency toward luxury — religious orders and others among the clergy and laity were criticized. Id. at 79-83. But compare Glover, The Attack on Big Business 148-152 (1954).

[17] Boulding, In Defense of Monopoly, 59 Q.J. Econ. 524 (1945); National Industrial Conference Board, Mergers in Industry 173 (1929). Compare Zimmerman, The Propensity to Monopolize 89-90 (1952); Spiegel, Current Economic Problems, 352 (The Blakiston Co. 1949).

[18] General Electric Co., 57th Ann. Rep. 3 (Schenectady, 1949); General Motors Corp., 40th Ann. Rep. 16-17 (New York City, 1949); National Biscuit Co., 1950 Ann. Rep. 11 (New York City, 1951); E. I. du Pont de Nemours & Co., 1948 Ann. Rep. 8 (Wilmington, 1949).

[19] Eastman Kodak Co., 1948 Ann. Rep. 27 (Rochester, 1949); National Dairy Products Corp., 30th Ann. Rep. 13 (New York City, 1954); Gulf Oil Corp., 1953 Ann. Rep. 25 (Pittsburgh, 1954); Thompson, Since Spindletop 57 (Gulf Oil Corp. 1951); Ohio Oil Co., 66th Ann. Rep. 9 (Findlay, 1954).

Note also that the big firms stress the large number of suppliers from whom they buy and retailers whom they provide with merchandise. General Motors Corp., 41st Ann. Rep. 9 (New York City, 1950); Kilgore Committee Hearings, pt. 1, at 345. In National Dairy Products Corp., 30th Ann. Rep. 15 (New York City, 1954) great emphasis was laid on large cash payments to farmers.

[20] Osborn, Efficiency and Profitability in Relation to Size, 29 Harv. Bus. Rev. No. 2, pp. 82, 93 (1951); Hower, History of Macy's of New York 144-145 (1943).

gold, oil, titanium and iron ore mining.[21]   One cannot help thinking that corporate wealth thus avoids many frictions otherwise inherent in the market place.   It saves, for example, the disastrous losses associated with bankruptcy: the concern is preserved as an existing entity though individual plants and processes are scrapped or sold.[22]   All the time and expense incident to "starting up" is saved and employees who become surplus on one task may readily be shifted to another.[23]   True, management can thus perpetuate itself in power despite many changes in the physical nature of the business conducted by the corporation.[24] At the same time, it still faces the test of profitability — unless the "responsibilities" undertaken by giant firms in the manner outlined above come to supplant the old objective of producing earnings for stockholders.

§8.5.   **Remedies for wealth.**   If we should decide to put a limit upon corporate wealth, a question would at once arise as to the appropriate means of effecting such an end.   One such remedy already in partial use is found in the corporate income tax.[1]   A progressive income tax upon corporations would operate impersonally and suggest to management the desirability of splitting great aggregations of business wealth into separate entities.[2]

[21] National Distillers Products Corp., 29th Ann. Rep. 10-11, 14-15, 17 (New York City, 1953); Kennecott Copper Corp., 1952 Ann. Rep. 13, 15, 17 (New York City, 1953); Borg-Warner Corp., 1952 Ann. Rep. 12 (Chicago, 1953). Compare the simple situation arising when the ore in one mine is exhausted, the equipment is salvaged and moved to another site and operations continued by the same company. Phelps Dodge Corp., 1953 Ann. Rep. 12 (New York City, 1954).

[22] Perhaps the phenomenon described in the text is merely another aspect of indivisibility. Note, however, that continuity of the corporation may result in an uneconomic allocation of resources. Boulding, The Organizational Revolution 139 (Federal Council of Churches of Christ in America, 1953).

[23] Hennipman, Monopoly: Impediment or Stimulus to Economic Progress, in Chamberlin, ed., Monopoly and Competition and Their Regulation 421, 438 (International Economic Assn. 1954).

[24] Robinson, Imperfect Competition Revisited, 63 Econ. J. 579, 582 (1953); Williamson, Winchester: The Gun That Won the West 211 (1952). But compare Hower, The History of an Advertising Agency 50, 150-151 (1939).

§8.5. [1] Int. Rev. Code of 1954, §11.

[2] Kaplan, Small Business: Its Place and Problems 174-175 (Committee for Economic Development, 1948).   Compare Buck and Schakelford, Retention of Earnings by Corporations Under the Income Tax Laws, 36 Va. L. Rev. 141, 323, 461, 470 (1950).

In Handler, The Legal Aspects of Industrial Mergers, in The Federal Anti-trust Laws 173, 199 (Handler ed. 1931), it was suggested:

". . . Taxation affords the best method of control and the easiest way of compelling a reorganization of the industrial structure.

"I advocate therefore a system of differential and graduated corporate taxation levied upon income and capitalization, authorized and actual, the rate of tax to increase with the size and percentage of control of the companies taxed. The tax would be measured by the capitalization of the company or degree of concentration, whichever yielded the larger tax."

How much "progression" would be required to effect dissolution could perhaps only be determined by experimentation: first, with lower rates and later, if necessary, with higher levies. Indeed, a good case can be made for the elimination of the corporate income tax upon all firms whose size does not appear to be offensive, since the tax, as a revenue measure, is difficult to justify by reference to any of the standard criteria.[3] On the other hand, we must recognize that any such scheme of graduated corporate income taxes would, at some levels, penalize efficiency and possibly curb growth.[4]

Other suggestions have involved direct limitations upon corporate activities such as once characterized the "private" law of corporations.[5] Professor Simons, for example, found no reason to permit corporations to hold stock in other corporations.[6] Others have suggested that the activities of the corporation be narrowly limited to those specified in its charter.[7] A flat limit on the dollar value of corporate assets has also been proposed.[8] None of the foregoing schemes, however, has much appeal. Several of them have been found wanting in the "private" law of corporations and all of them are open to the possibility of making the business corporation an inflexible device and reducing the rapidity with which its resources are located.[9] Professor Machlup cleverly suggested that members of the board of directors of a corporation be required to own more than half of its stock.[10] This proposal would, of course, cause a reduction in corporate wealth to bring it more closely into correlation with personal wealth.[11] It is not open to the objection of rigidity applicable to specific dollar values of assets and the like. On the other hand,

---

Professor Handler's proposal, as opposed to that set forth in the text, is directed at monopoly as well as at corporate wealth. Hence it involves the difficult problem of defining commodities and markets set forth in Chapter 3 *supra*.

[3] Machlup, The Political Economy of Monopoly 251-252 (1952); Shoup, Facing the Tax Problem 164-165 (Twentieth Century Fund, 1937); Ruml, Tomorrow's Business 201 (1945). Compare Colm, Conflicting Theories of Corporate Income Taxation, 7 Law & Contemp. Prob. 281, 288-289 (1940).

[4] Machlup, The Political Economy of Monopoly 251, 258, 261 (1952). Compare Blum and Kalven, The Uneasy Case for Progressive Taxation, 19 U. Chi. L. Rev. 417, 490 et seq. (1952).

[5] See §8.6 *infra*.

[6] Simons, Economic Policy for a Free Society 52, 59 (1948).

[7] Brandeis, J., dissenting in Louis K. Liggett v. Lee, 288 U.S. 517, 554 et seq. (1939); O'Mahoney Committee I, pt. 4, at 660.

[8] Simons, Economic Policy for a Free Society 59 (1948); Brandeis, J., dissenting in Louis K. Liggett Co. v. Lee, 288 U.S. 517, 550 et seq. (1933).

[9] See Dodge v. Ford Motor Co., 204 Mich. 459, 170 N.W. 668, 680 (1919).

[10] Machlup, The Political Economy of Monopoly 245 (1952); Celler Committee I, p. 2A, at 521.

[11] Hurff, Social Aspects of Enterprise in the Large Corporation 18, 24 (1950).

it appears to combine in its wealth-limiting feature a device to safeguard shareholders against lavish corporate expenditures. It is not clear, however, that the latter device is well conceived, since a board of directors holding 51 per cent of the outstanding stock might find it almost as easy to spend corporate funds and to place 49 per cent of the burden on the minority shareholders as if the percentages were reversed. In any event, it is not established that waste of corporate funds is now a problem needing such corrective action.

A proposal for curbing corporate wealth has been put forward by Mr. Raymond. Basically, he would limit corporations to a single location (plant) or to a specific number of employees, whichever was the larger.[12] Considerable leeway is, of course, found in the formula because it does not specify the number of employees. Such legislation would get directly to the root of the corporate wealth problem and avoid the controls which might otherwise be applied to big business.[13] It is a vivid suggestion which might open new opportunities to our citizens to become active managers of enterprises[14] without disastrous destruction of the existing economic system. It is, on the other hand, an arbitrary formula which could have adverse effects upon growth of the economy and which might considerably impair efficiency, particularly in the distribution rather than in the manufacture of goods.[15] Furthermore, it might be difficult to enforce,[16] although it could be combined with the tax adjustments outlined above and perhaps thus prove more workable in application.[17]

---

[12] Raymond, The Limitist (1947); Celler Committee I, pt. 2A, at 323, 521.

[13] Id. pt. 1 at 350-351, 369, 436.

[14] The concept of increasing personal opportunity is of course somewhat nebulous. Some persons want and perhaps deserve the opportunity to manage a really tremendous enterprise. Others have neither the desire nor the ability to undertake management responsibilities of any magnitude.

[15] Wright, Toward Coherent Anti-trust, 35 Va. L. Rev. 665, 684 (1949). Compare Glover, The Attack on Big Business 39 et seq. (1954). Another possibility is that no business enterprise should be allowed to attain or retain a size larger than that required by efficiency. The latter suggestion, of course, involves all the difficulty of measuring indivisibility discussed supra §§3.13 and 8.4.

[16] Markham, An Alternative Approach to the Concept of Workable Competition, 40 Am. Econ. Rev. 349 (1950). Among other things, limits upon corporate wealth would have to be designed to prevent stockholders organizing affiliated corporations which would act in concert with the curbed company. Just what might constitute "affiliation" would not be easy to establish. With the passage of time, however, the various corporate entities would no doubt grow apart.

[17] It should also be noted that plans for limiting corporate wealth would not necessarily affect the problem of monopoly. Business enterprises entrenched in a dominant position in local areas, for example, would probably go untouched under a prescription such as that proposed by Mr. Raymond.

It is apparent, therefore, that views with respect to corporate wealth involve many of the fundamental issues of political science facing our polity today. How much equality we crave and the price we are willing to pay for it are obviously inherent in any proposal to curb corporate size. To the extent that big business provides continuity and stability for its employees and the like, a challenge to its size involves the age-old controversy between freedom and security.[18] If it is argued that the charitable and other functions now performed by giant enterprise could be undertaken by government, we test our faith in the whole democratic process and in the scope of activity which we believe government can properly perform. Surely, this is no field for dogmatic assertion.[19] Indeed, the topic is closely related to the very existence of artificial persons and the powers and duties of such entities under the "private" law of corporations.

§8.6. The "private" law of corporations. In our polity, business corporations are most often creatures of the several states. General statutes permit the formation of such artificial persons with few limitations, and the conduct of their affairs is subject to controls exercised chiefly for the benefit of the stockholders. This state of affairs has been the source of frequent and important complaint. Professor Simons thought that the almost unlimited grant of powers to corporate bodies constituted one of the greatest sins of government against the free enterprise system.[1] He was not alone in his belief. Many years ago one of the leading courts of the land wrote:

> It is not a sufficient answer to say that similar results may be lawfully accomplished; that an individual having the necessary wealth might have bought all these refineries, manned them with his own

[18] Whether corporations exist for the benefit of their stockholders or some other group such as employees, consumers, or management has been the subject of a lively debate reviewed in Gower, Corporate Control, 68 Harv. L. Rev. 1176, 1189 et seq. (1955). We have not mentioned in our analysis the contention that big business is afflicted with a greedy materialism. We are not aware that either greed or materialism are limited to large scale enterprise; indeed, there are reasons for supposing that the truly giant concerns are somewhat less greedy than their less conspicuous rivals. But compare Glover, The Attack on Big Business, c. 6 (1954).

[19] Some years ago a careful student wrote: "Those who now take a positive stand of any sort on public policy with respect to big business and industrial markets must do so on a basis of faith rather than knowledge of market results, or on broader grounds of relations between concentration of private power and political and economic democracy." Wallace, Industrial Markets and Public Policy, in Public Policy 59, 98 (Friedrich and Mason ed. 1940).

§8.6. [1] Simons, Economic Policy for a Free Society 52 (1948). See also Burns, The Decline of Competition 9 (1936).

chosen agents, and managed them as a group, at his sovereign will; for it is one thing for the state to respect the rights of ownership and protect them out of regard to the business freedom of the citizen and quite another thing to add to that possibility a further extension of all those consequences by creating artificial persons to aid in producing such aggregations. The individuals are few who hold in possession such enormous wealth, and fewer still who peril it all in a manufacturing enterprise; but if corporations can combine, and mass their fortunes in a solid trust or partnership, with little added risk to the capital already embarked, without limit to the magnitude of the aggregation, a tempting and easy road is open to enormous combinations, vastly exceeding in number and strength and in their power over industry any possibilities of individual ownership. . . .[2]

Note also that for many years it was the policy of the common law and of statutes in the several states not to permit corporations to own real property beyond that necessary for the transaction of their businesses.[3] Furthermore, in the early history of this nation corporate charters were strictly construed: a company authorized to operate a railway from X to Y could not "divert" capital from the objects contemplated by the charter and continue the line to Z.[4] The doctrine of ultra vires was strictly applied to limit corporations to the businesses spelt out in their charters.[5]

[2] People v. North River Sugar Refining Co., 121 N.Y. 582, 24 N.E. 834, 840-841 (1890). As early as 1830, fears were expressed that the granting of corporate charters for manufacturing would gather wealth into large aggregations and make it impossible for the independent mechanic to enter into competition. Dodd, American Business Corporations Until 1860, 415 (1954). Note also that the traditional remedy for the forfeiture of a corporate charter is a petition in the nature of quo warranto and that the judgment therein is ouster. This, of course, is closely akin to remedies available under the antitrust laws. Hale, The Law of Private Corporations in Illinois §181 (1916). Compare §10.3 infra.

[3] People ex rel. Moloney v. Pullman's Palace Car Co., 175 Ill. 125, 142-143, 51 N.E. 664 (1898); National Home Building Association v. Home Savings Bank, 181 Ill. 35, 41-42, 54 N.E. 619 (1898); 2 Davis, Essays in the Earlier History of American Corporations 317 (1917); Hale, A Field for Corporate Law Revision — Collateral Attack, 11 Ill. L. Rev. 1, 8-9 (1916).

[4] Pearce v. Madison & Indianapolis Railway Co., 62 U.S. 441, 443-444 (1858). Compare Ramsey v. Tod, 95 Tex. 614, 69 S.W. 133 (1902); Williams v. Citizens' Enterprise Co., 25 Ind. App. 351, 57 N.E. 581 (1900); Marion Bond Co. v. Mexican Coffee Co., 160 Ind. 558, 65 N.E. 748 (1902). Earlier history is recounted in 1 Davis, Essays in the Earlier History of American Corporations 429 (1917); 2 id. at 22-23, 318-319, 380; Keasbey, New Jersey and the Great Corporations, 13 Harv. L. Rev. 198, 203 (1899). Near the end of the last century Mr. Morawetz could still write: "When the legislature incorporates an association for the purpose of carrying on a particular business in a particular manner, it thereby grants permission to the association to act in a corporate capacity for the purpose of prosecuting the particular enterprise described, and no other." Morawetz, Private Corporations 23 (1882). Compare Chapter 6 supra.

[5] Cherokee Iron Co. v. Jones, 52 Ga. 276 (1874); People ex rel. Peabody v. Chicago Gas Trust Co., 130 Ill. 268, 22 N.E. 768 (1889); Commercial Casualty Co. v. Daniel

Later there was a swing away from the narrow and restrictive views which formerly obtained as to the scope of corporate powers. The doctrine of ultra vires was found to work gross injustice,[6] and statutes were amended to prevent third parties from questioning the existence of corporate powers.[7] Dissatisfaction with the system of special charters granted by state legislatures led to the adoption of general statutes permitting anyone to form a corporation and making the issuance of charters a ministerial duty of state officers.[8] Amendments, under the new legislation, became easy and a corporation formed for one purpose could

---

Russell Boiler Works, 258 Mass. 453, 155 N.E. 422 (1927); People ex rel. Moloney v. Pullman's Palace Car Co., 175 Ill. 125, 51 N.E. 664 (1898). In the last case the Pullman Company was prohibited from engaging in the housing business, even though, as a later observer found, the construction of Mr. Pullman's model town was a practical necessity if there was to be a factory fifteen miles from Chicago at all, since there were no other quarters for the employees. Pullman, Inc., 17 Fortune No. 1, pp. 39, 102 (1938). Some courts displayed a trifling leniency in favor of temporary and incidental deviation from strict charter construction. E.g., Brown v. Winnisimet Co., 93 Mass. 326, 333 (1865).

[6] Hale, A Field for Corporate Law Revision — Collateral Attack, 11 Ill. L. Rev. 1, 2 et seq. (1916); Stevens, A Proposal as to the Codification and Restatement of the Ultra Vires Doctrine, 36 Yale L.J. 297, 299-300 (1927); Carpenter, Should the Doctrine of Ultra Vires Be Discarded? 33 Yale L.J. 49, 64 (1923).

[7] E.g., Illinois Business Corporation Act §8, Ill. Rev. Stat., c. 32, §157 (1957). Discussion of the ultra vires problem and the relaxation of the former rules was carried on largely in disregard of the question of monopoly. Thus a leading student wrote: "The mere fact that a corporation acts in excess of its charter powers does not mean that its action is adverse to public interest. To say that there is a public policy in favor of keeping the corporation within its charter limits is vague and in most cases is untrue. As to whether the action is adverse to public interest the same test should be applied to the corporate person as to the natural person." Carpenter, Should the Doctrine of Ultra Vires Be Discarded? 33 Yale L.J. 49, 64 (1923). To the same effect see Thompson, The Doctrine of Ultra Vires in Relation to Private Corporations, 28 Am. L. Rev. 376, 396 et seq. (1894).

[8] Dodd and Baker, Cases on Business Associations 20 (1940); Keasbey, New Jersey and the Great Corporations, 13 Harv. L. Rev. 198, 205 (1899). Statutes controlling the incorporation of banks, insurance companies and public utility ventures often contain narrower powers and restrict corporate activity to limited fields. E.g., Illinois Insurance Code §4.9, Ill. Rev. Stat., c. 73, §613 (1957). Those limitations, however, have almost invariably been motivated by a desire to protect creditors or customers. Thus it has been said: "The manifest purpose of the legislature in excepting banking, insurance, real estate brokerage and other corporations from the provisions of the act authorizing incorporation of companies for other lawful purposes, was, that these excepted corporations should be restrained by more strict requirements, securing the safe conduct and correct administration of their affairs." People ex rel. Kasson v. Rose, 174 Ill. 310, 316, 51 N.E. 246 (1898). See also Dyer v. Broadway Central Bank, 225 App. Div. 366, 233 N.Y. Supp. 96, 97 (1st Dept. 1929); Patterson, The Insurance Commissioner in the United States 204 et seq. (1927). On the other hand it should, of course, be noted that making the issuance of corporate charters a ministerial duty negatives the element of monopoly formerly inherent in the special charter. Compare Dodd, American Business Corporations Until 1860, 31, 126 (1954). Freedom to incorporate, in other words, may be an important element in the promotion of competition.

readily acquire authority to engage in other lines of activity.[9]   At one time the holding of stock in other corporations was rigidly prohibited[10] but this limitation too slipped away and today it is common to allow the formation of subsidiary and affiliated corporations.[11]   It was obvious that the foregoing changes in the private law of corporations would affect the power of artificial persons to acquire great aggregations of wealth.   Little consideration, however, appears to have been given to that aspect of the problem.[12]

In our law, the corporation as an artificial person is not distinguished from the natural person.   It follows that a corporation under the antitrust laws is not considered a "combination" in restraint of trade.   This is the famous "single trader" doctrine.[13] That doctrine, however, has never been applied so rigidly as to permit a state charter to shelter what would otherwise constitute an illegal monopoly.[14]   And in recent years there have been suggestions that the corporate entity should be disregarded for antitrust purposes.[15]   Such proposals, however, overlook the great utility of corporations in permitting individual investors to overcome indivisibility by joining their capital in a single fund

[9] Dodd, Statutory Developments in Business Corporation Law, 50 Harv. L. Rev. 27, 33, 37 (1936).

[10] People ex rel. Moloney v. Pullman's Palace Car Co., 175 Ill. 125, 159, 51 N.E. 664 (1898); Golden v. Cervenka, 278 Ill. 409, 116 N.E. 273 (1917); Hale, The Law of Private Corporations in Illinois §77 (1915).

[11] E.g., Illinois Business Corporation Act §5(g), Ill. Rev. Stat., c. 32, §157 (1957). See Hall v. Woods, 325 Ill. 114, 130, 156 N.E. 258 (1927); Roth v. Ahrensfeld, 300 Ill. App. 312, 321, 21 N.E.2d 21 (1939), aff'd, 373 Ill. 550, 27 N.E.2d 445 (1940); Keasbey, New Jersey and the Great Corporations, 13 Harv. L. Rev. 198, 207 (1899); Bonbright and Means, The Holding Company 64 (1932).   Such exceptions as remain pertain chiefly to public utility, banking, insurance and a few other types of business.   E.g., Steckler v. Pennroad Corp., 44 F. Supp. 800, 803 (E.D. Pa. 1942); Public Utility Holding Company Act of 1935, §9, 49 Stat. 803, 15 U.S.C.A. §79.

[12] Compare Simons, Economic Policy for a Free Society 59 (1948).

[13] See §3.9 supra; Walker, History of the Sherman Law 13 (1910); Stockton v. American Tobacco Co., 55 N.J. Eq. 352, 36 Atl. 971, 976 (1879).   But compare 2 Davis, Essays in the Earlier History of American Corporations 12-13 (1917).

[14] Northern Securities Co. v. United States, 193 U.S. 197, 332-333, 344-345, 350 (1904); Ford v. Chicago Milk Shippers' Assn., 155 Ill. 166, 180, 39 N.E. 651 (1895); Distilling & Cattle Feeding Co. v. People ex rel. Moloney, 156 Ill. 448, 491, 41 N.E. 188 (1895); Hale, The Law of Private Corporations in Illinois §232 (1916).

[15] Celler Committee I, pt. 5, at 44; Rahl, Conspiracy and the Anti-trust Laws, 44 Ill. L. Rev. 743, 756 et seq. (1950); §3.9 supra.   Compare Atty. Gen. Nat. Com. Rep. 36, (2).   It is of some interest to note that in 1938 the United States Steel Corporation had about 150 subsidiaries, many of which were later dissolved.   On that subject an officer of the company testified: "At the time of the TNEC investigations . . . those questions of the number of subsidiaries came up and we found we had a great many companies that served no purpose and we tried to eliminate and dissolve and get rid of all those unnecessary companies.   Many of them were companies only in name.   They had no assets, no business, did nothing." Celler Committee I, pt. 4A, at 474.

and the frictions eliminated by corporate continuity. We find, therefore, no reason to prohibit the use of the corporate form in business enterprises; nevertheless, some adjustment of the private law of corporations to the wealth problem may be indicated.[16]

[16] To the extent such adjustment is feasible. As indicated in this section, earlier efforts to control the size and activities of business corporations through the "private" law of the several states were not successful. Further, as indicated in prior sections, there may be reasons why wealth should not be curbed. To destroy giant corporations without some adjustment of federal taxes on natural persons, for example, would probably leave many charitable enterprises without support. Furthermore, in our federal system wherein corporate charters are granted by state law, uniformity would be difficult to achieve. Compare the proposal for federal "licensing" of corporations in §10.12 *infra*. Note also the discussion in §11.4 *infra*.

CHAPTER 9

Attempts to Monopolize

§9.1. Attempts as an antitrust problem. Many of the statutes, both state and federal, affecting the monopoly problem are criminal in character. It is an elementary principle of the common law that an attempt to commit a crime is in itself criminal.[1] Besides that, Section 2 of the Sherman Act, the principal statute with which we are here concerned, specifically makes an attempt to monopolize any part of the trade or commerce among the several states a misdemeanor.[2] Accordingly, a treatise on the law of monopoly is scarcely complete without some reference to attempted monopolization.

Such attempts are, of course, different from, but closely akin to, the abuses examined above. As we have seen, "attempts" and "abuses" enjoy many aspects of similarity. The concepts are, however, technically different and their legal content may vary perceptibly.[3]

It should also be noted that all the questions concerning the ultimate crime of monopolization are also involved in defining an attempt to monopolize. In previous chapters[4] we have examined at length the concept of monopoly and suggested the considerations logically applicable to a determination that a defendant has "monopolized" in violation of the Sherman Act or some similar statute. We shall not here set forth again all the suggested tests of illegality together with the infirmities applicable to each. In short, in discussing attempts to monopolize, we shall omit all the numerous difficulties (discussed above) involved in ascertaining what "monopolize" means.

§9.2. Acts which may constitute attempts. Two elementary principles common to all attempts should be mentioned. In the first place, no attempt can be criminal unless the act attempted

§9.1. [1] 22 C.J.S. 138.
[2] Section 2 of the Sherman Act reads in part as follows: "Every person who shall monopolize, or attempt to monopolize . . . any part of the trade or commerce among the several States . . . shall be deemed guilty of a misdemeanor . . ."
[3] See §§2.6, 2.9 *supra*.
[4] See Chapters 2, 3, 4, 5, 6 and 7.

itself constitutes a crime. As applied to the antitrust laws, this means simply that an attempt to monopolize cannot be unlawful unless monopolization itself is beyond the law.[1] We have, of course, assumed for present purposes that such monopolization is illegal. In the second place, by definition, an attempt involves a failure to achieve the completed act. Thus one who has successfully monopolized cannot be guilty of an attempt to monopolize: the very concept of attempt involves failure.[2]

Many attempts might also constitute infractions of other statutes. Consider, for example, Section 1 of the Sherman Act. An attempt to monopolize may constitute a restraint of trade within the meaning of that section.[3] Many of the practices forbidden by the Clayton Act could, if indulged in with the requisite specific intent, constitute attempts to monopolize.[4] Similarly, violations of Section 5 of the Federal Trade Commission Act might well overlap into the field of attempts.[5] Indeed, almost any act could constitute part of an attempt to monopolize. Presumably, all the abuses cataloged in a prior chapter could be so characterized.[6] Price discrimination, exclusive arrangements, acquisition of rival firms, and the like might all form the foundation of an illegal

§9.2. [1] Sayre, Criminal Attempts, 41 Harv. L. Rev. 821, 839 (1928). But compare United States v. Columbia Steel Co., 334 U.S. 495, 529, 531-532 (1948).

[2] Sayre, Criminal Attempts, 41 Harv. L. Rev. 821, 838 (1928). But compare United States v. Columbia Steel Co., 334 U.S. 495, 532 (1948). It is, however, clear that the impossibility of completing the intended crime, unknown to the defendant or otherwise, cannot of itself bar criminality for the attempt. Id. at 854. Recently an authority on the subject wrote: ". . . when it has been established that there was the intent to commit a specific crime and to carry out this intent an act or acts were committed, which caused damage or sufficient danger of damage, the fact that for some reason it is impossible to complete the intended crime should not be, and is generally held not to be, a defense to a prosecution for the attempt." Keedy, Criminal Attempts at Common Law, 102 U. Pa. L. Rev. 464, 489 (1954).

[3] Standard Oil Co. of New Jersey v. United States, 221 U.S. 1, 61 (1911). Other cases are collected *supra* §3.9. A good example of activities which apparently violated both §1 of the Sherman Act and constituted an attempt to monopolize will be found in U.S. Leather, 11 Fortune No. 2, pp. 56, 96 (1935). Compare Times-Picayune Publishing Co. v. United States, 345 U.S. 594, 608-609 (1953); Ware-Kramer Tobacco Co. v. American Tobacco Co., 180 Fed. 160, 165 (E.D.N.C. 1910). On the other hand the concept of attempts may include acts not within the prohibitions of §1 of that Act. Lorain Journal Co. v. United States, 342 U.S. 143, 153-154 (1951); United States v. Columbia Steel Co., 334 U.S. 495, 531-532 (1948).

[4] Compare McAllister, Where the Effect May Be to Substantially Lessen Competition or Tend to Create a Monopoly, Proceedings A.B.A., Section of Antitrust Law, 124 (Aug. 27, 1953).

[5] Thus it has been said: "It was . . . one of the hopes of those who sponsored the Federal Trade Commission Act that its effect might be prophylactic and that through it attempts to bring about complete monopolization of an industry might be stopped in their incipiency." Fashion Originators' Guild v. FTC, 312 U.S. 457, 466 (1941).

[6] See §§2.10 et seq. *supra*.

attempt.[7] Presumptively, all the business torts such as disparagement and harassment could similarly constitute attempts.[8]

There must, of course, be some limit to the misdemeanor: not every act can constitute an attempt. The act of the defendant must be dangerous or potentially dangerous. There must be a showing of some imminent probability that the purpose of the defendant can be realized.[9] Thus it seems doubtful whether a so-called "invasive" sales policy, whereby delivery of bits was made directly to customers on their oil drilling locations so that the salesmen could visit the drilling rig rather than merely make calls at warehouses, could constitute in and of itself an attempt to

---

[7] E.g., Lorain Journal Co. v. United States, 342 U.S. 143, 152-153 (1951); Southern Rendering Co. v. Standard Rendering Co., 112 F. Supp. 103 (E.D. Ark. 1953). Compare Atty. Gen. Nat. Com. Rep. 27, d.

[8] See §2.22 supra. The various business "shapes" described in Chapters 5, 6 and 7 have also been considered at various times to constitute attempts to monopolize. Various forms of patent ownership and use come close to such attempts. Compare Atty. Gen. Nat. Com. Rep. 226, 1. Even the use of trade-marks and the enforcement of rights therein have been subsumed under the rubric of an attempt. California Fruit Growers' Exchange v. Sunkist Baking Co., 166 F.2d 971, 974-975 (7th Cir. 1947); Pattishall, Trade-Marks and the Monopoly Phobia, 50 Mich. L. Rev. 967, 974, 977 (1952). Obviously it is impossible to anticipate every "predatory" act which one competitor might use against another; the instances given are illustrative therefore rather than exhaustive.

[9] Bender v. Hearst Corp., 152 F. Supp. 569, 578 (D. Conn. 1957). There must be either damage (or a sufficient danger of damage) before the attempt becomes a crime. Furthermore, the danger must be actual and not merely apparent. Thus a toy gun in the hands of the defendant would lay an insufficient foundation for an indictment for attempted murder. Keedy, Criminal Attempts at Common Law, 102 U. Pa. L. Rev. 464, 468-469, 471 (1954). On the other hand, where dangerous means are used (such as a real pistol mistakenly loaded with blank bullets) an attempt may be found, even though the result intended could not possibly be achieved. Sayre, Criminal Attempts, 41 Harv. L. Rev. 821, 849 et seq. (1928). Compare note 2 supra. As applied to an antitrust situation, it would appear to follow that a defendant who has attempted to monopolize by running his rivals out of business could not be convicted of that crime on evidence that he had raised prices and thus made his product less attractive to buyers than those of his competitors. As a leading practitioner put the matter: ". . . attempt to monopolize requires proof of a specific intent to bring about a monopolization of some appreciable segment of interstate commerce. While intent to monopolize is the distinguishing characteristic of this offense, it is obvious that there must be a showing of some reasonable probability that the purpose of the defendant can be realized and, generally, some overt acts in furtherance of the projected monopolization." Johnston, Monopolize or Attempt to Monopolize, Proceedings A.B.A., Section of Antitrust Law, 72, 76 (Aug. 26, 1953). In Northern Securities Co. v. United States, 193 U.S. 197 (1904), Mr. Justice Holmes, dissenting, said at page 409: ". . . in my opinion there is no attempt to monopolize . . . until something is done with the intent to exclude strangers to the combination from competing with it in some part of the business which it carries on." On the other hand, it has been said that a dangerous probability of resultant harm will give rise to a finding of an attempt within the meaning of §2 of the Sherman Act. Swift & Co. v. United States, 196 U.S. 375, 396 (1905).

monopolize.[10] On the other hand, the more serious the crime attempted, the further back in the series of acts leading up to the consummated crime should the criminal law reach in holding the defendant guilty of an attempt.[11]

That the act of the defendant must connote some dangerous probability of successfully accomplishing the attempted crime is another way of referring to the matter of impossibility. It follows that the defendant must possess a considerable degree of economic power. That power, unlike the requisite degree of market control under the abuse theory of monopoly,[12] is not necessarily derived from the business which the defendant desires to monopolize. The defendant's economic power may consist only in wealth.[13] He must, however, if he is rational, possess some such superior economic resources before he can logically attempt to monopolize any part of the trade or commerce among the several states.[14]

§9.3. Intent to attempt monopolizing. As in the case of most crimes, an attempt consists of two parts: the prohibited act and the requisite intent to commit the attempted crime. Intent, therefore, is essential to the illegality of an attempt.[1] Furthermore, the intent required is specific and not general.[2] Just what

---

[10] Hughes Tool Co. v. Ford, 114 F. Supp. 525, 554 (E.D. Okla. 1953), *rev'd*, 215 F.2d 924 (10th Cir. 1954), *cert. denied*, 348 U.S. 927 (1955). Compare Note, Morton Salt v. Suppiger, 50 Colum. L. Rev. 476, 480 (1950). But see Shawnee Compress Co. v. Anderson, 209 U.S. 423, 433 (1908) (attempt found without convincing demonstration of ability to monopolize). Perhaps the Hughes Tool case illustrates the minority view that a proven intent should make illegal tactics of an "unfairly exclusive" character regardless of the effect or lack thereof upon competition in the market. Kahn, Standards for Anti-trust Policy, 67 Harv. L. Rev. 28, 54 (1953).

[11] Sayre, Criminal Attempts, 41 Harv. L. Rev. 821, 845 (1928).

[12] See §2.28 *supra*.

[13] See Chapter 8. Compare Willett v. Herrick, 242 Mass. 471, 136 N.E. 366, 369-370 (1922).

[14] But compare United States v. Klearflax Looms, Inc., 63 F. Supp. 32 (D. Minn. 1945). There is perhaps a tendency to elide the necessary ability to carry out an attempt into the concept of intent. Note, for example, the following language: "When the intent to monopolize and the consequent dangerous probability that monopoly will result exist, then an attempt to monopolize is established." Johnston, Monopolize or Attempt to Monopolize, Proceedings A.B.A., Section of Anti-trust Law, 72, 76 (Aug. 26, 1953). Such reasoning, proceeding on the reasonable premise that one who intends to commit an attempt has the means to do so, does not, however, take account of irrational behavior which, owing to various market imperfections, is not uncommon in actual business life.

§9.3. [1] Swift & Co. v. United States, 196 U.S. 375, 396 (1905).

[2] Thus, in Times-Picayune Publishing Co. v. United States, 345 U.S. 594 (1953), the Court said at page 626: "While the completed offense of monopolization under §2 demands only a general intent to do the act, 'for no monopolist monopolizes unconscious of what he is doing,' a specific intent to destroy competition or build

constitutes such a "specific" intent may not be easy to state. A leading authority on the criminal law has pointed out that what must be specific is the crime which is intended.[3] In the present case the defendant must have intended to monopolize; it does not suffice that he intended to do some other wrongful act. Furthermore, we should carefully distinguish intent from motive, desire and expectation.[4]

Establishing the wrongful intent may be considerably more difficult than stating the necessity thereof. In a number of cases the courts have found that the conduct of the defendant was such that it demonstrated his wrongful purpose.[5] Departures from the competitive norm may indicate a specific intent to commit the crime of monopolization.[6] Particularly important is the temporary nature of a business practice, such as cutting prices, which may suggest an unlawful purpose.[7] On the other hand, it

---

monopoly is essential to guilt for the mere attempt now charged." *Accord:* Kansas City Star Co. v. United States, 240 F.2d 643, 663 (8th Cir. 1957). See also Atty. Gen. Nat. Com. Rep. 61, c.; Johnston, Monopolize or Attempt to Monopolize, Proceedings A.B.A., Section of Antitrust Law, 72, 75 (Aug. 26, 1953). As for the necessity of specific intent under the abuse and structure tests of monopoly, see §§2.29, 3.18 *supra.* Note, too, the interesting effect of proof of specific intent upon such problems as the definition of the commodity, indivisibility, and the like; when specific intent is established, the defendant's own conduct may suffice to resolve such otherwise insoluble issues.

3 Keedy, Criminal Attempts at Common Law, 102 U. Pa. L. Rev. 464, 468 (1954). Compare §2.30 *supra.* It is interesting to speculate on the relationship between specific intent, the general prohibitions of the Sherman Act, and the detailed proscriptions of the Clayton Act. In general, it may be true that the more specific the acts forbidden by statute, the less specific need be the intent accompanying them.

4 Id. at 466-467. Some of the common law business torts such as disparagement and conspiracy require a showing of "malice." Zephyr American Corp. v. Bates Mfg. Co., 59 F. Supp. 573, 575 (D.N.J. 1945); Meadowmoor Dairies, Inc. v. Milk Wagon Driver's Union, 371 Ill. 377, 382, 21 N.E.2d 308 (1939), *aff'd,* 312 U.S. 287 (1941). The exact content of "malice" is not clear. Handler, Unfair Competition, 21 Iowa L. Rev. 175, 197 (1936). In any event, there is nothing to indicate that malice must be shown to sustain allegations of attempted monopolization.

5 United States v. American Tobacco Co., 221 U.S. 106, 182 (1911); United States v. Besser Mfg. Co., 96 F. Supp. 304, 313 (E.D. Mich. 1951), *aff'd,* 343 U.S. 444 (1952). Compare People v. American Ice Co., 140 App. Div. 912, 125 N.Y. Supp. 1136 (1st Dept. 1910).

6 Compare Handler, Unfair Competition, 21 Iowa L. Rev. 175, 182 (1936). Compare the doctrine of tort law that one who intentionally harms the business of another must justify his conduct by showing a privilege to do so. Holmes, Collected Legal Papers 124 (1920). For discussion of the doctrine of res ipsa loquitur, see §2.30 *supra.* If the defendant has kept his conduct a secret (as by organizing a bogus independent), an inference of intent may legitimately be drawn. On the other hand, there are instances in which a desire to protect trade secrets or anxiety lest Robinson-Patman litigation be stirred up may explain such secrecy. See §2.30 *supra.*

7 See Dunshee v. Standard Oil Co., 152 Iowa 618, 132 N.W. 371, 376 (1911); 3 Restatement of Torts §709; Handler, Unfair Competition, 21 Iowa L. Rev. 175, 181 (1936). In People v. American Ice Co., 135 App. Div. 180, 120 N.Y. Supp. 41, 433 (1st Dept. 1909), *aff'd mem.,* 140 App. Div. 912, 125 N.Y. Supp. 1136 (1910),

is not every injury to a competitor which will establish the defendant's specific intent for present purposes.[8] Indeed, it may be difficult to distinguish vigorous competition from an attempt to monopolize. The cutting of prices, for example, is as consistent with a desire to increase the defendant's own volume of business as it is with a malevolent motive toward a competitor.[9] Indeed, so difficult is the distinction that a court once wrote:

> An attempt by each competitor to monopolize a part of interstate commerce is the very root of all competition therein. Eradicate it, and competition necessarily ceases — dies. Every person engaged in interstate commerce necessarily attempts to draw to himself, and to exclude others from, a part of that trade; and, if he may not do this, he may not compete with his rivals, all other persons and corporations must cease to secure for themselves any part of the commerce among the states, and some single corporation or person

a different view was taken. In that case the court said that continued underselling of independent dealers by the defendants could provide the jury with evidence of a design and purpose to drive the competitors out of business. The question probably is: How long is "temporary"? In cases of common law harassment (threats of patent litigation and the like), the test is usually one of good faith. 120 N.Y. Supp. at 443, 453. *Accord:* Adriance, Platt & Co. v. National Harrow Co., 121 Fed. 827, 829-830 (2d Cir. 1903); Celite Corp. v. Dicalite Co., 96 F.2d 242, 250-251 (9th Cir. 1938); Johnson Laboratories v. Meissner Mfg. Co., 98 F.2d 937, 948-949 (7th Cir. 1938); Betmar Hats, Inc. v. Young America Hats, Inc., 116 F.2d 956, 957 (2d Cir. 1941); Dixie Cup Co. v. Paper Container Mfg. Co., 169 F.2d 645, 652 (7th Cir. 1948); Sun-Maid Raisin Growers v. Avis, 25 F.2d 303, 304 (N.D. Ill. 1928); Salem Engineering Co. v. National Supply Co., 75 F. Supp. 993, 1001 (W.D. Pa. 1948).

[8] Times-Picayune Publishing Co. v. United States, 345 U.S. 594, 622 et seq. (1953). Compare Virtue v. Creamery Package Mfg. Co., 227 U.S. 8, 37-38 (1913); Oil Conservation Co. v. Brooks Co., 52 F.2d 783, 786 (6th Cir. 1931).

[9] Wilcox, Competition and Monopoly in American Industry 6 (TNEC Monograph No. 21, 1940). In United States v. Morgan, 118 F. Supp. 621 (S.D.N.Y. 1953), the court said at page 754: ". . . the Sherman Act makes no distinction between competitive effort to keep business and competitive effort to take business away from someone else. These are but two sides of the same coin." See §2.30 *supra.* In Windsor Theatre Co. v. Walbrook Amusement Co., 94 F. Supp. 388 (D. Md. 1950), aff'd, 189 F.2d 797 (4th Cir. 1951), the lower court found that the defendant had not been guilty of an attempt to monopolize in operating a second motion picture theater near that of the plaintiff. That result was reached in part on a finding that the second theater, alleged to have been a "fighting theater," had actually operated at a profit. 94 F. Supp. at 391. On the other hand, in United States v. Great Lakes Towing Co., 208 Fed. 733 (N.D. Ohio, 1913), it appears that the fact that the defendants had made profits was held indicative of an intent to monopolize. Id. at 744. An economist recently wrote: "The conclusion is that, if there is free or relatively free entry, the entrepreneur, if he is to avoid schizophrenia, will plan to charge a price yielding only a normal profit, save to the extent that he is aware of possessing an advantage peculiar to himself, will plan to have equipment on a scale that gives the lowest cost for producing what he can sell at such a price, and having acquired the equipment will sell at that price, even though the short period marginal revenue yielded by such a policy is less than the marginal cost." Harrod, Economic Essays 151 (1952). See §2.27 *supra.*

must be permitted to receive and control it all in one huge monopoly.[10]

The analogy between the race and the fight suggested in a prior chapter[11] may prove helpful but it does not solve all problems, for the basic question is one of distinguishing "hard" from "soft" competition. On the other hand, proof of specific intent in a case charging a defendant with attempted monopoly may be no more elusive than in any other case of an attempt to commit a wrongful act. Cutting prices may be equivocal but so is buying arsenic.[12]

§9.4. **Analysis of attempts.** It might be assumed that society could safely punish every attempt to monopolize. The very statement of such a conclusion of law almost suffices to establish its soundness. As we have seen, however, attempts to monopolize may be elusive in character. In the first place, we have ample difficulty in defining monopolization itself. In the second place, the difficulty in ascertaining the intent of the defendant — which is, as we have seen, requisite to the commission of the crime — may give rise to miscarriages of justice. As we have further seen, punishment of attempts to monopolize may constitute a prohibition upon competition itself; it may therefore curb growth and penalize efforts to expand production. Hence punishment of attempts to monopolize may slide easily into protectionism. It is easy enough to say that if society does not protect rival firms from predatory practices, they will disappear and then the defendant will easily monopolize the trade. The trouble is that it

---

[10] Whitwell v. Continental Tobacco Co., 125 Fed. 454, 462 (8th Cir. 1903). The mere fact that the defendant possesses either monopoly power or wealth will not, of course, establish a wrongful intent; otherwise there could be no such thing as a "good" trust.

[11] §2.30 *supra*. The reference there was to McLaughlin, Legal Control of Competitive Methods, 21 Iowa L. Rev. 274 (1936). In that article Professor McLaughlin wrote at page 280: "It is possible to distinguish between a competitive race and a competitive fight. If the large concern can run away from its competitors by reason of greater efficiency, no policy involved in the Sherman Act is violated by its successful issue from the race, but if the large competitor chooses to take advantage of its greater weight to spike or slug its competitor, the government should intervene as a referee and rule it from the track. It is with some such conception that the idea has developed that a trust be dissolved if it acts improperly, otherwise not." Compare Callmann, The Essence of Anti-Trust, 49 Colum. L. Rev. 1100, 1109 (1949).

[12] In the common law tort of harassment the defendant can establish good faith if he proves that he consulted counsel before doing the acts complained of. Gibson v. Smoot Engineering Corp., 50 F.2d 203, 205 (D. Del. 1931); Derman v. Stor-Aid, Inc., 52 F. Supp. 387, 392 (S.D.N.Y. 1943), *aff'd*, 141 F.2d 580 (2d Cir. 1944); A. Hollander & Son, Inc. v. Imperial Fur Corp., 2 N.J. Eq. 235, 66 A.2d 319, 324 (1949). There is, however, no indication that such evidence would be considered either relevant or conclusive if offered by a defendant charged with an attempt to monopolize.

becomes easy to anticipate the exit of the rivals and to turn the antitrust laws into a program of sheltering the inefficient.

One may well inquire why a defendant should ever attempt to monopolize.   In the absence of some barrier to entry into business, it is scarcely conceivable that an attempt to monopolize can be successful.   Repeated purchases of rival firms, for example, will not lead to monopoly if new firms can spring up overnight; and if prices are raised after the "monopoly" is attained, the self-corrective feature of the market will assure the reappearance of competition.[1]   As we have seen, if entry into competition is sufficiently easy, no degree of "monopoly" may be meaningful. Accordingly, an attempt to monopolize is irrational unless the defendant is somehow assured of natural or artificial barriers to entry into competition.[2]   It does not necessarily follow, however, that attempts to monopolize should not be punished, even though irrational in character.[3]   Such attempts may disturb the commercial peace of the land and cause dislocations simply by reason of fears that they may prove successful.[4]

§9.4.   [1] See §2.26 *supra.*

[2] Adelman, Integration and Dissolution of the A & P Company, 29 Ind. L.J. 367, 368 (1954).   Compare Bain, Conditions of Entry and the Emergence of Monopoly, in Chamberlin, ed., Monopoly and Competition and Their Regulation 215, 230, 237 (International Economic Assn. 1954).   See §3.12, *supra,* with respect to the effect of easy entry upon the structure theory of monopoly.   It may follow that repressing attempts to monopolize is comparable to public utility regulation, for the existence of barriers suggests that the defendant himself enjoys a degree of monopoly power arising out of indivisibility or some other imperfection.

[3] Because barriers to entry or other imperfections do not exist.

[4] Compare Sayre, Criminal Attempts, 41 Harv. L. Rev. 821, 849 (1948).   We believe a different rule may well apply in the antitrust field from that usually pronounced with respect to torts involving bodily injury.   Although a complaining witness once sought to have the grand jury of Cook County indict his enemy for an attempt to assault him with a deadly weapon, namely, a broom, the general public knows that brooms are relatively harmless.   The same is not necessarily true of some commercial activities, such as cutting prices.   Just how easy entry into competition may be in any given line of business at a specific time is not simple to determine.   It depends upon the information available to bankers and investors as well as the attitude of would-be entrants.

C H A P T E R   1 0

Remedies

§10.1.   Scope of this chapter.   Substantive legislation can be no
more effective than the remedies afforded litigants.   Accordingly,
it is appropriate to survey briefly the adjective devices for carrying
into effect our antimonopoly policy.   In doing so we shall make
no attempt to outline the whole topic of enforcement and administration of the antitrust laws.   Many of the remedies relate
to the whole field of trade regulation or, indeed, to the entire
law.[1]   It may, however, be worth while to mention the surprisingly wide variety of enforcement procedures available to curb
monopoly, placing emphasis on those not otherwise generally
applicable to antitrust proceedings.[2]

§10.2A.   Criminal enforcement.   It must never be forgotten
that many of our antimonopoly statutes, both state and federal,
carry criminal penalties.   Thus Section 2 of the Sherman Act
may be enforced by imprisonment for one year, a fine of as much
as $50,000, or both.[1]   Similar penalties are provided in state
legislation.[2]   Various minor means of enforcement are also

§10.1.   [1] Note, for example, that §12 of the Clayton Act makes special provision
for venue in antitrust cases.   15 U.S.C.A. §22.   A recent survey of some of the
principal enforcement problems will be found in Atty. Gen. Nat. Com. Rep., c. 8.
Compare Carman, Analysis of Chapter VIII [of Report *supra*], Proceedings A.B.A.,
Section of Antitrust Law, 148 (Aug. 22, 1955).   It has been said that the statutory
remedies made available under the antitrust statutes are exclusive in character.
See Geddes v. Anaconda Copper Mining Co., 254 U.S. 590, 593 (1921).   Numerous
remedies are available under state statutes and it has not been found feasible to
detail them all herein.

[2] Some discussion with respect to possible remedies for wealth will be found
supra §8.5.

§10.2A.   [1] 15 U.S.C.A. §2, as amended, c. 281, 69 Stat. 282.   Note also §73 of the
Wilson Tariff Act, 28 Stat. 570 (1894), as amended, 37 Stat. 667, 15 U.S.C.A. §8.   By
§14 of the Clayton Act, officers and directors of a corporation adjudged guilty of
violating the penal divisions of the antitrust laws are themselves guilty of a misdemeanor and may be imprisoned and fined.   15 U.S.C.A. §24.   The propriety
of enforcing such poorly understood legislation by criminal means has been questioned.   Cahill, Must We Brand American Business by Indictment as Criminal?
Proceedings, A.B.A., Section of Antitrust Law, 26 (Sept. 17, 1952).   As to the constitutionality of the vague prohibitions in the antitrust laws, see §11.4 *infra*.

[2] E.g., Illinois: An Act to Provide for the Punishment of Persons, Copartnerships
or Corporations Forming Pools, Trusts and Combines. . . .   (June 11, 1891), Laws

available, including the whimsical device of forbidding the use of the Panama Canal to violators of the antitrust laws.[3]

§10.2B. **Patents.** While the treatment accorded patents by courts in civil cases is not technically part of the criminal sanctions imposed for violation of antimonopoly statutes, it may be convenient to mention it here. Without relying on statutory provisions permitting the confiscation of property,[1] the courts have nearly accomplished the same thing so far as patents are concerned. In a number of antitrust cases defendants have been compelled to offer their patents freely to all comers, the amount of royalties being fixed by the courts. The phrase usually employed is that the royalties must be "reasonable."[2] An active question exists as to the propriety of requiring royalty-free licensing of patents.[3] In any event it is plain that compulsory licensing, with or without a court-determined royalty, is a partial or total confiscation of the value of the patent property. Rarely, if ever, have courts deprived antitrust defendants of other types of property. Just why patents should be singled out for such

---

1891, p. 206, Ill. Rev. Stat., c. 38, §§569 et seq. (1957). The Illinois legislation has several interesting features. The amount of the fine which may be levied progresses for second and subsequent offenders (§§3, 4); fines may be recovered in a civil action, and a preponderance of the evidence is sufficient to support a verdict (§7). Furthermore, an informer who instigates such litigation is entitled to one fifth of the fines recovered (§8). Note also the Illinois law of March 27, 1874, Ill. Rev. Stat., p. 348 (1874), Ill Rev. Stat., c. 38, §139, (1957) providing a five-year penalty for conspiracy to boycott or to induce a person not to compete. It is widely assumed that state legislation has fallen into disuse. Note, Illinois Anti-Trust Act Disinterred, 43 Ill. L. Rev. 205, 218 (1948). But see New York Times, Jan. 27, 1956, p. 1, col. 5.

3 Panama Canal Act §11, 15 U.S.C.A. §31. Note the statutory penalty providing that property owned by a combination violating §1 of the Sherman Act may be forfeited if in process of transportation from one state to another or found in the import trade contained in §6 of the Sherman Act and §76 of the Wilson Tariff Act. Section 313 of the Communications Act of 1934 provides that those guilty of violating the antitrust laws shall lose their broadcasting licenses. 47 U.S.C.A. §313.

§10.2B. 1 Atty. Gen. Nat. Com. Rep. 255.

2 United States v. National Lead Co., 332 U.S. 319, 350-351 (1947); United States v. United States Gypsum Co., 340 U.S. 76, 94 (1950); United States v. Imperial Chemical Industries, Ltd., 105 F. Supp. 215, 222 (S.D.N.Y. 1952); United States v. United Shoe Machinery Corp., 110 F. Supp. 295, 354 (D. Mass. 1953), aff'd per curiam, 347 U.S. 521 (1954). Compare Atty. Gen. Nat. Com. Rep. 255. As to nonenforcement of patent rights when there have been abuses or violations of the antitrust laws, see §10.5 infra. Note also that courts have compelled disclosure of secret technology as well as licensing of patents. United States v. National Lead Co., 332 U.S. 319, 358 (1947); United States v. Imperial Chemical Industries, Ltd., 105 F. Supp. 215, 227 (S.D.N.Y. 1952).

3 United States v. General Electric Co., 82 F. Supp. 753 (D.N.J. 1949), 95 F. Supp. 165 (1950), 115 F. Supp. 835, 843 (1953); Morison, The Patent Grant and Free Enterprise, 38 A.B.A.J. 739, 798 (1952). But compare Hartford-Empire Co. v. United States, 323 U.S. 386, 415 (1945), clarified, 324 U.S. 570 (1945); United States v. Imperial Chemical Industries, Ltd., 105 F. Supp. 215, 223-224 (S.D.N.Y. 1952).

drastic treatment by the courts is not wholly clear; indeed, there is something reminiscent of the old law of deodand[4] in this aspect of antitrust enforcement.

§10.3. Dissolution. Among the public remedies — as opposed to those designed merely to compensate private persons for damages sustained by them — none is more important to enforcement of an antimonopoly policy than dissolution.[1] Sometimes dissolution is distinguished from "divestiture" or "divorcement." Actually, the three concepts are identical in all but the mechanics of separation. In each a physical division is required of the adjudged monopoly. Dissolution contemplates that the corporation which has constituted the monopoly be dissolved and replaced by successor entities. Divorcement and divestiture, on the other hand, suggest respectively a separation of two or more not wholly integrated entities and the forced sale of physical assets of the adjudged monopoly.[2] While the varying methods of effecting a division of the monopoly may become important in specific cases, we shall discuss here the broad problems of achieving compliance with antimonopoly policy without distinguishing between the different types of separation.

Under state law, dissolution can be effected under the ancient writ of quo warranto. Most corporations are, of course, creatures of state statutes and most antitrust defendants are organized in corporate form. It follows that in proceedings under state law to dissolve a monopoly the writ of quo warranto is available and the judgment of ouster can be entered.[3] Such a judgment

---

[4] 2 Pollock and Maitland, History of English Law 473 (2d ed. 1899).

§10.3. [1] There is no specific statutory authority for the dissolution of monopolies. Proceedings looking to that end, however, can be founded either upon §4 of the Sherman Act or §15 of the Clayton Act, both of which authorize the Attorney General to institute proceedings in equity to restrain violations of the antitrust statutes. 15 U.S.C.A. §§4, 25. It is unusual for a court to decree dissolution at the suit of a private party. But compare Dunbar v. American Telephone & Telegraph Co., 238 Ill. 456, 488, 87 N.E. 521 (1909); Harding v. American Glucose Co., 182 Ill. 551, 55 N.E. 577 (1899). Indeed, there appears to be no compelling reason why the remedy of dissolution should not be available to a private litigant.

[2] United States v. Corn Products Refining Co., 234 Fed. 964 (S.D.N.Y. 1916); United States v. Eastman Kodak Co., 226 Fed. 62 (W.D.N.Y. 1915), 230 Fed. 522 (W.D.N.Y. 1916), *appeal dismissed*, 255 U.S. 578 (1921); Hale, Trust Dissolution, 40 Colum. L. Rev. 615, 628-629 (1940); Oppenheim, Economic Background, 19 Geo. Wash. L. Rev. 147 (1950).

[3] Distilling & Cattle Feeding Co. v. People ex rel. Moloney, 156 Ill. 448, 41 N.E. 188 (1895); State v. Nebraska Distilling Co., 29 Neb. 700, 46 N.W. 155 (1890); People v. North River Sugar Refining Co., 121 N.Y. 582, 24 N.E. 834 (1890); State ex Information Major v. International Harvester Co., 237 Mo. 369, 141 S.W. 672 (1911); see Stockton v. American Tobacco Co., 55 N.J. Eq. 352, 36 Atl. 971, 981 (1897); Hale, The Law of Private Corporations in Illinois §181 (1916); Dodd, American Business Corporations Until 1860, 58 (1954). In Harding v. American Glucose Co., 182 Ill. 551, 55 N.E. 577 (1899), the court directed the entry of a decree setting aside a deed whereby one of the constituent companies of the glu-

compels forfeiture of corporate rights and could have a drastic effect upon the value of the corporation's property.[4] As a practical matter, however, the ease with which a new corporation can be formed under modern general statutes should permit transfer of the property to a number of such new entities without heavy sacrifices by stockholders.

Since federal law does not often call into existence the corporate defendants in antitrust cases, the remedy of quo warranto is rarely available and the lack of explicit provision for dissolution in the federal antitrust legislation gives rise to a question as to the appropriateness of that remedy in national proceedings.[5] Many decades ago, however, that question was resolved in favor of the existence of the remedy and it has often been applied in subsequent years. Indeed, the Supreme Court was able to say a few years ago:

> The Court has quite consistently recognized in this type of Sherman Act case that the government should not be confined to an injunction against further violations. Dissolution of the combination will be ordered where the creation of the combination is itself the violation.[6]

Decrees of dissolution (or divorcement or divestiture) have been entered in litigation involving the oil, tobacco, blasting powder, farm implement, glucose, photographic equipment, motion picture and railroad industries.[7] In most of the opinions granting

---

cose "trust" conveyed its factory to the corporation formed to acquire the businesses of various competitors notwithstanding the fact that the new corporation had been in operation for at least several months. Id. at 644. Note also that the remedy of ouster is available against foreign corporations admitted to do business within a state. State v. Creamery Package Manufacturing Co., 110 Minn. 415, 126 N.W. 126 (1910); State ex rel. Attorney General v. International Harvester Co., 81 Kans. 610, 106 Pac. 1053, 1056 (1910). In the latter case the court declined to enter the judgment of ouster partly because the result merely would have been to shut off a supply of harvesting machinery from the state.

4 Compare State v. Standard Oil Co., 49 Ohio St. 137, 30 N.E. 279 (1892), in which the judgment of ouster was not entered but dissolution of the trust was nevertheless ordered.

5 Langdell, The Northern Securities Case, 16 Harv. L. Rev. 539, 549 (1903).

6 United States v. Crescent Amusement Co., 323 U.S. 173, 189 (1944). The leading decision on the subject is Standard Oil Co. of New Jersey v. United States, 221 U.S. 1 (1911). Presumably authority for such a decree is found in §4 of the Sherman Act, but the courts have not been overly explicit on that subject.

7 Hale, Trust Dissolution, 40 Colum. L. Rev. 615, 617 et seq. (1940); United States v. Paramount Pictures, Inc., 334 U.S. 131 (1948); United States v. Pullman Co., 50 F. Supp. 123 (E.D. Pa. 1943), 53 F. Supp. 908 (E.D. Pa. 1944), 64 F. Supp. 108 (E.D. Pa. 1946), aff'd per curiam, 330 U.S. 806 (1947). Dissolution is proper in a federal antitrust case, even though it appears to conflict with the granting of a charter by a state. Northern Securities Co. v. United States, 193 U.S. 197 (1904). Oddly enough, the power of the Federal Trade Commission was narrowly construed in FTC v. Eastman Kodak Co., 274 U.S. 619 (1927).

such relief the courts have taken the position that dissolution is necessary to neutralize the force complained of; in other words, that no other remedy is adequate to establish competition.[8] In other opinions retribution forms a ground for the decree of dissolution; the courts speak of preventing the defendant from enjoying the "fruits" of illegal behavior.[9] As the Supreme Court said some years ago,

> Divestiture or dissolution must take account of the present and future conditions in the particular industry as well as past violations. It serves several functions: (1) it puts an end to the combination or conspiracy when that is itself the violation. (2) It deprives the anti-trust defendants of the benefits of their conspiracy. (3) It is designed to break up or render impotent the monopoly power which violates the Act.[10]

Even in instances wherein defendants have been found guilty of monopolizing, however, the courts have sometimes refused to decree dissolution. Such refusals are often based on the ground that to do so would disrupt an essentially indivisible organization. Thus, in the long litigation involving the Aluminum

---

[8] Standard Oil Co. of New Jersey v. United States, 221 U.S. 1, 77-78 (1911); United States v. Paramount Pictures, Inc., 334 U.S. 131, 152-153 (1948); United States v. E. I. Du Pont de Nemours & Co., 188 Fed. 127, 153-154 (C.C.D. Del. 1911), *modified*, 273 Fed. 869 (D. Del. 1921); United States v. Corn Products Refining Co., 234 Fed. 964, 1018 (S.D.N.Y. 1916); United States v. New England Fish Exchange, 258 Fed. 732, 750-751 (D. Mass. 1919), 292 Fed. 511 (D. Mass. 1923); United States v. Pullman Co., 53 F. Supp. 908 (E.D. Pa. 1944), *aff'd per curiam*, 330 U.S. 806 (1947); United States v. Imperial Chemical Industries, Ltd., 105 F. Supp. 215, 237 (S.D.N.Y. 1952).

[9] In United States v. Crescent Amusement Co., 323 U.S. 173 (1944), the Court directed the separation of the corporate and individual defendants linked by stock ownership. Id. at 185 et seq. In the course of the opinion it was said at page 189: "The Court has quite consistently recognized in this type of Sherman Act case that the government should not be confined to an injunction against further violations. Dissolution of the combination will be ordered where the creation of the combination is itself a violation. . . . Those who violate the Act may not reap the benefits of their violations. . . ." See also United States v. Great Lakes Towing Co., 208 Fed. 733, 747 (N.D. Ohio, 1913), 217 Fed. 656 (N.D. Ohio, 1914).

[10] Schine Chain Theatres, Inc. v. United States, 334 U.S. 110, 128-129 (1948). In that case the Court also said at page 128: "In this type of case we start from the premise that an injunction against future violations is not adequate to protect the public interest. If all that was done was to forbid a repetition of the illegal conduct, those who had unlawfully built their empires could preserve them intact. They could retain the full dividend of their monopolistic practices. . . ." In United States v. General Electric Co., 82 F. Supp. 753 (D.N.J. 1949), 115 F. Supp. 835 (D.N.J. 1953), the court said: "There would appear to be no case in which divestiture was ordered where there were no recognizable fruits of behavior illegal under the antitrust acts and where the divestiture consisted of splitting a defendant which was a corporate and economic entity. Nevertheless, the various opinions in the Aluminum Company litigation indicate that under certain circumstances such divestiture would be appropriate." 115 F. Supp. at 866.

Company of America, the court finally concluded that dissolution should not be decreed: that Alcoa's entity with respect to both production and technological research contained important elements of indivisibility.[11]　Another court reached similar conclusions with respect to the research facilities of the General Electric Company's lamp department.[12]　In other instances the courts have balked at dissolution on the ground that it was a "harsh" remedy, and the Supreme Court itself has said:

> Since divestiture is a remedy to restore competition and not to punish those who restrain trade, it is not to be used indiscriminately, without regard to the type of violation or whether other effective methods, less harsh, are available.[13]

In other instances the courts have declined to dissolve monopolies for less articulate reasons, perhaps feeling that the judiciary is poorly equipped to rearrange the economic structure of the nation, or that some ill-defined harm might be worked by breaking up a going concern.　In an important case the Supreme Court wrote:

> It is not for the courts to realign and redirect effective and lawful competition where it already exists and needs only to be released from restraints that violate the antitrust laws.　To separate the operating units of going concerns without more supporting evidence than has been presented here to establish the need for, or

11 United States v. Aluminum Co. of America, 91 F. Supp. 333, 417 (S.D.N.Y. 1950).　A similar result was reached in Gamco, Inc. v. Providence Fruit & Produce Building, Inc., 194 F.2d 484 (1st Cir. 1952), cert. denied, 344 U.S. 817 (1952); United States v. United Shoe Machinery Corp., 110 F. Supp. 295, 348 (D. Mass. 1953), aff'd per curiam, 347 U.S. 521 (1954).　In the same case, however, some of the diversified activities of the defendant were divested on the theory that to do so would reduce monopoly power, and in apparent disregard of whatever elements of indivisibility may have affected that situation.　110 F. Supp. at 351.

12 United States v. General Electric Co., 82 F. Supp. 753 (D.N.J. 1949), 115 F. Supp. 835, 868, 870-871 (D.N.J. 1953).　In some instances the elements of indivisibility have been so obvious that dissolution has not even been discussed.　E.g., Associated Press v. United States, 326 U.S. 1 (1945); United States v. Pullman Co., 50 F. Supp. 123 (E.D. Pa. 1943), 53 F. Supp. 908 (E.D. Pa. 1944), 64 F. Supp. 108 (E.D. Pa. 1946), aff'd per curiam, 330 U.S. 806 (1947).

13 Timken Roller Bearing Co. v. United States, 341 U.S. 593, 603 (1951).　In the same opinion the majority wrote at pages 602-603: "There are no specific statutory provisions authorizing courts to employ the harsh remedy of divestiture in civil proceedings to restrain violations of the Sherman Act.　Fines and imprisonment may follow criminal convictions . . . and divestiture of property has been used in decrees, not as punishment but to assure effective enforcement of the laws against restraint of trade."　See also United States v. Paramount Pictures, Inc., 66 F. Supp. 323, 353 (S.D.N.Y. 1946), rev'd, 334 U.S. 131 (1948).　Compare United States v. International Harvester Co., 274 U.S. 693, 704 (1927) (dissolution would not be decreed when competitive conditions were in fact restored after the passage of time).

the feasibility of, such separation would amount to an abuse of discretion.[14]

Not enough precedents have accumulated to warrant codification of the rules utilized in splitting up monopolies. Perhaps there is a tendency to divide the "trust" into three parts of approximately equal size.[15] It is difficult, however, to determine the standards employed by the courts with respect to horizontal size, since questions of "shape" are often involved. Thus elements of vertical integration have been chopped from the limbs of Sherman Act defendants in proceedings which also involved monopoly itself.[16] Such an application of sanctions can, of course, decrease the over-all size (wealth) of the corporation without necessarily achieving a comparable reduction in monopoly power. It has also been thought necessary to impose restrictions upon shareholders of newly created entities in order to prevent them from collaborating in such a manner as to achieve substantially the same results as the existence of the monopoly

[14] United States v. National Lead Co., 332 U.S. 319, 353 (1947). An attempt was made to explain the quoted language in Schine Theatres, Inc. v. United States, 334 U.S. 110, 128 (1948), on the grounds that the factories involved in the lead case had neither been unlawfully acquired nor used in a manner violative of the antitrust laws. Query whether the distinction can be supported. Other cases evidencing a reluctance to decree dissolution are United States v. American Can Co., 230 Fed. 859, 903-904, 234 Fed. 1019, 1020 (D. Md. 1916), appeal dismissed, 256 U.S. 706 (1921); United States v. Great Lakes Towing Co., 208 Fed. 733 (N.D. Ohio, 1913), 217 Fed. 656 (N.D. Ohio, 1914); United States v. Aluminum Co. of America, 44 F. Supp. 97, 223 (S.D.N.Y. 1941), rev'd, 148 F.2d 416 (2d Cir. 1945). In Northern Securities Co. v. United States, 193 U.S. 197 (1904), Mr. Justice Holmes, dissenting, wrote at pages 407 and 411:

". . . the act of Congress will not be construed to mean the universal disintegration of society into single men, each at war with all the rest, or even the prevention of all further combinations for a common end. . . .

"I am happy to know that only a minority of my brethren adopt that interpretation of the law which in my opinion would make eternal the bellum omnium contra omnes and disintegrate society so far as it could into individual atoms. If that were its intent I should regard calling such a law a regulation of commerce as a mere pretense. It would be an attempt to reconstruct society."

See also Atty. Gen. Nat. Com. Rep. 353, b.

[15] United States v. American Tobacco Co., 221 U.S. 106 (1911); United States v. E. I. Du Pont de Nemours & Co., 188 Fed. 127 (C.C.D. Del. 1911), modified, 273 Fed. 869 (D. Del. 1921). The cases up to that time are surveyed in detail in Hale, Trust Dissolution, 40 Colum. L. Rev. 615, 623 (1940). Note that the degree of monopoly permissible by an unconvicted firm is not necessarily determinative of the remedy to be applied after violation of §2 of the Sherman Act has been found. United States v. Aluminum Co. of America, 91 F. Supp. 333, 346 (S.D.N.Y. 1950).

[16] United States v. Corn Products Refining Co., 234 Fed. 964 (S.D.N.Y. 1916); United States v. Paramount Pictures, Inc., 85 F. Supp. 881, 895-896 (S.D.N.Y. 1949), aff'd per curiam, 339 U.S. 974 (1950). See Hale, Trust Dissolution, 40 Colum. L. Rev. 615, 624 et seq. (1940); Chapters 5, 6, 7 supra. Note the interesting provision in United States v. Pullman Co., 53 F. Supp. 908 (E.D. Pa. 1944), aff'd per curiam, 330 U.S. 806 (1947), in which the defendant was permitted to elect which end of a vertically integrated business it would retain.

permitted.[17] Again, however, the instances are too scattered to permit generalization as to the manner in which the courts' discretion will be exercised.[18] It is interesting to note that the courts do not appear to have utilized a statutory provision permitting reference of such issues to the Federal Trade Commission as a master in chancery.[19]

§10.4. **Analysis of dissolution.** What one concludes with respect to the desirability of dissolution as a remedy depends upon what theory one uses in approaching the monopoly problem. Under the old abuse doctrine, an injunction prohibiting the defendant from engaging further in predatory practices would appear to be adequate.[1] Once one adopts the structure test, however, it logically follows that dissolution is the appropriate remedy. For under the structure theory, the whole point is that the public is unwilling to wait for natural correction of the market; if government insists upon immediate short-term relief, then, under the structure test, mere injunctions against abuses can never be adequate.[2] Failure to dissolve monopoly under the structure theory merely leaves the defendant in a position where it cannot possibly obey the law, since its continued existence can only be accompanied by the full exercise of its charter powers. Indeed, governmental control of output and prices is the only alternative:

> Concentrations of power . . . are inherently dangerous . . . in the absence of this protective mechanism, the demand for public regulation, public ownership, or other drastic measures would become irresistible. . . . Dispersal of private economic power is

---

[17] Harriman v. Northern Securities Co., 197 U.S. 244 (1905); United States v. Union Pacific Railroad Co., 226 U.S. 61, 96-97 (1912); United States v. Lehigh Valley Railroad Co., 254 U.S. 255, 270-271 (1920); Continental Insurance Co. v. United States, 259 U.S. 156 (1922). See Hale, Trust Dissolution, 40 Colum. L. Rev. 615, 630-631 (1940). Compare United States v. Aluminum Co. of America, 91 F. Supp. 333 (S.D.N.Y. 1950).

[18] It follows that trial courts enjoy considerable discretion in the framing of remedial decrees. See United States v. National Lead Co., 332 U.S. 319, 334 (1947); Brown, Injunctions and Divestiture, Proceedings A.B.A., Section of Antitrust Law, 129, 133 (Aug. 18, 1954). But compare Hartford-Empire Co. v. United States, 323 U.S. 386 (1945), *clarified,* 324 U.S. 570 (1945).

[19] Federal Trade Commission Act §7, 15 U.S.C.A. §47.

§10.4. [1] See United States v. Corn Products Refining Co., 234 Fed. 964, 1015 (S.D.N.Y. 1916).

[2] See United States v. United States Steel Corp., 223 Fed. 55, 64 (D.N.J. 1915), *aff'd,* 251 U.S. 417 (1920); United States v. Great Lakes Towing Co., 208 Fed. 733, 746-747 (N.D. Ohio, 1913), 217 Fed. 656 (N.D. Ohio, 1914); Mund, Open Markets 255 (1948); Timberg, Some Justifications for Divestiture, 19 Geo. Wash. L. Rev. 132, 134, 136 (1950). As Professor Timberg points out, intent is logically irrelevant in thus choosing the remedy of dissolution. Id. at 137.

thus one of the ways to preserve the system of private enterprise. . . .[3]

As we have noted, however, courts often hesitate to dissolve defendants found guilty of monopolizing. They fear that such a decree might impair efficiency: in other words, that elements of indivisibility are present in the defendants' enterprises and hence that the separation might provide only temporary relief.[4] A judgment of ouster under state law could result in a forced sale of corporate assets and large financial losses.[5] It does not appear, however, that dissolution has usually been accompanied by such disasters and it seems likely that devices have been and can be found to overcome frictions involved in separating the constituent elements of a monopoly.[6] Nevertheless, careful students, like cautious courts, hesitate to wield the hammer of atomization. Thus it was recently said:

> . . . enforced dissolution is justifiable only as a last resort. The free enterprise system would have little to recommend it — indeed the very reason for its being would be destroyed — if continual reorganization under government attack were required to keep it competitive. Freedom of enterprise is a futile concept if it excludes freedom to expand and to grow. . . .[7]

No doubt much of the hesitation to decree dissolution results from refusal to adopt the whole of the structure theory of monopoly and its implications.[8] Moreover, if an attempt is made to change the "shape" of the monopolist by eliminating vertical integration and the like, other complex problems may arise. In the first place, a presumption of indivisibility at an earlier stage may block an otherwise advisable degree of horizontal dissolution. If, for example, economies of scale with respect to access to capital markets result in part from a vertical amalgamation, re-

[3] United States v. United Shoe Machinery Corp., 110 F. Supp. 295, 347 (D. Mass. 1953), aff'd per curiam, 347 U.S. 521 (1954).

[4] The classic example is United States v. Terminal Railroad Assn. of St. Louis, 224 U.S. 383 (1912). Compare United States v. Aluminum Co. of America, 91 F. Supp. 333 (S.D.N.Y. 1950); Stocking and Watkins, Monopoly and Free Enterprise 563 (Twentieth Century Fund, 1951); §3.13 supra. "The character and incidence of advantages of scale are complicated and are variegated as among concentrated industries. Pending a development of regulatory law not yet attained, deconcentration measures ought to be highly selective and perhaps hand-tailored." Bain, Advantages of the Large Firm, 20 J. Marketing 336, 346 (1956).

[5] Hale, The Law of Private Corporations in Illinois §299 (1916).

[6] Hale, Trust Dissolution, 40 Colum. L. Rev. 615, 623 (1940); Faulkner, The Decline of Laissez Faire 31 (1951).

[7] Kaplan, Big Enterprise in a Competitive System 226 (Brookings Institution, 1954); see also Van Cise, Limitations upon Divestiture, 19 Geo. Wash. L. Rev. 147, 150, 152-153 (1950); Atty. Gen. Nat. Com. Rep. 353, b; Dewey, Romance and Realism in Antitrust Policy, 63 J. Pol. Econ. 93, 95 et seq. (1955).

[8] Infirmities inherent in the structure theory are outlined in Chapter 3.

duction of that integration may render horizontal division more costly or impossible. In the second place, if competition is desired among the successor units, then at least some degree of diversification and dispersion may become necessary in order to achieve that result: otherwise the newly created firms will each operate in its own geographic or product sphere, insulated from the rivalry of the others.[9]

§10.5. **Injunctive relief.** Statutory provisions are clear to the effect that injunctive relief may be obtained in federal antitrust litigation.[1] The courts have been liberal in fashioning such decrees. Trial courts are not limited to enjoining specific acts proven in furtherance of the illegal monopoly. They may range broadly through the practices connected with acts actually found to be illegal.[2] On the other hand, an injunction must be specific in terms and describe the prohibited acts in detail. It cannot be so sweeping as to outlaw the defendants and put them in a class different from other people.[3] In addition to the substantive prohibitions contained in such decrees it is common to provide that representatives of the Attorney General may inspect the defendants' files and interview the defendants' personnel during a period of years in the future.[4] Indeed, in some instances, the courts have in effect undertaken to supervise the conduct of the defendants by retaining jurisdiction for a period of years in order to hear applications for modification of the final decree.[5]

[9] Hale, Trust Dissolution, 40 Colum. L. Rev. 615, 626 (1940). Compare Edwards, Maintaining Competition 113 (1949); see Chapters 6 and 7 *supra.* Note also that dissolution may pose difficult tax questions and that penalties prescribed by the Internal Revenue Code may be applied to dissolution decrees wholly apart from the relief required under the antitrust laws.

§10.5. [1] Both §4 of the Sherman Act and §15 of the Clayton Act authorize the issuance of injunctions. 15 U.S.C.A. §§4, 25. Note also §5 of the Federal Trade Commission Act. 15 U.S.C.A. §45. Injunctive relief for private parties is made available by §16 of the Clayton Act. 15 U.S.C.A. §26. See Bedford Cutstone Co. v. Journeymen's Stonecutters Assn., 274 U.S. 37, 54-55 (1927). The procedure to be followed with respect to injunctive relief and the enforcement thereof is set forth in §§17-26 of the Clayton Act. 15 U.S.C.A. §§27-36.

[2] United States v. United States Gypsum Co., 340 U.S. 76, 88-89 (1950); FTC v. National Lead Co., 352 U.S. 419 (1957).

[3] Hartford-Empire Co. v. United States, 323 U.S. 386, 409-410 (1945), *clarified,* 324 U.S. 570 (1945); Schine Chain Theatres, Inc. v. United States, 334 U.S. 110, 126 (1948); United States v. National City Lines, 134 F. Supp. 350, 355, 359 (N.D. Ill. 1955). But compare FTC v. Ruberoid Co., 343 U.S. 470, 476 (1952). Compare Timberg, Equitable Relief Under the Sherman Act, 1950 U. of Ill. L. Forum 629, 633 et seq.

[4] United States v. United States Gypsum Co., 340 U.S. 76, 95 (1950); Lorain Journal Co. v. United States, 342 U.S. 143, 156 (1951); United States v. General Electric Co., 115 F. Supp. 835, 877 (D.N.J. 1953).

[5] United States v. Aluminum Co. of America, 91 F. Supp. 333, 418 (S.D.N.Y. 1950); United States v. Imperial Chemical Industry, Ltd., 105 F. Supp. 215, 220 (S.D.N.Y. 1952). In a proceeding in the nature of quo warranto in the state courts a judgment of conditional ouster can be entered having the same effect as a reservation

In substance, the decrees entered against monopolists have
prohibited a wide variety of abuses, attempts[6] and practices.
Thus, in the recent litigation involving the United Shoe Machinery Corporation, the leasing practice found to be so deleterious
was strictly curbed in the final decree. In the same case, the
defendant was forbidden to purchase any shoe machinery business for more than $10,000.[7] Decrees have also been entered
against discriminatory pricing practices[8] as well as "tie-ins" and
other "restrictive" agreements.[9] Competitive bidding has been
urged[10] and tried as a remedy for monopoly, with only indifferent results.[11] Even more drastic decrees have required de-

---

of jurisdiction. State ex rel. Sager v. Polar Ice Co., 259 Mo. 578, 169 S.W. 126, 135
(1914). It has been said, however, that a permanent receivership is not a proper
remedy in an antitrust proceeding. Hartford-Empire Co. v. United States, 323
U.S. 386, 411 (1945), clarified, 324 U.S. 570 (1945).

In the last two decades considerable use has been made of consent decrees as a
means of enforcing the antitrust laws. Consult Donovan and McAllister, Consent
Decrees in the Enforcement of the Federal Anti-Trust Laws, 46 Harv. L. Rev. 885
(1932); Isenbergh and Rubin, Antitrust Enforcement Through Consent Decrees,
53 Harv. L. Rev. 386 (1940); Katz, Consent Decrees in Antitrust Administration,
53 id. 415 (1940). Consent decrees no doubt expedite the disposition of litigation
and save much expense for all parties. On the other hand fears have been expressed lest a consent decree program deteriorate into codes of the NRA variety
or public utility type controls. Id. at 446-447; Birnbaum, The Auto-Finance Consent Decree, 24 Wash. U.L.Q. 525, 547-548 (1939). Compare Handler, A Study of
the Construction and Enforcement of the Federal Anti-Trust Laws 98, TNEC
Monograph No. 38 (1941).

[6] Lorain Journal Co. v. United States, 342 U.S. 143, 153 (1951).

[7] United States v. United Shoe Machinery Corp., 110 F. Supp. 295, 352, 354 (D.
Mass. 1953), aff'd per curiam, 347 U.S. 521 (1954). In the same case, ¶13 of the
decree forbade the defendant to acquire patents from any person other than one
of its own employees. Id. at 354. It is proper to enjoin a defendant from acquiring further physical facilities. Schine Chain Theatres, Inc. v. United States, 334
U.S. 110, 130 (1948). Use of trade-marks has been enjoined. United States v.
General Electric Co., 115 F. Supp. 835, 858 (D.N.J. 1953). It has even been suggested that advertising expenditures should be limited by such decrees. Dirlam
and Kahn, Fair Competition 162-163 (1954).

[8] United States v. Paramount Pictures, Inc., 334 U.S. 131, 154 (1948); United States
v. United Shoe Machinery Corp., 110 F. Supp. 295, 322, 353 (D. Mass. 1953), aff'd
per curiam, 347 U.S. 521 (1954); State ex rel. Attorney General v. International
Harvester Co., 81 Kan. 610, 106 Pac. 1053, 1054 (1910).

[9] Chorak v. RKO Radio Pictures, Inc., 196 F.2d 225, 229 (9th Cir. 1952), cert.
denied, 344 U.S. 887, 910 (1952); United States v. United Shoe Machinery Corp.,
110 F. Supp. 295, 352 (D. Mass. 1953), aff'd per curiam, 347 U.S. 521 (1954); see
Times-Picayune Publishing Co. v. United States, 345 U.S. 594, 608 (1953).

[10] Mund, Open Markets 238 et seq. (1948); see also Appendix A infra.

[11] Compare United States v. Pullman Co., 64 F. Supp. 108, 113 (E.D. Pa. 1946),
aff'd per curiam, 330 U.S. 806 (1947), with United States v. Paramount Pictures, Inc.,
334 U.S. 131, 165 (1948). There is, of course, no novelty in the use of the injunctive process. It has frequently been used in nonstatutory proceedings as, for example, in the common law tort of harassment. E.g., Emack v. Kane, 34 Fed. 46,
50 (N.D. Ill. 1888); Adjusta Co. v. Alma Mfg. Co., 36 F.2d 105 (S.D.N.Y. 1929);
Thomas French & Sons v. Carleton Blind Co., 34 F. Supp. 850 (E.D.N.Y. 1940).

fendants to sell their products to all comers or permit use of facilities by all who desire access thereto.[12] Retention of jurisdiction has also suggested a measure of judicial supervision, perhaps involving regulation of prices and production, as in some of the compulsory licensing patent cases.[13]

Those who believe in the abuse theory of the antitrust laws should be content with the entry of decrees of the type just mentioned. On the other hand, for those adhering to the structure view, mere injunctions will always seem inadequate.[14] Presumably those who would test monopoly by its "performance," or perhaps "workability," would tend to regard dissolution and injunction as alternative remedies to be applied as circumstances suggest. Those who prefer the injunction, however, must be prepared to accept its implications. When courts require defendants to serve all applicants and even go so far as to fix prices at which they may sell, government has intervened in the operation of the economy to a degree far beyond that found in a decree of dissolution. Indeed, such regulation is hard to distinguish from that applied in the public utility field.[15] Dean Levi has suggested that such decisions imply enforcement of the antitrust laws at several levels.[16] Presumably, extremely large monopolies would be dissolved. Those in a middle category would be sub-

[12] United States v. Terminal Railroad Assn. of St. Louis, 224 U.S. 383, 397, 401, 411 (1912); United States v. Great Lakes Towing Co., 208 Fed. 733 (N.D. Ohio, 1913), 217 Fed. 656, 661 (N.D. Ohio, 1914); Gamco, Inc. v. Providence Fruit & Produce Bldg., Inc., 194 F.2d 484, 487-488 (1st Cir. 1952), cert. denied, 344 U.S. 817 (1952); United States v. New England Fish Exchange, 258 Fed. 732, 748 (D. Mass. 1919), 292 Fed. 511 (D. Mass. 1923); United States v. United Shoe Machinery Corp., 110 F. Supp. 295, 353 (D. Mass. 1953), aff'd per curiam, 347 U.S. 521 (1954).

[13] See §10.2B supra. Compare Oppenheim, ed., Lectures on Federal Antitrust Laws 68-69 (University of Michigan, 1953). A requirement that a defendant sell its machines outright as well as lease them involves, of course, some judicial regulation of the sales price; otherwise the decree can easily be avoided.

[14] E.g., Berge, Some Problems in the Enforcement of the Antitrust Laws, 38 Mich. L. Rev. 462, 469 (1940).

[15] See the penetrating dissenting opinion of Swan, J., in United States v. Associated Press, 52 F. Supp. 362, 375, 376-377 (S.D.N.Y. 1943), aff'd, 326 U.S. 1 (1945). The Supreme Court flatly denied the validity of the analysis offered by Judge Swan. 326 U.S. at 19, 21. It is respectfully submitted, however, that the views of Judge Swan were correct. In State ex rel. Attorney General v. International Harvester Co., 81 Kan. 610, 106 Pac. 1053 (1910), the court said at page 1056: ". . . the volume of business in harvesting machinery transacted in this state by the defendant [is] sufficiently large to make it a matter of public concern and a proper subject for regulation." Note the use of the word "regulation." Compare Van Cise, Limitations Upon Divestiture, 19 Geo. Wash. L. Rev. 147, 152 (1950). For a discussion of the "voluntary" assumption of public utility status by big business, see §8.2 supra; TNEC Hearings, pt. 19, at 10,529.

[16] Levi, A Two Level Anti-Monopoly Law, 47 Nw. U.L. Rev. 567 (1952). Competitive bidding of course is ineffective against monopoly: it merely reduces imperfections.

jected to a court-controlled public utility type regulation. Small firms would be free of both remedies. A question may arise as to whether our economy can march in step thus half free and half regulated; that question, however, already exists with respect to the large areas wherein public utility measures have previously been enacted.

§10.6. **Rights of non-parties.** From the description of the broad relief available in antimonopoly proceedings set forth above, it is obvious that rights of non-parties are frequently affected. Minority stockholders, bondholders, mortgagees and other creditors may suffer when decrees of dissolution are entered.[1] Injunctions prohibiting the performance of existing contracts may obviously prejudice the rights of parties thereto.[2] Nevertheless, the courts have rarely hesitated to enforce the antitrust laws, even though severe hardship might thus be worked upon persons who have had no opportunity to be heard. Perhaps the most spectacular decision involved a decree requiring Imperial Chemical Industries to breach a contract with British Nylon Spinners, Ltd., a British corporation not before the United States court in which the relief was afforded. Subsequently courts of the United Kingdom refused to honor the United States court's decree for obvious reasons.[3] Absent such territorial (international) complications, however, the courts have usually prevailed in their position that the rights of third parties may be dealt with harshly in antitrust decrees.

If non-parties are to be adversely affected by a decree of dissolution or injunction, they may well consider resort to intervention. Under the present Federal Rules of Civil Procedure, intervention is mandatory when representation of the applicant's interest by existing parties is or may be inadequate. Intervention

----

§10.6. [1] United States v. Crescent Amusement Co., 323 U.S. 173, 190 (1944); Continental Insurance Co. v. United States, 259 U.S. 156, 171 (1922); United States v. E. I. Du Pont de Nemours & Co., 188 Fed. 127, 155 (C.C.D. Del. 1911), *modified*, 273 Fed. 869 (D. Del. 1921); Hale, Trust Dissolution, 40 Colum. L. Rev. 615, 630 (1940).

[2] United States v. Paramount Pictures, Inc., 66 F. Supp. 323, 347 (S.D.N.Y. 1946), *rev'd on other grounds*, 334 U.S. 131 (1948); United States v. United Shoe Machinery Corp., 110 F. Supp. 295, 353 (D. Mass. 1953), *aff'd per curiam*, 347 U.S. 521 (1954).

[3] United States v. Imperial Chemical Industries, Ltd., 105 F. Supp. 215, 230 (S.D.N.Y. 1952); Haight, International Law and Extraterritorial Application of the Antitrust Laws, 63 Yale L.J. 639, 642 (1954). Note also that a third party who hopes to recover treble damages under the provisions of §4 of the Clayton Act, partly in reliance upon the prima facie effect of a decree entered in a suit brought by the Attorney General under the provisions of §5 of the Clayton Act, may be prejudiced if the Attorney General's action is mishandled. His grievance, however, seems somehow less serious than those of third parties injured in the manner suggested in the text.

is discretionary with the court when the applicant's claim or defense and the main action have a question of law or fact in common.[4] Despite the explicit language of the rules, courts have been reluctant to permit intervention of private parties in government antitrust litigation.[5] In view of the hardships inflicted upon persons having no right otherwise to be heard in the antitrust proceedings, however, such an interpretation of the rules of procedure seems unwarranted.

§10.7. Non-enforceability of contracts. We turn now to remedies available to private litigants. First, at common law and under various specific state statutes, illegal bargains cannot be enforced in the courts.[1] Violations of antimonopoly statutes constitute, of course, illegal transactions, and it follows that a contract to monopolize cannot be enforced against a defaulting party.[2] Indeed, from the year 1415 to the enactment of the Sherman law in 1890, the defense of illegality was the principal means of enforcing antimonopoly policy in Anglo-Saxon jurisprudence.[3] Such decisions, of course, reflect the established rule of law that the courts will not lend their aid to the enforcement of agreements which violate the policy of the state.[4]

Several exceptions, however, may be stated to the foregoing rule. In the first place, if the transaction is technically executed,

[4] Fed. R. Civ. P. 24.

[5] United States v. Bendix Home Appliances, 10 F.R.D. 73, 75, 76-77 (S.D.N.Y. 1949). Compare United States v. Paramount Pictures, Inc., 334 U.S. 131, 177-178 (1948). *Contra:* United States v. Vehicular Parking, Ltd., 7 F.R.D. 336 (D. Del. 1947).

§10.7. [1] 2 Restatement of Contracts §598. Note the interesting provisions of §§5 and 6 of the Illinois Act of June 11, 1891, Laws 1891, p. 206, Ill. Rev. Stat., c. 38, §§569 et seq. (1957).

[2] Central Ohio Salt Co. v. Guthrie, 35 Ohio St. 666, 672 (1880); Georgia Fruit Exchange v. Turnipseed, 9 Ala. App. 123, 62 So. 542 (1913); Bassett v. Heiens, 307 Ill. App. 426, 30 N.E.2d 528 (1940); Grand Prize Distributing Co. v. Gulf Brewing Co., 267 S.W.2d 906 (Tex. Civ. App. 1954). Among the federal decisions are Continental Wallpaper Co. v. Louis Voight & Co., 212 U.S. 227 (1909); McConnell v. Camors-McConnell Co., 152 Fed. 321 (5th Cir. 1907); United Cigar-Whelan Stores Corp. v. H. Weinrich Co., 107 F. Supp. 89, 92 (S.D.N.Y. 1952); Re American Fuel & Power Co., 122 F.2d 223, 229 (6th Cir. 1941). Compare Standard Fashion Co. v. Magrane Houston Co., 251 Fed. 559 (1st Cir. 1918), 259 Fed. 793, 799 (1st Cir. 1919), *aff'd,* 258 U.S. 346 (1922); Bruce's Juices, Inc. v. American Can Co., 330 U.S. 743 (1947).

[3] Lockhart, Violation of the Anti-trust Laws as a Defense in Civil Actions, 31 Minn. L. Rev. 507, 512-513, 515 (1947); Note, Illinois Anti-trust Act Disinterred, 43 Ill. L. Rev. 205, 209 (1948).

[4] An analogous situation is found in the patent law where the courts have refused relief to patentees who have "misused" their patents. E.g., Mercoid Corp. v. Mid-Continent Co., 320 U.S. 661 (1944); F. C. Russell Co. v. Comfort Equipment Corp., 97 F. Supp. 784 (N.D. Ill. 1951), *aff'd,* 194 F.2d 592 (7th Cir. 1952); Note, Contributory Infringement and Misuse, 66 Harv. L. Rev. 909, 912 (1952). See also §10.2B *supra,* regarding compulsory licensing and dedication of patents as a remedy in antitrust litigation.

yet in practical effect still executory, a court of equity may decree
cancellation of the illegal agreement.[5]   In the Restatement of the
Law this principle, obviously designed to afford protection to the
innocent party, was given a larger scope.   Thus, in the Restatement of Contracts, it was said:

> If refusal to enforce or to rescind an illegal bargain would pro-
> duce a harmful effect on parties for whose protection the law
> making the bargain illegal exists, enforcement or rescission, which-
> ever is appropriate, is allowed.[6]

Then, too, there are questions of separability.   One who buys
from a monopolist and fails to pay the purchase price may apparently be compelled to meet his obligation despite a judicial
finding that the plaintiff has violated antitrust statutes.[7]

Perhaps future years will see some trend away from the rule
that the contracts of a monopolist cannot be enforced.   Such a
remedy is arbitrary in that it bears no relationship to the offense
of monopolization.   A trifling violation of the antitrust statutes
may result in substantial pecuniary losses; at the same time flagrant breaches of statutory duty can result in trifling penalties
under the nonenforceability rule.   Thus nonenforceability is not
a sanction designed to meet antitrust objectives — to make the
punishment fit the crime.[8]

§10.8.   **Treble damages.**   We cannot endeavor here to treat all
the questions of law which may arise in a suit for damages arising
out of a violation of antimonopoly statutes.   We merely attempt
to point out a few features peculiar to recovery in antitrust cases.
Perhaps most important are those statutory provisions permitting
the trebling of damages established in such a suit.   Since 1623,
various British and American statutes have permitted recovery of
three times the actual damages sustained by the plaintiff.[1]   In

---

[5] Cleveland Railway v. Hirsch, 204 Fed. 849 (6th Cir. 1913); Meredith v. Fullerton,
83 N.H. 124, 139 Atl. 359 (1927); see Stockton v. American Tobacco Co., 55 N.J. Eq.
352, 36 Atl. 971, 980 (1897); 6 Williston Law of Contracts §1787 (rev. ed. 1937).

[6] 2 Restatement of Contracts §601.   Compare Lockhart, Violation of the Antitrust Laws as a Defense in Civil Actions, 31 Minn. L. Rev. 507, 530 (1947).   Reliance upon a distinction between malum prohibitum and malum per se has not
proven fruitful.   Note, Enforceability of Contracts Which Violate the Robinson-
Patman Act, 55 Yale L.J. 820, 822 (1946).

[7] Bruce's Juices, Inc. v. American Can Co., 330 U.S. 743, 755 (1947).   But compare Patrizi v. McAninch, 269 S.W.2d 343 (Tex. 1954).   See Wood, Unenforceable
Contracts and Other Consequences, Proceedings A.B.A., Section of Antitrust Law,
159, 160 et seq. (Aug. 18, 1954).

[8] But compare Lockhart, Violation of the Anti-Trust Laws as a Defense in Civil
Actions, 31 Minn. L. Rev. 507, 572-573 (1947).

§10.8.   [1] Dana, "Monopoly" under the National Anti-trust Act, 7 Harv. L. Rev.
338, 342 (1894).

addition, the modern provision in the Clayton Act permits taxing of a reasonable attorney's fee as cost of suit.[2] Another adjective advantage available under federal legislation is the right to introduce a decree or judgment entered in a suit brought by the United States as prima facie evidence against the alleged monopolist in a private suit.[3] Furthermore, the running of the statute of limitations is tolled during the period wherein the suit brought by the United States is pending.[4]

In the language of the statute, anyone injured in his trade or business may bring such a treble damage suit. It is incumbent upon the plaintiff to establish the fact of injury. Furthermore, and closely connected therewith, the plaintiff must establish that the defendant's wrong was the proximate cause of the injuries suffered by him.[5] Such requirements, of course, are normal in the law of torts.

[2] The treble damage remedy is now contained in §4 of the Clayton Act. 15 U.S.C.A. §14. Section 7 of the Sherman Act, now repealed, formerly contained a similar remedy. A parallel provision is found in §77 of the Wilson Tariff Act, 28 Stat. 509 (1894), as amended, 37 Stat. 667, 15 U.S.C.A. §15. State statutes are less likely to contain treble damage provisions but some provide for informers' fees. Note, Illinois Anti-trust Act Disinterred, 43 Ill. L. Rev. 205, 219 (1948). Many other federal statutes contain treble damage clauses. E.g., §35 of the Act of July 5, 1946 (Lanham Trade-Mark Act), 60 Stat. 441, 15 U.S.C.A. §1051.

[3] The provision mentioned in the text is found in §5 of the Clayton Act. 15 U.S.C.A. §15. A private litigant, however, cannot take advantage of a consent decree or a judgment entered on a plea of nolo contendere. Pfotzer v. Aqua Systems, 162 F.2d 779, 784 (2d Cir. 1947).

[4] The provision tolling the statutes of limitations is also contained in §5 of the Clayton Act.

[5] Hunter Douglas, Inc. v. Lande Products, Inc., 120 F. Supp. 635, 638 (N.D. Cal. 1952), modified, 215 F.2d 372 (9th Cir. 1954). Compare Story Parchment Co. v. Paterson Parchment Paper Co., 282 U.S. 555 (1931); Bigelow v. RKO Pictures, Inc., 327 U.S. 251, 264 (1946); Landstrom v. Thorpe, 189 F.2d 46, 54 (8th Cir. 1951), cert. denied, 342 U.S. 819 (1951). See Doyle, Treble Damages and Counsel Fees, Proceedings A.B.A., Section of Antitrust Law, 142, 147 (Aug. 18, 1954); Proof Requirements in Anti-Trust Suits, 18 U. Chi. L. Rev. 130, 133 (1950); Antitrust Enforcement by Private Parties, 61 Yale L.J. 1010, 1017 (1952).
While the statute plainly refers to the fact of injury as sufficient ground for the maintenance of suit, the courts have sometimes tended to create arbitrary classifications of proper parties plaintiff. Thus it has been held that an officer and a shareholder of a corporation injured by the defendants' violation of an antitrust statute cannot recover damages in a suit brought by him. Barish v. Chrysler Corp., 141 Neb. 157, 3 N.W.2d 91 (1942); Martens v. Barrett, 245 F.2d 844 (5th Cir. 1957); Walder v. Paramount Public Corp., 132 F. Supp. 912, 916 (S.D.N.Y. 1955) (also creditor and corporate officer). Similar holdings have involved patentees, suppliers and would-be contractors. Productive Inventions v. Trico Products Corp., 224 F.2d 678 (2d Cir. 1955), cert. denied, 350 U.S. 936 (1956); Snow Crest Beverages v. Recipe Foods Inc., 147 F. Supp. 907, 909 (D. Mass. 1956); Miley v. John Hancock Mutual Life Ins. Co., 148 F. Supp. 299, 302-303 (D. Mass. 1957), aff'd, 242 F.2d 758 (1st Cir. 1957), cert. denied, 355 U.S. 828 (1957). A vigorous controversy has raged over the standing of landlords, e.g., Melrose Realty Co. v. Loew's, Inc., 234 F.2d 518 (3d Cir. 1956), cert. denied, 352 U.S. 890 (1956); Congress Building Corp. v. Loew's, Inc., 246 F.2d 587 (7th Cir. 1957). The last-cited opinion contains a care-

Two measures of damages have commonly been employed in antitrust cases.[6]   The first and best-accepted measure is profits which the plaintiff lost as a result of the defendant's monopoly.[7] It is well established, however, particularly in the earlier decisions, that the plaintiff's increased costs are likewise a proper measure of his recovery.   Thus, if the plaintiff can establish what the "normal" price of a commodity would have been in a free-market situation, and then prove the price he actually paid to a monopolist, he may recover the difference between those two figures.[8]   More troublesome has been the problem of establishing the amount of the lost profits to be recovered.   In some of the earlier cases emphasis was laid upon the requirement of certainty, the courts saying that remote and speculative damages could not be recovered.[9]   In recent years those requirements have been relaxed and lack of precise proof is no longer an insuperable obstacle to private recoveries.   Usually the yard stick employed is the profits earned by the plaintiff before the defendant entered

---

ful review of the authorities and adopts the better view (i.e., that a landlord has standing to sue).   Compare Note, Stockholders' Derivative Suits for Treble Damages Under the Anti-Trust Laws, 49 Nw. U.L. Rev. 383 (1954).   Consult Doyle, Treble Damages and Counsel Fees, Proceedings A.B.A., Section of Anti-trust Law, 142, 145 (Aug. 18, 1954); Whipple, Plaintiff's Treble Damage Suits, Proceedings, A.B.A., Section of Antitrust Law, 27, 33 (Apr. 5, 1956); Note, Antitrust Enforcement by Private Parties, 61 Yale L.J. 1010, 1020 (1952).   As to the possibility of class suits, see Daniel, Enforcement of the Sherman Act by Actions for Treble Damages, 32 Va. L. Rev. 910, 924 (1948).   Compare Kainz v. Anheuser Busch, Inc., 194 F.2d 737 (7th Cir. 1952).

6 We cannot here, of course, discuss the entire law of damages.   We mention only those aspects of that branch of the law which are peculiar to recovery from a monopolist.

7 E.g., Frey & Son v. Welch Grape Juice Co., 240 Fed. 114, 117 (4th Cir. 1917). See Clark, The Treble Damage Bonanza, 52 Mich. L. Rev. 363, 367 (1954); Note, The Proof of Damages Under the Anti-Trust Laws, 41 Ill. L. Rev. 462, 463 (1946). Compare 4 Restatement of Torts §912, Comment e.

8 Chattanooga Foundry v. City of Atlanta, 203 U.S. 390, 396 (1906); Thomsen v. Cayser, 243 U.S. 66, 88 (1917); Peto v. Howell, 101 F.2d 353, 361-362 (7th Cir. 1939). See Donovan and Irvine, Proof of Damages Under the Anti-Trust Law, 88 U. Pa. L. Rev. 511, 514, 517 (1940); Clark, The Treble Damage Bonanza, 52 Mich. L. Rev. 363, 404 (1954); Note, Proof Requirements in Anti-Trust Suits, 18 U. Chi. L. Rev. 130, 135 (1950).   Compare the distinction between "general" and "special" damages applied throughout the law of torts.   4 Restatement of Torts §904.

It has been suggested that the profits enjoyed by the defendant as a result of the unlawful monopoly might afford a third measure of damages whereby the defendant would account to the plaintiff for his "unjust enrichment."   McConnell, The Treble Damage Action, 1950 U. of Ill. L. Forum 659, 668.   Such an accounting has been held proper in various common law business torts such as harassment.   E.g., Adriance, Platt & Co. v. National Harrow Co., 121 Fed. 827, 831 (2d Cir. 1903).   But see Fargo Glass & Paint Co. v. Globe American Co., 201 F.2d 534, 540-541 (7th Cir. 1953), cert. denied, 345 U.S. 942 (1953); Clark, The Treble Damage Bonanza, 52 Mich. L. Rev. 363, 384-385 (1954).

9 Central Coal & Coke Co. v. Hartman, 111 Fed. 96, 98-99 (8th Cir. 1901); Donovan and Irvine, Proof of Damages Under the Anti-trust Law, 88 U. Pa. L. Rev. 511 (1940).

upon his illegal course of conduct. In some instances, however, that method of establishing the amount of lost profits has proven unsatisfactory, and various other means of fixing upon the amount of recovery have been allowed, including evidence as to the profits earned by an unaffected operator of a similar business.[10] One who has never been in business and whose entry into the field was blocked by the defendant's monopoly can, of course, scarcely establish his prior earnings as a basis for a treble damage recovery. Nevertheless, the courts have not been willing to support substantial awards for such would-be entrants into the competitive arena,[11] nor have they always taken adequate account of the possibility that the plaintiff's profits, although higher than before the defendant violated the law might — absent such violation — have been even greater during the monopoly period. Another difficult issue revolves around the question of the time during which the damages should be computed. Normally, of course, the plaintiff may only recover damages sustained by him since the defendant violated the law (or the statute of limitations ran) and until suit was brought. Under that formula, for example, the defendant might be liable for plaintiff's prospective profits during a period of, say, two or four years.[12] If, however, the plaintiff's business has been permanently impaired, there seems to be no compelling reason why he should not recover the capitalized value of his business loss.[13] The problem of course is intertwined with that of res judicata: if recovery of capitalized values were permitted, then one suit should preclude the bringing of subsequent actions for recovery of profits during later periods.

§10.9. "Passing on." Plaintiffs seeking to recover damages for losses sustained by reason of monopolistic activities of defendants must clear several hurdles beyond those customary in the law of

[10] Bigelow v. RKO Pictures, Inc., 327 U.S. 251 (1946); McConnell, The Treble Damage Action, 1950 U. of Ill. L. Forum 659, 664; Note, Anti-Trust Enforcement by Private Parties, 61 Yale L.J. 1010, 1025 (1952); Note, Proof Requirements in Anti-Trust Suits, 18 U. Chi. L. Rev. 130, 132 (1950); Clark, The Treble Damage Bonanza, 52 Mich. L. Rev. 381 (1954).

[11] Roseland v. Phister Mfg. Co., 125 F.2d 417, 420 (7th Cir. 1942); Peller v. International Boxing Club, 227 F.2d 593, 596 (7th Cir. 1955); Note, Proof of Damages Under the Anti-Trust Laws, 41 Ill. L. Rev. 462, 463-464 (1945); Note, Proof Requirements in Anti-Trust Suits, 18 U. Chi. L. Rev. 130, 131-132 (1950).

[12] Lawlor v. Loewe, 235 U.S. 522, 536 (1915); Eastman Kodak Co. v. Southern Photo Materials Co., 273 U.S. 359, 377 (1927); Central Coal & Coke Co. v. Hartman, 111 Fed. 96, 98 (8th Cir. 1901).

[13] Perhaps the suggestion in the text is supported by the language in Story Parchment Co. v. Paterson Parchment Paper Co., 282 U.S. 555, 567 (1931). As to depreciation, see Donovan & Irvine, Proof of Damages Under the Anti-Trust Law, 88 U. Pa. L. Rev. 511, 524 (1940). But compare Frey & Son v. Cudahy Packing Co., 243 Fed. 205, 206 (D. Md. 1917); Connecticut Importing Co. v. Frankfurt Distilleries, Inc., 101 F.2d 79, 81 (2d Cir. 1939).

torts. One such extraordinary requirement is the necessity of establishing that the plaintiff has not passed on to his customers the burdens imposed upon him by the defendant. It starts with the concepts of causation and the necessity of proving the fact of injury. Unless the plaintiff has been injured and unless the defendant's violations of the law constituted the proximate cause of such injury, the plaintiff may not recover.[1] In a series of decisions following the *Madison Oil* case[2] the courts held that retailers or other distributors who had passed on illegally high prices to their customers could not recover from the persons found to have violated the Sherman Act in the proceedings initiated by the Attorney General. In each case, the plaintiff bought petroleum products from the defendants for resale. The plaintiff invariably alleged that he had paid a higher price than would have obtained in a free market. He failed, however, to establish that his own selling prices had not been affected by the illegal activities of the defendants. Accordingly, the courts in a series of decisions held that such plaintiffs could not recover. In one case, for example, it was said:

> Plaintiff . . . apparently believed that proof of increased costs, due to an illegal fixing of prices . . . was sufficient to justify recovery of damages . . . without showing whether it had in fact escaped damage by fixing equivalently larger selling prices, thus passing on the increased cost to its purchasers. . . .
>
> In other words the Clayton Act does not permit recovery by plaintiff in causes such as this for unlawful prices as such but authorizes recovery only of pecuniary loss to property or business. . . . He may recover from any member of the conspiracy, if he shows that the direct effect is to injure him in his business or property and produces facts from which such injury may be ascertained. Inasmuch as plaintiff has wholly failed to prove any loss to its property or business but rather has shown, by all reasonable inferences, that the increased cost of which it complained was passed on to the ultimate consumer, the court rightfully directed a verdict for the defendant. . . .[3]

§10.9. [1] Hunter Douglas Corp. v. Lando Products, Inc., 102 F. Supp. 635, 638 (N.D. Cal. 1952), *modified,* 215 F.2d 372 (9th Cir. 1954); Note, Proof of Damages Under the Anti-Trust Laws, 41 Ill. L. Rev. 462, 463 (1946).

[2] United States v. Socony-Vacuum Oil Co., 310 U.S. 150 (1940).

[3] Northwestern Oil Co. v. Socony-Vacuum Oil Co., 138 F.2d 967, 969, 971 (7th Cir. 1943), *cert. denied,* 321 U.S. 792 (1944). Other cases in chronological sequence are Twin Ports Co. v. Pure Oil Co., 119 F.2d 747, 750 (7th Cir. 1941), *cert. denied,* 314 U.S. 644 (1941); Miller Oil Co. v. Socony Vacuum Oil Co., 37 F. Supp. 831 (E.D. Mo. 1941); Leonard v. Socony-Vacuum Oil Co., 42 F. Supp. 369, 370 (W.D. Wis. 1942), *appeal dismissed,* 130 F.2d 535 (7th Cir. 1942); Clark Oil Co. v. Phillips Petroleum Co., 148 F.2d 580 (8th Cir. 1945), *cert. denied,* 326 U.S. 734 (1945); McCain v. Socony-Vacuum Oil Co., 64 F. Supp. 12, 14 (W.D. Mo. 1945); Wolfe v. National Lead Co., 225 F.2d 427, 433 (9th Cir. 1955). See Clark, The Treble Damage Bonanza, 52 Mich.

The rule preventing recovery by a plaintiff who has passed on higher prices to his own customers has been the subject of frequent adverse comment. It is said, in the first place, to be inconsistent with those decisions permitting the plaintiff to measure his damages by his increased costs rather than by his lost profits, and undoubtedly the rule is open to that criticism.[4] It is also said that the rule has been repudiated in later decisions, although such repudiation has not been express in character.[5] Undoubtedly the courts were somewhat influenced by the erroneous concept that one who merely distributes a product and does not fabricate it is not entitled to much protection from monopolistic practices: this is the old prejudice against the middleman, who is thought to add nothing to the value of a commodity but merely to make a dubious profit by effortless trading. The rule is most vulnerable, however, by reason of its assumption that the plaintiff in a treble damage suit has lost no volume through the increase in price effected by the defendant's illegal activities.[6] Whether such a loss of volume has occurred will depend upon the

---

L. Rev. 363, 405 (1954); Day, Trial, Proceedings A.B.A., Section of Antitrust Law, 65, 96 (Aug. 18, 1954); Doyle, Treble Damages and Counsel Fees, id. at 142, 148.

[4] Note, Proof Requirements in Anti-Trust Suits, 18 U. Chi. L. Rev. 130, 136 et seq. (1950).

[5] Note, Anti-Trust Enforcement by Private Parties, 61 Yale L.J. 1010, 1023 (1952). The cases commonly cited in support of the repudiation theory are Alden-Rochelle, Inc. v. ASCAP, 80 F. Supp. 888 (S.D.N.Y. 1948); Pfotzer v. Aqua Systems Inc., 162 F.2d 779 (2d Cir. 1947); Volk v. Paramount Pictures, Inc., 91 F. Supp. 902 (D. Minn. 1950). About all one can conclude from those decisions is that the "increased cost" measure of damages is still available to plaintiffs. Thus, in Alden-Rochelle the court said at page 898: "None of the cases hold that those who have paid a monopolist a price for its product, may claim that the extent of their damage is the full amount paid. The amount of any overcharge may be recovered, but the purchaser should offer some evidence from which the trial court may reasonably approximate the overcharge. The fact that the thing sold is something intangible, a right instead of merchandise, does not alter the requirement of the anti-trust laws that the plaintiff must show that he has been injured. The burden of proof is on plaintiff to show that part of his case by a fair preponderance of the evidence. When it comes to proving the extent of his damage the burden a plaintiff carries in an anti-trust action is lighter; all he need prove are the basic facts from which the court may reasonably approximate the amount of the damages. A plaintiff does not satisfy that burden by offering no proof at all, except what he paid the violator." Note also the more recent decision in Wolfe v. National Lead Co., 225 F.2d 427, 433 (9th Cir. 1955).

[6] Note, Proof Requirements in Anti-Trust Suits, 18 U. Chi. L. Rev. 130, 136 (1950). But compare Anniston Mfg. Co. v. Davis, 301 U.S. 337 (1937). In that case, the Court sustained the validity of a statute providing that there should be no refund of taxes collected under an unconstitutional statute if the taxpayer had passed on the burden thereof to his customers. In the opinion it was said at page 348: "So far as petitioner's contention may be taken to be that it is entitled to recover by reason of the invalidity of the tax, although in fact its burden has been 'passed on' to another, the contention cannot be sustained. While the taxpayer was undoubtedly hurt when he paid the tax, if he has obtained relief through the shifting of its burden, he is no longer in a position to claim an actual injury and the refusal of a refund in such a case cannot be regarded as a denial of constitutional right."

slope of the demand curve facing the particular plaintiff. If demand is inelastic, it may be true that the distributor has actually sustained little or no loss. If, on the other hand, demand is elastic, it follows that the plaintiff's volume has contracted and hence that an injury has actually been sustained. Furthermore, courts have probably been casual in permitting proof of "passing on." On the other hand, as Professor Clark suggested, the "passing on" rule may merely affect the burden of proof with respect to the establishment of damages.[7]

§10.10. **Injury to the public interest.** Another trap for the unwary antitrust plaintiff lies in the doctrine that his suit must plead and prove an injury to the public interest and not merely private damage. Many of the cases so holding have arisen out of the termination of distribution arrangements. In a typical situation the plaintiff is a retailer or wholesaler who has no contractual right to continue to deal in the products of the defendant manufacturer. A defendant stops selling to the plaintiff, choosing a new distributor for his products, and the plaintiff brings suit. In many instances the courts have refused to allow recovery on the ground that the plaintiff had failed to establish an injury to the public interest, even though his evidence had shown both injury to himself and violation of the antitrust laws by the defendant.[1]

The rule that the plaintiff must establish a public injury as well as private damages arises out of litigation of recent years and is

---

[7] Clark, The Treble Damage Bonanza, 52 Mich. L. Rev. 363, 405 (1954). Compare Alden-Rochelle, Inc. v. ASCAP, 80 F. Supp. 888, 898 (S.D.N.Y. 1948). Under the Robinson-Patman Act, damages are usually measured merely by the amount of the price discrimination involved. See Bruce's Juices, Inc. v. American Can Co., 330 U.S. 743, 757 (1947). But compare Sun Cosmetic Shoppe, Inc. v. Elisabeth Arden Corp., 178 F.2d 150, 153 (2d Cir. 1949). It follows that the defense of "passing on" may not be available in actions brought under §2 of the Clayton Act as amended by the Robinson-Patman law. See Clark, The Treble Damage Bonanza, 52 Mich. L. Rev. 363, 407 et seq. (1954).

§10.10. [1] Shotkin v. General Electric Co., 171 F.2d 236 (10th Cir. 1948); Feddersen Motors Inc. v. Ward, 180 F.2d 519 (10th Cir. 1950); Emich Motors Corp. v. General Motors Corp., 181 F.2d 70, 75 (7th Cir. 1950), modified, 340 U.S. 558 (1951); Hudson Sales Corp. v. Waldrip, 211 F.2d 268, 274 (5th Cir. 1954), cert. denied, 348 U.S. 821 (1954); Dublin Distributors v. Edward & John Burke, Ltd., 109 F. Supp. 125, 127-128 (S.D.N.Y. 1952); Northern California Assn. v. Interment Assn., 120 F. Supp. 93, 95 (N.D. Cal. 1954). But see United States v. Borden Co., 347 U.S. 514, 518 (1954). An injury to the public must be spelled out in the complaint and not left to mere inference in the pleadings. Thus, in Kinnear-Weed Corp. v. Humble Oil & Refining Co., 214 F.2d 891 (5th Cir. 1954), cert. denied, 348 U.S. 912 (1955), the court said at page 893: "Public injury alone justifying the threefold increase in damages and being an indispensable constituent of a claim for violation of the antitrust laws, a general allegation of such injury is not sufficient. It is essential that the complaint allege facts from which it can be determined that the conduct charged to be in violation of the antitrust laws was reasonably calculated to prejudice the public interest by unduly restricting the free flow of interstate commerce. . . ."

difficult to analyze. Perhaps it is worth noting that some of the strongest cases on the subject appear to be based on the theory that a distributor is always replaceable; that the public interest does not suffer when a manufacturer substitutes a third party for the plaintiff in the handling of his goods in any specific territory. Thus, in one case the plaintiff alleged that he was the wholesaler of lamps and similar products and that the defendant manufacturers thereof had conspired to run him out of business in order to monopolize the trade therein in his area; that in furtherance of that effort to monopolize, the defendant Westinghouse had refused to sell the plaintiff any further lamps. The plaintiff's complaint was dismissed by the trial court and the Court of Appeals affirmed, saying:

> Founded upon these broad concepts of public policy, the Act is limited in operative scope and effect to combinations, agreements, or concerts which tend to prejudice the public interest by unduly restricting competition or unduly obstruct the due course of trade, or which because of their evident purpose or inherent nature injuriously restrain trade in the competitive markets. . . . A common form of such combination, agreement, or concert is one having for its purpose or tendency the dividing of territories, or one having for its purpose or tendency the apportionment of customers, or one having for its purpose or tendency the controlling or narrowing of outlets in order to raise or maintain prices.

The court went on:

> . . . the complaint failed to allege facts from which it could be determined as a matter of law that a combination or conspiracy was entered into which brought about an increase in prices to the consuming public, a diminution in the volume of merchandise in the competitive markets, a deterioration in the quality of the merchandise available in the channels of commerce, or any other like evil consequence in the free flow of interstate commerce. Instead, the pleading bore clear internal indications of a personal grievance on the part of plaintiff based solely and exclusively upon the declination of the defendant Westinghouse . . . further to transact business with him as an outlet for its manufactured merchandise, with no evil consequence to the consuming public.[2]

On the other hand, the courts have refused to apply the public interest rule — or, to put it another way, have found an injury to

---

[2] Shotkin v. General Electric Co., 171 F.2d 236, 238, 239 (10th Cir. 1948). See also Feddersen Motors, Inc. v. Ward, 180 F.2d 519, 522 (10th Cir. 1950); Hudson Sales Corp. v. Waldrip, 211 F.2d 268, 273 (5th Cir. 1954), cert. denied, 348 U.S. 821, (1954); Arthur v. Kraft-Phenix Cheese Corp., 26 F. Supp. 824, 828 (D. Md. 1938); Riedley v. Hudson Co., 82 F. Supp. 8 (W.D. Ky. 1949).

the public interest — when the plaintiff has been "foreclosed" from a market. Perhaps some significance should be attached to the fact that plaintiffs thus successfully meeting the public interest requirement have often been manufacturers,[3] as opposed to mere distributors, although persons engaged in rendering services[4] have also been able to meet its demands. On the other hand, in some opinions the plaintiffs have been held ineligible for recovery even though all sources of supply or avenues of sale were closed to them by action of the defendant. In one case the plaintiff held insurance policies protecting it against risks of loss by fire. A fire occurred and then the defendant circulated a report indicating that the plaintiff was a bad insurance risk; thereafter the plaintiff found that it could not buy fire insurance from any company. Despite this "foreclosure" the plaintiff's case for the recovery of damages was held not to comply with the public interest rule. On that subject the District Court said:

> Defendants' motion to dismiss the complaint for failure to state a claim must be granted. It is clear from the allegations of the complaint that plaintiff is concerned only with a single isolated incident involving plaintiff and defendants, and has completely failed to sufficiently plead that the public has been, or may be, affected in any way by defendants' alleged conduct. No valid reference is made in the complaint relating to the general market conditions for fire insurance or for the manufacture and distribution of clothing. There is no allegation of conduct on the part of defendant that would tend to inhibit competition among the defendants for the market for fire insurance. There is nothing in the complaint to indicate that the inception, purpose, intent or intended consequence of defendants' conduct was to affect market prices. . . . the net effect of the entire complaint is that the defendants have succeeded in boycotting a single business concern and have eliminated competition among themselves only insofar as it relates to the sale of fire insurance to that one business concern.[5]

---

[3] National Used Car Market Report v. National Auto Dealers Assn., 200 F.2d 359, 360 (D.C. Cir. 1952); Southern Rendering Co. v. Standard Rendering Co., 112 F. Supp. 103, 109 (E.D. Ark. 1953); Boerstler v. American Medical Assn., 16 F.R.D. 437, 444 (N.D. Ill. 1954).

[4] Darnell v. Markwood, 220 F.2d 374, 376 (D.C. Cir. 1954); Noerr Motor Freight Inc. v. Eastern Railroad Presidents Conference, 113 F. Supp. 737, 744 (E.D. Pa. 1953). Compare Revere Camera Co. v. Eastman Kodak Co., 81 F. Supp. 325, 332 (N.D. Ill. 1948).

[5] Ruddy Brook Clothes, Inc. v. British Insurance Co., 103 F. Supp. 290, 291 (N.D. Ill. 1951), aff'd, 195 F.2d 86 (7th Cir. 1952), cert. denied, 344 U.S. 816 (1952). See to the same effect Abouaf v. Spreckels Co., 26 F. Supp. 830, 834 (N.D. Cal. 1939); Neuman v. Bastian-Blessing Co., 70 F. Supp. 447, 449 (N.D. Ill. 1947). Compare the interesting opinion in Interborough News Co. v. Curtis Publishing Co., 127 F. Supp. 286 (S.D.N.Y. 1954). In the decision the court wrote at page 301: "The final test to be applied to . . . determine whether §1 of the Sherman Act was violated

It must be admitted that the delineation of the public interest rule is difficult if not impossible. One might imagine that injury to consumers must be shown by way of increased prices and the like.[6] The whole history of the antitrust laws, however, suggests that an immediate detriment to consumers has never been a requirement of antitrust violation. Local price-cutting, for example, gives consumers short-run benefits but may still be illegal.[7] Access to markets is a subject often dwelt upon under the antitrust laws[8] but, as we have seen, the public interest rule cases are not uniform on that subject. Ease of entry into competition may be an important factor in applying the rule. The notion that a distributor is readily replaceable and hence that his injury causes no public harm reflects an understanding that entry into competition at that level normally does not involve heavy capital requirements or advanced technological skills.[9] The whole notion of injury to the public interest mirrors the thought that under the Sherman Act there must be injury to competition and not merely to a competitor; in short, the requirement seeks to impose a "hard" rule of competition as opposed to a "soft" regime of protectionism; in this connection it is interesting to note that the requirement of injury to the public interest does not obtain in suits founded upon violations of the Robinson-Patman Act.[10]

§10.11. **Unclean hands.** One hurdle which plaintiffs need no longer clear in antitrust litigation is found in the ancient rule of pari delicto.[1] Under the accepted doctrine of earlier years, a

---

is whether the defendants' several refusals to deal with plaintiff necessarily had or will have any substantial pernicious effect on the commerce concerned in the sense that an adverse effect therefrom will be felt by the public. No such element of public injury is proven . . . I am not persuaded that as a result of defendants' conduct, the purchasing public had to pay any increase in price, suffered any diminution in the quality or kind of service prevalent in the market prior to the defendants' acts complained of, or that there was any effect resultant from defendants' act detrimental to any person but the plaintiff."

[6] E.g., Shotkin v. General Electric Co., 171 F.2d 236, 239 (10th Cir. 1948).

[7] See §2.10 *supra*. Compare Darnell v. Markwood, 220 F.2d 374 (D.C. Cir. 1954).

[8] E.g., Eastern States Retail Lumber Assn. v. United States, 234 U.S. 600 (1914); United States v. Griffith, 334 U.S. 100, 107 (1948).

[9] Compare United States v. Columbia Steel Co., 334 U.S. 495, 528 (1948); United States v. American Can Co., 234 Fed. 1019, 1021 (D. Md. 1916), *appeal dismissed*, 256 U.S. 706 (1921); United States v. Quaker Oats Co., 232 Fed. 499, 503 (N.D. Ill. 1916); see §3.12 *supra*.

[10] Midland Oil Co. v. Sinclair Refining Co., 41 F. Supp. 436, 438 (N.D. Ill. 1941); Myers v. Shell Oil Co., 96 F. Supp. 670, 674-675 (S.D. Cal. 1951). Compare Reid v. Doubleday & Co., 109 F. Supp. 354, 356-357 (N.D. Ohio, 1952).

§10.11. [1] The general law is illustrated by Johnson Laboratories v. Meissener Mfg. Co., 98 F.2d 937, 948-949 (7th Cir. 1938). See A. Hollander & Son, Inc. v. Imperial Fur Corp., 2 N.J. Eq. 235, 66 A.2d 319, 324 (1949); 6 Williston, Law of Contracts §1787 (rev. ed. 1937).

plaintiff who himself was guilty of violating the antitrust laws could not recover damages sustained by reason of a similar violation by the defendant. In recent years the courts, however, have swept the rule of pari delicto from the antitrust scene. The leading case involved a suit for treble damages brought by distributors of alcoholic beverages. They alleged that the defendants had agreed to fix maximum prices at the wholesale level and refused to sell to the plaintiffs because of their unwillingness to hold prices down to those figures. The defendants pleaded that the plaintiffs themselves had engaged in a price-fixing conspiracy in their resale of the same products. A demurrer to the plea was sustained, the court holding that the defense of unclean hands was no longer available in suits to recover damages for breaches of the antitrust laws.[2] Possibly a few exceptions may be stated in which pari delicto may still be well pleaded. Thus it has been intimated that if the parties have entered into an arrangement on terms of economic equality, one may still plead the unclean hands of the other in litigation over the same subject matter.[3]

A minor hurdle which may be faced by some plaintiffs is found in the compulsory counterclaim provisions of the Federal Rules of Civil Procedure.[4] If the monopolist, for example, has previously brought "fair trade" litigation against the plaintiff, and the plaintiff has therein failed to assert damages by way of counterclaim, he may be barred from further prosecuting a suit for treble dam-

---

[2] Kiefer-Stewart Co. v. Joseph E. Seagram & Sons, Inc., 340 U.S. 211, 214 (1951); Moore v. Mead Service Co., 184 F.2d 338, 340 (10th Cir. 1950), *vacated,* 340 U.S. 944 (1951), *rev'd,* 190 F.2d 540 (10th Cir. 1951). Compare Trebuhs Realty Co. v. News Syndicate Co., 197 F. Supp. 595, 598 (S.D.N.Y. 1952). See Wood, Unenforceable Contracts and Other Consequences, Proceedings A.B.A., Section of Antitrust Law, 159, 171 (Aug. 18, 1954); Note, Unclean Hands in Antitrust Cases, 48 Nw. U.L. Rev. 619 (1953). But compare Bushby, The Unknown Quantity in Private Antitrust Suits — The Defense of Pari Delicto, 42 Va. L. Rev. 785, 795 (1956), indicating that the law is less clear than stated in the text.

[3] Pennsylvania Water Co. v. Consolidated Gas Co., 209 F.2d 131, 133 (4th Cir. 1953), *cert. denied,* 347 U.S. 960 (1954). It has also been held that unclean hands with respect to the same subject will bar a plaintiff. Louisiana Petroleum Retail Dealers, Inc. v. Texas Co., 148 F. Supp. 334 (W.D. La. 1956). Compare Cleveland Railway v. Hirsch, 204 Fed. 849, 855-857 (6th Cir. 1913); Meredith v. Fullerton, 83 N.H. 124, 139 Atl. 359, 365 (1927).

A reverse development appears to have occurred in the field of patent law. The old rule was that a defendant to a patent infringement suit might not successfully plead that the plaintiff was party to an unlawful combination. Later it was decided that no relief would be allowed a patentee who had misused his patent rights. Radio Corp. of America v. Hygrade Sylvania Corp., 10 F. Supp. 879, 881 (D.N.J. 1934); Morton Salt Co. v. G. S. Suppiger Co., 314 U.S. 488 (1942). Compare United States v. Imperial Chemical Industries, Ltd., 105 F. Supp. 215, 224 (S.D.N.Y. 1952). But see Automatic Radio Co. v. Hazeltine Research, Inc., 176 F.2d 799, 805 (1st Cir. 1949), *aff'd,* 339 U.S. 827 (1950).

[4] Fed. R. Civ. P. 13(a).

ages founded upon the defendant's monopoly of a particular market.[5]

§10.12. **Conclusion with respect to antitrust remedies.** From time to time considerable dissatisfaction has been expressed concerning the efficacy of existing remedies, and particularly those applicable to monopoly. There are, of course, those who advocate widespread governmental intervention: direct control of prices and production throughout the economy. No doubt such steps would effectively foreclose whatever need there may be for additional antitrust remedies or, indeed, for enforcement of antimonopoly legislation in any form.[1] A less drastic proposal, often advanced, is that the federal government should license all enterprises engaged in interstate commerce.[2] This suggestion, of course, merely reaches the adjective aspects of monopoly: it does not offer guidance as to who should be allowed a license.[3] On the other hand, should the Congress deem that the courts have been too timid in utilizing the weapon of dissolution, a licensing provision might effect an atomization of industry not heretofore achieved under existing antitrust remedies.

Another proposal often heard is that government, and particularly the federal government, should directly enter into competition with private business in order to afford a yardstick of costs and prices. The suggestion is, of course, that direct enforcement of the antitrust laws has failed and that only through such vigorous measures can the existence of monopoly be demonstrated. This is not the place to enter into a discussion of the merits of such a sweeping proposal. We may, however, pause to point out the sorry record of the TVA in furnishing a yardstick for private electric power companies.[4]

[5] E. J. Korvette Co. v. Parker Pen Co., 17 F.R.D. 267, 268-269 (S.D.N.Y. 1955). But compare Mercoid Corp. v. Mid-Continent Investment Co., 320 U.S. 661, 670-671 (1944); Switzer Bros. v. Locklin, 207 F.2d 483, 488 (7th Cir. 1953); Douglas v. Wisconsin Alumni Research Foundation, 81 F. Supp. 57, 170 (N.D. Ill. 1948).

§10.12. [1] Hale and Hale, Monopoly and Mobilization, 47 Nw. U.L. Rev. 606 (1952). A less drastic proposal, frequently made through the years, is that adjudication of antitrust cases should be focused in a specialized tribunal. Donovan, The Need for a Commerce Court, 147 Annals 138 (1938); Commission on Organization of the Executive Branch of the Government, Legal Services and Procedure 86 (Mar. 28, 1955). If the suggestion is that ordinary federal judges cannot understand the antitrust laws as presently interpreted, a question at once arises as to how common citizens could be expected to comply therewith.

[2] E.g., TNEC, Final Rep. 24-25.

[3] Smith, Legislative Proposals for Federal Incorporation and Licensing of Interstate Corporations, Symposium, N.Y. State Bar. Assn., Section on Antitrust Law, 65, 66 (CCH, 1950).

[4] Haskins and Sells, Revolving Funds and Business Enterprises of the Government 90, 147 (Report to Commission on Organization of Executive Branch of the Govern-

As suggested in the foregoing discussion, the choice of remedy against monopoly will be largely determined by the legal theory of monopoly which is ultimately adopted. If the structure test is written into Section 2 of the Sherman Act, it will be logical to require more frequent use of dissolution decrees. If, on the other hand, the old abuse test or some newer concept of "performance" should prevail, then regulation by injunction is to be expected. That, however, is a simplified statement, since judicial control of abuses and practices so readily leads to interventionist techniques and a regime of protectionism. In any event, there is little to be done with respect to the improvement of antitrust remedies until we sharpen our picture of antitrust goals. If it were possible for the Congress to issue clear and concise instructions to the courts on substantive issues, no great difficulty would be experienced in fashioning appropriate remedies. Our difficulties in enforcing antimonopoly policy do not derive from lack of effective sanctions but from flaws in the policy itself.[5]

---

ment, 1949); Roberts, Certain Aspects of Power, Irrigation and Flood Control Projects 18 (Report to Commission on Organization of Executive Branch of the Government, 1949); Abrams, Fact and Fancy, 25 Barron's No. 7, p. 15 (1955); Callman, The Law of Unfair Competition and Trademarks §14 (1945). Another proposal frequently advanced is that the federal government should guarantee long-term loans to small business and otherwise promote new ventures. E.g., House Select Committee on Small Business, Review of Small Business, H.R. Rep. No. 2513, 82d Cong., 2d Sess. 93 (1952).

[5] It is fashionable to complain that the antitrust laws have not been enforced adequately. E.g., House Committee on Small Business, United States v. Economic Concentration and Monopoly, Staff Report Pursuant to H. Res. 64, 79th Cong. 11, (1947). Few such comments, however, have taken into account the inadequacy of substantive law mentioned in the text.

CHAPTER 11

In Ending

§11.1. **A backward glance.** In Chapter 2 of this work we examined the "abuse" theory of monopoly. We listed various types of conduct which could amount to an abuse, we examined the necessary intent to infringe the statutory prohibitions and we analyzed the abuse theory from both a legal and an economic point of view. In Chapter 3 we attempted a comparable survey of the "structure" theory of monopoly. Again we examined the decisions in order to ascertain how that theory had been applied by the courts, and we analyzed the results thereof in the light of both economic and legal concepts. Finding serious deficiencies in both the abuse and the structure doctrines, we turned, in Chapter 4, to various other proposals. We there touched on the "performance" test of monopoly and the theory of "workable" competition. In the absence of a scientific standard for the measurement of monopoly power,[1] however, we were unable to approve any of the suggested methods of applying the antitrust laws to the activities of single traders. We went on in Chapters 5, 6 and 7 to examine various "shapes" of business entities. We looked at vertical integration, diversification and dispersion, recording the attitude of the courts toward each of these forms of enterprise and analyzing the results of the decisions. We found that although various shapes had often been the subject of adverse criticism, both in the courts and elsewhere, there was, on analysis, little validity to such charges. Most of the conclusions in those chapters were negative and we had little to suggest of a constructive character. In Chapter 8, discussing corporate wealth, we did attempt to point out the possibility of placing an absolute limit

§11.1. [1] Chamberlin, Measuring the Degree of Monopoly, in Chamberlin, ed., Monopoly and Competition and Their Regulation 255, 258, 267 (International Economic Assn. 1954); see §4.14 *supra*. It has frequently been suggested, of course, that monopoly should be curbed upon moral or ethical grounds. E.g., Schumpeter, History of Economic Analysis 60-61 (1954); Dirlam and Kahn, Fair Competition 39 (1954). Criteria of "fairness," however, are scarce. Possibly "fairness" means giving recognition to seniority, which may be another way of spelling protectionism. In any event we have been unable to discover helpful guideposts in the writings of moralists and philosophers. See §1.10 *supra*.

upon the size of corporations instead of curbing their share of a particular market.   On the whole, however, the impression of the previous chapters is that those who enforce the antitrust laws sail on largely uncharted seas.   The reader may therefore well be reminded of the language of Omar:

> Myself when young did eagerly frequent
> Doctor and Saint, and heard great argument
> About it and about: but ever more
> Came out by the same door where in I went.

> With them the seed of Wisdom did I sow,
> And with mine own hand wrought to make it grow;
> And this was all the Harvest that I reaped —
> "I came like Water and like Wind I go." [2]

We shall not quarrel with the reader who utters such a complaint.
    It is true, on the other hand, that economic theories are not all at war; not every school of economics is in conflict with all the propositions of every other.[3]   Furthermore, it is not impossible that an intelligent choice of theories could be made, at least for individual situations.[4]   A great deal depends upon whether we

[2] The Rubáiyát of Omar Khayyám, Stanzas XXVII, XXVIII (Fitzgerald ed. 1858). As early as 1552 a British statute specifically acknowledged the confusion surrounding the crimes of forestalling, engrossing and regrating which had been known to the common law then for about two hundred years. Adler, Monopolizing at Common Law, 31 Harv. L. Rev. 246, 253 (1917).   The lawyer who desires to deride the contribution of the economist can easily find examples of "learning" upon which to expend his wit.   Take, for example, the following discussion: "The existence of monopolies is theoretically compatible with the competitive mechanism, provided competition prevails between the monopolies themselves.   Thus it is by changes in the supply or demand curves that the possibilities of a better adaptation of production to the wants of consumers become apparent even to firms enjoying a monopoly. Similarly, the expectation of increased profits induces even the monopolies to put such possibilities into practice.   On the other hand, we must not overlook the fact that the existence of monopolies impairs the competitive system to a certain extent." Johr, Regulation of Competition, in Chamberlin, ed., Monopoly and Competition and Their Regulation 338, 339 (International Economic Assn. 1954).

[3] Compare, for example, Wright, Toward Coherent Anti-Trust, 35 Va. L. Rev. 665, 691 (1949); MacLaurin, Technological Progress in Some American Industries, 44 Proceedings Am. Econ. Assn. 178, 182 (1954); Edwards, Maintaining Competition 108 (1949); Simons, Economic Policy for a Free Society 87 (1948).   Professor Simons wrote: "I am, indeed, not much distressed about private monopoly power . . . the ways of competition are devious, and its vengeance — government intervention apart — will generally be adequate and admirable."   Id. at 87.   The literature is well summarized in Hoover, The Relevance of the Competitive, Laissez-Faire Economic Model to Modern Capitalistic National Economics, 8 Kyklos No. 1, 40 (1955).

[4] In United States v. Winslow, 195 Fed. 578 (D. Mass. 1912), aff'd, 227 U.S. 202 (1913), the lower court wrote at page 589: "The . . . expression 'rule of reason' . . . was merely a short way of expression to the effect that the present state of the common law on that topic is the result of development along reasonable lines, and hand in hand with modern commercial advance."   On the other hand, in United

seek immediate short-run results or whether we are content to await developments in the long term.[5] That is something like determining how much of our national income should be saved each year and invested in productive facilities for future generations. Besides, there is some value in setting forth the applicable legal doctrines and their economic counterparts in an orderly fashion. Yet it must be admitted there is much room for cynicism and doubt as to the enforcement of antimonopoly policy today.[6] For, whether we desire it or not, current antitrust enforcement appears to be based less upon rational rules of law than upon a judicial desire to reduce disparities in economic advantage.[7]

§11.2. **Presumptions.** Inability to formulate satisfactory proposals for the substantive law of monopoly has led some observers to retreat into an adjective position. They would create presumptions of illegality from various manifestations of possible monopoly. Thus Professor Kales advocated that the horizontal size of a corporation (under the structure theory) should give

---

States v. National Lead Co., 63 F. Supp. 513 (S.D.N.Y. 1945), aff'd, 332 U.S. 319 (1947), the trial court wrote at page 525: "The economic theory underlying the Sherman Act is that, in the long run, competition is a more effective prod to production . . . than even an enlightened combination." Economic counterparts for such views can readily be found. E.g., Maclaurin, Invention and Innovation in the Radio Industry 251 (1949); Bowman, Toward Less Monopoly, 101 U. Pa. L. Rev. 577, 630 (1953).

[5] In United States v. Addyston Pipe Co., 85 Fed. 271 (6th Cir. 1898), aff'd, 175 U.S. 211 (1899), Judge Taft wrote in the Court of Appeals at page 284: "The public policy embodied in the common law requires the discouragement of monopolies, however temporary their existence may be. The public interest may suffer severely while new competition is slowly developing." On the other hand, antitrust suits are notoriously protracted in character. United States v. National City Lines, 334 U.S. 573, 590 (1948); House Select Committee on Small Business, Review of Small Business, H.R. Rep. No. 2513, 82d Cong., 2d Sess. 286 (1952). If a decade or more is consumed in an effort to dissolve a monopoly which might otherwise be eroded through natural forces in the same length of time, little will have been accomplished.

[6] It is, of course, well recognized that businessmen often conduct themselves in such a way as to discourage additional governmental intervention. E.g., Lauterbach, Discussion, 45 Proceedings Am. Econ. Assn. 555, 556 (1955). The well-advised businessman will also, of course, take careful heed of the pressures of partisan politics, often reflected in the institution of antitrust litigation. E.g., Associated Press v. United States, 326 U.S. 1 (1945).

[7] See §8.3 supra. Note also the suggestion that antitrust enforcement could be carried out on three levels. There would be regulated public utilities at the largest level; freely competitive small units at the other extreme and quasi-regulated concerns in the middle category. Such quasi-regulation would reflect business goals including "responsibility" to employees, suppliers and consumers, as well as investors. It would also involve compliance with statutes such as the Robinson-Patman Act (§2 of Clayton Act, as amended). Levi, A Two Level Anti-Monopoly Law, 47 Nw. U.L. Rev. 567 (1952); Kaplan, Big Enterprise in a Competitive System 57 (Brookings Institution, 1954). See §10.5 supra.

rise to a presumption of illegality which could be rebutted by the defendant. His language was:

> It is sufficient protection to the public and a sufficient concession to the possible abuse of power by combinations, and any bias against them, that every combination having a preponderant position at the time it is organized must sustain the burden of rebutting a *prima facie* inference of excluding purposes and unlawful excluding practices.[1]

Such presumptions might also be based upon various market practices such as maintaining prices below free-market levels and consequent rationing of output; refusals to deal might form another foundation for a rebuttable presumption of infringement of the statute.[2]

To date the courts have not seen fit to spell out any doctrine of presumption; yet it is surprising how frequently they have actually employed that technique. Take, for instance, the old case involving the Eastman Kodak Company. The court there started out by suggesting that control of from 75 to 80 per cent of the industry therein defined constituted a monopoly. But it went on to say that the burden then shifted to the defendants to justify that combination, as by showing that it resulted from lawful normal growth and the like.[3] In a recent decision even the word "presumption" was used.[4]

Clearly, however, any such presumption must meet the constitutional test of a rational connection between the fact proven and the ultimate fact presumed.[5] Thus a statute creating a pre-

§11.2. [1] Kales, Contracts and Combinations in Restraint of Trade §92 (1918). See also id. §§62, 91; Stocking and Watkins, Monopoly and Free Enterprise 553 (Twentieth Century Fund, 1951); Bowman, Toward Less Monopoly, 101 U. Pa. L. Rev. 577, 613 (1953).

[2] Id. at 616; Rahl, Conspiracy and the Anti-Trust Laws, 44 Ill. L. Rev. 745, 758 (1950). Compare Rostow, Monopoly Under the Sherman Act, 43 id. 745, 754 et seq. (1949). Almost any of the tests of monopoly set forth in this chapter could be made the basis of such a presumption.

[3] United States v. Eastman Kodak Co., 226 Fed. 62, 79-80 (W.D.N.Y. 1915), *decree*, 230 Fed. 522 (W.D.N.Y. 1916), *appeal dismissed*, 255 U.S. 578 (1921). Compare American Column & Lumber Co. v. United States, 257 U.S. 377, 409 (1921); Harding v. American Glucose Co., 182 Ill. 551, 620, 55 N.E. 577 (1899); Kales, Contracts and Combinations in Restraint of Trade §65 (1918).

[4] United States v. United Shoe Machinery Corp., 110 F. Supp. 295, 342 (D. Mass. 1953), *aff'd per curiam*, 347 U.S. 521 (1954). Compare United States v. Pullman Co., 50 F. Supp. 123, 132 (E.D. Pa. 1943), *aff'd per curiam*, 330 U.S. 806 (1947); Gamco, Inc. v. Providence Fruit & Produce Building Inc., 194 F.2d 484, 487-488 (1st Cir. 1952), *cert. denied*, 344 U.S. 817 (1952); Bowman, Toward Less Monopoly, 101 U. Pa. L. Rev. 577, 583-584 (1953).

[5] Morgan, Federal Constitutional Limitations upon Presumptions Created by State Legislation, in Harvard Legal Essays 323 (1934). Thus, in Tot v. United States, 319 U.S. 463 (1943), the Court wrote at page 467: "Under our decisions, a statutory

sumption of monopoly out of proof of keeping part of a plant idle was held unconstitutional on the ground that no such rational connection had been established.[6] From the discussion set forth in this work, however, it is apparent that several types of proven facts could rationally give rise to presumptions of monopolization. Indeed, the existence of excess capacity may itself rationally suggest that monopoly elements may be present in the industry. So long, therefore, as the presumption is rebuttable, there would appear to be no constitutional or other legal obstacle to its employment, provided that such rationality exists.[7]

The difficulty, of course, is that the presumption merely shifts the burden of proof and contributes little to our understanding of the substantive law. Wisely used, such a presumption might furnish a framework for rational consideration of the problems discussed throughout this book. It might constitute a device for focusing attention on the really relevant criteria. To suppose, however, that it may work some magic in the resolution of substantive questions of the type herein outlined would be fanciful in the extreme.[8]

§11.3. Freedom vs. security. Even if we could devise a scientific test to determine whether a noxious amount of monopoly were present in any market situation, enforcement of the antitrust laws would continue to involve basic elements of conflict. The attempt to compel businessmen to compete ends inevitably in curbs upon competition. In larger terms this is the struggle between freedom and security, between opportunity and equality. It is evidenced in the antitrust laws by the conflicting aims of rewarding victory and penalizing success. Competition itself is a cause of monopoly. As Mr. Justice Holmes wrote many decades ago:

---

presumption cannot be sustained if there be no rational connection between the fact proved and the ultimate fact presumed, if the inference of the one from the proof of the other is arbitrary because of lack of connection between the two in common experience."

[6] McFarland v. American Sugar Refining Co., 241 U.S. 79, 81, 86 (1916).

[7] Query, however, whether such a presumption should be created in criminal cases arising under the antitrust laws. Compare Cahill, Must We Brand American Business by Indictment as Criminal? Proceedings A.B.A., Section of Antitrust Law, 26 (Sept. 17, 1952).

[8] In United States v. Pullman Co., 50 F. Supp. 123, 132 (E.D. Pa. 1943), aff'd per curiam, 330 U.S. 806 (1947), the lower court, for example, took the high prices charged by the defendant as indicative of the existence of a monopoly. In effect, therefore, it was following a presumption technique. The difficulty, of course, is that there was no showing of why the prices were considered high. Compare §4.10 supra. Furthermore, there was nothing to indicate that whatever prices prevailed should be attributed to the existence of monopoly power. This example merely illustrates that the device of a presumption is no substitute for genuine analysis of situations alleged to be monopolistic.

It is plain from the slightest consideration of practical affairs, or the most superficial reading of industrial history, that free competition means combination. . . .[1]

The basic inconsistency of antitrust enforcement was echoed in the following statement from another court:

The evils sought to be averted by the act are those which spring from monopoly. Competition is the antithesis of monopoly. In a sense any elimination of competition is a movement in the general direction of monopoly. But competition is, in its very essence, a contest for trade and any progress or victory in such contest must lessen competition. Competition must always bear in itself the seed of its own alteration or even destruction.[2]

On the one side the statutes appear to demand a regime of "hard" competition. Let competition be full, fair and free, the statutes appear to say, and the devil take the hindmost. Thus one court wrote:

The national will has not declared against elimination of competitors when they fail from their inherent industrial weakness. On the contrary, it has declared with great emphasis against any methods by which such weaknesses might be concealed. . . .[3]

But to political ears the pleasure of consumers is a distant tinkle of cash registers, and the distress of rivals a close bellow of anguish. As we have seen,[4] the antitrust laws are frequently applied so as to protect competitors; to afford a measure of security against the more alert, more efficient and more industrious rival. For candidates, capitalist or collectivist, the cry for shelter has strong appeal.[5]

§11.3. [1] Vegelahan v. Guntner, 167 Mass. 92, 44 N.E. 1077, 1081 (1896) (dissenting opinion). The inherent inconsistency of monopoly legislation is not unique. Every statute creating a crime represents a compromise between our craving for individual freedom and security for our fellow citizens. The difference is only that the crime of monopolization is so much more difficult to define than such tangible offenses as burglary.

[2] United States v. Standard Oil Co., 47 F.2d 288, 297 (E.D. Mo. 1931). Martin Luther condemned both monopolies and high prices, believing in the "just price." Followers of Calvin punished both monopolists and userers in much the same vein. Tawney, Religion and the Rise of Capitalism 85, 105 (Mentor ed. 1947). Lack of consistency is not solely a modern vice.

[3] United States v. Corn Products Refining Co., 234 Fed. 964, 1015 (S.D.N.Y. 1916). Indeed, it is difficult to envision a free-market economic system in which businessmen are not encouraged to exploit market "impurities" and "imperfections" to the best of their honest ability.

[4] §§2.31, 3.20 supra.

[5] The National Association of Manufacturers, for example, once strongly affirmed its belief in competition and opposition to monopoly but asked for relief from "excessive" competition. O'Mahoney Committee I, pt. 4, at 392. It has been said that cartels are not formed to exploit consumers but to achieve security for themselves.

From a purely economic standpoint it would appear preferable to pay direct subsidies to those deemed worthy of such shelter. By doing so we should avoid what amounts to an annoying degree of intervention in the free-market system. The amount of the subsidy would be plainly exposed to public view and we could then determine in a more rational fashion whether the "security" thus afforded inefficient business units was worth its cost. Psychologically and politically, however, such a subsidy would be unacceptable. The sheltered businessman does not wish to admit that he needs a subsidy. The notion is that he is "independent": a citizen standing on his own feet and needing the aid of no one. A direct subsidy from the public treasury would destroy that illusion. Hence it appears likely that enforcement of any antimonopoly policy will involve contradictions, confusion and inconsistencies. A line must be drawn between liberty and regimentation and it will not always be straight. If we can

---

Schneider, Real Economies of Integration, in Chamberlin, ed., Monopoly and Competition and Their Regulation 203, 207 (International Economic Assn. 1954). For such reasons a prominent student recently wrote: "Finally, genuinely easy entry has its political dangers, especially if slow exit is found in the same industries. A small margin of long-run excess profit coupled with 'a little monopoly' may be a reasonable price to pay for diminishing the force and effectiveness of pressures for state-sponsored cartelization. But the limits of 'a little monopoly' should be carefully drawn." Bain, Conditions of Entry, id. at 240. Perhaps the change from "hard" enforcement of the antitrust laws to the more recent "soft" tendencies parallels the change in the meaning of the word "liberal" from one who believes in free-market pricing to one who believes in state intervention. Protectionism is not novel; the medieval guilds were monopolistic in character; usury was widely denounced in sixteenth-century England and attempts were made to repress it. In Elizabethan days the state used its power to protect the small outmoded producer (both the farmer and weaver) from innovations, and the religious thought of the Reformation was based upon medieval concepts wherein the owner of property was a trustee for society who should not raise rents even if the free market would permit him to do so. Tawney, Religion and the Rise of Capitalism 32, 128, 131, 140 (Mentor ed. 1947). The cautious businessman today does not raise his prices without a lengthy statement blaming someone else for the higher costs which require him to advance his sales figures. E.g., Cassady, Price Making and Price Behavior in the Petroleum Industry 130, 265n (Petroleum Monograph Series No. 1, 1954). Ethical concepts have not proven of much assistance. Compare Dirlam and Kahn, Fair Competition 206 (1954). It is easy to say that the law must do "equity" but query what is that? Injury to the established firm, whether through predatory practices, innovation or plain competition, is always tangible and obvious. Injury to the public, when deprived of competition or innovation, is often obscure. It is no mere accident, however, that those who have sought to impose collectivist economic principles upon society have always laid great stress upon "equity" and the equalization of natural advantages. Socialism and protectionism, in other words, have always been closely linked. E.g., Dicey, Law and Public Opinion in England 216, 226, 234, 270, 275 (2d ed. 1914). In the last few years there may have been some trend away from collectivism in religious and ethical thinking. Katz, Natural Law and Human Nature, 3 U. Chi. L. School Rec. No. 3, pp. 1, 17 (1954); Riesman, Individualism Reconsidered 26 (1954). In other words, there are ethical concepts which justify "hard" competition as well as the "soft" variety.

decide how much competition we want and what we wish it to
accomplish for us,[6] we may be able to march along a somewhat
steadier path but complete consistency appears unattainable.[7]

§11.4. **Constitutionality.** Amid so much uncertainty and
doubt as to the meaning of our antimonopoly statutes, the question of whether such legislation, particularly when accompanied
by criminal penalties, affords due process of law is a serious one.
True, the United States Supreme Court has declared that the
Sherman Act is not too vague and that its prohibitions are not so
scattered as to lead to criminal convictions without adequate
warning.[1] As the Supreme Court noted, many other statutes are
also extremely vague and the modern trend in constitutional
doctrine with respect to statutes controlling businessmen is surely
far on the "liberal" side.[2]

From what has been set forth above, however, it is plain that
compliance with antimonopoly statutes is difficult in the extreme.
So loose has been their construction that there is a constant stream
of complaint on the subject. Even among the experts there is
disagreement and one specialist may refer to the ignorance of
another.[3] More than four decades ago a court declared:

> There is such a chaos of decisions in reference to the Sherman
> Anti-Trust Act, and such a chaos of understanding or misunder-
> standing thereto . . . that any conclusions a single judge may
> reach may prove of very little importance.[4]

Indeed, so great has been the uncertainty with respect to the application of the Sherman Act that it is frequently urged that its

---

6 Adelman, Business Size and Public Policy, 24 J. Business 269, 279 (1951); Clark,
Competition and the Objectives of Government Policy, in Chamberlin, ed., Monopoly
and Competition and Their Regulation 317 (International Economic Assn. 1954).
Compare Palamountain, The Politics of Distribution (1955).

7 The task of framing rational public policy is surely made no easier when public
opinion is inflamed by demagogues careless of fact and casual of conscience. E.g.,
2 Nevins, Study in Power 144 (1953).

§11.4. 1 See Nash v. United States, 229 U.S. 373, 377 (1913).

2 Boyce Motor Lines v. United States, 342 U.S. 337 (1952); Yakus v. United States,
321 U.S. 414 (1944). Compare Lockhart and McClure, Obscenity in the Courts, 20
Law & Contemp. Prob. 587, 595-596 (1955).

3 Dirlam and Kahn, Anti-Trust Law and the Big Buyer, 60 J. Pol. Econ. 436, 439
(1952); Dirlam and Kahn, Reply, 61 id. 441 (1953). But Dirlam and Kahn do not
recommend curbs upon corporate wealth. Id. 284.

4 United States v. Winslow, 195 Fed. 578, 580 (D. Mass. 1912), aff'd, 227 U.S. 202
(1913). In a later case involving the same defendant a judge wrote: "In connection
with the Sherman Act, it is delusive to treat opinions written by different judges at
different times as pieces of a jig-saw puzzle which can be, by effort, fitted correctly
into a single pattern." United States v. United Shoe Machinery Corp., 110 F. Supp.
295, 342 (D. Mass. 1953), aff'd per curiam, 347 U.S. 521 (1954).

enforcement has been heavily weighted by partisan political considerations.[5]

Our federal legislation is penal in character. It is generally accepted doctrine that a person should not be put in peril of imprisonment by statutes so vague that their prohibitions cannot be ascertained by reasonable diligence. Legislation of a comparable character has been held beyond the pale.[6] Note too the comment of Professor Freund, a great student of statutory regulation:

> The history of the criminal enforcement of the Sherman Anti-Trust Act should prove another principle, namely, that penal legislation ought to avoid elastic prohibitions where the difference between the exercise of a valuable right and the commission of a proposed criminal offense is entirely one of degree and effect. . . .
> The Act of 1890 creates a crime of monopolizing an industry which no one as yet has been capable of defining.[7]

In these circumstances, and particularly with increased awareness of the difficulties inherent in antitrust interpretation, it is indeed doubtful whether the statute should be considered constitutional to the extent it carries criminal punishment. On the other hand there is little present prospect that the courts will reconsider the issue.

§11.5. **Recommendations.** We have indicated our feeling that it is difficult to administer Section 2 of the Sherman Act

---

[5] E.g., Benton, The Sherman or Anti-Trust Act, 18 Yale L.J. 311, 325 (1909). The discretion of prosecuting officers has been greatly broadened by recent decisions which, if literally applied to other cases, would seem to outlaw a large proportion of the business transacted in the United States. E.g., United States v. Griffith, 334 U.S. 100 (1948); Timken Roller Bearing Co. v. United States, 341 U.S. 593 (1951). There has, of course, been much complaint with respect to the uncertainty of all the antitrust laws. E.g., Jacoby, Anti-trust Policy Reexamined, 58 J. Pol. Econ. 61, 62 (1950); O'Mahoney Committee I, pt. 4, at 666; Fairless, Guilty Before Trial 6-7, 14 (United States Steel Corp., May 18, 1950).

[6] International Harvester Co. v. Kentucky, 234 U.S. 216, 222-223 (1914); United States v. L. Cohen Grocery Co., 255 U.S. 81, 89, 92 (1921); Cline v. Frink Dairy Co., 274 U.S. 445, 457-458, 460 (1927); People v. Building Maintenance Assn., 41 Cal. 2d 719, 264 P.2d 31, 35 (1953). All the foregoing decisions except United States v. L. Cohen Grocery Co. involve antitrust statutes of one type or another. Note also that we have acquired a good deal of (negative) learning with respect to the inherent difficulties of an antimonopoly policy since the decision in Nash v. United States, 229 U.S. 373 (1913). But compare Jordan v. de George, 341 U.S. 223, 231 n.15 (1951).

[7] Freund, Standards of American Legislation 222 (1917). *Accord:* Cahill, Must We Brand American Business by Indictment as Criminal? Proceedings A.B.A., Section of Antitrust Law, 26 (Sept. 17, 1952). It is customary for proponents of the legislation to suggest, by way of analogy, that it is foolish to walk on the very edge of a precipice. But the very meaning of a line in the law is that you may intentionally go as close to it as you can. See Atlantic Coastline R.R. v. Phillips, 332 U.S. 168, 172-173 (1947).

upon a scientific basis. We have even cast doubt upon the constitutionality of that measure in view of its vagueness and uncertainty. Our contribution, if such it can be called, is heavily on the negative side; for we urge again and again that this theory and that should not be applied in antitrust enforcement. Hence we may be obliged to state our recommendations affirmatively. We can only do so on faith: science provides no ultimate answers. Thus what follows makes no pretension to that rationality which we have sought to infuse into the analysis of preceding chapters.

Since we regard efforts to improve our economy through enforcement of Section 2 of the Sherman Act as something like trying to repair a watch with a steam shovel, we should prefer to abandon that legislation.[1] We believe it more satisfactory to take explicit account of whatever judicial trend toward a curb on corporate wealth may be found in recent decisions.[2] A limit upon the over-all size of business enterprise would achieve far more than antimonopoly legislation. From a political and sociological point of view such a limit would reduce the public prejudice against a free-enterprise system and make possible the reduction of intervention and its burdens.[3] Partisan politics would play a lesser role, since limitations upon wealth (such as a progressive corporate income tax) — as opposed to those on monopoly — can be made explicit and relatively free from dubious interpretation. True, a limitation upon wealth does nothing to disturb monopoly. For monopoly may be enjoyed by concerns of relatively small absolute size. But the whole argument of this book is that rational limitation upon monopoly is impossible: hence abandonment of the effort would constitute no loss. At the same time, by expressly attacking pure size, we should bring into the open the criterion which courts are actually applying in the guise of enforcing the antitrust laws. We should, indeed, be making explicit the egalitarian rationale of some recent judicial pronouncements.[4]

In making the foregoing recommendation, we fully realize that curbs upon corporate wealth might well themselves involve dis-

§11.5. [1] Compare Machlup, The Political Economy of Monopoly 232 (1952); Burns, The Decline of Competition 17 (1936).

[2] See §8.3 *supra*.

[3] In Dirlam and Kahn, Fair Competition 17 (1954) the authors wrote: "Clearly we are not devoted to a competitive system only for 'economic' reasons. It is also associated with such social and political ideals as the diffusion of private power and maximum opportunities for individual self-expression. If the economy will run itself, governmental interference in our daily life is held to a minimum."

[4] No doubt such a change would require legislative action. But compare the judicial enactment of the rule against perpetuities. Kales, Contracts and Combinations in Restraint of Trade §91 (1918).

economies.[5] It is simply our belief, which we cannot support by scientific standards, that on balance an over-all limitation upon size of business enterprise would afford a larger degree of freedom and opportunity to our citizens at a lower cost in terms of living standards than can be achieved under existing legislation.

At the same time we do not favor repeal of Section 1 of the Sherman Act. Retention of Section 1 would not be based upon any notion of effecting retribution on knowing wrongdoers. Those who combine to restrain trade, however, by their own acts eliminate many of the gross uncertainties involved in a prohibition against monopoly on the part of a single entity. Persons actually engaged in trade have unique opportunities to judge market conditions. When they take action by way of combination they eliminate many of the obstacles to rational enforcement of a limitation upon monopoly itself. One example may suffice: since the defendants do not merge their separate businesses into a single trader unit but merely effect a loose combination, they thereby admit that in their judgment no element of indivisibility is present.[6] Accordingly, it is unlikely that enforcement of the statute will adversely affect economies of scale.

If, however, the choice is between public utility type regulation (or outright socialization) and enforcement of existing statutes, our choice is clearly to continue our efforts, however wobbly, to destroy monopoly. We do not contend that competition is a perfect regulator of the economy. Obviously, it is a device afflicted with much waste. It is simply our belief, again unsupported by scientific proof, that it offers a higher standard of living and greater individual freedom than interventionist systems. It is consistent with our traditions and it affords greater insulation from partisan political pressures.[7] Like the whole

5 See §8.4 *supra*.

6 The term "loose combination" as used in the text probably requires definition. A combination to engage in research activities might reflect indivisibility without indicating that a combination of all production was required. Compare United States v. Line Material Co., 333 U.S. 287, 310 (1948). Note also that a merger might have been prevented by §7 of the Clayton Act.

7 A court once wrote: "Monopoly in trade . . . is odious to our form of government . . . its tendency is . . . destructive of free institutions, and repugnant to the instincts of a free people, and contrary to the whole scope and spirit of the federal constitution. . . ." Richardson v. Buhl, 77 Mich. 632, 43 N.W. 1102, 1110 (1889). Compare Hale and Hale, Monopoly and Mobilization, 47 Nw. U.L. Rev. 606 (1952). Note the close connection between monopoly and socialization in British and Italian experience. Allen, Monopoly and Competition in the United Kingdom, in Chamberlin, ed., Monopoly and Competition and Their Regulation 88, 89 (International Economic Assn. 1954); Vito, Monopoly and Competition in Italy, id. at 43, 56-57. A well-known philosopher wrote that society, that it might live better, creates the state; then the state gets the upper hand and society has begun to live for the state; the people are converted into fuel to feed the mere machine which is the state.

concept of political democracy, an antimonopoly policy is afflicted with many weaknesses. Compared, however, with the rigidity and veniality of an interventionist state, it appears far more attractive.

The case in favor of the continued enforcement of Section 2 of the Sherman Act rests upon the hope that conscientious judges can, in specific cases brought before them, take account of the various considerations rationally affecting the existence of monopoly. A judge who has renounced partisan politics and personal ambition may be able to weigh and give effect to such factors as ease of entry, indivisibility and the like, in the light of evidence adduced before him.[8] We have here, indeed, provided something like a qualitative analysis of monopoly: we know what elements enter into its composition and our deficiency lies in our inability to make a quantitative analysis. Which theory of monopoly — whether structure,[9] performance[10] or another — should be utilized in that effort is perhaps not of great importance, although the structure test is perhaps most compatible with the foregoing approach. And, as we have said on a prior page,[11] no antimonopoly policy can be effective or complete unless many other fields of law are brought into coordination therewith.

We close with the customary recommendation for further study. As Mr. Justice Holmes wrote many decades ago,

> It does not follow, because we are all compelled to take on faith at second hand most of the rules upon which we base our action and our thought, that each of us may not try to set some corner of his world in the order of reason or that all of us collectively should

---

The skeleton eats up the flesh around it. The scaffolding becomes the owner and tenant of the house. Ortega, The Revolt of the Masses 89 (Mentor ed. 1950). Note that our system of political democracy is also afflicted with much confusion. One votes, for example, for a member of Congress; many issues are involved and the result of the election is scarcely a barometer of public opinion on any one of them.

[8] Compare the proposal that antitrust litigation be focused in a specialized court. §10.12.1 *supra.*

[9] Rostow, Market Organization and Stabilization Policy, in Income Stabilization for a Developing Economy 439, 510-511 (Millikan ed. 1954).

[10] Mason, The Current Status of the Monopoly Problem in the United States, 62 Harv. L. Rev. 1265, 1282 (1949).

[11] §1.2 *supra.* Compare Gray, Income Tax Deductions as a Means of Effectuating Governmental Policies, 2 Wash. & Lee L. Rev. 191, 193 (1941); Lintner and Butters, Effect of Taxes on Concentration, in Business Concentration and Price Policy 239, 275 (Stigler ed. 1955); Whitney, Vertical Disintegration in the Motion Picture Industry, 45 Proceedings Am. Econ. Assn. 491, 498 (1955). Note, however, that there may be tangible reasons for a monopolistic policy in the labor and farm segments of the economy. There the supply factor may be highly inelastic, and if wages are reduced, hours of work may actually be increased. Clark, Competition: Static Models and Dynamic Aspects, 45 Proceedings Am. Econ. Assn. 450, 462 (1955).

not aspire to carry reason as far as it will go throughout the whole domain.[12]

Every chapter, every section of this book opens possibilities of deeper probing. Empirical investigation is desirable at every point.[13] It may be expensive to mobilize the resources necessary for such thorough studies, since we believe a team composed of persons trained in many disciplines would constitute the most effective task force. Furthermore, it is far easier to call for empirical investigation than to produce statistics of real relevance. Nevertheless, we can but plod onward, utilizing our ingenuity at every turn to pry open the secrets of human action.[14] As the novelist wrote,

> We work in the dark — we do what we can — we give what we have. Our doubt is our passion and our passion is our task. The rest is the madness of art.[15]

12 Holmes, Collected Legal Papers 185 (1920).

13 Triffin, Monopolistic Competition and General Equilibrium Theory 189 (1940); Jacoby, Anti-Trust Policy Reexamined, 58 J. Pol. Econ. 61, 65-66 (1950). Investigations conducted under governmental auspices, however, have not proven fruitful. E.g., Galbraith, Monopoly and the Concentration of Economic Power, in Ellis, ed., A Survey of Contemporary Economics 99, 122 et seq. (American Economic Assn. 1949).

14 We venture the suggestion that most of the progress in understanding antitrust policy in the next few decades will involve a searching out and identification of various "imperfections." Note, for example, the long time lag which elapsed before commercial banks lent their depositors funds for the financing of automobile purchases.

15 James, The Middle Years.

Appendixes

A P P E N D I X   A

Market Imperfections: Enforcement of the Antitrust Laws in a Friction-afflicted Economy[*]

INTRODUCTION

In analyzing the nature of monopoly economists distinguish between market "impurities" and "imperfections." "Pure" competition is a simple concept: there must be many buyers and many sellers, no one of whom can affect prices. Since the sales or purchases of each trader are small, each seller is faced with a perfectly elastic demand curve for his product.[1] A second requirement of market "purity' is that the commodity must be homogeneous.[2] When the two foregoing conditions for "purity" have been achieved, all monopoly elements have been removed from the market.

"Perfect" competition is a residual concept. All obstacles to an economic allocation of resources other than monopoly are referred to as "imperfections."[3] Time lags, immobility of capital and labor,

---

[*] Reprinted, with minor changes, from 102 University of Pennsylvania Law Rev. 157 (1953).

This paper was presented to the antitrust seminar conducted by the University of Chicago Law School on June 17, 1953. The authors gratefully acknowledge the helpful suggestions made by the seminar participants upon that occasion.

[1] Chamberlin, The Theory of Monopolistic Competition 7 (5th ed. 1946); Chamberlin, Monopolistic or Imperfect Competition? 51 Q.J. Econ. 557, 566 (1937); Robinson, The Economics of Imperfect Competition 88-89 (1936); Robinson, What Is Perfect Competition? 49 Q.J. Econ. 104, 105 (1934); Machlup, Monopoly and Competition: A Classification of Market Positions, 27 Am. Econ. Rev. 445, 451 (1937); Triffin, Monopolistic Competition and General Equilibrium Theory 138 (1940). Cf. Kaldor, Professor Chamberlin on Monopolistic and Imperfect Competition, 52 Q.J. Econ. 513, 516 (1938).

[2] Chamberlin, The Theory of Monopolistic Competition, c. 1 (5th ed. 1946); Machlup, Monopoly and Competition: A Classification of Market Positions, 27 Am. Econ. Rev. 445, 448 (1937). Difficulty in defining commodities has been, of course, a major problem in the attempt to achieve "pure" competition. §3.5 supra.

[3] Haney, History of Economic Thought 695 (4th ed. 1949); Chamberlin, The Theory of Monopolistic Competition 6, 206 (5th ed. 1946); Machlup, Monopoly and Competition: A Classification of Market Positions, 27 Am. Econ. Rev. 445 (1937); Knight, Risk, Uncertainty and Profit 76-79 (1921).

ignorance on the part of producer or consumer, the irrational decisions by buyers and sellers are prominent examples of imperfections.[4] As we shall see, commodities must also be homogeneous in order to avoid market imperfections; thus there is an overlap between the concepts of "purity" and "perfection." [5]

This study examines the nature of imperfections and suggests their application in the enforcement of the antitrust laws.[6] In a free-market economy allocation of resources is guided by consumer demand. Frictions and imperfections which reduce mobility of capital and labor or cloud the reign of consumer sovereignty may be just as injurious to the economy as monopoly itself.[7] In addition, such frictions and

[4] As stated by Professor Knight, the condition of perfect competition ". . . assumes complete absence of physical obstacles to the making, execution and changing of plans at will; that is there must be 'perfect mobility' in all economic adjustments, no costs involved in movements or changes. To realize this ideal all the elements entering into economic calculations — effort, commodities, etc. — must be continuously variable, divisible without limit. Productive operations must not form habits, preferences, or aversions, or develop or reduce the capacity to perform them. In addition the production process must be constantly and continuously complete; there is no time cycle of operations to be broken into or left incomplete by sudden readjustments. Each person continuously produces a complete commodity which is consumed as fast as produced. The exchange of commodities must be virtually instantaneous and costless." Id. at 128. Cf. Haney, Value and Distribution 149 (1939). Imperfections prevent application of the "profits" test to determine the existence of monopoly. High profits, in other words, may reflect merely frictions in the market place and not monopoly power. Knight, Risk, Uncertainty and Profit 19 (1921); Machlup, Monopoly and Competition: A Classification of Market Positions, 27 Am. Econ. Rev. 445, 448 (1937); Robinson, What Is Perfect Competition? 49 Q.J. Econ. 104, 107 (1934).

[5] Differentiation of products is a way of avoiding pure competition. Hence the existence of homogeneous commodities is a necessary condition of purity. Chamberlin, The Theory of Monopolistic Competition 7 (5th ed. 1946); Robinson, The Economics of Imperfect Competition 90 (1936); Triffin, Monopolistic Competition and General Equilibrium Theory 133 (1940); Samuelson, Economics: An Introductory Analysis 492 (1948); Haney, Value and Distribution 146n (1939). Cf. Kaldor, Professor Chamberlin on Monopolistic and Imperfect Competition, 52 Q.J. Econ. 513, 517 (1938). Many subtle forms of product differentiation impair commodity homogeneity. Delivery service, extension of credit and the privilege of returning merchandise are three prominent examples. Robinson, The Economics of Imperfect Competition 89, 90 (1936); Copeland, Competing Products and Monopolistic Competition, 55 Q.J. Econ. 1, 30 (1940). Standardization of commodities is also important in the concept of "perfect" competition. Without such standards it is impossible for buyers to identify what they are paying for. Id. at 32. Cf. Lyon, The A.B.C. of the N.R.A. 173, 174, 177, 178 (1934) (Code provisions under the NRA). Such standardization, however, can be carried so far as to deny consumers any real choice. At that point there may be conflict between the requirements of "purity" and "perfection" and of consumer sovereignty. Chamberlin, Monopolistic or Imperfect Competition? 51 Q.J. Econ. 557, 577 (1937); Stocking and Watkins, Monopoly and Free Enterprise 508 (1951).

[6] The basic federal statute is the Sherman Act. 26 Stat. 209 (1890), 15 U.S.C. §1 (1946). Supplementary legislation is collected in the first part of Title 15 of the United States Code. Similar legislation exists in most of the states and was collected in Martin, ed., State Anti-Trust Laws (WPA, 1940). The common law of the several states should also be considered.

[7] Lindhahl, The Federal Trade Commission Act as Amended in 1938, 47 J. Pol. Econ. 497, 504 (1939); Garver and Hansen, Principles of Economics 58 (3d ed. 1947).

imperfections may themselves give rise to a degree of monopoly power: if Ivory is the only brand of soap known to a housewife, its maker can monopolize her trade.[8] This discussion suggests that in some instances monopoly elements in effect merely eliminate imperfections which may be more disruptive to the economy than the impurities which they create. In any antitrust case, therefore, not only the monopolistic tendencies, but also the imperfections which they tend to remove must be examined and weighed in order to obtain an economically sound result.

I. THE NATURE OF MARKET IMPERFECTIONS

Immobility is an obvious imperfection. Workers may hesitate to leave family and friends in order to secure higher wages in a distant area.[9] Space itself is an imperfection[10] and likewise gives rise to part of the problem of mobility.[11] Similarly, time lags prevent a perfect

---

Imperfections may seriously distort the economy. Machlup, Monopoly and Competition: A Classification of Market Positions, 27 Am. Econ. Rev. 445, 451 (1937). Consumer sovereignty is, of course, also thwarted by monopoly. Hildebrand, Consumer Sovereignty in Modern Times, 41 Am. Econ. Rev. 19, 21 (Supp. 1951) (Proceedings American Economic Assn.).

[8] Robinson, What Is Perfect Competition? 49 Q.J. Econ. 104, 106 (1934); Lyon and Abramson, The Economics of Open Price Systems 64 (1936); Borden, The Economic Effects of Advertising 182 (1942); Wright, Toward Coherent Anti-Trust, 35 Va. L. Rev. 665, 678 (1949).

[9] Cf. Knight, Risk, Uncertainty and Profit 177 (1921); Chamberlin, Monopolistic or Imperfect Competition? 51 Q.J. Econ. 557, 564-565 (1937); Haney, Value and Distribution 151 (1939); Wilcox, Competition and Monopoly in American Industry 2 (TNEC Monograph No. 21, 1940); Gregory, Fashion and Monopolistic Competition, 56 J. Pol. Econ. 69, 73 (1948). Such imperfections are often equivalent to those economies of scale which stand in the way of pure competition. Kaldor, Professor Chamberlin on Monopolistic and Imperfect Competition, 52 Q.J. Econ. 513, 521 (1938). Query whether differences in managerial ability should be considered imperfections. In United States v. Aluminum Co. of America, 148 F.2d 416, 431 (2d Cir. 1945), one of the elements of monopolization mentioned was that the defendant had kept the elite of personnel in its industry available for production of its goods. Note also the following statement: "Small business by its very nature — the low financial requirements, easy entry, attractiveness to the individual — invites entrants without management experience while it is usually unable to contain within itself the elements of good management in the way of accountants, financial experts, fact finding, and so on." Waxman, Financial Advice and Guidance for Small Business, 11 Law & Contemp. Prob. 334, 336 (1945).

[10] Stated differently: The fact that all economic activity does not occur at one place is in itself an imperfection.

[11] Marshall, Principles of Economics 324-325 (8th ed. 1922); Knight, Risk, Uncertainty and Profit 79 (1921); Robinson, The Economics of Imperfect Competition 89 (1936); Garver and Hansen, Principles of Economics 61 (3d ed. 1947); Hotelling, Stability in Competition, 39 Econ. J. 41, 44 (1929); Lerner and Singer, Some Notes on Duopoly and Spatial Competition, 45 J. Pol. Econ. 145, 186 (1937); Weintraub, Price Theory 277, 278, 285 (1949); Smithies, Optimum Location in Spatial Competition, 49 J. Pol. Econ. 423, 434 (1941); Copeland, Competing Products and Monopolistic Competition, 55 Q.J. Econ. 1, 29 (1940). From another point of view, the factor of space simply differentiates products and hence constitutes an impurity rather than an imperfection. §3.7 *supra;* Enke, Space and Value, 56 Q.J. Econ. 627,

allocation of resources: even though a new product is not protected by patent some delay normally ensues before the innovator is challenged by competition.[12]

Inertia is an important imperfection.[13] Many economic decisions are the result of habit and custom rather than rational choice. We do not and we could not pause to re-examine every day the quality of the commodities which we buy.[14] The man who has always driven a Buick may purchase another car of that make to save an afternoon of shopping around in order not to miss his game of golf. Closely akin to inertia are the emotional barriers to a free flow of resources.[15] Sec-

637 (1942); Sraffa, The Laws of Returns Under Competitive Conditions, 36 Econ. J. 535, 544 (1926); Chamberlin, Monopolistic or Imperfect Competition? 51 Q.J. Econ. 557, 562 (1937); Lerner and Singer, Some Notes on Duopoly and Spatial Competition, 45 J. Pol. Econ. 145 (1937); Weintraub, Price Theory 272, 284n (1949). For a discussion of how competitors behave in relation to the impurity or imperfection of space, see Copeland, Competing Products and Monopolistic Competition, 55 Q.J. Econ. 1, 29 (1940); Lerner and Singer, Some Notes on Duopoly and Spatial Competition, 45 J. Pol. Econ. 145, 151, 154 (1937); Smithies, Optimum Location in Spatial Competition, 49 J. Pol. Econ. 423, 430, 432, 436 (1941). Retail market areas, of course, vary in size and economic importance. Waite and Cassady, The Consumer and the Economic Order 234 (1939).

12 Marshall, Principles of Economics 330 (8th ed. 1922); Haney, History of Economic Thought 707 (4th ed. 1949); Wilcox, Competition and Monopoly in American Industry 2 (TNEC Monograph No. 21, 1940); Waite and Cassady, The Consumer and the Economic Order 254n (1939); Chamberlin, The Theory of Monopolistic Competition 6 (5th ed. 1946); Burns, The Decline of Competition 29 (1936). Some variations in price on a seasonal or other basis reflect changes in demand rather than imperfections. The August fur sale, the higher price of hair cuts on Saturday and the lower telephone rates available in the evenings are examples of such changes in demand corresponding to time periods. Oxenfeldt, Industrial Pricing and Market Practices 240 (1951). The passage of time is important, however, to a study of monopoly proper even though most observers to date have contented themselves with "static" analyses. Haney, History of Economic Thought 709, 713 (4th ed. 1949); Chamberlin, An Experimental Imperfect Market, 56 J. Pol. Econ. 95, 108 (1948).

13 Robinson, The Economics of Imperfect Competition 89 (1936); Haney, History of Economic Thought 702 (4th ed. 1949).

14 Knight, Risk, Uncertainty and Profits 210 (1921); Gordon, Economics for Consumers 7, 66 (2d ed. 1944); Mack, Economics of Consumption, in A Survey of Contemporary Economics 42 (Haley ed. 1952). A vivid illustration of the force of habit is found in consumers' attachment to particular brands of goods. Oxenfeldt, Industrial Pricing and Market Practices 140 n.64, 146 (1951). But cf. Nichol, Edgeworth's Theory of Duopoly Price, 45 Econ. J. 51, 62-63 (1935); Roper, The Fortune Consumer Outlook, 40 Fortune No. 3, pp. 57, 60 (1950). The very notion that consumers may exercise freedom of choice is a modern one. In earlier ages consumer sovereignty was unknown and even the amount of food to be eaten by the citizenry was prescribed closely by governmental decree. Gordon, Economics for Consumers 599 (2d ed. 1944).

15 Differences in tastes vary greatly among consumers. Mack, Economics of Consumption, in A Survey of Contemporary Economics 62, 63 (Haley ed. 1952); Robinson, The Economics of Imperfect Competition 89 (1936). Unequal distribution of income is, of course, responsible for a large part of (but not all) taste variations. Mack, Economics of Consumption, in A Survey of Contemporary Economics 40, 45, 53, 55, 63-64, 67, 68, 71 (Haley ed. 1952). Consumers are often motivated by a desire for display and to acquire the latest fashions. Gordon, Economics for Con-

tional, social, family and religious considerations make markets rigid. Racial prejudice warps employment and other transactions. Hopes and habits, customs and conventions often prevent consumers from acting in a manner which others might consider rational.[16]

Government action in the nature of intervention — control over prices and the rationing of commodities — should be considered as an impurity.[17] Other types of governmental action may, however, well result in imperfections. Thus taxes levied on particular products such as gasoline and cigarettes tend to distort consumer demand for those commodities.[18] In the short run, police power regulation de-

---

sumers 64, 98, 291 (2d ed. 1944); Borden, The Economic Effects of Advertising 655 (1942); Hoyt, Consumption in Our Society 78 (1938); Gregory, Fashion and Monopolistic Competition, 56 J. Pol. Econ. 69, 70 (1948) (pointing out the relationship between fashion and that product differentiation which characterizes monopolistic competition). Cf. FTC v. Algoma Lumber Co., 291 U.S. 67, 78 (1934); Eastern Wine Corp. v. Winslow-Warren Ltd., 137 F.2d 955, 958 (2d Cir. 1943) (quoting FTC v. Algoma Lumber Co. *supra*). Some commodities are sold in conventionalized price "lines" which are maintained even when competition takes the form of changes in quality. Nelson and Keim, Price Behavior and Business Policy 75 (TNEC Monograph No. 1, 1941).

[16] Scoville, Revolution in Glassmaking: Entrepreneurship and Technological Change in the American Industry, 1880-1920, 284-290 (1948); Ward, The American Economy — Attitudes and Opinions 10 (1955); Knight, Risk, Uncertainty and Profit 78 (1921); Boulding, Welfare Economics, in A Survey of Contemporary Economics 31 (Haley ed. 1952); Mitchell, The Backward Art of Spending Money, in American Standards and Planes of Living 377, 388 (Eliot ed. 1931); Mack, Economics of Consumption, in A Survey of Contemporary Economics (Haley ed. 1952); Galbraith, Rational and Irrational Consumer Preference, 48 Econ. J. 336 (1938); Gordon, Economics for Consumers 43, 70, 72, 291, 507 (2d ed. 1944). Even on the assumption that consumers act purely "rationally," many imperfections must be recognized. Thus it has been said: "Consumers tend to choose wisely, but because they have so many alternatives before them they need help in discriminating on the actual market. We have only 24 hours a day, and we cannot spend the whole 24 weighing potatoes, burning silk, experimenting with coffee grinders and feeding guinea pigs." Hoyt, Consumption in Our Society 79 (1938). Another observer said: "To learn really to select wisely among the many items in order to build a program of consumption would be a life's work. To learn, in addition, to choose the best value among the many qualities in which each item is offered at different prices would take the proverbial nine lives of a cat. . . ." Vaile, Consumption, The End Result of Marketing, 209 Annals 14, 21 (1940).

[17] Statutes illustrating this type of government action are: 49 Stat. 543 et seq. (1946), as amended, 54 Stat. 919 (1940), 49 U.S.C. §§301 et seq. (1946) (Part II of the Interstate Commerce Act); 52 Stat. 977 et seq. (1938), as amended, 49 U.S.C. §§401 et seq. (Supp. 1951) (Civil Aeronautics Act); 49 Stat. 2036-2039 (1936), as amended, 41 U.S.C. §§35-41 (Supp. 1951) (Walsh-Healey Act). See Fisher, Anti-Trust During National Emergencies, 40 Mich. L. Rev. 969, 1167 (1942); Hale, Principles of Free Enterprise, 1 Bill of Rights Rev. 186, 193 (1941); Hale, Monopoly and Mobilization: The Conflict Between Direct Control and the Anti-Trust Laws, 47 Nw. U.L. Rev. 606 (1952). Cf. Sargent, Economic Hazards in the Fair Labor Standards Act, 6 Law & Contemp. Prob. 422, 429 (1939). But cf. Chamberlin, The Theory of Monopolistic Competition 47 (5th ed. 1946).

[18] See Int. Rev. Code of 1954, §§4081, 5701. Steeply progressive income taxes may impair incentives and hence constitute imperfections. Stigler, The Economics of Minimum Wage Legislation, 36 Am. Econ. Rev. 358, 364 (1946); Boughner, Methods of Reducing Excess Profits Taxes, 32 Chi. B. Record 453, 456 (1951). Restraints

signed to protect public health and safety[19] may have some similar effect. A statute requiring theaters to be constructed with a minimum number of fire exits may make it more expensive to erect such structures and hence discourage entry. In the long run, however, statutes designed in good faith[20] to protect public health and safety should not be considered imperfections because the barriers which they create will be counterbalanced by subsequent savings to society. In such instances the burden of regulation can be justified if the countervailing savings actually exist. Contrariwise, even statutes designed to protect investors from fraud[21] may be administered in such a manner as to handicap small and growing business[22] to the point where resources are allocated imperfectly.

---

have sometimes been imposed upon the extension of credit. Federal Reserve System Regulation No. 10, 16 Fed. Reg. 1586 (1951) (Regulation 10, Real Estate Credit). It is not clear whether such restrictions should be regarded as market imperfections.

[19] Examples of this type of regulation are: 49 Stat. 546, 557 et seq. (1935), as amended, 49 U.S.C. §§304(a)(2), 315 et seq. (1946); Ill. Rev. Stat., c. 95½, §§240 et seq. (1949) (Truck Act); 52 Stat. 977 et seq. (1938), as amended, 49 U.S.C. §§401 et seq. (Supp. 1951); Ill. Rev. Stat., c. 127½, §§6 et seq. (1949) (fires — investigation and prevention). See Brownfield, Compulsory Liability Insurance for Commercial Motor Vehicles, 3 Law & Contemp. Prob. 571, 574 (1936); 1 Sharfman, The Interstate Commerce Commission 245, 248 (1931).

[20] It is a commonplace, of course, that police power regulation may be diverted to interventionist ends. Edwards, Maintaining Competition 313 (1949); cf. American Trucking Assn., Inc. v. United States, 344 U.S. 298 (1953). Many statutes fall near the border line. E.g., Ill. Ann. Stat., c. 48, §36 (Supp. 1952) (semimonthly payment of wages); Ill. Rev. Stat., c. 74, §§1 et seq. (1949) (regulation of rate of interest). For the history of statutes regulating hours of work and the like, see Reisenfeld and Maxwell, Modern Social Legislation 598 et seq. (1950).

[21] E.g., 17 C.F.R. §240.14a (1949) (SEC, Regulations X-14).

[22] Celler Committee I, pt. 2-A, at 468. Friends of the Securities and Exchange Commission have attempted to minimize the impact of its regulation upon small business. Id. at 686-688; Loss, Securities Regulation 246-247 (1951). Practitioners familiar with the field have not been impressed by the Commission's defense. Cf. Margraf, Does Securities Regulation Hinder Financing Small Business? 11 Law & Contemp. Prob. 301, 302, 308 (1945); Burns, The Decline of Competition 419 (1936). Other examples of police power regulation which may handicap small business are found in the fields of sanitation, small loan regulation, control of insurance company investments and the like. Matthews, Guinea Pigs No More 138 (1936); Robinson and Nugent, Regulation of the Small Loan Business 120, 135, 174 (1935); Ill. Rev. Stat., c. 73, §737(1)(h), (3), (4)(a) (Insurance Code). Complicated tax legislation may have a similar effect, e.g., Int. Rev. Code of 1954, §401; Kaplan, Small Business: Its Place and Problem 68, 106, 174 (1948). As Professor Kaplan suggests, legislation of a manifestly interventionist type places a particularly heavy burden upon small and growing business. Hale, Monopoly and Mobilization: The Conflict Between Direct Controls and the Anti-Trust Laws, 47 Nw. U.L. Rev. 608, 614 (1952).

II. Indivisibility and Ignorance: The Grand Imperfections

We have scant data with respect to economies of scale.[23] We do not, for example, know precisely how large a steel manufacturing company should be to attain maximum of efficiency. Within limits, however, the effects of economies of scale are obvious. Hospitals are not built for a mere five beds: the minimum operating room, laboratories, kitchen, and the like can serve many more patients. A small town may well support one bank, one motion picture theater and one hotel, but not two. In manufacturing, indivisibility goes hand in hand with interchangeable parts and mass production;[24] it is reflected, too, in public utilities, wherein a "natural monopoly" is deemed to exist.[25] In distribution it fixes limits upon department store and specialty shop alike, with important repercussions upon manufacturers who need channels to reach consumers.[26] Indivisibility takes a slightly different form when risks are so great that no single investor is willing to incur them or when a customer insists upon multiple sources of supply so as to reduce the hazards created by fires, strikes and the like.[27] Economies of scale also have much to do with difficulty of entry into competition and hence upon innovation.[28] In short, as stated by Professor Knight,

It is universally recognized that effective competition calls for "fluidity," the perfect divisibility and mobility of all goods and services entering into exchange. The limited extent to which this assumption fits the facts of life sets limits to the "tendency" of actual competition, which in many cases nullify the principle. . . .[29]

Lack of knowledge is surely also an important imperfection and perhaps the underlying cause of some of those listed above. Upon the part of producers, ignorance of demand and costs is the most damaging.[30] A taxi driver sinks the savings of a lifetime in a chicken

[23] See §3.13; Smith, Survey of the Empirical Evidence on Economics of Scale, in Business Concentration and Price Policy 213, 229-230 (Stigler ed. 1955).

[24] E.g., Kilgore Committee, pt. 6, at 2529.

[25] E.g., id. at 2630-2631.

[26] E.g., Loehwing, Drive, Drive-Ur-Self, 35 Barron's No. 36, p. 3 (1955).

[27] E.g., Kilgore Committee, pt. 6, at 2535; Chamberlin, The Product As an Economic Variable, 67 Q.J. Econ. No. 1, p. 22 (1953).

[28] E.g., Chamberlin, Tomorrow's Factories, 34 Barron's No. 11, pp. 3, 25 (1954); Monsanto Chemical Co., 52d Ann. Rep. 19 (St. Louis, 1954); Kilgore Committee, pt. 6, at 2739.

[29] Knight, The Ethics of Competition 50 (1935).

[30] For a detailed analysis of the problem mentioned in the text, see Knight, Risk, Uncertainty and Profit 86, 198, 213, 225, 226, 230, 252, 253, 254, 260, 263 (1921). Many observers have recognized the problem, e.g., Pigou, The Economics of Welfare 356 (4th ed. 1932); Samuelson, Economics: An Introductory Analysis 38-39 (1948); Oxenfeldt, Industrial Pricing and Market Practices 123 (1951); Lyon and Abramson, The Economics of Open Price Systems 7 (1936). For examples of ignorance even upon the part of large business men, see The Scrap Men, 39 Fortune No. 1, pp. 80, 88 (1949); Knight, The Ethics of Competition 50 (1935).

farm; but his location is too distant from urban markets to permit profitable operation.[31] At great effort an inventor develops a method of fixing nitrogen only to find that the cost of manufacture by his process is prohibitive.

Consumer ignorance is a far more important cause of market imperfections.[32] Faced with a vast selection of goods and imprisoned by prejudice, habit and emotion, it is next to impossible for the average consumer to buy intelligently.[33] Family units are not sufficiently large and their requirements are too varied to allow a detailed investigation of all the goods purchased.[34] Exhaustive laboratory tests are necessary to determine the relative merits of goods offered in the market place.[35] Even governmental and industrial buyers are not always able to determine precisely which product is the most satisfactory.[36] As a result, correlation between price and quality is often loose.[37] Rainboots selling for eighty-eight cents a pair were found better than another brand of the same commodity retailing for $1.85.[38]

[31] Marketing research has now been refined to a point where it is able to give producers considerable help in determining the nature of consumer demand. Testing devices indicate the preferences of consumers for various types of products and the marketing methods which will be most effective. See Brown, Marketing and Distribution Research 16 (1949); Cowan, The Function of Management in Marketing, 209 Annals 71, 74 (1940). It appears likely, however, that marketing research is employed only by large and perhaps medium size firms. Small producers appear not to have utilized such techniques. Smith, Increasing Distribution Efficiency by Better Organized Research, 17 J. Marketing 233, 234 (1953); Oxenfeldt, Industrial Pricing and Market Practices 130 (1951); Mulvihill, Marketing Research for the Small Company, 16 J. Marketing 179 (1951). Cf. Knight, Risk, Uncertainty and Profit 254 (1921).

[32] Sorenson, The Consumer Movement 8-9 (1941).

[33] Mitchell, The Backward Art of Spending Money, in American Standards and Planes of Living 377, 380 (Eliot ed. 1931); Hoyt, Consumption in Our Society 78, 109 (1938); Haley, Value and Distribution, in A Survey of Contemporary Economics 1, 6 (Ellis ed. 1948); Alderson, The Consumer Market — Income, Expenditure and Saving, 209 Annals 1 (1940).

[34] Mitchell, The Backward Art of Spending Money, in American Standards and Planes of Living 377, 379 (Eliot ed. 1931); Edwards, Competition in Selling Consumer Goods, in Social Meaning of Legal Concepts No. 4, pp. 353, 359 (Cahn ed. 1952); Robinson and Nugent, Regulation of the Small Loan Business 89 (1935) (old-time loan sharks operated in secrecy). Compare Strodtbeck and Sussman, Of Time, the City and the "One-Year Guaranty," 61 Am. J. Sociol. 602 (1956).

[35] Nelson and Keim, Price Behavior and Business Policy 60 (TNEC Monograph No. 1, 1941); cf. Gordon, Economics for Consumers 8, 12, 221 (2d ed. 1944). Just as names are convenient to identify persons, uniform labels for commodities are important to the exercise of rational choice by consumers. See Kaidanovsky, Consumer Standards 141, 339 (TNEC Monograph No. 24, 1941).

[36] Id. at 167. Cf. Nelson and Keim, Price Behavior and Business Policy 68 (TNEC Monograph No. 1, 1941).

[37] Knight, The Economic Organization 69 (1951); Chase and Schlink, Consumers in Wonderland, in American Standards and Planes of Living 804, 806 (Eliot ed. 1931); Nelson and Keim, Price Behavior and Business Policy 78 (TNEC Monograph No. 1, 1941); Oxenfeld, Consumer Knowledge: Its Measurement and Extent, 32 Rev. Econ. & Stat. 300 (1950); Stewart and Dewhurst, Does Distribution Cost Too Much? 310 (1939); TNEC Hearings, pt. 8, at 3322.

[38] Rainboots for Women, 30 Consumers' Research Bull. 17, 18 (Aug. 1952). See also The New Carpets, 30 id. 13, 16, 17 (Sept. 1952); Vacuum Cleaners, 30 id. 5,

Product differentiation and the difficulty of evaluating credit, delivery and installation services render it almost impossible for the domestic consumer to achieve rational results in buying.[39]

Advertising is frequently seen as an important cause of consumer ignorance and hence of imperfections in the market place.[40] Advertising assists in the differentiation of otherwise identical commodities and thus permits sellers to discriminate among groups of buyers. Identical goods are sold to different groups at widely varying prices when advertised under different trade-marks.[41] So heavy have been the expenditures for advertising of cigarettes and tooth paste and so great is the attachment of consumers to the established brands[42] that it has become more difficult and expensive for new producers to enter those fields.[43] Finally, it is urged that advertising, when not

---

8-9 (Nov. 1952); 1952 Automobiles, 29 id. 5, 6 (June, 1952); TNEC Hearings, pt. 8, at 3331; Borden, The Economic Effects of Advertising 305 (1942). Indeed, observers have often noted that consumers frequently take price as an index of quality: the higher the price, the better the quality. Corey, Fair Trade Pricing: A Reappraisal, 30 Harv. Bus. Rev. No. 5, 47, 52 (1952); cf. Gordon, Economics for Consumers 13 (2d ed. 1944); cf. Robinson, The Economics of Imperfect Competition 89 (1936). Price reductions are sometimes avoided for fear that buyers, ignorant of quality, will assume a deterioration has taken place in manufacture. Edwards, Competition in Selling Consumer Goods, in Social Meaning of Legal Concepts No. 4, pp. 353, 361 (Cahn ed. 1952).

[39] Cf. Mack, Economics of Consumption, in A Survey of Contemporary Economics 61 (Haley ed. 1952); Oxenfeldt, Consumer Knowledge: Its Measurement and Extent, 32 Rev. Econ. & Stat. 300, 313 (1950). However, it has proven difficult or impossible to determine the quantitative importance of the problem. Ibid. Consumer ignorance can have broad effects upon the economy generally. It raises questions as to the whole doctrine of consumer sovereignty. See id. at 312, 313; Hildebrand, Consumer Sovereignty in Modern Times, 41 Am. Econ. Rev. 19, 21 (Supp. 1951) (Proceedings American Economic Assn.); Clark, An Appraisal of Certain Criticisms of Advertising, 15 id. 5, 13 (Supp. 1925) (Proceedings American Economic Assn.); Gordon, Economics for Consumers 7, 13 (2d ed. 1944). As to the relationship between consumer ignorance and standardization suggested in the text, see Wilcox, Competition and Monopoly in American Industry 2 (TNEC Monograph No. 21, 1940); Montgomery, Consumer Standards and Marketing, 209 Annals 141, 143 (1940); Edwards, Maintaining Competition 33 (1949); TNEC Hearings, pt. 8, at 3346.

[40] Knight, Risk, Uncertainty and Profit 185 (1921); Nelson and Keim, Price Behavior and Business Policy 55 (TNEC Monograph No. 1, 1941); Brown, Advertising and the Public Interest, 57 Yale L.J. 1165, 1171, 1173 (1948); Borden, The Economic Effects of Advertising 21, 322 (1942).

[41] See Nelson and Keim, Price Behavior and Business Policy 80 (TNEC Monograph No. 1, 1941); Timberg, Trade-Marks, Monopoly and the Restraint of Competition, 14 Law & Contemp. Prob. 323, 341 (1949); Celler Committee I, ser. 12, at 462. But cf. Knight, Risk, Uncertainty and Profit 262 (1921). From time to time the courts have had to determine whether a brand designation distinguished otherwise identical commodities. §§3.4, 3.5 supra.

[42] Pigou, The Economics of Welfare 356 (4th ed. 1932); Oxenfeldt, Industrial Pricing and Market Practices 140 (1951); Gordon, Economics for Consumers 253 (2d ed. 1944).

[43] TNEC Hearings, pt. 8, at 3399. As to the existence of monopolistic profits in such situations, compare Nelson and Keim, Price Behavior and Business Policy 81 (TNEC Monograph No. 1, 1941) with Borden, The Economic Effects of Advertising 175, 176 (1942). As stated in the text, heavy advertising expenditures

downright dishonest and misleading,[44] appeals to the emotions[45] more than the intellect and hence contributes to the irrationality of consumer behavior.[46] If the seller of a face cream does not promise to rejuvenate beauties faded with the passage of years, he may nevertheless murmur sweet nothings in their ears until his product is on their faces.[47]

can raise barriers to entry into competition. Stewart and Dewhurst, Does Distribution Cost Too Much? 227 (1939); Oxenfeldt, Industrial Pricing and Market Practices 283 (1951); Stocking and Watkins, Monopoly and Free Enterprise 75, 164 (1951); Simons, Economic Policy for a Free Society 71, 72 (1948); Borden, The Economic Effects of Advertising 859 (1942). Such advertising may also force competitors into defensive and retaliatory measures of the same type. Oxenfeldt, Industrial Pricing and Market Practices 224 (1951). Note, for example, the following comment appearing in an annual report: "Quality of product, although all important, is only a starting point. Unless the consumer is repeatedly convinced through advertising and merchandising, as well as by experience, that the Company's products offer the best value, sales volume will drop." The Best Foods, Inc., Ann. Rep. 5 (New York City, 1951). It is probably true, however, that the foregoing effects of advertising operate only in the short run. Borden, The Economic Effects of Advertising 860 (1942).

44 Compare Borden, id. at 808 (1942).

45 Borden, id. at 604 (1942); Oxenfeldt, Industrial Pricing and Market Practices 205 (1951); Gordon, Economics for Consumers 182-183 (2d ed. 1944).

46 It is argued that advertising is merely persuasive and not informative and that trade-marks are not a scientific mechanism to identify product quality. Clark, An Appraisal of Certain Criticisms of Advertising, 15 Am. Econ. Rev. 5 (Supp. 1925) (Proceedings American Economic Assn.); Robinson, The Economics of Imperfect Competition 90 (1936); Nourse, Price Making in a Democracy 248 (1944); Wilcox, Brand Names, Quality and Price, 173 Annals 80, 82 (1934). Advertising is often designed merely to catch the attention of consumers so that they may receive a message of persuasion. Thus a cigarette manufacturer may employ well-known theatrical performers for its radio broadcasts simply to assure a large audience for its commercial. See, e.g., P. Lorillard Co., 1950 Ann. Rep. 13 et seq. (New York City).

47 See Charles of the Ritz Distributors Corp. v. FTC, 143 F.2d 676 (2d Cir. 1944). It is sometimes argued that advertising can actually create demand. E.g., Shove, The Imperfection of the Market, 43 Econ. J. 113, 124 (1933). Such a view would compel sweeping revision of the whole theory of consumer sovereignty. Stocking, Modern Advertising and Economic Theory, 21 Am. Econ. Rev. 43, 44, 50, 53 (1931). But see Hotchkiss, An Economic Defense of Advertising, 15 Am. Econ. Rev. 14-6 (Supp. 1925) (Proceedings American Economic Assn.). Similarly, it is sometimes urged that advertising can shift consumer demand from one brand or product to another. E.g., Mack, Economics of Consumption, in A Survey of Contemporary Economics 59 (Haley ed. 1952). It is often urged that such advertising is merely persuasive and hence wasteful in character. Brown, Advertising and the Public Interest, 57 Yale L.J. 1165, 1169 (1948); Simons, Economic Policy for a Free Society 71 (1948). But see Borden, The Economic Effects of Advertising 165, 168, 313 (1942). It was reported, for example, that parent-teacher associations had induced school boards to remove candy vending machines from schoolhouses. So successful had the campaign been that only 5 per cent of the schools had such machines as against 80 per cent before the campaign started. Candy distributors proposed a campaign to remedy the situation by advertising candy as a food contributing to health and good spirits. Opportunities and Dangers Ahead, 10 Southern Candy Jobber 10, 13 (Dec. 1951). Whether advertising can create demand or not, it is often credited with an ability to influence demand and much money is spent in reliance on such beliefs. Borden, The Economic Effects of Advertising 337, 380 (1942); The Lambert Co., 1950 Ann. Rep. 2 (Jersey City, 1951); Gulf Presents a New TV Show, 10 Orange Disc 21, 22 (Sept.-Oct. 1952).

On the other hand, advertising and trade-marks serve as devices to remove imperfections in that they inform buyers of the existence of products and their prices.[48] Classified advertising in newspapers surely constitutes an important element looking to the reduction of consumer ignorance. Mail order catalogs supply a host of information concerning products, their quality and prices.[49] Trade-marks identify goods by reference to standards of quality which have been tested and approved by consumers.[50] Newly developed products are quickly brought to the attention of consumers through advertising[51] and thus achieve a volume of sales which permits mass production and hence low prices far more rapidly than would otherwise be possible.[52]

[48] Knight, Risk, Uncertainty and Profit 261 (1921); Gordon, Economics for Consumers 69, 155, 156, 165 (2d ed. 1944); Hotchkiss, An Economic Defense of Advertising, 15 Am. Econ. Rev. 15, 17 (Supp. 1925) (Proceedings American Economic Assn.); Borden, The Economic Effects of Advertising 27, 169, 415 (1942); Stocking and Watkins, Monopoly and Free Enterprise 72, 73 (1951); Brown, Advertising and the Public Interest, 57 Yale L.J. 1165, 1168 (1948). How salesmen overcome inertia, as well as ignorance, is described in $1,000,000 A Year Insurance Men, 40 Fortune No. 1, pp. 79, 81 (1949); Sales People Aren't Selling, 40 id. 3, p. 78 (1949).

[49] Gordon, Economics for Consumers 154 (2d ed. 1944); Borden, The Economic Effects of Advertising 668 (1942). Note the important role played by display advertisements inserted in newspapers by department stores and chain groceries. TNEC Hearings, pt. 8, at 3290.

[50] Hotchkiss, An Economic Defense of Advertising, 15 Am. Econ. Rev. 14, 21 (Supp. 1925) (Proceedings American Economic Assn.); Auerbach, Quality Standards, Informative Labeling, and Grade Labeling as Guides to Consumer Buying, 14 Law & Contemp. Prob. 362, 381 (1949); Wilcox, Brand Names, Quality and Price, 173 Annals 80, 83 (1934); Borden, The Economic Effects of Advertising 23, 25 (1942); TNEC Hearings pt. 8, at 3442. But see id. at 3325; Robinson, The Economics of Imperfect Competition 89 (1933); Borden, The Economic Effects of Advertising 25 (1942). Note the following comment by a well-known proponent of protection for consumers: "It isn't possible to draw sweeping conclusions that a well known brand is necessarily the consumer's guarantee of a high-quality product. Sometimes it is an important safeguard to assure at least reasonable quality, but it all depends on the sense of public responsibility of the company's management, and not at all on the volume or character of its advertising." Schlink, Off the Editor's Chest, 30 Consumers' Research Bull. 2, 18 (Oct. 1952).

[51] Hotchkiss, An Economic Defense of Advertising, 15 Am. Econ. Rev. 14, 20 (Supp. 1925) (Proceedings American Economic Assn.); Brown, Advertising and the Public Interest, 57 Yale L.J. 1165, 1177 (1948); Stocking and Watkins, Monopoly and Free Enterprise 164 (1951); Gordon, Economics for Consumers 155 (2d ed. 1944); Oxenfeldt, Industrial Pricing and Market Practices 230 (1951). But see the factors of jealousy and greed mentioned in Vaile, Consumption, The End Result of Marketing, 209 Annals 14, 18 (1940). All that is new does not glitter. See, e.g., No Cure-All for Wet Basements, 30 Consumers' Research Bull. 28 (July 1952).

[52] Clark, An Appraisal of Certain Criticisms of Advertising, 15 Am. Econ. Rev. 5, 7 (Supp. 1925) (Proceedings American Economic Assn.); Borden, The Economic Effects of Advertising 173, 409, 436, 502 (1942); What's the Matter with American Salesmanship? 40 Fortune No. 3, pp. 67, 68 (1949); Tosdal, The Advertising and Selling Process, 209 Annals 62, 66 (1940); Gordon, Economics for Consumers 165 (2d ed. 1944). Query whether advertising has an effect upon the number of producers in an industry. Clark, An Appraisal of Certain Criticisms of Advertising, 15 Am. Econ. Rev. 5, 9 (Supp. 1925) (Proceedings American Economic Assn.); TNEC Hearings, pt. 8, at 3298; §6.26 supra.

Without advertising, many American women might still be deprived of a Toni permanent.[53]

Many private weapons in addition to advertising are employed in the struggle against ignorance. Producers commonly employ "market research" as a device to ascertain the rough outlines of consumer demand.[54] Mass merchandisers seek constantly to inform themselves as to product quality and market conditions.[55] Both sellers and buyers are aided in securing knowledge of market conditions by employment agencies, real estate brokers, trade journals and similar services.[56] Trade associations and professional societies engage in standardization and testing activities.[57] Specialized services exist to advise domestic consumers of the relative merits of products offered for consumption in the home.[58] Because, however, the tastes and subjective values of consumers vary widely, the services rendered by organizations such as Consumers' Research fall considerably short of removing all the ignorance and irrationality with which purchasers are afflicted.[59]

[53] It is sometimes suggested that advertising might be able to smooth out hourly, daily, seasonal or longer fluctuations in business volume. Advertising, for example, might induce housewives to buy their groceries earlier in the week when stores are not operating at capacity levels. Shifts in Advertising Sought for Weekly "Second Food Day," 20 Am. Baker 50 (Jan. 1952). See What's the Matter with American Salesmanship? 40 Fortune No. 3, pp. 67, 69 (1949). Query whether such an effect should be deemed the removal of an imperfection or an effort to alter demand.

[54] Jeuck, Marketing Research — Milestone or Millstone? 17 J. Marketing 381 (1953); Borden, The Economic Effects of Advertising 127 (1942).

[55] Stocking and Watkins, Monopoly and Free Enterprise 316 (1951); White, Marketing Research, 209 Annals 183, 185 (1940); Kaidanovsky, Consumer Standards 306, 311 (TNEC Monograph No. 24, 1941). But see id. at 323. Even relatively small retailers sometimes approach market studies. A highly amusing account of the efforts of a dealer in infants' wear to secure the names of potential customers before its competitors will be found in Watson, "Crib of the Month" Club Plan Rocks Miami, 6 Juvenile Merchandising 60 (Jan. 1952).

[56] Lyon, and others, Government and Economic Life 216n (1939); Our Market Opinion, The Cheese Reporter 5 (Jan. 18, 1952); Lampson, Fraser & Huth, Inc., March Sapphire Sale, 18 Fur. J. 9 (March-April 1952); Loeser, The Over-the-Counter Securities Market, cc. 1-4 (1940); Wexman, Financial Advice and Guidance for Small Business, 11 Law & Contemp. Prob. 334, 338 (1945); Kaplan, Small Business: Its Place and Problems 119 (1948). Even managers of steel mills find it advantageous to utilize the services of brokers in buying scrap iron. The Scrap Men, 39 Fortune No. 1, pp. 86, 88 (1949).

[57] Gordon, Economics for Consumers 517, 519 (2d ed. 1944); Kaidanovsky, Consumer Standards 211 (TNEC Monograph No. 24, 1941). But see TNEC Hearings, pt. 8, at 3380 (complaint that "Good Housekeeping" seal of approval granted too liberally).

[58] Kaidanovsky, Consumer Standards 312 (TNEC Monograph No. 24, 1941); Sorenson, The Consumer Movement 33 (1941). An example of significant service rendered by such organizations in bringing new products to the attention of consumers is found in Plastic Dishes, 30 Consumers' Research Bull. 10 (July 1952). Some observers have held high hopes for consumer advisory services, e.g., Simons, Economic Policy for a Free Society 73, 85 (1948); Stewart and Dewhurst, Does Distribution Cost Too Much? 350, 352 (1939); Oxenfeldt, Consumer Knowledge: Its Measurement and Extent, 32 Rev. Econ. & Stat. 300, 306, 312, 313 (1950).

[59] Mitchell, The Backward Art of Spending Money, in American Standards and Planes of Living 377, 384 (Eliot ed. 1931); Montgomery, Consumer Standards and Marketing, 209 Annals 141, 142 (1950); Lyon, and others, Government and Economic

Hence private efforts have not been wholly successful in overcoming such frictions.[60]

III. Statutory Efforts to Reduce Imperfections

Much governmental activity has been directed at the reduction of frictions in the market place.[61] Establishment of uniform weights and measures by statute has contributed immensely to the smooth flow of commerce.[62] Many agencies and particularly those of the federal government, such as the Departments of Agriculture and Commerce, are constantly engaged in the collection and dissemination of information concerning crops, minerals, finished products and their prices.[63] The whole census of manufactures can be regarded as an

---

Life 235 (1939); Borden, The Economic Effects of Advertising 646 (1942); Beem, Consumer-Financed Testing and Rating Agencies, 16 J. Marketing 272, 274, 278 (1952). In part the difficulty arises from an attempt to determine which commodity is "best" for everyone and hence, in some degree, to limit consumer sovereignty. But see Clark, An Appraisal of Certain Criticisms of Advertising, 15 Am. Econ. Rev. 5, 11 (Supp. 1925) (Proceedings American Economic Assn.); Duesenberry, Income, Saving and the Theory of Consumer Behavior 1 (1949). Attempts to avoid the standardization inherent in an effort to specify which commodity is "best" encounter the obstacle of consumer failure to understand the technical problems involved. Beem, Consumer-Financed Testing and Rating Agencies, 16 J. Marketing 272, 280 (1952); Kaidanovsky, Consumer Standards 351 (TNEC Monograph No. 24, 1941). Take, for example, Administrator, Production and Marketing Division, U.S. Dept. of Agriculture, U.S. Standards, Fruit Preserves, 17 Fed. Reg. 11,683 (1952). In §52.30.333(f)(4) of that Regulation, the Administrator was attempting to specify grades of jams. His method was to weigh various factors. The "flavor" was given a weight of 40 per cent. In the discussion of flavor, however, all the Administrator could say was that it should be "good" and "characteristic" of the kind of fruit involved.

[60] It has sometimes been urged that consumers be organized for political purposes into pressure groups. Gordon, Economics for Consumers 291, 397, 518, 592 (2d ed. 1944). On the other hand, it appears that agencies purportedly representing the interest of consumers have sometimes held other objectives. Such political objectives have probably hindered the agencies in the accomplishment of their ostensible purposes. Sorenson, The Consumer Movement 127, 226 (1941); TNEC Hearings, pt. 8, at 3381 et seq.

[61] Interventionist measures adopted by government should, of course, be distinguished from activity designed to reduce imperfections. Some legislation may fall on the border line. Take, for example, the prescription of minimum wages and the prohibition of usury. 52 Stat. 1062 (1938), 29 U.S.C. §206 (1946), as amended, 63 Stat. 912 (1949), 29 U.S.C. §206 (Supp. 1952); Illinois Act to revise the law in relation to the rate of interest, Ill. Rev. Stat. c. 74, §1 (1957). If free-market prices are above the minima prescribed by the wage legislation or below the rates fixed by the usury statutes, then governmental action merely removes imperfections in that it protects ignorant workers and borrowers who are unfamiliar with market values.

[62] Lyon, and others, Government and Economic Life 217 (1939); Kaidanovsky, Consumer Standards 20 (TNEC Monograph No. 24, 1941). Similarly, our whole system of commercial law has a like purpose.

[63] Lyon, and others, Government and Economic Life 240, 243, 245 (1939); Gordon, Economics for Consumers 570 (2d ed. 1944).

effort to improve our knowledge of industry and hence to reduce imperfections arising out of ignorance.   In the labor field, establishment of an employment service on a national basis at public expense reflects a congressional desire to assist both employers and employees through the rapid dissemination of information concerning the availability of jobs and workers.[64]

Misrepresentations, of course, are a prime source of ignorance in the market place.   Although the rule of caveat emptor may still hold some sway, the common law has always protected buyers against active deceit.[65]   In recent years statutory regulation, both state and federal, has gone far to protect buyers against positive misstatements.   Measures to protect the public against adulterated and misbranded foods have long enjoyed popularity and recent amendments have made those measures more effective.[66]   Regulation has not been limited, however, to situations in which public health and safety are affected.   Several federal statutes require affirmative labeling of goods in the market place.   The names which can be applied to furs, for example, are now controlled under statutory authority.[67]   In the sale of securities governmental requirements are particularly strict and detailed.   "Blue Sky" legislation compels sellers of stocks and bonds to make full disclosure of all pertinent facts to their customers.[68]

[64] 48 Stat. 114, 29 U.S.C. §49(b) (1946) (Federal Employment Service).   But see Simons, Economic Policy for a Free Society 61 (1948); Lyon, and others, Government and Economic Life 241 (1939).   Particular attention has been devoted to supplying information to small business.   H.R. Rep. No. 2513, 82d Cong., 2d Sess. 31 (1952) (Select Committee on Small Business, Final Report); 56 Stat. 351 (1942), 50 U.S.C. §1101 (1946) (small business mobilization).   But see 53 Stat. 1435 (1939), 44 U.S.C. §§301 et seq. (1946), as amended, 63 Stat. 381 (1949), 44 U.S.C.A. §§301 et seq. (Supp. 1952); 1 Sharfman, The Interstate Commerce Commission 22, 284 (1931) (requirement that railroad tariffs be published).

[65] Kittelle and Campbell, Power of the Federal Trade Commission to Require Informative Labeling of Textiles, 20 B.U.L. Rev. 23, 29 (1940); 3 Restatement of Torts §525.
The whole law of fraud is a recognition of the desirability of suppressing intentional consumer ignorance.

[66] Illinois, An Act to Prevent Untrue, Deceptive or Fraudulent Advertising, Ill. Rev. Stat., c. 38, §249a (1957); 34 Stat. 1260 (1907), 21 U.S.C. §71 (1946) (meat inspection); 61 Stat. 163 (1947), 7 U.S.C. §135 (Supp. 1952) (Federal Insecticide, Fungicide and Rodenticide Act); 52 Stat. 1040 (1938), 21 U.S.C. §§301 et seq. (1946) (Federal Food, Drug and Cosmetic Act); Handler, The Control of False Advertising under the Wheeler-Lea Act, 6 Law & Contemp. Prob. 91 (1939); Legis., The Federal Trade Commission Act of 1938, 39 Colum. L. Rev. 259, 263 (1939); Lindhahl, The Federal Trade Commission Act as Amended in 1938, 47 J. Pol. Econ. 497 (1939). But see Schlink, What Government Does and Might Do for the Consumer, 173 Annals 125, 127, 135, 137 (1934).

[67] 65 Stat. 175 (1951), 15 U.S.C.A. §69 (Supp. 1952) (Fur Products Labeling Act); 54 Stat. 1128 (1940), 15 U.S.C. §68 (1946) (Wool Products Labeling Act); 49 Stat. 977 (1935), 27 U.S.C. §201 (1946) (Federal Alcohol Administration Act); Kaidanovsky, Consumer Standards 94, 96, 158, 235 (TNEC Monograph No. 24, 1941).   Activities of the National Bureau of Standards in cooperation with trade associations to encourage use of more informative labeling are described in Briggs, Services of the National Bureau of Standards to Consumers, 173 Annals 153, 156 (1934).

[68] Note also the legislation compelling disclosure in the solicitation of proxies

It has often been urged that governmental action should go far beyond mere prohibitions of misrepresentation. As indicated above, the standardization of commodities is necessary for them to achieve that homogeneous character requisite for both pure and perfect competition. Buyers cannot act rationally if they do not identify goods by precise quality standards. Therefore it has been urged that statutes should authorize the standardization and "grade labeling" of all commodities.[69] Standardization and grading activities, however, are subject to several objections. Complicated machines, for example, reflect a series of compromises among various engineering aims and it would be difficult to grade them in terms which would be significant and meaningful to all buyers.[70] Similarly, standardization could be carried so far as to limit consumer choice unduly and hence to defeat the very consumer sovereignty which a free-market economy seeks to achieve.[71] Again, standardization and grading activities might be subject to political pressures of a monopolistic character and for that reason — if for no other — might tend to curb innovation and stultify the economy.[72] Nevertheless, we find a number of statutes which do require governmental action looking to the standardization and grading of commodities. Most of them fall in the field of agriculture and were designed primarily for the promotion of producers' interests.[73] The

---

and the like. 15 U.S.C. §78 (1946) (Securities Exchange Act of 1934); Loss, Securities Regulation 492, 523 (1951). Similarly, attempts have been made to compel issuers of securities to sell them on a basis of competitive bidding. Id. at 264.

[69] Sen. Doc. No. 35, 77th Cong., 1st Sess. 447 (1941); Hoyt, Consumption in our Society 110 (1938); Agnew, The Movement for Standards for Consumer Goods, 173 Annals 60 (1934); Auerbach, Quality Standards, Informative Labeling, and Grade Labeling as Guides to Consumer Buying, 14 Law & Contemp. Prob. 362, 366 (1949). Earlier literature is summarized in Kaidanovsky, Consumer Standards 355, 361 (TNEC Monograph No. 24, 1941).

[70] Stocking and Watkins, Monopoly and Free Enterprise 509, 510 (1951); Watkins, Public Regulation of Competitive Practices in Business Enterprise 132 (National Industrial Conference Board, 3d ed. 1940).

[71] Stocking and Watkins, Monopoly and Free Enterprise 508 (1951); Watkins, Public Regulation of Competitive Practices in Business Enterprise 124 (National Industrial Conference Board, 3d ed. 1940). But see Mack, Clothing and Household Goods for Consumers, 173 Annals 35, 42 (1934); Lyon, and others, Government and Economic Life 236 (1939).

[72] Note, for example, the authoritarian overtone in Sorenson, The Consumer Movement 24 (1941). Congressional reaction to OPA efforts looking to the standardization of commodities is illustrative of such fears. Auerbach, Quality Standards, Informative Labeling, and Grade Labeling as Guides to Consumer Buying, 14 Law & Contemp. Prob. 362, 374 (1949).

[73] See, e.g., Int. Rev. Code of 1954, §4854; 42 Stat. 1517 (1923), 7 U.S.C. §§52, 56 and 57 (1946) (United States Cotton Standards Act); 37 Stat. 250 (1912), 21 U.S.C. §20 (1946) (an act to establish a standard barrel and a standard grade for apples); 42 Stat. 1435 (1923), 7 U.S.C. §93 (1946) (Naval Stores Act); 39 Stat. 482, 483 (1916), 7 U.S.C. §§74, 76 (1946) (United States Grain Standards Act); Lyon, and others, Government and Economic Life 227, 230 (1939). An example of a recently promulgated standard will be found in Administrator, Production and Marketing Division, U.S. Dept. of Agriculture, U.S. Standards, Cauliflower, 17 Fed. Reg. 11,137 (1952). A detailed account of federal activity in the field of standard-

present Food, Drug and Cosmetic Act,[74] however, has a broader purpose and it has been applied so as to prohibit the production and sale of wholesome and honestly labeled food. Such utilization of the statute was approved by the Supreme Court on the express ground that the intent of the Congress was to protect consumers against a confusing variety of products through exercise of a standardization power. In the case referred to, the Quaker Oats Company was prevented from marketing a type of farina enriched with certain vitamins. The Quaker product was unacceptable because it was neither plain farina nor enriched with all the vitamins prescribed in the governmental standard for "enriched farina." [75] Whether such statutory restrictions are desirable may be open to debate. Their existence does indicate a congressional intent to reduce the imperfection of ignorance through administrative standardization.

IV. Effects upon Interpretation of the Antitrust Statutes

Antitrust decisions have always taken account of market imperfections.[76] There has, however, been little if any explicit discussion of such frictions in antitrust opinions. It is thus possible that the role of imperfections has not received due recognition: judicial zeal to extirpate "impurities" may have been so powerful as to blind the courts to the desirability of curbing market frictions. No doubt such frictions are present in every situation from which an antitrust case arises. In subsequent paragraphs we shall only consider decisions in which the role of imperfections has been most obvious.[77]

Trade Commission activities against fraud. There has been much dissatisfaction with the performance of the Federal Trade Commis-

---

ization will be found in Kaidanovsky, Consumer Standards 14, 23, 77, 93, 97, 111, 197 (TNEC Monograph No. 24, 1941).

[74] 52 Stat. 1040 et seq. (1938), 21 U.S.C. §§301, 401, 403(h)(1) (1946) (Federal Food, Drug and Cosmetic Act).

[75] Federal Security Administrator v. Quaker Oats Co., 318 U.S. 218, 226, 230, 231 (1943).

Is it correct to say that the task (role) of the entrepreneur is to minimize imperfections? to reduce ignorance? to cut down indivisibility (find smallest investment which will be productive)? to abolish inertia? to reduce immobility? Such may be the result, but it may in the short run be to his advantage to confuse the consumer by advertising and to promote inertia when he is established. He may start with the least amount of capital, but will probably increase his capital as a means of getting bigger or staying bigger. This is more the role of the organized market than of individual producers.

[76] But see Oppenheim, Federal Antitrust Legislation: Guideposts to a Revised National Antitrust Policy, 50 Mich. L. Rev. 1139, 1151, 1154 (1952).

[77] Many other examples could be cited in which imperfections have played a role, e.g., United States v. United Shoe Machinery Corp., 110 F. Supp. 295, 336 (D. Mass. 1953); 2 Restatement of Contracts §516(a). Indeed, the whole problem of entry into competition may be profoundly affected by the imperfections of inertia and ignorance. See Wright, Some Pitfalls of Economic Theory as a Guide to the Law of Competition, 37 Va. L. Rev. 1083 (1951).

sion.[78] As many observers have noted, the Commission was expected to take vigorous action against monopoly but has devoted most of its attention to the suppression of misrepresentations in trade. That shift in emphasis has been the subject of many biting comments. Mr. Henderson rebuked the Commission for wasting time "upon petty squabbles and dishonesties." [79] Even so sophisticated a jurist as Mr. Justice Brandeis did not believe that the Federal Trade Commission Act was designed directly to protect consumers.[80] A statutory amendment in 1938 [81] was required before the courts recognized that misrepresentations may be harmful even though no competitor is directly affected.[82] Sophisticated sneers greeted the opinion in the *Standard Education Society* case,[83] in which one court finally permitted the Commission to pursue a stringent antifraud policy. Most lawyers preferred the opinion of Judge Learned Hand in the court below and agreed that the Commission's "trivial niceties" were "too impalpable for practical affairs." [84]

[78] The organic statute is the Federal Trade Commission Act, 15 U.S.C. §41 (1946). Section 45(a), as amended, provides: "Unfair methods of competition in commerce, and unfair or deceptive acts or practices in commerce, are declared unlawful."

[79] Henderson, The Federal Trade Commission 339 (1925). See Watkins, An Appraisal of the Work of the Federal Trade Commission, 32 Colum. L. Rev. 272, 277 (1932); Watkins, Public Regulation of Competitive Practices in Business Enterprise 125 (National Industrial Conference Board, 3d ed. 1940); Committee on Independent Regulatory Commissions, Report to the Commission on Organization of the Executive Branch of the Government 119, 120 (1949); Stocking and Watkins, Monopoly and Free Enterprise 548 n.7 (1951); H.R. Rep. No. 2513, 82d Cong., 1st Sess. 278 (1952).

[80] FTC v. Klesner, 280 U.S. 19, 27, 28 (1929). Cf. FTC v. Gratz, 253 U.S. 421, 427 (1920); American Washboard Co. v. Saginaw Manufacturing Co., 103 Fed. 281, 284, 285 (6th Cir. 1900); Allen B. Wrisley Co. v. FTC, 113 F.2d 437, 442 (7th Cir. 1940). See Handler, The Jurisdiction of the Federal Trade Commission over False Advertising, 31 Colum. L. Rev. 527, 529, 533 (1931); Handler, Unfair Competition and the Federal Trade Commission, 8 Geo. Wash. L. Rev. 399, 401 (1940).

[81] The 1938 amendment to the Federal Trade Commission Act, 52 Stat. 111.

[82] Scientific Manufacturing Co. v. FTC, 124 F.2d 640, 643 (3d Cir. 1941); Pep Boys v. FTC, 122 F.2d 158, 160 (3d Cir. 1941). Compare FTC v. Standard Education Society, 302 U.S. 112, 116 (1937). See Handler, The Control of False Advertising under the Wheeler-Lea Act, 6 Law & Contemp. Prob. 91, 96 (1939); Handler, Unfair Competition and the Federal Trade Commission, 8 Geo. Wash. L. Rev. 399, 404 (1940); Kittelle and Campbell, Power of the Federal Trade Commission to Require Informative Labeling of Textiles, 20 B.U.L. Rev. 23, 27 (1940); Legis., The Federal Trade Commission Act of 1938, 39 Colum. L. Rev. 259, 261, 262 (1939).

[83] FTC v. Standard Education Society, 302 U.S. 112 (1937). Cf. (earlier cases) FTC v. R. F. Keppel and Bro., Inc., 291 U.S. 304 (1934); FTC v. Algoma Lumber Co., 291 U.S. 67, 81 (1934). *Accord* (later cases): Book-of-the-Month Club, Inc. v. FTC, 202 F.2d 486 (2d Cir. 1953); Rothschild v. FTC, 200 F.2d 39 (7th Cir. 1952); R. J. Reynolds Tobacco Co. v. FTC, 192 F.2d 535 (7th Cir. 1951); P. Lorillard Co. v. FTC, 186 F.2d 52 (4th Cir. 1950); Carlay Co. v. FTC, 153 F.2 493 (7th Cir. 1946); Gulf Oil Corp. v. FTC, 150 F.2d 106 (5th Cir. 1945); Charles of the Ritz Distributors Corp. v. FTC, 143 F.2d 676, 679 (2d Cir. 1944); Moretrench Corp. v. FTC, 127 F.2d 792, 795 (2d Cir. 1942); Ford Motor Co. v. FTC, 120 F.2d 175, 182 (6th Cir. 1941).

[84] FTC v. Standard Education Society, 86 F.2d 692, 696 (2d Cir. 1936). See Allen B. Wrisley Co. v. FTC, 113 F.2d 437, 440 (7th Cir. 1940). See also Watkins, Public

It may be conceded that the Commission could easily push its powers too far. Elimination of all puffing and a requirement of absolute truth in advertising could result in a bureaucratic paternalism of dangerous proportions.[85] Any such program would probably exceed the needs of the market place. If consumer ignorance, however, contributes as greatly to market imperfections as this study indicates, the position of the Federal Trade Commission may be more rational than heretofore supposed. Common law remedies are often inadequate,[86] and without expressing a view as to any particular decision, we may well find ourselves sympathetic to the position taken by the Commission.[87] Similarly, there may be more justification than has heretofore been recognized for the affirmative labeling requirements contained in various trade practice conference rules of the Commission. Those advisory interpretations of the Commission's organic act have often been regarded as ultra vires to the extent that they imposed an affirmative duty upon sellers of labeling goods.[88] For reasons expressed above, we may well hesitate to endow the Commission with broad powers to standardize goods.[89] To the extent that such regula-

---

Regulation of Competitive Practices in Business Enterprise 152 (National Industrial Conference Board, 3d ed. 1940).

[85] Watkins, Public Regulation of Competitive Practices in Business Enterprise 141, 146 (National Industrial Conference Board, 3d ed. 1940). See Borden, The Economic Effects of Advertising 760, 774 (1942); Gordon, Economics for Consumers 198 (2d ed. 1944).

[86] Watkins, An Appraisal of the Work of the Federal Trade Commission, 32 Colum. L. Rev. 272, 276 (1932); Lyon, and others, Government and Economic Life 318 (1939).

[87] Professor Handler is one of the few experts in the field who has vigorously approved the Commission's activities in the area of misrepresentation. Handler, The Control of False Advertising Under the Wheeler-Lea Act, 6 Law & Contemp. Prob. 91, 98 (1939); Handler, Unfair Competition and the Federal Trade Commission, 8 Geo. Wash. L. Rev. 399, 405, 406, 418, 420 (1940). To the same general effect see Stocking and Watkins, Monopoly and Free Enterprise 351 (1951); Knight, Risk, Uncertainty and Profit 78 (1921); Miller, Unfair Competition 115 (1941). It should be recorded, however, that few voices were raised in support of the Commission's position at the University of Chicago's antitrust seminar on June 17, 1953.

[88] Atty. Gen. Comm. Ad. Proc., FTC, Sen. Doc. No. 186, pt. 6, 76th Cong., 3d Sess. 31 (1940); Hale, Agreements Among Competitors, 33 Minn. L. Rev. 331, 335 (1949); Note, Federal Trade Commission Cosmetic Trade Practice Rules, 65 Harv. L. Rev. 1261, 1262 (1952); 16 C.F.R. §§204.2, 204.5 (Cum. Supp. 1952) (FTC; rayon and acetate textile industry). See also Kittelle and Campbell, Power of the Federal Trade Commission to Require Informative Labeling of Textiles, 20 B.U.L. Rev. 23, 26, 34, 36 (1940); Kittelle and Mostow, A Review of the Trade Practice Conferences of the Federal Trade Commission, 8 Geo. Wash. L. Rev. 427, 439, 446 (1940).

[89] See Alberty v. FTC, 182 F.2d 36 (D.C. Cir. 1950), cert. denied, 340 U.S. 818 (1950); Scientific Manufacturing Co. v. FTC, 124 F.2d 640 (3d Cir. 1941). But cf. Perma-Maid Co. v. FTC, 121 F.2d 282 (6th Cir. 1941). Instances may arise in which the expense of precise labeling is more costly than the imperfections which would thereby be removed, e.g., Gimbel Bros., Inc. v. FTC, 116 F.2d 578 (2d Cir. 1941); Kaidanovsky, Consumer Standards 350 (TNEC Monograph No. 24, 1941). It is also not impossible that regulation of the type in question could take on an interventionist character. Thus the following statement was found in a trade journal: "After considerable discussion it was the general opinion that the Fur Products

tion removes market imperfections, however, it may contribute to an economic allocation of resources.[90]

Horizontal size. We experience great difficulty in defining a monopoly. It is hard to say how small firms must be in order to avoid "impurities." [91] In that effort account should be taken of the often repeated view that small firms are more likely to deceive their customers than large enterprises.[92] No positive proof of that tendency

---

Labeling Act held great promise of eliminating a substantial part of the unfavorable competition from low grade pelts and means were agreed upon to advance this project as fast as expedient." National Board of Fur Farm Organizations, Report of Meeting of Executive Committee, 19 Fur J. 11 (Sept.-Oct. 1952). See Hamilton, The Ancient Maxim of Caveat Emptor, 40 Yale L.J. 1133, 1138, 1148, 1152 (1931); Miller, Unfair Competition 113 (1941).

[90] Lotteries have been forbidden as a means of selling goods. FTC v. R. F. Keppel and Bro., Inc., 291 U.S. 304 (1934); Deer v. FTC, 152 F.2d 65 (2d Cir. 1945); Handler, Unfair Competition and the Federal Trade Commission, 8 Geo. Wash. L. Rev. 399, 415 (1940). Elimination of the lottery feature in a sale constitutes standardization and to that extent appears to be meritorious. The Commission's activities in the field of commercial bribery and false disparagement of competitors can likewise be supported as tending to remove market imperfections. Id. at 408; Perma-Maid Co. v. FTC, 121 F.2d 282 (6th Cir. 1941); Nims, Unfair Competition by False Statements or Disparagement, 19 Cornell L.Q. 63 (1933); Oxenfeldt, Industrial Pricing and Market Practices 254 (1951). But see Henderson, The Federal Trade Commission 216 (1924). Query, however, whether the Commission should be empowered to prevent firms from advertising, or to control the manner in which business is solicited. Cf. New Jersey Asbestos Co. v. FTC, 264 Fed. 509, 511 (2d. Cir. 1920). See Henderson, The Federal Trade Commission 224 (1924).

[91] See §§3.8, 3.10 *supra.*

[92] Oxenfeldt, Industrial Pricing and Market Practices 255 (1951); Stocking and Watkins, Monopoly and Free Enterprise 317 (1951); Celler Committee I, ser. 12, at 493; TNEC Hearings, pt. 8, at 3336; Loss, Securities Regulation 380 (1951).

Many judicial findings could be cited to the same effect. Thus, in Radio Shack Corp. v. Radio Shack, Inc., 180 F.2d 200, 202 (7th Cir. 1950), it was said: "Some 22 years after plaintiff herein was organized, and long after the plaintiff had widely used its corporate name as its trade name, defendants deliberately went into direct competition, using for all practical purposes the identical corporate and trade name. For some four years prior to incorporation of the defendant company at least one of its officers had knowledge of the plaintiff and of the operation of its business."

As to the importance of integrity upon the part of producers and distributors, see Borden, The Economic Effects of Advertising 678 (1942).

Considerable thought has been given to the possibility of a survey which would test the suggestion made in the text that small firms are more likely to deceive their customers than large ones. It was proposed, for example, to select five scattered volumes of Federal Trade Commission decisions and to determine whether more cease and desist orders had been entered against small producers and distributors than against their larger competitors. Aside from the merely mechanical difficulties of ascertaining the size of the various firms against which the Commission has entered orders over the years, several insuperable obstacles have prevented the making of such a survey. One obvious difficulty is that the Federal Trade Commission's jurisdiction extends only to interstate commerce. In earlier years particularly, that restriction upon its activities might result in the elimination of many smaller firms from its purview. A second obstacle lies in the fact that there are degrees of misrepresentation. If it appeared that small firms engage in flagrant frauds while their larger competitors merely fail to make information in their hands available to their customers, the action taken by the Commission in such cases would scarcely be comparable in character. For these reasons it is not now known how the com-

has been found, nor can any specific size be named as indicative of questionable representations. It is true, however, that the extensive services offered by large concerns to teach consumers how to use their products and the like, could scarcely be offered by their smaller competitors.[93] Mass merchandisers can inspect the goods they offer for sale to the ignorant consumer with much greater care and expert knowledge than small independent merchants. Indeed, some of the largest distributing concerns maintain their own laboratories for the benefit both of consumers and producers.[94] It follows that the confidence which consumers have placed in such large-scale distributors, evidenced by acceptance of their private brands (often available at

parative integrity of small business can be tested. It is probable that imperfections play a considerably more important role in the determination of appropriate size than indicated in this study. It is hoped that the topic may be expanded in future research.

[93] Gordon, Economics for Consumers 508 (2d ed. 1944). In many instances, large firms insist that their salesmen enjoy considerable technical ability, e.g., Minneapolis-Honeywell Regulator Co., 1950 Ann. Rep. 15 (Minneapolis, 1951); Parke, Davis & Co., 84th Ann. Rep. 10 (Detroit, 1951). A flour miller conducts a cooking school with a tremendous registration, develops and promulgates new recipes, and broadcasts the information over a radio network of 187 stations. General Mills, Inc., 20th Ann. Rep. 38 (Minneapolis, 1948). A public utility concern conducted a cooking school with over 9000 home demonstrations given during a single year. Its electricians worked with architects and contractors to make recommendations for the wiring of residential and commercial buildings. Ohio Edison Co., 1950 Ann. Rep. 7 (Akron, Ohio, 1951). Metropolitan Life Insurance Company engages in activities designed to promote public health, and also conducts a nursing service for some of its policyholders. TNEC Hearings, pt. 12, at 5838, 5840. A firm which the Attorney General seeks to break into five separate competing companies produced six motion pictures in 1950 showing customers how to carve meat and how to cook foods. Armour & Co., 1950 Ann. Rep. 3, 5 (Chicago, 1951). A company engaged in the lending of money has published a number of helpful pamphlets telling its patrons how to buy intelligently. The pamphlets appear to be reliable and to give sound, nonpolitical advice which should be of considerable assistance to consumers. Household Finance Corporation, Better Buymanship: Meat, Fish, Poultry and Eggs (1951); Household Finance Corporation, Money Management: Your Home Furnishings Dollar (1952). Note also the activities of large firms as buyers. They conduct extensive investigations, standardize the commodities they require, and probably thus contribute in an important manner to the reduction of market imperfections at that level. Kaidanovsky, Consumer Standards 191, 192 (TNEC Monograph No. 24, 1941). Such benefits may reflect the balancing of monopoly with monopsony which has, of course, effects in the realm of "impurities." It has been suggested that large firms are more likely to indulge in undesirable types of advertising than small ones. See Stocking and Watkins, Monopoly and Free Enterprise 73 (1951). If that assertion can be proven, it may relate only to very large firms and not to those of middle size. Another factor worthy of mention is that firms may be too small to comply with regulations designed to remove market imperfections. Take, for example, the case of a firm desiring to raise a small amount of capital by public sale of its securities. See page 424 supra, note 68.

[94] Stocking and Watkins, Monopoly and Free Enterprise 316 (1951); Gordon, Economics for Consumers 511 (2d ed. 1944); Sears, Roebuck & Co., 1952 Ann. Rep. 15-9 (Chicago, 1953). The catalog published by the rival mail order firm of Montgomery Ward & Company is famous for its detailed information on various products such as radios, hot-water tanks and so forth.

prices below those established for heavily advertised brands of the same commodities), may not be misplaced.[95]

Recognition of market imperfections will not, in all likelihood, lead to any alteration in our notions as to an acceptable size for manufacturing concerns. As just indicated, however, mass merchandisers render services to consumers of a type which little merchants cannot match. Display advertising of chain and department stores in metropolitan newspapers is often highly informative.[96] It is clear, also, that some degree of size is necessary to permit sellers to engage in those market research activities which we have noted as important in the reduction of ignorance of demand.[97] Thus it is possible that a desire to reduce market imperfections could affect the problem of horizontal size in the field of distribution.

Trade-mark "monopolies." In recent years the view has often been expressed that trade-marks are monopolistic in character. Judge Jerome Frank, perhaps the most active proponent of that point of view, has stated that legal protection of trade names does not engender competition but, on the contrary, creates lawful monopolies.[98] A producer seeking to enjoin use of his trade-mark on goods sold to the same type of consumers through identical channels of distribution was rebuked by the Court of Appeals for the Seventh Circuit, which referred to "[t]he unconscionable efforts of the plaintiffs to monopolize the food market by their monopoly of the word Sunkist."[99] A more sophisticated view finds trade-marks objectionable in that they permit that product differentiation utilized by oligopolists to avoid the impact of pure competition.[100] Upon whatever ground, some of the literature can be read as an argument in favor of the abolition of trade-marks and similar identifying mechanisms.[101]

[95] Edwards, Maintaining Competition 368 (1941); Sorenson, The Consumer Movement 11 (1941); Borden, The Economic Effects of Advertising 42, 605 (1942). It does not follow, of course, that the private brand of merchandise is always of the highest available quality. 1953 TV Receivers, 30 Consumers' Research Bull. 5, 8 (Dec. 1952). As to the value of endorsements by publishers of magazines and the like, some information will be found in Hearst Magazines, Inc., 32 F.T.C. 1440 (1941).

[96] Note also that mass merchandisers may be able to reduce advertising costs. Borden, The Economic Effects of Advertising 465, 470, 483 (1942). Compare Nelson and Keim, Price Behavior and Business Policy 88 (TNEC Monograph No. 1, 1941).

[97] White, Marketing Research, 209 Annals 183, 184 (1940).

[98] Eastern Wine Corp. v. Winslow-Warren, Ltd., 137 F.2d 955, 957, 958, 959 (2d Cir.), *cert. denied*, 320 U.S. 758 (1943); Standard Brands, Inc. v. Smidler, 151 F.2d 34, 38 (2d Cir. 1945) (concurring opinion). See Stocking and Watkins, Monopoly and Free Enterprise 509 (1951); Pattishall, Trade-Marks and the Monopoly Phobia, 50 Mich. L. Rev. 967, 968 n.3, 974, 976 (1952).

[99] California Fruit Growers Exchange v. Sunkist Baking Co., 166 F.2d 971, 975 (7th Cir. 1947).

[100] Timberg, Trade-Marks, Monopoly, and the Restraint of Competition, 14 Law & Contemp. Prob. 323, 325 (1949). Cf. Consolidated Book Publishers, Inc. v. FTC, 53 F.2d 942 (7th Cir. 1931), *cert. denied*, 286 U.S. 553 (1932).

[101] See Brown, Advertising and the Public Interest, 57 Yale L.J. 1165, 1190 (1948); Timberg, Trade-Marks, Monopoly, and the Restraint of Competition, 14 Law & Contemp. Prob. 323, 326 (1949); Miller, Unfair Competition 116 (1941). As Mr. Timberg points out, trade-marks can be used as vehicles for both horizontal and

Supporters of trade-marks point out the difference between a patent or a copyright and a mere trade-mark.[102] Resources of the language, they argue, are inexhaustible and the existence of 6000 brands of shoes and 10,000 brands of wheat flour is cited as evidence of that fact.[103] Trade-marks, they urge, are mere means of identification and do not in themselves confer any monopoly in the commodities to which they are attached.[104] In some degree, at least, trade-marks constitute a certificate of quality[105] and the fact that the Federal Trade Commission has moved against those using the trade-marks of others indicates that infringement of a mark constitutes a positive misrepresentation.[106] In short, if the courts refused to enjoin the use of trade-marks by those not entitled to them under the established law of unfair competition,

---

vertical price-fixing schemes. Timberg *supra*, at 328, 352. It is also true, as indicated in the text, that if a commodity becomes known only by its brand name, the producer using that mark will gain a monopoly advantage. Id. at 324; Montgomery, Consumer Standards and Marketing, 209 Annals 141, 144 (1950); Stocking, Modern Advertising and Economic Theory, 21 Am. Econ. Rev. 43, 52 and n.17 (1931). At that point, however, the mark has ceased to distinguish the brand of the commodity in question from other brands of the same commodity. It becomes descriptive in character and hence is denied protection. 3 Restatement of Torts §735; Callmann, The Law of Unfair Competition and Trade-Marks §74.1 (1945); Oppenheim, The Public Interest in Legal Protection of Industrial and Intellectual Property, 40 Trade-Mark Rep. 613, 625, 626 (1950). But see Timberg *supra*, at 332 (expensive to litigate issue of loss of distinctiveness).

[102] Pattishall, Trade-Marks and the Monopoly Phobia, 50 Mich. L. Rev. 967, 971 (1952); Oppenheim, The Public Interest in Legal Protection of Industrial and Intellectual Property, 40 Trade-Mark Rep. 613, 614 (1950); Oppenheim, Federal Antitrust Legislation: Guideposts to a Revised National Antitrust Policy, 50 Mich. L. Rev. 1139, 1217 (1952).

[103] Wilcox, Brand Names, Quality and Price, 173 Annals 80, 82 (1934); Borden, The Economic Effects of Advertising 633 (1942); see Best & Co. v. Miller, 167 F.2d 374, 378 (2d Cir. 1948) (Judge Clark's dissenting opinion).

[104] Rogers, The Lanham Act and the Social Function of Trade-Marks, 14 Law & Contemp. Prob. 173, 176-177 (1949). Cf. Mishawaka Rubber Co. v. S. S. Kresge Co., 316 U.S. 203, 205 (1942). Query whether trade-marks could survive governmental grade-labeling. See Agnew, The Movement for Standards for Consumer Goods, 173 Annals 60, 66 (1934).

[105] Borden, The Economic Effects of Advertising 23, 629, 631-632 (1942). Note the following statement: "CR Bulletins have often mentioned the desirability of knowing by what manufacturer an article has been produced, and the need, as a practical matter, and for very good reasons, of avoiding the purchase of any important food, beverage, or other article or appliance of unknown origin." Clinical Thermometers, 31 Consumers' Research Bull. 24 (Jan. 1953). But see Gordon, Economics for Consumers 247 (2d ed. 1944).

[106] Juvenile Shoe Co. v. FTC, 289 Fed. 57 (9th Cir. 1923); Pep Boys v. FTC, 122 F.2d 158 (3d Cir. 1941); FTC v. Real Products Corp., 90 F.2d 617 (2d Cir. 1937); Henderson, The Federal Trade Commission 169, 170 (1924); Watkins, Public Regulation of Competitive Practices in Business Enterprise 184 (National Industrial Conference Board, 3d ed. 1940); Chamberlin, The Theory of Monopolistic Competition, App. E (5th ed. 1946). But cf. FTC v. Klesner, 280 U.S. 19 (1929). See also Handler, The Jurisdiction of the Federal Trade Commission over False Advertising, 31 Colum. L. Rev. 527, 538 (1931). In the Lanham Act it was specifically provided that a false designation of origin should be considered a tort. 15 U.S.C. §1125 (1946).

their decisions would tend to promote rather than suppress market imperfections.

The conflict between those who would curb impurities and those who would suppress imperfections through restricting or encouraging the use of trade-marks comes to a focus in cases wherein it must be decided how far trade-mark protection shall be extended. The most ardent "restrictionist" (with the exception of those who would abolish trade-marks altogether) would not permit a second user of the mark to apply it to identical goods. He would, however, deny the trade-mark owner injunctive relief in cases wherein the infringer is not a competitor. Apparently that view is based on the belief that such protection of the trade-mark against "dilution" encourages a persuasive rather than an informative use of advertising. Informative advertising is recognized as desirable in that it reduces consumer ignorance. Mere persuasive advertising is, however, identified with product differentiation and hence with monopoly.[107]

Historically, the basic principle of the law of unfair competition has been protection of the consumer from confusion.[108] That view is, of course, closely related to the suppression of market imperfections. Undoubtedly, a narrow scope of legal protection would weaken the persuasive force of trade-marks. Tiffany, the jeweler, would not have sought an injunction against the use of his name in the production of motion pictures[109] had he not believed that such use would detract from his good will;[110] and if advertising which is merely persuasive in character is a principal weapon of the oligopolist, then refusal to issue the injunction against a noncompetitor may contribute in some degree to the enforcement of our antitrust policy. On the other hand, if likelihood of confusion[111] can be proven even in a minor

[107] Timberg, Trade-Marks, Monopoly and the Restraint of Competition, 14 Law & Contemp. Prob. 323, 351 (1949); Brown, Advertising and the Public Interest, 57 Yale L.J. 1165, 1184, 1194 (1948). The proprietor of a trade-mark which has achieved public acceptance may well wish to use it in the promotion of other or new goods. See, e.g., Sunbeam Corp., Ann. Rep. 3 (Chicago, 1953); Borden Co., 1950 Ann. Rep. 5 (New York City, 1950). See also 3 Restatement of Torts §731. Hence the problem may become one of diversification. See §6.7 *supra.*

[108] Oates, Relief in Equity Against Unfair Trade Practices of Non-Competitors, 25 Ill. L. Rev. 643, 655 (1931). See Callmann, The Law of Unfair Competition and Trade-Marks §3.4 (1945).

[109] See Tiffany & Co. v. Tiffany Productions, 264 N.Y. Supp. 459 (1932), *aff'd,* 237 App. Div. 801, 260 N.Y. Supp. 821 (1st Dept. 1932), *aff'd,* 262 N.Y. 482, 188 N.E. 30 (1933); Callmann, Trade-Mark Infringement and Unfair Competition, 14 Law & Contemp. Prob. 185, 189 (1949).

[110] Development of the view that a trade-mark is property and should be protected even on noncompeting goods can be traced in Schechter, Fog and Fiction in Trade-Mark Protection, 36 Colum. L. Rev. 60, 84 (1936); Oates, Relief in Equity Against Unfair Trade Practices of Non-Competitors, 25 Ill. L. Rev. 643, 650 (1931); Lunsford, Trade-Mark Infringement and Confusion of Source: Need for Supreme Court Action, 35 Va. L. Rev. 214, 217 (1949); Note, Trade-Marks, Unfair Competition and the Courts: Some Unsettled Aspects of the Lanham Act, 66 Harv. L. Rev. 1094 (1953).

[111] 3 Restatement of Torts §730; Note, Trade-Marks, Unfair Competition and the

degree, the court denying injunctive relief may be striking a feeble blow against market impurities while adding in considerable measure to market imperfections.

Cooperation among competitors. Trade associations often promulgate codes of ethics and take similar action against misrepresentation and other forms of activity regarded as unfair competition. Support of "better business bureaus" and of the Federal Trade Commission's trade practice conferences constitute conspicuous examples of such trade association practices.[112] Whether such groups should be permitted to curb style piracy, protect the public against indecency and prohibit the practice of medicine by corporations[113] is, of course, debatable. To the extent, however, that such activity reduces fraud and unethical practices in the market place, it should at least receive the sympathetic consideration of the courts.[114]

Trade associations also engage in market research activities[115] and particularly in the gathering and dissemination of trade statistics.[116] Over the years the permissible boundaries of such trade association activity have been delineated with reasonable clarity.[117] The courts have, for example, insisted that the information circulated should be made available to purchasers and the public at large as well as to producers.[118] Such restrictions are highly desirable because publication of trade statistics has often formed a convenient vehicle for price-

---

Courts: Some Unsettled Aspects of the Lanham Act, 66 Harv. L. Rev. 1094, 1096 (1953). But cf. Miller, Unfair Competition 116 (1941).

[112] Henderson, The Federal Trade Commission 181 (1924); Pearce, Trade Association Survey 345 (TNEC Monograph No. 18, 1941); Lyon, The A.B.C. of the N.R.A. 175-180 (1934); Hale, Agreements Among Competitors, 33 Minn. L. Rev. 331, 349 (1949); Sorenson, The Consumer Movement 11, 198-199 (1941); Gordon, Economics for Consumers 516, 517 (2d ed. 1944); TNEC Hearings, pt. 10, at 4634; 16 C.F.R. §135.1(c) (2d ed. 1949) (silk industry rule).

[113] Fashion Originators' Guild, Inc. v. FTC, 312 U.S. 457 (1941); American Medical Assn. v. United States, 317 U.S. 519 (1943); Hale, Agreements Among Competitors, 33 Minn. L. Rev. 331, 352, 375, 377, 379 (1949); Comment, 40 Colum. L. Rev. 736, 739 (1940).

[114] A leading authority said some years ago: "Regulation of unfair and deceptive competitive practices, the arbitration of commercial disputes, the standardization of identity and quality of products, the improvement of conditions of labor, the registration of trade-marks and original styles and designs, the conservation of natural resources, the elimination of wasteful practices, and the promotion of efficiencies in production and distribution are only a few of the fields in which trade associations perform a distinct social service." Handler, A Study of the Construction and Enforcement of the Federal Antitrust Laws 28 (TNEC Monograph No. 38, 1941).

[115] White, Marketing Research, 209 Annals 183, 186 (1940); Gordon, Economics for Consumers 508 (2d ed. 1944); Kaplan, Small Business: Its Place and Problems 124-125, 132 (1948).

[116] Pearce, Trade Association Survey, c. 5 (TNEC Monograph No. 18, 1941); Miller, Unfair Competition 285 (1941).

[117] Handler, A Study of the Construction and Enforcement of the Federal Antitrust Laws 18 (TNEC Monograph No. 38, 1941); Comment, 18 U. Chi. L. Rev. 380 (1951).

[118] See Tag Manufacturers Institute v. FTC, 174 F.2d 452, 462 (1st Cir. 1949). But cf. Sugar Institute, Inc. v. United States, 297 U.S. 553, 604 (1936); Handler,

fixing conspiracies.[119] Those who take the extreme position of advocating abolition of such activities,[120] however, apparently overlook the contribution they make to the reduction of imperfections. Mr. Justice Brandeis argued that the Sherman Act did not require competition to be pursued blindly and Mr. Justice Holmes suggested that the ideal of commerce was an intelligent interchange made with full knowledge of the facts as a basis for a forecast of the future.[121] It is true that governmental agencies do provide much the same service in the agricultural field which, presumably, could be extended to those areas now served by trade associations.[122] Any extension of such governmental activity, however, carries its own hazards of the development of intervention, and in any event the trade associations perform an important role during a period when such public service is undeveloped.

As we have noted, standardization of commodities is important for the suppression of both impurities and imperfections in competition. Unless the product is homogeneous, pure competition cannot exist. Similarly, a bewildering array of differentiated goods may so confuse consumers as to prevent them from exercising their sovereignty in the market place.[123] Trade associations have played a prominent role in the standardization and simplification of many types of goods. They have formulated standards of quality and "simplified" products to eliminate large numbers of shapes, sizes and models felt to be unnecessary. In some instances, associations have "graded" merchandise and applied certification marks thereto.[124] As the record of antitrust litigation shows, it is possible for groups of competitors to cloak price-fixing and similar activities in the raiment of standardization and simplification.[125] For such reasons Section 14(d) was inserted in the

---

A Study of the Construction and Enforcement of the Federal Antitrust Laws 21 (TNEC Monograph No. 38, 1941).

[119] American Column & Lumber Co. v. United States, 257 U.S. 377 (1921); Edwards, Maintaining Competition 26 (1949); Comment, 18 U. Chi. L. Rev. 380, 381 (1951).

[120] Some observers take the position that all price-reporting systems, by their very nature, tend to eliminate competition. Fly, Observations on the Anti-Trust Laws, Economic Theory and the Sugar Institute Decisions, 45 Yale L.J. 1339, 1345 (1936); Oxenfeldt, Industrial Pricing and Market Practices 318 (1951).

[121] See American Column & Lumber Co. v. United States, 257 U.S. 377, 412, 415-416 (1921) (dissenting opinion). See Maple Flooring Manufacturers Assn. v. United States, 268 U.S. 563, 582-583 (1925); Sugar Institute, Inc. v. United States, 297 U.S. 553, 598 (1936); Handler, A Study of the Construction and Enforcement of the Federal Antitrust Laws 22 (TNEC Monograph No. 38, 1941); Lyon and Abramson, The Economics of Open Price Systems 88 (1936).

[122] Mund, Open Markets 246 (1948); Stocking and Watkins, Monopoly and Free Enterprise 255 (1951).

[123] But see Marshall, Principles of Economics 325 (8th ed. 1920).

[124] Kaidanovsky, Consumer Standards 193, 196, 198, 201, 225 (TNEC Monograph No. 24, 1941); Hale, Agreements Among Competitors, 33 Minn. L. Rev. 331, 362 (1949); Agnew, The Movement for Standards for Consumer Goods, 173 Annals 60, 66 (1934); TNEC Hearings, pt. 8, at 3421, 3428. Professional and technical societies engage in similar activities. Kaidanovsky, supra, at 210, 224.

[125] C-O-Two Fire Equipment Co. v. United States, 197 F.2d 489, 493 (9th Cir.), cert. denied, 344 U.S. 892 (1952). See also TNEC Hearings, pt. 8, at 3420, 3430;

Lanham Act to provide for cancellation of certification marks if used to restrain trade or to discriminate against producers.[126]   On the whole, however, there has been widespread acceptance of the desirability of such standardization programs.   Unless used as a cloak for direct restraints of trade or carried to the extent where consumer sovereignty is effectively suppressed, most observers have found standardization and simplification to be meritorious.[127]   In that connection it is interesting to note that the governmental programs of the same type often lean heavily upon trade standards previously adopted by private groups.[128]

Exchanges.   Unities of time and place are achieved when traders gather in organized markets.   Imperfections can be removed from the flow of commerce when all trading is focused on a single exchange. Economists are agreed upon the desirability of such institutions,[129] and in many decisions over the decades the courts have approved them.[130]   Indeed, the courts have permitted members of the exchanges

---

Edwards, Maintaining Competition 29 (1949); Pearce, Trade Association Survey 84 (TNEC Monograph No. 18, 1941); Hale, Monopoly and Mobilization: The Conflict Between Direct Controls and the Antitrust Laws, 47 Nw. U.L. Rev. 606, 631 (1952).

[126] 60 Stat. 433 (1946), U.S.C. §1064(d) (1946) (Lanham Act).   See Callmann, The Law of Unfair Competition and Trade-Marks §68.3 (1945); Timberg, Trade-Marks, Monopoly and the Restraint of Competition, 14 Law & Contemp. Prob. 323, 343, 352 (1949); Diggins, The Lanham Trade-Mark Act, 35 Geo. L.J. 147, 182 (1947); Sen. Doc. No. 35, 77th Cong., 1st Sess. 304 (1941).   An example of desirable certification is found in Kaidanovsky, Consumer Standards 233 (TNEC Monograph No. 24, 1941).

[127] Hale, Agreements Among Competitors, 33 Minn. L. Rev. 331, 365 (1949); Edwards, Maintaining Competition 194 (1949); Tag Manufacturers Institute v. FTC, 174 F.2d 452, 462 (1st Cir. 1949).   But cf. Paramount Famous Lasky Corp. v. United States, 282 U.S. 30, 41 (1930).

[128] Kaidanovsky, Consumer Standards 16 (TNEC Monograph No. 24, 1941); Lyon, and others, Government and Economic Life 231 (1939); TNEC Hearings, pt. 8, at 3437, 3484.   See Atlas Powder Co. v. Ewing, 201 F.2d 347 (3d Cir. 1953).

[129] Robinson, The Economics of Imperfect Competition 51 (1948); Harrod, Doctrines of Imperfect Competition 48 Q.J. Econ. 442, 445 (1934); Sen. Doc. No. 35, 77th Cong., 1st Sess. 403 (1941).   But see Chamberlin, An Experimental Imperfect Market, 56 J. Pol. Econ. 95 (1948).   A particularly vigorous advocacy of organized exchanges will be found in Mund, Open Markets 212, 234-235, 238, 244, 257 (1948). An example of the market place in action is reported in To Market, To Market, 40 Fortune No. 1, p. 87 (1949).

[130] In United States v. New York Coffee and Sugar Exchange, Inc., 263 U.S. 611, 619 (1924), it was said: "The usefulness and legality of sales for future delivery, and of furnishing an Exchange where under well-defined limitations and rules the business can be carried on, have been fully recognized by this court. . . .   The machinery of such an Exchange has been at times made the means of promoting corners . . . thereby restraining and obstructing foreign and interstate trade.   In such instances, the manipulators subject themselves to prosecution and indictment under the Anti-Trust Act. . . .   But this is not to hold that such an Exchange with the facilities it affords for making contracts for future deliveries is itself a combination and conspiracy thus to restrain . . . trade."   See Anderson v. United States, 171 U.S. 604, 616 (1898); Board of Trade v. Christie Grain and Stock Co., 198 U.S. 236, 249 (1905); New York and Chicago Grain and Stock Exchange v. Board of Trade, 127 Ill. 153, 161, 19 N.E. 855, 858 (1889); State v. Duluth Board of Trade,

to agree not to trade with nonmembers and even to fix the rate of commission which should be charged for dealings in the organized market. In the early *Anderson* case, the Court examined such an exclusive trade arrangement and found "there is no feature of monopoly in the whole transaction." [131] In the famous *Chicago Board of Trade* case, Mr. Justice Brandeis wrote an opinion sustaining a rule of that body prohibiting a change in the price of grain after the close of trading and until the exchange opened the following morning.[132] Recent legislation appears to approve such rules of organized exchanges, at least if governmental supervision be exercised over them.[133]

Transactions in restraint of trade can, of course, be carried out through the facilities of an organized exchange. Similarly, such an institution may be used as a cloak for price-fixing or other undesirable practices.[134] It was, however, disturbing when the Supreme Court of the United States recently cast doubt on prior favorable decisions.[135] That doubt arises from an assertion that the older cases rested upon the ground that only local commerce was involved.[136] The statement was made in a case involving real estate brokers, who are not, of course, traders on organized exchanges. Such agents, however, perform essentially the same service as brokers upon stock and grain exchanges. It is true that an agreement among such brokers looking to the fixing of commission rates flies in the face of the rule that price-fixing is illegal *per se* under the antitrust laws. If, however, the informal exchanges operated by real estate and similar brokers be properly credited with the important role they play in diffusing information to both buyers and sellers,[137] a different result may well follow. Experience

---

[107] Minn. 506, 521, 121 N.W. 395, 401 (1909). The importance of organized exchanges to the economy is recognized in the Commodity Exchange Act §§3, 4a, 4d, 4e, 4h, 6(b), 42 Stat. 999-1002 (1922), as amended, 7 U.S.C. §§2, 5, 6, 9 (1946). Note that §4b of that statute is aimed at gambling on organized markets, a practice which has been suppressed by private exchanges with judicial approval in the past. Moore v. New York Cotton Exchange, 270 U.S. 593 (1926); Board of Trade v. Christie Grain and Stock Co., 198 U.S. 236, 252 (1905) (by implication).

[131] Anderson v. United States, 171 U.S. 604 (1898); cf. Hopkins v. United States, 171 U.S. 578 (1898).

[132] Board of Trade v. United States, 246 U.S. 231 (1918). Other illuminating opinions were prepared in Chamber of Commerce of Minneapolis v. FTC, 13 F.2d 673 (8th Cir. 1926); State v. Duluth Board of Trade, 107 Minn. 506, 121 N.W. 395 (1909). But cf. United States v. New England Fish Exchange, 258 Fed. 732 (D. Mass. 1919); State v. Wilson, 73 Kan. 334, 80 Pac. 639 (1906).

[133] 15 U.S.C. §78f(d) (1946); 15 U.S.C. §78s(d) (1946).

[134] See United States v. New York Coffee and Sugar Exchange, Inc., 263 U.S. 611, 619 (1924).

[135] United States v. National Assn. of Real Estate Boards, 339 U.S. 485 (1950).

[136] Id. at 492. There is language in Hopkins v. United States, 171 U.S. 578, 588 (1898), which supports the recent statement made by the Court. But cf. id. at 592; Anderson v. United States, 171 U.S. 604, 615-616 (1898); Stafford v. Wallace, 258 U.S. 495, 524 (1922); Mandeville Island Farms, Inc. v. American Crystal Sugar Co., 334 U.S. 219, 229-230 (1948).

[137] See Lyon and Abramson, The Economics of Open Price Systems 9 (1936); Atkinson, Fundamentals of Real Estate Practice 291, 295, 309 (1946); Mund, Open Markets 244 (1948).

appears to indicate that fixing of commission rates on organized exchanges is essential to facilitate the fast flow of transactions. In informal markets similar considerations may apply. Fixing of rates of commission, of course, diverts competition among the brokers into service channels.[138] While in the field of industry as a whole such diversion may be undesirable, it is entirely possible that buyers and sellers of the commodities dealt in by brokers benefit from the commission fixing. In other words, it may be more important for the vendor or purchaser of real estate to secure service competition in the making of a sale or purchase rather than some small concession from the broker's normal rate of commission. If that is true, considerable question is cast upon the merits of cases holding that brokers of real estate, sugar and insurance cannot agree upon rates of commission.[139]

CONCLUSIONS

In the nature of things, we cannot assess the relative importance of impurities as against imperfections in the total commerce of the nation. Hence no firm suggestion can be made to a court trying a particular case as to the relative weight to attach to those two obstacles to an economic allocation of resources. Within the boundaries of a single suit, however, it is conceivable that calculations roughly approximating quantitative appraisals might be possible. Economists should

[138] State v. Duluth Board of Trade, 107 Minn. 506, 551, 121 N.W. 395, 414 (1909). A vivid illustration of service competition by a real estate broker is furnished in a direct mail advertising circular published by A. H. Gruetzmacher & Co. of 29 S. LaSalle Street, Chicago (1953). In that circular the broker offered to have a picture taken of the owner's premises by a professional photographer and to mail a brochure containing that photograph to 25,000 prospective purchasers. He also offered to furnish the picture and a listing of property to 2500 brokers, place advertisements in the newspapers and render other services all at no cost whatever to the property owner and at no increase in commission above the standard rate charged in the city.

[139] On such an exchange, all terms of trade except price must be fixed (the commodities must be rigidly defined and standardized to permit pure price-trading). It follows that if one term, the amount of broker's commission, is variable, the whole system breaks down; for the price quoted is subject to an explanation (amount of commission absorbed by broker) and hence is not a firm basis for further quick transactions. But cf. United States v. Sugar Institute, Inc., 15 F. Supp. 817, 903 (S.D.N.Y. 1934), aff'd, 297 U.S. 553, 587-589 (1936). See United States v. Southeastern Underwriters Assn., 322 U.S. 533 (1944). A question may arise as to whether the foregoing reasoning can be applied to the "fair trade" statutes so as to afford economic justification for those measures. Comment, Resale Price Maintenance and the Anti-Trust Laws, 18 U. Chi. L. Rev. 369 (1951); Hearings Before the Antitrust Subcommittee of the House Committee on the Judiciary on H.R. 4365, H.R. 4593, H.R. 4662, H.R. 6367, 82d Cong., 2d Sess. (1952). For several reasons it is believed that the arguments applicable to organized and informal exchanges should not be extended to all retail trade. "Fair trade" statutes protect retailers who take title to the goods they sell and thus incur risks in reselling them. Brokers by definition merely act as agents for the trading parties. Hence there is a marked distinction between the retail druggist, for example, on the one hand, and the real estate broker on the other. There are several other reasons why the argument advanced in the text should not be applied to justify resale price maintenance.

be able to make an informed guess as to the cost of monopolistic factors in a given situation. Similarly, the expense of continuing those market imperfections which a trade practice seeks to suppress could be appraised in some rough form. If a court were considering, for example, the validity of commission-fixing by real estate brokers, it would not be too difficult to make an estimate of the additional expense resulting therefrom. Perhaps more difficulty would be encountered in assessing the countervailing cost of lethargy in service competition. If, however, markets could be found where commissions had not been so fixed by agreement among the brokers, testimony as to experience in those areas might be helpful in assessing the relative merits of the two systems.

It is submitted that the antitrust laws cannot be enforced without taking account of frictions in the market place. A blind zeal to remove all monopoly elements in the economy might well result in a less efficient allocation of resources than previously obtained.[140] What we are urging is, of course, little more than a formalized application of the familiar rule of reason;[141] and the fact that quantitative standards for its application may often be lacking cannot excuse a refusal to consider the impact of judicial action upon the economy as a whole. Extension of the doctrine of violations *per se* is not, in other words, a rational approach to the solution of most antitrust problems.

[140] Compare Edwards, Maintaining Competition 30-49 (1949) with Nelson and Keim, Price Behavior and Business Policy 56-57 (TNEC Monograph No. 1, 1941).

[141] Oppenheim, Federal Antitrust Legislation: Guideposts to a Revised National Antitrust Policy, 50 Mich. L. Rev. 1139, 1145, 1156 (1952); United States v. Morgan, 118 F. Supp. 621, 687, 689 (S.D.N.Y. 1953).

APPENDIX B

Monopoly in Motion: Dynamic
Economics in Antitrust Enforcement*

INTRODUCTION

At the core of most antitrust problems lies the difficulty of defining monopoly. Some decades ago there was little doubt as to the meaning of that term. Further study, however, has made us realize more and more acutely how little we know about the actual working of our economy and, hence, how poorly prepared we are to formulate a rational application of the statutes.

Often the courts define monopoly by the "structure" of the market: by counting the number of sellers and gauging their relative size.[1] One difficulty with that method of measuring monopoly is that we cannot fix with any degree of certainty the boundaries of the "market" within which "structural" tests should be applied. Until we learn how to measure cross-elasticities of demand in practical situations, the problem of defining markets and commodities will constitute a tremendous barrier to the rational definition of monopoly. In the second place, the "impurities" of monopoly are inextricably intertwined with the "imperfections" of a friction-afflicted economy. Indivisibility, ignorance, immobility, and inertia all play important roles in the allocation of resources. In some measure, these imperfections constitute impediments to the removal of impurities through enforcement of the antitrust laws.[2]

A third difficulty encountered in the identification of monopoly lies in the fact that the economy is not standing still, but is constantly in motion. People, prices, and products are continually on the move. We must make sure that our concepts take that important fact into account; hence this study attempts to outline the principal considerations involved in a moving or "dynamic" analysis of monopoly.

* This appendix appeared in article form in 41 Virginia Law Review 431 (1955). It is republished here with only slight additions. Cf. Clark, Competition: Static Models and Dynamic Aspects, 45 Proceedings Am. Econ. Assn. 450 (1955).

[1] United States v. United Shoe Machinery Corp., 110 F. Supp. 295, 345 (D. Mass. 1953), aff'd per curiam, 347 U.S. 521 (1954); Rostow, The New Sherman Act: A Positive Instrument of Progress, 14 U. Chi. L. Rev. 567, 585 (1947).

[2] See Appendix A, page 426.

The law, of course, has not overlooked such an obvious fact as the constant change which characterizes our economy. Those who urge the "abuse" test of monopoly in lieu of that based upon "structure" are motivated in part by a desire to avoid the difficulties inherent in "static" analysis.[3] Again, those who propose a "performance" test of business enterprise, with emphasis upon technological progress, have dynamic factors in mind.[4] For the most part, however, the courts have failed to deal with such matters explicitly. Accordingly, we turn first to economic theory to discover what light it may shed upon legal problems. We next examine the real world of industry and commerce in an effort to test the validity of that body of theory. In the light of considerations thus developed, we then discuss their effects upon the enforcement of the antitrust laws, and particularly upon the definition of monopoly.

Our study is limited to the antitrust laws. Many other statutes affect the economy and are of great importance in analyzing its "dynamic" character. The tariff, for example, so often denounced as the "mother of trusts," has been supported as the shelter of "infant industries." Our Internal Revenue Code contains a host of provisions profoundly affecting the growth of new enterprise.[5] It would be foolish to adjust enforcement of the antitrust laws to the "dynamic" considerations here outlined, without, at the same time, making similar changes with respect to other legislation. The character of those other changes, however, is beyond the compass of this study.

I. ECONOMIC THEORIES

A. "Static" and "Dynamic" Analyses of Monopoly

Neoclassic economic theory is grounded in "static" analysis. It argues that the actions of businessmen may be validly, if not completely, described by analysis of the incentives to action which can be supposed to exist when the general conditions of demand and supply remain unchanged. A stationary state theory, its core is the proposition that whenever conditions change, there exists a constant tendency for output to be such that marginal cost is equal to price;[6] that "supply is equal to demand."

---

[3] Johnston, Monopolize or Attempt to Monopolize, A.B.A. Proceedings, Section of Antitrust Law, 72, 74-75 (Aug. 26, 1953).

[4] Oppenheim, Economic Background, 19 Geo. Wash. L. Rev. 120, 127-128 (1950).

[5] H.R. Rep. No. 2513, 82d Cong., 2d Sess. 8 (1952); Celler Committee I, ser. 14, pt. 2-B, at 1034, 1035; Committee for Economic Development, Taxes, National Security and Economic Growth 5, 23 (Jan. 1954); Machlup, The Political Economy of Monopoly 253 (1952); Wright, Democracy and Progress 97 (1948).

[6] Abramovitz, An Approach to a Price Theory for a Changing Economy 11 (1939). It is true that in the "cobweb" theory, neoclassic analysis has recognized the process of fixing prices by trial and error, whereby overestimates of production and the

Insofar as neoclassic theory takes account of the problem of innovation, it finds in competition the principal stimulant: it is the hot breath of the competitor on his neck which spurs the businessman to install new methods and reduce his costs.[7] Monopoly, on the other hand, is viewed as the cause of stagnation and as a curb upon growth and change.   In thus preferring the stick to the carrot as a means of inducing businessmen to adopt new methods, neoclassic economists urge that the natural tendency of the monopolist is to restrict production in order to maintain profits.   Any innovation which could increase the quantity of goods offered in the market will be shunned by one enjoying monopoly power.[8] Investment will be curtailed [9] because "big business" is comfortably ensconced in sheltered positions and is likely to let well enough alone.[10] In the language of Judge Learned Hand, they believe that immunity from competition is a narcotic and rivalry is a stimulant to industrial progress.[11] Further-

---

like can lead to subsequent underestimates and the possibility that equilibrium will never be attained. Id. at 26, 32, 53, 59-60. Another example of the recognition of change is found in the "theory of games." See Morgenstern, Oligopoly, Monopolistic Competition, and the Theory of Games, 38 Am. Econ. Rev. 10 (1948).

7 Clark, Social Control of Business 160, 162 (1926); Abramovitz, Economics of Growth, in 2 A Survey of Contemporary Economics 132-163 (Haley ed. 1952); Bowman, Toward Less Monopoly, 101 U. Pa. L. Rev. 577, 629 (1953); Higgins, The Theory of Increasing Under-Employment, 60 Econ. J. 255, 274 (1950); Terborgh, Capitalism and Innovation, 40 Am. Econ. Rev. 118, 120 (Supp. 1950).

8 Evans, The Entrepreneur and Economic Theory: A Historical and Analytical Approach, 39 Am. Econ. Rev. 336, 343 (1949); Higgins, The Theory of Increasing Under-Employment, 60 Econ. J. 255, 268-269 (1950); Hildebrand, Monopolization and the Decline of Investment Opportunity, 33 Am. Econ. Rev. 591, 593 (1943); Hoover, Capital Accumulation and Progress, 40 Am. Econ. Rev. 124, 126 (Supp. 1950). Something may depend upon the slope of the demand curve. See Kaysen, A Dynamic Aspect of the Monopoly Problem, 31 Rev. Econ. & Stat. 109, 110-111 (1949).

9 Domar, Investment, Losses and Monopolies, in Income, Employment and Public Policy 33, 51 (1948); Ellis, Monetary Policy and Investment, 30 Am. Econ. Rev. 27, 33 (Supp. 1940); Kaysen, A Dynamic Aspect of the Monopoly Problem, 31 Rev. Econ. & Stat. 109, 110 (1949).

10 Clark, Social Control of Business 436 (1926); Barnard, The Entrepreneur and Formal Organization, in Change and the Entrepreneur 1, 9 (1949); Ellis, Monetary Policy and Investment, 30 Am. Econ. Rev. 27, 33 (Supp. 1940); Rothschild, Price Theory and Oligopoly, 57 Econ. J. 299, 310 (1947); Hennipman, Monopoly: Impediment or Stimulus to Economic Progress, in Chamberlin, ed., Monopoly and Competition and Their Regulation 421, 432, 433 (International Economic Assn. 1954). An old enterprise, regardless of its size, may be less likely to take risks than a new one. See Rostow, The Process of Economic Growth 99 et seq. (1952); Abramovitz, Monopolistic Selling in a Changing Economy, 52 Q.J. Econ. 191, 210 (1938).

11 United States v. Aluminum Co. of America, 148 F.2d 416, 427 (2d Cir. 1945). On the other hand, it has been contended that big business, despite the rigidity and cumbersomeness of the bureaucracy it breeds, is in a position to be much more daring than its smaller counterparts. Bernstein, Profit Theory — Where Do We Go from Here? 67 Q.J. Econ. 407, 412 (1953). It is sometimes urged that a monopolist will be guided by a desire to protect his existing investment in plant and machinery, and hence will reject suggestions for change. Clark, Social Control of Business 436 (1926); Hansen, Fiscal Policy and Business Cycles 363-364 (1941); Higgins, The Theory of Increasing Under-Employment, 60 Econ. J. 255, 268 (1950). But cf.

more, the existence of monopoly can constitute a barrier against the entry of others.[12]

Many students have deplored the inadequate nature of "static" analysis of economic phenomena. They have pointed out the failure of neoclassic doctrines to take account of expectations, of the interdependence of various factors assumed to remain constant, and of the continual fluctuation in national income and in demand.[13] Many claim that static analysis is simply not useful because it fails to take account of so many important changes actually occurring in the economy.[14]

Most economists today would probably concede that analysis should take account of dynamic factors. Such a statement is easy to make. It is all very well to say that theory is not weaponless in the face of changes in data;[15] but it is much more difficult to introduce so many variables into the equations. As a consequence, there exists little general agreement as to the content of dynamic economic theory.[16] A few hesitant steps have been taken. They go beyond recognition of imperfections like immobility and ignorance. They attempt to take account of the passage of time, and to treat economic society as a living organism which grows and functions by unceasing adaptation to an ever-changing environment.[17]

Schumpeter, Capitalism, Socialism and Democracy 97 (3d ed. 1950); Kaysen, A Dynamic Aspect of the Monopoly Problem, 31 Rev. Econ. & Stat. 109, 111 (1949).

[12] Machlup, The Political Economy of Monopoly 65 (1952); Simons, Economic Policy for a Free Society 117-118 (1948); Domar, Investment, Losses and Monopolies, in Income, Employment and Public Policy 33, 51 (1948).

[13] Abramovitz, Monopolistic Selling in a Changing Economy, 52 Q.J. Econ. 191, 195 (1938); Kaysen, A Dynamic Aspect of the Monopoly Problem, 31 Rev. Econ. & Stat. 109 (1949). Thus Professor Roos said: "The principle [sic] economic theories, both old and new, have been based mainly upon a static view of economic phenomena, that is, upon a view which, as a matter of principle, does not take into account variations of economic situations with time. Such theories are concerned chiefly with a hypothetical state of equilibrium and the inter-relations of prices, demand, supply, and so forth, when equilibrium has been attained. As a result economic theory is today essentially an analysis of invariability and identity and of a fixed standard of elements." Roos, Dynamic Economics 3 (1934). To the same effect, see Hurff, Social Aspects of Enterprise in the Large Corporation 123 (1950).

[14] Thus Professor Harrod said: "Static assumptions are often made so far-reaching in recent discussions that a law based upon them seems incapable of having any application to the world of reality." Harrod, Towards a Dynamic Economics 4 (1948).

[15] Schumpeter, The Theory of Economic Development 62 (1951).

[16] Harrod, Towards a Dynamic Economics 9 (1948).

[17] Id. at 6; Hicks, Value and Capital 115 (1939); Lipson, A Planned Economy or Free Enterprise 16 (1944). We cannot pause here to examine all the elaborate theories which have been developed with respect to dynamic economics. It has been suggested, for example, that one of the principal forces affecting the economy is man's belief that he can control his environment. Again, it has been suggested that growth can be explained by the principle of "nucleation," which is expanded into "heterogeneous nucleation," or the "pinocchio principle." Rostow, The Process of Economic Growth 77 (1952); Boulding, Toward a General Theory of Growth, 19 Can. J. Econ. & Pol. Sci. 326, 333-334 (1953). There has been much discussion, too, of the role of equilibrium in a dynamic economy. Knight, The Ethics of

Dynamic theory does not deal with great upheavals which may occur against the background of the chronic imbalance of an economic system,[18] but it specifically recognizes the existence of change and attempts to cope with an economy in which rates of output are changing.[19] It deals, too, with problems of transition from one pace to another.[20] It takes account of expectations and of changes in the rate of expectation.[21] It seeks a solution to the riddle of capital in the community's propensities to invest and to save.[22] It connects those propensities with the rate of profit,[23] and it focuses sharply on levels of national income and shifts in demand.[24] It notes, for example, a change in the national diet away from fats and starches toward proteins, reflected in the demand for cheeses and skim milk.[25] Particular attention is paid to the role of inventions and of innovation in general.

Competition 184 (1935); Merlin, The Theory of Fluctuations in Contemporary Economic Thought 11, 13 (1949).

[18] Id. at 14. Professor Merlin attempted to summarize the subject as follows: "In the dynamic theory an attempt is made to bring factors formerly regarded as indeterminate within the scope of equilibrium analysis. These factors relate to estimates of the future made by individual firms and consumers, when prices and the data change, and to the process of (supply and demand) adjustment undertaken on the basis of such estimates. More generally, dynamic theory deals with economic variables relating to different points of time and with hypotheses regarding casual [sic] connections between such variables." Id. at 12.

[19] Harrod, Towards a Dynamic Economics 4 (1948). But cf. Robinson, Mr. Harrod's Dynamics, in 2 Readings in Business Cycles and National Income 233 (Hansen and Clemence ed. 1953); Wright, Mr. Harrod and Growth Economics, in 1 id. at 220, 228; Yeager, Some Questions About Growth Economics, 44 Am. Econ. Rev. 53 (1954); Roos, Dynamic Economics 13 (1934). Mrs. Robinson concluded that Mr. Harrod's milieu was so far removed from reality that his policy conclusions could not be useful. See Robinson, supra at 248. Cf. the statements of Mr. Harrod about static analysis, supra note 14.

[20] Merlin, The Theory of Fluctuations in Contemporary Economic Thought 43 (1949); Boulding, Toward a General Theory of Growth, 19 Can. J. Econ. & Pol. Sci. 326, 339 (1953).

[21] Harrod, Towards a Dynamic Economics 8 (1948); Hicks, Value and Capital 117, 119 (1939); Merlin, The Theory of Fluctuations in Contemporary Economic Thought 42-43 (1949).

[22] Hansen, Fiscal Policy and Business Cycles 381 (1941); Harrod, Economic Essays 265 (1952); Domar, Expansion and Employment, 37 Am. Econ. Rev. 34 (Supp. 1947); Harrod, An Essay in Dynamic Theory, in Readings in Business Cycles and National Income 200, 201, 210 (Hansen and Clemence ed. 1953); Higgins, Concepts and Criteria of Secular Stagnation, in Income, Employment and Public Policy 82, 85 (1948).

[23] Cf. Mill, Principles of Political Economy 484-485 (1869); Ricardo, Principles of Political Economy and Taxation 289 (Sraffa ed. 1951).

[24] Wright, The Economics of Disturbance 34-35 (1947); Burck and Parker, The Changing American Market, 48 Fortune No. 2, p. 98 (1953); Slichter, The Conditions of Expansion, 32 Am. Econ. Rev. 1, 16 (1942). But cf. Roos, Dynamic Economics 8 (1934); 1 Schumpeter, Business Cycles 73 (1939).

[25] Borden Co., 1952 Ann. Rep. 9, 11, 16 (New York City, 1953); see also Pittsburgh Plate Glass Co., 69th Ann. Rep. 14 (Pittsburgh, 1953). The magnitude of such fluctuations in demand is suggested by the statement that between 1950 and 1952 the output of rayon textile yarn by all producers in the United States declined by 40 per cent because styles of women's fashions changed. See American Viscose Corp., 1952 Ann. Rep. 13 (Philadelphia, 1953).

In the words of one of the most important students of the subject: "But what dominates the picture of capitalistic life . . . is innovation, the intrusion into the system of new production functions which incessantly shift existing cost curves." [26]

[26] 1 Schumpeter, Business Cycles 91 (1939). See also Hansen, Fiscal Policy and Business Cycles 352 (1941); Harrod, Towards a Dynamic Economics 21 (1948); Schumpeter, Capitalism, Socialism and Democracy 82-83 (3d ed. 1950); Slichter, The Conditions of Expansion, 32 Am. Econ. Rev. 1, 11 (1942). It cannot be claimed that recognition of innovation is a novelty introduced by dynamic economics. It receives considerable attention, for example, in the works of John Stuart Mill. Mill, Principles of Political Economy 485, 488, 495 (1869). See Higgins, Concepts and Criteria of Secular Stagnation, in Income, Employment and Public Policy 82, 85 (1948).

Perhaps it is desirable to indicate that the word "innovation" is not used in a uniform sense by all students of the subject. It includes business ideas and other novelties for which no patent can be granted under the terms of our present patent law. See 35 U.S.C. §101 (1952). As used here, it also includes more than that "development" upon which Professor Schumpeter laid so much stress. By "development," Professor Schumpeter meant only such changes in economic life as are not forced upon it from without, but arise by their own initiative from within. "Development" in his sense was a distinct phenomenon, entirely foreign to what may be observed in the circular flow or tendency toward equilibrium. It was a spontaneous and discontinuous change in the channels of the flow, a disturbance of equilibrium which forever alters and displaces the equilibrium state previously existing. Schumpeter, The Theory of Economic Development 63, 64 (Opie transl. 1934).

It must not be thought that the text above exhausts the topics considered under the heading of dynamic economics. Many other principles and concepts are involved. Among these are time lags, the role of foreign investment, the encouragement of pure science, and the like. See Harrod, Towards a Dynamic Economics 106 (1948); Higgins, What Do Economists Know? 112 (1951); Ortega y Gasset, The Revolt of the Masses 78 (Mentor ed. 1950); Rostow, The Process of Economic Growth 82 (1952); Schumpeter, Capitalism, Socialism and Democracy 103 (3d ed. 1950); Abramovitz, Economics of Growth, in 2 A Survey of Contemporary Economics 132, 142 (Haley ed. 1952); Hicks, Mr. Harrod's Dynamic Theory, in Readings in Business Cycles and National Income 249, 254 (Hansen and Clemence ed. 1953). Economists have, of course, long studied the closely allied field of business cycles. There has been much debate as to the relationship between monopoly and fluctuations in economic activity. Economists do not agree on whether a competitive or a monopolistic economy would be most suitable for stabilizing economic activity at high levels of employment. See Rostow, Market Organization and Stabilization Policy, in Income Stabilization for a Developing Economy 444 (Millikan ed. 1954); Wallace, Industrial Markets and Public Policy: Some Major Problems, in 1 Public Policy 59, 115 (Friedrich and Mason ed. 1940); cf. Harrod, Doctrines of Imperfect Competition, 48 Q.J. Econ. 442, 465 (1934).

Some economists regard monopoly as an impediment to those price adjustments which will bring the economy into equilibrium again after a depression has started. Stabilization of particular prices through the exertion of monopoly power, in their view, merely shifts the burdens of the depression to other groups and increases the difficulty of monetary counteraction. Indeed, Professor Simons said that no amount of monetary or physical stimulation will give us adequate employment or investment if strategically situated unions and enterpriser monopolists insist upon utilizing improved demand conditions to increase their wages and prices, rather than to increase employment, investment and output. Simons, Economic Policy for a Free Society 111, 114-116 (1948); Rostow, Market Organization and Stabilization Policy, in Income Stabilization for a Developing Economy 451, 459, 471 (Millikan ed. 1954); accord: Hansen, Fiscal Policy and Business Cycles 312, 333 (1941); Nelson and Keim, Price Behavior and Business Policy xi (TNEC Monograph No. 1, 1940);

B. *Dynamic Theory Applied to the Monopoly Problem*

Some two decades ago, neoclassic economics brought forth the theory of monopolistic competition. According to its doctrines, elements of monopoly are found in many business situations. Markets dominated by a few sellers are termed "oligopolistic" in character. Analysis stresses the "structure" of the market which, in turn, involves counting the number of sellers.[27] Dynamic studies have taken a dim view of the orthodox theory of monopolistic competition.[28] Their authors believe that it takes no account of growth and change, and that the "pure" competition which it suggests is incompatible with the op-

---

Ellis, Monetary Policy and Investment, 30 Am. Econ. Rev. 27, 32, 37 (Supp. 1940); Higgins, Concepts and Criteria of Secular Stagnation, in Income, Employment and Public Policy 82, 86, 88 (1948). An example often pointed to is the maintenance of the price of steel rails during the depression of the thirties. The Steel Rails, 8 Fortune No. 6, pp. 42, 46 (1933). But cf. Galbraith, Monopoly and the Concentration of Economic Power, in A Survey of Contemporary Economics 99, 111 (Ellis ed. 1939); Wallace, Industrial Markets and Public Policy: Some Major Problems, in 1 Public Policy 59, 96-97 (Friedrich and Mason ed. 1940).

Other observers have seen monopoly as a stabilizing influence in the economy which might prove beneficial to everyone. Fellner, Competition Among the Few 289 (1949); Schumpeter, Capitalism, Socialism and Democracy 91 (3d ed. 1950); Wright, Capitalism 170 (1951); Rostow, Market Organization and Stabilization Policy, in Income Stabilization for a Developing Economy 452-453 (Milliken ed. 1954). A purported example of such stabilization is found in Reynolds, Future Trend of Trade, 169 Economist 989 (1953). Wholly different results, however, are reported in Rich, Tin Control, 169 id. 990 (1953). Cf. Bowman, Toward Less Monopoly, 101 U. Pa. L. Rev. 577, 625, 626-627 (1953); Robinson, Imperfect Competition Revisited, 63 Econ. J. 579, 589 (1953). Monopoly-fostered innovation is sometimes seen as the cure for secular stagnation. MacLaurin, Invention and Innovation in the Radio Industry 264-265 (1949); 1 Schumpeter, Business Cycles 100 (1939); Wright, Capitalism 164 (1951); Domar, Investment, Losses and Monopolies, in Income, Employment and Public Policy 33 (1948).

In any event, it appears generally agreed that monopoly is not the sole factor affecting business cycles, and that other policies must be utilized as well as those embodied in the antitrust laws if stabilization is to be achieved. Hansen, Fiscal Policy and Business Cycles 315 et seq. (1941); Machlup, The Political Economy of Monopoly 62-63 (1952); Simons, Economic Policy for a Free Society 108 (1948); Ellis, Monetary Policy and Investment, 30 Am. Econ. Rev. 27, 36 (Supp. 1940); Johr, Regulation of Competition, in Chamberlin, ed., Monopoly and Competition and Their Regulation 338, 348-349 (International Economic Assn. 1954).

[27] Chamberlin, The Theory of Monopolistic Competition (1933); Robinson, The Economics of Imperfect Competition (1933); Galbraith, Monopoly and the Concentration of Economic Power, in A Survey of Contemporary Economics 99-100, 103 (Ellis ed. 1949).

[28] Harrod, Towards a Dynamic Economics 7 (1948); Schumpeter, Capitalism, Socialism and Democracy 103 (3d ed. 1950); Chamberlin, The Impact of Recent Monopoly Theory on the Schumpeterian System, 33 Rev. Econ. & Stat. 133, 138 (1951); Harbeson, A New Phase of the Antitrust Law, 45 Mich. L. Rev. 977, 998 (1947); Mason, Price and Production Policies of Large-Scale Enterprise, 29 Am. Econ. Rev. 61 (Supp. 1939); Wallace, Industrial Markets and Public Policy: Some Major Problems, in 1 Public Policy 59, 66 (Friedrich and Mason ed. 1940).

eration of an economy in which living standards are constantly rising.[29]

One of the most important contributions of dynamic theory lies in the proposition that profits must exceed levels of pure competition in order to stimulate growth and innovation. Since many ventures fail, new products must yield a monopoly return over some period to cover costs and to achieve the ideal of competition.[30] Some influence over the market is, therefore, necessary to stimulate the introduction of new products and new services; mere maintenance of the marginal return of an established business will not suffice.[31] The late Professor Joseph A. Schumpeter was perhaps the leading exponent of the foregoing views. He believed that firms must have some insurance against the risks of long-term investment and, hence, must secure a monopolistic position in order to make it practical to adopt innovation.[32] In his own words,

. . . largest-scale plans could in many cases not materialize at all if it were not known from the outset that competition will be discouraged by heavy capital requirements or lack of experience, or that means are available to discourage or checkmate it so as to gain the time and space for further developments.

The introduction of new methods of production and new commodities is hardly conceivable with perfect — and perfectly prompt — competition from the start. And this means that the bulk of what we call economic progress is incompatible with it.[33]

In short, Professor Schumpeter argued that innovators required some protection from the competitive forcing of prices toward short-run marginal costs.[34]

[29] Brems, Product Equilibrium Under Monopolistic Competition 120 (1951); Chamberlin, The Impact of Recent Monopoly Theory on the Schumpeterian System, in Schumpeter: Social Scientist 83, 86-87 (Harris ed. 1951); Markham, An Alternative Approach to the Concept of Workable Competition, 40 Am. Econ. Rev. 349, 360-361 (1950); Wright, Toward Coherent Anti-Trust, 35 Va. L. Rev. 665, 668 (1949).

[30] Discussion, 44 Am. Econ. Rev. 63, 65 (No. 2, 1954). An interesting example of an entrepreneur who invested and lost many, many millions in a variety of ventures and finally backed a winner is found in Air Reduction, 8 Fortune No. 1, pp. 24, 26 (1933).

[31] Nourse and Drury, Industrial Price Policies and Economic Progress 265, 271-272 (Brookings Institution Pub. No. 76, 1938); Abramovitz, Economics of Growth, in 2 A Survey of Contemporary Economics 132, 139 (Haley ed. 1952); Jacoby, Antitrust Policy Re-Examined, 58 J. Pol. Econ. 61, 62 (1950); Terborgh, Capitalism and Innovation, 40 Am. Econ. Rev. 118, 120 (Supp. 1950); Wright, Toward Coherent Anti-Trust, 35 Va. L. Rev. 665, 669, 676 (1949); cf. Fellner, Competition Among the Few 284, 306 (1949).

[32] Schumpeter, Capitalism, Socialism and Democracy 88 (3d ed. 1950).

[33] Id. at 89, 105. By "perfect" competition, Professor Schumpeter referred to the phenomenon herein called "pure" competition. Cf. Hennipman, Monopoly: Impediment or Stimulus to Economic Progress, in Chamberlin, ed., Monopoly and Competition and Their Regulation 421, 450 (International Economic Assn. 1954).

[34] Higgins, The Theory of Increasing Under-Employment, 60 Econ. J. 255, 261 (1950); Hildebrand, Monopolization and the Decline of Investment Opportunity, 33 Am. Econ. Rev. 591 (1943); Mason, Schumpeter on Monopoly and the Large Firm, in Schumpeter: Social Scientist 89, 90 (Harris ed. 1951); cf. Wallace, Market Control

More than incentive is required. Once a new enterprise is launched, monopoly profits are necessary to finance its growth.[35] Professor Schumpeter remarked that purely competitive enterprise might never show excess capacity; it might also show much less utilized capacity, he argued, simply because only big business can create and build ahead of demand.[36] In this connection, stress is laid upon the necessity of accumulating ample funds for technological research. Those funds, it is argued, could not be generated in a purely competitive economy.[37]

Competition, however, would not be abolished; under dynamic theory, it would merely take a different form. Perpetual innovation would give rise to the process of "creative destruction," which is the most effective type of competition. Competition from makers of the same commodity who cut prices is not nearly so important as that derived from innovation.[38] In the language of Professor Schumpeter,

> . . . it is not that kind of competition [from the maker of an identical product] which counts but the competition from the new commodity, the new technology, the new source of supply, the new type of organization (the largest-scale unit of control for instance) — competition which . . . strikes not at the margins of the profits and the outputs of the existing firms but at their foundations and

in the Aluminum Industry 348-349 (1937); Boulding, Toward a General Theory of Growth, 19 Can. J. Econ. & Pol. Sci. 326, 334 (1953). Some observers regard labor unions as threats to innovation and technological progress by reason of their ability to take the profit out of change by exertion of wage pressures. See Bronfenbrenner, The Incidence of Collective Bargaining, 44 Am. Econ. Rev. 293, 305 (No. 2, 1954). Some antecedents for the foregoing views can be found in the comparatively early literature. See Ricardo, Principles of Political Economy and Taxation 120 (Sraffa ed. 1951).

35 Nourse and Drury, Industrial Price Policies and Economic Progress 265 (Brookings Institution Pub. No. 76, 1938); Roos, Dynamic Economics 127 (1934); Schumpeter, Capitalism, Socialism and Democracy 87 (3d ed. 1950). Professor Hart carried the argument even further. He said that the identity (existence) of a firm depended upon possession of some sort of restricted business opportunity (monopoly power); otherwise, he urged, the firm would sell its assets and leave the field. See Hart, Anticipations, Business Planning, and the Cycle, 51 Q.J. Econ. 273, 277 (1937). Cf. Hennipman, Monopoly: Impediment or Stimulus to Economic Progress, in Chamberlin, ed., Monopoly and Competition and Their Regulation 421, 424-425 (International Economic Assn. 1954).

36 Schumpeter, Capitalism, Socialism and Democracy 106 (3d ed. 1950).

37 Wallace, Industrial Markets and Public Policy: Some Major Problems, in 1 Public Policy 59, 111 (Friedrich and Mason ed. 1940). "Expenditure for research is an exceptionally risky type of investment which as a rule, needs to be written off immediately and cannot be financed through the ordinary channels of the capital market. Only firms enjoying considerable and relatively stable monopoly profits can therefore regularly afford the large-scale research often required for innovations under modern technological conditions." Hennipman, Monopoly: Impediment or Stimulus to Economic Progress, in Chamberlin, ed., Monopoly and Competition and Their Regulation 421, 429 (International Economic Assn. 1954).

38 Domar, Investment, Losses and Monopolies, in Income, Employment and Public Policy 33, 53 (1948); Mason, Schumpeter on Monopoly and the Large Firm, in Schumpeter: Social Scientist 89, 91 (Harris ed. 1951); cf. Brems, Product Equilibrium Under Monopolistic Competition 245 (1951); Adelman, Effective Competition and the Antitrust Laws, 61 Harv. L. Rev. 1289, 1303 (1948).

their very lives. This kind of competition is as much more effective than the other as a bombardment is in comparison with forcing a door. . . .[39]

Arguments such as those advanced by Professor Schumpeter have not met with universal acceptance. Many economists believe that monopoly profits are not a necessary incentive to innovation; they think of competition itself as providing whatever incentive is required for the creation of new products.[40] The argument that monopoly is required to provide funds for growth does not impress them. They believe that funds for that purpose can be raised from other sources.[41] It appears likely, however, that market imperfections may play a considerable role in the economy, and thus support Professor Schumpeter's theory that monopoly profits are the most convenient means of financing such growth.[42] Whether technological research could not be financed without monopoly profits is also the subject of dispute. It has been argued that such research should be subsidized by government, rather than by monopoly profits.[43]

[39] Schumpeter, Capitalism, Socialism and Democracy 84 (3d ed. 1950). Professor Schumpeter also said:

"The best way of getting a vivid and realistic idea of industrial strategy is indeed to visualize the behavior of new concerns or industries that introduce new commodities or processes (such as the aluminum industry) or else reorganize a part or the whole of an industry (such as, for instance, the old Standard Oil Company).

"As we have seen, such concerns are aggressors by nature and wield the really effective weapon of competition. Their intrusion can only in the rarest of cases fail to improve total output in quantity or quality, both through the new method itself — even if at no time used to full advantage — and through the pressure it exerts on the preexisting firms." Id. at 89.

Cf. Steindl, Maturity and Stagnation in American Capitalism 43 (Oxford University Institute of Statistics, Monograph No. 4, 1952); Nutter, Monopoly, Bigness and Progress, 64 J. Pol. Econ. 520 (1956).

[40] Bowman, Toward Less Monopoly, 101 U. Pa. L. Rev. 577, 623, 628-629 (1953); Hildebrand, Monopolization and the Decline of Investment Opportunity, 33 Am. Econ. Rev. 591, 594, 596 (1943); cf. Zimmerman, The Propensity to Monopolize 29, 31 (1952). Something may depend upon the motives attributed to corporate executives. See Hurff, Social Aspects of Enterprise in the Large Corporation 7-8 (1950).

[41] Bowman, Toward Less Monopoly, 101 U. Pa. L. Rev. 577, 623, 624 (1953).

[42] Indivisibility compels the making of additional investment in long "jumps." See Robinson, Imperfect Competition Revisited, 63 Econ. J. 579, 591 (1953); cf. Machlup, The Economics of Sellers' Competition 234 (1952); Abramovitz, Economics of Growth, in 2 A Survey of Contemporary Economics 132, 139 (Haley ed. 1952); Chamberlin, The Product As an Economic Variable, 67 Q.J. Econ. 1, 14 (1953). Ignorance upon the part of investors may make the raising of such relatively large sums of difficult task. Cf. Schumpeter, Capitalism, Socialism and Democracy 87-88 (3d ed. 1950).

[43] Discussion, 44 Am. Econ. Rev. 196, 200 (No. 2, 1954). It is usually recognized that indivisibility prevents very small firms from carrying on important technological research. See, e.g., Nourse and Drury, Industrial Price Policies and Economic Progress 266 (Brookings Institution Pub. No. 76, 1938). Note also the interesting suggestion that technological research should be considered a cost of operation, and that hence no monopoly profit is required to finance it. See Solo, Innovation in the Capitalist Process: A Critique of the Schumpeterian Theory, 65 Q.J. Econ. 417, 427 (1951).

More fundamentally, the neoclassic economist argues that the incentives produced by monopoly profits may simply lead to a less desirable allocation of resources than pure competition would accomplish. That venture capital has entered into a particular field in which rewards are rich does not mean that society as a whole will benefit. Greater production of established commodities may, for example, be more beneficial than the introduction of new gadgets.[44] There is nothing to indicate that innovation in and of itself is desirable — that is, that any particular innovation or invention constitutes a better allocation of resources than obtained prior to its introduction.[45]

To this old controversy over the relative efficacy of the carrot and the stick in the promotion of economic change, there is no theoretical answer.[46] We can point out that competition is a somewhat limited device for spurring the introduction of new products and new services. In other words, competition operates only upon the established firm and does not offer an incentive for innovation.[47] On the other hand, we can well agree with Professor Bowman, who said:

[44] Machlup, The Political Economy of Monopoly 66 (1952); Bowman, Toward Less Monopoly, 101 U. Pa. L. Rev. 577, 623 (1953); Stigler, Industrial Organization and Economic Progress, in The State of the Social Sciences 269 (White ed. 1956).

[45] Penrose, The Economics of the International Patent System 35 (1951); Plant, The Economic Theory Concerning Patents for Inventions, 1 Economica (N.S.) 30, 39-42 (1934). Professor Bowman said: "There just is no system of economic calculus which can prove that the social gain from new productive facilities and technical changes or innovations created by monopoly offsets the loss of other output." Bowman, Toward Less Monopoly, 101 U. Pa. L. Rev. 577, 629 (1953).

Many observers, however, would take the position that only innovation has raised living standards above the levels of a "bare hands" economy. Indeed, Professor Wallace went so far as to say that stimulation of industrial research and continuous adoption of improvements should probably be the most important objective of public policy. See Wallace, Industrial Markets and Public Policy: Some Major Problems, in 1 Public Policy 59, 120 (Friedrich and Mason ed. 1940). Innovation may also play an important role in preventing the "vesting" of economic interests and their entrenchment behind legal barriers. Cf. Wright, The Economics of Disturbance 90 et seq. (1947); Domar, Investment, Losses and Monopolies, in Income, Employment and Public Policy 33, 49-50 (1948).

[46] Machlup, The Political Economy of Monopoly 65 (1952); Mason, Schumpeter on Monopoly and the Large Firm, in Schumpeter: Social Scientist 89, 90 (Harris ed. 1951).

"In the basic doctrine of competitive-minded liberalism, the problem competition-monopoly-efficiency was centered around the behaviour of the individual firm or still more typically, the individual entrepreneur in person. The basic postulate runs along the line, that a donkey (the entrepreneur) is made more efficient by dangling a carrot (profits) in front of him and a whip (loss) on his back (the typical situation of competition), than by keeping him in a state of well-fed prosperity (under monopoly). As an argument ad moninem, one must admit that this view of human behaviour has a very strong appeal. But, as far as I know, it has not been possible to verify it by economic research. As stated in the liberal doctrine, the empirical tests would also rather have to be provided by psychological research. How it would stand up to such tests, I do not know." Svennilson, Monopoly, Efficiency, and the Structure of Industry, in Chamberlin, ed., Monopoly and Competition and Their Regulation 272-273 (International Economic Assn. 1954).

[47] Whether new firms should be encouraged to enter into business or old ones induced to manufacture new products and the like raises questions of diversification,

The amount of monopoly in the system has no fixed relationship to the "right" amount of investment, and no rule for determining the proper amount of investment in the absence of the standard of the market place has been forthcoming.[48]

What does seem clear is that the "dynamic" theorists stress long-term considerations. They are content, in the short run, with an economy characterized by a considerable degree of monopoly. Their opponents are more concerned with the short run, and worry less about long-term effects.[49]

II. Empirical Evidence

A. *In Support of Static Theory*

As indicated above, neoclassic economic theory envisages competition as the primary source of those innovations which raise living standards. It is easy to find examples of such effects flowing from competition. Indeed, it is a commonplace that competition is a force encouraging constant change; competitors are constantly watching their rivals and attempting to meet the threat of lower prices, new models, and the like. For example, the Texas Company at first shipped its oil abroad in packages, but later the competition from other suppliers forced it to set up bulk storage facilities in foreign areas.[50] A manufacturer of pharmaceutical products found that competition in its established drugs was intense; accordingly, from 45 to 73 per cent of its volume was pushed in the direction of "specialties" on which profit margins appeared to be larger.[51]

Businessmen recognize the force of competition as a stimulant to innovation. Thus it was recently said:

---

of the imperfections involved in the cost of entry into and exit from the market, and of wealth in that the corporate entity would be perpetuated.

[48] Bowman, Toward Less Monopoly, 101 U. Pa. L. Rev. 577, 624 (1953).

[49] Id. at 622. In the short run, sellers are supposed to respond to a change in price by making such alterations in their rate of output as they find worthwhile without changing their existing equipment and managerial personnel. In the long run, changes in output are considered free of these limitations. Abramovitz, An Approach to a Price Theory for a Changing Economy 13 n.5 (1939).

[50] Answer of Texas Company, ¶3, United States v. Standard Oil Co. of New Jersey, Civ. 86-27, S.D.N.Y.; defendants' answers filed Sept. 1, 1953; amended answer filed by Texas Company, Sept. 21, 1953.

[51] Sharp & Dohme, Inc., 1952 Ann. Rep. 12 (Philadelphia, 1953); *accord:* United States v. E. I. Du Pont de Nemours & Co., 118 F. Supp. 41, 186 (D. Del. 1953); American Brake Shoe Co., 1953 Ann. Rep. 26 (New York City, 1954); Carrier Corp., 1952 Ann. Rep. 4, 6, 13 (Syracuse, 1953); Gibb, The Saco-Lowell Shops 172, 597 (1950); Aluminum Company of America, 10 Fortune No. 3, pp. 46, 102 (1934); Gerschenkron, Economic Backwardness in Historical Perspective, in The Progress of Underdeveloped Areas 3, 10 (Houselitz ed. 1952). Possibly pressure from labor unions for high wage rates can also provide incentives to innovation. Phelps Dodge Corp., 1953 Ann. Rep. 5 (New York City, 1954).

The American economy is in a period of transition. . . . once again, competition is the spur which is urging business on in its never-ending pursuit for new products and better methods leading to an ever-growing standard of living.[52]

It is also easy to document the accusation that monopoly is often inert and slow moving. Thus an observer reported that the vast investment of the United States Steel Corporation had always worked against change, the chief energies of its management being devoted to the prevention of deterioration in its investment, and not to its rapid growth or development.[53]

Considerable evidence exists as to the source of innovation in the economy. As indicated above, dynamic theory requires the prospect of monopoly profit as an incentive to growth and change. Furthermore it demands high earnings as a condition precedent to the large investment requisite for growth. If all that is true, it is difficult to understand why wholly independent inventors so frequently are responsible for fundamental technological improvements.

For many years the Winchester Repeating Arms Company, a leading manufacturer of rifles and shotguns, depended heavily for new inventions on the Browning brothers. The Brownings were self-taught, untrained inventors who resided in the then remote region of Utah.[54] The solvent standardized for use in dry-cleaning establishments was not developed by the manufacturers of the liquids formerly used for that purpose. Instead, it was originated by the proprietor of a modest dry-cleaning establishment in Atlanta, Georgia.[55] In 1929, a relatively simple new idea for cementing shoes was offered to the great United Shoe Machinery Company. United Shoe would pay only $50,000 for the invention, and its sponsors refused to accept so low a figure. By 1932 the new idea was producing earnings of $124,000 per year.[56]

[52] Caterpillar Tractor Co. (California), 1953 Ann. Rep. 12 (Peoria, 1954). Another corporate report stated: ". . . competition stimulates improvements, increases research and lowers costs, all resulting in increased benefits to the consuming public." Pure Oil Co., 40th Ann. Rep. 2 (Chicago, 1954).

[53] Gibb, The Saco-Lowell Shops 402 (1950); Scoville, Revolution in Glass Making 240 (1948); 109 Degrees Below Zero, 6 Fortune No. 1, pp. 74, 82 (1932); U.S. Steel: I, 13 id. No. 3, pp. 59, 170 (1936).

[54] Williamson, Winchester: The Gun That Won the West 97 et seq. (1952).

[55] Osborne, This Business of Dry Cleaning, 11 Orange Disc 8, 9 (Gulf Oil Corp., Aug. 1953).

[56] And There's a Company Called Compo, 8 Fortune No. 3, pp. 42, 114 (1933); accord: Longstreet, A Century on Wheels 66 (1952); MacLaurin, Invention and Innovation in the Radio Industry 218 (1949); Markham, Competition in the Rayon Industry 8 (1952); Sherman and Sherman, The New Fibers 166 (1946); Wallace, Market Control in the Aluminum Industry 59 (1937); Perham, Ideas and Dollars, 34 Barron's No. 13, p. 3 (1954); cf. MacLaurin, Patents and Technical Progress, 58 J. Pol. Econ. 142, 148 (1950) (untrained farm boy from Idaho made spectacular advances in television with financial backing of individuals and an established firm). In a public lecture delivered at the University of Chicago Law School on May 13, 1954, Professor John Jewkes reported that research carried on by him had suggested results similar to those referred to above. His investigations, although based on a

Events of the type just related may have impressed Charles F. Kettering of the General Motors Corporation. He stated to a congressional committee that there were many brilliant inventors outside the General Motors laboratories. Indeed, he said, GM does not lock its laboratories because it would lock out so much more than it would lock in.[57]

Against the argument that large firms are required to finance important innovations, there can be cited instance after instance in which small, struggling firms without large financial resources have made striking contributions to the technological progress of the nation. Brushless shaving soaps, for example, did not originate with one of the leading manufacturers of shaving cream. Colgate, Palmolive, and the others slept while Barbasol introduced the new product.[58] Several of the most important innovations in aircraft engines were the work of new, small firms in the face of indifference or hostility on the part of industry leaders.[59] Radio Corporation of America, closely linked to both General Electric and Westinghouse, with a long head start and important patent rights, still was unable to keep up with its much smaller competitors.[60] The self-service supermarket, constituting the greatest innovation in the distribution of food products in many years, was not originated by the Great Atlantic & Pacific Tea Company or one of its major rivals. It was developed by independent food stores.[61]

Frequently, new ideas arise in the minds of customers or suppliers of established firms. Market research surveys were conceived not by manufacturers, but by a farsighted advertising agency.[62] The Pittsburgh Plate Glass Company, although committed to the reinvestment of its profits, permitted two highly important developments to originate outside its industry: the continuous process of making plate glass was started by Henry Ford, and an independent French chemist invented "safety" glass.[63]

---

qualitative rather than a quantitative plane, indicated that the "independent" inventor still plays a large role in technological advance.

[57] TNEC Hearings, pt. 2, at 351.

[58] Colgate-Palmolive-Peet, 13 Fortune No. 4, pp. 120, 144 (1936).

[59] Schlaifer, Big Business and Small Business: A Case Study, 28 Harv. Bus. Rev. No. 4, pp. 97, 98 (1950).

[60] Blue Chip, 6 Fortune No. 3, pp. 45, 102 (1932); Bethlehem Steel, 23 id. No. 4, pp. 61, 68 (1941).

[61] Fulda, Food Distribution in the United States, The Struggle Between Independents and Chains, 99 U. Pa. L. Rev. 1051, 1064 (1951); accord: Bright, The Electric-Lamp Industry 462 (1949); Cochrane, The Pabst Brewing Company 102 (1948); Gibb, The Saco-Lowell Shops 76-77, 314, 351 (1950); Hower, History of Macy's of New York, 1858-1919, at 21 et seq., 48, 50, 52, 119-120 (1943); MacLaurin, Invention and Innovation in the Radio Industry 23, 143 et seq., 186 et seq. (1949); Bright and MacLaurin, Economic Factors Influencing the Development and Introduction of the Fluorescent Lamp, 51 J. Pol. Econ. 429, 439, 449 (1943); In Television, Admiral's Hot, 39 Fortune No. 6, pp. 89, 128 (1949); United States Leather, 11 id. No. 2, pp. 57, 100 (1935).

[62] Hower, The History of an Advertising Agency 88-89 (1939).

[63] Life Goes On, 9 Fortune No. 1, pp. 42, 88 (1934); accord: Hower, The History of an Advertising Agency 96 (1939); Hower, History of Macy's of New York, 1858-1919, at 219-220 (1943); 1 Nevins, Study in Power 349 (1953). Occasionally university

Considerable evidence also can be mustered against the argument that large firms, financed by generous profits, are necessary to maintain those research laboratories which alone produce technological change. In many instances the results have been disappointing. Neither the cable nor the telegraph companies were interested in developing the wireless radio. Those firms were apparently preoccupied with perfecting existing mechanisms, and paid little attention to Marconi's great advance in communication.[64] We have a judicial finding to the effect that the Pullman Company displayed obdurate resistance to changes in the types of sleeping cars requested by railways.[65] The Bell Telephone Laboratories have been financed with generous appropriations over a long period of time; they have not, however, produced startling inventions.[66] Established manufacturers of carriages and bicycles played only a subordinate role in the development of the automobile, and makers of steam locomotives seem not to have participated at all.[67] In view of the meager results obtained from research in the laboratories of big business,[68] it has sometimes been argued that invention is purely an accident, a by-product of other efforts which cannot be purchased.[69]

---

laboratories, dedicated to "pure" science, are the birthplaces of commercial innovations. MacLaurin, Invention and Innovation in the Radio Industry 20, 183 (1949). In the nature of things, however, such innovations must be considered fortuitous in character.

[64] MacLaurin, Invention and Innovation in the Radio Industry 25 (1949).

[65] United States v. Pullman Co., 50 F. Supp. 123, 134 (E.D. Pa. 1943), aff'd per curiam, 330 U.S. 806 (1947).

[66] MacLaurin, Invention and Innovation in the Radio Industry 159-160 (1949); Adelman, Measurement of Industrial Concentration, 33 Rev. Econ. & Stat. 269, 279 (1951).

[67] Nevins, Ford: The Times, the Man, the Company, c. 8 (1954); accord: Bright, The Electric-Lamp Industry 455 (1949); Gibb, The Saco-Lowell Shops 149, 214 (1950); Gibb, The Whitesmiths of Taunton: A History of Reed & Barton 174-175, 190-191 (1943); Rostow, The Process of Economic Growth 48-49 (1952); Abramovitz, Monopolistic Selling in a Changing Economy, 52 Q.J. Econ. 191, 207 (1938); Schlaifer, Big Business and Small Business: A Case Study, 28 Harv. Bus. Rev. No. 4, pp. 97, 101 (1950); U.S. Steel: II, 13 Fortune No. 4, pp. 127, 128 (1936). The controversy as to whether the established firm or the independent inventor is responsible for more innovation goes back to the days of Adam Smith, who attributed invention to the specialization of labor (i.e., the established firm). See Plant, The Economic Theory Concerning Patents for Inventions, 1 Economica (N.S.) 30, ¶11 (1934).

[68] United States v. United Shoe Machinery Corp., 110 F. Supp. 295, 331, 337 (D. Mass. 1953), aff'd per curiam, 347 U.S. 521 (1954); Celler Committee I, ser. 14, pt. 2-A, at 319, pt. 2-B, at 931; Rostow, Market Organization and Stabilization Policy, in Income Stabilization for a Developing Economy 475 (Millikan ed. 1954).

[69] Cf. Gilfillan, The Prediction of Technical Change, 34 Rev. Econ. & Stat. 368, 369 (1952). A leading businessman has been quoted to the effect that you can influence research environmentally, but you cannot lead it; you must follow where research leads. General Mills, Inc., 20th Ann. Rep. 34 (Minneapolis, 1948). That statement, of course, reflects a somewhat different point of view from the one expressed in the text.

B. *In Support of Dynamic Theory*

On the other hand, many events of our commercial history support the thesis advanced by Professor Schumpeter. His doctrine of "creative destruction" is amply buttressed by evidence. That theory, as stated above, indicates that competition from established firms making identical products is vastly less important than the competitive effects of innovation.

Power tools directly driven by attached electric motors destroyed the "trust's" market for leather belting which had been used to connect overhead shafts with individual workbenches in factories.[70] When sales of rubber footwear declined drastically, the change was attributed to increased use of the automobile, and not to competition from new manufacturers of shoes.[71] Facilities for the manufacture and use of ice made from water were sharply reduced in value by the innovation of carbon dioxide (dry ice).[72]

Indeed, evidence is often available to show two stages of "creative destruction" operating in rapid sequence. For example, no sooner did solid carbon dioxide capture a foothold in the refrigeration business than a new method, employing silica gel, was developed and began to cut into its prospects.[73] In 1912, the Great Atlantic & Pacific Tea Company operated a prosperous chain of four hundred grocery stores. In that year John Hartford launched the "economy" self-service cash-and-carry store which rapidly took business away from both the regular A & P stores and their competitors. For several years the innovation was so successful that eight new "economy" stores were opened per day. Finally, however, in 1932, rivals opened "supermarkets" which cut prices below the costs of the A & P chain, and in turn drove the "economy" self-service stores from the field.[74] Any reasonable familiarity with business history indicates that Professor Schumpeter's "creative destruction" is a force at least as powerful as competition itself.[75]

---

[70] United States Leather, 11 Fortune No. 2, pp. 57, 100 (1935); cf. Hobby, Bottles or Cans, 34 Barron's, No. 42, p. 7 (1954).

[71] U.S. Rubber, 9 Fortune No. 2, pp. 52, 127 (1934); Pianos, 20 id. No. 2, p. 45 (1939). Cf. Steindl, Maturity and Stagnation in American Capitalism 41-42 (Oxford University Institute of Statistics, Monograph No. 4 (1952).

[72] 109 Degrees Below Zero, 6 Fortune No. 1, pp. 74, 82 (1932).

[73] Id. at 80.

[74] Biggest Family Business, 7 Fortune No. 3, pp. 52, 55, 128, 132 (1933).

[75] Balian Ice Cream Co. v. Arden Farms Co., 104 F. Supp. 796, 806 (S.D. Cal. 1952); United States v. Aluminum Co. of America, 44 F. Supp. 97, 355 (S.D.N.Y. 1941), *rev'd in part*, 148 F.2d 416 (2d Cir. 1945); Celler Committee I, ser. 14, pt. 2-B, at 814-815; Chute, Marketing Burned-Clay Products 73, 88, 284, 285 (1939); Diamond Match Co., 1948 Ann. Rep. 7 (New York City, 1949); Gibb, The Saco-Lowell Shops 539 (1950); United Fruit Co., 53d Ann. Rep. 19 (Boston, 1953); Wilcox, Competition and Monopoly in American Industry 308 (TNEC Monograph No. 21, 1940); Henle, Variety Chains, 34 Barron's No. 12, p. 19 (1954). But cf. Steindl, Maturity and Stagnation in American Capitalism 41 (Oxford University Institute of Statistics, Monograph No. 4, 1952).

In dynamic theory, monopolistic profits are required to call forth new inventions and growth in the economy. The earnings permitted business enterprise under a regime of "pure" competition would not, it is urged, suffice to encourage innovation. Considerable empirical evidence supports such views. In the first place, it is not difficult to find instances in which new ventures were induced by the prospect of substantial profits. So far as causation can be isolated in the actual business world, it appears that growth and change have often resulted from the hopes of investors for substantial returns.[76] It can also be shown that innovations have actually resulted in the past when business profits have been substantial. Thus the monopolistic profits earned by the Radio Corporation of America from its patent pool were used to defray the tremendous costs of developing television.[77] When enterprise has been unable to earn such handsome rewards, innovation has often been retarded.[78]

Another phenomenon worthy of note is the growth of business corporations through retention of earnings. The existence and retention of those earnings suggest that profits have been higher than would be permissible under a system of "pure" competition; that the growth of the firm has been induced by the carrot rather than the stick. Under present federal tax policies, of course, the retention of earnings by corporate enterprise is encouraged.[79] Long before those sections were inserted in the Internal Revenue Code, however, many prominent

[76] Gibb, The Whitesmiths of Taunton: A History of Reed & Barton 6-7 (1943); MacLaurin, Invention and Innovation in the Radio Industry 34 (1949); Minnesota Mining & Manufacturing Co., 1953 Ann. Rep. (St. Paul, 1954); Minnesota Mining in Motion, 39 Fortune No. 3, pp. 93, 96, 162 (1949). But cf. Penrose, The Economics of the International Patent System 39 (1951) (comparisons between nations with and without patent systems do not prove that patent reward is necessary for innovation). It is, of course, well understood that innovators have often made handsome profits. United States v. Aluminum Co. of America, 44 F. Supp. 97, 302 (S.D.N.Y. 1941), rev'd in part, 148 F.2d 416 (2d Cir. 1945); Gibb, The Saco-Lowell Shops 27 (1950); Scoville, Revolution in Glass Making 83 (1948). The existence of those magnificent returns is a matter of general knowledge, and hence can be taken as an inducement to new firms to enter other promising fields.

[77] United States v. Aluminum Co. of America, 44 F. Supp. 97, 309 (S.D.N.Y. 1941), rev'd in part, 148 F.2d 416 (2d Cir. 1945); Continental Can. Co., Inc., 1952 Ann. Rep. 7, 23 (New York City, 1953); Dow Chemical Co., 1953 Ann. Rep. 7 et seq. (Midland, 1953); Greyhound Corp., 1952 Report to Stockholders 5, 11 (Chicago, 1953); Bernstein, Profit Theory — Where Do We Go From Here? 67 Q.J. Econ. 407, 412 (1953; MacLaurin, Patents and Technical Progress — A Study of Television, 58 J. Pol. Econ. 142, 147 (1950); MacLaurin, Technological Progress in Some American Industries, 44 Am. Econ. Rev. 178, 186 (1954); Minnesota Mining in Motion, 39 Fortune, No. 3, pp. 93, 96 (1949); 2 NaCl+2 $H_2O \rightarrow 2$ Na(OH)+Cl_2+H_2, 3 id. No. 4, pp. 58, 158 (1931). But cf. Scoville, Revolution in Glass Making 271 (1948).

[78] MacLaurin, Invention and Innovation in the Radio Industry 149 (1949); American Sugar Refining Co., 7 Fortune No. 2, pp. 59, 60-61 (1933); MacLaurin, Patents and Technical Progress — A Study of Television, 58 J. Pol. Econ. 142, 150-151, 155 (1950); MacLaurin, Technological Progress in Some American Industries, 44 Am. Econ. Rev. 178, 187 (1954); cf. Adelman, The Large Firm and Its Suppliers, 31 Rev. Econ. & Stat. 113, 117 (1949).

[79] Int. Rev. Code of 1954, §34.

American concerns had prospered and grown large on earnings plowed back into the business. Such was the case, for example, with the Winchester Arms Company, the Ford Motor Company, the Pabst Brewing Company, the American Viscose Company, R. H. Macy & Company[80] and many others.[81] Those which did not rely wholly upon retained earnings may have done so in large measure, particularly in their earlier years.[82] The process of growth through retention of earnings continues into the present day.[83] Even mature, well-established firms find it desirable to enhance their assets through the retention of profits.[84] Indeed, lavish disbursement of earnings in the form of dividends is regarded with apprehension by investors.[85]

[80] Cochran, The Pabst Brewing Company 23, 66, 84 (1948); Hower, History of Macy's of New York, 1858-1919, at 228 (1943); Nevins, Ford: The Times, the Man, the Company 339, 490 (1954); Williamson, Winchester: The Gun That Won the West 48, 80, 209 (1952).

[81] Campbell and Hatton, Herbert H. Dow, Pioneer in Creative Chemistry 47 (1951); Cross, From Land, Sea and Test Tube 64 (1954); Gibb, The Whitesmiths of Taunton: A History of Reed & Barton 348 (1943); Hansen, Fiscal Policy and Business Cycles 367 (1941); Hower, The History of an Advertising Agency 51 (1939); Longstreet, A Century on Wheels 52 (1952); Markham, Competition in the Rayon Industry 16 (1952); 1 Nevins, Study in Power 74, 151 (1953); Wallace, Market Control in the Aluminum Industry 29 (1937).

[82] Bendix Aviation Corp., 1952 Ann. Rep. 9 (Detroit, 1953); Lion Oil Co., 30th Ann. Rep. 3 (Eldorado, Ark., 1954); Sylvania Electric Products, Inc., 1953 Ann. Rep. 6, 8 (New York City, 1954); cf. 1 Nevins, Study in Power 34, 58 (1953).

[83] Borg-Warner Corp., 1952 Ann. Rep. 8 (Chicago); Gulf Oil Corp., 1952 Ann. Rep. 4 (Pittsburgh, 1953); Merck & Co., 1948 Ann. Rep. 4 (Philadelphia, 1949); National Lead Co., 61st Ann. Rep. 10 (New York City, 1953); Socony-Vacuum Oil Co., 1952 Ann. Rep. 6 (New York City, 1953); F. W. Woolworth Co., Woolworth's First 75 Years 61 (1954). The following statement appeared in Minneapolis-Honeywell Regulator Co., 1952 Ann. Rep. 7 (Minneapolis, 1953): "Year after year through its history, Honeywell has retained in the business a very substantial share of earnings to finance its future capital requirements. In normal times that policy is sound; indeed it is basic in a growth company."

[84] Celanese Corp. of America, 1948 Ann. Rep. 7, 10 (New York City, 1949); General Motors Corp., 44th Ann. Rep. 32 (New York City, 1953); Gibb, The Saco-Lowell Shops 611-613 (1950); Gulf Oil Corp., 1952 Ann. Rep. 4 (Pittsburgh, 1953); National Biscuit Co., 1950 Ann. Rep. 7 (New York City); Radio Corp. of America, 1952 Ann. Rep. 7 (New York City, 1953); Standard Oil Co. of Indiana, 1952 Ann. Rep. 8 (Chicago, 1953); Wisconsin Power & Light Co., 1952 Ann. Rep. 4 (Madison, Wis.); Burlington Mills, 40 Fortune No. 1, pp. 82, 95, 110 (1949); Walton, U.S. Gypsum, 34 Barron's No. 8, pp. 23, 25 (1954). The following statement appeared in Gulf Oil Corp., 1953 Ann. Rep. 4 (Pittsburgh, 1954): "Being a growth company in a growth industry, Gulf for some time has followed the policy of financing its replacement and growth requirements out of retained earnings and plant exhaustion charges, thus avoiding expansion in its long-term debt or invasion of its high degree of liquidity. This form of financing has involved the re-investment of a substantial portion of net income. . . ." Cf. Thompson, Since Spindletop 49 (Gulf Oil Corp. 1951); Steindl, Maturity and Stagnation in American Capitalism 42 (Oxford University Institute of Statistics, Monograph No. 4, 1952).

[85] Gibb, The Saco-Lowell Shops 394 (1950); U.S. Rubber, 9 Fortune No. 2, p. 52 (1934). But cf. Hower, History of Macy's of New York, 1858-1919, at 110, 127 (1943). It can be argued that funds for the growth of enterprise should be obtained out of the general savings of the community; in other words, that successful corporations should resort to the flotation of securities and obtain their capital from the

Taking the foregoing factors into account, we cannot overlook the considerable evidence suggesting a positive correlation between growth, innovation and earnings above marginal standards. Quantitative proof of the connection has not been attempted, and would probably be impossible. Furthermore, the growth of firms with monopoly profits does not indicate that their industries or, indeed, the economy as a whole, has grown equally rapidly. There nevertheless remains an impression[86] supporting Professor Schumpeter's thesis that earnings above the normal interest rates assist in the process of innovation and in the encouragement of growth.

There is also evidence to support the thesis that big business spends large sums for technological research and receives a commensurate return. Some $5 billion is spent annually on industrial research in the United States, and it is claimed that the Du Pont Company alone spent $22 million to put a new fiber, orlon, on the market.[87] Many other tremendous expenditures are reported. The Standard Oil Company of New Jersey, for example, spent $18.2 million on research and development in 1947. That figure constituted 0.76 per cent of its sales. Other firms report even higher percentages.[88] A survey of 191 leading

---

savings of individuals, rather than from the retained earnings of their shareholders. Hurff, Social Aspects of Enterprise in the Large Corporation 93 (1950).

As a practical matter, however, market imperfections, meaning chiefly the ignorance of investors, make it more difficult to raise funds by such means. Robinson, Imperfect Competition Revisited, 63 Econ. J. 579, 583 (1953). In addition, and more importantly, neither investment bankers nor investors would look with favor upon a security issue unless it were amply buttressed by earnings. Air Reduction, 8 Fortune No. 1, pp 24, 118 (1933).

Accordingly, retention of profits within the corporation merely avoids the friction incidental to capital markets and permits original managers to retain control even through periods of depression. Gibb, The Saco-Lowell Shops 291 (1950); Chase, Danger at the A. O. Smith Corporation, 2 Fortune No. 5, pp. 62, 63 (1930); Osborn, Efficiency and Profitability in Relation to Size, 29 Harv. Bus. Rev. No. 2, pp. 82, 94 (1951). More closely related to the growth problem are the discussions in Buchanan, The Economics of Corporate Enterprise 256 (1940); Abramovitz, Economics of Growth, in 2 A Survey of Contemporary Economics 132 (Haley ed. 1952).

86 Perhaps it should be recorded that the authors have examined many business histories and annual reports of corporations which are not cited herein. To some extent, their "impressions" are derived in negative fashion from facts which did not appear in those materials. Cf. McLean and Haigh, How Business Corporations Grow, 32 Harv. Bus. Rev. No. 6, pp. 81, 82 (1954).

87 E. I. du Pont de Nemours & Co., Du Pont Stockholder 3 (Summer, 1950). See also United States v. Aluminum Co. of America, 44 F. Supp. 97, 143 (S.D.N.Y. 1941), rev'd in part, 148 F.2d 416 (2d Cir. 1945); Burns, The Decline of Competition 420 (1936); Terborgh, Capitalism and Innovation, 40 Am. Econ. Rev. 118, 120 (Supp. 1950); Walton, U.S. Gypsum, 34 Barron's No. 8, pp. 23, 25 (1954).

88 Corning Glass Works, 1953 Ann. Rep. 8 (Corning, 1954); E. I. du Pont de Nemours & Co., 1950 Ann. Rep. 8, 38 (Wilmington, 1951); Philco Corp., 59th Ann. Rep. 10, 22 (Philadelphia, 1951); Socony-Vacuum Oil Co., 1953 Ann. Rep. 10, 18 (New York City, 1954), 1952 Ann. Rep. 9, 19 (1953); Standard Oil Co. of Indiana, 1952 Ann. Rep. 14 (Chicago, 1953); Standard Oil Co. of New Jersey, 1948 Ann. Rep. 24-25, 30 (New York City, 1949, 1947 Ann. Rep. 15, 26 (1948). In the foregoing reports, research and development expenditures constituted respectively 3.5, 2.9, 2.1, .83, .74, .87, .61, and .76 per cent of sales. Note the approximately identical percentages in the oil industry. It is, of course, difficult to define the

companies showed that such expenditures ranged from 0.3 per cent for food and kindred products, up to 4.9 per cent in the drug industry.[89] As many as 1 out of every 10 employees of an established firm may be engaged in research and engineering activities.[90] Available evidence also suggests that such expenditures are concentrated in large firms. Thus a study showed that 92 per cent of the companies employing more than 5000 persons had laboratories, but that less than 10 per cent of the firms with only 500 employees had such facilities.[91]

Mere expenditure of money on technological research does not, of course, establish the proposition that large firms are more productive of innovation than small ones.[92] Only the results of such expenditures are strictly relevant to the proof of the proposition. Observers have detected a good many instances in which such results have been impressive. A careful investigator of the radio industry declared flatly that the research and development done by the large companies in that field substantiated Professor Schumpeter's theories.[93] Again, most inventions in the lamp industry since 1912 have come from the laboratories of the General Electric Company.[94] A trial court recently found that the research activities of the Du Pont Company had had significant results in the development of new products.[95] Rare is the annual re-

expenditures involved in "research and development." Cf. Dearborn, Kneznek, and Anthony, Spending for Industrial Research 1 (1953).

[89] Id. at viii. Comparable results were reported in Sherman, "Seed" Money, 34 Barron's No. 29, p. 11 (1954). Sherman's compilation of such expenditures by 34 well-known corporations showed a mean disbursement of 1.8 per cent of sales.

[90] Minneapolis-Honeywell Regulator Co., 1952 Ann. Rep. 14 (Minneapolis, 1953); Sylvania Electric Products, Inc., 1953 Ann. Rep. 14 (New York City, 1954); Minnesota Mining in Motion, 39 Fortune No. 3, pp. 93, 95 (1949).

[91] Dearborn, Kneznek and Anthony, Spending for Industrial Research 12 (1953); Adelman, Measurement of Industrial Concentration, 33 Rev. Econ. & Stat. 269, 278 (1951). See also United States v. Aluminum Co. of America, 91 F. Supp. 333, 383-386 (S.D.N.Y. 1950).

[92] Dearborn, Kneznek and Anthony, Spending for Industrial Research 1 (1953).

[93] MacLaurin, Invention and Innovation in the Radio Industry 154, 178, 196 (1949); 2 Nevins, Study in Power: John D. Rockefeller, Industrialist and Philanthropist 101 (1953).

[94] Bright, The Electric-Lamp Industry 449, 469 (1949); 2 Nevins, Study in Power 101 (1953).

[95] United States v. E. I. Du Pont de Nemours & Co., 118 F. Supp. 41, 74 (D. Del. 1953), aff'd, 351 U.S. 377 (1956); accord: United States v. United Shoe Machinery Corp., 110 F. Supp. 295, 330 (D. Mass. 1953), aff'd per curiam, 347 U.S. 521 (1954); United States v. Aluminum Co. of America, 44 F. Supp. 97, 207 (S.D.N.Y. 1941), rev'd in part, 148 F.2d 416 (2d Cir. 1945); TNEC Hearings, pt. 3, at 872 et seq., 899, 911-924, 949-958, 971-976; Gibb, The Saco-Lowell Shops 594-600 (1950); Gibb, The Whitesmiths of Taunton: A History of Reed & Barton 56-59, 72-75, 118-122, 327 (1943); Hansen, Fiscal Policy and Business Cycles 379-380 (1941); Hower, The History of an Advertising Agency 71-78, 161 (1939); Longstreet, A Century on Wheels 25, 69-70 (1952); Markham, Competition in the Rayon Industry 7 (1952); National Industrial Conference Board, Mergers in Industry 118-119 (1929); Sherman and Sherman, The New Fibers 71, 109-110, 183 (1946); Thompson, Since Spindletop 27 (Gulf Oil Corp. 1951); American Sugar Refining Co., 7 Fortune No. 2, pp. 59, 60 (1933); Chamberlin, Tomorrow's Factories, 34 Barron's No. 11, p. 3 (1954); Profits in Cans, 9 Fortune No. 4, pp. 76, 138 (1934); Nylon, 22 id. No. 1, p. 57 (1940).

port of a nationally known corporation that does not boast of its technological research and of the new products developed by it during the year under review.[96]

The argument that invention is a mere accident and cannot be the result of conscious purpose is at least partially refuted by industrial experience.[97] Large firms not only develop new products, they actually sell them. In 1948, for example, a company claimed that sales of products developed by its own research and either not in existence or having little or no commercial value two years before exceeded $9 million.[98] Other firms have reported from time to time that from 40 to 85 per cent of their sales was represented by products developed in their own research laboratories.[99] Such statistics are difficult to ignore, even though the degree of development added to the products by the concerns involved cannot be gauged. In some instances these figures form a striking comparison with comparable results achieved by small firms in industries more "purely" competitive in character.[100]

Observers have often suggested that large firms become complacent and passive.[101] If that is true, countervailing factors must be at work

[96] Continental Can Co., 1952 Ann. Rep. 8, 9 (New York City, 1953); Deere & Co., 1952 Ann. Rep. 7 (Moline, 1953); General Motors Corp., 44th Ann. Rep. 13, 15 (New York City, 1953), 40th Ann. Rep. 10, 15 (1949); Gulf Oil Corp., 1952 Ann. Rep. 18, 21 (Pittsburgh, 1953); Merck & Co., 1948 Ann. Rep. 4 (Philadelphia, 1949); National Biscuit Co., 1950 Ann. Rep. 8, 22 (New York City); Parke, Davis & Co., 82d Ann. Rep. 2, 8 (Detroit, 1949); Pittsburgh Plate Glass Co., 70th Ann. Rep. 8 (Pittsburgh, 1954); Radio Corp. of America, 1952 Ann. Rep. 13 et seq. (New York City, 1953); R. J. Reynolds Tobacco Co., 1952 Ann. Rep. 8 (Winston-Salem, 1953); Sterling Drug, Inc., 1952 Ann. Rep. 8 (New York City, 1953). In Borg-Warner Corp., 1952 Ann. Rep. 11 (Chicago, 1953) this statement was made: "The health of a corporation depends upon the acquisition of new products and the improvement of products which are already being manufactured. To this end, Borg-Warner's three-sided program of engineering research was enlarged and its scope broadened last year."

[97] Campbell and Hatton, Herbert H. Dow, Pioneer in Creative Chemistry 135 (1951); Sherman and Sherman, The New Fibers 37-38 (1946); Gilfillan, The Prediction of Technical Change, 34 Rev. Econ. & Stat. 368, 382 (1952).

[98] Minnesota Mining & Manufacturing Co., 1948 Ann. Rep. 10 (St. Paul, 1949); cf. National Lead Co., 61st Ann. Rep. 8 (New York City, 1953).

[99] Abbott Laboratories, Inc., 1949 Ann. Rep. 4 (North Chicago); E. I. du Pont de Nemours & Co., 1949 Ann. Rep. 13 (Wilmington, 1950); Merck & Co., 1948 Ann. Rep. 4 (Philadelphia, 1949); Minnesota Mining & Manufacturing Co., 1952 Ann. Rep. 2 (St. Paul); Monsanto Chemical Co., 51st Ann. Rep. 26 (St. Louis, 1953); Parke, Davis & Co., 86th Ann. Rep. 6 (Detroit, 1953). In E. I. du Pont de Nemours & Co., 1950 Ann. Rep. 7 (Wilmington, 1951), it was said that sales during 1950 were 35 per cent derived from facilities placed in operation after the end of World War II.

[100] Bright and MacLaurin, Economic Factors Influencing the Development and Introduction of the Fluorescent Lamp, 51 J. Pol. Econ. 429, 438-445 (1943); Galbraith, Monopoly and the Concentration of Economic Power, in A Survey of Contemporary Economics 99, 120 (Ellis ed. 1939); cf. Dearborn, Kneznek and Anthony, Spending for Industrial Research 13 (1953).

[101] Some observers have stressed the bureaucratic and conservative aspects of large organizations. Hurff, Social Aspects of Enterprise in the Large Corporation 123 (1950); Rostow, Market Organization and Stabilization Policy, in Income Stabilization for a Developing Economy 475 (Millikan ed. 1954). Others have suggested

in order to permit the rather impressive results of technological research by big business outlined above. One of those countervailing factors may be found in the indivisibility of research equipment: laboratories must be large to achieve efficiency.[102] Another aspect of indivisibility lies in the fact that modern technological research relies more and more heavily upon explorations in pure science. Accordingly, the company laboratory today cannot confine its activities to mere technological investigations.[103] It follows that the amount of technological research which can be done varies directly with over-all size, because the larger the research project, the further it will be removed from immediate application to any single product. As a result, the firm must be wealthy enough to produce many items in order to make discoveries in pure science of value to it.[104] Theoretically, perhaps, small concerns could "farm out" their research projects just as their legal and accounting problems can be delegated to independent firms. In actual practice, however, small companies apparently do not utilize to any great extent this method of coping with indivisibility,[105] although there are

---

that, as firms grow larger, their motives for further expansion and greater profits decline. Stability becomes more essential than new profit potentials. Attention has also been invited to the fact that many large corporations are now managed by persons who are not themselves substantial stockholders, and who are more interested in maximization of the present value of an indefinitely long series of secure and socially permitted profits, with their firm receiving its share, than in immediate large returns. American Viscose Corp., 1952 Ann. Rep. 16 (Philadelphia, 1953); Gibb, The Saco-Lowell Shops 298 et seq. (1950); Cole, Twentieth-Century Entrepreneurship in the United States and Economic Growth, 44 Am. Econ. Rev. 35, 47 (1954); Osborn, Efficiency and Profitability in Relation to Size, 29 Harv. Bus. Rev. No. 2, pp. 82, 93 (1951); U.S. Steel: 1, 13 Fortune No. 3, pp. 59, 173 (1936); Schneider, Real Economies of Integration and Large-Scale Production versus Advantages of Domination, in Chamberlin, ed., Monopoly and Competition and Their Regulation 203, 207 (International Economic Assn. 1954).

[102] Bowman, Toward Less Monopoly, 101 U. Pa. L. Rev. 577, 600 (1953). But cf. id. at 606-607. Factors of time and taxation also may be important. Celler Committee I, ser. 14, pt. 2-B, at 1034; Bright and MacLaurin, Economic Factors Influencing the Development and Introduction of the Fluorescent Lamp, 51 J. Pol. Econ. 429, 447 (1943). Note also the possible effects of a belief among business executives that there is no such thing as standing still in industry; that the corporation which takes a position that it will not expand will go downhill eventually, and that the morale of employees will decline unless each year records additional growth. Donald R. Booz, Interview (May 20, 1953); Doan, Remarks at 54th Meeting of Stockholders 5 (Dow Chemical Co., Aug. 22, 1951).

[103] MacLaurin, Invention and Innovation in the Radio Industry 166, 172 (1949); United States Steel Corp., 51st Ann. Rep. 14 (New York City, 1953).

[104] Cf. Dearborn, Kneznek and Anthony, Spending for Industrial Research 6 (1953).

[105] Id. at 7. "Innovations in industries with atomistic competition, on the other hand, are largely dependent on research carried on collectively by industrial institutes or trade associations, or by governmental agencies, and finally on possibilities created by other industries. This observation is valid, for instance, for the agricultural revolution of the last generation. It appears that pure, or near pure competition, although certainly not adverse to the energetic realization of innovation possibilities created elsewhere, is not so favourable a condition for evolving these possibilities by itself as a monopoly, at any rate some types of monopoly." Hennipman, Monopoly: Impediment or Stimulus to Economic Progress, in Cham-

firms which exist solely for the discovery of innovations and their licensing to concerns without such facilities.[106]

Much work must be done before an invention is ready for mass production and marketing. The device must not only work, it must work under adverse conditions and in the hands of untrained consumers. Such "development" of an invention may be extremely difficult and expensive.[107] After the invention of television, for example, enormous expenditures were still required before the sets were ready for the production line and distribution to consumers. An acute observer said of that situation:

> . . . the developmental problems have proved so difficult and expensive that the principal burden of translating these concepts into an operational product has had to be carried by the large industrial research laboratory.[108]

At the development stage, the individual inventor is supplanted by organized research teams, each member specializing in a particular aspect of the problem.[109]

It follows that only large firms are in a position to carry forward the development of highly technical innovations. In actual fact we find the large firm playing that role. Although the fluorescent lamp was inspired largely by European inventions, its practical development was brought about by General Electric, and the size of that concern in the lamp field made it the only effective agent, it has been said, for such activities.[110] The basic idea for the manufacture of cellophane

---

berlin, ed., Monopoly and Competition and Their Regulation 421, 430, 431 (International Economic Assn. 1954).

[106] Automatic Radio Mfg. Co. v. Hazeltine Research, Inc., 339 U.S. 827, 829 (1950); Hazeltine Corp., 1952 Ann. Rep. 8, 10 (Little Neck, N.Y.); Scoville, Revolution in Glass Making 96 et seq. (1948). Customers and suppliers sometimes perform such functions. Swift & Co., 1952 Year Book 11 et seq. (Chicago, 1952). Note the existence of vertical integration implied in the above discussion.

[107] Deller, Book Review, 60 Harv. L. Rev. 1366, 1367 (1947); cf. Higgins, What Do Economists Know? 74 (1951).

[108] MacLaurin, Invention and Innovation in the Radio Industry 191 (1949); accord: id. at xx, 88; TNEC Hearings, pt. 2, at 343; Abbott Laboratories, Inc., 1949 Ann. Rep. 10-11 (North Chicago); Campbell and Hatton, Herbert H. Dow, Pioneer in Creative Chemistry 135 (1951); Sharp & Dohme, Inc., 1952 Ann. Rep. 19 Philadelphia, 1953); Williamson, Winchester: The Gun That Won the West 100 (1952); In Debatable Air, 3 Fortune No. 5, pp. 53, 55 (1931); MacLaurin, Patents and Technical Progress — A Study of Television, 58 J. Pol. Econ. 142, 157 (1950); MacLaurin, The Sequence From Invention to Innovation and Its Relation to Economic Growth, 67 Q.J. Econ. 97, 107 (1953); Schlaifer, Big Business and Small Business: A Case Study, 28 Harv. Bus. Rev. No. 4, pp. 97, 103-104, 107 (1950). Part of the expense burden is attributable to the fact that so many projects do not prove feasible from a commercial point of view. See Monsanto Chemical Co., 51st Ann. Rep. 25 (St. Louis, 1953).

[109] MacLaurin, Invention and Innovation in the Radio Industry 215 (1949); MacLaurin, Patents and Technical Progress — A Study of Television, 58 J. Pol. Econ. 142, 150 (1950).

[110] Bright and MacLaurin, Economic Factors Influencing the Development and

was obtained from French sources, but the Du Pont Company expended much effort in its technological development in order to make the product acceptable to the United States market.[111] Thus we find the large firm playing an important role in the improvement of ideas which may originate with others. So important is this function that corporations have established separate divisions within their research organizations purely to forward the process of development.[112]

Again, the heavy expenditures required for development are not limited to the engineering aspects of innovation. The product must become acceptable in the market place, and this often requires tedious "missionary work" to give ill-informed consumers technical data about the performance of the product. In other instances, heavy advertising expenditures may be required, and new channels of distribution may have to be created.[113] Coca-Cola, for example, pushed the development of the soda fountain as a whole, its salesmen spreading the gospel of "cold and cleanliness," while the company was content to take its share of the resulting fountain sales.[114] When customers cannot be

---

Introduction of the Fluorescent Lamp, 51 J. Pol. Econ. 429, 437-438, 445 (1943); cf. Celler Committee I, ser. 14, pt. 2-A, at 319.

[111] United States v. E. I. Du Pont de Nemours & Co., 118 F. Supp. 41, 75 (D. Del. 1953); see United States v. United Shoe Machinery Co., 222 Fed. 349, 369-370 (D. Mass. 1915), aff'd, 247 U.S. 32 (1918); Bright, The Electric-Lamp Industry 449, 469 (1949); E. I. du Pont de Nemours & Co., Du Pont: The Autobiography of an American Enterprise 132 (1952); Gibb, The Saco-Lowell Shops 34 (1950); MacLaurin, Patents and Technical Progress — A Study of Television, 58 J. Pol. Econ. 142, 150 (1950).

[112] American Can Co., 1952 Ann. Rep. 22 (New York City, 1953); Weyerhaeuser Timber Co., 1952 Ann. Rep. 10 (Tacoma, 1953). "Independent" inventors may still carry on a part of the task of development. Wallace, Market Control in the Aluminum Industry 59 (1937). Heavy expenses incidental to development may explain why large firms sponsor fewer radical innovations than one might expect. Development is so expensive and slow that there is a limit to the amount of innovation that even a tremendous company can undertake; established firms are offered hundreds of ideas from which a selection must be made. See Dow Chemical Co., 1950 Ann. Rep. 13 (Midland, 1950); Schlaifer, Big Business and Small Business: A Case Study, 28 Harv. Bus. Rev. No. 4, pp. 97, 102 (1950).

[113] Machlup, The Political Economy of Monopoly 264 (1952); Nicols, The Development of Monopolistic Competition and the Monopoly Problem, 31 Rev. Econ. & Stat. 118, 122 (1949); Schlaifer, Big Business and Small Business: A Case Study, 28 Harv. Bus. Rev. No. 4, pp. 97, 107 (1950); Deller, Book Review, 60 Harv. L. Rev. 1366, 1367 (1947).

[114] United States v. Aluminum Co. of America, 44 F. Supp. 97, 176-177, 207 (S.D.N.Y. 1941), rev'd in part, 148 F.2d 416 (2d Cir. 1945); American Viscose Corp., 1948 Ann. Rep. 18 (Philadelphia, 1949); International Nickel Co. of Canada, Ltd., 1953 Ann. Rep. 13 (Copper Cliff, 1954); Element Number Forty-Two, 14 Fortune No. 4, pp. 105, 187, 194 (1936); Four Walls Around an Industry, 10 id. No. 2, p. 64 (1934); In Debatable Air, 3 id. No. 5, pp. 53, 55 (1931); To Pause and Be Refreshed, 4 id. No. 1, pp. 64, 110 (1931). Instances of advertising expenditures of the above type will be found in Hower, History of Macy's of New York, 1858-1919, at 54-55 (1943); Longstreet, A Century on Wheels 26 (1952); Swift & Co., 1952 Year Book 14 (Chicago, 1952); To Pause and Be Refreshed, 4 Fortune No. 1, pp. 64, 106, 110 (1931). It does not follow, of course, that large firms will necessarily employ their resources in such "missionary work." See Bright and MacLaurin, Economic

persuaded to try the new product, either by technical information or by bombasts of advertising, it may be necessary for the producer himself to fabricate or market it at retail.[115] In that way a measure of vertical integration is encouraged which, of course, imposes additional financial requirements upon the firm.

In the nature of things, we shall probably never be able to measure the empirical evidence available for testing the "dynamic" theories outlined above. We cannot compare the importance of different innovations. It would be difficult to distinguish between the "independent" inventor and the small firm which may, in its restricted field, be comparatively large. There is no proof that research by big business is more or less productive than that of smaller companies.[116] The problem is blurred by artificial industry boundaries[117] — a company may lag in one department and pioneer in another. From the qualitative materials available, however, it appears likely that both large and small firms play important roles in our economy. Somewhat paradoxically,[118] we must probably rely upon the "independent" elements in the economy for those long-range changes which revolutionize productive processes. As one observer put it,

. . . the natural source of most really radical innovations must be new, small firms founded with the development of some single innovation as their primary objective and with managements having complete — even if sometimes irrational — faith in the ultimate success of their particular innovations.[119]

Factors Influencing the Development and Introduction of the Fluorescent Lamp, 51 J. Pol. Econ. 429, 447 (1943).

[115] United States v. Aluminum Co. of America, 44 F. Supp. 97, 170, 185 et seq. (S.D.N.Y. 1941), rev'd in part, 148 F.2d 416 (2d Cir. 1945); Gibb, The Saco-Lowell Shops, 24 (1950); Swiss Family Dreyfus, 8 Fortune No. 4, pp. 51, 141 (1933).

[116] Mason, The Current Status of the Monopoly Problem in the United States, 62 Harv. L. Rev. 1265, 1271 (1949); Rostow, Market Organization and Stabilization Policy, in Income Stabilization for a Developing Economy 472, 476 (Millikan ed. 1954); Wallace, Industrial Markets and Public Policy: Some Major Problems, in 1 Public Policy 59, 105 (Friedrich and Mason ed. 1940); Hamberg, Book Review, 44 Am. Econ. Rev. 414, 418 (1954); Scoville, Revolution in Glassmaking: Entrepreneurship and Technological Change in the American Industry, 1880-1920, at viii (1948).

[117] Adelman, Symposium Review, 49 Nw. U.L. Rev. 155, 157 (1954).

[118] The paradox arises because static economics, under whose doctrines the smaller firm is encouraged at the expense of its larger rival, is usually considered to focus on short-run rather than long-term considerations.

[119] Schlaifer, Big Business and Small Business: A Case Study, 28 Harv. Bus. Rev. No. 4, pp. 97, 103 (1950); see Celler Committee I, ser. 14, pt. 2-A, at 319; MacLaurin, The Sequence From Invention to Innovation and Its Relation to Economic Growth, 67 Q.J. Econ. 107 (1953). In MacLaurin, Invention and Innovation in the Radio Industry 244 (1949) it was said: ". . . it is only the very large companies in the radio industry which have first-rate scientists in their employ. And it will be unfortunate if the translation of scientific advances into new products and new industries is left entirely to the great corporations. Any large, well-established institution almost inevitably tends to become somewhat bureaucratic. It develops fields of special interest; and no matter how hard it tries to be receptive to new

At the same time, the evidence suggests that we must depend on large firms for the "development" of highly technical devices,[120] just as we rely upon the universities and their scholars for leadership in the field of pure science.

III. EFFECTS OF DYNAMIC THEORY UPON ANTITRUST ENFORCEMENT

A. *Monopoly and Its Definition*

In the view of Professor Schumpeter, the Sherman Act and related statutes were out of step with the real requirements of the economy. He counted as destroyers of capitalism those enforcement officers who attempted the application of "pure" competition to American business.[121]   In the ensuing discussion, we shall examine the interpretation placed upon our antitrust statutes by the courts in an effort to determine how far, if at all, they deviate from the standards formulated by "dynamic" economic theory.

Under static economic doctrines, the existence of monopoly power can be determined, in theory, through the application of Lerner's formula to indicate the deviation of prices from marginal cost.   That formula, however, fails to take account of dynamic factors.[122]   Accordingly, Professor Schumpeter insisted that new methods of production and new commodities do not confer a lasting economic monopoly, and therefore should not be considered illegal.[123]

For the most part, the courts appear to have expressed views not in-

---

ideas, the radical notion and the new risk-taking approach are not always exploited. We can expect our great industrial corporations to take substantial risks and to be very forward-looking in many areas.   But some of the less obvious developments which are off the beaten track, and which are in the highly speculative stage where their potentialities cannot be visualized, are likely to be neglected."

[120] TNEC Hearings, pt. 1, at 90; Abbott Laboratories, Inc., 1949 Ann. Rep. 8 (North Chicago); Burns, The Decline of Competition 420 (1936); Abramovitz, Economics of Growth, in 2 A Survey of Contemporary Economics 132, 143 (Haley ed. 1952); Adelman, The Large Firm and Its Suppliers, 31 Rev. Econ. & Stat. 113, 117 (1949). An oil company has inaugurated an interesting program whereby independent inventors are encouraged to submit ideas for testing and development.   Some 6000 inquiries were received in the first nineteen months of the plan's operation, and apparently one idea was successfully developed.   See Sinclair Oil Corp., 1952 Ann. Rep. 18 (New York City, 1953).

[121] Mason, Schumpeter on Monopoly and the Large Firm, in Schumpeter: Social Scientist 89, 94 (Harris ed. 1951).

[122] Wallace, Industrial Markets and Public Policy: Some Major Problems, in 1 Public Policy 59, 107, 109 (Friedrich and Mason ed. 1940).

[123] Nourse and Drury, Industrial Price Policies and Economic Progress 270 (Brookings Institution Pub. No. 76, 1938); Schumpeter, Capitalism, Socialism and Democracy 102 (3d ed. 1950). Cf. the surprising views expressed in Kreps and Wright, Measurement of the Social Performance of Business 35 (TNEC Monograph No. 7, 1940), in which adverse criticism is offered of the tobacco industry because it produced more commodities with fewer employees, apparently as the result of installing new labor-saving machinery.

consistent with those of the "dynamic" economic theorists. Apart from a few decisions, innovators have not been condemned as monopolists under the Sherman Act, and the courts have tended to encourage, rather than to penalize, success and growth. Thus they have said:

"There is no limit under the American law to which a business may not independently grow," [124] and

". . . certainly improvement of business and its efficiency can be striven for without offense to the law." [125] Another court denied that the statutes were designed to restrict the growth of enterprise. It said: "It was never intended by Congress that the Trade Commission would have the duty and power to judge what is too fast a pace for merchants to proceed in business and to compel them to slow up. To do so would be to destroy all competition except that which is easy." [126]

Whatever apprehensions may be felt on the subject stem chiefly from Judge Learned Hand's decision in the *Alcoa* case. In holding that Alcoa constituted a monopoly within the prohibition of Section 2 of the Sherman Act, Judge Hand may have overlooked the fact that the defendant was an innovator; that it was promoting the use of a new product; that it had overcome tremendous technological problems; and that it had faced and largely overcome high barriers of consumer ignorance and inertia.[127] If such adverse criticism is justified, the decision stands nearly alone and presumably will not be followed. History indicates that the authors of the Sherman Act were content to let the

[124] United States v. International Harvester Co., 214 Fed. 987, 1000 (D. Minn. 1914), *appeal dismissed,* 248 U.S. 587 (1918).

[125] United States v. United Shoe Machinery Co., 247 U.S. 32, 53 (1918).

[126] National Biscuit Co. v. FTC, 299 Fed. 733, 739 (2d Cir.), *cert. denied,* 266 U.S. 613 (1924); *accord:* United States v. E. I. Du Pont de Nemours & Co., 118 F. Supp. 41, 217 (D. Del. 1953), *aff'd,* 351 U.S. 377 (1956); Commonwealth v. North Shore Ice Delivery Company, 220 Mass. 55, 107 N.E. 402 (1914). In American Tobacco Company v. United States, 328 U.S. 781, 786 (1946), the Court said: "The present cases are not comparable to cases where the parties, for example, merely have made a new discovery or an original entry into a new field and unexpectedly or unavoidably have found themselves enjoying a monopoly coupled with power and intent to maintain it." Cf. Timken Roller Bearing Co. v. United States, 341 U.S. 593, 603-604 (1951) (concurring opinion); Excelsior Motor Mfg. & Supply Co. v. Sound Equipment, Inc., 73 F.2d 725, 728 (7th Cir. 1934), *cert. denied,* 294 U.S. 706 (1935).

[127] United States v. Aluminum Co. of America, 148 F.2d 416, 430-431 (2d Cir. 1945); cf. the opinion below, 44 F. Supp. 97, 183 (S.D.N.Y. 1941), and the opinion on remand, 91 F. Supp. 333, 401 (S.D.N.Y. 1950). In Pearsall v. Great Northern Ry., 161 U.S. 646, 676 (1896), the Court said: "Owing to the greater speed and cheapness of the service performed by them, railways become necessarily monopolists of all traffic along their lines. . . ." This dictum has not been followed. Note, however, the interesting opinion in Peto v. Howell, 101 F.2d 353 (7th Cir. 1938), which is founded exclusively upon static concepts.

A different view, of course, has been applied to combinations of competitors under §1 of the Sherman Act. United States v. Patten, 226 U.S. 525 (1913). Interesting applications of such statutes to the problem of innovation are found in Hartford-Empire Co. v. United States, 323 U.S. 386, 400, 406, *clarified,* 324 U.S. 570 (1945); Slaughter v. Thacker Coal & Coke Co., 55 W. Va. 642, 47 S.E. 247 (1904).

entrepreneur of superior skill enjoy his reward[128] — he who is first in the field has a head start, and if such leadership should persist because others are slow, there is no reason to characterize it as an illegal monopoly.[129] Thus a court recently said:

> Being the first in an untried and doubtful risky field is neither inherently evil nor prohibited, even when the pioneer venture is crowned with success.[130]

In short, the factor of time should enter into the definition of monopoly, as do the concepts of commodities and geographic markets. How long the pioneer should be permitted to retain the fruits of his successful venture is a more difficult question.[131] If no artificial barriers to the entry of competitors can be found, however, perhaps it is the part of wisdom for courts to leave matters as they find them.[132] This, in short, is what the advocates of the abuse theory of monopoly have always taught.[133]

For the same reasons, the lone survivor in a once thickly populated industry should not be held an illegal monopolist. Such survivorship may be attributed principally to the skill and resources of the surviving enterprise. A decline in demand may hasten the process.[134] In either event, unless "soft" competition is to prevail, the survivor should not be held to have violated the statute. The courts have so stated,[135] and even Judge Learned Hand's opinion in the *Alcoa* case recognizes that a contrary construction of the statutes would be improper.[136]

---

[128] Walker, History of the Sherman Law 58 (1910). But cf. United States v. Aluminum Co. of America, 148 F.2d 416, 429 (2d Cir. 1945).

[129] Machlup, The Economics of Sellers' Competition 549 (1952); Smith, Effective Competition, 26 N.Y.U.L. Rev. 405, 414 (1951). Examples of such leadership will be found in United States v. Aluminum Co. of America, 91 F. Supp. 333, 379-380 (S.D.N.Y. 1950); Borden Co., 1952 Ann. Rep. 16 (New York City, 1953); Chase, Danger at the A. O. Smith Corporation, 2 Fortune No. 5, pp. 62, 102 (1930); Six in the Money, 40 id. No. 2, pp. 68, 71 (1949).

[130] United States v. Inter-Island Steam Nav. Co., 87 F. Supp. 1010, 1021 (D. Hawaii, 1950).

[131] Wright, Capitalism 178 (1951); Wright, Towards Coherent Anti-Trust, 35 Va. L. Rev. 665, 690 (1949).

[132] Cf. United States v. Aluminum Co. of America, 91 F. Supp. 333, 355 (S.D.N.Y. 1950).

[133] Johnston and Stevens, Monopoly or Monopolization, 44 Ill. L. Rev. 269, 282 (1949).

[134] Celler Committee I, ser. 14, pt. 6-A, at 772; Competition Not Cartelization, 6 Fortune No. 4, pp. 62, 64, 94, 96 (1932); $2NaCl + 2H_2O \rightarrow 2\,Na(OH) + Cl_2 + H_2$, 3 Fortune id. No. 4, p. 58 (1931); Robinson, Imperfect Competition Revisited, 63 Econ. J. 579, 592 (1953); The Steel Rail, 8 Fortune No. 6, pp. 42, 44-47 (1933).

[135] United States v. Pullman Co., 50 F. Supp. 123, 126-127 (E.D. Pa. 1943), aff'd per curiam, 330 U.S. 806 (1947); United States v. Aluminum Co. of America, 44 F. Supp. 97, 154-161 (S.D.N.Y. 1941), rev'd in part, 148 F.2d 416 (2d Cir. 1945). But cf. Times-Picayune Publishing Co. v. United States, 345 U.S. 594, 626 (1953).

[136] United States v. Aluminum Co. of America, 148 F.2d 416 (2d Cir. 1945). In that opinion, Judge Learned Hand wrote: ". . . persons may unwittingly find themselves in possession of a monopoly, automatically so to say: that is, without having intended either to put an end to existing competition, or to prevent com-

Dynamic theory, however, would go a good deal further. It would protect not only innovators and survivors. It would question whether any monopoly should be destroyed or regulated, for in dynamic theory the threat of new processes and products provides a stimulus to make businessmen behave as if conditions were purely competitive. The entrepreneur, dynamic theorists contend, is not motivated exclusively by the desire to reap short-run profits. He looks to the maintenance of his business over a period of years.[137] As stated by Mrs. Robinson;

> . . . the most valid simple generalisation is that the aim of the entrepreneur is for the firm first to survive, and secondly to grow. To this end he must pursue profit, but he must avoid action which, though profitable in the present, will damage his future position. . . .[138]

In a dynamic economy, for example, sellers with monopoly power do not necessarily set prices at the high levels which would maximize short-run profits. They desire to give their customers an impression of stability, and to encourage wider use of their products.[139] They also may wish to discourage entry by competitors.[140] Accordingly, prices

---

petition from arising when none had existed. . . . Since the Act makes "monopolizing" a crime . . . it would be not only unfair, but presumably contrary to the intent of Congress, to include such instances. . . . there may be changes in taste or in cost which drive out all but one purveyor. . . . In such cases a strong argument can be made that, although, [sic] the result may expose the public to the evils of monopoly, the Act does not mean to condemn the resultant of those very forces which it is its prime object to foster. . . . The successful competitor, having been urged to compete, must not be turned upon when he wins." Id. at 429-430.

[137] Schumpeter, Capitalism, Socialism and Democracy 85, 102 (3d ed. 1950); Abramovitz, Monopolistic Selling in a Changing Economy, 52 Q.J. Econ. 191, 198 (1938); Kaysen, A Dynamic Aspect of the Monopoly Problem, 31 Rev. Econ. & Stat. 109, 110 (1949); cf. Gordon, Short-Period Price Determination in Theory and Practice, 38 Am. Econ. Rev. 265, 266 (1948).

[138] Robinson, Imperfect Competition Revisited, 63 Econ. J. 579, 582 (1953). See also Brems, Product Equilibrium Under Monopolistic Competition 116-117, 136 (1951); Rostow, The Process of Economic Growth 32 (1953); Bernstein, Profit Theory — Where Do We Go From Here? 67 Q.J. Econ. 407, 415-416 (1953); Rothschild, Price Theory and Oligopoly, 57 Econ. J. 299, 309 (1947); Wright, Some Pitfalls of Economic Theory As a Guide to the Law of Competition, 37 Va. L. Rev. 1083, 1086-1087 (1951); cf. Clark, Social Control of Business 157 (1926); Gordon, Short-Period Price Determination in Theory and Practice, 38 Am. Econ. Rev. 265, 269 (1948).

[139] American Viscose Corp., 1948 Ann. Rep. 13 (Philadelphia, 1949); Hart, Anticipation, Business Planning and the Cycle, 51 Q.J. Econ. 273, 285 (1937); Robinson, The Impossibility of Competition, in Chamberlin, ed., Monopoly and Competition and Their Regulation 245, 248 (International Economic Assn. 1954); cf. Brems, Product Equilibrium Under Monopolistic Competition 238-240 (1951); Nourse and Drury, Industrial Price Policies and Economic Progress 269 (Brookings Institution Pub. No. 76, 1938); Evans, The Entrepreneur and Economic Theory: A Historical and Analytical Approach, 39 Am. Econ. Rev. 336, 344 (May 1949).

[140] Harrod, Economic Essays 146-147 (1952); Gordon, Short-Period Price Determination in Theory and Practice, 38 Am. Econ. Rev. 265, 277 (1948); cf. Bain, Conditions of Entry and the Emergence of Monopoly, in Chamberlin, ed., Monopoly and Competition and Their Regulation 215, 232 (International Economic Assn. 1954).

are held below the levels which would be fixed by supply and demand,[141] and sales are made to customers of long standing even though profits are forfeited thereby.[142] Of such factors the courts have yet to take account,[143] for the views of the dynamic school of economists go beyond the limitations of the abuse theory of the law.[144]

Even more drastic consequences flow from dynamic theory. Professor Schumpeter and others of his school believed that monopoly is a self-correcting phenomenon. It is true that static theory also recognizes a strong element of self-correction in the economy. According to its doctrines, monopoly profits will attract additional competitors unless some artificial factors, meaning chiefly governmental intervention, restrict the process. Professor Simons, a vigorous champion of the competitive system, said:

> I am . . . not much distressed about private monopoly power. . . . the ways of competition are devious, and its vengeance — government intervention apart — will generally be adequate and admirable.[145]

Examples of the dramatic effect of competition are easy to find. Penicillin was a relatively novel product in 1949, yet during the twelve months of that year so many new producers entered the field that its price fell an average of 55 per cent.[146] The experience of the American

[141] United States v. Aluminum Co. of America, 44 F. Supp. 97, 302 (S.D.N.Y. 1941), rev'd in part, 148 F.2d 416 (2d Cir. 1945); Celler Committee I, ser. 14, pt. 6-A, at 823, 838, 944-945; Hower, The History of an Advertising Agency 25 (1939); United States Steel Corp., Business . . . Big and Small . . . Built America 70-71 (1950); Four Walls Around an Industry, 10 Fortune No. 2, pp. 64, 102 (1934); Just About All About Cellophane, 5 id. No. 2, pp. 74, 101 (1932); Thompson, Address to Shareholders 3 (International Nickel Co. of Canada, Ltd., Toronto, April 25, 1951); cf. United States v. Aluminum Co. of America, 91 F. Supp. 333, 356 (S.D.N.Y. 1950); Wright, Capitalism 175 (1951).

[142] United States v. Aluminum Co. of America, 91 F. Supp. 333, 384 (S.D.N.Y. 1950); Celler Committee I, ser. 14, pt. 2-A, at 558. Economists have devoted much attention to the closely related problem of how prices will be fixed in an oligopolistic industry. See, e.g., TNEC Hearings, at 10679; Machlup, The Economics of Sellers' Competition (1952); Abramovitz, Monopolistic Selling in a Changing Economy, 52 Q.J. Econ. 191, 197 (1938); Kaysen, A Dynamic Aspect of the Monopoly Problem, 31 Rev. Econ. & Stat. 109, 112 (1949).

[143] Kiefer-Stewart Co. v. Joseph E. Seagram & Sons, Inc., 340 U.S. 211 (1951); United States v. Trenton Potteries Co., 273 U.S. 392, 396-401 (1927); cf. Dodge v. Ford Motor Co., 204 Mich. 459, 170 N.W. 668 (1919).

[144] Schumpeter, Science and Ideology, 39 Am. Econ. Rev. 345, 357-358 (1949).

[145] Simons, Economic Policy for a Free Society 87 (1948); see Celler Committee I, ser. 14, pt. 2-A, at 539; Wilcox, Competition and Monopoly in American Industry 314-315 (TNEC Monograph No. 21, 1940). But cf. Robinson, Imperfect Competition Revisited, 63 Econ. J. 579, 592 (1953).

[146] Abbott Laboratories, Inc., 1949 Ann. Rep. 2, 4, 8 (North Chicago, 1950); Argus Research Corp., Ethical Drug Industry (1952); Parke, Davis & Co., 86th Ann. Rep. 3-4 (Detroit, 1953); No. 1 Threat to Du Pont's Cellophane, 8 Fortune No. 4, pp. 144, 145 (1933); 109 Degrees Below Zero, 6 id. No. 1, pp. 74, 78 (1932); Six in the Money, 40 id. No. 2, pp. 68, 72 (1949). Petroleum was discovered in Pennsylvania in 1859; by 1874, competition had become so fierce that overproduction was rampant. See 1 Nevins, Study in Power 15, 195 (1953).

Can Company is illustrative.   That combination paid extravagant
prices to gather up practically all the canmaking plants in the country.
In order to remain solvent, it then had to raise prices, whereupon new
competitors sprang up at once.   The combination tried to buy them
all out, but found the process too expensive; and finally prices came
down.[147]   Few of the great "trusts" formed at the turn of the century
now possess anything approaching monopoly power.[148]

But Professor Schumpeter went further.   He declared that long-run
monopoly simply could not exist.   Oblivious of the short term, he did
not conceive of monopoly as a reality in a dynamic economy.[149]   His
theory of "creative destruction," as we have seen, is amply supported by
evidence in the commercial history of modern times, and it strongly
suggests that no market position can long be held without governmental
intervention.[150]   Needless to say, the courts have not accepted such an
extreme argument;[151] to do so would leave no room for the operation
of the Sherman Act.   Perhaps executive officers have taken some account
of such dynamic theories in refusing to prosecute monopolists whose
position might be undermined by natural forces before litigation could
be terminated, but there is no record of their having done so.

As indicated above, the technological research carried on by large
firms plays an important role in dynamic economic theory.   On the
other hand, under static doctrines it can be urged that a leading firm

147 United States v. American Can Co., 87 F. Supp. 18, 23 (N.D. Cal. 1949); United
States v. American Can Co., 230 Fed. 859, 879-881, 234 Fed. 1019 (D. Md. 1916),
appeal dismissed, 256 U.S. 706 (1921); cf. Paper & Power, 1 Fortune No. 5, pp. 65,
69-70 (1930).

148 Adams, Is Bigness Bad? 19 et seq. (Republic Steel Corp, 1950); Big Business:
Its Growth and Place 101-102 (Bernheim ed. 1937); Scoville, Revolution in Glass
Making 219 et seq. (1948); Wilcox, Competition and Monopoly in American Industry
309 (TNEC Monograph No. 21, 1940); A Bicycle Rampart, 8 Fortune No. 3, pp. 49,
51 (1933); Nicholls, Some Economic Aspects of the Margarine Industry, 54 J. Pol.
Econ. 221, 233-234 (1946); Patinkin, Multiple-Plant Firms, Cartels, and Imperfect
Competition, 61 Q.J. Econ. 173, 201 (1947); U.S. Rubber, 9 Fortune No. 2, pp. 52,
54 (1954); Water Still Freezes, 7 Fortune No. 5, pp. 73, 75 (1933).   Neither wealth
nor prestige necessarily produces profitable results.   American Home Products Corp.,
28th Ann. Rep. 5 (New York City, 1954); U.S. Corporate Management, 7 Fortune
No. 6, p. 47 (1933).

149 Schumpeter, Capitalism, Socialism and Democracy 99 (3d ed. 1950); Hildebrand,
Monopolization and the Decline of Investment Opportunity, 33 Am. Econ. Rev. 591,
592 (1943); Mason, Schumpeter on Monopoly and the Large Firm, in Schumpeter:
Social Scientist 89, 93 (Harris ed. 1951).

150 See, e.g., the impact of radio and television upon newspapers as noted in Times-
Picayune Publishing Co. v. United States, 345 U.S. 594, 604 (1953).   But cf. Reynolds,
The Canadian Baking Industry, 52 Q.J. Econ. 659, 672 (1938).

151 Cf. United States v. Aluminum Co. of America, 148 F.2d 416, 422-427 (2d Cir.
1945).   But see Standard Oil Co. of New Jersey v. United States, 221 U.S. 1, 55 (1911),
where the Court said: "It is remarkable that nowhere at common law can there be
found a prohibition against the creation of monopoly by an individual.   This would
seem to manifest, either consciously or intuitively, a profound conception as to the
inevitable operation of economic forces and the equipoise or balance in favor of the
protection of the rights of individuals which resulted."   As indicated above, a good
deal depends upon whether short-run or long-term considerations are involved.
See Bowman, Toward Less Monopoly, 101 U. Pa. L. Rev. 577, 622 (1953).

should not be permitted to continue technological research, because in that way it might perpetuate its position at the expense of potential competition. For such reasons, the Attorney General argued in the *United Shoe Machinery* case that technological research carried on by that concern was designed to anticipate competitors, to forestall competition, and hence to violate the antitrust laws.[152] And in one recent decision, a trial court held that an intensive scientific and engineering research program was not "acceptable," and, apparently, that is constituted an attempt to monopolize within the meaning of the antitrust laws.[153] On the other hand, one of the principal factors which saved the Aluminum Company from dissolution was the indivisibility of its technological research. The court thought that breaking up Alcoa's research department might have an adverse effect upon the whole aluminum industry.[154] Similar considerations have motivated those who have urged "performance" tests for the existence of monopoly.[155]

Dynamic theory also affects a problem which lies at the heart of the static analysis of monopoly, the problem of defining commodities.[156] In neoclassic theory the problem of defining commodities admittedly exists, but more emphasis is placed upon product differentiation as a tool of monopoly power[157] than upon tests of substitutability. In other words, the neoclassic doctrine takes a relatively narrow view of the scope of the relevant commodity. Dynamic theory would agree that differentiation should not be confused with innovation. Its interest in growth, however, would lead to the encouragement of all change in the hope that innovation would result. Since such innovation is conceived of as the source of really important competition ("creative destruction"),[158] it is apparent that the process of innovation and the definition of a commodity are closely linked. Take, for example, the effects of the introduction of substitutes recorded in the following quotation:

> Manufacturers of floor and wall tile, whose products sell in close conjunction with the sanitary fixtures for installation in kitchens, toilet rooms . . . etc. have experienced an avalanche of competition. A former executive of the Trade Association in that field

[152] United States v. United Shoe Machinery Corp., 110 F. Supp. 295, 329, 330, 345 (D. Mass. 1953), aff'd per curiam, 347 U.S. 521 (1954).

[153] Hughes Tool Co. v. Ford, 114 F. Supp. 525, 552 (E.D. Okla. 1953), rev'd, 215 F.2d 924 (10th Cir. 1954). See Investigations of Concentration of Economic Power 138 (TNEC, Final Rep. of Exec. Secy.).

[154] United States v. Aluminum Co. of America, 91 F. Supp. 333, 416-417 (S.D.N.Y. 1950); cf. United States v. Line Material Co., 333 U.S. 287, 310 (1948).

[155] Mason, The Current Status of the Monopoly Problem in the United States, 62 Harv. L. Rev. 1265, 1281 (1949); cf. Harbury and Raskind, The British Approach to Monopoly Control, 67 Q.J. Econ. 380, 382 (1953).

[156] See §3.5 supra.

[157] Chamberlin, The Theory of Monopolistic Competition 56 et seq. (3d ed. 1938). Differentiation can, of course, lead to competition in quality. Brems, Product Equilibrium Under Monopolistic Competition 243 (1951); Chamberlin, The Product As an Economic Variable, 67 Q.J. Econ. 1 (1953).

[158] Schumpeter, Capitalism, Socialism and Democracy 85 (3d ed. 1950).

furnished a list of 119 substitutes for burned-clay tile as illustrative of the competitive condition. . . . some of these wall "tile" are glass units in metal frames. . . . others are units of asbestos or wallboards or sheet-metal units marked and enameled to resemble tile. Floor tile finds competition in rubber "tile" and in numerous types of composition floors.[159]

To date, however, dynamic factors have received little, if any, recognition in the decisions dealing with the problem of defining commodities and industries.[160] As in the case of the self-corrective character of monopoly in general, a dynamic definition of commodities would result in such broad concepts that the notion of monopoly itself would be almost obliterated.[161]

A further striking contrast between the static and dynamic theories is found in their treatment of limitations upon the horizontal size of business firms. In neoclassic theory, monopoly will not be achieved by a successful competitor unless some imperfection (such as indivisibility) is present; in that case, monopoly is "natural" and regulation is prescribed. The firm which grows more rapidly than its rivals and comes to dominate its field is suspected of attempting to monopolize by expanding ahead of demand.[162] Long before Professor Schumpeter's time, however, lawyers were pointing out that absolute ceilings upon corporate size would discourage growth and deprive competition of its incentive to progress.[163] Most of the older decisions, based upon the "abuse" theory, were in accord with the dynamic view. The courts refused to hold that mere horizontal size fell within the Sherman Act,

[159] Chute, Marketing Burned-Clay Products 285 (1939). But cf. Steel Rails, 8 Fortune No. 6, p. 42 (1933).

[160] Cf. Eastman Kodak Co. v. FTC, 158 F.2d 592, 594 (2d Cir. 1946), cert. denied, 330 U.S. 828 (1947).

[161] Take, for example, the situation in which competition left but two producers of women's seamless hosiery (Burlington Mills, 40 Fortune No. 1, pp. 82, 109 (1949)) and the situation in which a new firm introduced acetate (as opposed to viscose) rayon (Swiss Family Dreyfus, 8 id. No. 4, pp. 50, 51, 54 (1933)). Obviously, it is difficult to distinguish product differentiation from innovation. Again, whether the product is regarded as one or the other may depend upon such "imperfections" as consumer ignorance and the like.

[162] Machlup, The Economics of Sellers' Competition 234-235 (1952); cf. Levi, The Antitrust Laws and Monopoly, 14 U. Chi. L. Rev. 153, 156 (1947). But see Robinson, Imperfect Competition Revisited, 63 Econ. J. 579, 592 (1953), where it is said: "The chief cause of monopoly (in a broad sense) is obviously competition. Firms are constantly striving to expand, and some must be more successful than others. It is easier to defend a position once gained than to conquer, so that the most successful firms grow the most rapidly."

[163] Markham, Competition in the Rayon Industry 205 (1952); Clark, The Orientation of Antitrust Policy, 40 Am. Econ. Rev. 93, 96-97 (1950); Dana, "Monopoly" Under the National Anti-Trust Act, 7 Harv. L. Rev. 338, 353 (1894); Johnston and Stevens, Monopoly or Monopolization, 44 Ill. L. Rev. 269, 289-290 (1949); Pope, The Legal Aspect of Monopoly, 20 Harv. L. Rev. 167, 188 (1907); Smith, Effective Competition, 26 N.Y.U.L. Rev. 405, 406 (1951). As to "building ahead of demand," see Dow Chemical Co., 1953 Ann. Rep. 11 (Midland, 1953); Gulf Oil Corp., 1952 Ann. Rep. 10 (Pittsburgh, 1953); Schumpeter, Capitalism, Socialism and Democracy 105 (3d ed. 1950).

saying that it would penalize competition itself to prohibit growth in that manner.[164]   Even within the last few years, the courts have frequently denied that any rule of law prohibits the expansion of business enterprise.   Thus, in the *Columbia Steel* case the Supreme Court said:

> . . . no direction has appeared of a public policy that forbids, *per se,* an expansion of facilities of an existing company to meet the needs of new markets of a community. . . .[165]

Undoubtedly, such sentiments represent the overwhelming weight of authority.

On the other hand, observers have been alarmed by a few recent decisions.   In the *Aluminum* case, the trial court found that the defendant had expanded ahead of demand, buying up water power sites and other facilities in prudent anticipation of future needs.   In that connection it said:

> . . . if a business man be accorded, as I think he must be accorded, the right to look far ahead in conducting his business, the quantity of power Alcoa acquired on the Saguenay can [not] properly be characterized as in excess of what was reasonable.[166]

In the Court of Appeals, however, the trial court's ruling was reversed. On the subject of business growth, Judge Learned Hand wrote:

> It insists that it never excluded competitors; but we can think of no more effective exclusion than progressivley to embrace each new opportunity as it opened, and to face every newcomer with new capacity already geared into a great organization, having the ad-

---

[164] United States v. United States Steel Corp., 251 U.S. 417, 450 (1920); United States v. Standard Oil Co. of New Jersey, 47 F.2d 288, 297 (E.D. Mo. 1931); United States v. United Shoe Machinery Co., 222 Fed. 349, 357 (D. Mass. 1915), *aff'd,* 247 U.S. 32 (1918); Dodge v. Ford Motor Co., 204 Mich. 459, 170 N.W. 668, 673, 681 (1919).

[165] United States v. Columbia Steel Co., 334 U.S. 495, 526 (1948). In United States v. Inter-Island Steam Nav. Co., 87 F. Supp. 1010, 1016-1017 (D. Hawaii, 1950), the court said:

"There is nothing in the statute to prevent a corporation from entering a virgin field, and, through a subsidiary or otherwise, engaging in a pioneer enterprise. . . .

"The antitrust laws were enacted to promote and not to retard the economic growth of the nation.

"In a word, the Sherman Act is not an instrument of stagnation."

And again:

". . . the Act does not penalize business efficiency, unless it be accompanied by some unlawful act." Id. at 1021.

Accord: United States v. E. I. Du Pont de Nemours & Co., 118 F. Supp. 41, 215 (D. Del. 1953), *aff'd,* 351 U.S. 377 (1956); Hughes Tool Co. v. Cole, 113 F. Supp. 519, 523 (W.D. Okla. 1953), *rev'd on other grounds,* 215 F.2d 924 (10th Cir. 1954); Windsor Theatre Co. v. Walbrook Amusement Co., 94 F. Supp. 388, 393 (D. Md. 1950), *aff'd,* 189 F.2d 797 (4th Cir. 1951); cf. United States v. National Lead Co., 332 U.S. 319, 352-353 (1947).

[166] United States v. Aluminum Co. of America, 44 F. Supp. 97, 144 (S.D.N.Y. 1941), *rev'd,* 148 F.2d 416 (2d Cir. 1945); see also id. at 125, 248.

vantage of experience, trade connections and the elite of personnel.[167]

There is evidence suggesting that decisions of that type — or, more properly, the anticipation of such decisions — have had the effect of putting a voluntary ceiling upon the horizontal size of some of the largest firms in the United States.[168] Whether such ceilings are desirable or catastrophic depends, again, upon whether one takes a static or a dynamic point of view. Perhaps, however, the contrast is less vivid than it appears on the surface. Even under the most advanced dynamic doctrine, the firm which has grown large by reason of governmental intervention, market imperfections, and the like would not be protected. The dynamic economist believes merely that the innovating firm should not be penalized for its expansion.[169] Furthermore, the growth which the court curbed in the *Aluminum* case was not new; decades had passed since the expiration of the chief Alcoa patent. Possibly subsequent cases will attach some importance to that factor and refuse to strike down the innovator who has not had an opportunity to exploit the market he has created. Finally, if the courts revert to the abuse theory of the Sherman Act, it is less likely that a conflict between static and dynamic concepts will arise.[170]

[167] United States v. Aluminum Co. of America, 148 F.2d 416, 431 (2d Cir. 1945); cf. United States v. New York Great A & P Tea Co., 173 F.2d 79 (7th Cir. 1949); Hughes Tool Co. v. Ford, 114 F. Supp. 525, 544 (E.D. Okla. 1953), *rev'd on other grounds,* 215 F.2d 924 (10th Cir. 1954).

[168] United States v. United States Steel Corp., 223 Fed. 55, 149 (D.N.J. 1915), *aff'd,* 251 U.S. 417 (1920); Brief for Appellants, p. 97, International Harvester Co. v. United States, 248 U.S. 587 (1918); Allis-Chalmers Manufacturing Co., 1948 Ann. Rep. 14 (Chicago); American Can Co., 1952 Ann. Rep. 16 (New York City, 1953); General Motors Corp., 44th Ann. Rep. 8 (New York City, 1953), 41st Ann. Rep. 10 (1950); Wright, Capitalism 192 (1951); Bleiberg, Amazing Shortage, 34 Barron's No. 30, pp. 3, 16 (1954); Hoover, Some Institutional Factors in Business Investment Decisions, 44 Am. Econ. Rev. 201, 212 (1954). But cf. Diamond Match Co., 1948 Ann. Rep. 5 (New York City, 1949).

Some of the foregoing annual reports suggest that companies have been afraid to expand production of their original products, and hence have diversified into other industries in order to grow. In that way, innovation may be fostered by a ceiling upon size.

[169] Cf. Adelman, Business Size and Public Policy, 24 J. Bus. U. Chi. 269, 274 (1951).

[170] Cf. United States v. Eastman Kodak Co., 226 Fed. 62 (W.D.N.Y. 1915), *decree entered,* 230 Fed. 522 (W.D.N.Y. 1916), *appeal dismissed,* 255 U.S. 578 (1921). The following language appeared in the trial court's opinion: "There is no limit in this country to the extent to which a business may grow, and the acquisitions of property in the present case, standing alone, would not be deemed an illegal monopoly; but when such acquisitions are accompanied by an intent to monopolize and restrain interstate trade by an arbitrary use of the power resulting from a large business to eliminate a weaker competitor, then they no doubt come within the meaning of the statute." Id. at 80.

Public policy, as expressed in §7 of the Clayton Act, 15 U.S.C. §18 (1952), has long discouraged growth by acquisition as opposed to "internal" expansion. In part, that policy reflects experience with the "trusts" of the last century. 1 Nevins, Study in Power 256, 285 (1953). It also reflects fears of "concentration" arising from such acquisitions. FTC, Report on the Merger Movement 5 (1948). But cf. Lintner and

B. *Other Antitrust Effects*

In neoclassic eonomic theory, only a monopolist can discriminate in price; furthermore, a monopolist will discriminate among his customers in order to maximize his revenues. Accordingly, the existence of price discrimination has been treated as evidence of monopoly power, and its prohibition has been encouraged as a proper means of promoting competition. Such views have found ready, and even zealous, acceptance in legislative quarters.[171] Under dynamic doctrines, however, underselling is frequently a helpful tool to open new markets and encourage the acceptance of innovations.[172] In order to spread the uses of a new product, it may be necessary to make drastic price reductions.[173] Those reductions, however, need not be made available to every consumer in order to stimulate growth; hence, discriminatory prices may be charged.[174] It follows that price discrimination may be an important means of fostering economic progress. As a result, dynamic economic theory furnishes additional reasons for the repeal of the Robinson-Patman Act.[175]

Butters, Effect of Mergers on Industrial Concentration, 32 Rev. Econ. & Stat. 30, 31-32 (1950). Similar views have obtained under the Sherman Act. Standard Oil Co. of New Jersey v. United States, 221 U.S. 1, 32, 45 (1911); United States v. United Shoe Machinery Corp., 110 F. Supp. 295, 312 (D. Mass. 1953), aff'd per curiam, 347 U.S. 521 (1954); United States v. American Can Co., 230 Fed. 859, 861, 866, 902, 234 Fed. 1019 (D. Md. 1916), appeal dismissed, 256 U.S. 706 (1921). But cf. United States v. United States Steel Corp., 251 U.S. 417, 452, 460-461 (1920).

On the other hand, circumstances may arise under which acquisition may prove considerably cheaper than "internal" growth. For example, savings may be realized in acquiring a going concern, equipped with personnel and technology, at a distress price. See Cross, From Land, Sea and Test Tube 38-39 (1954); Gibb, The Whitesmiths of Taunton: A History of Reed & Barton 120-121 (1943); Mathers, Scott Paper Company 8-9 (1953); cf. Bowman, Toward Less Monopoly, 101 U. Pa. L. Rev. 577, 610-611 (1953). If, therefore, growth is deemed as important as Professor Schumpeter would have it, doubt is cast upon the rule embodied in §7 of the Clayton Act.

171 Rowe, Price Discrimination, Competition, and Confusion: Another Look at Robinson-Patman, 60 Yale L.J. 929 (1951).

172 Clark, Alternative to Serfdom 79-80 (1948); Nourse and Drury, Industrial Price Policies and Economic Progress 254-255 (Brookings Institution Pub. No. 76, 1938); Schumpeter, The Instability of Capitalism, 28 Econ. J. 361, 380-381 (1928); Wright, Some Pitfalls of Economic Theory As a Guide to the Law of Competition, 37 Va. L. Rev. 1083, 1091 (1951).

173 Brems, Product Equilibrium Under Monopolistic Competition 138 (1951); Monsanto Chemical Co., 51st Ann. Rep. 22 (St. Louis, 1953); Nevins, Ford: The Times, the Man, the Company 282 (1954); Wallace, Market Control in the Aluminum Industry 256 (1937). But cf. Williamson, Winchester: The Gun That Won the West 179 (1952).

174 Wallace, Market Control in the Aluminum Industry 14-15, 390, 392-393 (1937); Air Reduction, 8 Fortune No. 1, pp. 24, 117 (1933).

175 Levi, The Robinson-Patman Act — Is It in the Public Interest? Proceedings A.B.A., Section of Antitrust Law, 60 (Sept. 17, 1953); cf. United States v. New York Great A & P Tea Co., 67 F. Supp. 626, 664 et seq., 678 (E.D. Ill. 1946), aff'd, 173 F.2d 79 (7th Cir. 1949); United States v. Aluminum Co. of America, 44 F. Supp. 97, 218-219 (S.D.N.Y. 1941), rev'd, 148 F.2d 416 (2d Cir. 1945). Note the effect of imperfec-

A firm launching a new product may have to overcome formidable obstacles. The ignorance and inertia of investors and consumers may require much "selling" of the product.[176] To provide an incentive for such sales effort, it may be desirable to give the local distributor exclusive rights in a limited territory. Otherwise he may not find it worth his while to expend effort in "missionary" work. Similarly, the producer may benefit from requirements contracts whereby the distributors agree not to deal in rival products. Such exclusive agreements have recently been frowned upon by the courts under both the Sherman Act [177] and the Clayton Act.[178] Adoption of dynamic economic theory might well result in re-examination of those authorities.

Contractual arrangements may not prove adequate to the task of securing consumer acceptance for a new product. When potential customers did not know how to fabricate aluminum, their inertia and ignorance were overcome by the Aluminum Company of America itself entering into fabrication of its ingots.[179] A similar tale has been told of magnesium: the Dow Chemical Company had hoped to confine itself to the manufacture of ingots, but potential customers did not know how to utilize the new metal and would not take the risks involved in exploiting it. Accordingly, a measure of vertical integration became necessary.[180] In recent years, however, the courts, and more particu-

tions like time lags. See Dirlam and Kahn, Price Discrimination in Law and Economics, 11 Am. J. Econ. & Soc. 281, 291 (1952).

[176] What Man Has Joined Together . . . , 13 Fortune No. 3, pp. 69, 150 (1936). In many instances, heavy advertising expenditures may be required to secure consumer acceptance. See MacLaurin, Invention and Innovation in the Radio Industry 148 (1949); R. J. Reynolds Tobacco Co., 1950 Ann. Rep. 13 (Winston-Salem, 1951). But cf. Brown, Advertising and the Public Interest: Legal Protection of Trade Symbols, 57 Yale L.J. 1165 (1948).

[177] Times-Picayune Publishing Co. v. United States, 345 U.S. 594, 608-609 (1953); United States v. Columbia Steel Co., 334 U.S. 495, 523-524 (1948); International Salt Co. v. United States, 332 U.S. 392 (1947); United States v. National City Lines, Inc., 186 F.2d 562, 567 (7th Cir.), cert. denied, 341 U.S. 916 (1951). But cf. Virtue v. Creamery Package Mfg. Co., 227 U.S. 8, 32-33 (1913); Bascom Launder Corp. v. Telecoin Corp., 204 F.2d 331, 335 (2d Cir.), cert. denied, 345 U.S. 994 (1953); Fargo Glass & Paint Co. v. Globe American Corp., 201 F.2d 534 (7th Cir.), cert. denied, 345 U.S. 942 (1953); United States v. Imperial Chemical Industries, Ltd., 105 F. Supp. 215, 244 (S.D.N.Y. 1952); United States v. Bausch & Lomb Optical Co., 45 F. Supp. 387, 399 (S.D.N.Y. 1942), aff'd as modified, 321 U.S. 707, 728 (1944); Chamberlain, Tomorrow's Factories, 34 Barron's No. 11, pp. 3, 25 (1954).

[178] Standard Oil Co. of California v. United States, 337 U.S. 293 (1949); cf. FTC v. Motion Picture Advertising Serv. Co., 344 U.S. 392 (1953); Excelsior Motor Mfg. & Supply Co. v. Sound Equipment, Inc., 73 F.2d 725, 728 (7th Cir.), cert. denied, 294 U.S. 706 (1934); Lockhart and Sachs, The Relevance of Economic Factors in Determining Whether Exclusive Arrangements Violate §3 of the Clayton Act, 65 Harv. L. Rev. 913 (1952). But cf. Wayne-Monroe Telephone Co. v. Ontario Telephone Co., 60 Misc. 435, 112 N.Y. Supp. 424, 426 (Wayne County, 1908); Ives v. Smith, 3 N.Y. Supp. 645, 654, aff'd per curiam, 55 Hun 606, 8 N.Y. Supp. 46 (App. Div., 1st Dept. 1889).

[179] Wallace, Market Control in the Aluminum Industry 9 et seq., 349-350 (1937); The Aluminum Company of America, 10 Fortune No. 3, pp. 46, 50 (1934).

[180] Campbell and Hatton, Herbert H. Dow, Pioneer in Creative Chemistry 149

larly the enforcement agencies, have dealt harshly with such integration.[181] Now observers recognize that vertical integration can offer a dynamic contribution to the development of the economy.[182]

Another form of business integration may be encouraged by dynamic doctrines. For the successful introduction of liquid petroleum gas into Brazil, the Standard Oil Company found it necessary also to distribute stoves, water heaters, and other devices which consume the product.[183] Again, technological research carried on by an existing firm frequently leads to discoveries in other fields. Diversification of the firm's production may be the inevitable result.[184] Indeed, growth of business enterprises is frequently associated with diversification because additional facilities do not precisely duplicate those formerly in existence.[185] It follows that decisions frowning upon diversification[186] are open to question if dynamic economic theory is accepted.

Static economic theory has long taken a dim view of the patent system. It has been argued, for example, that the patent affords its owner a considerable amount of time in which to become entrenched in a dominant position; smaller competitors are kept out of markets by extensions of the original patent term by improvement patents, grant-backs, and the like.[187] Dynamic doctrine, on the other hand, affords

---

(1951); Gibb, The Saco-Lowell Shops 39 (1950); International Minerals & Chemical Corp., 39th Ann. Rep. 8-9 (Chicago, 1948); Dow Chemical, 3 Fortune No. 4, pp. 58, 61 (1931); Minnesota Mining in Motion, 39 id. No. 3, pp. 93, 172 (1949); United Shoe Machinery, 8 id. No. 3, pp. 34, 41 (1933); Dow Goes Down to the Sea, 26 id. No. 6, pp. 111, 192 (1942).

181 United States v. Yellow Cab Co., 332 U.S. 218 (1947); United States v. New York Great A & P Tea Co., 173 F.2d 79 (7th Cir. 1949); Hughes Tool Co. v. Ford, 114 F. Supp. 525, 544, 551, 553 (E.D. Okla. 1953); United States v. Richfield Oil Corp., 99 F. Supp. 280, 292 (S.D. Cal. 1951), aff'd per curiam, 343 U.S. 922 (1952).

182 See §5.9.15 supra; Kahn, A Legal and Economic Appraisal of the "New" Sherman and Clayton Acts, 63 Yale L.J. 293, 300 n.43, 309, 345 (1954).

183 Standard Oil Co. of New Jersey, 1947 Ann. Rep. 15 (New York City, 1948); §6.7 supra.

184 Corn Products Refining Co., 43d Ann. Rep. 8 (New York City, 1950); Socony-Vacuum Oil Co., 1949 Ann. Rep. 13 (New York City, 1950); cf. Elgin National Watch Co., 88th Ann. Rep. 2, 11 (Elgin, 1953); Parke, Davis & Co., 86th Ann. Rep. 3 (Detroit, 1953); Adelman, Business Size and Public Policy, 24 J. Bus. U. Chi. 269, 276 (1951).

185 See E. I. du Pont de Nemours & Co., 1952 Ann. Rep. 7 (Wilmington, 1953); Gibb, The Saco-Lowell Shops 63, 90, 405 (1950); Hower, History of Macy's of New York, 1858-1919, at 107 (1943). A copper producer, possibly finding its markets shrinking, has entered into the production of gold, oil, titanium, aluminum, and phosphates. See Kennecott Copper Corp., 39th Ann. Rep. 3, 9, 12, 20 (New York City, 1954). Note the implications for corporate wealth and perpetuation inherent in that decision.

186 See §6.4 supra.

187 United States v. United Shoe Machinery Corp., 222 Fed. 349, 414 (D. Mass. 1915), aff'd, 247 U.S. 32 (1918); Investigation of Concentration of Economic Power 137 (TNEC, Final Rep. of Exec. Secy.); MacLaurin, Invention and Innovation in the Radio Industry 260 (1949); Markham, Competition in the Rayon Industry 16 (1952); Penrose, The Economics of the International Patent System 12 et seq. (1951); Wallace, Market Control in the Aluminum Industry 101 (1937); Abramson, The

strong support for the patent system. Incentive is required to bring innovations into the economy, and it finds the patent's grant an ideal method of affording shelter from the perennial gale of competition. Even a system of government subsidies would not, in dynamic theory, be as helpful to the economy as a whole, and to small business and the independent inventor in particular, as the statutory monopoly embodied in the patent system.[188]

In recent years, however, the courts have shown marked hostility to patents. Standards of patentable invention have been raised, the Supreme Court declaring that the inventor's claim ". . . must reveal the flash of creative genius. . . ."[189] All kinds of abuses have been found in patent licenses.[190] The grant itself, arising from a statute of equal dignity, was formerly considered beyond the purview of the antitrust laws, and it was thought that mere exercise of rights granted by the patent could not infringe the Sherman Act.[191] More recently, however, the courts have suggested that even the narrowest interpretation of patent privileges may conflict with statutes designed to curb monopoly.[192] Those who accept the doctrines of dynamic economics must regard the recent decisions as unfortunate and open to review when the courts attain a broader understanding of our economic machinery. Indeed, under those doctrines it would be desirable to extend the scope of patent protection to business ideas and other innovations not now within its scope.[193]

Economic Bases of Patent Reform, 13 Law & Contemp. Prob. 339, 341 et seq. (1948). But cf. Nevins, Ford: The Times, the Man, the Company 442 (1954).

[188] TNEC Hearings, pt. 2, at 262, 332, 344; MacLaurin, Invention and Innovation in the Radio Industry 258-259 (1949); Schumpeter, Capitalism, Socialism and Democracy 88 (3d ed. 1950); Gilfillan, The Prediction of Technical Change, 34 Rev. Econ. & Stat. 368, 371, 376 (1952); Prager, Standards of Patentable Invention From 1474-1952, 20 U. Chi. L. Rev. 69, 92 (1952); cf. Plant, The Economic Theory Concerning Patents for Inventions, 1 Economica (N.S.) 30, ¶9 (1934).

[189] Cuno Engineering Corp. v. Automatic Devices Corp., 314 U.S. 84, 91 (1941); see Great Atlantic & Pacific Tea Co. v. Supermarket Equipment Corp., 340 U.S. 147, 154-155 (1950); Marconi Wireless Telegraph Co. v. United States, 320 U.S. 1, 32 (1943); Prager, Standards of Patentable Invention From 1474-1952, 20 U. Chi. L. Rev. 69, 78 (1952). But cf. Pacific Contact Laboratories, Inc. v. Solex Laboratories, Inc., 209 F.2d 529, 532-533 (9th Cir.), cert. denied, 348 U.S. 816 (1954).

[190] Folk, The Relation of Patents to the Antitrust Laws, 13 Law & Contemp. Prob. 278, 285, 287 et seq. (1948); Notes, Contributory Infringement and Misuse — The Effect of Section 271 of the Patent Act of 1952, 66 Harv. L. Rev. 909, 910, 913-914 (1953); Patent Abuses and Antitrust: The Per Se Rule, 64 Harv. L. Rev. 626, 627, 629 (1951).

[191] Patterson v. United States, 222 Fed. 599, 625, 646 (6th Cir.), cert. denied, 238 U.S. 635 (1915); cf. United States v. National Lead Co., 332 U.S. 319, 359 (1947).

[192] Kobe, Inc. v. Dempsey Pump Co., 198 F.2d 416 (10th Cir.), cert. denied, 344 U.S. 837 (1952); Hughes Tool Co. v. Ford, 114 F. Supp. 525, 553-554 (E.D. Okla. 1953); Oppenheim, ed., Lectures on Federal Antitrust Laws 53 (University of Michigan, 1953). But cf. Foundry Services v. Beneflux Corp., 110 F. Supp. 857 (S.D.N.Y.), rev'd on other grounds, 206 F.2d 214 (2d Cir. 1953).

[193] Great Atlantic & Pacific Tea Co. v. Supermarket Equipment Co., 340 U.S. 147, 153 (1950); cf. Moore v. Ford Motor Co., 43 F.2d 685, 686 (2d Cir. 1930); 4 Restate-

Conclusion

Full acceptance of Professor Schumpeter's dynamic doctrines would necessitate repeal of the antitrust laws by Congress. Whether the intermediate suggestions for the enforcement of the antitrust laws outlined above should be adopted by the courts depends upon how much faith we place in the not yet fully developed dynamic theories of economic progress. It is true that dynamic and static doctrines are not wholly at odds. Economists of the dynamic persuasion would not countenance a monopolist who sat idly by and reaped his profits; they would insist that he use them for progressive purposes. In the language of Professor Wright, "We need enough market control for incentives, but not so much as to make for social ossification." [194] Economists of the static persuasion likewise recognize the importance of improving technology and stimulating research.[195]

In the end, however, the courts must choose. At least they must place more emphasis in one direction than the other. Today most decisions are grounded in static analysis. As indicated above, however, the dynamic view is often persuasive and finds considerable support in empirical evidence.[196] To give weight to factors encouraging growth and progress is no novelty in the law. Long ago it was said:

> . . . the . . . expression "rule of reason" . . . was merely a short way of expression to the effect that the present state of the common law on that topic is the result of development along reasonable lines and hand in hand with modern commercial advance.[197]

---

ment of Torts §757; Handler, Unfair Competition, 21 Iowa L. Rev. 175, 192 (1936); Havighurst, The Right to Compensation for an Idea, 49 Nw. U.L. Rev. 295, 297 (1954). Note the interesting development of "clearances" in the motion picture cases. See United States v. Paramount Pictures, Inc., 334 U.S. 131, 145 (1948); cf. Laren, Food Fair, 34 Barron's No. 28, p. 15 (1954).

[194] Wright, Some Pitfalls of Economic Theory As a Guide to the Law of Competition, 37 Va. L. Rev. 1083, 1093 (1951). See also MacLaurin, Technological Progress in Some American Industries, 44 Am. Econ. Rev. 178, 182 (1954); Wright, Toward Coherent Anti-Trust, 35 Va. L. Rev. 665, 691 (1949). Query whether horizontal size, as opposed to wealth, is necessary to technological development under dynamic doctrines. But wealth may merely reflect a monopoly profit of the past.

[195] Edwards, Maintaining Competition 108 (1949); Simons, Economic Policy for a Free Society 87 (1948).

[196] MacLaurin, Invention and Innovation in the Radio Industry 251 (1949). But cf. Bowman, Toward Less Monopoly, 101 U. Pa. L. Rev. 577, 630 (1953).

[197] United States v. Winslow, 195 Fed. 578, 589 (D. Mass. 1912), aff'd, 227 U.S. 202 (1913). But cf. United States v. National Lead Co., 63 F. Supp. 513, 525 (S.D.N.Y. 1945), aff'd, 332 U.S. 319 (1947). It must be recognized that dynamic economic doctrines suggest the adoption of "performance" tests of monopoly. A sharp conflict of view exists as to whether such tests are meaningful. See Mason, The Current Status of the Monopoly Problem in the United States, 62 Harv. L. Rev. 1265, 1282 (1949); Rostow, Market Organization and Stabilization Policy, in Income Stabilization for a Developing Economy 510-511 (Millikan ed. 1954).

A good deal will depend upon whether the courts believe that the antitrust laws are designed to protect the economy in the short run, as well as in the long term. It is true that proceedings to enforce the Sherman Act and kindred legislation are notoriously protracted.[198] Little can be gained by instituting lengthy litigation to correct situations which, through the natural operation either of competition or of "creative destruction," will be as soon remedied if left alone. On the other hand, a wise judge once declared:

> . . . the public policy embodied in the common law requires the discouragement of monopolies, however temporary their existence may be. The public interest may suffer severely while new competition is slowly developing.[199]

We offer, therefore, no facile formula for the adjustment of conflicting views. If it is true that some measure of both the carrot and the stick is needed to make our economic machine march forward rapidly, the problem becomes one of delicately balancing these factors in particular cases. Perhaps something is gained by identifying and naming the factors. We can suggest to a court that it take account of growth and change along with the orthodox antitrust ingredients, just as we can tell a cook that a cherry pie must be baked of cherries, sugar, flour, water, and shortening. What we cannot do is provide a precise recipe for the mixing of those ingredients. Whether to use a pound of cherries and a cup of sugar or some other mixture must be left to the discretion of the chef. We can, however, insist that the courts, in their zeal to extirpate impurities from the market place, take care not to crush that growth and innovation which alone have made possible our rising standards of living.[200]

---

[198] Final Report of the Select Committee on Small Business, H.R. Rep. No. 2513, 82d Cong., 2d Sess. 286 (1952).

[199] United States v. Addyston Pipe & Steel Co., 85 Fed. 271, 284 (6th Cir. 1898), aff'd, 175 U.S. 211 (1899).

[200] Other factors should be considered, of course. For example, there are political dangers in any measure of antitrust enforcement. See Bain, Conditions of Entry and the Emergence of Monopoly, in Chamberlain, ed., Monopoly and Competition and Their Regulation 215, 240 (International Economic Assn. 1954).

Table of Cases

TABLE OF CASES

A

Bibliography

BIBLIOGRAPHY

Abramovitz, An Approach to a Price Theory for a Changing Economy (1939)

Ackley, Spatial Competition in a Discontinuous Market, 56 *Q.J. Econ.* 212 (1942)

Adelman, Acquire the Whole or Any Part, Proceedings A.B.A., Section of Antitrust Law, 111 (Aug. 26, 1953)

————, The A & P Case: A Study in Applied Economic Theory, 63 *Q.J. Econ.* 238 (1949)

————, Business Size and Public Policy, 24 *J. Business* 269 (1951)

————, Concept and Statistical Measurement of Vertical Integration, in Business Concentration and Price Policy 281-322 (Stigler ed. 1955)

————, Effective Competition and the Antitrust Laws, 61 *Harv. L. Rev.* 1289 (1948)

————, Federal Trade Commission Report on Changes in Concentration in Manufacturing, 50 *J. Am. Stat. Assn.* 660-664 (1955)

————, Integration and Antitrust Policy, 63 *Harv. L. Rev.* 27 (1949)

Adler, Monopolizing at Common Law and under Section Two of the Sherman Act, 31 *Harv. L. Rev.* 246 (1917)

Attorney General's National Committee to Study the Antitrust Laws, Report of the (1955)

Bailey, Price and Output Determination by a Firm Selling Related Products, 44 *Am. Econ. Rev.* 82 (1954)

Bain, Barriers to New Competition (1956)

————, Conditions of Entry and the Emergence of Monopoly, in Monopoly and Competition and Their Regulation: Papers and Proceedings of a Conference Held by the International Economic Assn. 215-241 (Chamberlin ed. 1954)

————, Economies of Scale, Concentration, and the Condition of Entry in Twenty Manufacturing Industries, 44 *Am. Econ. Rev.* 15-39 (1954)

————, The Profit Rate as a Measure of Monopoly Power, 55 *Q.J. Econ.* 271-293 (1941)

————, Workable Competition in Oligopoly: Theoretical Considerations and Some Empirical Evidence, 40 Proceedings Am. Econ. Assn. 35 (1950)

Barber, Refusals to Deal under the Federal Anti-Trust Laws, 103 *U. Pa. L. Rev.* 847 (1955)

Beckman and Nolen, The Chain Store Problem (1938)

Bernstein, Profit Theory — Where Do We Go from Here? 67 *Q.J. Econ.* 407-422 (1953)

Bicks, Mergers and Acquisitions, 11 Proceedings A.B.A., Section of Antitrust Law, Report 20 (1957)

Birch, A Revised Classification of Forms of Competition, 20 *Can. J. Econ. & Pol. Sci.* 157-165 (1954)

Bishop, Elasticities, Cross-Elasticities, and Market Relationships, 42 *Am. Econ. Rev.* 779-803 (1952)

Bladen, Monopoly and Competition in Canada, in Monopoly and Competition and Their Regulation: Papers and Proceedings of a Conference Held by the International Economic Assn. 3-20 (Chamberlin ed. 1954)

Blair, The Relation between Size and Efficiency of Business, 24 *Rev. Econ. Stat.* 125-135 (1942)

Boulding, In Defense of Monopoly, 59 *Q.J. Econ.* 524 (1945)

———, The Organizational Revolution (1953)

Bowman, Toward Less Monopoly, 101 *U. Pa. L. Rev.* 577 (1953)

———, Tying Arrangements and the Leverage Problem, 67 *Yale L.J.* 19 (1957)

Brems, Product Equilibrium under Monopolistic Competition (1951)

Brown, Injunctions and Divestiture, Proceedings A.B.A., Section of Antitrust Law, 129 (Aug. 18, 1954)

Buchanan, The Economics of Corporate Enterprise (1940)

Burling and Sheldon, Price Competition as Affected by the Robinson-Patman Act, 1 *Wash. & Lee L. Rev.* 31 (1939)

Burns, The Decline of Competition: A Study of the Evolution of American Industry (1936)

Cahill, Must We Brand American Business by Indictment as Criminal? Proceedings A.B.A., Section of Antitrust Law, 26 (Sept. 17, 1952)

Callmann, The Essence of Anti-Trust, 49 *Colum. L. Rev.* 1100 (1949)

Carson, Corporate Mergers, in How to Comply with the Antitrust Laws 279 (Van Cise and Dunn ed. 1954)

Cassady, Price Making and Price Behavior in the Petroleum Industry, Petroleum Monograph Series No. 1 (1954)

Chaffetz, The Antitrust Laws and Small Business, Proceedings A.B.A., Section of Antitrust Law, 77 (April 1, 1953)

Chamberlin, Elasticities, Cross-elasticities and Market Relationships, 43 *Am. Econ. Rev.* 910 (1953)

———, Measuring the Degree of Monopoly and Competition, in Monopoly and Competition and Their Regulation: Papers and Proceedings of a Conference Held by the International Economic Assn. 267 (Chamberlin ed. 1954)

———, The Product as an Economic Variable, 67 *Q.J. Econ.* 1 (1953)

———, Product Heterogenity and Public Policy, 40 Proceedings Am. Econ. Assn. 85 (1950)

———, Proportionality, Divisibility and Economies of Scale, 62 *Q.J. Econ.* 229 (1948)

———, The Theory of Monopolistic Competition (6th ed. 1948)

Chapin, The Optimum Size of Institutions, 62 *Am. J. Sociol.* 449 (1957)

Clark, Homer, The Treble Damage Bonanza, 52 *Mich. L. Rev.* 363 (1954)

Clark, J. M., Competition and the Objectives of Government Policy, in Monopoly and Competition and Their Regulation: Papers and Proceedings of a Conference Held by the International Economic Assn. 317-337 (Chamberlin ed. 1954)

———, Competition: Static Models and Dynamic Aspects, 45 Proceedings Am. Econ. Assn. 450 (1955)

———, The Orientation of Antitrust Policy, 40 Proceedings Am. Econ. Assn. 93 (1950)

Dean, Supervision of Selling, Proceedings N.Y. State Bar Assn., Section on Antitrust Law, 5th Annual Meeting, 201 (1953)

Director and Levi, Trade Regulation, 51 *Nw. U.L. Rev.* 281 (1956)

Dirlam and Kahn, Price Discrimination in Law and Economics, 11 *Am. J. Econ. & Sociol.* 281 (1952)

Edwards, Conglomerate Bigness as a Source of Power, in Business Concentration and Price Policy 331-352 (Stigler ed. 1955)

———, Issues in the Monopoly Problem, in Monopoly and Competition and Their Regulation: Papers and Proceedings of a Conference Held by the International Economic Assn. 188-200 (Chamberlin ed. 1954)

———, Maintaining Competition: Requisites of a Governmental Policy (1949)

———, Public Policy and Business Size, 24 *J. Business* 280 (1951)

Enke, Resource Malallocation within Firms, 63 *Q.J. Econ.* 572-576 (1949)

———, Space and Value, 56 *Q.J. Econ.* 627 (1942)

Federal Trade Commission, The Concentration of Productive Facilities, 1947 (1950)

———, Corporate Mergers and Acquisitions (1955)

Fellner, Collusion and Its Limits under Oligopoly, 40 Proceedings Am. Econ. Assn. 54 (1950)

———, Competition Among the Few: Oligopoly and Similar Market Structures (1949)

———, Elasticities, Cross-Elasticities and Market Relationships, 43 *Am. Econ. Rev.* 898 (1953)

———, Prices and Wages under Bilateral Monopoly, 61 *Q.J. Econ.* 503-532 (1947)

Friedmann, ed., Anti-Trust Laws: A Comparative Symposium, University of Toronto Faculty of Law, Comparative Law Series, Vol. 3 (1956)

Galbraith, American Capitalism (1952)

———, Monopoly and the Concentration of Economic Power, in A Survey of Contemporary Economics 99 (Ellis ed. 1949)

Glover, The Attack on Big Business (1954)

Griffin, An Economic Approach to Antitrust Problems (1951)

Hale, Principles of Free Enterprise, 1 *Bill of Rights Rev.* 186 (1941)

Hamilton and Till, Antitrust in Action (TNEC Monograph No. 16, 1941)

Handler, Antitrust in Perspective (1957)

————, The Legal Aspects of Industrial Mergers, in The Federal Antitrust Laws 173 (Handler ed. 1931)

————, Monopolies, Mergers and Markets (1954)

————, A Study of the Construction and Enforcement of the Federal Antitrust Laws (TNEC Monograph No. 38, 1941)

————, Unfair Competition, 21 *Iowa L. Rev.* 175 (1936)

Harrod, Doctrines of Imperfect Competition, 48 *Q.J. Econ.* 442-470 (1934)

————, Toward a Dynamic Economics (1949)

Hawkins, Methods of Estimating Demand, 21 *J. Marketing* 428 (1957)

Henderson, The Theory of Duopoly, 68 *Q.J. Econ.* 565 (1954)

Hennipman, Monopoly: Impediment or Stimulus to Economic Progress, in Monopoly and Competition and Their Regulation: Papers and Proceedings of a Conference Held by the International Economic Assn. 421-456 (Chamberlin ed. 1954)

Hines, Effectiveness of "Entry" by Already Established Firms, 71 *Q.J. Econ.* 132 (1957)

Hoover, The Location of Economic Activity (1948)

Hurff, Social Aspects of Enterprise in the Large Corporation (1950)

James, Welsh and Arneson, Industrial Concentration and Tariffs (TNEC Monograph No. 10, 1940)

Johnston, Monopolize or Attempt to Monopolize, Proceedings A.B.A., Section of Antitrust Law, 72 (Aug. 26, 1953)

Johnston and Stevens, Monopoly or Monopolization — A Reply to Professor Rostow, 44 *Ill. L. Rev.* 269 (1949)

Kahn, Standards for Antitrust Policy, 67 *Harv. L. Rev.* 28 (1953)

Kales, Contracts and Combinations in Restraint of Trade (1918)

Kaplan, Big Enterprise in a Competitive System (1954)

————, The Influence of Size of Firms on the Functioning of the Economy, 40 Proceedings Am. Econ. Assn. 74 (1950)

————, Small Business: Its Place and Problems (1948)

Keyes, The Shoe Machinery Case and the Problem of the Good Trust, 68 *Q.J. Econ.* 287-304 (1954)

Knauth, Monopoly Reconsidered, 60 *Pol. Sci. Q.* 563 (1945)

Knight, The Economic Organization (1951)

————, Risk, Uncertainty and Profit (1921)

Letwin, Congress and the Sherman Antitrust Law, 23 *U. Chi. L. Rev.* 221 (1956)

————, The English Common Law Concerning Monopolies, 21 *U. Chi. L. Rev.* 355 (1954)

————, The Origins of Antitrust Policy, 64 *J. Pol. Econ.* 156-159 (1956)

Levi, The Antitrust Laws and Monopoly, 14 *U. Chi. L. Rev.* 153 (1947)

————, A Two Level Anti-Monopoly Law, 47 *Nw. U.L. Rev.* 567 (1952)

Lintner and Butters, Effect of Mergers on Industrial Concentration, 32 *Rev. Econ. & Stat.* 30 (1950)

Lovell, Sales Below Cost Prohibitions: Private Price Fixing Under State Law, 57 *Yale L.J.* 391 (1948)

Lyon, Watkins and Abramson, Government and Economic Life (1939)

Machlup, Characteristics and Types of Price Discrimination, in Business Concentration and Price Policy 397 (Stigler ed. 1955)

——, The Economics of Sellers' Competition (1952)

——, Monopoly and the Problem of Economic Stability, in Monopoly and Competition and Their Regulation: Papers and Proceedings of a Conference Held by the International Economic Assn. 385-397 (Chamberlin ed. 1954)

——, The Political Economy of Monopoly (1952)

McLaren, Related Problems of "Requirements" Contracts and Acquisitions in Vertical Integration under the Anti-Trust Laws, 45 Ill. L. Rev. 141 (1950)

McLaughlin, Legal Control of Competitive Methods, 21 Iowa L. Rev. 274 (1936)

McLean and Haigh, The Growth of Integrated Oil Companies (1954)

Markham, An Alternative Approach to the Concept of Workable Competition, 40 Am. Econ. Rev. 349-361 (1950)

Mason, The Current Status of the Monopoly Problem in the United States, 62 Harv. L. Rev. 1265 (1949)

——, Economic Concentration and the Monopoly Problem (1957)

——, Price and Production Policies of Large-Scale Enterprise, 29 Proceedings Am. Econ. Assn. 61 (1939)

——, Workable Competition vs. Workable Monopoly, Proceedings N.Y. State Bar Assn., Section on Antitrust Law, Symposium, 67 (1951)

Meade, Planning and the Price Mechanism (1949)

Miller, Measures of Monopoly Power, in Business Concentration and Price Policy 119 (Stigler ed. 1955)

Mund, Government and Business (2d ed. 1955)

——, Open Markets (1948)

Nelson and Keim, Price Behavior and Business Policy (TNEC Monograph No. 1, 1940)

Nicols, The Development of Monopolistic Competition and the Monopoly Problem, 31 Rev. Econ. & Stat. 118 (1949)

Nutter, The Extent of Enterprise Monopoly in the United States, 1899-1939 (1951)

——, Monopoly, Bigness and Progress, 64 J. Pol. Econ. 520 (1956)

Oliver, Pure Competition and Coercion, 57 Ethics 65 (1946)

Oppenheim, Federal Antitrust Legislation, 50 Mich. L. Rev. 1139 (1952)

Oppenheim, ed., Lectures on Federal Antitrust Laws (1953)

Oxenfeldt, Industrial Pricing and Market Practices (1951)

Palmer, Economic and Social Aspects of Chain Stores, 2 J. Business 272 (1929)

Papandreou and Wheeler, Competition and Its Regulation (1954)

Patinkin, Price Flexibility and Full Employment, 38 Am. Econ. Rev. 543-564 (1948)

Pattishall, Trademarks and the Monopoly Phobia, 50 *Mich. L. Rev.* 967 (1952)

Penrose, Limits to the Growth and Size of Firms, 45 Proceedings Am. Econ. Assn. 531 (1955)

Pigou, The Economics of Welfare (4th ed. 1932)

Pope, Alexander H., Vertical Forestalling under the Antitrust Laws, 19 *U. Chi. L. Rev.* 583 (1952)

Pope, Herbert, The Legal Aspect of Monopoly, 20 *Harv. L. Rev.* 167 (1907)

Prais, The Financial Experience of Giant Companies, 67 *Econ. J.* 249 (1957)

Rahl, Antitrust Policy in Distribution, 104 *U. Pa. L. Rev.* 185 (1955)

Raymond, The Limitist (1947)

Robinson, The Economics of Imperfect Competition (1933)

———, Imperfect Competition Revisited, 63 *Econ. J.* 579 (1953)

———, The Impossibility of Competition, in Monopoly and Competition and Their Regulation: Papers and Proceedings of a Conference Held by the International Economic Assn. 245-254 (Chamberlin ed. 1954)

Rosenbluth, Measures of Concentration, in Business Concentration and Price Policy 57 (Stigler ed. 1955)

Rostow, Eugene, Market Organization and Stabilization Policy, in Income Stabilization for a Developing Economy, c. 10, p. 439 (Millikan ed. 1954)

———, Monopoly under the Sherman Act: Power or Purpose? 43 *Ill. L. Rev.* 745 (1949)

———, The New Sherman Act: A Positive Instrument of Progress, 14 *U. Chi. L. Rev.* 567 (1947)

———, Problems of Size and Integration, Proceedings N.Y. State Bar Assn., Section on Antitrust Law, 3d Annual Meeting, 117 (1951)

Rostow, W. W., The Process of Economic Growth (1952)

Schneider, Real Economies of Integration and Large-Scale Production versus Advantages of Domination, in Monopoly and Competition and Their Regulation: Papers and Proceedings of a Conference Held by the International Economic Assn. 203-214 (Chamberlin ed. 1954)

Schumpeter, Capitalism, Socialism and Democracy (3d ed. 1950)

———, History of Economic Analysis (1954)

Scitovsky, Economic Theory and the Measurement of Concentration, in Business Concentration and Price Policy 101 (Stigler ed. 1955)

Simon, The Case against the FTC, 19 *U. Chi. L. Rev.* 297 (1952)

Simons, Economic Policy for a Free Society (1948)

Smith, Survey of the Empirical Evidence on Economies of Scale, in Business Concentration and Price Policy 213 (Stigler ed. 1955)

Solo, Innovation in the Capitalist Process: A Critique of the Schumpeterian Theory, 65 *Q.J. Econ.* 417-428 (1941)

Sprunk, Intra-Enterprise Conspiracy, Proceedings A.B.A., Section of Antitrust Law, IX, Report 20 (1956)

Stewart and Turner, The Significance of Oligopoly in Acquisitions and Exclusive Dealing Situations under the Clayton Act, 25 *U. Cin. L. Rev.* 427 (1957)

Stigler, The Economist Plays with Blocs, 44 Proceedings Am. Econ. Assn. 7 (1954)

———, The Extent and Bases of Monopoly, 32 *Am. Econ. Rev.* Supp. No. 2, 1 (1942)

———, Mergers and Preventive Antitrust Policy, 104 *U. Pa. L. Rev.* 176 (1955)

———, Monopoly and Oligopoly by Merger, 40 Proceedings Am. Econ. Assn. 23-34 (1950)

———, Notes on the Theory of Duopoly, 48 *J. Pol. Econ.* 521 (1940)

———, The Theory of Price (rev. ed. 1952)

Stigler, ed., Business Concentration and Price Policy, A Report of the National Bureau of Economic Research (1955)

Stocking and Watkins, Monopoly and Free Enterprise (1951)

Triffin, Monopolistic Competition and General Equilibrium Theory (1940)

Van Cise, Understanding the Antitrust Laws (1955)

Villard, The Social Cost of Corporate Monopoly Profits, 72 *Pol. Sci. Q.* 380-387 (1957)

Viner, Cost, 4 Encyc. Soc. Sci. 466 (1931)

Wallace, Industrial Markets and Public Policy, in Public Policy 59 (Friedrich and Mason ed. 1940)

———, Monopolistic Competition and Public Policy, in Readings in the Social Control of Industry 263 (Hoover and Dean ed. 1942)

Watkins, Trusts, 15 Encyc. Soc. Sci. 115 (1935)

Weston, The Role of Mergers in the Growth of Large Firms (1953)

Wilcox, Competition and Monopoly in American Industry (TNEC Monograph No. 21, 1940)

———, On the Alleged Ubiquity of Oligopoly, 40 Proceedings Am. Econ. Assn. 67 (1950)

Williams, The Compleat Strategyst (1954)

Wold, Demand Analysis (1953)

Zimmerman, The Propensity to Monopolize (1952)

Index

INDEX